AFRICAN HISTORICAL DICTIONARIES
Edited by Jon Woronoff

1. *Cameroon*, by Victor T. LeVine and Roger P. Nye. 1974. Out of print. See No. 48.
2. *The Congo*, 2nd ed., by Virginia Thompson and Richard Adloff. 1984. Out of print. See No. 69.
3. *Swaziland*, by John J. Grotpeter. 1975.
4. *The Gambia*, 2nd ed., by Harry A. Gailey. 1987.
5. *Botswana*, by Richard P. Stevens. 1975. Out of print. See No. 70.
6. *Somalia*, by Margaret F. Castagno. 1975.
7. *Benin [Dahomey]*, 2nd ed., by Samuel Decalo. 1987. Out of print. See No. 61.
8. *Burundi*, by Warren Weinstein. 1976.
9. *Togo*, 3rd ed., by Samuel Decalo. 1996.
10. *Lesotho*, by Gordon Haliburton. 1977.
11. *Mali*, 3rd ed., by Pascal James Imperato. 1996.
12. *Sierra Leone*, by Cyril Patrick Foray. 1977.
13. *Chad*, 2nd ed., by Samuel Decalo. 1987.
14. *Upper Volta*, by Daniel Miles McFarland. 1978.
15. *Tanzania*, by Laura S. Kurtz. 1978.
16. *Guinea*, 3rd ed., by Thomas O'Toole with Ibrahima Bah-Lalya. 1995.
17. *Sudan*, by John Voll. 1978. Out of print. See No. 53.
18. *Rhodesia/Zimbabwe*, by R. Kent Rasmussen. 1979. Out of print. See No. 46.
19. *Zambia*, by John J. Grotpeter. 1979.
20. *Niger*, 3rd ed., by Samuel Decalo. 1996.
21. *Equatorial Guinea*, 2nd ed., by Max Liniger-Goumaz. 1988.
22. *Guinea-Bissau*, 2nd ed., by Richard Lobban and Joshua Forrest. 1988.
23. *Senegal*, by Lucie G. Colvin. 1981. Out of print. See No. 65.
24. *Morocco*, by William Spencer. 1980. Out of print. See. No. 71.
25. *Malawi*, by Cynthia A. Crosby. 1980. Out of print. See No. 54.
26. *Angola*, by Phyllis Martin. 1980. Out of print. See No. 52.
27. *The Central African Republic*, by Pierre Kalck. 1980. Out of print. See No. 51.
28. *Algeria*, by Alf Andrew Heggoy. 1981. Out of print. See No. 66.
29. *Kenya*, by Bethwell A. Ogot. 1981.
30. *Gabon*, by David E. Gardinier. 1981. Out of print. See No. 58.
31. *Mauritania*, by Alfred G. Gerteiny. 1981. Out of print. See No. 68.

64. *Uganda,* by M. Louise Pirouet. 1995.
65. *Senegal,* 2nd ed., by Andrew F. Clark and Lucie Colvin Phillips. 1994.
66. *Algeria,* 2nd ed., by Phillip Chiviges Naylor and Alf Andrew Heggoy. 1994.
67. *Egypt,* by Arthur Goldschmidt, Jr. 1994.
68. *Mauritania,* by Anthony G. Pazzanita. 1996.
69. *Congo,* 3rd ed., by Samuel Decalo, Virginia Thompson, and Richard Adloff. 1996.
70. *Botswana,* 3rd ed., by Jeff Ramsay, Barry Morton, and Fred Morton. 1996.
71. *Morocco,* 2nd ed., by Thomas K. Park. 1996.

HISTORICAL DICTIONARY OF CONGO

Samuel Decalo,
Virginia Thompson,
and Richard Adloff

African Historical Dictionaries, No. 69

The Scarecrow Press, Inc.
Lanham, Md., and London

SCARECROW PRESS, INC.

Published in the United States of America
by Scarecrow Press, Inc.
4720 Boston Way
Lanham, Maryland 20706

4 Pleydell Gardens, Folkestone
Kent CT20 2DN, England

Copyright © 1996 by Samuel Decalo

British Cataloguing-in-Publication Information Available

Library of Congress Cataloging-in-Publication Data

Decalo, Samuel.
Historical dictionary of Congo / Samuel Decalo, Virginia Thompson,
Richard Adloff.
p. cm. — (African historical dictionaries)
Rev. ed. of: Historical dictionary of Congo / by Virginia Thompson
and Richard Adloff.
Includes bibliographical references.
1. Congo (Brazzaville)—History—Dictionaries. I. Thompson,
Virginia McLean, 1903– . II. Adloff, Richard. III. Title.
IV. Series
DT546.215.D4 1996   967.24'003—dc20   95-50638   CIP

ISBN 0-8108-3116-3 (cloth: alk. paper)

♾ ™ The paper used in this publication meets the minimum requirements of
American National Standard for Information Sciences—Permanence of
Paper for Printed Library Materials, ANSI Z39.48—1984.
Manufactured in the United States of America.

Contents

Editor's Foreword

Since its independence nearly four decades ago, Congo's history has been characterized more by movement than progress. One of Africa's most unstable states, it has swung from the right to the left of the political spectrum and finally back closer to the middle. While not quite democratic to begin with, it has undergone a bout of centralized leadership that surely convinced the population that democracy was not the worst system. After priding itself on socialist purity, in theory more than practice, Congo has had to scrap a sinking state sector and rebuild an economy. Privatization is only one of many steps needed. Meanwhile, the new government must make exceptional efforts to attain the degree of unity of purpose and national harmony that existed four decades ago.

The past is, admittedly, the past. What about the future? Surely, the Congolese desire — and perhaps deserve — better. And it is in the interest of all Africa and the outside world that this time there be more progress and less movement. But it will take much hard work and discipline to ensure political stability, strengthen national unity and promote economic development. Just how hard that will be is intimated by the historical portions of this book which relate the many false starts and failures. But there are also glimmers, here and there, of causes for hope. Indeed, if the Congolese could survive such a harsh past they may be able to create a better future.

The first two editions of the *Historical Dictionary of Congo* were written by Virginia Thompson and Richard Adloff, pioneers in African studies with a particular interest in Francophone Africa. They described the first, more promising decades. Samuel Decalo has brought the story up to date, with an analysis of the times when things went wrong and now again a period of modest promise. Professor Decalo is already well known to readers of this series as author of the Benin, Chad, Niger and Togo volumes. But he has written much more broadly, including such books as *Coups and Army Rule* and *Psychoses of Power* as well as his forthcoming *The Stable Minority: Civilian Rule in Africa*.

Jon Woronoff
Series Editor

Acknowledgments

In revising the second edition of the *Historical Dictionary of Congo,* originally prepared by Virginia Thompson and Richard Adloff, while including much new material and a lengthier bibliography, I decided to retain in edited and updated form, many of the comprehensive thematic entries that gave this seminal reference work the holistic approach that was its strength. Also, many of the original entries were retained, in updated form. The end result is that this third edition is somewhat of a hybrid, reflecting both the style of the original authors and my own, and is really the product of all three scholars. In recognition of this, I think it only appropriate that this third edition is dedicated to Virginia Thompson and Richard Adloff, two of the pioneers of modern African Studies.

Recent Chronology

May 15, 1957	Investiture of the Conseil de Gouvernement under Vice-president J. Opangault.
Sept. 28, 1958	Admission of the Congo to the Franco-African Community as an autonomous state.
Nov. 28, 1958	Proclamation of the republic.
Dec. 8, 1958	Investiture by the legislative assembly of Abbé Fulbert Youlou as prime minister and head of government.
June 14, 1959	Election of the National Assembly.
Nov. 21, 1959	Election of Fulbert Youlou as president of the republic.
Aug. 15, 1960	Proclamation of independence.
Aug. 13–15, 1963	Riots at Brazzaville during the celebration of "Les Trois Glorieuses"; overthrow of the government; resignation of Fulbert Youlou; dissolution of the National Assembly; formation of a temporary government under Massamba-Débat.
Dec. 8, 1963	Legislative elections and approval by referendum of a new constitution.
Dec. 19, 1963	Election of Massamba-Débat as president of the republic.
Dec. 24, 1963	Formation of the first government of the second Congo Republic.
July 1964	The MNR becomes Congo's single party.
Apr. 1, 1965	Escape of Youlou to Léopoldville.
June 1966	Unsuccessful military coup against Massamba-Débat.
Aug. 23, 1967	Reorganization of the country into nine regions.
July 31–Aug. 3, 1968	Unrest among army officers because of the arrest of Marien Ngouabi; they act to overthrow Massamba-Débat.
Aug. 1, 1968	Massamba-Débat orders the disolution of the MNR.
Aug. 5, 1968	Formation of a National Council of the Revolution (CNR) and of a temporary government.

Aug. 14, 1968	The CNR, under the chairmanship of Capt. Marien Ngouabi, abrogates the constitution and replaces it by a Fundamental Act.
Sept. 4, 1968	Resignation of President Massamba-Débat.
Sept. 5, 1968	Capt. Alfred Raoul becomes acting head of state.
Dec. 31, 1968	The CNR replaces the MNR and becomes highest organ of the state.
Jan. 1, 1969	Marien Ngouabi becomes head of state, replacing Raoul, who becomes vice-president and premier.
August 1969	The JMNR becomes the UJSC, which declares that it will participate in the economic reconstruction of the country.
Dec. 29–31, 1969	Creation of the constituent congress of a vanguard revolutionary Parti Congolais du Travail (PCT).
Dec. 30, 1969	Adoption of a new constitution changing the name of the country to République Populaire du Congo (People's Republic of the Congo) and of a new national emblem, slogan, and anthem, as well as new state institutions.
Jan. 3, 1970	Promulgation of the new constitution.
Mar. 23, 1970	Failure of a raid on Brazzaville by commandos led by Kikanga.
November 1971	The army subdues student (UGEEC) strikers.
December 1971	Purge of the Maoist faction of the PCT.
Feb. 22, 1972	Abortive putsch by Ange Diawara.
Dec. 27–31, 1972	Holding of an extraordinary PCT congress, during which party institutions are modified and a new constitution is drafted.
Dec. 31, 1972	Breaking of diplomatic relations with Israel.
June 24, 1973	The new constitution is approved by referendum.
July 1973	Ngouabi decrees worker participation in state and parastate enterprises.
November 1973	New regional institutions are set up.
December 1974	Endorsement by the PCT congress of a development program (1975–77) as prelude to the first development plan.
Dec. 30, 1974	The PCT unanimously elects Ngouabi president of the PCT central committee and consequently president of the republic for five years.
Jan. 9, 1975	Major Ngouabi is invested as president of the republic; Henri Lopès forms a new government.

Dec. 8–12, 1975	Extraordinary session of the PCT central committee, followed by a declaration of Dec. 15; resignation of the PCT politburo, creation of a special revolutionary *état major*.
March 1976	Arrest of trade-union leaders on the charge of fomenting a general strike.
Mar. 18, 1977	Assassination of Ngouabi, followed shortly by the murder of Cardinal Biayenda; the PCT forms an 11-member military committee of the party with full powers.
Apr. 5, 1977	Col. Yhomby Opango is named chief of state, a new government is formed, and a Fundamental Act is promulgated.
Sept. 9, 1977	The French and Congolese governments decide to liquidate the Compagnie des Potasses du Congo.
Sept. 22, 1977	Several thousand alien Africans are expelled from the Congo.
Feb. 8, 1978	Trial of Ngouabi's assassins; ten death sentences are passed.
Dec. 30, 1978	Col. Yhomby Opango is promoted to the rank of general.
Feb. 5, 1979	The PCT military committee hands over its powers to the central committee; day-to-day affairs are turned over to the government under Premier Goma.
Feb. 8, 1979	The PCT central committee names Col. Denis Sassou Nguesso chief of state.
Feb. 12, 1979	The 1973 constitution is abrogated in part.
Mar. 26–30, 1979	Holding of the third extraordinary congress of the PCT; Col. Nguesso is named head of the PCT and of the state; Yhomby Opango is arrested.
May 12, 1979	Reestablishment of full diplomatic relations with the United States after a 12-year hiatus (1965–77).
July 8, 1979	Adoption of a new constitution and elections to a people's national assembly and to regional and local councils.
Aug. 14, 1979	Nguesso takes the oath of office and becomes the republic's third president, for a five-year term.
Oct. 3, 1980	Celebration of the centenary of Brazzaville's founding.
December 1981	Adoption by the National Assembly of the 1982–86 socioeconomic plan.

Oct. 10–11, 1982	State visit by President Mitterrand of France.
January 1983	Visit to Brazzaville by the Chinese premier.
April 1983	Curtailment of the 1982–86 development plan because of the fall in revenues.
Oct. 27, 1983	Georges Marchais, secretary-general of the French Communist Party, visits Brazzaville.
Nov. 23–25, 1983	State visit by the King and Queen of Spain
Dec. 19–20, 1983	Nguesso elected president of the UDEAC for 1984.
Dec. 23, 1983	Submission by the government to the National Assembly of the 1984 budget, totaling 412.4 billion CFA francs.
June 1984	Army called in to collect Sangha's cocoa harvest as rural apathy leaves the crop rotting in the fields.
June 20–30, 1985	The PCT Central Committee, in examining the horrendous fiscal losses of the State sector, resolves that as a "Socialist state" Congo can do nothing on the matter.
June 30, 1985	PCT Central Committee scraps the 1982–86 Development Plan, and announces a massive austerity plan, in an attempt to meet IMF restructuring conditionalities. France refuses to reschedule Congo's debt.
November 1985	Congo's debt servicing burden rises to 55% of the recurrent budget.
November 11, 1985	Students riot with anti-government slogans as the regime announces it will restrict scholarships for higher education.
December 1985	Major cabinet reshuffle.
March 1986	The recurrent budget for 1986 is again reduced to 46% of the 1985 amount, due to a 60% fall in oil prices.
June 1986	Compulsory 5% levy announced on all top salaries.
August 3, 1986	Trial of Ndalla and Thystère-Tchicaya for plotting and several mysterious bombings.
May 1987	PCT reluctantly decrees some privatizations.
July 1987	Twenty Congolese officers, some senior, arrested for an alleged coup plot.
September 6, 1987	Troops, including seconded Cubans, sent to arrest Captain Anga, who accuses Sassou Nguesso of the murder of Ngouabi. Fighting in the center of Owando.

July 1988	Major scandal erupts, leading to dismissal of cabinet ministers conniving to import, for burial in Congo, of toxic waste.
September 1988	Second compulsory levy on all civil service salaries of 10% stuns the country.
September 1988	Secret negotiations in Brazzaville to resolve the Angola/Namibia/South African conflict and Cuba's military involvement. Congo pledges that if withdrawn from Angola, Cuban troops will not regroup in Congo.
May 1989	5,000 Zairiens expelled from Congo.
May 19, 1989	Attempted assassination plot against Sassou Nguesso linked to Ngouabi's mother. Earlier, a kidnap plot against his son-in-law is foiled by Cuban intelligence officers.
July 26, 1989	PCT Congress held, resulting in a major reshuffle to allow new moderate membership in both the Central Committee and the Politburo.
December 1989	The end to Hydro-Congo's monopoly on petroleum distribution announced, together with large redundancies in the State sector. Few of these are implemented, and instead a new paramilitary force is recruited from Brazzaville's unemployed.
July 4, 1990	PCT announces it will transform itself into a mass party; Socialism will remain the state objective, multipartyism to be investigated.
July 1990	Increasing pressures for a National Conference.
September 7, 1990	The country's CSC trade union confederation calls for a national conference.
September 14, 1990	The government dismisses the CSC's leaders, and the confederation announces an unlimited general strike. After two weeks the government capitulates. New political parties emerge.
October 1990	The CSC strikes for two weeks in Pointe Noire and Brazzaville, over the planned redundancies of 650 workers at Hydro-Congo. The government capitulates. The strikes spread into other sectors weary at the regimen of austerity, and continue into 1991.
December 1990	The PCT disassociates itself from Marxism-Leninism. The name, flag and anthem of Congo are replaced. Mass resignations of former leading PCT politicians takes place.

January 15, 1991	Though bankrupt, the regime agrees to pay rises in order to end the strikes. The government also agrees to hire unemployed graduates, increasing the civil service from 77,000 to 83,000, and shelves plans to privatize or restructure Hydro-Congo.
February 1991	Foreign capital continues to enter the country to purchase some bankrupt/closed down state enterprises. Vehement trade union demands that full complements of the original force be hired (as opposed to the 40–60% judged adequate) blocks several deals.
February 25, 1991	The National Conference convenes in Brazzaville with 1,100 delegates, 700 from the ranks of the opposition. Early squabbles lead to adjournment until mid-March.
March 15, 1991	The National Conference reconvenes and elects the (southern) Bishop of Owando as its President. As many as 77 political parties are registered.
March 17, 1991	Sassou Nguesso is several times (including by Yhomby Opango) accused publicly and to his face of Ngouabi's murder, other killings, and the parlous state of the economy.
April 26, 1991	In a televised speech Sassou Nguesso acknowledges serious abuses of power and wastage of resources under his aegis, and requests indulgence. An opposition leader retorts, "We are not a Catholic Church here."
May 18, 1991	A 153-person HCR is set up as the interim Assembly under the Bishop of Owando.
June 10, 1991	The National Conference ends with the election of a 25-man transitional government headed by Prime Minister Milongo, with Sassou Nguesso staying on as interim President. Milongo wins on the 4th ballot against Pascal Lissouba. Sassou Nguesso and Yhomby Opango publicly embrace and make up.
August 22, 1991	Diplomatic relations with Israel resumed by Congo.
August 23, 1991	New ministers vote themselves salary increases of up to 80%
November–December 1991	Massive expulsions of non-nationals, including 30,000 Zairiens.

November 1991	Referendum on a new Constitution and elections postponed due to lack of money.
January 15, 1992	Week-long army mutiny caused by efforts to re-structure commands in the military.
March 15, 1992	Referendum (with foreign funds) takes place, approving by 93.63% a new Constitution, in a 70.93% electoral turnout.
May 3, 1992	Local and municipal elections take place. Electoral fraud leads to the dismissal of six mayors and all nine regional prefects on June 12th.
June 29, July 2, 1992	Legislative elections bring Lissouba's UPADS party 39 seats and Kolelas' MCDDI 29. The PCT trails in third place. A total of 101 parties at one time or another since 1991 sought registration.
July 26, 1992	Senate elections take place in which UPADS wins 23 of the 60 seats, the MCDDI 13, the PCT a distant third.
August 2, 1992	First round of the Presidential elections give Lissouba 35.89% of the vote and Kolelas 22.89%. Sassou Nguesso is eliminated from the next round.
August 16, 1992	Second round of the elections see Lissouba win 61.3% of the vote.
August 31, 1992	Lissouba is sworn in as President, and gives Sassou Nguesso immunity from future prosecution. In the new National Assembly the PCT is supportive of UPADS. Bongho-Nouarra is Prime Minister.
October 31, 1992	In a parliamentary rift the PCT shifts support to the MCDDI, and a no-confidence vote passes, leading to the fall of the Bongho-Nouarra government. Parliamentary embroglio ensues when Lissouba announces new legislative elections to give him a majority.
November 30, 1992	Inter-ethnic violence erupts in Brazzaville.
December 6, 1992	Da Costa appointed interim Prime Minister.
December 8, 1992	Segment of the CSC secedes. Civil service salaries now regularly being paid in arrears.
March 3, 1993	Families of Captain Anga and others killed in Owando in 1987 sue Sassou Nguesso despite his immunity.
May 6, June 6, 1993	New elections produce a slim majority for UPADS, but several results are disputed by the opposition. New broadly based government is set

	up under Prime Minister Yhomby Opango. Riots again erupt in Brazzaville, and continue intermittently through 1995.
July 1993	Chief of Staff Mokoko, who does not recognize Yhomby Opango's authority, is dismissed.
July 16, 1993	State of emergency declared.
July 29, 1993	Mediation agreement in Libreville produces agreement to repeat the contested elections on October 15th.
June 1994	Armed clashes by groups loyal to Lissouba and to Kolelas continue in Brazzaville. Youthful private militias fight across barricades, with the northern army siding with Kolelas. An estimated 1,000 people have died so far.
June 30, 1994	After three years of dragging its heels on the privatization of State enterprises, Congo finally bows to IMF pressure and receives 18.5 billion CFAF in credits.
July 16, 1994	Kolelas elected mayor of Brazzaville.

TABLE 1. FOREIGN TRADE

	1985	1986	1987	1988	1989	1990	1991	1992	1993
Exports f.o.b.	514.3	233.0	263.5	251.2	368.4	431.0	311.1	343.0	320.2
Imports f.o.b.	283.1	177.5	126.2	155.7	160.3	190.0	199.6	190.2	168.2
BALANCE	231.2	55.5	137.3	95.5	208.1	241.0	111.5	152.8	152.0

In billions of CFAF.

TABLE 2. MAIN EXPORTS

	1985	1986	1987	1988	1989	1990
Oil	439.9	170.7	211.5	185.7	279.5	340.0
Timber & products	12.4	29.0	31.0	43.2	49.7	51.0

In billions of CFAF.

TABLE 3. DIRECTION OF TRADE

Exports to:	1985	1990	1992	Imports from:	1985	1990	1992
USA	60	37	36	France	46	42	37
Italy	2	25	13	USA	7	14	9
France	11	13	8	Italy	8	10	10
Benelux	1	10	23	Hong Kong	—	4	8
Spain	3	7	10				

In percentages of total trade.

TABLE 4. GROSS DOMESTIC PRODUCT

	1985	1986	1987	1988	1989	1990
GDP @ current prices	970.8	640.4	690.6	659.6	773.5	798.3
GDP @ constant prices	416.7	388.2	390.9	391.7	406.2	415.1
Real change as %	-1.2	-6.8	0.7	0.2	3.7	2.2
In billions CFAF						
GDP per capita						
@ current prices	500.4	320.2	335.2	309.4	351.6	351.7
@ constant prices	214.8	194.1	189.7	183.9	184.6	182.9
Real change as %	-4.2	-9.6	-2.3	-3.1	0.4	-0.9
In thousands CFAF						

TABLE 5. OIL PRODUCTION AND EXPORTS

	1986	1987	1988	1989	1990	1991
Production	5,951	6,317	7,038	7,962	8,029	8,020
Export	5,416	5,749	6,701	7,424	7,425	7,328

In thousands of tons.

TABLE 6: GOVERNMENT ACCOUNTS

	1987	1988	1989	1990
Revenues	135.5	125.4	167.1	209.4
Expenditures	224.5	244.6	244.6	268.8
of which salaries	83.7	81.2	78.5	79.5
of which interest	45.8	54.1	56.0	79.5
Balance	−89.0	−119.2	−77.5	−59.4

In billions of CFAF.

TABLE 7: EXTERNAL DEBT

	1986	1987	1988	1989	1990
Total Debt	3,482	4,351	4,161	4,326	5,118
Debt servicing	384	446	415	324	300
Debt as % of GNP	184.9	213.0	218.2	204.1	203.6

In millions of US $.

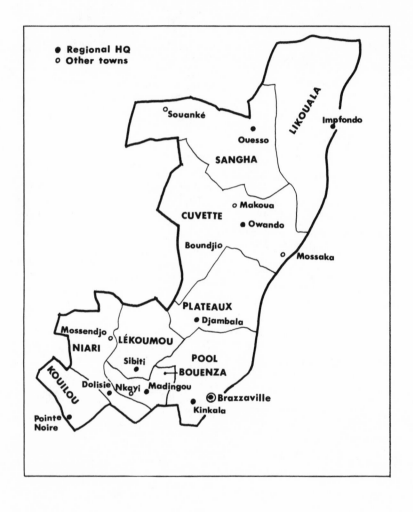

- ● Regional HQ
- ○ Other towns

Souanké

Ouesso

LIKOUALA

Impfondo

SANGHA

○ Makoua

● Owando

CUVETTE

Boundjio

○ Mossaka

PLATEAUX

● Djambala

Mossendjo ○ LÉKOUMOU

NIARI

Sibiti

POOL

BOUENZA

KOUILOU

Dolisie Nkayi Madingou

◉ Brazzaville

Kinkala

Pointe
Noire

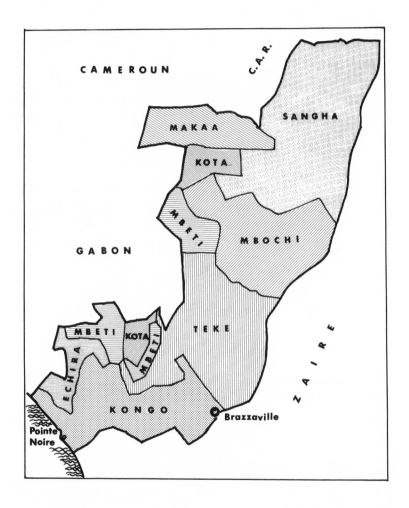

Abbreviations and Acronyms

ACCF	Agence Centrafricaine des Communications Fluviales
ACI	Agence Congolais d'Information
AEC	Association des Etudiants Congolais
AFRICAPLAST	Industrie Africaine des Plastiques
AIPFL	Association International des Parlementaires de Langue Française
ALUCONGO	Société pour la Transformation de l'Aluminium et Autres Métaux du Congo
ANAC	Agence Nationale de l'Aviation Civile
AND	Alliance Nationale pour la Démocratie
ANP	Assemblée Nationale Populaire
APN	Armée Populaire Nationale
ARR	Action de Rénovation Rurale
ASECNA	Agence pour la Sécurité de la Navigation Aérienne
ATC	Agence Transcongolaise des Communications
ATEC	Agence Transéquatoriale des Communications
ATEC	Agence des Transports des Etats d'Afrique Centrale
BAB	Boissons Africaines de Brazzaville
BCA	Banque Commerciale Africaine
BCB	Bureau Congolais du Bois
BCC	Banque Commerciale Congolaise
BCCO	Bureau pour la Création, le Contrôle, et l'Orientation des Entreprises et Exploitations de l'Etat
BCEAE	Banque Centrale des Etats de l'Afrique Equatoriale
BCEOM	Bureau Central d'Etudes pour les Equipements d'Outre-Mer
BDPA	Bureau pour le Développement de la Production Agricole
BEAC	Banque des Etats d'Afrique Centrale
BIAO	Banque Internationale pour l'Afrique Occidentale

BIDC	Banque Internationale du Congo
BMR	Brigades Mobiles Rurales
BNCI	Banque Nationale pour le Commerce et l'Industrie
BNDC	Banque Nationale de Développement du Congo
BRGM	Bureau de Recherches Géologiques et Minières
BRP	Bureau des Recherches Pétrolières
BUMCO	Bureau Minier du Congo
CAC	Chantiers et Ateliers du Congo
CACP	Centre d'Animation du Cinéma Populaire
CAIEM	Complexe Agro-Industriel de l'Etat de Montsumba
CATC	Confédération Africaine des Travailleurs Croyants
CBI	Congolaises des Bois Impregnés
CBMA	Commission des Biens Mal-acquis
CCA	Caisse Congolaise d'Amortissement
CCCE	Centre Congolais du Commerce Extérieur
CCSL	Confédération Congolaise des Syndicats Libres
CCSO	Compagnie Commerciale Sangha-Oubangui
CDC	Caisse des Depots et Consignations
CDC	Centre Démocratique Congolaise
CEEAC	Communauté Economique des Etats de l'Afrique Centrale
CENAGES	Centre National de Gestion
CENAR	Centre National d'Administration Routière
CFA	Colonies Françaises d'Afrique (franc)
CFA	Communauté Financière Africaine (franc) (after May 12, 1962)
CFA	Compagnie Forestière Africaine
CFAO-Congo	Compagnie Française de l'Afrique Occidentale-Congo
CFCO	Chemin de Fer du Congo-Océan
CFHBC	Compagnie Française du Haut et Bas Congo
CFTC	Confédération Française des Travailleurs Chrétiens
CGAT	Confédération Générale Africaine du Travail
CGOT	Compagnie Générale des Oléagineux Tropicaux
CGTAE	Compagnie Générale des Transports en Afrique Equatoriale
CHACONA	Chantiers de Constructions Navales
CIB	Société Congolaise Industrielle des Bois
CIDOULOU	Cimentérie Domaniale de Loutété
CMCF	Compagnie Minière du Congo Française

CMP	Comité Militaire du Parti
CNAR	Centre National d'Administration Routière
CNC	Comité Nationale de la Cellulose
CNOC	Conseil Nationale de l'Opposition Congolaise
CNPS	Caisse Nationale de Prévoyance Sociale
CNR	Conseil National de la Révolution
CNSEE	Centre National de la Statistique et des Etudes Economiques
COMILOG	Compagnie Minière de l'Ogooué
COPARCO	Société Congolaise de Parfumérie et de Cosmétiques
COPEMAR	Congolaise de Pêches Maritimes
CORAF	Congolaise de Raffinage
CPC	Compagnie des Potasses du Congo
CRETH	Centre de Recherches, d'Etudes Techniques et de l'Habitat
CSC	Confédération Syndicale Congolaise
CTFT	Centre Technique Forestier Tropical
DGSE	Direction Générale de la Securité de l'Etat
DRM	Direction de Renseignements Militaires
EMSR	Etat-Major Spécial Révolutionnaire
ENELCO	Energie Electrique du Congo
ENI	Ente Nazionale Idrocarburi
ENSET	Ecole Nationale Supérieure de l'Enseignement Technique
ERAP	Entreprise de Recherches et d'Activités Pétrolières
ESACC	Ecole Supérieure Africaine des Cadres de Chemin de Fer
FAC	Fonds d'Action Conjoncturelle et d'Equilibre Régional
FAC	Fonds d'Aide et de Coopération
FAPLA	Forces Armées Populaires de Libération de l'Angola
FEA	French Equatorial African Federation
FED	Fonds Européen de Développement
FESAC	Fédération de l'Enseignement Supérieur en Afrique Centrale
FIDA	Fonds International de Développement Agricole
FIDES	Fonds d'Investissement pour le Développement Economique et Social
FLEC	Front de Libération de l'Enclave de Cabinda
FPA	Fabrique de Peinture en Afrique
FSN	Fonds de Solidarité Nationale
GP	Garde Présidentielle

HCR	Haut Conseil de la République
HUILKA	Huilérie de Nkayi
HYDROCONGO	Société Nationale de Recherche et d'Exploitation
IMPRECO	Impressions de Textiles de la République Populaire du Congo
INRAP	Institut National de Recherche et d'Action Pédagogique
IRHO	Institut de Recherches pour les Huiles et les Oléagineux
IRSC	Institut de Recherches Scientifiques au Congo
ISSE	Institut Supérieur des Sciences d'Education
JMNR	Jeunesse du Mouvement National de la Révolution
LAPCO	Laboratoire Pharmaceutique du Congo
LINA-CONGO	Lignes Nationales Aériennes du Congo
M-22	Mouvement du 22 Février
MAAC	Manufacture d'Art et d'Artisanat du Congo
MAB	Minotérie-Aliments de Bétail
MACC	Manufacture d'Armes et de Cartouches Congolaises
MCDDI	Mouvement Congolais pour la Démocratie et le Développement Integrale
MFC	Messagéries Fluviales de la Cuvette Congolaise
MNR	Mouvement National de la Révolution
MOLICA	Mouvement de Libération pour le Cabinda
MPC	Mouvement Patriotique Congolaise
MPLA	(People's Movement for the Liberation of Angola)
MSA	Mouvement Socialiste Africain
NAP	Nouvelle Agence de Presse
NIBOLEK	Niari, Bouanza, Lékoumou
OAU	Organization of African Unity
OBAEF	Office des Bois de l'A.E.F.
OCAM	Organisation Commune Africaine et Malgache (until July 1, 1963); Organisation Commune Africaine et Mauricienne
OCB	Office Congolais des Bois
OCC	Office du Café et du Cacao
OCF	Office Congolais des Forêts
OCH	Office Congolais d'Habitat
OCMC	Office Congolais des Matériaux de Construction
OCO	Office Congolais de l'Okoumé
OCT	Office Congolais du Tabac

OCV	Office des Cultures Vivrières
ODI	Office de Développement Industriel
OFNACOM	Office National de Commerce
OGB	Office du Gros Betail
ONACI	Office National du Cinéma
ONAKO	Organisation National du Kouilou
ONCPA	Office National de la Commercialisation des Produits Agricoles
ONIVEG	Office National d'Importation de Viande en Gros
ONLP	Office National des Librairies Populaires
ONO	Office National de l'Okoumé
ONPT	Office National des Postes et Télécommunications
ONUDI	Organisation des Nations Unies pour le Développement Industriel
OPMA	Office de Petite Motorisation Agricole
ORSTOM	Office de la Recherche Scientifique des Territoires d'Outre-Mer
PAM	Programme Alimentaire Mondial
PCR	Parti Congolais de Renouveau
PCT	Parti Congolais de Travail
PDC	Parti Démocratique Congolais
PDR	Projet de Développement Rural du Pool
PLACONGO	Société des Placages au Congo
PLC	Parti Liberal Congolais
PPC	Parti Progressiste Congolais
PPSDR	Parti Populaire pour la Démocratie Sociale et la Defence de la République
PRP	Parti du Renouvellement et du Progrès
PT	Parti du Travail
RASD	République Arabe Sahraoui Démocratique
RDA	Rassemblement Démocratique Africain
RDC	Radiodiffusion-Télévision Congolaise
RDD	Rassemblement pour la Démocratie et le Développement
RDPCC	Rassemblement pour la Defence des Pauvres et des Chomeurs au Congo
RDPS	Rassemblement pour la Démocratie et le Progrès Sociale
RNPC	Régie Nationale des Palmeraies du Congo
RNTB	Régie Nationale des Transports Brazzavillois
RNTTP	Régie Nationale des Transports et des Travaux Publics
RPF	Rassemblement du Peuple Français

SARIS-CONGO	Société Agricole pour la Raffinage du Sucre
SAVONCONGO	Savonnérie du Congo
SCBK	Société Congolaise des Brasseries Kronenbourg
SCEI	Société Centrale d'Echanges Internationaux
SCGI	Société Congolaise des Gaz Industriels
SCKN-Congo	Société Commerciale du Kouilou-Niari-Congo
SCT	Société Congolaise de Transit
SECC	Société d'Etude de la Cellulose du Congo
SEN	Société Equatoriale de Navigation
SEPAC	Société Economique de Pêche, d'Armements, et de Conserverie
SFIO	Section Française de l'Internationale Ouvrière
SGBC	Société Générale de Banques au Congo
SIA-Congo	Société Industrielle et Agricole du Congo
SIACIC	Silos à Ciments au Congo
SIAP	Société Industrielle d'Articles en Papier
SIAT	Société Industrielle et Agricole du Tabac Tropical
SIBC	Société Internationale des Brasseries du Congo
SICAPE	Société Italienne-Congolaise d'Armements et de Pêche
SIDETRA	Société Industrielle du Déroulage et de Tranchage
SIP	Société Indigène de Prévoyance
SITRACO	Société d'Importation Alimentaire du Congo
SLNA	(Angola National Liberation Front)
SMDR	Société Mutuelle du Développement Rural
SMIG	Salaire Minimum Interprofessional Garanti
SMM	Société Minière de M'Passa
SMOL	Société Minière Ogooué-Lobaye
SNDE	Société Nationale de Distribution des Eaux
SNE	Société Nationale d'Electricité
SNE	Société Nationale d'Energie
SNEA	Société Nationale Elf-Aquitaine
SNEB	Société Nationale d'Exploitation des Bois
SNTI	Société Nationale de Transports Interrégionaux
SOCALA	Société Congolaise Arabe Libyenne de l'Agriculture
SOCALIB	Société Congolaise Arabe-Libyenne
SOCICO	Société Cimentière du Congo
SOCIMPEX	Société Congolaise d'Import et d'Export
SOCOBOIS	Société Congolaise de Bois
SOCODI	Société Congolaise du Disque
SOCOFROID	Société Congolaise de Conserverie et de Congélation

SOCOMAB	Société Congolaise de Manutention des Bois
SOCOME	Société Congolaise de Meubles
SOCOREM	Société Congolaise de Recherches et d'Exploitation Minières
SOCOTEX	Société Congolaise de Textiles
SOCOTON	Société Cotonnière Congolaise
SOCOTR	Société Congolaise de Transit
SODETRAF	Société de Développement et Transport Aérien en Afrique
SOMANGOL	(Angola National Oil Company)
SONACO	Société Nationale de Construction
SONAMIF	Société Nationale des Mines de Mfouati
SONAMINES	Société Nationale des Recherches et d'Exploitations Minières
SONAMIS	Société Nationale de Sounda-Makamoueka
SONATRAB	Société Nationale de Transformation des Bois
SONEL	Société Nationale d'Elevage
SOPHOSCO	Société Mixte Bulgaro-Congolaise de Recherches et d'Exploitation des Phosphates
SOPROGI	Société de Promotion et de Gestion Immobilière
SOSUNIARI	Société du Sucre du Niari
SOTEXCO	Société des Textiles du Congo
SOVERCO	Société des Verreries du Congo
SPA	Société des Produits Agricoles
SPAEF	Société des Pétroles d'Afrique Equatoriale Française
SPAFE	Société des Pétroles d'Afrique Equatoriale
SUCO	Sucreries du Congo
UAIC	Unité d'Afforestation Industrielle du Congo
UAM	Union Africaine et Malgache
UBC	Usine de Broyage de Calcaire
UCB	Union Congolaise des Banques
UCC	Union Ecologique du Congo
UDC	Union Démocratique Congolais
UDC	Union pour la Démocratie Congolaise
UDDIA	Union Démocratique pour la Défense des Interêts Africains
UDE	Union Douanière Equatoriale
UDEAC	Union Douanière et Economique de l'Afrique Centrale
UDPS	Union pour le Développement et le Progrès Sociale
UDR	Union pour la Démocratie et la République
UEAC	Union des Etats de l'Afrique Centrale

UFA	Unités Forestières d'Aménagements
UGEEC	Union Générale des Eleves et Etudiants Congolais
UJC	Union de la Jeunesse Congolaise
UJSC	Union de la Jeunesse Socialiste Congolaise
UMC	Union de Moyen-Congo
UNAJOC	Union Nationale des Journalistes Congolais
UNDP	Union Nationale pour la Démocratie et le Progrès
UNEAC	Union Nationale des Ecrivains, Artistes et Artisans du Congo
UNICONGO	Union Patronale Interprofessionelle du Congo
UNJSC	Union Nationale de la Jeunesse Socialiste Congolaise
UNRFC	Union Nationale Révolutionnaire des Femmes Congolaises
UNTC	Union Nationale des Tradipraticiens Congolais
UP	Union de Progrès
UP	Union pour le Progès
UPADS	Union Panafricaine pour la Démocratie Sociale
UPDP	Union Patriotique pour la Démocratie et le Progrès
UPPC	Union pour le Progrès du Peuple Congolais
UPRN	Union Patriotique pour la reconstruction nationale
UPSD	Union pour le Progrès Social et la Démocratie
URD	Union pour le Renouveau Démocratique
URFC	Union Révolutionnaire des Femmes du Congo
URPP	Union Républicaine pour le Progrès
UTS	Usine de Textiles Synthetiques

Introduction

Geography and Resources

Congo, formerly the People's Republic of Congo, straddles the Equator covering an area of 342,000 sq. km. (132,042 sq. mi.), with a maximum length of 1,006 km. (625 mi.), a width of 225 km. (140 mi.), and a 150 km. coastline on the Atlantic Ocean. The country is bounded in the north by Cameroun and the Central African Republic, to the west by Gabon, to the east by Zaire, and to the south by the Cabinda enclave. Roughly 1,000 kms. of the country's eastern boundary is along the Zaire (ex-Congo) river. It is along that river and its affluents that under conditions of high water that Bangui, capital of the landlocked Central African Republic, has vital access to Brazzaville, and via the Congo-Ocean railway, to Congo's Atlantic port of Pointe Noire.

The country is composed of three main natural regions. The immediate coastal zone (where offshore are found Congo's substantial oil deposits), is sandy in the north though progressively swampy beyond Kouilou. The narrow low-lying coastal plain's weather is moderate due to the effects of cool Ocean currents in the region. Two spurs of the Mayombe escarpment, east of the plain, emerge on the coast at Pointe Noire and Pointe Indienne. The well-forested ridges of the Mayombe (with its valuable timber resources) that parallel the coast and attract heavy rainfall, have a maximum altitude of 800 meters (2625 ft.) and culminate in the Chaillu massif in the north and the Bateke plateau in the east, between which are found the gorges of the Kouilou and Niari rivers, natural hydro-electric power sites. At Holle, at the western foot of the range and conveniently close to the coast, are found massive phosphate deposits, whose exploitation had to be terminated in the mid-1970's due to flooding in the mines. The Niari valley, with a lower elevation and more fertile soils, has sustained a wide variety of commercial crops including coffee, cocoa, sugar, tobacco, palm oil and maize, and allowed the development of much of Congo's agro-industry. The Chaillu massif, another heavy rain-forested range, is the Zaire basin's western watershed, beyond which, to the northeast, is found the much drier Bateke plateau that gradually descends to the Zaire River, where it forms cliffs on both banks and rapids in its bed.

1

The Bateke plateau, extending north of Brazzaville, the capital, has an average altitude of 600–700 meters, and is cut by a number of dry valleys. Among the main rivers that join either the Zaire or the Oubangui are the partly navigable Alima, Motaba, Sangha and Likouala. The northeast of the country, flanking the right bank of the Oubangui and Zaire rivers, is part of the huge Zaire water basin. It is a large low alluvial plain, crisscrossed by a multitude of rivers that are stagnant during the dry season, and contains large inaccessible swamps. Indeed fully a quarter of Congo's land-area is covered by swamps, nearly half by dense equatorial forests, with much of the rest grasslands. Between the Oubangui and the Likouala, the swamp area includes forest galleries along the river banks, separated by vast stretches of inundated prairies. Trees dot the savanna areas of the south but not those of the sandy Bateke plateau. The dense forest is dispersed between the Mayombe escarpment, the Chaillu massif, and the northwestern Sangha region. In the more accessible zones intensive felling of the more valuable species of trees has given rise to secondary forests of pines and other commercially-planted varieties, such as eucalyptus trees near Pointe Noire.

Congo has an equatorial climate that is moderated by altitude and by the cold Benguela current off the coast. It has two dry and two wet seasons, that are more clearly marked in the north than in the south of the country. At Brazzaville (at the country's southeast extremity) the main dry season is from mid-May to the end of September, with the "small" dry season occurring for about a month starting in mid-December. The long rainy season is between mid-January and mid-May, while the small rainy season is from October to mid-December. The country's average temperature is 25° C. though along the coast the climate is cooler (and drier) due to the cold offshore current.

The country abounds with many, valuable, and large natural resources, from timber through phosphates to oil, and new deposits are discovered nearly every year. However the exorbitant cost of their exploitation, given the rudimentary state of the country's communications, Congo's combative trade unions, and until recently the political uncertainties posed by one of the continent's most vehemently-vocal People's Republics, has severely limited their development, and by extention the country's economic growth. Since the 1970's oil has been Congo's main export, replacing the country's early reliance on timber exports. But increasing oil exports have not been a panacea. Global market-price vicissitudes together with Congo's tendency to rely on overly optimistic projections of future revenues for purposes of sustaining a large civil service and a highly inefficient State sector, have regularly caused fiscal imbalances that finally virtually bankrupted the economy in the late 1980's.

Early History

Little is known about the early history of Congo. Although evidence of early settled life has come to light near Brazzaville and Pointe Noire and in the Niari valley, they relate to only about a tenth of the country's total area and precludes accurate classification concerning age and origin. The basic assumption is, however, that the major ethnic groups that came to populate Congo—notably the Bakongo, Bateke and the Mbochi—encountered on their arrival a territory largely uninhabited except for the Pygmies, remnants of whom are still found in small and inaccessible bands in the Far North of the country.

There have always been major demographic disparities among Congo's various regions, and these have been greatly exacerbated since independence. Nearly eighty percent of the country's two and a half million people currently reside in the south between Brazzaville and Pointe Noire, part of a demographic shift that commenced even before independence. Indeed in 1994 over 40 percent of the population resided in the capital, Brazzaville, that in three decades mushroomed from a picturesque small town into a sprawling urban conglomeration. The sparsely populated northwestern two-thirds of the country, poor, undeveloped, unhealthy, with few means of communications (except riverine) and services, currently contains twenty percent of the population. Apart from the regional North-South demographic shift, that acquired further momentum during the lengthy northern military reign (1968–1992) that expanded employment opportunities for Northerners in the South, there has also been a massive rural-urban exodus that made Congo one of the continent's most urbanized countries. This brought about a host of concomitant negative repercussions, amongst which one could note a declining agricultural output that has necessitated large purchases overseas of basic staple foodstuffs, and insistent urban pressures for employment, education and social services.

Of the country's three main ethnic groups the Bakongo (or Kongo) historically arrived from the northeast, from the Chad basin area, to reach the coastal regions early in the 15th century where a loose but large kingdom was formed. When in 1484 the Portuguese Diego Cao explored the region (to discover the mouth of the Congo/Zaire river), the largest Kongo concentration was in what is today northern Angola. There the Kongo had their capital, Mbanza-Kongo, that was to be baptized San Salvador by the Portuguese. Most of the history of the Kongo kingdom had little to do with Congo, except that with the subsequent disintegration of the kingdom a number of groups migrated northwards and/or established their autonomy from Mbanza-Kongo.

Among the Kongo groups that migrated north were the Vili, who crossed the Zaire River to progressively occupy the coastal regions of today's Congo as far as Cap Sainte Catherine, and the immediate hinterland to the Mayombe foothills. Their kingdom, Loango, with its capital in what is today a small village north of Pointe Noire, was divided into seven provinces and headed by a king called the Ma Loango. It reached its apogee at the end of the 17th century when Loango was a major slave-trading center, attracting Portuguese, Dutch, British and French ships and traders, and to which trade and slave-caravans gravitated overland from the Bateke plateau. Loango was also the early site of Catholic missionaries evangelizing groups in the interior of the country. Under demographic pressures from non-Vili groups arriving from Gabon, Loango progressively lost control over its northern dominions, and entered a period of decline.

Beyond the Mayombe escarpment the Bateke people were settled. Considerably less detail is known about their origins, despite the fact that they occupied a large area extending from the Mayombe to the plateau north of Brazzaville, and were one of the oldest groups inhabiting the region. Organized in a decentralized kingdom headed by a Makoko, mining ores at Boko-Sangho and Mindouli, and controlling trade between riverine groups and the coastal Vili (both via the Pool region and through caravan routes reaching directly to the coast), evidence suggests a common origin (even if in the distant past) with the Kongo. The Bateke also came under population pressures in their plateau from the Kongo exodus from the south, and especially from the aggressive expansion southwards of the Mbochi, more recent arrivals in Congo.

Latecomers to northern Congo, the Mbochi (composed of several subgroups) spread throughout the Likouala-Mossaka basin along its rivers only at the end of the 18th century. Their pressure on the Bateke forced the latter out of some territory and loosened their grip over several tributary groups, though the Bateke continued to resist the southward expansion of the Mbochi, retaining a monopoly over trade between the North and the Pool, that was at the time a major trade entrepot and meeting-place of caravans from Loango and from upriver. By the mid-19th century, despite a continuing dynamic tug-of-war, Congo's main ethnic groups inhabited much of the territory they occupy today.

The abolition of the slave trade (in which the Vili were especially engaged), and the 1849 founding of Libreville (in contemporary Gabon) by France as a haven for freed slaves gave the latter a base for the exploration of the interior. No European had penetrated the hinterland beyond the Mayombe mountains until 1875, when Savorgnan de Brazza commenced the first of his three explorations from Libreville. Five years later he managed to reach the Zaire River and signed a treaty with the Makoko who placed the by-now much-weakened Bateke under French protection. The latter also ceded to France at that time the site of what in due course was to become the town of Brazzaville. Possession of this area enabled France to frustrate the attempt on the right bank of the river by

Stanley to extend the domain of King Leopold of Belgium. In 1883, joined by his lieutenant, Albert Dolisie (who had been signing treaties with ethnic groups in the lower Oubangui), Brazza explored the country as far as the west coast where a similar protectorate treaty was signed with the Ma Loango, who ceded to France outright the area known as Pointe Indienne.

The Colonial Era

In 1885 the Act of Berlin formalized various European territorial claims in the region. France lost direct access to the mouth of the Zaire River, but retained possession of the Niari basin and the areas explored by Brazza. The Act was followed by a series of bilateral treaties that demarcated the frontiers of the new colonies. An administrative reorganization of France's equatorial possessions united them in a single colony called Congo Français, but between 1906 and 1910 France's equatorial dominions were again reorganized as the French Equatorial African Federation (FEA), composed of the four colonies of Congo (then called Moyen-Congo), Oubangui-Chari (the future Central African Republic), Gabon and Chad. Brazzaville became the capital of both Moyen-Congo and the Federation, that was headed by a governor-general appointed by France.

In theory each colony retained economic and administrative autonomy, though power was in reality strongly centralized in the hands of governors-general. Ruling by decree and disposing funds allocated for all the FEA, governors-general set general policies, carried out programs to develop education, health services, judicial systems, and public works on a federation-wide basis with little control from the distant metropole or effective opposition from territorial governors. In the process, Moyen-Congo received preferential treatment, being provided with the only railroad and deep-water port in the entire Federation, and Brazzaville's public buildings, schools, law courts, trading firms, telecommunications and medical services soon surpassed by far their counterparts in all the other territorial capitals of the federation. Moyen-Congo's pre-eminence, achieved in part with manpower and funds from other colonies (as when massive forced labor was recruited from as far-afield as Chad to help construct the Congo-Ocean railroad), caused resentment among all its neighbors. At the same time Brazzaville's transformation into the federation's capital set the stage for the rural-urban exodus, creating a large civil service not needed, but impossible to prune, after the colonial federation fell apart at independence.

Two other colonial era by-products unique to French Equatorial Africa that deeply influenced Moyen-Congo's development were the rise of messianic movements in the region and the concessionary system set up by France. Catholic missionaries, first to evangelize and educate in Congo, soon encountered competition from Protestants and strong opposition from socio-political protest movements that developed into messianic cults. With the progressive liberalization in the post-1946 era these became potent political forces, and they still play a very vibrant role in the country today as was cogently manifest during the 1993 Presidential elections where all southern candidates tried to tap the allegiances of the messianic cults.

The concessionary-companies, on the other hand, chartered by France in 1899, were in part an effort to circumvent the agreed-upon economic nondiscrimination of the signatory powers of the Berlin Act. At the same time, the parcelling out of Equatorial Africa to private French concessions was rationalized as a step towards economizing on the cost of administering large undeveloped and underpopulated regions. Some 40 companies with a registered capital of 59.5 million francs were granted 30-year monopolies to exploit and administer for France 650,00 sq. km. in the Zaire basin. The consequences of this policy were disastrous in both financial and human terms, inasmuch as a systematic and brutal plunder of the concessions was by far the most common outcome. Cost-benefit considerations reigned supreme as often undercapitalized companies employed unqualified personnel and/or adventurers who lived off the land while stripping their concessions of all possible riches. Ivory and rubber virtually disappeared from the concessionary areas; indigenous populations were decimated by brutal forced labor, disease, and maladministration, and some fled to neighboring colonies; the French government lost more money than it gained in rents and taxes; and French public opinion was shocked by reports of the wide-scale brutalities which the system had given rise. By 1930 most of the concessionary companies had gone bankrupt and the practice was largely liquidated.

When the Second World War broke out the FEA was dramatically transformed from a minor colonial backwater into Free France's bastion in sub-Saharan Africa. In August 1940, Moyen-Congo joined Chad to declare for General de Gaulle in London, who rewarded Felix Eboué (a French Guyanese who was the sole African colonial governor to rally behind Free France) with the post of governor-general of the FEA. Moyen-Congo's contribution to the Allied war effort as a base and transit area, with Pointe Noire port and the Congo-Ocean railroad operating to capacity provisioning troops and shipping out FEA's produce, further improved the colony's infrastructure and expanded its modern urban labor force.

The colonial reforms that followed at the end of the Second World War saw the abolition of forced labor, and the implementation of freedom of association, a uniform code of law, and elective institutions at three levels. Under the 1946 constitution, Moyen-Congo's restricted electorate, voting as separate colleges of European and African citizens, chose four representatives to the three parliamentary bodies of France, five to the Grand Council of FEA, and 30 to its own territorial assembly. Ten years later the *loi-cadre* (Enabling Act) of June 23, 1956 eliminated the dual-college system and the federal government-general, expanded the electorate to encompass all adult Congolese, and augmented the territorial assembly's economic and fiscal powers to include a share in the executive authority. The 45-man assembly elected in 1957 chose from its ranks the members of a new government council, whose vice-president became prime minister of Moyen-Congo in all but name.

In 1958, General de Gaulle's return to power in France accelerated Congo's political evolution via the referendum on a constitution for the Fifth French Republic, in which France's dependencies were asked to choose between maintaining the status quo, independence without further French aid, or membership as autonomous republics in a federal Franco-African Community. On September 28, Moyen-Congo recorded the highest proportion of affirmative votes (339,436) to negative ones in the FEA, and two months later its assembly voted to join the Community as the autonomous Congo Republic. On August 15, 1960, Congo took the final step of proclaiming its independence, after signing agreements for defense and cooperation with France.

The span of 14 years during which Congo moved from the status of a colony without any elective bodies to a sovereign state was too short for the development of more than nominally democratic institutions. Inevitably, Congo's first constitutions, political parties, and labor unions were based on French models, though they were progressively "Congolized" as ties with France loosened. Congo's constitution of March 2, 1961, did not survive the downfall of its author, President Fulbert Youlou; the constitution of December 8, 1963, sponsored by his successor, Massamba-Debat, was likewise replaced by the Fundamental Act of August 14, 1968 after Marien Ngouabi's coup d'etat; on June 24, 1973 the latter set up a People's Republic with different structures, and when the experiment came to an end under Sassou-Nguesso in 1992, a new constitution, Congo's current one, was again promulgated and ratified by referendum.

In like manner the parties that emerged during the postwar decade were in reality ethnic and regional groupings, with today's more numerous political groupings likewise reflecting ethnic and regional sentiments. In all elections between 1946 and 1956, the large Lari clan of the Bakongo (centered around the Brazzaville region, and one of the most modern groups in the country) either refused to participate electorally or inscribed on the ballots the name of their dead messianic leader, André Matsoua, expecting him to return to restore their former ascendancy over other Congolese groups, Kongo and non-Kongo. Their political abstention left the field open for the rise to political paramountcy of the country's two other ethnically-based parties, of approximately equal strength, that dominated the Congolese political scene until 1956. These were Felix Tchicaya's PPC, coalescing the Vili of the Pointe Noire area, and Jacques Opangault's MSA, that grouped the northern Mbochi. The support Tchicaya received by the powerful inter-territorial RDA more than offset that given to Opangault by the French Socialist party, so that the PPC had an edge over its rival until 1956. But in that year, a defrocked Lari priest, Fulbert Youlou, convinced his fellow kinsmen that he was Matsoua's political and religious heir, winning their allegiance for his new party, the UDDIA.

The Civilian Era: Youlou and Massamba-Debat

It took four years, marked by acute interethnic strife, for Youlou to eliminate his rivals either by force or by bribery and to become successively vice-president of the government council (1958) and president of the republic (1959). During this time he overtly and consistently favored the Lari over all other ethnic groups in the country, showed his disdain for Northerners, and even suggested that Northern Congo might possibly better belong within an expanded Central African Republic.

Youlou, moreover, had no economic plan for dealing with the country's flagging economy, and his government was both venal and corrupt. He became absorbed in unpopular foreign ventures that antagonized his neighbors, was obsessed by fear of Communism, and rapidly alienated the burgeoning youth in Congo's urban centers with his pro-French, ultra-conservative policies, and corrupt administration. Youlou's attempt to establish total paramountcy in Congo through the creation of a single political party and a single trade union confederation dominated by the Lari united against him all ethnic and ideological opposition, and finally spelled his doom. In August 1963 large demonstrations in Brazzaville, spearheaded by labor leaders and unemployed youths, for three days paralyzed all government activity.

With Youlou's fledgling armed forces (still commanded by French officers) refusing to support him by dispersing the mobs, and De Gaulle in Paris unwilling to rescue his administration, what was later to be sanctified as Congo's greatest civil holiday, "Le Trois Glorieuses"—the three days of urban unrest—finally brought about Youlou's resignation. Placed under house arrest, he was in due course spirited out of the country by supporters in the gendarmerie. Refused asylum by France, he settled in Spain, where he was eventually to die. In the interim a Conseil National de la Révolution (CNR) government was set up headed by the Bakongo Alphonse Massamba-Debat, a former schoolteacher, Socialist and former Youlou minister who had acquired a rare reputation for moral probity by resigning from the cabinet over Youlou's policies.

Massamba-Debat's government of largely apolitical technocrats in many ways marked a far sharper break with the past than did Youlou's with the colonial administration. Massamba-Debat deliberately set Congo on a new course of closer relations with the Socialist bloc; imposed state control over organized labor and segments of trade, transport, and natural resources; and established domination of the government by the new single party, the Mouvement National de la Révolution (MNR). He was careful, however, not to alienate the West, whose flow of technical and financial aid was vital to Congo; or to antagonize private investors by nationalizing existing business enterprises; or to permit the MNR's extremist elements, who had formed paramilitary groups, to estrange the armed forces. In essence Massamba-Debat engaged in an increasingly difficult balancing act for over three years, allowing radicals (including his own Prime Ministers) to freely express their Socialist vituperations, while pursuing in fact relatively moderate policies. This policy of "rhetoric-reality" was to become in many ways the hallmark of Congolese policy until the onset of "normalization" in the 1990's.

Massamba-Debat came to power sustained by a wide coalition of forces, all claiming to be Marxist or nationalist, but whose sole common ground was opposition to Youlou. Within a few weeks, riots and violence at Brazzaville, perpetrated by armed youths and some army officers whose targets were the Lari and Western businessmen, indicated the regime's authority was weak. To restore order and win the support of radical youth and labor leaders, Massamba-Debat forcibly merged them into single organizations called, respectively, the Jeunesse du Mouvement National de la Révolution (JMNR) and the Confédération Syndicale Congolaise (CSC). He made both the JMNR and CSC branches of the single party. In so doing, however, he in reality allowed extremists to effectively absorb and take over the Catholic labor unions, mission schools, and youth groups, and to form a militia and a civil defense corps that rapidly became competitive with the armed forces.

Massamba-Debat's decision to allow Cuban military instructors to train not only Congo's paramilitary forces, but also guerrilla groups planning to overthrow the governments of neighboring Cameroun, Angola, and Congo-Kinshasa, increasingly strained Congo's international relations with these countries, and especially the latter. Indeed, in retaliation Mobutu allowed Massamba-Debat's Lari and Youlouist opponents to use Kinshasa as a staging base for armed raids against Brazzaville, just across the river. The numerous commando attacks that ensued over the years were abortive, but each served to undermine Massamba-Debat's authority, to strengthen demands by MNR militants for a radicalization of the "revolution" under "scientific socialism," and to eliminate Lari conservatives in the administration and gendarmerie.

Despite very strident left-wing pressure on him, Congo remained a member of both the UAM and the UDEAC, and negotiated new aid treaties with the EEC and with Israel. Counterbalancing these, Congo accepted large loans from the Soviet Union, China and other Communist states. To redress Congo's disastrous financial situation Massamba-Debat did all he could to encourage large-scale foreign private investments such as those that eventually were attracted into potash mining (at Hollé), and in developing sugar plantations (SIAN). He also tried to eliminate some of the economic inequities that were one cause of ethnic antagonisms in the country, but was unable to move much to appreciably alleviate the grievances of the peasantry or of the urban unemployed that had been so instrumental in creating the revolutionary context that propelled him to power.

Indeed, most state enterprises that were set up in fields not directly competitive with private enterprises were from outset total financial failures because Congo lacked adequate indigenous cadres, experience, organization and monitoring personnel to assure their efficiency. They rapidly became deficitory, distinguished primarily by their overbloated personnel rolls, and bouts of embezzlement. Massamba-Debat was well aware that pruning or closing them down was ideologically (in a Socialist country) impossible, and, within the context of a country with few employment options, playing with fire. In like manner the heavily overstaffed civil service was largely left untouched (and, indeed, was grossly expanded later when the North rose to political imminence), setting the pattern for three decades of unsustainable State expenditures on nonproductive sectors of society that finally brought the Congolese economy to its knees.

Personally lacking both charisma and a firm ethnic or regional political base, and too realistic and intellectually honest to act demagogically, Massamba-Debat, and what were perceived as his half-measures, failed to satisfy either conservatives or radicals in Congo. He was progressively marginalized, loosing the reigns of power. He juggled the various factions in the MNR by frequently reshuffling his government, promoting and demoting leaders of various groups. But the JMNR and paramilitary gained such ascendance over the party, taunting the army as "un-revolutionary" that in June 1966 the armed forces' Kouyou troops mutinied.

A compromise was reached between the military and the government, and the JMNR was reined in until December 1967, when Massamba-Debat was forewarned that its leaders were preparing a coup d'etat. Convinced now that no *modus vivendi* with the intransigent radicals was possible, Massamba-Debat moved sharply to the right. His regime became more oppressive and arbitrary, and when in July 1968 he arrested the popular Kouyou paratrooper commander, Captain Marien Ngouabi, for subversive activities, the army's opposition was added to that of his ideological opponents. Militant students and other youthful radicals, in conjunction with the army, sparked demonstrations that led to Massamba-Debat's downfall exactly five years after Youlou had been overthrown. Realizing that he lacked the support required to re-establish his authority, Massamba-Debat resigned as president of the Republic, to leave his mutually antagonistic adversaries to fight over the succession. By the end of August 1968 the army under Marien Ngouabi had won in a brief but violent trial of strength with the JMNR, and a Northern military government succeeded the previous ones of Lari and Bakongo civilians. Northern military and political supremacy was to last for the next twenty-four years.

The Ngouabi Era

Ngouabi's rule rested primarily on (a) his control of the largely Northern armed forces, aggravated by a decade of Southern rule, (b) his personal charisma, that tied the different ethnic strands within the armed forces together, preventing the kind of falling apart between the Mbochi and the Kouyou that was to develop after his death, and (c) the more stridently radical ideology he enunciated that appealed to many of the more volatile groups in the country at the time. But it is important to note, along the rhetoric-reality point made earlier, that personal loyalty to him (and later to his successor, Sassou-Nguesso), and considerations relating to the stability of the regime always took precedence over ideology or Socialist rectitude, something that explains the zigzag course of the Congolese "revolution."

Ngouabi had concluded that only a radical single party based on Marxist-Leninist principles could bridge the conflicts between Congo's ethnic groups and build a strong state based on scientific socialism. On December 30, 1969, a Fundamental Act created a new single Parti Congolais du Travail (PCT), complete with its mass organizations for youth, women, and labor, structured like the MNR. Under its aegis the country's name was changed to the People's Republic of the Congo and its official policy was proclaimed to be Marxism-Leninism. In another radical step, also designed to placate the hard-core left, Ngouabi nationalized the SIA-CONGO company, which was widely viewed by Congolese as a symbol of neocolonialism.

Virtually simultaneously Congo adopted its third constitution since independence, increasing the president's powers. The next day, January 4, 1970, Ngouabi was sworn in as head of state for five years and also as head of the PCT central committee, with Alfred Raoul, a loyal officer from Cabinda head of the state council. The dual executive system introduced by Massamba-Debat's constitution of December 8, 1963 was perpetuated, but the former distinction between party and government was abolished, as were existing elective bodies, and considerable changes were made in the local administration. The government of President Ngouabi and Vice-President Ange Poungui and the twelve heads of its major services was clearly subordinated to a 40-member PCT central committee and its five-man politburo. Party militants had already gained control of the civil service, and the legislature was a rubber stamp for the executive.

All politically conscious Congolese, including Ngouabi (who, based on an examination of his early speeches knew little on the subject) proclaimed themselves Marxist-Leninists, as all the outward trappings and nomenclature of a People's Republic were decreed and implemented. The stated goal of the regime was to make Congo truly economically and politically independent of "neo-colonialism" and free from the control of foreign capitalists. This was seen as attainable by renouncing Massamba-Debat's "half-hearted" approaches and developing a greater and more sincere alignment with the East, a further diversification of the country's sources of international aid, a more systematic nationalization of the means of production, and the erection of a multitude of new State enterprises especially aimed at reviving peasant agriculture and regionally redistributing economic development, catering to perennial urban unemployment, addressing social and gender issues, and developing the country's infrastructure to better bind the country together. (Until the early 1980's when the first paved roads were built, communications between Brazzaville and with the North were difficult or impossible except by river or air.)

Because Ngouabi was operating from a different ethnic base and had the army's support, he was able to move further and faster along the Socialist path originally charted by Massamba-Debat. Initially he also used many of the same individuals and institutions as had his predecessor, but progressively discarded them when they no longer served to consolidate his power and indeed threatened to undermine it. In December 1968, for example, the two Lari ministers were dropped from the government, accused of subversive activities. Others cabinet leftovers from the Massamba-Debat era were replaced with personally loyal (and notably non-Marxist!) military officers (such as Captains Raoul and Yhomby-Opango), efficient civilians (such as Nzé, Lopes), or leftist leaders with significant sway among students, youth, labor, and the armed forces (Ndalla, Diawara, Lekounzou). Some of these were to turn against him (notably Diawara), citing the same charges made against Massamba-Debat—ideological insincerity.

As for the political institutions inherited from the preceding regime, the CSC's structure was retained but its elected leaders were replaced by handpicked party men in 1968; the MNR and CNR respectively, became the PCT and its central committee in 1969, and in the latter year the JMNR was renamed the UJSC, after its militia (along with the civil-defense corps) had been absorbed into the regular army and thus placed under military subordination. Some of the changes were triggered by Ngouabi's suspicions of disloyalty of his appointees while others were prompted by actual plots against him (e.g., the commando raid of March 1970; the Diawara abortive putsch of February 1971; the UGEEC strike of November 1971, etc.).

Ngouabi easily survived the threats posed by organized labor and by the Lari conservative and Youlouist Mouzabakany, Kolelas, and Kikanga, during the period that has been referred to as "the era of permanent plots." But the neutralization of his conservative opposition by early 1971 made him more vulnerable to attacks from his "Maoist" opponents, especially those from former paramilitary leaders who had been absorbed into the armed forces and also held key posts in the government and party (Diawara, Ndalla, Noumazalaye), that were by far more dangerous to his political hegemony.

In November 1971, the army subdued student strikers in Brazzaville and Pointe Noire, and the Maoist faction of the PCT was largely purged in December of that year. Two months later its leading theoretician, Lieutenant Ange Diawara, mounted a cunning putsch that failed only due to the unswerving personal loyalty to Ngouabi of the "rightist" Major Yhomby-Opango, who for his efforts was rewarded with the highest rank in the Congolese army. After failing to overthrow the People's Republic, which he accused of resting on an ethnically based army and conservative administrative bourgeoisie, Diawara and some of his key lieutenants were able to elude arrest for fourteen months, indicating the Ngouabi regime, for all its ability to ward off armed attacks, had numerous dedicated domestic foes.

Although all the plotters were eventually tracked down and killed, including in due course Diawara, their left-wing origin caused Ngouabi to devise ways to counter the appeal of Congolese radical extremists while making his administration more populist. A new constitution was promulgated on June 24, 1973, in which an elective national assembly of 115 members was reinstated, the former state council reappeared as a ministerial cabinet, and the post of prime minister was created. The June 24, 1973 constitution restored the distinction between government and party, though the PCT not only kept intact its authority as the country's sole policymaking body, but added to it that of selecting candidates for election to the legislature and also to the new local councils. Henri Lopes proved to be an adroit Prime Minister who had influence with the PCT cadres and enough army support to enforce the party's decisions. By scrapping the authoritarian 1970 constitution and replacing it with one that combined the principle of popular elections at the central and local-government levels with strict party controls, lip service was paid to democratic procedures, the rural population again participated in the process of government (if only to a limited degree), and the PCT's authority remained intact.

Elections for the Congo's second national assembly since 1963 were duly held, and new faces appeared in the Lopes government of August 26, 1973. An amnesty saw the return to Brazzaville of many political exiles such as Gilbert Pongault. And new revenues that began to flow into the treasury from the recently productive offshore oil deposits allowed a stabilization of the regime through more popular policies such as more rapid industrialization, the forced Congolization of all personnel in local trading firms, and a decree that Congo would accept foreign investments and technicians only in selected areas pending their replacement by Congolese funds and cadres. Yet despite these reforms, ongoing radical-conservative, northern-southern and civil-military tug-of-war underscored the tenuous nature of Ngouabi's base of support. Ngouabi's efforts to further consolidate the regime's legitimacy possibly through a swing to the right, further civilianization and/or a sharing of power with Southerners (the precise causes are still not fully known), adequately alarmed a section of the armed forces leading to a plot in which a military suicide squad assassinated him in 1977.

Yhomby-Opango and Sassou-Nguessou

The immediate aftermath of Ngouabi's assassination saw the mysterious liquidation, by different factions, of all those individuals directly involved in Ngouabi's killing and of those who were in contact with him just prior to his death (e.g. Cardinal Biayenda, who was abducted and murdered). Two trials, the first one of which (a court-martial) took place in great haste, saw Massamba-Debat's rapid condemnation and execution for Ngouabi's murder, allegedly sealing the matter. But to this day, however, most accusations lay the blame for Ngouabi's assassination at the door of Denis Sassou-Nguesso and a group of military hard-liners, who were allegedly unwilling to see their individual, and/or the army's, center-stage role in power diluted, and Northern hegemony in Congo arrested. Indeed, in the 1990's, after the civilianization of Congo, the same charges resurfaced in public in the national assembly.

However that may be, Ngouabi's successor, chosen in April 1977 by the PCT after a tug-of-war, was Yhomby-Opango, the most senior officer in the army, well-known for his easy-going life and lack of commitment to anything resembling Marxism-Leninism. In reality, however, a troika was set up, in which Yhomby-Opango was hemmed in by his Vili (i.e. Southerner, and hence not a real threat) Prime Minister Major Sylvain Goma, and Denis Sassou-Nguesso. Two years later, Yhomby-Opango, who—nicknamed "the Czar of M'Pila" after the quarter where he lived—had become extremely widely detested in southern urban centers for his pro-French policies and hedonistic personal excesses (including a private zoo of exotic animals), and whose tenure coincided with a downturn in the Congolese economy, was surprisingly easily, and bloodlessly, unseated by Sassou-Nguesso. Yhomby-Opango was subsequently dismissed from the PCT party, demoted to the ranks (though in due course rehabilitated), had his property confiscated, and he was also placed under house arrest. The latter was necessary because, though clearly his personal stock was low and the more sophisticated, debonair, and radical Sassou-Nguesso was the overwhelming choice of the PCT, a growing Kouyou-Mbochi split in the armed forces (to become more serious subsequently) had created an opening that Yhomby-Opango's Mbochi origins could tap.

Sassou-Nguesso immediately proceeded to satisfy the radical wing of the party by a renewal of Leftist policies ignored for long, including forging tighter relations with most Communist nations. Cuba in particular came to play a larger role, providing Sassou-Nguesso with a large praetorian guard that on several instances alerted him of plots in the armed forces and even helped quell them. (He also fell into the habit of wearing a bullet-proof vest beneath his Pierre Cardin suits.) Cuba also used Congo as its rear base for its large expeditionary force in Angola, something that alarmed both South Africa and the United States. He also gave a powerful thrust to basic and cherished Congolese planks that greatly solidified his reign—improving the country's communications network (especially paving the trunk road North from Brazzaville); attempting to revitalize conditions in the countryside in an effort to arrest the monumental population drift into cities, and especially Brazzaville; commencing an extremely ambitious Five Year Plan that greatly expanded the State sector and civil service; and re-invigorating the PCT and party control of the countryside, all policies that though "Socialist" had the additional sweet portent of the creation of thousands of new jobs, and huge governmental expenditures that were indeed forthcoming.

Such extravagant outlays were possible due to a major upswing that developed in global oil prices, and Congo's progressively higher output of crude oil, that brought into the Congolese treasury large unanticipated oil-revenues. This also allowed the mending of the always turbulent aid-related Franco-Congolese relations. Indeed in October 1980 Congo "celebrated" in pomp, with the French Ambassador as Dean of the diplomatic corps, the centenary of its colonization, a fact that brought a stern rebuke from the Soviet Union about the inappropriate nature of the event being celebrated.

Yet, notwithstanding Congo's increasingly doctrinaire Socialist policies, including *inter alia* a new constitution (in July 1979) that for the first time formally institutionalized Marxism, and legislation placing *all* of the country's resources under national control, the rhetoric emanating from Brazzaville was completely negated by the reality that existing risk capital in the country's prime industries—oil and timber—*virtually the only ones profitable,* remained foreign.

As in the previous decade, sharp vicissitudes of global oil market prices played havoc with Congolese finances. Inevitably after the boom years that brought massive unanticipated revenue bonanzas, came the bust years of major fiscal shortfalls. And again as in the Ngouabi era, the regime was caught grossly unprepared and over-extended, with an onerous and unmanageable wage-bill for a bloated civil service, huge annual operating deficits on its State enterprises, and numerous costly developmental projects half-completed. (The regime nevertheless decided to continue one of the costliest—paving the North-South artery, a pet Northern plank.) And as in yesteryear the financial calamity that threatened to greatly contract the economy demanded a search for external scapegoats, for clearly there was a "conspiracy" aimed at preventing Congo's economic independence—international capitalism, France, the foreign oil companies, etc.

However this time the quest for ideological scapegoats was simply not enough. The much larger Congolese civil service and over-extended economy could not weather the crisis without massive fiscal infusions or severe pruning. A desperate attempt to avoid falling into the clutches of the IMF/World Bank by imposing internal austerity via a "domestic" structural adjustment (including pay-cuts) proved both inadequate and impossible to execute with the labor movement, youth, and party ideologues flexing their muscles. In 1986 the civil service numbered 73,000 workers (a quarter of the labor force!), up from the 3,300 in Youlou's days and the 25,000 in Ngouabi's, and this not counting some 20,000 members of the parastatals, party, and armed forces. The number of state employees was also increasing annually, with university students routinely joining the civil service on graduation, an established tradition. There were now also eight-five State enterprises (the vast majority deficitory) in contrast to the sixty-odd at the time of Ngouabi's assassination, and the budget deficit consumed around 18% of the GDP, with the *accumulated* Congolese foreign debt in 1980 matching the country's GDP (to double and become the highest per capita in the world by 1990). Already by the mid-1980s some parastatals had closed down as the State's parlous finances afforded no succor. Congo had no choice but to turn to the IMF, signing its first agreement in July 1986, pledging to cut the national budget by half and privatizing the economy—pledges clearly it had neither the resolve nor ability to execute. Indeed right into the mid-1990's neither the budget, civil service nor state sector was pruned to the degree deemed necessary by the World Bank.

The crumbling and eventual collapse of the Congolese economy led to the erosion of the regime itself. A very reluctant Sassou-Nguesso and PCT dismantled Congolese Marxism-Leninism (that in 1989 lost its global mentor), the single party State and military rule in 1990–1992, directly eliminating the northern political hegemony that had reigned since Massamba-Debat's ouster in 1968. Robbed of the glue of patronage Sassou-Nguesso's regime suffered numerous assaults against its legitimacy. The Vili, Bateke, and progressively other groups strained at Northern *de facto* political hegemony; the large Bakongo and Lari groups were already alienated, completely marginalized in the political system, including in Brazzaville that now had large northern population concentrations; the issue of the true conspirators behind Ngouabi's assassination (allegedly including Sassou-Nguesso)—always not far from the political surface—re-emerged in the form of Captain's Anga's armed revolt, that led to many deaths and arrests, and underscored the final rupture of the Kouyou-Mbochi alliance in the armed forces.

On July 4, 1990 the PCT abandoned Marxism-Leninism, transformed itself into a mass party of all political persuasions, and announced that the government would move to multipartyism. Aware of the North's minority status, and the many enemies made during the lengthy military era, Sassou-Nguesso attempted to control the pace of reform, and its outcome, by prevarications and delaying tactics. This was thwarted when the CSC—by now virtually autonomous of the government—declared a general strike, forcing the immediate legalization of political parties and accelerated preparations for a national conference to decide Congo's political future. Intermittent strikes became a regular pattern now, mostly over basic bread and butter issues, forcing the completely powerless government to concede wage increases and to halt the restructuring of the State sector, efforts that inevitably held the prospects of mass layoffs and/or closures.

Over a hundred political parties were formed in anticipation for the national conference that finally took place in February 1991. Though a good number of these parties were personalist and/or ephemeral groupings, some fifty proved their staying powers. The conference, convening under the "neutral" Chair of the Bishop of Owando, lasted three months (rather than the originally scheduled two weeks), proceeded to declare itself sovereign, and acted as a constitutional convention. Sassou-Nguesso was roundly lambasted for corruption, mismanagement, and he was moreover publicly accused of complicity in Ngouabi's murder, and of scores of others including those associated with the brutal putting down of Captain Anga's 1987 rebellion. (Towards the end of the conference a repentant Sassou-Nguesso apologized for all "errors" committed under his aegis.) The conference concluded its sessions with the election of André Milongo, a former World Bank official as interim head of government until the scheduled local, legislative, and presidential elections of mid-1992.

The period leading up to the elections, the elections themselves, and their aftermath cogently attest how little has changed in Congo since colonial days. Over a dozen presidential hopefuls, and a large number of parties—ethnic, regional and personalist—contested the elections, often in the form of electoral compacts. Ethnicity and regionalism remained the prime polarizing feature of Congo, with every ethnic group closing ranks behind "its" ethnic or regional candidate or party. Three major political formations emerged: (a) Pascal Lissouba, who was eventually elected President, coalesced behind his candidacy and his party alliance (UPADS) the growing political and economic weight of the non-Lari southwest, defeating the (b) PCT's Sassou-Nguesso, who retained his favorite-son role in the North (though ceding the Kouyou vote, now alienated, to Yhomby-Opango and his political formation) and (c) Bernard Kolelas who, to some extent using Matsouanist symbols, won over the Brazzaville region Lari vote to his MCDDI party.

And, as if to underscore how pragmatic political alliances can be, the Lari's "loss" of the presidency resulted in a powerful *de-facto* legislative (and military) coalition between Kolelas (eventually Mayor of Brazzaville) and his former tormentor Sassou Nguesso, while Lissouba, trying to project a "national" coalition, has joined forces with, *inter alia,* the Kouyou under Yhomby-Opango, who now serves as Prime Minister of Congo!

All is not well in Congo today, however. Since civilianization Sassou-Nguesso remains in his native North surrounded with the rump of a personally loyalist army, leaving President Lissouba the task of creating a new security force, while in Brazzaville Kolelas has also organized youthful Bakongo into armed militias to defend his turf. Right through 1995 intermittent but at times fierce battles have been fought in downtown Brazzaville between these three forces, popularly named Cobras, Ninjas and Zoulous. In the economic domain also, the country is barely limping. Some state companies have been sold to foreign investors, whose first act, fiercely resisted by unionists, has been to trim manpower by 60%, underscoring the degree to which they had in the past served as tools of social (rather than economic) policy (averting unemployment). Others have simply shut down, while others resist, with vociferous union pressures for government restructuring. Neither the civil service, the budget or its massive deficits, nor levels of fraud have been trimmed anywhere near the degree demanded by overseas donors, with Congo surviving fiscally only due to large French subventions. Shortages are endemic, the State has been unable to regularly meet its civil service payroll, or issue subsistence grants to its university students, triggering intermittent urban unrest. In 1995, indeed, the regime closed down all ministerial checking accounts in an effort to curb routine unauthorized overexpenditures that were thwarting fiscal discipline. The country has thus a long way to go yet before it can attain either economic or political stability.

The Dictionary

-A-

ABIBI, DANIEL, 1942– . Former minister of higher education and Rector of Marien Ngouabi University. A Mbochi born on March 13, 1942 in Allad in the Sangha region, Abibi studied at Souanké and Brazzaville before going to France for his higher education. He attended the University of Grenoble completing his PhD in Mathematics, following which he taught at the University of Paris (1975–78) and University of Brazzaville (1978–79). An ally of Sassou Nguesso he was promptly promoted to rector of the university in 1979 and served in that capacity until 1983. During this period, as a militant PCT member, he was elected to the party's Central Committee, serving for a while as PCT secretary for foreign affairs. During the period 1979–1984 he was also Cultural Advisor to the Head of State, and joined the cabinet as minister of Information (1983–84) and secondary and higher education (1984–85), partly to solidify support in Sangha behind the regime. Though dropped from the cabinet he remained in the Central Committee and was PCT secretary for education since 1984.

ADADA, RODOLPHE. Former cabinet minister. A Mbochi from the north, Adada first came into prominence in February 1976 when he was appointed head of the newly created department of scientific research and member of the state council with the rank of cabinet minister. In January 1977 he joined the government as minister of mines and energy, retaining his post as head of scientific research until 1984.

ADMINISTRATIVE ORGANIZATION. Congo is divided administratively into nine regions and 45 districts and communes. The regions and districts (with regional headquarters in brackets) are *Kouilou* (Pointe Noire), with the districts of Madingo-Kayes, Mvouti, Loandulu; *Niari* (Loubomo), with the districts of Divinié, Mayoko, Kibangou, Mossendjo, Loubomo, Kimonko; *Lékoumou* (Sibiti), with the districts of Komono, Bambama, Zananga, Sibit; *Bouénza* (Madingou), with the districts of Loudima, NKayi, Madingou, Mouyondzi,

19

Boco-Songo, Mfouati; *Pool* (Kinkala), with the districts of Kindamba, Mayama, Ngabe, Mindouli, Kinkala, Ngamaba, Boko; *Cuvette* (Owando), with the districts of Mbomo, Kelle, Makoua, Ewo, Boundji, Owando, Mossaka, Loukolele, Okoyo; *Plateaux* (Djambala), with the districts of Abala, Lekana, Djambala, Gamboma; *Sangha* (Ouesso), with the districts of Souanké, Sembé, Ouesso; and *Likouala* (Impfondo), with the districts of Dongou, Epena, Impfondo. The regions are corporate entities, with financial autonomy. During the PCT era, each region was administered by elected people's councils, and the PCT was also represented by political commissars.

AFIA. See KYEBE-KYEBE.

AFRIQUE ÉQUATORIALE AFRICAINE (AEF). French Equatorial Africa, one of France's two colonial federations (the other being French West Africa, AOF). The AEF was constituted on June 26, 1908, originally composed of Moyen Congo, Gabon and "Oubangui-Chari-Tchad," with, at the federal level a Governor General in Brazzaville, assisted by a nominated government council, with a monopoly of civil and military power, and Lt. Governors aided by nominated administrative councils in each of the constituent territories. Over time the boundaries of the AEF changed (e.g. after the 1911 major Franco-German territorial adjustments; as a result of the first world war); as well as those of its constituent parts, as when Chad emerged in 1920 as a separate colony. Moreover, during the global recession the AEF's population (3 million) was judged too small to merit a top-heavy administration and between 1930 and 1937 the AEF became a unitary colony with 20 departments (in 1936 increased to 34) grouped into regions (conforming to the former federated territories). After WW II territorial assemblies were set up in each colony providing (progressively enhanced) elected representation for Africans via a double electoral college, leading to universal single-roll franchise in 1956. See also FRENCH EQUATORIAL AFRICA, GOVERNORS OF.

AGENCE CONGOLAISE D'INFORMATION (ACI). Congo's official information agency, that issues a daily news bulletin and several number of other publications. In the late 1980's severe fiscal austerity caused the agency to stop most publications, including its daily, for 19 months, recommencing operations only in May 1989. Scheduled for privatization, in mid-1994 the cash-strapped Congolese government instead decided to close down four other publications, leaving the ACI as the sole news publisher in the country.

AGENCE TRANSCONGOLAISE DES COMMUNICATIONS (ATC). In 1959, the four territories of the A.E.F. created an Agence

Transequatoriale des Communications (ATEC), that was placed under a board of directors responsible for managing the communications network for the common benefit of member states. ATEC was charged with managing the railroad in Congo (CFCO) running from Brazzaville to Pointe Noire (and the link to the outside world for the Central African Republic, and, until recently, an evacuation route for Gabonese manganese through Congo, and southern Chad trade via Bangui), the Congolese Atlantic port of Pointe Noire and the river ports of Brazzaville and Bangui that are linked by barges plying the Congo and Oubangui rivers.

With the rise of a more militant regime in Congo, Brazzaville unilaterally revoked the agreement in October 1969 and nationalized ATEC assets in its territory, placing them under a new national organization, the Agence Transcongolaise des Communications (ATC), under the overall responsibility of the Congolese ministry of transport and public works. After prolonged negotiations, the nationalizations were reluctantly accepted by the former ATEC member-states, with ATC buying out some private companies (such as the CGTAE, CFHBC, Messageries Fluviales, MVC, and SEN, or absorbing what had previously been neighboring territories' organizations), ending up with overall control and responsibility for coordinating riverine/rail services of vital interest to Congo's neighbors, and coordinating communication links with Zaire. ATC has expanded the three monopolies it acquired over CFCO, the port of Pointe Noire, and the navigable waterways and river ports, but has not excluded private companies from using the Congolese rivers and ports.

Between 1970 and 1975, the ATC invested 32.5 billion CFA francs, and even larger sums in the subsequent decade, from its own resources, from funds provided by the EEC and the World Bank. Its activities consisted of building, expanding, and improving river ports, the CFCO, and the key outlet to the Atlantic Ocean, the port of Pointe Noire. It also spent considerable resources in improving transport services and training railroad personnel. By 1980 the ATC was carrying half of the more than 220,000 tons of interstate river traffic, and the combined tonnages of the CFCO and Comilog railroads (linking Gabon with the CFCO in Congo), from which it derived up to 80 percent of its local resources. ATC's revenues have fluctuated over the years, depending upon the amounts and kinds of freight carried (exports, mostly timber from the C.A.R., agricultural products, and mineral products, including large amounts of manganese from Gabon; imports, for domestic use and especially for the R.C.A., of food, fuel, and manufactured goods), with on the whole, surpluses accruing on its running operations' budget.

Though considered for some time as one of the better-managed Congolese state enterprises, the reality was quite different. For the

ATC, controlled by Brazzaville, too large to be effectively monitored, and influenced by powerful unionists, suffered from many of the same profligate and overstaffing policies practiced in other state companies, especially where the railroad was concerned. Maintenance and technical innovations (except in the port of Pointe Noire) were deferred or ignored, salary hikes and an increasing labor force were financially covered by increases in haulage and transshipment charges passed on to Gabon, Chad and the CAR, and operating deficits increased, and got out of hand. In 1933, for example, the losses amounted to one billion CFAF, and the company's inefficiency was threatening the viability of the important timber sector of northern Congo.

In the mid-1980's Congo entered a prolonged period of increasingly severe liquidity and budgetary crisis (that continues to this day) that reduced funds that could be allocated from the Congolese budget for state companies including the ATC. (In 1994 the ATC budget had to be sharply slashed, repercussions notwithstanding, from its 1993 sum of 32 billion CFAF to 24.5 billion.) This coincided with the absolute necessity of the ATC to mount costly much-postponed maintenance, renovation and new railbed construction on the by-now rundown CFCO, where major delays and hauling blockages had become the norm, with hundreds of thousands of tons stockpiled waiting shipment at both Pointe Noire and Brazzaville. The ATC was also faced by the imminent loss of a major source of revenue as Gabon neared completion of its own Transgabonaise railroad that would syphon the huge tonnage of manganese ore hitherto passing through the CFCO to Gabon's own port of Owando.

As early as 1986, and again in 1988, the regime in Brazzaville considered breaking up the ATC into its component parts, and involving private capital in some, in order to promote greater accountability and efficiency. Such trial balloons were strongly resisted by organized labor. In the interim the ATC proceeded with some maintenance and construction work lest the entire communications system grind to a complete halt. Costly new rail had to be laid to bypass (and provide a short-cut) a section of the original track running through rough country that the ageing trains could no longer traverse except at snail's pace. However many of the CFCO's 28 locomotives were functionally inoperative for technical reasons, standing idle while 14,000 tons of goods waited shipment (in 1993) in Pointe Noire and 200,000 cubic meters of timber in Brazzaville (for over two years). (And, to operate a normal service at least 54 locomotives were needed.) The problem of barge traffic along the river connecting Brazzaville and upriver ports and ultimately Bangui, always unreliable and slow (especially in the dry season or periods of drought when parts of the Oubangui were too shallow to allow navigation), also called for a solution since six month delays in the arrival of imports were intolerable to land-locked Central African Republic. (In 1993 Congo took delivery of some hydrofoils to service urgent upriver needs.) By January 1993, with four of Congo's eight northern logging companies either operating at lower capacity or actually closed down, the regime was apprised that unless an urgent overhaul and streamlining of the ATC (and in particular the CFCO) were undertaken, all evacuation of timber from north Congo might grind to a halt. Measures to that end were again mounted later that year, calling for a measure of privatization.

AGENCE TRANSEQUATORIALE DES COMMUNICATION (ATEC). See AGENCE TRANSCONGOLAISE DES COMMUNICATION (ATC).

AGIP RECHERCHES CONGO. Subsidiary of the Italian oil giant AGIP, with a 20% Congo state equity. The company is one of the two major explorers and producers of oil in Congo. See also PETROLEUM.

AGRICULTURE. More than half of Congo's total surface is covered by equatorial forest, and about one third consists of poor, sandy soil. Of the area considered arable, only about 55 percent is actually cultivated. Agriculture accounts for less than 10 percent of GNP. And although some 40 percent of the population is still engaged in farming and related activities, foodstuffs are one of Congo's main imports at an astronomical cost.

The disaffection of farmers with agriculture has multiple causes. Some of these include the fact that only meager profits are possible from the sale of crops, whose yield is small and of mediocre quality because of antiquated farming methods and the primitive equipment used. There is also the problem of transport and evacuation of rural produce to major urban centers (where high prices are obtainable) via rough track or slow and unreliable river transport, something only prioritized by the government in the early 1980's when flush with oil-royalties some major advances were made. Moreover, agriculture is practiced primarily by women and older men, since for five decades youth has been deserting the countryside in one of the largest rural-urban exoduses in Africa. (It is estimated that at current levels by the year 2000 fully 70% of the population will reside in urban areas.) They flock to the southern towns (especially Brazzaville, that is literally bursting at its seams) or regional centers, where civil service and parastatal jobs are theoretically available, and even if not, where life is at least more amenable than in the countryside where (especially in the north) transport by dugout canoe is still common. Farming is also universally associated with traditional life, not with modernity. Only on state farms and in export-oriented agro-industrial enterprises are modern cultivation techniques employed, livable wages obtainable, and intermittently some agricultural advances, fleeting as they may be, made. The net result is that in 1995, despite massive expenditures in capital, little of much import has transpired in Congo's agriculture. Production levels of staple crops have only kept apace with population growth, but reach urban areas in such small quantities (being consumed in rural areas) that Congo even has to import from neighboring states commodities produced by her own farmers in tens or hundreds of thousands of tons. When it comes to cash crops, while some have grown in tonnage, this has as often as not been followed by subsequent sharp declines, piling up deficits on costly State processing plants forced to remain idle, or production levels have declined to levels below those attained during the colonial era. With a growing population estimated in 1994 at 2.42 million people, and ever-mushrooming urban growth needing foodstuffs, Congo finds itself both subsidizing a non-productive rural sector and importing over three-quarters of its foodstuffs. In 1990 the cost of the latter was over 45 billion CFAF.

Despite some concerted efforts, both during the colonial era and after it (especially by the Ngouabi regime), neither the rural-urban exodus, nor increased agricultural output have been attained. During the colonial era the administration organized the Sociétés de Prevoyance (STP), Sociétés Mutuelles du Développement Rural (SMDR), paysannats, and cooperative societies, as well as scientific research and agricultural stations. Four regions were chosen for the implementation of the 1947–52 plan for intensive development: the Sangha for cocoa, tobacco, and oil palms; the Bateke plateau for tobacco and mixed farming; Mayombe for bananas and cocoa; and the Niari valley for peanuts, cotton, fruit, food crops, and sugar cane. That plan's only notable success was in developing industrial crops in the Niari valley, which had several advantages to start with: unusual soil fertility; the Congo-Ocean railroad that ran through the valley (allowing for easy and fast evacuation of perishable crops); and the fact that initially involved in the cultivation were enterprising French immigrant farmers that attracted large-scale investments of French capital.

Since independence, successive Congolese governments have tried to exert more control over agriculture and make farming more productive and remunerative to Congolese peasants. A price-support fund for agricultural products was created in 1963; a monopoly of the sale of all crops produced in the north was given to a state organ, ONCPA; more state farms were formed and in 1964 a number of state companies engaged in agricultural products were formed.

Ever-increasing imports of foodstuffs continued in the 1970's through the 1990's though there were some improvements in certain local crops, especially those produced in large estates, such as sugar, cocoa, and coffee, though all, moving from depressed levels, soon stabilized, or fell back. Both the Ngouabi and the Sassou Nguesso regimes moved energetically to revitalize agricultural production, with the goal of self-sufficiency in foodstuffs, higher living standards for the rural population, and the expansion of crops for processing and export, but to no avail. In the 1980's an ambitious road paving program in the north was commenced (with several segments completed before the budgetary crisis cut it short), model farms were started (supplementing those at Mantsoumba and Kombe erected in the 1970's), and the state created experimental stations and nurseries for fruit trees (at Loudima), cocoa (at Elongo, Bondika, Mandou, and M'Foutou), oil palms (Ouesso, Oweno, and Sangha), and coffee (at Komoro).

However, all along Brazzaville's stress has been on export crops, with those in the Pool and Niari accorded greater attention, and those of Likouala and Lekousso the least. The traditional agrarian economy was not particularly targeted for massive upliftment; later, when more radical action was deemed necessary, only those regions producing lesser food crops but still with some export potential (peanuts) received any specific official encouragement until a "transitional program" for 1975–77. At the same time, however, some of the unusual obstacles to agrarian revitalization in Congo was underscored by the revelation that some 70% of the country's 1,400 agronomists and rural "animateurs," supposed to be in the field guiding and supervising agrarian activity, were instead permanently resident in Brazzaville; and their combined annual payroll and fringe benefits exceeded the entire agrarian output of the country.

As to consumption crops, tubers and root crops, plantain bananas, paddy, and corn, are the Congo's basic foods. Of the 160,000 hectares planted with these crops, 145,000 hectares are devoted to cassava, whose production has been rising at the rate of 3 percent a year, to roughly 800,000 tons. Produced in small family plots dispersed throughout the country, notably in the Pool region (where 26 percent of the total is grown), cassava is sold in very limited amounts to city dwellers, who increasingly prefer rice. On the other hand, two food crops encouraged by the government—potatoes and white beans— showed some production improvements, though the tonnage produced is objectively small. Banana production suffered sharply in the 1970s due to a plant disease, only recovering after a new variety was planted in southern Congo.

Peanuts fall into a special category because of their dual role as both a food, and as a source of edible oil. Peanuts were originally grown by four French mechanized companies, but now this is a Congolese crop. Strong government support in the late 1960's and early 1970's brought mixed results: failure in the Bateke plateau, but success in the Niari valley. Overall, after increasing fourfold between 1968 and 1971, production declined throughout the region the crop is planted, including in Bouenza, Niari, Lekoumou, and the Pool, where peanuts were grown on nearly 19,000 hectares by traditional methods and where they were also largely consumed. This has had repercussion on the Huilka mill (with a crushing capacity of 6,000 tons), that started recording major deficits as it worked at well below capacity. In 1981, for example, it produced only 1321 tons of oil, and soon had to be restructured and privatized.

In 1979 Sassou-Nguesso, disappointed with the mediocre results of the transitional 1975–77 program, created an Office des Cultures Vivrières (OCV) as the successor to ONCPA, that was dissolved in 1978. OCV was charged with the development of food crops by new methods, concentrating successively on increasing the production of corn, paddy, peanuts, beans, and potatoes by training farmers in new techniques, collecting their output, conducting campaigns against plant pests, reviving or building rice and oil mills, and promoting units of production destined to become cooperative societies. This ambitious mission of OCV was taken over by the government under the 1982–86 development plan and was given a subsidy of 2.3 billion CFA francs for its execution, but again in midstream the country's fiscal crisis caused the regime to terminate many scheduled expenditures. Export crops in any case followed the same melancholy history of growing local consumption and declining domestic production, despite successive price increases to growers in 1981–1987.

The 1982–86 development plan had tried to revive the output of the rural sector, targeting now oil palms and sugar cane. As early as 1946, SIAN had planted 50 hectares to cane near Loudima. This plantation was gradually extended, and by 1960 cane was grown on 2,400 hectares, and processed by SIAN's mill. Four years later, a bigger plantation was started and a refinery was built at Nkayi, by SIAN's subsidiary, SOSU-NIARI. By the end of the 1960's Congo was producing annually over 96,000 tons of raw sugar and 51,000 tons of refined sugar. In 1970 labor difficulties and militancy afflicted SIAN-SOSUNIARI's 7,000-odd workers and the refineries experienced major drops in output, causing the government to replace the companies that year by SIA-Congo. The new company failed to increase production, and by 1978 raw sugar production had fallen to 5,700 tons, a level not only uneconomical for the mills (they rarely made a profit) but threatening their closure. The regime formed still another state company, the Sucreries du Congo (SUCO), to take over SIA-Congo, notably its plant at Mantela. However SUCO was unable to improve performance, or even produce enough sugar to meet domestic demand, utilizing barely 11.5 percent of refinery capacity, bringing about a major governmental rehabilitation program. Under the 1982–86 plan, based on massive new oil revenues, investments amounting to 12.8 billion CFA francs were scheduled to raise processed sugar to 75,000 tons from 750,000 tons of cane grown on some 15,000 hectares, and in 1982 a large French loan was secured (72 million French francs) to renovate the Nkayi refinery, but again with mixed results.

As to palms, during the colonial era palm kernels and palm oil were Congo's prime agricultural export: the colony's 1938 tonnages of oil (6,000) and kernels (14,000) have not since been surpassed. After World War II, all oil-palm products exported came from the palms grown at the Sibiti experimental station, built by TRHO in 1946. By far the most productive area is the Sangha, where the French company CFHBC began scientific and mechanized culture of oil palms on its 3,000-hectare plantation, and their processing in oil mills. Oil palms were considered so important a national resource that in 1961, the conservative regime of Youlou formed the Regie Nationale des Palmeraies du Congo (RNPC) which took over the eighteen privately owned oil mills and all of the CFHBC's operations, providing more than 27 million CFA francs to promote production.

Oil-palm production nevertheless declined steadily throughout the three decades following independence, partly due to the shrinkage in producing areas and the aging of the palms. By the end of the 1970s, exploitable oil-palm groves covered only 5,875 hectares, of which some 1,800 were in the Sangha and 4,000 in the Cuvette. By 1980, fewer than 2,000 tons of oil were sold, and the sale of kernels totaled only about 700 tons, none coming from the Sangha and 90% produced in Kouilou and Niari. To finance a revival of the RNPC's Ouesso grove, BAD granted two loans to Congo, one of which was to be devoted to renovating and enlarging the Ouesso-Makolo oil mill, and the government itself undertook to reorganize the RNPC. Under the 1982–86 plan, BAD and Congo were to jointly invest 2.1 billion CFAF for a revival of the palm-oil industry, and an agreement was made with the French agro-industrial firm SOCFINO to initiate and guide it. The Sangha part of the project included the planting of 10,000 hectares (2,000 per year), the renovation of existing groves, and building or repair of mills, with the goal of a total production of 32,500 tons of oil and 7,000 tons of kernels a year by 1995. The new building involved in this project included a mill at Brazzaville capable of producing 4,000 tons of cake as well as 8,000 tons of oil, and soap factories at Komo and Loloaumou. Like other projects, these were not concluded due to the collapse in the mid-1980's of oil-revenues.

Coffee and cocoa have also not fulfilled early post-World War II hopes. Both crops suffered from labor shortages. Cocoa was first planted in the Sonaké district in 1947, and by 1960 was also grown in Likouala, M'Vouti, and Kayes. A pilot project, financed in part by the EEC and supervised by the ORSTOM, was launched soon after independence, with the aim to increase the area planted to cocoa and make Ouesso "the cocoa capital of Congo." Because the expansion failed to materialize, the operation was entrusted in 1980 to the newly created Office du Cafe et du Cacao (OCC), with a mandate to clear 1,600 hectares of forest land, of which 1,000 were to be planted with cocoa and 600 with coffee. On some 3,500 hectares, mainly in the Niari, coffee (of both the robusta and the arabica varieties) has been the recipient of official aid in the form of technical advice and of bushes grown at the Sibiti station. However, production and exports of both cocoa and coffee have declined to less than 2,500 tons a year, and because of their dispersed production, lack of care of the plants, and their excessive age, there is little hope of marked improvement in either their quality or their quantity. Indeed, in 1984 peasant apathy was so high in Sangha that the army had to be dispatched there to harvest the cocoa crop.

Tobacco is the third industrial crop introduced in the late 1940's in the Congo. The French tobacco monopoly, finding the indigenous tobacco too heterogeneous for its use, encouraged African farmers to plant the Kentucky and Maryland varieties, but the results were disappointing. In 1948 SIAT, a local subsidiary of the big French company Job, built a cigarette factory at Brazzaville. Initially it absorbed about half of the 3-400 tons of tobacco produced annually from imported stock planted in the Niari valley, the Bateke plateau, and Alima-Lefini. In the 1960s, tobacco production soared to some 700 tons, and with periodic declines, reflecting a shrinkage in the area planted with tobacco, has remained more or less stable. A sharp fall in output in 1977 prompted the authorities to organize an Office Congolais des Tabacs (OCT) and to seek a loan from France to carry out an expansion. To entice the 8,000 African peasants involved in tobacco planting to increase their output and improve its quality, a higher price was paid for their crops, new varieties of tobacco were introduced, and more capital, trucks, and experts were placed at their disposal in 1981–82, but results have been erratic.

Congolese exports of mangoes, pineapples, and citrus fruits date from the beginning of World War II. They were developed by a cooperative society, the Union Fruitiere du Pool, to about 1,700 to 1,800 tons a year, but their volume declined markedly in the 1960s due to lack of care and low rainfall. Nothing came of a project to grow fruit to supply a plant making juice and preserves, but the government did create a Station Fruitiere de Loudima (STAFRUIT) to promote fruit production in the Pool and Bouenza.

During World War II, wild rubber was collected from Congo's forests, and in 1946, 300 hectares were planted with hevea. In 1954, a processing plant was built at Komono in Lekoumou, and the next year, Congo exported 25 tons of rubber. Within two years of independence, Congo sold 247 tons, after which production rapidly dwindled, and by 1965 the hevea plantations were abandoned. Aiming to encourage all potentially exportable crops that could earn foreign currency for Congo, the 1982–86 development plan allotted 1.3 billion CFA francs to revive the plantations in Lekoumou, the Cuvette, and Kouilou—most not actually spent.

In sum, despite considerable expenditures the government has not been able to make commercial agriculture more than a marginal national activity, with consistent decline in volume (and variety) of the country's exports of oleaginous products, sugar, coffee, cocoa, tobacco, and fruit. On the other hand, production of staple foodstuffs (tubers and root plants) have kept pace with the increase in the rural population, but it does not meet the needs of the mushrooming urban population. All of Congo's governments, regardless of political orientation, have been eager but unable to increase food exports or to decrease imports of foodstuffs from abroad; nor to stem the rural exodus, or in promoting farming as a solution for growing unemployment, all deeply intertwined problems. Beginning in 1964 Congo's successive socialist regimes expanded the state sector of the economy as the solution for the problem of declining agricultural output. They multiplied the number of official organizations to control or monopolize production and marketing of commodities. When these failed in their mission, they were broken down and new organizations were formed to take over their various functions, with fresh funding. To Congolese administrators of that era the only remedy for a visibly ineffective official promotion of a crop, was even tighter state controls. For the first time in Congolese history, the country's spurting oil revenues between 1979 and 1982 made it possible for Sassou-Nguesso to enforce such controls in carrying out the 1982–86 plan. By 1981 the state sector had taken over 29 percent of cultivated land, and under the Price Stabilization Fund, fixed prices were set for both growers and consumers of local agricultural produce. By 1983, however, it became clear that the basic agricultural situation remained unchanged, and Congo remained a weak agrarian producer and a voracious foodstuffs consumer, at huge cost to state coffers. All the "solutions" espoused at home and abroad had been found wanting: neither new seeds, new crops, better technical assistance, more extension workers, nor massive state funding, or tighter control via state corporations.

With the disengagement of the State from the economy in the 1990's the basic dilemma remains: how to attain a modicum of self-sufficiency in foodstuffs in light of a progressively depopulated countryside where agricultural activity is both detested and practiced mostly by old people and women. The paradoxes of Congolese agriculture were noted in 1989 by a foreign observer in the far north. Despite the availability of adequate arable land, plenty of rain, and the fact that every imaginable crop grew wild in abundance, no one was interested in agriculture or even in harvesting the untended wild crops. State plantations were neglected and mismanaged as managers and laborers alike worked casual hours, going about their private affairs in Ouesso or traveling to Brazzaville for prolonged periods of absence. No consumption goods could be found in local stores of Ouesso except for fish and imported goods, mostly canned. Other foodstuffs consumed in the region were brought in from Brazzaville. And in Ouesso—the cocoa capital of Congo—powdered chocolate, consumed daily by an urban population that had internalized this Western habit, all came from neighboring Cameroun, smuggled across the border.

AISSI, ANTOINE-MARIE, 1944– . Academic. Born in 1944 and educated in France where he obtained a PhD in history, Aissi teaches at Marien Ngouabi University in Brazzaville.

AKA. Pygmies, which see.

AKOLA, EKONDI. Former opposition leader in self-exile in Paris. An advisor of Yhomby Opango, Akola fled abroad after the latter's ouster by Sassou-Nguesso in the late-1970's. There he set up an opposition group called the Mouvement Patriotique Congolais. A moderate Marxist movement calling for Yhomby Opango's return to power, the MPC was split into two wings due to conflict between Akola and co-leader Moudileno-Massengo.

AKOUANGO, EDOUARD ROGER, 1942– . Teacher and administrator. Born on April 6, 1942 in Ongondza, Akouango was educated in Boundji, Makoua, and at the Dolisie Teachers Training College (1970–73) serving as headmaster in several schools. In 1975 he became administrative secretary in INSSED as well as director of administration at Marien Ngouabi University.

ALANGAMOYE BAKARY, BENOIT, 1942– . Former MNR militant and Member of the National Assembly. Born on October 9, 1934 in Ouesso in northern Congo, and by profession a teacher, Alangamoye Bakary was trained at the Makoua and Owando Teachers

Training Colleges. In June 1973, as an MNR militant and member of the Ouesso MNR executive committee, he was elected to the National Assembly. When the PCT party was formed he joined it and continued on as a militant in the Ouesso district.

ALIHONOU, EMMANUEL, 1942– . Jurist and administrator. Born in Pointe Noire on June 25, 1942 and educated in Brazzaville, Alihonou then went to the University of Bordeaux where he studied law. In 1971 he returned to Congo, joined the party and was named to the Brazzaville High Court as a magistrate. The next year he was appointed government commissioner to the Court of Revolutionary Justice, and in 1975 assumed the position of secretary-general of the ministry of foreign affairs, a position he held until 1984.

ALIMA. Congo affluent in the Cuvette region that is navigable for 390 kms.

ALLIANCE NATIONALE POUR LA DEMOCRATIE (AND). A broad coalition of 43 anti-PCT political parties (many including former PCT members bolting the latter when multipartyism was allowed) emerging in 1991, with its coordinator being Stéphane Bongho-Nouarra.

AMBOULOU, DANIEL, 1948– . Academic. Born on November 17, 1948 and obtaining a PhD in Nutritional Science in France, Amboulou is deputy head of the Institute for rural development at Marien Ngouabi University in Brazzaville.

ANCESTOR WORSHIP. Despite the heavy inroads of urbanization and modernization in Congo, ancestor worship is still practiced in rural areas. Ancestors are viewed as elders, individuals linked by kinship to those still alive, and hence meriting occasional ritual offerings, in exchange for which they exercise their special powers against enemies of those still living.

ANGA, PIERRE (Lieutenant), 1940–1988. Architect of the largely **Kouyou** attempted coup of 1987. An uncle of both **Marien Ngouabi** and Sassou-Nguesso, Anga had been Ngouabi's loyal aide-de-camp at the time of the latter's 1977 assassination. After Yhomby-Opango's rise to power, he was appointed member of the PCT military committee, and ideological commissar of the Brazzaville military zone. When two years later Yhomby-Opango was ousted by Sassou-Nguesso, Anga was imprisoned for several years and then placed under house arrest. Imprisoned again under suspicion of another conspiracy, he was released after pressure from family members and ethnic elders. Implicated, together with Yhomby Opango, in the largely-Kouyou July 1987 conspiracy against Sassou-Nguesso, he refused to surrender to government troops when they arrived in Owendo on September 6, 1987 to escort him to Brazzaville. Publicly accusing Sassou Nguesso of being behind the 1977 killings of both Ngouabi and Cardinal Biyenda. He and a small group of followers had a shoot-out with government troops in the streets of Owendo before escaping into the bush. According to official reports he was finally tracked down and killed in another shoot-out on July 7, 1988; in rumor-prone Brazzaville, however, it is claimed that Anga escaped to Zaire where he was captured, handed over to Sassou Nguesso by Zaire's President Mobutu and secretly executed.

ANGOR, LEON ROBERT, 1928– . Diplomat, union leader, and former president of the national assembly. Born July 13, 1928 in Brazzaville, of northern origin, and an accountant by profession, Angor came to prominence through his trade union leadership. Resentful of the excessive southern influence in Congo, Angor was at one time a pro-China MNR militant. He was elected president of the national assembly in January 1964, and was reelected in March 1965. He was, however, increasingly isolated in the party, and though he threatened revolutionary opposition unless reelected, he was not successful in his bid for a third term in April 1966. He also fell afoul of the **JMNR** in August 1966 (he had been their advocate in the past) and was even briefly imprisoned by them. Appointed by Ngouabi to the central organ of the **CNR** in August 1968, he was dropped from that body two months later, and was sent abroad as Congo's ambassador, first to the U.A.R. (1969–1971) and then to Gabon and Equatorial Guinea.

ANIMAL HUSBANDRY. Starting from a few hundred head of undernourished cattle and several thousand scrawny poultry in the period before World War II, animal husbandry has developed considerably in Congo. As yet, however, it falls far short of filling domestic needs for meat, milk, and eggs and is far below the country's potential. Meat imports, largely beef, come mainly from Chad, and until 1988 in unmarked planes from South Africa ("Botswana beef"). Their cost to consumers has been subsidized by the government. Both government and private companies have been successful in promoting animal husbandry by importing breeding stock, developing ranches, and encouraging mixed farming. However, Congo's pastoral vocation is handicapped by lack of natural pastures and of land capable of being enriched for cattle husbandry, by the prevalence of trypanomiasis, to which cattle in particular are vulnerable.

Sheep and goats are exclusively reared by Congolese peasants in their villages: goats predominate in the Pool and on the Bateke plateau, whereas less numerous sheep are found in the Niari as well as the Pool. Although the rearing of hogs has been officially encouraged since Congo became independent, their number has been stagnant. An even greater effort has been made on behalf of poultry in areas near Brazzaville and Pointe Noire, and by now large numbers are raised all over the southern regions.

To supply more protein for a generally undernourished population and to reduce beef imports, the colonial administration imported in 1932 tsetse-resistant N'Dama and Lagoon cattle, and via a private company—Société Africaine d'Elevage (SAFEL)—created two cattle ranches in southern Congo. A form of metayage was also introduced whereby farmers who accepted the loan of small herds of pigs or cattle became "state herders," reared the animals according to official directives and eventually returned to the state the same number of living animals as they had received. As a means of popularizing animal husbandry and increasing the amount of meat available to rural Congolese, this form of pig and cattle lend-lease proved successful. By 1980, the number of animals "on loan" totaled 22,000, twice the number a decade earlier. Indeed, in thirty years since independence Congo's cattle herds have more than quadrupled, and though the number of sheep and goats has grown modestly, the number of poultry has also quadrupled. Meat production in 1990 amounted to 6246 tons (roughly half supplied by farmers), and the rest more or less equally by privately owned farms and by state farms.

In the nationalizations initiated by Massamba-Debat, the government bought out SAFEL in 1966 and transformed it into the Société Nationale d'Elevage (SONEL), which by 1985 owned 62,000 head of cattle. By the 1980's there were a dozen cattle ranches, of which two were state-owned (at M'Passa and M'Kenke). SONEL managed two farms at Loamba and Massangui; and there existed seven other similar enterprises in private or semiprivate hands. Today cattle husbandry is concentrated in two regions: 79 percent in Bouenza, and 23.5 percent in the Pool. In 1970 it was decided to create a model cattle ranch in the hope of eliminating all beef imports within a generation. The 30,000 hectare ranch at Dihesse was inaugurated in May 1974. Raising the funds for a herd of 6,000 cattle, and the staff to manage them took six years, and it was only in 1980 that the Dihesse ranch got under way. An appreciable increase in beef production then ensued, though unanticipated problems were also encountered.

ANZIKA. Another name for the Batéké kingdom in central Congo. See BATEKE.

ANZIMBA. One of the numerous religious sects in Congo. Former President Yhomby Opango was one of its prophets, using it as a stepping-stone to power. In 1984 ugly rumors circulated that Bakongo children were being kidnapped in Brazzaville for sacrifice in the northern part of Tai-Langai by members of the sect in order to assure political power did not slip from northern hands. The matter caused such unease in the capital that president Sassou Nguesso was forced so squash the rumor over the radio. However, the next year, in November 1985, after the urban student riots, that brought in demonstrations on the part of the many religious sects, Anzimba and many other movements were formally banned, with the regime issuing a list of only eight recognized religious movements.

APANOU, GABRIEL OBA. PCT militant and former minister of youth and employment. He was dropped from the cabinet in December 1990 after the 4th extraordinary PCT congress of that month that tried to revamp the party along more acceptable lines in preparation for multi-party elections. Apanou's main disadvantage was that he had adopted a firm line vis-a-vis the constantly unruly students and youth, who in the forthcoming elections played a decisive role.

ARMED FORCES. In 1960 Congo inherited a small French-trained armed force, with few local officers (most Bakongo) and a largely northern rank and file, still-commanded by expatriate French commanders, a fact explaining their general apolitical timidity at the time of the unrest that led to President Youlou's ouster in 1963 (See COUP D'ETAT OF 1986) that they only presided over. Massamba-Debat, who succeeded Youlou, Africanized the officer corps, and expanded the security forces by forming, or integrating several paramilitary groups that had spontaneously risen to "protect" the revolution. These included the People's Militia, the unruly and highly independent **JMNR**, and the civil-defense corps, all of which were later collectively to be known as the People's National Army (ANP).

Massamba-Debat's own ouster in 1968 (see COUP D'ETAT OF 1968) was a direct result of multiple challenges to his authority by a number of armed assaults from Youlouist elements and left-wing pressures from an increasingly radicalized youth, in the midst of which he insisted on civilian supremacy over the military. This led to two confrontations with the military, whose own corporate monopoly over armed force was challenged by the paramilitary structures, especially the JMNR. Clashing twice with the army (including demoting and then arresting the popular Mbochi paratrooper, Captain Marien Ngouabi), Massamba-Debat sealed his own fate.

With Ngouabi's rise to power a major transformation of the armed forces took place, as Bakongo began to be replaced—many after a series of plots or attempted coups that they supported—by northern Mbochi and Kouyou officers, and a similar influx of northerners took place in the government. Northerners, originally with few educational qualifications, had traditionally supplied the bulk of the recruits for Congo's rank and file, but now began to be promoted to command positions. During Ngouabi's presidency, military service was made obligatory, political indoctrination was introduced—providing stepping stones to power as manifest by the 1972 left-wing attempted putsch by **Ange Diawara**—and the country was divided into seven defense zones, of which Brazzaville was the smallest but most important.

After the military regime had firmly entrenched itself in office in the early 1970s, disputes began to erupt over the division of political power between army officers, first at a low level and later in the higher echelons, and some of these were translated into attempted putsches, conspiracies and plots. A lot of the criticism of large-scale torture, political arrests, and detention without trial in Congo (and especially the role of the Direction Générale de Sécurité de l'Etat) took place during this period. There was a tug-of-war mostly between northerners and southerners, the latter aware of their decreasing role in the army and government; but many were the result of personality and ideological differences, the latter since the Ngouabi regime was regarded by the ultra-Left (then largely pro-Chinese, see M-22) as not adequately committed to a real "people's revolution" and too responsive to French sensitivities. By the mid-1970's Ngouabi's main role was that of juggling various ideological and personality cliques, alternately purging left- and right-wing officers, trying to preserve his own centrist (broadly Marxist) role. Additional intra-military divisions began to crop up in the officer corps, however, that meshed with the other sources of conflict, leading to the assassination of Ngouabi. The masterminds behind the latter event have never been definitively identified. The liquidation of the "suicide squad" that perpetrated the assassination, and the execution of individuals who could have thrown light on the event, have assured that the true sequence of events still remains speculative. However, Sassou-Nguesso, who succeeded Ngouabi after the brief "rightist" interlude of the Yhomby Opango presidency, has constantly been linked (see for example PIERRE ANGA) to a falling apart in the officer corps—between the Mbochi and the Kouyou (Sassou Nguesso's ethnicity), over an alleged Ngouabi "opening" up to civilians (Massamba-Debat) and Bakongo in general, which a hard-line military clique was determined to prevent.

Until the post-1990 civilian era brought some changes, the Congolese army was dominated by northern officers (both Mbochi and Kouyou) with only a minority of other ethnic groups (usually Batéké), and specifically few Bakongo. Already in 1984 the sole senior Lari was arrested for plotting, and retired though never put to trial. On the other hand, the technical services, secret services, other security bodies remained dominated by southerners, but denied access to the most secret documents. The secondment of Cuban security personnel to supervise, or parallel, the activities of the Congolese internal security activities, also exacerbated intra-ethnic resentments in the armed forces between southerners and northerners. A specially trained, well-armed and well-paid elite Presidential Guard (the Red Berets), whose importance grew after Ngouabi's assassination, was composed of handpicked northerners, bolstered by Cuban advisors and operational personnel. Cubans were progressively phased out of Congo starting in 1987, though replaced by (originally 20 wire-tapping intelligence specialists, later up to 200) security, intelligence and personal bodyguard officers from Morocco (see SAIDOU BADIAN). In 1990, as part of the overall settlement in Angola and Namibia all Cubans left Congo. The Cubans (and later Moroccans) were used not just to serve as a Presidential bodyguard (Sassou-Nguesso has also recruited an additional small unit from his home village), but also recruited to crush political opposition or demonstrations. At the height of Congo's financial crisis in 1989, and the major austerity and redundancy drives, Sassou Nguesso still found it possible to set up yet another new paramilitary force, drawn from unemployed northern youth and based at the Camp du 15 Aout, that by January 1990 was 400-strong. As many other military leaders, Sassou-Nguesso recruited and placed in key positions in the armed forces members from his own village (Oyo), region (Cuvette), ethnicity (Mbochi) and especially members of his own extended family. The military as a whole only reluctantly accepted democratization and political liberalization in 1991. They fiercely resisted efforts by the new government to control it, prune its size or benefits, and indeed on two occasions they forced a humiliating change of defence ministers in Brazzaville when the government's appointees were unacceptable to them.

The new Milongo and Lissouba governments thus inherited a northern army intrinsically neither reliable nor loyal, and later Lissouba also came to feel threatened by the police, supportive as the latter was of the Bakongo Bernard Kolelas. In January 1991 a week-long military mutiny that saw the capture of Brazzaville airport, radio and TV stations (and the broadcast of Milongo's ouster over his government's "politically-motivated transfers of commanding officers") indicated that civilian supremacy was still illusory. A request from France for military aid to retrain the army was rebuffed, so an Israeli military presence in the country was secured, to serve as both an interim mercenary buffer against the government's own army, and for retraining purposes. At the same time the Presidential Guard (under its northern Colonel Oba) became Sassou Nguesso's bodyguard; the State Security Service was dissolved, and all security services were centralized and coordinated through the Prime Minister's office (under a loyal appointee). In 1992 **Martin Mberi** was appointed interior minister, with the task of ethnically restructuring the police and the non-army security services. He proceeded with zeal, bypassing the police chain of command via a brother, Colonel Nguembo, who was given command of a new political police recruited mostly from Bembe and other **Nibolek** ethnic personnel. The command of the 400-man rural gendarmerie nationale was also passed to a Bembe, General Mankoumba N'Zambi, and a Bembe, Colonel Yves Ibala, was named head of a new Presidential Guard. Sassou Nguesso's political police head, the Batéké General Emmanuel Ngouelondele, was retrained by Lissouba, however, as his military aide-de-camp, being regarded as loyal.

The Israeli presence in Congo ultimately nudged a reluctant France, fearful of losing influence in the country, to dispatch a gendarmerie retraining mission in 1993, and new military aid was finally pledged for Lissouba's specialized loyal units.

In 1994 Congo's armed forces totalled some 17,000 men, having been augmented during 1980–1982, and again in 1987–1989. They include 8,700 in the regular armed forces, with 8,000 in the army, 500 in an air force with ten fighter planes, fifteen transport planes, five helicopters,and a navy of 200 men and 13 vessels, all patrol craft. The paramilitary units amounted to a force of 7,500 with a gendarmerie numbering 2,500 men, and an augmented militia of 5,000 men. These numbers had briefly topped 20,000 in 1990 but they slowly declined as some paramilitary units were disbanded. During the two austerity pay-cuts of 1986 (5% and 10% of salary) the military was spared; an effort in 1988 to bring their salaries under the ambit of the new austerity measures was quietly shelved when senior commanders advised Sassou Nguesso that the officer corps could not absorb such economies. Despite a variety of foreign aid programs in Congo during the country's Marxist phase, France was a major donor, and in 1988 even offered to increase its military aid by 30%.

The command of the armed forces has been shifted a number of times. On March 12, 1981, Lt. Col. Emanuel Elenga succeeded Lt. Col. Raymond Ngollo as head of the armed forces' general staff. Promoted to Colonel, he was replaced in July 1987 by Colonel Jean-Marie Mokoko, whose continued presence at the head of the armed forces was unacceptable to the new Milongo, and later Lissouba governments. Mokoko was replaced in 1993 by General Emmanuel Eta-Onka who is currently Congo's chief of staff. The presidential guard, drawn heavily from northern elements, became Sassou Nguesso's personal bodyguard, and have retained their commander, Oba. The relative professionalism of the armed forces has been badly eroded by the various armed conflicts in Brazzaville. However, interior minister Mberi's ethnic policies vis-a-vis the police since 1992 have also been cause for concern. General Ngollo, the minister of defence, has in general played a soothing role in civil-military relations, being both loyal to the civilian government while trusted and mindful of the interests of the northern army.

ASSEMBLEE NATIONALE. Congo's national assembly of 125 deputies. The country did not have an assembly between 1968, when Massamba-Debat was ousted, and 1973 when Ngouabi inaugurated the **Assemblée Nationale Populaire**. In the 1992 multiparty legislative elections no single formation secured a majority of the seats, though Lissouba's **UPADS** party gained the largest number of seats. As soon as an anti-Lissouba majority developed in the assembly (anchored in an unholy alliance of the two next-largest groups, headed by the Bakongo Kolelas and the Mbochi Sassou Nguesso) Lissouba was forced to broaden his cabinet to include a large number of ministers from the other political parties. In 1992 the array of power in the legislature was: UPADS, 39 seats; MCDDI, 29 seats; PCT, 19 seats; RDPS, 9 seats; RDD, 5 seats. See also LEGISLATURE.

ASSEMBLEE NATIONALE POPULAIRE (ANP). Congo's 1973–1992 legislature, elected from a single PCT party list. In 1989, faced by pressures for political liberalization the PCT nominated for the forthcoming elections a majority (74 out of 133) of members not from its own ranks. This was insufficient to block the pressure for multi-partyism, and after the national conference took place the ANP was replaced by the Assemblée Nationale. See also LEGISLATURE.

ASSEMEKANG, CHARLES, 1926–. President of the Supreme Court and former minister of foreign affairs. Born on June 16, 1926, at Souanké, and educated at the Institut des Hautes Etudes d'Outremer where he obtained a law degree, on his return to Congo Assemekang first taught at the University of Brazzaville before being appointed by Ngouabi in 1969 as minister of foreign affairs. In January 1970 he was named president of the supreme court, and remained on the bench though he was expelled from the PCT party in December 1971 for 'ideological insufficiency' and practicing occult sciences. In April 1973 he was named a member of the special revolutionary court that was set up to try the 1972 rebellion enemies of the state, and in December 1977 he was also appointed a member of a special court set up to try the alleged assassins of Ngouabi.

ASSOCIATION DES ETUDIANTS CONGOLAIS (AEC). Unofficial students' organization parallel to similar government-recognized associations. Founded after World War II by the handful of Congolese students studying in Paris, the AEC became affiliated with the militant **Federation des Etudiants de l'Afrique Noire Franc**, whose radical views were reflected in its bulletin, *Action Congolaise*. Although most of its members were Lari with tepid Marxist views, the AEC took a stand against the constitutional referendum of September 1958, and later opposed the pro-Western and reactionary policies of Fulbert Youlou who emerged President of Congo. By the late 1960s the AEC had grown to 1,000 members and had progressively radicalized. In 1968 it joined the **Union Générale des Eleves et Etudiants Congolais** in helping overthrow President Massamba-Debat, but rapidly became disenchanted with his successor, Marien Ngouabi, whom they viewed a pseudo-revolutionary. The AEC joined in FEANF's denunciation of Ngouabi's purge of the PCT radical wing and his use of the armed forces to break up the major student strike in November 1971. A year later there was a direct confrontation between the AEC and the regime when Brazzaville ordered all Congolese students not on state-scholarship to vacate the Maison des Etudiants Congolais in Paris, where both the AEC and FEANF had their headquarters.

Because of its anti-regime activities, and largely southern membership, the AEC was formally superseded by the government-controlled **UGEEC,** losing many members who needed government-sponsorship for their studies abroad. Later there was a direct confrontation between the AEC and the Congo authorities, in Paris, when the Congolese embassy ordered all students not holding state-scholarships to vacate the Maison des Etudiants Congolais. Both the AEC and FEANF protested since the building was their common headquarters. Among Congolese students abroad, the AEC was soon superseded by the UGEEC, and it did not reemerge until after that body was suppressed in 1974 (see UGEEC). The AEC's attempts to re-establish better relations with Ngouabi's successor, Sassou Nguesso, were not successful when the latter refused to meet with an AEC delegation when he visited Paris in November 1979. Angry at this rebuff, the AEC delegates distributed tracts hostile to the regime in the hotel lobby, for which they were beaten up by Nguesso's bodyguard. The AEC remained a largely Lari/Bakongo unofficial organization parallel to the UGEEC that by the 1980's had become an association of mostly northern students from the Cuvette.

ATONDI, JULIEN-LECAS. Journalist and ultra-Left militant. During the 1960's Atondi was general manager of the national library cooperative ONLP, concurrent with his journalistic activities, and already a radical Marxist. As an MNR activist linked with the extreme-left he was appointed editor in chief of the newspaper *Etumba*, a post he continued to occupy into the late-1980's, despite several arrests for involvement, or suspected involvement, in several plots against both Ngouabi and Sassou Nguesso. He was a founding member of Ngouabi's PCT and one of its first Central Committee members, being appointed political commissar responsible for rural affairs. He constantly fell afoul of whatever regime was in power in Brazzaville because of his feelings each had 'sold' out on ideological rectitude. In 1972, for example, while director of the National School of Administration he was arrested, imprisoned and sentenced to death for participation in the **Ange Diawara** putsch of February 22nd. His sentence was commuted to life imprisonment within a month, and he was later pardoned and bounced back to his editorial post. He was later twice more arrested on suspicion of plotting as an influential member of the (originally pro-Chinese, later pro-Soviet) M-22 pressure group. In July 1987, described as an 'incorrigible recidivist,' he was implicated in **Captain Anga's** conspiracy, and arrested.

ATONDI-MONMONDJO, LECAS see ATONDI, JULIEN-LECAS.

AUJOURD'HUI. New private daily set up on March 23, 1991 in Brazzaville after the liberalization of the freedom of the press in Congo. It is headed by Christian N'Dinga, former permanent undersecretary at the ministry of information, with the chief editor being Firmin Ayessa, a former PCT member.

AYA, JUSTIN (Major). Former director general of public security in the Sassou-Nguesso regime. He lost his post in August 1987, and was shunted to security duties in the north for not being alert enough in detecting the **Captain Anga** conspiracy of the former month.

AYAYEM, FRANCOIS (Colonel). A senior military officer, Ayayem was appointed Minister of Interior in December 1992 when Lissouba lost a confidence vote in the national assembly and was forced to accept an influx of PCT ministers into the government.

AYESSA, FIRMIN. Former PCT militant, since 1991 editor in chief of the new Brazzaville daily, *Aujourd'hui*.

-B-

BABACKAS, EDOUARD ABOUKA, 1933– . Former ambassador to France. Born on July 14, 1933 at Mossaka, Babackas received his pri-

mary schooling at the Catholic mission at Dolisie and Brazzaville, after which he studied law at the University of Nancy, graduating in
1960, and Customs administration in Paris. On his return to Brazzaville
in 1962 he was appointed chief inspector of the customs service. In August 1963 he was suddenly elevated to cabinet rank by Massamba-
Debat, becoming minister of transport and mines and, four months
later, minister of finance. He held that post until 1968, when he was
named minister delegate to the presidency, and a month later ambassador to France. He remained in Paris until December 1969 when he
was named head of the new Agence Transcongolaise des Communications. In October 1973, he was named deputy director of Air
Afrique, and in January 1974 was stationed at Abidjan.

BABASSANA, HILAIRE, 1943– . Economist. Born in 1943 and educated at home and in France, where he obtained a doctorate in Economics, Babassana returned to Congo to teach at the Marien Ngouabi
University where he eventually became head of the department of economics. In 1989 he joined Sassou Nguesso's last cabinet as minister
of fishing, industry, crafts and tourism.

BABINGA. See PYGMIES.

BACONGO. One of Brazzaville's two main African quarters, in the
southern part of the town. The oldest quarter, and smaller of the two,
Bacongo lies between the military airport and the Congo river.

BADIAN, SAIDOU. Former influential Special Advisor to Sassou
Nguesso. Badian was born in Mali, studied history, and became a close
and radical collaborator of President Modibo Keita, joining the latter's
cabinet in a variety of posts. After the 1968 coup in Bamako he was
jailed for eight years following which he moved to Senegal. After Sassou Nguesso's rise to power in 1979 he relocated to Brazzaville and
became the latter's main speech-writer, confidant and security adviser, living in the Cité des 17 Presidential complex. He developed a
network of political informers and spies drawn from among the West
African marabouts and traders in Brazzaville, who were promised in
exchange security from the periodic expulsions of illegal foreigners
from the country. Since 1985 Badian was instrumental in convincing
Sassou-Nguesso to shift ideologically to the right and improve
Congo's relations with the US. He was also the go-between in securing 20 officers and 100 troops from Morocco to replace Cuban troops
that began to be phased out of Congo; in 1990 the latter were completely replaced by a larger unit of Moroccan security officers with
wire-tapping equipment. In 1987 he also helped bring a diplomatic

rapprochement with Israel, leading to the latter's dispatch to Brazzaville of additional security specialists including an anti-terrorism contingent. As the dawn of the multipartyism reached Congo in the 1990's Badian disappeared, and is assumed to be in Senegal.

BADILA, LOUIS, 1930– . Director and chief editor of the Catholic weekly *La Semaine Africaine*. A Lari born in 1930 in Brazzaville, Badila was educated in Catholic missions and in due course became a priest. He became editor of the weekly in 1962.

BADJO, ANGUY. Author and poet. Better known under his pseudonym Auguste Badjokila, Badjo is trained in the natural sciences and teaches in a school in Brazzaville.

BADJOKILA, AUGUSTE see BADJO, ANGUY.

BAGNA, JEAN GESTON, 1920– . Administrator. Born on November 28, 1920 in Brazzaville, Bagna's career has been linked with that of **Stéphane Tchichéllé** whose personal and diplomatic aide he was, starting with the latter's term as vice-president of Congo. After the 1963 coup Bagna was appointed head of the division of cultural cooperation in the ministry of foreign affairs, a post he held until his retirement.

BAKALA, ADRIEN, 1935– . Diplomat. Born in Mouyondzi in 1935, and educated at the University of Caen and at IHEOM in Paris, Bakala returned to Brazzaville in 1965 to become director of the Administration and Cultural Affairs division of the ministry of foreign affairs. Between 1965 and 1968 he was secretary of the ministry of foreign affairs; and, between 1968 and 1970 director of the department of studies and documentation in that ministry, concurrent with an appointment between 1967–68 as permanent representative to the U.N., where he returned in 1970 as deputy head of the Congolese delegation to the General Assembly. He served for one year (1970) as Professor at the Ecole Nationale d'Administration, following which he was appointed ambassador to Egypt (1971–1973) and then to Italy.

BAKONGO. Congo's largest ethnic group, found in a broad arc in southern Congo (and across the border in Zaire and parts of Angola) between Brazzaville and the Atlantic Ocean. For their subdivisions see KONGO.

BAKOTA. See KOTA.

BAKOUMA, SERAPHIN (DR.) Since the early 1980's Bakouma, a Lari, has been the leader of the Paris-based opposition to Sassou

Nguesso, the Parti Démocratique Congolais, and a strong proponent of free enterprise.

BAMA, VICTOR, 1952– . Agricultural engineer. Born in 1952 and trained in France in agronomy, Bama has served in a variety of senior posts, including most recently as head of the Tubers Laboratory at the Agricultural Research Center at Loudima.

BANDOU, ANGELE. Political leader, founder in 1991 of the populist Rassemblement pour le défense des pauvres et des chomeurs au Congo (RDPCC).

BANKING. Before World War II, French Equatorial Africa's meager credit facilities were provided by three private banks—the Banque de l'Afrique Occidentale (BAO), the Banque Commerciale Africaine (BCA), and the Banque Belge d'Afrique. They concentrated on financing trade through short-term loans, while another bank, the Credit Agricole, was the only one offering—on a small scale—what was called "social credit." After World War II, local credit facilities were expanded and diversified. Independence brought in Congo changes in the names and operations of the four French banks, and the advent of new banking institutions created by the state.

In 1961 Congo's government became a minority shareholder in the BAO. This was the oldest and most important of the preindependence banks, although it had lost its note-issue privilege in 1941 to the newly created Banque Centrale des Etats de l'Afrique Equatoriale (BCEAE). Twenty years later, the BAO changed its name to the Banque Internationale pour l'Afrique Occidentale and took over the business of the BCA. The Banque Nationale pour le Commerce et l'lndustrie (BNCI), capitalized at 150 million CFAF and affiliated with the Banque Nationale de Paris, was outstanding among the post-World War II Congolese banks. It rapidly expanded its business in Congo by establishing branches at Brazzaville, Pointe Noire, and Dolisie, and it acquired Italian, American, and Swiss shareholders. In 1963, it changed the name of its Congolese affiliate to Banque Internationale pour le Commerce et l'lndustrie, but continued to maintain its majority interest under a reorganized local administration. The Société Générale of Paris was the second nationalized French bank after World War II to found a branch in Moyen-Congo, for which it supplied almost all its capital of 200 million CFAF. Like the BNCI, it attracted Western minority shareholders, and in 1963 it changed its name to Société Générale de Banques au Congo. Concessions to Congo's sovereign status was for long confined merely to a modified nomenclature, for the only one of the four French commercial banks operating in the country in which the state was the majority shareholder was the Banque Commerciale

Congolaise (BCC). Its parent organization, the Credit Lyonnais, broke new ground when it reduced its holding in the BCC to 49 percent of its stock, and later to even less.

To finance its first development plan, the independent Congolese government established a Banque Nationale de Développement du Congo in 1961. The state held 58 percent of its capital of 430 million CFAF, to which France added 32 million in 1963. In the latter year, an Office Congolais des Changes was created to apply the government's currency regulations. No additional state financial institutions were created until 1971, when a Caisse d'Amortissement was founded to handle government loans and manage the public debt.

In November 1972, the four French commercial banks that still financed Congo's foreign trade together formed an Association Professionnelle de Banque au Congo. This association's objective was to simplify and unify its member banks' procedures, negotiate collective agreements with their employees, and attract a larger local clientele in Congolese towns. A more cogent motivation for their solidarity was the difficulty being encountered by all the commercial banks in being profitable. Commercial banks in Congo felt poorly recompensed for their financing the country's foreign trade, especially as state enterprises were notoriously slow in repaying their debts, and the banks were hampered by inadequate resources. During Ngouabi's presidency, banking was limited by the small aggregate of deposits, by low interest rates on loans granted from their own resources, and from those borrowed from their parent organization in France, and also by the requirement that they buy each year a certain percentage of government bonds. Changes made in 1974 further restricted rather than liberalized the banking sector. The BCC absorbed the local branch of the BIAC, and the Union Congolaise de Banques was formed by a merger between the BICI-Congo and the Société Générale de Banques du Congo. This reduction in the number of banks operating in Congo was only partially offset by the opening in Brazzaville of a branch of the Banque de Développement des Etats d'Afrique Centrale in 1976. Two years later, banking operations on the whole again slumped, although deposits in commercial banks grew by 8.8 percent. Of the loans granted in 1978, only 51 percent went to the rural sector, whereas 31.3 percent were taken by industry and the largest share (56.4 percent) went to trade and transport. A third commercial bank, Banque Internationale du Congo, capitalized at 600 million CFAF (51 percent state-owned), was inaugurated in November 1983. As Congo launched in 1982 its ambitious five-year plan, there was a large demand for capital and increased banking activities. In July 1982, the demand for loans rose to 95.5 billion CFAF, although deposits that same month totaled no more than 82.4 billion. In 1983, public funds accounted for the bulk of the three Congolese banks' capital, or about 60.6 percent of the total, while French public funds approximated 25 percent, ranging from 10.6 percent of the capital in the BNDC to 24.87 percent by the Credit Lyonnais in the BCC and to 24.5 percent by the Société Générale in the UCB. The likelihood that the spurt in investments under the plan would be maintained prompted the government to approve the creation of a third commercial bank in 1983, the Banque Internationale du Congo (BIDC), with a Congolese president, and with capital of 600 million CFAF, divided between the state (51 percent), the BIAO (19 percent), Chemical Bank of Great Britain (10 percent), the Long-Term Credit Bank of Japan (10 percent), and Banco Central of Spain (10 percent). The BIAO headed the group of French bankers who at the end of 1982 loaned Congo 310 million French francs and offered the new bank its technical assistance, as evidence of foreign capitalists' confidence in the country's future.

The slump in oil revenues in the mid-1980's exacerbated the deficits most banks were accumulating due to sloppy business practices, non-repayment of debts by the State and public sector and policies of overstaffing under unionist pressures. By 1990 with two exceptions all banks were recording strong deficits, and all but the BIDC were virtually illiquid. In 1991 the national conference heard a report that total debts owing the banking sector was 202 billion CFAF, 70 billion of this owed by the State itself, and 47 billion by the private sector. The conference recommended reducing staff in all banks, unlinking their administration from the control of ministers, placing them in the hands of professionals, as well as closing down two banks and privatizing another. The country's strong trade unions, worried about job losses, prevented the implementation of this policy. In due course, however, the actual collapse of the banking sector brought about that result. The BNDC, described in 1991 as "in catastrophic conditions," had to close down due to the impossibility of its being rescued by private capital. The BNC was taken over by the BCEAC. And the BCC, the country's largest commercial bank, running out of banknotes and closing down in September 1992, went into receivership under interim control by Credit Lyonnais. In August 1994, after two years of negotiations, 619 employees were dismissed with redundancy payments. See also each bank's separate entry.

BANQUE CENTRALE DES ETATS DE L'AFRIQUE EQUATORIALE ET DU CAMEROUN (BCEAC) see BANQUE DES ETATS DE L'AFRIQUE CENTRAL.

BANQUE COMMERCIALE CONGOLAISE (BCC). The BCC commenced operations in June 1963 as a subsidiary of the Credit

Lyonnais, with a capital of 100 million CFAF. It soon became the Congo's premier commercial bank, in 1974 taking over the BIAO's agencies. Progressively its capital was augmented by the State that acquired a majority stake in it; by 1982 its capital had grown to 2 billion CFAF, of which the state and the BNDC jointly owned 63.7 percent, and Credit Lyonnais with its German and Italian associates the rest. Headquartered in Brazzaville, the BCC had a network of two agencies in Brazzaville, two in Pointe Noire, and five elsewhere in the country, accounting for 55% of the banking market. After the state acquired a majority stake BCC personnel zoomed up, reaching over 600 employees in 1982. Like much of the rest of the State-controlled banking community the BCC then lost profitability and fell into a severe liquidity crisis, the result of excessively high payrolls and unrepaid loans by parastatals and influential individuals. Losing over 6 billion CFAF in 1991, the bank ran out of cash in September 1992 and closed operations. The bank was rescued when Congo relinquished its majority position with Credit Lyonnais pumping in new capital as an interim measure. The equity was then readjusted to Credit Lyonnais (55%), the State (35%) and private shareholders (5%). Experiencing strong union resistance to a suggested 50% trimming of the bank's manpower, in August 1994 all 619 personnel were dismissed with redundancy payments.

BANQUE DES ETATS DE L'AFRIQUE CENTRAL (BEAC). Central bank of Chad, Gabon, Cameroun, the C.A.R. and Congo, all of whom share a common currency (the CFA franc) that is pegged to the French franc. Until 1973 known as the BCEAC and headquartered in Paris, the BEAC is now based in Yaoundé, Cameroun.

BANQUE INTERNATIONALE DU CONGO (BIDC). Set up in 1983 with over 2 billion CFAF in capital, with the State equity at 56.7%, the BIAO 21.1% and the rest owned by a Japanese/Spanish bank consortia. The bank was one of the few to control staff expenditures and loans, being the sole one in Congo constantly profitable. The BIDC recorded profits of 138 million CFAF in 1984 and 427 million in 1992 when other banks were going under.

BANQUE NATIONALE DE DEVELOPPEMENT DU CONGO (BNDC). Formed in 1961, and by 1979 capitalized at 1.087 million CFAF, with the state owning 78.5% of the equity, France's CCCE 10.6%, BEAC 8.3% and private sector organizations 2.6%. Its function was to finance Congo's development plan, especially its socioeconomic rural projects. By early 1981, its deposits totaled 2.43 billion CFAF, a 123 percent increase over the preceding year, and during that period it had granted loans amounting to 3.29 billion CFAF. Like much of the State-controlled banking community the BNDC collapsed due to excessively-high payrolls, mismanagement and unrepaid loans by parastatal organs. Losing 8.6 billion CFAF in 1990 alone the bank came to a virtual standstill in 1991 when its debt reached 12 billion CFAF, and it was estimated it needed an infusion of 28 billion CFAF to affectuate a turnaround. The national conference in 1991 agreed to close the bank but this was not done due to unionist pressures worried about the 163 jobs involved. The bank nevertheless closed down in July 1991. Under an agreement in 1992 its debt was taken over by the BEAC central bank and strict accounting and banking procedures were adopted. Its governor in 1993 was Felix Mamalépot.

BANSALI, ANNE MERCELLE, 1953– . Former URFC militant. Born in Brazzaville on October 4, 1953, and trained as a teacher, Bansali—who was URFC secretary general for Djambala, and a PCT Plateaux committee member—was elected to the national assembly in 1984, serving until 1989.

BANTHOUD, PAUL. Radical unionist constantly a thorn in the side of President Massamba-Debat. Succeeding Idrissa Diallo in April 1966 as president of the **CSC**, he went to study labor organization in the USSR, and on his return urged that all foreign banks and enterprises in Congo be nationalized. This led to the famous retort of Massamba-Debat that there was nothing to nationalize in the country. On December 20, 1967 he was dismissed as head of CSC, charged with mismangement of its funds; four months later, he played an active part in the strikes at Brazzaville. He participated in the revolt against the military authorities at the Biafra camp and on August 31, 1968, was arrested for possession of arms and incitement to revolt. Although sentenced to two years in prison, he was amnestied in May 1969. In the 1970's he became one of the second-echelon leaders in the radical M-22 movement.

BASSEKOUABO, FRANCOIS, 1945– . Director of the agricultural farm at Kinkala, and former deputy of the national assembly. Born on September 8, 1945 in the Pool region, and trained in agronomy, Bassekouabo had been head of the agricultural station at Ngabé, before assuming leadership of the Kinkala state farm. Head of the **CSC** single trade union branch for the Pool region, he was elected to the national assembly in 1984, serving until 1989.

BATANGA, ANDRE, 1932– . Lawyer and civil administrator. Born on April 4, 1932 in Moutsila, Batanga obtained a law degree from the University of Paris, studying also at IHEOM. On his return to Brazzaville he practiced law for a few years and was eventually appointed vice-president of the Congolese chamber of commerce, agriculture and industry. He also served as president and director-general of the Société Hoteliére et Immobiliére, and between 1972–73 as director-general of commerce. In 1974 he was named assistant director of the Société Générale des Banques au Congo.

BATANTU, BARTHELEMY. Archbishop of Brazzaville.

BATEKE (also TEKE). Major ethnic group in central Congo, with members found also across the border in Gabon. The name Téké or Batéké is a recent one, since in precolonial days the group was referred to by other names, notably Anziki. Divided into twelve clans, the most important of which are the Téké proper, the Téké-Lari (a mix of Téké and Lari), Koukouya, Gangoulou, Nzikou, Aboma, Njikini (a mixture of Téké and Mbochi) and the Tegué, it was with one of their kings, the **Makoko** of the Tio kingdom with its capital at Mbé, that Brazza signed the treaty that gave France control of the north bank of the Congo river, and land to set up what eventually became Brazzaville. Some evidence suggests a common origin for the Vili, Kongo and Batéké. They were living in the Batéké plateaus from at least 1507, as part of the decentralized **Kongo kingdom**. When the latter began to fall apart in the 17th century, the vice-royalty of Nzikou (or Anzika) asserted its independence, controlling both banks of the Congo river and a part of the Niari valley. The kingdom was also highly decentralized, with no central army and/or administration, and many of the sub-chiefdoms, nominally ruled in the name of the Makoko who retained the prerogative of appointing them, were virtually autonomous. Originally Mbé (now a small village) was a large settlement of great antiquity. It remained the political center of the kingdom, though the Pool region was the economic and trade hub, with caravans reaching it from **Loango** with European commodities, to trade for slaves captured by the Batéké and upriver forest goods. Encroachments by better organized and/or more aggressive riverine and other northern groups such as the Mbochi, who refused to pay transit tolls, led to Mbé's eclipse. For long controlling central Congo, the pressures from northern groups in the 19th century eroded their hegemony by the time of the arrival of the French. The last Makoko died in 1918, future leaders being appointed by the French as *chefs de canton,* residing in Ntsaa.

Though the normal habitat of the Batéké is in the center of the country, in the Plateaux region north of Brazzaville, many have migrated to the capital in search of work. Politically a swing group between the Mbochi-Kouyou in power under Presidents Ngouabi and Sassou Nguesso, and the Lari-Bakongo opposition, the Batéké were restless in the 1980's in light of purges of many of their leaders from the cabinet, leaving only two in place: Christophe Bouramoué and Raymond Damase Ngollo. A "liberation" group (FROLIBABA) was then set up to press for their ethnic needs. In 1992 estimates placed their number at around 14 percent of the country's population of roughly 2.6 million. See also POPULATION.

BATEKE PLATEAU. Geographic region with deep forested valleys through which Congo tributaries flow.

BATHEAS-MOLLOMB, STANISLAV CHARLES, 1941– . Former radical PCT Central Committee member. Born on August 13, 1941 in Botala, and educated in Makoua and Brazzaville, Batheas-Mollomb then proceeded to France to study philosophy at the University of Montpellier (1963–65), Aix-en-Provence (1965–66) and librarianship in Paris (1967–70). On his return to Brazzaville he was appointed director-general of Congo's Library, Archives and Documentation services. Joining the PCT party, he was elevated to the Central Committee, and in the 1980's served as Congo's ambassador to Ethiopia and Romania. On August 9, 1991, with the onset of multipartyism in Congo Batheas-Molomb set up a political party, the Parti populaire pour la démocratie sociale et la défense de la république (PPDSDR).

BATIMA, AUGUSTE. Former minister of primary and secondary education in the 1970's under President Ngouabi.

BATTAMBICA, MAURICE, 1930–1965. Editor and early literary figure. Born in Brazzaville in 1930, and educated at mission schools Battambica served for a few years as primary school supervisor for Catholic schools. Turning against the Church he entered commerce and it was during this period that he was attracted to theater and literary activities. He served on the editorial board of *Liaison,* through which he published several of his first poems, and later moved on to the editorial board of *Le Progrès.* He was constantly active in theater productions as actor, producer and author, dying at an early age in 1965.

BATUMENI, V. VICTOR, 1937– . Educator and former secretary-general of the National Popular Assembly. Born on July 12, 1937 and obtaining a PhD in History in France, Batumeni taught at Marien Ngouabi University, joined the PCT party and in 1985 was appointed the assembly's secretary-general.

BAYIZA, ALPHONSE, 1938– . Regional director of education, first of Lékoumo and then of the Pool region. Born in 1938 in Kinamana, and trained as a teacher, he was administrative secretary of the executive committee of the Pool region when elected in 1984 PCT deputy to the national assembly, serving until 1989.

BAYONNE, BERNADETTE, 1932– . PCT militant. Born in Brazzaville on September 12, 1932 and by profession a teacher and inspector of primary education. Bayonne joined the Union Révolutionnaire des Femmes des Congo (URFC) and in 1984 was elected to Congo's national assembly, serving one term until 1989.

BAZINGA, APOLLINAIRE, 1924– . Early political leader and diplomat. Born on January 2, 1924, at Impfondo, Bazinga attended a Catholic mission school and then entered government service as a pharmacist in 1952. In that year he was also elected deputy for Likouala at the colonial territorial assembly, serving until 1959 (between 1958–59 as its vice-president), as well as Grand Councilor of French Equatorial Africa. In 1959 he was tapped for higher office by President Fulbert Youlou, serving for one year as minister without portfolio, and in 1960 was appointed head of the information service. He took an active part in the negotiations for construction of the Kouilou dam. In 1965, Massamba-Debat appointed him ambassador to Peking, and he held that post briefly under Ngouabi. In January 1970, he was named ambassador to France and in 1971 Congo's permanent representative to UNESCO. He became ambassador to Zaire in December 1972, serving for three years until he was retired from the diplomatic service.

BEKATE, MEYONG, 1934– . Dramatologist. Born on November 20, 1934 and obtaining a doctorate in Theater Arts from the University of Paris, Bekate joined Marien Ngouabi University and is currently a productive dramatologist and head of the University's Faculty Theater.

BELVAIN, MICHEL see BEMBA, SYLVAIN.

BEMBA, SYLVAIN, 1934– . Former minister and one of Congo's towering literary figures. A Bayaka, born February 17, 1934 at Sibiti, and educated in Brazzaville and Dolisie, Bemba, who, coming from a modest family with a father who was a male nurse, did not proceed into higher studies, and joined the civil administration as a simple clerical officer, a post he occupied between 1955–1960. Writing short stories, plays, and articles in his spare time under the pseudonyms of Martial Malinda and Michel Belvain among others, in 1960 he was appointed cabinet director of the minister of Finance, and once his reputation as an author spread, he was appointed by President Youlou editor-in-chief of the Agence Congolaise d'Information (1962–63). After Youlou's overthrow he repeated this cycle, first as cabinet director of the minister of Justice (1963–1966) and then as Head of Press Services in the Ministry of information (1966–67), director of Information (1967–68), secretary-general for information (1968–1970) and director of the radio and television stations (1970–72). In 1972 he was director-general of cultural affairs and editor of the PCT party newspaper *Etumba*. In the government of January 7, 1973, he was given the information portfolio, but the following month he was arrested for complicity in the radical Maoist putsch of **Ange Diawara**. He admitted complicity at his trial in April 1973, and because of his international standing was only given a suspended three-year sentence. To earn a living he joined the staff of the library of Marien Ngouabi University, continuing his literary output. Widely regarded as one of the most talented Congolese writers, having written numerous plays, books and poems, and winner of a variety of literary prizes in 1977 Bemba was given a special award by the Congolese state in recognition of his attainments. For several years in self-exile abroad, mostly in Abidjan, in 1988 he set up a political party abroad—the Union pour la démocratie Congolais—together with many of former President Youlou's associates, calling for multipartyism, free enterprise and a capitalist economy. When Congo's political system liberalized in 1990 he returned to Brazzaville and competed under his party's banner in the forthcoming elections.

BEMBA-DEBERT, WA M'BANGUI. Prolific and well-known Congolese author and poet, though little-published abroad. In 1972 he won first prize in Congo's first public competition for poetry.

BEMBE. Bakongo agrarian clan living around the upper Bouénza river. It currently is the main group supportive of the Lissouba presidency, and has many key members in the government.

BETOU, GABRIEL. One of Massamba-Debat's key cabinet ministers, Betou served as minister of labor in October 1964, and between December 1965 and 1968 as minister of education. He was dropped from the government after Ngouabi's rise to power.

BIAYENDA, EMILE (CARDINAL), 1927–1977. Born in 1927 in Maléla-Bombé in the Pool region, Biayenda attended the Kindamba missionary school, the Saint-Paul secondary school in Mbamou, and then the Liberman seminary in Brazzaville studying philosophy and theology between 1950–1959. He was ordained a priest in October 1958, served as vicar in a number of localities until 1965 when he went to Lyon to complete his studies, obtaining a PhD in Political Science and a further degree in theology. He then continued on with a string of other appointments in Congo until receiving episcopal ordination in 1970, returning to Brazzaville as Cardinal. Biayenda was abducted and murdered by unknown assailants (allegedly, but not necessarily, by Ngouabi family members) shortly after the still mystery-shrouded assassination of President Ngouabi, with whom he had talked minutes before the military assault on the latter. The speculation is that he either (or both) saw, or was told, something by Ngouabi about the imminent assault, that could identify those behind Ngouabi's assassination, or that he was the go-between for a rumored Ngouabi political shift to greater moderation and re-integration of civilian elements in his government, including formerly deposed Massamba-Debat, a move opposed by radical hard-line high military officers. President Sassou-Nguesso, who assumed power after the Yhomby Opango interregnum in 1979, has been constantly mentioned, including by rebelling military elements, as directly implicated in both Ngouabi's and Biayenda's murders.

BIAYOULA, FULGENCE, 1936– . Early moderate trade union leader. A Bassoundi, Biayoula was born in Brazzaville's Poto-Poto quarter on October 30, 1936. He was trained as a carpenter at the Brazzaville Ecole de Formation Professionnelle Rapide, and became involved in CATC trade unionism. In 1958 he was a founder of an interprofessional school for manual workers, whose bulletin, *Le Travailleur Africain,* he edited. Persuaded by Pongault to resume his CATC activities, he played a major role in bringing about the overthrow of President Fulbert Youlou in 1963. He, however, rapidly fell afoul of the new regime that emerged in Brazzaville. As president of the CATC, he opposed the MNR's politicization of the labor movement, and was detained in prison for the "separatist" tendencies of his union. In 1965 he attempted to escape the country, with the aid of French missionaries, dressed as a woman, but was caught and imprisoned. After his release he faded into relative obscurity.

BICOUMAT, GERMAIN, 1906– . A Vili, born in the Pointe Noire region on April 20, 1906, after primary school he became an accountant for the Congo-Ocean Railroad. In due course he rose to become head of the public works service at Brazzaville, where he became a municipal councilor in 1958. He was a charter member of the PPC and leader of its left-wing faction. With the rise of the Youlou regime he was appointed minister in charge of the Office du Kouilou and Congo's operations in the ATEC (1960–1962). In Massamba-Debat's first government, he was minister of the interior and information, though towards the end of the latter's tenure he was demoted, due to his political moderation, to the post of President-delegate to the merchant marine. After Massamba-Debat's ouster he was very briefly reappointed to his former ministerial posts by President Ngouabi, but again his moderation brought about his eclipse. In April 1966 he was named ambassador to East Germany, and in April 1969, ambassador to West Germany, serving until 1970 when he was retired.

BIKINDOU, ROBERT. Former cabinet minister. An engineer in the public works service specializing in urban construction, Bikindou was appointed minister of town planning, housing and tourism in the Henri Lopes government of August 30, 1973, serving also as head of Congo's internal airline Lina-Congo. He was dismissed from his post by the PCT military committee in November 1977 for "inadequate ideological formation" because he had refused to have Lina-Congo's premises serve as headquarters of the PCT branch for public works and transportation workers, and was retired from the civil service.

BIKOUTA-MENGA, GASTON, 1935– . Author and playwright, better known as Guy Menga, and one of Congo's towering literary figures. Born in 1935 in Mankonongo, in the Pool region, after primary and secondary schooling in Brazzaville he was a teacher for five years until 1961 when he secured a grant to study telecommunications in France. Primarily a dramatologist, he scored his first major success in 1966 with his first play *La marmite de Koka-Mbala*. Other plays followed, some produced in Paris. In 1968 he published his first novel, *La Palabre sterile*. He is the author of numerous other works, many published in France. Much of his work deals with traditional-modern tensions in a changing society, in which he sides with the efforts of youth and women to break the chains of the past.

BILOUMBA-SAMBA, JEAN-BLAISE. Teacher and author who has written poetry both on the Marxist revolution and on more personal themes.

BIMBAKILA, CLAUDE see BIVOUA, CLAUDE.

BINDI, MICHEL. Former controversial general-director of security services. A Lari, Bindi was head of the security police throughout most of Massamba-Debat's administration. In late 1963, he actively aided in the escape of enemies of Zaire's Prime Minister Adoula when they fled from Kinshasa to Brazzaville. Highly unpopular because of his harsh measures as Security head, he was briefly kidnapped by the army mutineers in June 1966. In January 1968 Massamba-Debat appointed him minister of the interior. He joined the armed opposition of youthful militants to Ngouabi's regime late in August 1968, but escaped arrest when the Biafra camp of mutineers surrendered. He was finally captured in November 1968, and sentenced to ten years in prison on charges of smuggling firearms into Congo, and for several murders committed in 1965. After his release he faded from public view, living for some time in Zaire.

BITA, FRANCOIS. Former cabinet minister. With advanced training in Statistics, Bita served for five years (1969–74) as head of the Statistics and Economic accounts department in the ministry of Finance. An active PCT member, he then was appointed head of the Agence Transcongolaise des Communications, based in Pointe Noire, serving until 1989 when he was brought into Sassou-Nguesso's cabinet as minister of transport and civil aviation. He reverted to administrative duties after the advent of multipartyism.

BITOULOU, JOACHIM, 1927– . Former Head of Congo's radio station, La Voix de la Révolution. Born in 1927 of Bakongo ethnicity, and educated in Catholic mission schools, he taught in schools for several years before commencing in 1957 a radio career with Radio Afrique Equatoriale Française based in Brazzaville. After independence he proceeded twice abroad for specialized studies in telecommunications, and in September 1962 was appointed program-director of Radio Congo. He continued in his functions when the station's name was changed to La Voix de la Révolution, until reaching retirement age.

BITSINDOU, GERARD. One of former President Sassou Nguesso's prime civilian aides and confidants. A Lari, Bitsindou's informal influence stemmed from being during the 1980's the Presidential Office cabinet director and secretary-general.

BITUMEN. Though the presence of bitumen was known to exist in several locations in Congo, it was only in 1983 that major exploitable resources were discovered in Moyambé, 400 kms. southwest of Brazzaville. They contain at least 10% of ore content. Exploitation has not yet commenced.

BIVOUA, CLAUDE. Editor, journalist, author, poet and singer. Better known under his pseudonym Claude Bivoua, he is a graduate of the school of journalism at Strasbourg University. Bivoua served as a journalist and reporter on Radio Congo, and in 1982 was appointed editor of the newspaper *Mweti*. During his years at Radio Congo he blossomed as a singer as well, and this then led him into poetry. In 1977 his play *Maria-Vipère* won him a national prize as the best play of the year.

BIZENGA, MARTIAL, 1933– . Cartographer. Born in 1933 and trained in France in cartography, including aerial surveys, on his return to Congo he was appointed director of the Congolese Institute of Geography, where he has been responsible for many of the maps and geographical surveys of the country.

BOGUIELI see PYGMIES.

BOISSONS AFRICAINES DE BRAZZAVILLE (BAB). Manufacturer of carbonated drinks and syrups. Founded in Brazzaville in 1964 with 350 million CFAF in capital.

BOKILO, GABRIEL, 1938– . Director of the Banque des Etats de l'Afrique Centrale. Born in 1938, after secondary studies in Brazzaville, he earned law degrees from the universities of Bordeaux and Paris. Upon returning to Congo, he rose in the administrative hierarchy, becoming successively, subprefect of Gamboma, prefect of Nkayi, secretary-general of the Brazzaville municipality, and cabinet director to the ministers of civil service, labor, and justice. After working in the African Development Bank he was named in July 1973 the Congo's director of the BCEAE.

BOMBETE, JACQUES, 1944– . Trade union militant. Born in 1944 in Bokombo (Mossaka), his militant union activities rapidly made him secretary-general of FETRASSEIC and Permanent secretary of the Confédération Syndicale Congolaise. In 1984 he was elected to the national assembly, serving until 1989.

BONGHO-NOUARRA, STEPHANE MAURICE, 1937– . Former Prime Minister under President Lissouba. Born in 1937 at Ouesso in the Sangha region, and trained in France (1959–1962) as an agricultural engineer, Bongho-Nouarra worked as an engineer in the public-works service and in the ministry of agriculture in Brazzaville. In 1966 he served as chairman of the Chambre Economique de Congo-Brazzaville, and also chairman of the Union des Jeunes Chambres d'Expression Française. The same year he was appointed by Massamba-Debat president of Congo's Economic and Social Council. A close friend of Ngouabi, when the latter rose to power Bongho-Nouarra was named secretary of state of agriculture, then minister of public works. In September 1969, after the rise of the Ngouabi regime Bongho-Nouarra was retained in his post in the administration. He was arrested in August 1970 on charges of conspiring against the regime and was sentenced to ten years imprisonment. Freed in an amnesty in 1971 he went into self-exile in Paris, setting up a number of companies in Benin, Congo and Cote d'Ivoire. He returned to Congo to participate in the 1991 national conference that paved the road for the re-emergence of civilian multiparty politics. He was elected by the conference as one of its vice presidents, heading a newly formed political party, the PRDC. He later became General-Secretary of the **Alliance Nationale pour la Démocratie**, and coordinator of the broad anti-PCT grouping of 43 of the 70 political parties that were set up in Congo. Close to Pascal Lissouba, he supported Lissouba's emergence as President of Congo. On September 8, 1992 he was appointed Prime Minister of Congo, replacing the interim prime minister, André Milongo. On November 13, 1992 he and his government had to resign when a no-confidence motion succeeded in the national assembly. Lissouba, forced to appoint a new interim prime minister (Dacosta), retained Bongho-Nouarra as coordinator of the parties supporting UPADS,and as chairman of the cabinet advisory commission.

BONGO, OTTO. Influential Congolese businessman. Emerging in control over a business empire, and backed by Yhomby-Opango, a close friend, Bongo played a major role in facilitating the diplomatic talks between the USA and Angola that led to the resolution of the conflicts in Angola and Namibia, and the eventual withdrawal of Cuban troops from the entire region, including Congo. Involved in unofficial (but well-known) meat imports from South Africa, his links with that country allowed him also to bring in South African negotiators in the above-noted talks in Zaire and Congo, leading to the early Congo-South Africa diplomatic rapprochement.

BONGOU, CAMILLE. Powerful former Secretary-general of the PCT Politburo, head of the PCT Permanent Secretariat, and hard-line key leader of the Marxist-Leninist Mouvement du 22 Fevrier (M-22), that, during the days of **Ange Diawara** was pro-Chinese, but later "moderated" to pro-Soviet postures. Educated at the Chaminade seminary in Brazzaville, Bongou was part of the triumvirate at the pinnacle of power in the 1980's, the regime's de facto number two man, and acting head of state during Sassou-Nguesso's travels abroad. Aware of the fact that the Vili **Thystére-Thicaya** had higher party rank than him, Bongou forcefully tried to assure that power did not slip from northern hands. Relations between the two were always poor, and Bongou was also at loggerheads with some other Sassou-Nguesso appointees, including the latter's cousin, in charge of the UJSC youth movement. Bongou's uncompromising political and ideological stands finally brought about his eclipse in July 1989 when Sassou Nguesso, aware that pragmatism and moderation were imperative in light of the economic crisis and changing political conditions, jettisoned him from the top PCT hierarchy. Dismissed also as permanent secretary of the PCT, Bongou was dispatched as ambassador to Nigeria.

BONGOU, LEON AUGUSTIN, 1927– . Town planner and civil engineer. Born in Brazzaville on April 4, 1927, and trained in town planning and engineering, Bongou has been Congo's long-term director of construction, town planning and housing improvements (1967–1973), and since 1973 director of the Office Congolais de l'Habitat. He was retired in 1985.

BOUBANGUI. Small northern ethnic group comprising some 4 percent of the population of Congo, and subdivided into a number of clans, the most important of which are the Boubangui, Bondjo, Mondjombo, Bondongo, Bomitaba, Bandja and Babolé. They arrived into Congo from regions in what is now the Central African Republic, their spread further southward blocked in the 19th century by the Mbochi.

BOUENZA. Congolese region southwest of the Pool with administrative headquarters in the town of Madingou, and comprising the districts of Madingou, NKayi, Loudima, Mouyondzi, Boco-Songo and Mfouati. Encompassing an area of 13,000 sq. kms. and 219,822 (making it the fourth largest in Congo) Bouenza includes rich agrarian land along the Niari river that produces sugar, tobacco, coffee and a variety of staple crops. It includes an array of peoples among which are the Bembe, Batéké, Bassoundi and Lari. Bouenza is also the site of a hydro-electric station, some 300 kms. south of Brazzaville, originally built with Chinese assistance. In 1987 Sassou-Nguesso secured an additional Chinese commitment to dispatch 33 technicians for four months to bring about an overhaul of the station that is a major producer of hydro-electric power (74,000 kW), most going to the port of Pointe Noire.

BOUITI, DR. JACQUES, 1922– . Surgeon and politician. Born on December 14, 1922 in Kouilou, Bouiti gained a medical degree, specializing in surgery, and opened his practice in Pointe Noire, where he was elected mayor. Joining the PCT, and elected to the latter's Central Committee he was named minister of health in January 1968 by President Ngouabi. He was utilized by Ngouabi on several diplomatic missions as in September 1968, to explain the military takeover to the presidents of Chad and the Central African Republic, and in November 1969, when he accompanied Raoul on a mission to Peking. He was removed from his cabinet post in March 1970, and a year later was also removed from the PCT's Central Committee on the grounds of "practicing occult sciences," a general catch-all accusation usually signifying ideological immaturity. Bouiti continued his medical practice in Brazzaville until he went into retirement in the early 1980's.

BOUITI, JEAN-PAUL, 1949– . Sociologist. Born in Brazzaville on July 5, 1949, and trained in France in Sociology, Bouiti has been head of the department of Sociology at Marien Ngouabi University in Brazzaville since December 1979.

BOUKAKA, SAMUEL, 1934– . Civil engineer. Born in 1934, and trained in civil engineering and town planning in France, Boukaka has been in charge of several major engineering projects, and between 1970 and his retirement in 1989 he was director of air bases at the Agence Nationale de l'Aviation Civile, based in Brazzaville.

BOUKAMBA-YANGOUMA, JEAN-MICHEL. Former key hardline PCT member and powerful union leader. In the mid-1970's Boukamba-Yangouma was named Secretary-general of the CSC single trade union confederation, and he kept the union in line behind the Sassou Nguesso regime, at times against opposition from within the rank and file. On February 3, 1979, he was named president of the sociocultural committee of the preparatory committee for the third extraordinary party congress, and a few months later replaced Goma as one of the three leaders most influential in the Congo. In January 1980 it was Boukamba-Yangouma, representing "the workers" who made the key speech at a meeting commemorating Sassou-Nguesso's takeover from Yhomby Opango. He has been a member of the PCT inner circle, the Politburo, and the latter's secretary in charge of party organization. He remained a hard-liner to the end, vehemently defending the PCT and opposing multipartyism as late as 1990. However when multipartyism triumphed he joined with Poungui to form a new party—Union pour le progrès social et démocratie (UPSD)—that stood for private enterprise and personal freedom. Later the same year, he led a breakaway faction out of the party to found the Union pour le développement et le progrès social (UDPS).

BOUKAMBOU, JULIEN, 1917– . One of the founders of modern Congolese trade unionism. A Bassoundi, born on April 17, 1917 at Mindouli, Boukambou attended a Catholic mission primary school, following which he became a primary school monitor in Brazzaville (1935–50), and an agent with Air France's office in Brazzaville. After being dismissed from his job with Air France in 1952 for disseminating Communist propaganda, he was unemployed until he became general secretary of the **Conféderation Générale Africaine de Travail**. A former left-wing militant in the Parti Progressiste Congolais, he was defeated in the Brazzaville municipal elections of 1956, but as leader of CGAT he secured backing from the French Communist Party to travel to France and Eastern Europe for training. On his return to the Congo in 1960 he was arrested for these travels. He was active in the 1963 trade union demonstrations that led to the coup that toppled President Fulbert Youlou. After the upheaval Boukambou was elected to the national assembly and became its first Vice-President under the Lissouba government of President Massamba-Debat. He also became administrative secretary of the Politburo's new party then set up, the MNR. In his various capacities he visited Peking in 1964, and helped in the gradual radicalization of Congo. After Ngouabi's coup d'etat he was appointed to the interim CNR, and from March 1970 to August 1971 he served as the Congo's ambassador to the USSR. By now old and ailing, his remarkable career ended shortly after this appointment.

BOULAMBA, JOACHIM, 1942– . Militant trade union leader. Born in Loukelo (Loudima) on May 22, 1942, and trained as a teacher, Boulamba joined trade union activities, and as member of the regional PCT bureau was elected communal and regional councilor of Niari. He also served as secretary-general of the Niari branch of the Confédération Syndicale Congolaise. In the 1984 legislative elections he was elected to the national assembly, serving until 1989.

BOUNDJI. District in the Cuvette region with administrative headquarters at a town with the same name that is 60 kms. from Owando, the region's capital.

BOUNGOU-BALENDET, LAZARE, 1948– . Economist. Born on May 31, 1948 in Mandou, Madingou, and educated in a Catholic school and at the Lycée Chaminade in Brazzaville, after further technical studies in Brazzaville (1966–69) he proceeded for higher studies at the Gorky State University in Kharkov (1969–70) and Kiev State University (1970–74) in the Soviet Union. On his return to Brazzaville he was appointed director of Surveys and Planning in the Ministry of the Plan, preparing many of the technical and statistical reports of that ministry. In 1980 he was appointed director-general of industry, remaining in that post until 1985 when he returned to his technical duties in the ministry of the Plan.

BOURAMOUE, DR. CHRISTOPHE, 1941– . A Batéké born on September 22, 1941 and educated locally at the Chaminade seminary in Brazzaville, Bouramoué studied medicine at the University of Montpellier, specializing in cardiology and internal medicine and receiving his final degree in 1968. On returning to Congo he rapidly became Chief Medical Doctor at the Brazzaville Hospital, Professor of Cardiology at the Marien Ngouabi University, and eventually Rector of the university. The author of over forty scientific articles and papers, founder of the *Revue Medicale du Congo* (1981), and a member of numerous medical associations in Africa and in France, Bouramoué was politically radical. On his return to Congo he joined the PCT party (within which he was promoted to the Politburo) but also was a key member of the hardline pro-Soviet M-22 pressure group outside the PCT. He was integrated into Sassou-Nguesso's cabinet as minister of health and social affairs. In 1986 he was reshuffled to head the ministry of scientific research and the environment, despite his known feelings that the regime was increasingly too pragmatic, largely because of his Bateke ethnicity in a cabinet and PCT Politburo increasingly dominated by northerners. On the advent of multipartyism he was briefly one of the leaders of the new Union des Forces Démocratiques (UDF), but together with eight other founding members he resigned from the party in 1993 in disgust over its "lethargy" and conservative policies, and rejoined the PCT party.

BOUSSOUKOU-BOUMBA, PIERRE DAMIEN, 1945– . Vice President of the Association of African Historians and former cabinet minister. Born in 1945 and educated at the University of Toulouse (1970) and Paris, where he secured a PhD in History (1977). He was head of the department of history at Marien Ngouabi University since 1977, but in 1980 he was brought into Sassou Nguesso's government as minister of health, and in August 1984 was reassigned to the ministry of scientific research. In 1986 he left the cabinet.

BRASSERIE DE BRAZZAVILLE. Manufacturer of beer and soft drinks. Founded in Brazzaville in 1968 with 1,250 million CFAF in capital, and employing 360 workers.

BRAZZA, PIERRE SAVORGNAN DE, 1852–1905. Explorer and French colonial governor-commissioner. Born January 25, 1852, in Rome, Brazza came from an aristocratic Italian family. After attending school in Paris, he was admitted to the French Naval School in 1868, and served as midshipman in the French North Sea fleet during the 1870–71 Franco-Prussian war. After a voyage to the coast of Gabon, where he explored the Ogooué river, he submitted to the French Minister of the Navy and of Colonies a project for exploring Gabon. The project was officially approved on February 25, 1875, by which date Brazza had become a naturalized French citizen. On September 10, 1880, he raced against Stanley into the interior of central Africa and signed, among others, a treaty with the Batéké king (Makoko), giving France rights over the north bank of the Congo river, even though the Batéké by that time were a spent force, and the Makoko only ruled over a small dominion. After further explorations this treaty gave birth to the French Congo, of which Brazza became general commissioner for much of the period between 1883 and 1898. Brazza's expeditions were very popular in France, and accelerated the scramble of other European powers for colonial territories in Africa. An explorer and pacifier of central Africa rather than a conqueror, Brazza was profoundly distressed by the concessionary-company exploitation system France established in the Congo basin area. In 1905 he was charged by the French government to investigate various brutal scandals in Congo, but died at Dakar on September 14 of that year before completing his mission.

BRAZZAVILLE. Burgeoning capital of Congo, nerve-center of the country's economy, politics, education and culture, and major riverain port. Founded in 1880 on a site ceded to France by the paramount chief (Makoko) of the Batéké who controlled the region, the settlement (originally Nkuma) was later renamed by the French Geographical Society in honor of the explorer Savorgnan de Brazza who had signed the treaty on behalf of France. It is situated 350 km. from the mouth of the Congo River and extends for 7 km. along the right bank of Stanley Pool. On the opposite side of the Pool, at a distance of 24 km., is Kinshasa, Zaire's capital. Troubled diplomatic relations between the two countries ever since independence have as often disrupted the crossing (by ferry) between these two capitals, and for much of the remaining period the ferry was restricted to nationals only.

Brazzaville's administrative center is called the Plateau; its commercial district, the Plain; its industrial zone, M'Pila; and its two best known quarters, Poto-Poto and Bacongo. Poto-Poto, founded in 1900, is the older, more populous and more heterogeneous of the two, and it contains the cathedral of Sainte Anne-du-Congo and a school of painting which together have made Poto-Poto widely known in artistic circles abroad. Bacongo, smaller and more recently founded, is inhabited almost wholly by Lari, whereas Poto-Poto's more mixed population is by now predominantly Mbochi and Batéké. During the recent (1992–1994) in-fighting in Brazzaville, youth militias shelled each other in these quarters.

Although Brazzaville replaced Libreville as capital of French Congo in 1903 and became that of the newborn French Equatorial Africa Federation in 1910, its population, which then numbered only 4,000, did not grow appreciably until World War II when a massive rural-urban demographic shift began, still unabated. Under Governor-general Eboué, it became headquarters of Free France in Black Africa, and in 1944 was the site of a historic conference chaired by General de Gaulle. The loss of its status as federal capital when the government-general disappeared in 1959 did not retard Brazzaville's rapid numerical growth or deflect its political and cultural evolution. Still a small town of 135,000 in 1962, twenty years later Brazzaville's population had grown to 420,000 (more than twice the size of the second largest city, Pointe Noire), although its resident European component remained fairly stationary at some 6,000. A continuation of the drift into the capital increased its population further, to 585,812 in 1985, and again to an incredible 909,542 (or 850,000, as different estimates exist) in 1992.

This burgeoning population has been a persistent problem for all administrations. Apart from the need to provide at least minimal and costly urban services, constantly needing to be expanded, that the State has not been able to keep pace with, it has caused massive educational shortages, large classrooms, and eroding educational standards. Moreover, the regime has had to face increasing unemployment, estimated in 1992 at a staggering 50%; a restless youthful unemployed population that can be mobilized around populist slogans and platforms, and a civil service jealously guarding its privileges, foremost among them their tenure, that has been at the core of Congo's slide into fiscal bankruptcy in the 1980's.

Urbanization plans drafted in the 1920s were never fully carried out, but over the years the city acquired a large and well-equipped modern hospital, university buildings, a stadium, an enlarged river port, and an international-class airport (Maya-Maya). In 1971, the government began paving about 50 km. of the city's streets and raised a loan to improve the capital's water-distribution system. By way of celebrating the city's centenary on October 3, 1980, a large modern hotel, the Meridien, was inaugurated and a boulevard was built connecting Bacongo with Poto-Poto, thus embellishing the city as well as adding to its conveniences. Further improvements and urban renovations (including the river-port, bursting at its seams) came in the late-1970's and early 1980's when the regime of Sassou-Nguesso, flush with windfall oil-royalties allocated large sums of money for a variety of projects.

Since rapids and other impediments on the Congo prevent river transport downriver to the Atlantic Ocean, most imports and exports move along the (currently greatly dilapidated and slow) 509 kms.-long **Ocean-Congo railroad** that connects Pointe-Noire with Brazzaville. Exports from the landlocked countries upriver (the Central African Republic, and to a certain extent Chad) use barges on the Oubangui river (which in the dry season, and in times of drought, is too shallow for this purpose) and the Congo river to link up with the railroad at Brazzaville, with imports following the reverse route. The port of Brazzaville has been expanded several times in order to accommodate its increasing loads, and now has over 1,310 meters of quais. The tonnage of goods it handles has varied with the levels of the Congo river and its affluents, since at times levels are so low that barge-traffic is at a standstill for months on end. In recent years it has handled 500,000 million tons, with twice as much flowing downstream (i.e. to Brazzaville and on to the coast by rail) than upstream. Timber logs, floating downstream, represent over 50% of this traffic.

Brazzaville is also connected by road to Loubomo (380 kms. by road; Pointe Noire, 599 kms.; and Owando, 523 kms.) Until the 1980's all travel upcountry was difficult and unreliable since much of the road-system was not paved. And, despite subsequent very costly paving of some of the roads in the early-1980's, their poor quality and the eroding effects of heavy rainfall and little maintenance still makes trips upcountry difficult.

Brazzaville has been unique among African capitals in its development as a bastion of Franco-Congolese cultural collaboration, that was not affected much, except through censorship during the Marxist phase of the country. Under the aegis of world-famous authors such as Henri Lopes, Thystère-Tchicaya, Emmanuel Dadet, and Tchicaya U Tamsi it has gained an enviable literary distinction. Long famous for its important Poto-Poto school of painting, the city boasts an annual book fair, a People's (since 1990, "National") Library, a national music festival, and an association of extremely prolific Congolese writers and poets.

BUALI. Royal capital of the historic kingdom of **Loango**, and residence of the **Ma Loango**, north of the contemporary Pointe Noire. In the late 18th century a very large town (relative to other Vili settlements of 100–500 people) of 15,000 (compared by one European trader to Amsterdam), today it is a very small village. A few miles away, at Loangele (or Loangiri), is the burial site of the kingdom's Ma Loango rulers.

BUNKULU, BENJAMIN. Minister of foreign affairs, cooperation and hydrocarbons, since August 1992. Bunkulu is a technocrat, and a loyalist to President Lissouba.

BUREAU DE RECHERCHES GEOLOGIQUES ET MINIERES (BRGM). French organ set up in 1959 to carry on the work of the former Bureau Minier de la France d'Outre-Mer, created in 1948 to promote the prospecting and development of mineral deposits in France's overseas dependencies. The BRGM mounted numerous details surveys of Congo's mineral resources, and helped open up the Hollé potash deposits (that had to close down in 1977), and held 36.12 percent of the shares in the Compagnie des Potasses du Congo, and 22 percent of those in COMILOG, which operates the manganese mines in Franceville in Gabon. In 1970, its prospecting operations in Congo were taken over by the newly created Bureau Minier Congolais (BMC), though with the continued technical assistance and cooperation of BRGM.

BUREAU MINIER CONGOLAISE see BUREAU DE RE-CHERCHES GEOLOGIQUES ET MINIERES (BRGM).

BUREAU POUR LA CREATION, CONTROLE, ET ORIENTA-TION DES ENTREPRISES D'ETAT (BCCO). Ambitious state organ set up in 1965 to promote investment and implement the development plan. Though patently incapable of performing these tasks, with the radicalization of Congo in 1968 its duties were expanded to include the control of existing state companies, including hotels, a cement plant, electric-power plants, riverboats etc. After several costly efforts to improve its operations, the BCCO was closed down in May 1972.

BUREAU POUR LE DEVELOPPEMENT DE LA PRODUCTION AGRICOLE (BDPA). French scientific organization that has helped Congo in the promotion of market gardening and other agricultural projects.

-C-

CACAO. Over 80% of Congo's cacao is grown in the Sangha region on 8,000 hectares, efforts to expand the crop in the Cuvette largely failing. Mass apathy to agrarian work has often left Sangha's plantations under-manned: in 1984 the army had to be dispatched to collect the harvest. Production fell to 900 tons in 1986, from 1981's 1,900. See also AGRICULTURE.

CAISSE CENTRALE DE LA FRANCE D'OUTRE MER (CC-FOM) see CAISSE CENTRALE DE COOPERATION ECONO-MIQUE (CCCE).

CAISSE CENTRALE DE COOPERATION ECONOMIQUE (CCCE). Without counterpart elsewhere, this is the French government's highly autonomous investment and development bank, or as one observer referred to it, a mini-World Bank à la francaise. Insofar as Francophone Africa is concerned, the CCCE is the agency through which France has, since 1958, channeled, banked and administered her aid to her former colonies, as well as funds dispersed by the Economic Development Fund of the EEC. The CCCE also extends credit and medium and long-term loans. The CCCE is the successor of the antecedent Caisse Centrale de la France d'Outre Mer (CCFOM).

CAISSE DES DEPOTS ET CONSIGNATIONS (CDC). Official French agency that serves as banker, administrator, and manager of Francophone Africa's pension, national security, and other social welfare programs and benefits.

CARAVAN ROUTES. In pre-colonial days **Stanley Pool** was a major commercial entrepot, with Vili caravans from **Loango** converging on it bringing salt and European goods from the Atlantic coast, and Batéké caravans coming from the interior. Other caravans, notably of slaves, plied routes north or south of the Pool.

CASSAVA. See AGRICULTURE.

CATHOLICS. The dominant faith in Congo, with around 125,000 adherents. See RELIGION.

CENTRE DEMOCRATIQUE CONGOLAISE (CDC). New political grouping formed in January 1993 out of the merger of six small parties. The CDC attempted to take a middle position between the UPADS coalition and the URD opposition alliance, that between them controlled most of the parties that had secured seats in the national assembly. It was, however, too small to play a significant role. Member parties were the MPC, URD (a small party with the same acronym as the Kolelas alliance), RNDP, RAD, MOLIDE and the RDC.

CENTRE D'ENSEIGNEMENT SUPERIEURE DE BRAZZAVILLE. See UNIVERSITE DE BRAZZAVILLE.

CFA FRANC. Formerly the Colonies Françaises d'Afrique franc, changed in 1962 to the Communauté Financiere Africaine franc, this is the common currency of the associated states of the former AEF and the AOF in West Africa, except for those (such as Mali) that opted for their own separate currency. The CFAF is pegged to the French franc, giving it hard-currency convertability. For many years valued at 50 CFAF to one French franc, in early 1994 the rate of exchange was halved. See also BANKING; CURRENCY.

CHAMINADE SEMINARY. Prestigious Catholic seminary in Brazzaville, nationalized together with most other educational institutions in 1965. Paradoxically a large number of the more radical Congolese political leaders were trained in Chaminade, giving rise in the Pool area of the term "the Chaminade Mafia" referring, inter alia, to Camille Bongou, Christophe Bouramoué, Okandza, Elenga-Ngaboro, Noumazalaye, Thystère-Tchicaya and Tati-Loutard.

CHEMIN DE FER CONGO-OCEAN (CFCO). French Equatorial Africa's sole railroad, connecting Brazzaville with its Atlantic Ocean port of Pointe Noire 509 kms. away. Built between 1922–1934 at great cost (231 million gold francs) and forced labor (120,000 workers drawn from as far away as Chad, of whom between 10–25% died). In 1962 a 286 km. long branch line was added to M'Binda at the Gabonese border, to accept COMILOG's Gabonese manganese destined for export via Pointe Noire. By 1970 the CFCO was carrying 3.1 million tons annually, much of it Gabonese manganese, compared to 655,000 tons in 1958, mostly Congolese timber. In 1969 Congo nationalized the CFCO, all river transport (linking Brazzaville with land-locked Bangui, in the Central African Republic), and the port of Pointe Noire, and set up the Agence Transcongolaise des Communications (ATC) to administer the integrated transportation network.

Because of constant bottlenecks on one section of CFCO, in 1976 the realignment of an 88 kms. stretch of track connecting Bilinga and Loubomo was commenced. It was finally inaugurated on August 15, 1986, nine years later, a delay of six full years due to technical difficulties. The final cost was 107 billion CFAF, more than triple the original estimate of 32.7 billion, making it the costliest rebuilding project in the world. Most of the work was on 1,964 meters of bridges (the longest, 221 meters) and three tunnels for a total of 4,523 meters. With this new track the CFCO was expected to double transport capacity to 10,000 tons, without the previous frequent derailments on the steeper and tighter curves on the old track. The next stage was supposed to be renovating the 342 km. Brazzaville-Loubomo section (during 1987–1991) and electrifying the whole network with the final aim of boosting capacity to 15 million tons a year. However, renovation of the second stage was postponed due to shortage of funds, and due to Gabon's plans to divert its manganese exports to its own new Transgabonaise railway, that greatly decreased the capacity needed on the CFCO. And since the electrification of the CFCO assumed construction of the Moukoukoilou and Imbouli dams, on which a start had not even been made, nothing came out of this project. Gabonese exports via Congo ended in 1991, and precipitated an inter-state crisis as Congo requisitioned all rail material and equipment worth 60 billion CFAF belonging to **COMILOG** that had become redundant.

Traffic on the CFCO in 1991 was 1,087,000 tons of freight and 2,323,000 passengers. Of the freight 385,569 tons were of timber and 25,961 tons of SARIS-Congo sugar. The railroad generated 20 billion CFAF in revenue but remained, as in the 1970's, under major cost pressures due to inefficiency, frequent costly derailments, gross over-staffing (5,000 employees), high staff salaries, and a go-slow work-ethic of its demoralized labor force, constantly under threat of having their ranks thinned out, but always successful in warding off these threats.

The CFCO has always been plagued with such difficulties, especially high operating costs and inefficiency. With most funds devoted to paying its bloated manpower, little was channeled to normal upkeep of rail or equipment, that deteriorated. By 1993 the CFCO's catastrophic state of operations, despite the early 1980's track realignment, was threatening logging operations in northern Congo. Four of the eight private companies there had suspended operations, and the other four were experiencing cash-flow problems, with over 200,000 cubic meters of their logs stockpiled in Brazzaville for over two years waiting for transshipment on the CFCO that, with little operational moving stock, was unable to cope with the demand. In that year the CFCO had only half the locomotives needed to assure adequate service, with 28 costly new ones urgently needed: moreover even many of the existing engines in operation (that were not standing idle) were in need of routine maintenance that was only intermittently supplied, with the result that many breakdowns, derailments, costly communication disruptions and delays continued unabated. See also TRANSPORTATION; AGENCE TRANSCONGOLAISE DES COMMUNICATIONS.

CHIEFS. See LOCAL ADMINISTRATION.

CHINA. See FOREIGN RELATIONS.

CHURCH OF CHRIST ON EARTH. Name of the **Kimbangouist** Church in Congo. See RELIGION.

CIMENTERIE DOMANIALE DE LOUTETE (CIDOLOU). Former state cement factory established in Loutété in 1968 and capitalized at 900 million CFAF. With a productive capacity of 80,000 tons of building material, CIDOLOU's output plummeted to 28,000 tons in 1983 after a fire. Despite rebuilding, the company could not operate profitably and closed down in 1987. It was later privatized with Norwegian capital and renamed SOCICO which see.

CITE DE 16. Name of the Presidential guesthouse in Brazzaville.

CIVIL SERVICE. Part of Congo's parlous public finances has been linked to its burgeoning civil service, a large number of which is unnecessarily located in Congo's urban areas, and most of whom are inefficient. In 1984 it was estimated that half the force could be trimmed with no decline in service, assuming the rest were in place throughout the country instead of in Brazzaville, and trimming the civil service budget by 40% has been one of the conditions demanded by donor agents for further structural adjustment aid to Congo.

Congo inherited from colonial days an overstaffed and privileged bureaucracy, whose upper echelons were highly paid and were originally recruited in France. Brazzaville, as the federal capital of Afrique Equatoriale Française had 17,200 government employees, whose trade union was the strongest group of organized wage earners in AEF. The departure of French civil servants in 1960 created a void that was filled at the outset by Lari and non-Congolese nationals. The Youlou government, far from reducing the size, pay, or perquisites of the Congolese civil servants, created new administrative departments, and between 1960 and 1963 their salaries were raised by 40 percent. By 1964 Congo's civil service, less than one percent of the total population, was absorbing about 62 percent of the national revenue.

During the Massamba-Debat presidency, the government's attitude toward the bureaucracy only slightly changed. Although Massamba-Debat continued to favor the civil service, as a bulwark vis-a-vis the increasingly threatening military, he was forced, for financial reasons, to take timid steps to discipline them. This took the form of frequently and arbitrarily transferring provincial and municipal administrators to other posts, and appointing MNR militants to supervise their activities. In 1967, non-nationals were largely eliminated from government service by an obligatory "Congolization" of the civil service. However, no real effort was made to cut the cost of the civil service as a percentage of total public expenditures, since Massamba-Debat was well-aware of the role of their trade unions in the previous upheaval that had toppled Youlou. Moreover, in the absence of real administrative controls, the government's policy of freezing the size of the civil service was impossible to implement, with division heads appointing new staff at will.

With the rise to power of Ngouabi, the composition of the civil service started to change, though not its size. As a northern military officer, Ngouabi felt no compulsion to be indulgent toward southern elites, whom he viewed as intrinsically opposed to both northern military rule and the Marxist system he imposed on Congo. Moreover, thanks to the spread of educational facilities throughout the country, and, to the recently founded National School of Administration, Ngouabi had a wider pool of candidates for the civil service, including those from the north. When the civil servants went on strike in 1969 because their pay was in arrears, he did not hesitate to break up their union and to accuse them of laziness, incompetence, and lack of zeal. The next year, he required all civil servants to undergo special training in Marxist-Leninist doctrine and all aspirants to government service to produce a party certificate attesting to their revolutionary ardor. In March 1970, the participation of civil servants in the Kikanga attempted putsch led Ngouabi to dismiss eighty government employees, and in October 1971 he had eighteen magistrates arrested on the grounds of corruption and made embezzlement a criminal offense. The fact that **Ange Diawara's** rebellion in 1972 included elements from the civil service further triggered official animosity toward the bureaucracy.

Notwithstanding its financial burden, and various purges on the grounds of political disloyalty or corruption, the civil service—including employees of the newly nationalized state enterprises—rapidly rose to over 25,000, and their salary complaints were addressed. Northerners began to be appointed to high positions in the bureaucracy, and an effort was made to assure also new northern recruits. The second PCT congress in December 1974 voted the civil service substantial pay increase, ranging from 60 percent for the lowest-ranking employees to 7 percent for the highest.

Later, as Congo's oil revenues started falling, recriminations against the "overprivileged and overpaid" Brazzaville elite (still the backbone of the bureaucracy) led to the creation in September 1975 of a committee to purge it of "irrecuperable cadres." In 1976, the recent increase in the size of the Congolese foreign service and its costs (the number of Congolese embassies had grown to 20 with a staff of 194, whose annual salaries, not counting various perquisites, totaled 690 million CFAF) was whittled down. But offsetting these economies was a reintegration into the civil service of "repentant" individuals previously purged. This practice of periodically cutting the bureaucracy and its costs, and then offsetting the resultant economies by fresh recruitments and pay raises was seen as politically justified in order to compensate southerners for their loss of political power since 1968.

In 1977 in the aftermath of Ngouabi's assassination Yhomby Opango dismissed all civil servants at the prefectoral level, replacing them by "special delegates." Those who remained in the service were not only subjected to disciplinary punishments but, for lack of funds, were also deprived of part of their salaries for months at a time. Paradoxically, on a tour in 1978 through Likouala and Sangha, he was to complain of the north's "abandonment and underadministration," proposing as a remedy, inter alia, a periodic recycling of those civil servants who remained at their posts, and more thorough training of future cadres.

After Sassou-Nguesso ousted Yhomby Opango in February 1979, the latter's "special delegates" were replaced by PCT appointees, and the pendulum swung toward institutionalized decentralization. Government servants were given the task of preparing the population for eventual elections to a series of councils to be formed at the regional, district, and communal levels. Once again the bureaucracy was disparaged in official publications as a "political and economic plague," in much the same terms as the radical intelligentsia used in castigating the bourgeoisie as being out of touch with the masses and intent on usurping the people's power. By then, all elements of the urban population were suffering from acute inflation, and their reciprocal reproaches ceased only later in 1979 when resurgent oil revenues brought regular pay to the civil servants, leading to somewhat better relations with the government. This only lasted for a few years, however. By the early 1980's once again falling oil-revenues, coupled with the need to service a huge national debt—largely incurred on the expectation of continuing boom revenues—brought relations between the government and the civil service to a new nadir.

By now, however, the size of the civil service had mushroomed to 50,000, and together with personnel in the state economy over 75,000 were on the governmental payroll. The latter figure, plus the security services, amounted to a staggering 25% of the entire adult workforce in the country. The civil service payroll had more than doubled between 1980 and 1985 from 35.7 billion CFAF to 75.7 billion, at a rate of 20% per year. By 1988 the civil service payroll (78.3 billion CFAF), was second only in the budget after the public debt at 127 billion, and far ahead of social services at 5.8 billion. Trimming the civil service was virtually impossible for the Sassou-Nguesso regime, since patronage appointments had been the cement that had stabilized it, while a long-standing practice assured university graduates (up to 2,000 a year) civil service appointments. Already in 1984 a government announcement that there would be competitions for university scholarships and that entry to the civil service would not be automatic had triggered vicious student demonstrations. Unwilling to bend to the harsh dictates of a civil service cut called for by the World Bank, Sassou-Nguesso attempted austerity measures: the first, a 5% pay-cut in 1986, and the second in September 1988, a more significant 10% cut on salaries and a 50% cut in allowances and 13th month bonuses. However, since only 15,000 of the workforce of 75,000 were affected, and many evaded it, the total savings were not significant enough to affect the state of the budgetary deficit.

Indeed not only were there no cuts in the civil service but later, in the transitional phase before Sassou-Nguesso handed over power, an additional 5,000 new civil service appointments were made, to "recompense" in advance northerners for the pending handover of power to the south. By the late-1980's the country had no choice but to accept a commitment to radically restructure the deficitory state sector (via privatization), with implicit manpower reductions. For this reason all efforts to set the Congolese budget and economy on an even keel were hampered by adamant trade unions protests, that prevented a number of reforms by Sassou-Nguesso, and later by both the interim Milongo and the Lissouba governments. The current regime in Brazzaville has so far trimmed several thousand non-existent "phantom" positions, and has cracked down on (1,600) absentee employees, but is facing the same vehement opposition from all quarters against a serious cutback in personnel expenditures, possible only with massive layoffs. Some of these were indirectly attained when the bankrupt state sector was allowed to close down, and/or through privatization (that led to instant reduced manpowers of 40–60%) but the civil service payroll still continues to drag the Congolese economy.

COFFEE. Grown solely on 3,500 hectares in Niari, production dropped to 2,500 tons in 1985. See AGRICULTURE.

COLONIAL CONQUEST. Though the French were to claim control over what became Congo on the basis of their treaties with the Batéké (signed by their Makoko), and the coastal Vili (signed by the Ma Loango), various groups resisted the French entry into their areas, and the colony was not fully occupied (or, as the French put it, "pacified") until virtually 1920. The northern Mbochi, in the late 19th century in the process of an aggressive expansion southwards (pressing against the Batéké) had actually blocked Brazza's first explorations in their regions in the 1880's, and offered resistance later, in 1902, when French armed columns were dispatched to the Gagna plains. Earlier, in 1887, during the French attempt to secure the axis connecting Nkuma (the future Brazzaville) with Loango, the Sundi (a Bakongo clan) resisted French power for several months in the vicinity of Mindouli. Between 1902–1904 the Bakwélé likewise resisted the French intrusion in their lands, as did the Bémbé in the Haut Louessé in 1907. Harsh **concessionary company** rule and brutalities triggered revolts of the Sembé in 1910, of the populations of the Bouénza valleys and Upper Niari in 1911, and in 1913 in the Likouala-Mossaka region.

COMBO-MATSIONA, BERNARD. Former radical Marxist and member of the PCT Central Committee. A Lari, Combo-Matsiona came to prominence when he was appointed Secretary-general of the Union of Congolese Youth (the reincarnation of the JMNR) where he undertook to politicize and indoctrinate youth. In January 1970 he publicly denounced French neocolonialism and urged breaking off relations with Paris. Utilizing his hold over Brazzaville youth as a pressure group against the Ngouabi regime, he was finally purged from the PCT central committee in December 1971, and in February 1972 he was sentenced to death for participating in the **Diawara** putsch. His sentence was commuted the following month to life imprisonment, and he was later amnestied. After the assassination of Ngouabi his career took an upward turn as he joined the national assembly and on December 28, 1980 was appointed by Sassou-Nguesso as minister of labor, civil service and social insurance, later minister of health and social affairs, a position he held until 1989. A prominent member of the pro-Soviet M-22 clique, for years he remained the only Lari member in a largely northern cabinet, his hard-line positions tolerated primarily for that reason. On October 25, 1989 he was elected President of the national assembly, though he lost that post with the advent of multipartyism.

COMITE ISLAMIQUE DU CONGO. See ISLAM.

COMITE NATIONAL DE LA CELLULOSE (CNC). High-level committee set up in 1984 under President Sassou-Nguesso's direct supervision, charged with overseeing the implementation of one of Congo's most ambitious projects, the eucalyptus forestry and large paper mill project. Since it was soon clear the massive project could not be implemented, the committee was disbanded in 1987. See also EUCALYPTUS PROJECT.

COMITES DE VIGILANCE. Spontaneously-emerging vigilante youth groups that sprang up throughout Congo in the aftermath of the overthrow of President Fulbert Youlou to safeguard the revolution. Found at prefectural and subprefectural levels, they met very intermittently, had no real structures, engaged in harassment of chiefs and casual passers-by, leading to efforts by President Massamba-Debat to bring them under central control via the **JMNR** that was set up in the summer of 1964.

COMMISSION DES BIENS MAL-ACQUIS (CBMA). Special investigatory commission set up in mid-1991 to investigate all ill-gotten gains of the Sassou-Nguesso regime. Since just about everyone had been tarnished during the preceding decades the commission fell prey to internal squabblings, with only two prominent figures to date arrested or imprisoned, the presidential brother Maurice Sassou Nguesso, and Lekoundzou.

COMMUNICATIONS see TRANSPORTATION.

COMPAGNIE COMMERCIALE SANGHA-OUBANGUI. French trading company which operated in both Congo and the Central African Republic until 1971, when its activities were restricted to the former country. It owned a retail store in Brazzaville ("'Parisangha'") and garages in Brazzaville, Pointe Noire, and Dolisie.

COMPAGNIE DES POTASSES DU CONGO (CPC). Large company formed in April 1964, with a mining concession covering 1,300 sq. km. astride the Congo-Ocean Railroad, and capitalized at 2.5 billion CFA francs. The State originally held 15 percent of its stock, and the Bureau de Recherches Geologiques et Minieres (BRGM), the Mines Domaniales des Potasses d'Alsace, and the SPAFE, 12.75 percent each. By 1970, the CPC had become the single most important industrial enterprise in the country with installations capable of producing 500,000 tons of potash a year, wage expenditures exceeding 800 million CFA francs annually, and investments totalling 28 billion CFA francs. The CPC employed 200 Europeans and 700 Congolese, for whom lodgings, a hospital, a school, a shopping center, and a meeting hall were built at St. Paul Holle. The CPC's mineral port, three km. from Pointe Noire, could receive freighters up to 70,000 tons and stock 65,000 tons of ore.

The CPC turned out to be the first of many industrial disappointments in Congo. By 1971, only two years after it began mining potash, the CPC was in such technological and financial trouble that its French shareholders (who had provided all the CPC's capital of 2.5 billion CFA francs except for the 15 percent owned by the Congo government and the $30 million loaned by the World Bank in 1967), wanted to withdraw from that company. Production and exports had proved very disappointing, potash reserves were smaller than originally estimated, and the company's annual deficit already approximated two billion CFA francs. The next few years brought no improvement in the CPC's situation, even though the company cooperated with the Congo government to improve living and working conditions at the mine and experimented with mining the adjacent sylvanite and carnallite deposits so as to compensate for the steadily decreasing production of potash.

Early in 1977, moves by the CPC (by then, five billion CFA francs in debt) to close down the mine and dismiss its employees precipitated visits to CPC headquarters at St. Paul-Holle by indignant Congolese politicians, headed by President Ngouabi, and there was an exchange of recriminations. The French shareholders accused the Congolese of waste and corruption, and the latter charged France with trying to undermine the country's economy and to sabotage the Congolese revolution, simply because both parties had become disillusioned. Production during the nine years of the CPC's operations totaled 3.11 million tons, whereas an annual output of over 800,000 tons had been expected, with potash accounting for an ever-smaller percentage of Congo's total exports, falling from 13.6 percent in 1971 to 9.4 percent in 1977. Technical difficulties delayed further mining of sylvanite and carnallite, although Congolese deposits were of exceptionally high metal content. Moreover, there seemed to be no way of providing substitute jobs for the 1,300-man work force, much of it idle, that had been assembled at Holle by the CPC. The problem suddenly resolved itself on the eve of Yhomby Opango's visit to Paris in June 1977, when the mines were flooded due to an unsuspected geological fault, leading to their closure and the dismissal of the work force. Prolonged negotiations between the shareholders and their governments led to a compromise agreement in September 1979 whereby Congo, unable to finance a revival of potash mining by itself, accepted the French terms. These included repayment of the CPC's accumulated debt (by now nine billion CFA francs), compensation for the discharged workers, indemnification of the Congolese government for its losses, and the financing of the construction of a spur of the Congo-Ocean railroad to serve the Holle area. In 1985 the Congolese government, unable to accept the closedown of Holle, set up the Société de Potasses Congolaises with 51% state participation and 49% shares in the hands of the Alsace Potassium Mining Co., to mount new explorations to locate additional exploitable deposits of Congo's known one billion tons of potassium.

COMPAGNIE FRANCAISE DU HAUT ET BAS CONGO (CFHBC). Concessionary company formed by the Freres Trechot, with a 30-year exploitation monopoly over an area covering 70,000 sq. km. granted in 1899. It began planting selected oil palms in 1920 and was among the few concessionary companies that survived the interwar period. Increasing financial difficulties after World War II led to its acquisition by the Banque de l'Indochine. This gave the CFHBC only a temporary respite, for in 1961 and again in 1964 it had to seek aid from the Congolese government, which agreed to take it over. CFHBC shareholders, having received no dividends since 1960, had refused to provide finance for further production, although the company was then producing nearly one-third of Congo's edible oils and operating a fleet of river boats in the Congo basin. The government in 1964 organized the Regie Nationale des Palmeraies (RNP) to take over the CFHBC's 2,118 hectares of productive oil-palms, three oilmills, hospital, and school. Since then, the RNP has been in charge of CFHBC's production; the ONCPA of its sales of kernels and oil; and the Société Nationale des Transports Fluviaux, created in 1965, operated its river boats until it was superseded by the ATC in 1970.

COMPAGNIE GENERALE DES OLEAGINEUX TROPICAUX (CGOT). Created in 1948 with a capital of 300 million francs for the purpose of increasing, industrializing, and coordinating the production of oils and fats throughout the French Union.

COMPAGNIE GENERALE DES TRANSPORTS EN AFRIQUE EQUATORIALE (CGTAE). Originally known as the Compagnie Générale des Transports en Afrique (CGTA), this was a private French company formed in 1910 to operate a service on the Oubangui-Congo River. In 1954, it increased the traffic carried by 7,000 tons when it acquired from the CFHBC a second monopoly—that of transport on the Sangha River—which brought the total tonnage handled that year to 104,000 tons. After World War II, CGTA had to be repeatedly prodded by the federal authorities before it improved its services in 1955 by acquiring 20 diesel-powered tugs and 100 large barges and reduced its high rates for transporting cotton and coffee. In 1956, it increased its capital from 982 million to 1,179 million CFAF. Seven years later it changed its name to Compagnie Générale des Transports en Afrique Equatoriale. The CGTAE's monopoly and remarkable prosperity made its nationalization inevitable. In 1970 it was taken over by the ATC. (See AGENCE TRANSCONGOLAISE DE COMMUNICATIONS.)

COMPAGNIE INDUSTRIELLE DES BOIS (CIB). Private logging company, the largest in Congo, that in 1984 produced some 82,000 c.m. of timber, one quarter of the country's total.

COMPAGNIE MINIERE DE L'OGOOUE (COMILOG). COMILOG was founded in 1953 to study the manganese deposits, estimated at 200 million tons, that had been discovered before World War II at Moanda, 50 km. west of Franceville in Gabon. A 76 km. aerial cableway (the longest in the world) was built to carry the ore from these deposits, situated 350 km. from the coast, to the frontier of Congo at M'Binda. From M'Binda 286 km. of tracks were constructed between 1959 and 1962 to join up with the **Congo-Ocean Railroad,** at a point 200 km. from Pointe-Noire.

Although the COMILOG is controlled by French and American capital and its mining operations are carried out in Gabon, the revenues derived from the transport of its ores (nearly 2 million tons annually) and their shipment from Pointe Noire are of prime importance to the Congolese economy. However in the 1980's Gabon commenced construction of its ambitious Transgabonaise railroad that reached Franceville in 1988, and manganese shipments via Congo to Pointe Noire stopped in 1991, with the ore transported over the Transgabonaise to Gabon's own port near Libreville. The pullout of the large tonnage of manganese from the Congo-Ocean railroad adversely affected its finances, while leaving the country with a useless track.

Congo promptly expropriated some 60 billion CFAF worth of rails and equipment on its territory belonging to COMILOG, while on the other side of the border the 76 km. aerial cableway was dismantled in 1993 for sale to South Korea.

COMPLEXE AGRO-INDUSTRIEL D'ETAT DE MANTSOUBA. State agro-industrial holding company for several farms and processing units mainly in the southern part of the country. In 1986 the company started a project of mechanized cultivation of manioc and cassava with mixed results.

CONCESSIONARY COMPANIES. The original vast Moyen Congo colony was at outset parcelled out by France into forty concessions, granted to private companies, some hastily assembled, under-financed and recruiting avaricious personnel concerned solely with private profit. Thirteen of the concessions were in the area currently in Congo. The zones of exploitation that were granted covered large areas: in Congo some were over 4 million hectares in size. In return for an annual fee paid to the government, the companies both exploited all the natural resources in their concessions and administered their regions. The system of brutal pillage that followed in many of these concessionary zones, as finally brought to the attention of public opinion in France in the 1920's and in particular by the author André Gide (who travelled to the AEF), led to tighter control over the companies, and later the scrapping of the system altogether. In Congo the concessionary system ended by 1920, much earlier than elsewhere.

CONFEDERATION AFRICAINE DES TRAVAILLEURS CROYANTS (CATC). See LABOR.

CONFEDERATION CONGOLAISE DES SYNDICATS LIBRES (CCSL). See LABOR.

CONFEDERATION GENERALE AFRICAINE DES TRAVAILLEURS. See LABOR.

CONFEDERATION SYNDICALE CONGOLAISE (CSC). Congo's former unified, and still largely intact trade union confederation. See LABOR.

CONFERENCE NATIONALE. As in Francophone countries, this was the venue that produced regime-change in Congo, transferring power from a military one-party system to a civilian multi-party government. The progressive erosion of Congo's economy in the 1980's until the country was virtually bankrupt, growing domestic unrest and union pressures, and the changed international environment, led the Sassou-Nguesso regime to relax its political monopoly, renounce Marxism-Leninism, and convene a conference in Brazzaville with representatives of all opposition and self-exiled groups. The final straw may have been the mid-September 1990 call for an unlimited general strike by the CSC trade-union confederation (over delays and non-payment of salaries) coupled with a declaration of disengagement from the ruling PCT party, and a demand for a national conference. After two weeks Sassou Nguesso agreed to convene the national conference, leading to the emergence of numerous new political parties in the country, many formed by former PCT leaders.

The conference was a lengthy one, lasting three months, and with hefty per-diem allowances for its participants (who may have prolonged the meeting out of self-interest) cost nearly $12 million. It convened on February 25, 1991 with between 1,000–1,200 delegates representing around 108 political parties/factions, organizations and corporate groups of civil society, with the participation of PCT loyalists and the military/northern membership artificially padded. During the first week there was a deadlock over prime minister Goma's suggestion that a 25-man commission be selected to preside over the conference. Re-convened in mid-March, the conference promptly declared itself sovereign and its decisions legally binding. On March 14th the Bishop of Owando, Mgr. Ernest Kombo, was elected President and three of the vice-presidents of the conference went to opponents of the PCT. A High Council of the Republic of 153 deputies was elected as the interim legislature pending local, legislative and presidential elections, and later a 25-member interim government was likewise selected, to be headed by **André Milongo** who won the post in the fourth ballot when he defeated Pascal Lissouba (later to emerge President of Congo) by a vote of 454 to 419. The conference ended on June 10th: it reinstated Congo's old flag and name (Republic of Congo), adopted a new anthem, witnessed Sassou-Nguesso's public apology for the previous regime's sins of omission and commission, and saw the reconciliation of Sassou-Nguesso with Yhomby Opango, who publicly embraced.

Notwithstanding the resolution of some basic issues at the national conference, that led to the civilianization of politics and the promised elections, the transition in Congo has been difficult, and as of mid-1994 still not definitive. Hard-line factions in the PCT, military, and among northerners, unhappy with the shift of power to both civilian politicians and southerners, and the existence of privately-controlled armed militias in Brazzaville (see NINJAS; ZOULOUS) led to constant armed confrontations, shoot-outs, and bombardments of "enemy" quarters, keeping the situation tense throughout.

CONGO-BRAZZAVILLE. This is the unofficial name of the country known successively as Congo Français, Moyen-Congo, République du Congo (September 28, 1958), République Populaire du Congo (December 30, 1969), and with the eclipse of Marxism-Leninism again République du Congo. When Congo sought admission as a sovereign state to the United Nations in September 1960, the former Belgian Congo had already that July been admitted to membership in that body as the République du Congo. Inasmuch as neither of the governments concerned was willing to yield its name, and the existence of two countries bearing the same name was likely to cause confusion, the United Nations proposed the following compromise: until some negotiated settlement of the question was reached, the two states should be known as the Republic of Congo-Brazzaville and the Republic of Congo-Leopoldville. (On August 1, 1964, the latter took the name of Republique Democratique du Congo; and on October 27, 1971, it was renamed the Republique du Zaire.) Today the name Congo-Brazzaville is still occasionally used in referring to Congo, despite the fact that the "second" Congo (i.e., Zaire) no longer exists.

CONGO-OCEAN RAILROAD. See CHEMIN DU FER CONGO-OCEAN.

CONGO RIVER. Known also as the Zaire river. Brazzaville is located on the Congo river at Stanley Pool, a riverine lake 28 km. long and 24 km. wide, with Kinshasa, capital of Zaire on the other bank. Upriver of Brazzaville the Congo flows for some 200 kms. to where a major affluent, the Oubangui, branches off, providing (depending on water-levels) river access to Bangui, capital of the Central African Republic. Downriver of Brazzaville the river flows for an additional 300 kms. to the Atlantic Ocean. The presence of rapids on this stretch makes access to the coast by the river impossible. Both Congo and Zaire have their own national railways to the coast, as well as roads. Zaire's Atlantic port is Matadi, on the river mouth, while Congo's is Pointe Noire, north of it.

CONGOLAISE DES PECHES MARITIMES (COPEMAR). Mixed economy fishing company that in 1983 replaced **SICAP**. COPEMAR also imports and markets fish for the domestic market.

CONGOLAISE DE RAFFINAGE (CORAF). Former state-controlled oil refining facilities in Pointe Noire, with a processing capacity of one million tons a year, built with an investment of 33 billion CFAF, 60% from **Hydro-Congo** and 40% from the French oil company Elf-Aquitaine. Shortly after being opened, and processing 600,000 tons in 1986, its operating costs proved exorbitantly expensive, and the plant closed down. Various plans for the privatization of the plant were debated since 1988.

CONGOLAISES DES BOIS IMPREGNES (CBI). Mixed economy enterprise founded in Pointe Noire in 1986 with 800 million CFAF in capital with Ambroise Noumazalay as its president. The company produces electricity poles from eucalyptus trees originally planted in the vicinity for the paper mill project that was never established. See EUCALYPTUS PROJECT.

CONGOLAISES INDUSTRIELLE DE BOIS (CIB). Congo's largest private timber company, capitalized at 2 billion CFAF of which a German group owns 51% equity, a Swiss one 42% and the World Bank 7%. Cutting an annual 150,000 metric cubes of timber in north Congo, an annual turnover of 6 billion CFAF, and 300 workers, the company was forced to suspend operations and dismiss its 196 employees in September 1992 due to currency fluctuations in South Europe to which most of its products are exported, opposition of ecological groups to forest depletion, on top of the traffic bottlenecks on the CFCO that resulted in sales being consummated over four years after logging. See also CHEMIN DE FER CONGO-OCEAN.

CONSEIL CONSTITUTIONEL. Constitutional council set up after the 1979 modification of the Congolese constitution, with Louis Sylvain Goma as its president. The council supplanted Congo's supreme court as the ultimate arbiter of the constitutionality of government laws, and was also charged with supervising the country's elections.

CONSEIL D'ETAT. Under the constitution of 1973 the Conseil d'Etat was the locus of power, the meeting point of the executive, the party, and the legislature. It was a presidential council composed of the head of state (who was also head of the PCT party), the four members of the PCT political bureau, the five executive officers of the legislature and the prime minister.

CONSEIL NATIONALE DE L'OPPOSITION CONGOLAISE (CNOC). Moribund opposition party set up in 1980 in Paris by self-exiled former Colonel David Mountsaka.

CONSEIL REPRESENTATIF. Colonial assembly created in October 1946 and sitting in Brazzaville until January 1, 1950 when it relocated to Pointe Noire. Members were elected from a **double electoral college** for a term of five years. It was originally composed of 12 members elected by the first (mostly French) electoral college (or one deputy per 750 inhabitants) and 18 from the second electoral college (one per 37,500 inhabitants), with the franchise progressively expanded.

CONSEIL SUPERIEUR DE LA REPUBLIQUE (CSR). Congo's interim legislature headed by Bishop Ernest Kombo, that in 1991 replaced the Assemblée Nationale Populaire. The CSR was a body of 153 members, elected from members in the **national conference**, to serve until competitive elections produced a new national assembly. While Sassou-Nguesso was retained as titular head of state (with reduced powers), the CSR's head of government and interim prime minister was **André Milongo** who won on the fourth ballot over 19 other candidates, including Pascal Lissouba.

CONSEILS MUNICIPAUX. Municipal councils, set up in Congo's main cities, differing in size: Brazzaville's and Pointe Noire's were the largest with 41 members.

CONSEILS POPULAIRES DE REGIONS. Regional councils, set up by the constitution of 1973. Their size differed from that of the Pool and Kouilou regions (41 members), to those in Niari, Cuvette, Plateaux and Bouénza (36) to those in Sangha and Lekounou (32).

CONSTITUTIONS. (1) February 23, 1959. This constitution gave the autonomous Congo Republic a parliamentary government. Deputies were elected to the legislature by universal adult suffrage for a five-year term. The majority-party leader of the assembly was chosen by, and was responsible to the legislature, and he appointed and could dismiss the ministers and secretaries of state who formed his cabinet. (2) March 2, 1961. A presidential-type government, similar to those of the other Francophone equatorial states, was instituted by Fulbert Youlou and was accepted in a referendum. Elected by universal adult suffrage for a five-year term, Congo's president was both head of state and head of government, as well as commander-in-chief of the armed forces. His cabinet and the vice-president were appointed by the president and responsible to him alone. As before, the legislature was elected for five years by direct universal suffrage, but from a single national list of candidates. The deputies' legislative powers were limited to certain domains, and their authority could be by-passed if the president chose to submit any question to a direct popular vote. This constitution provided for the establishment of a supreme court and a social and economic council. (3) December 8, 1963. Drafted as a compromise between a parliamentary and a presidential regime, Massamba-Debat's constitution also provided for a social and economic council and a high court of justice. Deputies, elected from a single list drawn up by the new party, the MNR, were to serve for five years, as was the president of the republic, but he was to be chosen by an electoral college composed of deputies and local/government councilors. The president was authorized to elect and dismiss his premier and ministers, and under certain circumstances could dismiss the unicameral assembly and rule by decree for a limited time. The president was also, ex-officio, chairman of the CNR, which was to coexist with the government and guide its policy for an indefinite period. The most important innovations introduced by this constitution were the post of prime minister, the elimination of salaries for deputies, and the institution of an executive body parallel to the government. (4) On August 14, 1968, the CNR abrogated this constitution and replaced it with a Fundamental Act. Six months later, that Act was modified, the CNR became the supreme organ of the state, and it named Major Marien Ngouabi head of state. (5) January 3, 1970. The congress that set up the PCT as the single national party adopted on December 30, 1969 a draft constitution giving the country a new flag, anthem, and name—Republique Populaire du Congo. On January 3, 1970, this constitution was promulgated. The PCT, as repository of the people's sovereignty, elected for five years the president of the republic, who was concurrently chairman of the PCT central committee. Executive power was vested in a state council (conseil d'état), whose members were directly or indirectly named by the president of the republic. All elective bodies were eliminated. (6) June 24, 1973. This constitution revived the elected national assembly (115 members) and the post of prime minister, charged with executing the PCT's decisions. A revised state council, still the supreme organ of state under the PCT president, now comprised the PCT politburo, officials of the national assembly, and the prime minister. Councilors were to be elected at the regional, district, and communal levels from among candidates chosen by the PCT, and were to be given limited powers over local affairs and a degree of financial autonomy. Following the assassination of Ngouabi on March 15, 1977, the 1973 constitution was suspended. (7) July 8, 1979. The new constitution set up by referendum, established a president of the republic, elected for five years by the PCT congress, who was both chairman of the party's central committee and the embodiment of national unity. He had the duty of ensuring respect for the constitution and the proper functioning of its institutions. The cabinet became Congo's supreme executive body, and the prime minister, as head of the government, guided and controlled his ministers' actions. The people's national assembly, elected by universal suffrage for a five year term, represented the state's highest authority. The partially decentralized communes and regions were to be administered by people's councils, which had a legal status and financial autonomy. The PCT was defined as a proletarian party guided by Marxist-Leninist principles in leading the Congolese to national liberation and the practice of scientific socialism. The supreme policy-making body was the

PCT's national congress, meeting at least every five years. Its central committee functioned in its place between congress sessions, just as the politburo acted for that committee on occasion. The 1979 constitution marked a return to the elective system and, to a limited degree, decentralized authority, but it was regarded by its sponsors as a first step toward constructing a Marxist-Leninist Society in Congo. However, only in so far as it aimed to change the PCT from a mass party to one of handpicked membership did it differ radically from its predecessors. (8) March 15, 1992. The constitution currently governing Congo was approved by a referendum (by 96.32% of the vote) postponed from November 1991 due to lack of funds in the treasury. It provides for a strong president with 'proven moral probity' within a parliamentary multiparty system. The president appoints a prime minister from the winning majority in a new bicameral system of a national assembly and a senate. The prime minister directs the work of the government via a cabinet, and is the Chief of Staff of the armed forces. Both he and the national assembly are limited to two terms of five years. The senate members cannot be below the age of 50 and are elected for a six-year term.

COUP D'ETAT OF AUGUST 1963. Celebrated as "Les Trois Glorieuses," a reference to the three days of civil unrest that dislodged Congo's first president **Fulbert Youlou**, the upheaval is also referred to as Congo's revolution. Strictly speaking neither a coup nor a revolution, Youlou's conservative and venal regime's efforts to impose trade union unity and a single-party system triggered large demonstrations during August 13–15, 1963, with the military, still under the command of French officers, conspicuous to the end for their noninvolvement. When a last-minute appeal for military support from General de Gaulle was turned down, a military delegation obtained Youlou's resignation.

COUP—ATTEMPTED—OF FEBRUARY 1969. Amateurish counterrevolutionary conspiracy by a group headed by **Major Mouazabakany**, that was nipped in the bud.

COUP—ATTEMPTED—OF MARCH 13, 1970. Pro-Youlouist armed assault on Brazzaville mounted from across the river by Lieutenant Kinganga, who received passive, and some active support from some units of the gendarmerie that were still staffed by Bakongo, and chafing under the northern military regime. The assault was rebuffed, however, and in its aftermath the gendarmerie was re-organized and shackled to the armed forces.

COUP—ATTEMPTED—OF FEBRUARY 1972. Dangerous attempted left-wing coup against Ngouabi masterminded by the "Maoist" **Lt. Ange Diawara**, political commissar of the armed forces. Seizing power during a period of multiple assaults on the regime from all directions, Diawara cunningly proclaimed he was protecting the regime by forestalling an alleged right-wing coup by Major Yhomby-Opango. Diawara's ploy caused much confusion and fence-straddling by several key military units, aggravated by the seizure of all communications in the capital. His power grab was blocked by Yhomby-Opango's decisive military action, though at the time an order for his arrest had been issued by Ngouabi, who had been misled by Diawara's ploy. After the putsch failed Ange Diawara was able to evade security forces for over a year, sheltered by allies, until finally caught in an ambush and killed.

COUP—ATTEMPTED—OF JULY 1987. A conspiracy involving a large number of senior officers, mostly Kouyou from the north, allegedly including also General Yhomby Opango, against the Mbochi Sassou-Nguesso, who they maintained was behind the 1977 intra-military tug-of-war that led to President Ngouabi's assassination. The plot was discovered by the security apparatus, and many of the officers involved were arrested. Among them were Colonel Eboundit, Major Obombo, and several Captains. **Captain Pierre Anga**—related to both Sassou Nguesso and Ngouabi, but loyal to the latter—escaped to Owando with some of his supporters where he resisted efforts of troops sent to arrest him and escort him to Brazzaville. On September 6th larger contingents re-entered the town and in a shootout Anga was killed. (Other versions exist about how he died.) The other plotters were in due course rehabilitated.

COUR REVOLUTIONNAIRE DE JUSTICE (CRJ). Special court established on February 7, 1969. Initially it was charged with trying all individuals threatening the public order; its mandate was later expanded to include all civil servants accused of corruption and embezzlement. These new fields were removed from its competence and handed back to lower courts in July 1975, but in August 1976 Congo's assembly once again empowered the CRJ to try fiscal cases, especially acts of economic sabotage. In August 1984 these areas were once more withdrawn from the court's mandate.

CROIX-KOMA. Anti-sorcery movement, with some similarities to **Mounkoungouna**, using faith and herbal remedies to eliminate from its members maladies caused by sorcerers and spirits.

CUBA. Cuba, starting as somewhat of a surrogate for the mainstream Communist powers, eventually acquired a unique role and a permanent military presence in Congo during the country's revolutionary era. This presence had two aspects: one local and the other regional. Several hundred Cuban troops, at times estimated at over one thousand, have been directly involved in training the Congolese armed forces and paramilitary hierarchies, and providing specialized personnel to the Congolese internal security services, including between twenty and a hundred to the presidential bodyguard. Through a system of spies and informers they provided the regime information about internal threats, especially within the Congolese armed forces, riddled by internal personal and ethnic dissensions. As late as May 1989, for example, it was Cuban intelligence officers who forewarned President Sassou Nguesso of several plots against him, two of which indeed materalized, with those captured in the assaults passed over to Cuban officers in the Presidential Guard for interrogation. Cuban troops have also been used to beef up various operational sorties mounted by the Congolese armed forces. The last instance was when troops and officers were involved in the 1987 confrontation with **Captain Anga** and his followers at Owando. Despite this long-standing and invaluable security assistance for Ngouabi, and later Sassou Nguesso's regimes, Cuba has also been supportive of more militant factions in Congo, including the M-22 and clandestine Parti Communiste Congolais.

Other Cuban units, estimated at several thousand in the mid-1980's, have been stationed in the Pointe Noire region since 1977 in support of (and as a rear base for) units in Angola backing the MPLA's struggle against South African/U.S.A. backed Savimbi. The elimination of this Cuban presence in Africa had been a prime plank of US foreign policy in Africa. It was only attained on April 5, 1991 when the last 1,500 Cuban troops left their bases in Pointe Noire after a political solution to the Angolan conflict was reached. Congo had played a role in mediating Namibia-Angola-South Africa negotiations starting in 1988, pledging that Cuban troops withdrawn from Angola would not simply regroup in Congolese rear bases.

Non-military cooperation between Cuba and the Congo took place in a variety of domains, notably in the area of public health, technical assistance and implementation of several agrarian and industrial projects in fields Cuba had particular expertise, and in the fields of culture and education. In the late-1970's, for example, hundreds of Congolese youth, many Bacongo and allegedly involuntarily, were sent to Cuba for ideological indoctrination. See also FOREIGN RELATIONS.

CURRENCY. In pre-colonial trade and commerce, apart from barter, there were a variety of currencies in use in what was to become

French Congo. Among the most commonly used were copper, brass and lead ingots/rods, several cloth units, as well as shells. The most important of these was the brass rod, called *mitako,* of 3-5 mm. in diameter, and of variable length (10-65 cms.) depending on location and year. Though the rate of exchange fluctuated, an indication of their value in the 1880's in the Pool region can be gleaned from the fact that one mitako would buy a fowl, a bag of salt or a liter of palmwine; an entire buffalo, or a female slave cost 400 and 460 *mitako* respectively. (Male slaves were more normally exchanged for guns, powder or cloth.) Local currencies remained prevalent for several decades after the imposition of French colonial rule, competing with France's currency that was the legal tender in Congo. A local franc was created in 1941, that remained the currency of the AEF until the CFA franc (originally, Colonies Française d'Afrique franc) was created in 1945, pegged to the French franc. After three devaluations, in 1948, 1950,and 1969, the CFA franc was for thirty-five years valued at 0.02 French francs, or 50 CFAF per one French franc. The CFAF remained the legal tender in Congo, despite frequent warnings during the revolutionary era that it would be replaced by a national currency. In 1994, shortly after the death of Ivorien president Houphouet-Boigny, France devalued the CFAF franc by 50%, to 100 CFAF to the French franc, triggering a massive outcry in all Francophone states.

CUVETTE. Northern region of Congo with administrative headquarters in Owando, and composed of the districts of Mbomo, Kelle, Makoua, Ewo, Boundji, Owando, Mossaka, Loukoléla and Okoyo. The Cuvette is a very sparsely populated region with dense vegetation and many rivers (e.g. Congo, Sangha, Kouyou, Likouala, Likouala-aux-Herbes, N'Deko) only in the mid-1980's linked by a paved road to the south. In 1992 its estimated population was 151,539, Congo's sixth largest. The region is the principal habitat of the Mbochi ethnic group, Congo's third-largest, that includes the Mbochi proper and the Kouyou, many members of which have flocked south depopulating the Cuvette of young educated people.The region is one of Congo's poorest: its major products are tobacco, palm oil, smoked fish, coffee, manioc, bananas, with some gold deposits in the area. There is big wild game in the region, including elephants, and the Parc National d'Odzola (30 kms. by track from Libango) is of interest to tourists. During the revolutionary military era a large number of the key ministers, senior civil servants, military officers and PCT central committee members came from the Cuvette, and their influence in Congo is still great. It is from the Cuvette, for example, that Ngouabi, Sassou-Nguesso and Yhomby Opango all originate.

-D-

DACKEY, DR. REMY, 1923– . World Health Organization administrator. Born on September 23, 1923 in Dangi, Togo, of Congolese nationality, and trained in medicine in Dakar, Montepellier, Marseilles and Paris (1943–55) specializing in malariology, Dackey served for several years in various WHO positions in Togo, before returning to the Congo in 1969 as advisor to the WHO regional office in Brazzaville.

DA COSTA, CLAUDE-ANTOINE. Temporary Prime Minister of Congo. An agronomist by training, and of Cabinda origins, and hence neutral in the north-south ethnic tug-of-war in Congo, Da Costa served in a variety of posts in the governments of Massamba-Debat and Ngouabi: head of the political police under Lissouba's prime ministership in 1963, minister of defence in 1965; minister of transport and public works later the same year; and under the Nouamzalaye government as minister of agriculture. He then joined the Food and Agricultural Organization and World Bank, returning to Congolese politics to become, on December 6, 1992 President Lissouba's compromise Prime Minister after the fall of the Bongho-Nouarra government forced by the bolting of the PCT (then in alliance with Lissouba's UPADS) to join the MCDDI opposition. Da Costa tried, with only limited success, to implement the austerity drives, civil service cuts and privatization demands by the World Bank, but immediately ran afoul of the country's trade unions. He was in any case a temporary compromise candidate with no political support of his own, and was replaced a few months later by Yhomby Opango. His younger brother, Jean Da Costa, was appointed in 1992 to train young **Nibolek** youths in commando and urban warfare tactics, supplementing the spontaneous **Zoulous** formations that sprang up in Brazzaville to defend the regime of Pascal Lissouba against Lari/Bakongo attacks.

DADET, EMMANUEL. 1916–1973. Former ambassador to the United States. Born in Impfondo in 1916, Dadet acquired French citizenship and rose to the level of prefect in the colonial administration. He wrote for the local press and radio and also produced a novel set in French Equatorial Africa entitled *Congolila,* which was published in 1950. Having resigned from the PPC in 1949, he was badly defeated when he sought reelection to the French Union Assembly in 1953. Two years later, he founded the short-lived Front Démocratique Congolais, and in 1956, he joined the UDDIA. He was rewarded by being named to its executive committee and to various ministerial posts from 1958 to 1960. In 1961 he was named ambassador to the United States and United Nations. Dadet died at Pointe Noire on March 14, 1973. At that time, his son, Cesar Mompolo-Dadet, was director of President Ngouabi's presidential cabinet, later to became minister plenipotentiary.

DENGUET, ALEXANDRE. Former cabinet minister. Originally a councilor of the Economic and Social Council of the Congo, Denguet was political officer at the Congolese Embassy in Paris from February 1970 to December 1971. In the latter month, he was named a member of the PCT central committee and minister of labor. In the Lopes cabinet of August 30, 1973, he added the justice portfolio to that of labor, serving until 1975. He was then dropped from the PCT central committee and appointed to a variety of administrative duties.

DEVELOPMENT PLAN (1982–1986). See ECONOMY.

DHELLO, DR. THOMAS ALPHONSE FELICIEN, 1941– . State prosecutor. Born on February 27, 1941 in Pointe Noire, and educated at a lycée in France followed by legal studies at the Universities of Caen (1959–62) and Paris (1962–1972), during which time he was treasurer-general of the Fédération des Etudiants d'Afrique Noire, and president of the Congolese Students' Association in France. After obtaining his doctorate, Dhello returned to Brazzaville to join the High Court as state prosecutor.

DIALLO, IDRISSA, 1932– . Former union leader. Born on August 25, 1932 in Brazzaville, the son of a Senegalese father and a Congolese mother. Diallo entered the postal service in 1952 and became secretary of its CGAT union. In December 1964 he was elected first general secretary of the CSC. He held that post until April 1966, when he was dismissed and charged with embezzlement.

DIATA, HERVE, 1951– . Academic. Born on December 9, 1951 and obtaining a doctorate from the University of Grenoble (1976) in economics, Hervé is currently head of the Social and Economic research unit at Marien Ngouabi University in Brazzaville.

DIATOULOU, HENRIETTE, 1942– . Magistrate. Born in Brazzaville on August 26, 1942, and with legal training, Diatoulou served concurrently as judge and regional president for Kouilou of the Union Révolutionnaire des Femmes du Congo. In 1984 she was elected to the national assembly.

DIAWARA, ABDOUL KADER. Brother of **Ange Diawara**. Director of the Brazzaville general hospital since July 1971, at the time of the 1972 attempted putsch he was imprisoned and only released once his brother had died. He was then reassigned Director of Forests. A member of the **M-22**, he was again arrested by Sassou-Nguesso in May 1988 for membership in the illegal Communist Party of Congo, the PCC.

DIAWARA, ANGE, 1941–1973. Radical populist, and possibly Congo's only true revolutionary leader, who mounted the dangerous 1972 attempted putsch against Ngouabi. Born in 1941 in the Pool region, to a Malian father and a Lari mother, he earned a master's degree in political economy and briefly studied in the USSR and Cuba. Returning to Congo, he became commander of the civil-defense corps, and utilizing this as a stepping stone, was elected in July 1967 to the five-man executive committee of the JMNR. He was sent by Ngouabi on a good-will mission to Mali and Guinea, and in September 1968 was named a vice-president of the CNR directorate. A month later, he was also appointed secretary of state for defense with the rank of a second lieutenant, later minister of development in charge of water and forestry. In February 1969 he was also named political commissar of the reorganized people's army, in charge with indoctrinating it with Marxist ideology. Diawara was credited with defeating an attempted assault from Zaire of Youlouist supporters in March 1970, and became a pillar of the regime, an important member of the PCT politburo, and one of the party's leading Maoists. His constant prodding the regime to shift further to the left, and complaints from the army at his excessive ideological zeal, brought about his purge from his cabinet portfolio in December 1971, though he was too powerful to be excised as political commissar of the armed forces. On February 22, 1972, cunningly claiming he was acting to defend the regime against a rightist coup by **Yhomby Opango**, he mounted a putsch against Ngouabi, that nearly succeeded. It was only forestalled by the loyalty to Ngouabi of Colonel Yhomby Opango who rallied his forces to block Diawara's move. Diawara escaped with some of his followers to be sheltered by supporters in Brazzaville itself. He was the object of a massive and increasingly paranoid manhunt for over a year, evading all the dragnets set up by Ngouabi, but was finally discovered and killed in a shootout with the army in April 1973. An alternate version has him being captured by Mobutu in Zaire, and returned for execution in Brazzaville in exchange for Congo's extradition of Pierre Mulele to Zaire.

DIOB-KEGNI, ALPHONSE, 1954–1978. Author and poet. Born on December 25, 1954 in M'Bay near Mossenjo, Diob-Kegni pursued a teaching career while writing a number of acclaimed poems, and serving on the Cercle Culturel Congolais.

DIOSSO. Site, 29 kms. north from Pointe Noire, of spectacular semi-circular red gorges and cliffs facing the Atlantic Ocean.

DIPANDA. Organ of the JMNR.

DIRECTION GENERALE DE LA SECURITE DE L'ETAT (DGSE). During the military era in Congo the DGSE was the notorious security service charged with ferreting out political opposition to the regime. Large-scale political arrests and torture in Congolese jails were a regular feature of life in the country between 1977–1979, and again starting with 1982.

DJAMBALA. District in the Plateaux region with administrative headquarters in the town of the same name. The district comprises 16,250 sq. kms. and two plateaux (Djambala and N'Sah) reaching an altitude of 832 meters where the small town of Djambala is located. The district is inhabited by a number of ethnic groups, especially Batéké.

DJOMBO, HENRI, 1952– . Former cabinet minister. Of Impfondo origins, born in 1952 in Enyelle, Djombo was educated locally before proceeding to study forestry in Leningrad (1971–76). On his return to Brazzaville he became advisor to the minister of rural economy (1977), director of studies and planning (1977–79) and then general director (1979–80) of the ministry of rural economy, before being appointed to the newly created portfolio of waterways and forests in the cabinet of December 28, 1980. A member of the PCT since 1979, he joined its Central Committee in 1982. He remained in his cabinet post until 1985 when he was reassigned to administrative duties. A year later he was appointed head of SUCO, Congo's state sugar company.

DJOUBOUE, JEAN BARON, 1929– . Former PCT militant and administrative head of the district of Ouesso. Born on November 25, 1929 in Ouesso, and educated as a sanitary technician, Djoumboué served with the infirmary of the CFCO and as head infirmary officer of a hospital in Pointe Noire. An active PCT member he returned to his home-town as administrative head, and president of the party branch of Ouesso. In 1984 he was also elected deputy to the national assembly.

DOLISIE see LOUBOMO.

DOLISIE, ALBERT, 1856–1899. Colonial explorer and administrative officer. According to many deserving equal credit with **de Brazza** as the founder of French Congo, and after whom the town of Dolisie (now Loubomo) is named, Dolisie was born on December 22, 1856 in Mutzig (Lower Rhine) and became an artillery officer in the French army. He started his explorations of Congo in August 1886, and in December 1888 was assigned administrative duties in the territory. He was repatriated to Paris when he became very sick in 1893, but returned to serve as Lt. Governor of Congo in April 1894.

DONGALA, EMMANUEL BOUNDZEKI, 1941– . One of Congo's greatest poets and authors, and a Chemistry professor at Marien Ngouabi University in Brazzaville. Born to a Congolese father and a Central African mother on July 16, 1941 in Alindao (C.A.R.), Dongala pursued scientific studies in the United States, and at Montpellier University in France where he earned his doctorate. Teaching organic chemistry at Marien Ngoaubi University in Brazzaville, his true avocation is literature. Equally at home with novels, poetry and plays, he is the author of numerous works which are widely cited and for which he has been awarded several international prizes, most recently in 1988.

DONGOU. Large (32,000 sq. kms.) very sparsely populated northernmost district in Congo, with administrative headquarters in the town with the same name, that is 950 kms. from Brazzaville. The district borders the Central Africa Republic, and is part of the Likouala region. The district is dominated by three rivers that run through it, the Oubangui and two affluents, the Motoba and the Ibenga. All villages in Dongou are found on the banks of these rivers. Every two months goods produced in the region (some palm products and coffee) are collected by the central government.

DOUBLE ELECTORAL COLLEGE. Under the 1946 French constitution a territorial assembly was set up in Congo (and other colonies), deputies being elected through two electoral colleges. The first electoral college, that was very small, was composed of French citizens (including Africans who had attained that civil status) who elected 13 deputies; the second electoral college, nearly all African, elected 24 deputies. This system was in effect until the *loi cadre* (enabling Act) of 1956 that saw the elimination of the double electoral college. In the interim the franchise was progressively extended. See also ADMINISTRATION.

DOULOU, VICTOR, 1947– . Physiologist. Born in 1947, after securing a first degree at Marien Ngouabi University in 1971, Doulou went to Toulouse where he earned his doctorate in the physiology of nutrition. He returned to Congo to head various research divisions in the several government ministries, and has been the leader of several agricultural research projects in Congo, on which he has written scientific reports. He has also been involved in formulating sections of the country's development plans and between 1986 and 1988 was also vice-president of the international council coordinating a UNESCO program in Congo.

DOUMANGUELE, HENRI MARCEL. Politician who in 1991 set up the political party Parti du renouvellement et du progres.

DOUNIAM, OSSEBI, 1940– . Doctor and PCT militant. Born in Ossio (in the district of Gamboma) on August 14, 1940,and educated in medicine, Douniam entered Brazzaville's general hospital and by 1980 was its director-general. A PCT militant he was also a deputy to the national assembly and after the 1984 elections became its first vice-president. He was appointed in 1986 minister of forestry but was dropped from the cabinet later when he was involved in soliciting bids from European consortia for toxic waste disposal in Congo.

-E-

EASTERN EUROPE see FOREIGN RELATIONS.

EBA, SAMUEL. A cousin of Sassou Nguesso. He was appointed secretary-general of the Brazzaville mayor's office in 1980 to monitor developments in the capital. He lost his post in 1991 with the onset of multipartyism and the rise of Bakongo power through Bernard Kolelas' MCDDI party.

EBA, SYLVAIN RAPHAEL (Captain), 1949– . PCT militant and former member of the national assembly. Related to Sassou Nguesso, Eba was born in Okassa (Abala) on April 14, 1949 and joined the Congolese armed forces. He held various appointments including Commander of the School for Revolutionary Cadets, regional commissioner of the Pioneers, and secretary of the central committee of Congo's youth organization, the **UJSC.** A member of the PCT central committee, in 1984 he was elected to the national assembly, serving until 1989.

EBAKA, JEAN-MICHEL (Lt. Colonel). A Kouyou military officer from northern Congo, originally promoted by President Ngouabi. A member of the PCT military committee and president of its control and verification committee, as well as in the 1980's director of security services under Sassou Nguesso, Ebaka was arrested in July 1987 for complicity in the Kouyou anti-government conspiracy of **Captain Anga**. He did not benefit from an amnesty for political prisoners next year, and was only released from prison in 1989.

EBOKI, PATRICK BENJAMIN. Newly appointed (1993) editor-in-chief of Congo's television services.

EBOUE, FELIX, 1884–1944. Former Governor-general of French Equatorial Africa. Born December 26, 1884, in Cayenne, French Guiana, Eboué was educated in France and entered the colonial administration as governor of Chad. After the outbreak of World War II, he was the sole colonial governor to declare for Free France in 1940, and in November 1941, General de Gaulle rewarded him by naming him governor-general of the FEA federation. His role in the resistance and the reforms in colonial policy that he carried out made him a major figure in French colonial history, and he was given a prominent burial place in Paris.

EBOUKA-BABAKAS, EDOUARD, 1933– . Cabinet minister under several different administrations. Born on July 14, 1933 in Mossaka in northern Congo, Ebouka-Babakas studied law and economics at the University of Nancy, joining the Congolese civil service as principal inspector of customs in 1962, later becoming technical advisor in the ministry of finance. A moderate, Ebouka-Babakas was promoted after the 1963 coup d'etat as minister of finance. He remained throughout Massamba-Debat's reign, at one point expanding his ministry to include the budget and mines portfolios. In October 1968 he was appointed ambassador to France, following which he was reassigned to various other administrative duties. He came again into the limelight when he was appointed to the 1991 interim Milongo government, the only new minister with any prior cabinet experience.

EBOUNDIT, ELENGA (Colonel). See ELENGA-YOKA, HENRI EBOUNDIT.

ECONOMY. Congo, possessing one of Africa's most youthful, educated, upward-mobile and urbanized populations, and a remarkable array of exploitable natural resources, has never been able to balance its aspirations with its resources, its Marxist phase being an aggressive nationalist approach to breach the gap. Yet, despite the massive transformation of the weak Congolese economy of the Youlou era, to a multifaceted one under Sassou-Nguesso, the vastly increased royalties flowing into the treasury have been squandered by corruption, embezzlement and the erection of a large inefficient, deficitory State sector, and a civil service estimated in 1990 as 100 percent larger than the country's population and services warranted. The net result has been even greater budgetary deficits and a huge national debt mortgaging future income to pay for the excesses of the past, placing Congo into greater dependence on Western donor-agents.

Congo's budgetary deficits and acute dependence on foreign aid has always been greatly aggravated by the decline in Congo's agricultural sector and output, a massive rural-urban exodus and growing urban unemployment (estimated in 1990 at 50%) and the proliferation of unviable state enterprises catering to labor's needs for jobs at any cost. To this could be added the country's chronic instability and former radical rhetoric that kept much investment capital away. Notwithstanding this, Congo's economy has been one of Africa's most developed ones; already in 1970, before the onset of rapid petro-dollar income, the country's GNP stood at 50 billion CFAF, already placing Congo among the top twelve African states with a per capita income of $300 or more.

Although in the early 1970s Congo's economy was threatened by a decline in oil production, blamed by the regime on Western efforts to choke off the Congolese revolution, the discovery of new offshore oil deposits in the late 1970s and increases in global oil prices brought Congo massive unprecedented royalties that bolstered the economy. Congo also began to attract Western private investment, as the regime succeeded to convince entrepreneurs that private capital was sacrosanct notwithstanding the contrary radical rhetoric emanating from Brazzaville.

In the early 1980s oil and oil royalties became by far the dominant factor in Congo's economic evolution, depressing the role of other resources, such as timber, that had played an important role in the 1960's. This turn-around, occurring shortly after the rise to power in 1979 of Sassou-Nguesso stabilized the latter's military regime and enabled it to finance the first stages of an ambitious 1982–86 development plan, designed to lay the foundations for economic independence. By the end of 1982, however, the high hopes of the leadership were, for the second time, dashed by a rapid and drastic fall in global oil prices. Capital that had recently flocked to Congo melted away. Expectations of large budgetary resources proved illusory, and the weakness of Congo's economy and timidity of the foreign oil companies in Congo became obvious. Many projects of the 1982–86 development plan were cancelled, and its scope was sharply curtailed in April 1983. By July Congo's resources were so depleted the regime was forced to seek foreign loans to meet operating expenses. The 20th anniversary of Congo's "Les Trois Glorieuses" was celebrated without the usual fanfare.

By the mid-1980's Congo was virtually bankrupt living a hand-to-mouth existence. The regime, hoping to avoid turning to the IMF, that would have imposed harsh conditions, tried an "internal" adjustment program in mid-1980's, with severe spending cuts, including two cuts on civil service salaries (first 5%, then another 10%), aimed at financial equilibrium. But the austerity measures produced modest results, hampered as they were by the crippling deficits piled up by the state sector, where only two companies were operating at a profit, and the government's own decision to complete the ambitious road-paving program in the north. By 1985 Congo had no option but to sign a SAP agreement with the IMF, ending all expenditures on the 1982–1986 development plan, and pledging a 50% cut in the national budget within two years. The second pay cut of 10% in late 1988, and a 50% cut of bonuses/allowances were not sufficient to enable Congo to meet the IMF conditions it had contracted, and relations with the IMF soon came to a standstill. In 1989 the regime began to liberalize the political system in an effort to stabilize itself in face of growing civic disenchantment, and periodic demonstrations. By then the building sector, a barometer of economic activity, had shrunk by 21.3 percent, GDP had shrunk by 30 percent since 1985 alone, commerce and industry was stagnant due to a fall in domestic demand, and total government receipts were down by a staggering 41 percent.

The civilian regime that came to power in 1991 inherited the economic morass, but despite draconian policies was unable to ameliorate the situation. In September 1992 interim prime minister Milongo announced a progressive pruning of the civil service. Though this policy was continued by the successor Lissouba regime in 1993, the only posts eliminated through 1994 were 6,000 phantom workers whose salaries had been pocketed by division heads and/or political barons, and jobs that became vacant as some state enterprises closed down bankrupt. Attempts to prune Congo's manpower were resisted by the trade unions, forcing back-pedalling of the policy by a civilian government still threatened by PCT and military elements not reconciled with civilianization. Milongo's 1992 decree that the hitherto very lax collection of income taxes and customs duties would be tightened up (in the past wide-scale evasions resulted in only modest revenue from such sources) simply led to new forms of evasion, and few new revenues, that coupled with the country's bankruptcy resulted in prolonged delays in the paying of salaries. It was against this background that the Lissouba government contracted forward-selling of oil from the Yombo-marine concession, to avert confiscation of Congo's foreign assets abroad by creditors demanding debt-repayment, and to obtain some much-needed funds for its payroll.

Though IMF credits were finally reinstated in 1994, demands for the privatization of much of Congo's state sector, including Hydro-Congo, and a 50% cut in the civil service eludes the Lissouba government just as it eluded Sassou-Nguesso when the IMF first raised this as a condition for future fiscal assistance. To get a better perspective on the monumental drag Congo's state sector has exerted on the economy, one could note that between 1982 and 1986 over 300 billion CFAF were poured into the country's state sector, merely in an effort to keep it afloat, without success, the enterprises remaining deficitory to this day. Many were to either close down, or are slowly being privatized, despite vehement union protests, with 40–50% cutbacks in their original manpower complements. See also AGRICULTURE; BANKING; CURRENCY; FINANCES; FORESTRY; INDUSTRY; LABOR; MINING; PETROLEUM; PLANNING, TRADE.

EDUCATION. In the late nineteenth century, Catholic missions in Congo pioneered education for boys and girls. Their schools stressed literacy in French, vocational training, and religious instruction. It was not until after World War II that state schools finally surpassed mission schools in the number of their pupils, of teachers, salaries, and in level of instruction offered. Under the postwar French administration, mission schools were complementary to the public schools rather than competitive with them, and had identical curricula and examinations, but they charged small fees for attendance and depended heavily on government grants. In 1965, mission schools were nationalized and missionary teachers were replaced by Congolese and foreign laymen, of whom 323 were French and 83 were Soviet citizens in 1972. Among those nationalized was the **Chaminade seminary** in Brazzaville, that paradoxically trained a broad array of what was to become Congo's Marxist elite.

Attendance in Congo's primary schools is mandatory for children between the ages of 6 and 16. Primary-school attendance has been rising at the rate of 5.1 percent a year, or faster than the growth rate of the entire population, which is expected to top 3 million in the year 2000. In secondary schools the number of students has been increasing annually by 20.3 percent; in technical schools, by 16 percent; and in the university, by 17.9 percent. In 1987 there were 800,000 students in primary and secondary schools (with just over 10,000 at Marien Ngouabi university and some 3,500 abroad), with Congo having an inordinately high level (97%) of scholarization, and also, the highest percentage in the world of students as compared to total population. Instruction at all levels is provided without charge by the state, and French is used as the sole instructional language, although in 1981 the study of the two most widespread vernacular languages, Lingala and

Koutouba, was made obligatory in secondary schools. Some extremely disturbing aspects of education in Congo have always been the high levels of violence, indiscipline and absenteeism (including of teachers) in schools, declining educational standards as reflected, in part, by the average number of years it takes to graduate, the mean age of high school pupils that is very high, and acute overcrowding of 80-100 pupils per class.

Congo's student population has increased at all levels, regardless of changes in Congo's political orientation, and/or the problems afflicting it. Among the practical problems, the more serious have been the shortage of teachers, of jobs for school graduates, and of sufficient funds. In the psychological category, the most acute problem has been, and still is, the adversary relationship that has developed between students and all governments, today as in the days of the military interregnum, or for that matter during the Youlou and Massamba-Debat reigns. This chronic tension has erupted in violence especially in 1971, 1974, 1984, and again in the 1990's, and is in many ways (except when ideologically motivated) a basic function of the government being seen as unable to provide the jobs youth expect at the end of their educational career, in a country where jobs other than in the public sector are very few.

By far the most serious student demonstrations took place on November 11, 1984 as Brazzaville's secondary schools erupted in violence that spread throughout the city as students ransacked shops and destroyed cars. The upheaval was over the government's decision to hold competitions in the future, to decide which of the graduates would proceed to university—as opposed to automatic entry to all graduates. Since a university degree in turn conferred automatic entry to a decent civil service appointment, the government decision affected career expectations of every secondary school student. Yet the government decision was inevitable, not only because of the extreme fiscal shortfalls experienced in the 1980's, but also because at the time fully 650,000 students were attending school (or over one-third of the population), with the secondary school population also burgeoning and the impossibility of the regime, even in the best of times, to either admit that many students to university, and later recruit that many new personnel into the civil service. The riots were repeated again in December 1986, and student unrest continued during that remainder of the decade, as on February 22, 1989 over their scholarship arrears. Even after the political normalization of the 1990's that brought about a largely southern multiparty leadership to power, student unrest has been as visible as before, though not with the same intensity. On October 23, 1991, for example, student riots occurred again, over their non-payment of their grants.

Teacher shortages in Congo concerns both numbers and qualifications and exists at both ends of the educational spectrum — in the technical schools and the university as well as in the rural primary schools. The main weaknesses of the school system inherited from the colonial administration and perpetuated in independent Congo are the large percentage of school dropouts and the alienation of literate Congolese from their rural milieu. In an attempt to remedy these defects, the Ngouabi government, in 1972, required all civil servants who had been teachers to resume their former occupation and those who held university degrees (including members of the military) to teach in secondary schools. The ineffectiveness of these measures was indicated in a speech made two years later by Ngouabi. In reporting that half the students in primary grades, 30 to 40 percent of those in secondary schools, 65 percent in technical courses, and 70 percent in the university were dropouts, he termed the state of education catastrophic. He attributed this dismal situation to absenteeism and negligence on the part of students and teachers alike, rowdiness, anarchy and violence in classrooms, and he specifically charged teachers with favoritism in grading pupils according to their own self-interests. Because the 500 baccalaureate degrees awarded in 1974 were found to be "substandard," their holders would not, as before, receive scholarships but be compelled to teach in primary schools. The requirement that school teachers, along with their pupils, participate manually in agricultural projects hardly contributed to that profession's popularity.

Such drawbacks might have been acceptable had they been accompanied by higher salary inducements, but the appreciable budget allocations — 26 percent of the total revenues for education as compared with 16.5 percent for the armed forces in 1974 — even though they were supplemented by foreign contributions, were insufficient to meet the expenditures necessitated by the steady growth in the number of students, school buildings, and equipment needs. In 1976, the regime announced that 1,200 teachers holding certain brevets would be recruited to meet the primary-school requirements; 420 teaching posts in secondary schools (along with a special honorarium) would be awarded to university students working for their master's degree; and the Ecole Normale Superieure would provide the candidates necessary to replace foreign incumbents in the university faculty. With regard to training Congolese to take over posts still filled by foreigners in the civil service and the education system, and renaming the university (for Marien Ngouabi) and the lycees for revolutionary heroes or dates (the Lycee Savorgnan de Brazza became the Lycee de la Liberation), the PCT leaders encountered no opposition. Indeed, the nationalistic Congolese were pleased by the burgeoning in 1974–75 of technical schools and vocational training centers. The Ecole Polytechnique at

Brazzaville, the Technical Institute at Pointe Noire, the Ecole des Eaux et Forets in the Niari region, the Centre de Formation Agricole at Boko, a center for economic planning and management, and even a chair of Marxist philosophy at the university were all founded during Ngouabi's presidency. (The university itself underwent various metamorphoses since its founding in 1973 after the dissolution of the FESAC, or Fondation de l'Enseignement Superieur en Afrique Centrale.)

It was not until the authorities, in their determination to "change the Congolese mentality" and especially the Congolese attitude toward education, made radical changes in the curriculum, notably in requirements for the baccalaureate degree, that strong opposition arose, and it came from diverse quarters. The changes most strongly resented were the addition of an oral examination to the written test for graduation from secondary schools and the suppression of automatic admission to the civil service of all holders of the baccalaureate. Furthermore, those Congolese who had earned degrees under the old French system felt that their credentials had been downgraded, and students who aspired to graduate study in European universities realized that the new Congolese diplomas would not gain them admission there without additional study. From the opposite quarter came objections from "Maoist" students who urged that the entire existing system be abolished and be replaced by a genuine "people's school" (or ecole du progrès) in which the curriculum would be wholly revolutionary and the sole language a national dialect.

Under the ambitious 1982–86 plan education was allocated 22.7 billion CFAF, of which the largest single share (9.1 billion) was for the university with the balance earmarked for improving the quality of instruction throughout the system so that it could keep pace with its numerical expansion. The PCT leadership was particularly concerned to deflect Congolese students from the study of law, which attracted over 1,000 of the over 10,000 university students in the late 1980's, the rest being dispersed between the two other departments (economics and liberal arts). Steps were also taken to increase the number of teaching posts and to enhance the authority of the university administration by giving stronger disciplinary powers to the Conseil Superieur dominated by two left-wing party ideologues, Martin Mberi and J. P. Thystere-Tchicaya.

Paradoxically, Congo, that has invested huge sums of money in education at all levels, and has recorded the highest rates of increase of African states in primary and secondary education, has reaped mixed benefits, with the negative repercussions being the creation of a bloated and highly redundant civil service, and continued expectations on the part of graduates of government jobs, precisely when Congo is compelled to undertake a massive pruning of its existing manpower.

Moreover, with the quality of education progressively declining, the school cycle has progressively grown longer. In 1990 students graduated from school at the average age of twenty-four years, and the percentage of students sitting for the baccalaureate exams and passing them has been extremely low. A very large percentage of students dropped out from high school after 3–5 years of study because they remained virtually illiterate. In the same year out of 17,113 candidates for graduation only 92 passed the written tests and 2,400 the oral tests, all with very low averages. In 1991 over 103,000 students in the entire country were repeating their previous year.The fact that over 60% of these students were over 20 years of age, indicated the educational system disguised widespread latent unemployment in the country.

Secondary school enrollment figures peaked in 1982, slowly declining for the rest of the decade. In 1986, for example, secondary school students numbered 26,823 (down from 31, 943 in 1982) while professional and technical school registrations stood at 39,835 (down from 39,965). In that year, however, Marien Ngouabi University had its highest enrollment ever, 11,000 students. In 1990, private schools were legalized again, as part of the political liberalization in the country. There were, at that time, 502,918 pupils enrolled in primary school, 17,026 in general secondary schools, 11,112 in vocational schools, 199 in teacher training colleges, 10,671 at Marien Ngouabi University and up to 200 additional ones in foreign universities. In that year the International Labor Office reported Congo held the global record with over 35% of its entire population attending school. And, according to UNESCO, adult illiteracy was 43.3% (30% for males, 56.1% for females), one of the lowest rates in Africa. Government spending on education amounted to 37,899 million CFAF, or 14.4% of the national budget.

EGLISE EVANGELIQUE DU CONGO. Congo's main Protestant Church. In 1991 it was estimated there were around 120,000 Protestants in Congo, with their head being Reverend Jean Mboungou. See also RELIGION.

EKAMBA ELOMBA, NICODEME. Radical union leader and former General-secretary of the Union of Workers in State Enterprises, and co-leader of the Confédération Syndicale Congolaise. Ekamba-Elomba was integrated in March 1970 into the PCT Central Committee, and in December 13, 1971, was appointed to head the newly created Commission pour l'Organisation de la Propagande of the PCT. He was eliminated from the latter position in January 1973, though retained membership in the Central Committee. In July 1973 he was appointed national propaganda commissar of the Workers' Militia, but his support for an abortive general strike in March 24, 1976, led to his arrest, ouster from the CSC ruling body and interdict against ever seeking elective office in the labor organization. In November 1977, he became head of the radio station "La Voix de la Revolution Congolaise," a post he also lost a few years later.

EKONDY, AKALA, 1938– . Banker. Born in Pointe Noire, after secondary school in his home town Ekondy studied at the university of Neuchatel in Switzerland. On his return home he joined the foreign ministry, and served at the UN offices in New York and Bruxelles. He then joined president Ngouabi's staff as economic councillor, and continued on as Yhomby Opango's political councillor. In 1979 he was appointed director-general of the Banque Commerciale Congolais, but resigned for personal reasons in 1982 returning to get a PhD in economics from his alma mater, following which he became an international administrator.

ELECTIONS OF SEPTEMBER 24, 1989. Last elections under the aegis of the PCT for the national popular assembly. They were somewhat anachronistic since pressures for democratization were buffeting Congo, and were shortly to bring the dissolution of the 1989 assembly. In the elections 135 parliamentarians were elected on a single PCT list, though fully 74 were not PCT members, since the party opted for a corporatist approach to stave off multipartyism.

ELECTIONS (LEGISLATIVE) OF 1992. These were Congo's first competitive elections since independence, coming after the PCT's monopoly of power had been broken by the **national conference**. A large number of political formations (as many as 115) emerged in 1990–1992, some to disappear before the elections, others to merge, and yet others to join in alliances and coalitions before and/or after the elections. (See POLITICAL PARTIES). A staggering 1,000 candidates ran for the 125 seats in the first round, and 300 for the 57 seats in the second round, with the elections confirming the continued hold of ethnicity in the country, since each party emerged victorious in its own ethnic stronghold, securing only a minority of the vote in other regions. This included the PCT, that though discredited for its ruinous reign nevertheless garnered the majority of the Mbochi vote in the north, ceding the Kouyou vote to Yhomby Opango's RDD. On the average 81% of the vote in each region went to leaders originating from that area, reflecting what may be called a tendency towards regional single-partyism. The largest number of the assembly's 125 seats were ultimately captured by Lissouba's UPADS (39), based on its **Nibolek** constituency, followed by Kolelas' MCDDI (29), that scored heavily among the Bakongo/Lari in the south, and the PCT (18), that gained support from the Mbochi. After these three large parties came a number of smaller groups, including Thystère-Tchicaya's Vili-based RDPS (9) and Yhomby Opango's Kouyou-based RDD (5). The rest of the seats were won by smaller parties, including the USD (3), the UPSAD (2), eleven other parties, each winning one seat, and six independents. Post-election maneuverings briefly resulted in a Presidential Tencency coalition of an absolute majority of the seats, but this was shattered by the PCT bolting from its original alignment with UPADS to the opposition of MCDDI, forcing Lissouba to broaden his cabinet to avert another parliamentary no-confidence vote such as ousted his first prime minister Bongho-Nouarra.

ELECTIONS (LOCAL AND MUNICIPAL) OF MAY 3, 1992.
These local/municipal elections, the country's first competitive multiparty ones since independence, produced the following results for the main parties.

449 seats were won by Pascal Lissouba's UPADS alliance party. UPADS won most of the seats in the Nkayi, Bouenza and Moussendjo districts, and over half of the seats of the Niari, Bouenza and Lekoumou regions, its stronghold.

297 seats were won by the MCDDI coalition (including Milongo and Kolelas), with the latter emerging mayor of Brazzaville. The MCDDI won heavily in the Pool region, its stronghold, carrying six of its seven districts and more than three-quarters of its seats, and also won 15 of Brazzaville's seats.

193 seats were won by Sassou Nguesso's PCT. The party won outright only one district, Talangai, where it obtained seven seats, and only secured the regional council of the Plateaux region. It obtained only four of the 13 seats in Ouesso, and was beaten in the Cuvette by Yhomby Opango's Kouyou party, the RDD, that secured 15 of its 31 seats.

86 seats were won by Thystère-Tchicaya's RDPS mainly in his fief of Kouilou and home-town Pointe Noire, but in all instances did less well than expected, especially in Kouilou where the AND, a party allied to Pascal Lissouba's UPADS, won 12 of the 31 seats.

The elections themselves passed without any incident, though in the distant and isolated Likouala the elections had to be held on May 6th, and the election results were disputed by the PCT, citing various deficiencies. Members elected in turn elected the mayors of the country's municipalities, regional and district prefects.

ELECTIONS (PRESIDENTIAL) OF AUGUST 1992. These elections were the first completely free and competitive presidential elections in post-independence Congo, following the national conference that laid the foundation for a constitutionalized multiparty democracy. The elections had two rounds, the first on August 2nd, when sixteen candidates presented their candidacies; and, in the absence of an absolute majority vote for any one of these, on August 16th the two candidates with the highest vote in the first poll squared off against each other. Sassou Nguesso was humiliatingly ousted in the first round, reflecting both his minority ethnic status, and widespread hatred in the south of the authoritarian regime erected under his aegis. The vote for the top five candidates in the first round was: Pascal Lissouba 35.89%; Bernard Kolelas 22.89%; Denis Sassou Nguesso 16.87%; André Milongo 10.18%; Thsytère-Tchicaya 5.78%. In the second round, which saw those excluded shifting their support towards one of the two contenders, Lissouba obtained 61.3% of the vote to Kolelas who secured 38.6%.

ELECTIONS (SENATE) OF JULY 26, 1992. Elections for Congo's 60-man senate, a novel structure set up by Congo's new **constitution** took place on July 26, 1992 with the following results: Pascal Lissouba's UPADS alliance secured 23 seats; Bernard Kolelas' MCDDI secured 13; Yhomby Opango's RDD gained 8; Sassou Nguesso's PDT won 3; and Milongo's FPC one. The remaining seats were won by independents with regionalist or personalist strengths.

ELECTRICITY. Electricity was more widely distributed in Moyen-Congo than in any other AEF territory because of its more extensive urbanization and means of communication. Before World War II, both Brazzaville and Pointe Noire had small generating plants, and the distribution of their output (at very high rates) was monopolized by a private French company, the Energie Electrique du Congo (ENELCO). After the war, the demand for power rose rapidly, and a 15,000-kw hydroelectric dam was built near Brazzaville at Djoué and small diesel-powered plants at Dolisie and Jacob. In the late 1950s and early 1960s, the government placed its hopes for industrializing the Pointe Noire region on building a hydroelectric dam on the Kouilou River, where it flowed through the Sounda gorge, 75 km. from the sea.

Technical studies were begun in 1954, and work on an access road four years later, when an Office National du Kouilou was set up, but the estimated cost (80 billion CFAF in 1958) prevented its realization. Between 1965 and 1969, 3.4 billion CFAF were invested in increasing Congo's production of energy,and in 1967 the monopoly for its distribution was taken from the ENELCO and entrusted to a new state company, the Société Nationale d'Electricité (SNE).

SNE, with a capital of 3,268 million CFAF and a total generating capacity of 125 megawatts, employed over 1750 persons. It had difficulty meeting its payroll and repaying its other debts (which totaled 6.3 billion CFAF in the early 1980's), because a large proportion of is 60,000-odd clients were slow in paying their bills. Most of SNE's current was generated at two hydroelectric plants, at Djoué on the Congo River and at Moukoulou on the Bouénza (which began operating in 1953 and 1980 respectively) and at thermal plants situated in Congo's four largest towns. The balance came from smaller thermal generators, which supplied current during four to five hours to Impfondo, Ouésso, Owando, Djambala, and some rural settlements. The hydroelectric power now available at Brazzaville, Pointe Noire, and, in lesser amounts, in Loubomo and Nkayi (despite the variations due to differences between high and low water levels), has virtually eliminated the frequent breakdowns caused by obsolete equipment that long hampered industrial output in Congo's southern towns. Still, Congo's generating capacity does not meet its needs (124.5 million kWh in 1981; 175 million kWh in 1990). Under the 1982–86 plan, the regime allocated investments amounting to 83.4 billion CFAF for the production of a total of 232 megawatts. To attain the plan's goal, the capacity of the existing facilities was to be increased, from four new sources: dams scheduled to be built at Imbolou on the Lefini River (75 megawatts; at Kandeno and Assoumoundele, both on the Sangha River (three megawatts together); and at Etoumbi (or Adinga) in the Cuvette area (four megawatts). Altogether, by 1986, Congo was scheduled to have available enough electric energy not only to meet its own needs, including the electrification of the smallest villages, but also to export to Angola, Cabinda, Gabon,and Cameroun. As with other scheduled industrial projects, the economic slowdown of the economy in the mid-1980's arrested most of these high-cost plans, with the result that many had to postponed or scrapped.

ELENGA, EMMANUEL (General), 1938– . Former general chief of staff of the Congolese armed forces. Born on October 1, 1938 in Pointe Noire, and rapidly progressing up the ranks especially under Sassou Nguesso, Elenga was appointed chief of staff in 1984 when he was also elected as PCT deputy to the national assembly. In 1987 he was replaced as chief of staff by Colonel Jean-Marie Makoko and joined the government as minister of defence and security. He served in that capacity until July 1988 when he was named Inspector-General of the Army. In 1991 he left the armed forces.

ELENGA-NGAPORO, JOSEPH, 1940– . Academic and former cabinet minister. Born on June 25, 1940 in the north, and related to Sassou Nguesso, Elenga-Ngaporo studied at the Chaminade Seminary in Brazzaville before going to France to major in economics and sociology. On his return to Brazzaville he joined Marien Ngouabi University, and for a time he was also an economic adviser to Yhomby

Opango. A radical and influential member of the Mouvement du 22 Fevrier (M-22), after Yhomby Opango's ouster he was briefly director of the presidential office. He then joined the cabinet as minister of commerce on April 4, 1979, and in August 1984 was shifted to head the ministry of energy and water power. In the reshuffle of December 1985 he was replaced by Basile Ikouébé and returned to academic duties.

ELENGA-YOKA, HENRI EBOUNDIT (Colonel). Former deputy chief-of-staff of the Congolese armed forces, PCT member and member of the national assembly. Of Kouyou ethnicity, Elenga-Yoka was arrested together with a number of other senior officers in July 1987 in connection with the anti Sassou-Nguesso plot of **Captain Anga**. Never put on trial he was only amnestied in mid-1990 at the end of the Sassou Nguesso era.

ELENGUE, JEAN-MARIE. Former ambassador to France. Elengué, Sassou Nguesso's uncle, and close collaborator in the PCT party, was replaced as ambassador in December 1992.

ELF-CONGO. Subsidiary of the French oil company Elf-Aquitaine, and largest producer of oil in Congo. Elf-Congo, founded in Brazzaville and Pointe Noire in 1969, is capitalized at 5 billion CFAF in which the State has a 20% equity. See also PETROLEUM.

ELF-AQUITAINE. See PETROLEUM.

EMOUENGE, GABRIEL, 1945– . Former mayor of Brazzaville. Born in 1945, and a member of the PCT central committee, Emouengé was elected in 1984 to the national assembly.

EMPANA, ALPHONSE CLAUDE. Former minister of health between January 7, 1972 and January 1976, when he was demoted to administrative duties in the ministry he headed.

ENERGIE ELECTRIQUE DU CONGO (ENELCO). Subsidiary of the French Union Electrique d'Outre-Mer, based in Paris, holding a monopoly for electric-power generation and distribution in Brazzaville until nationalized in June 1967. See ELECTRICITY.

ENO. See PETROLEUM.

EPENA. Large very sparsely populated swampy district of 18,000 sq. kms. in Congo's northernmost, isolated Likouala region, with headquarters in the village of the same name. On the banks of the Likouala river, the district has no distinguishing relief, being essentially composed of savanna and forests that are inundated during the September–December rainy season when the Likouala regularly overflows its banks. Sightings of "prehistoric dinosaurs" have been recorded in the region between Epena and Dongou, by both (recently) pygmies, and historically, by missionaries. Scientific expeditions to the region have uncovered nothing, but the area is so large and inaccessible, that even they have not definitively ruled out the persistent stories are false.

ESSAKOMBA, JACQUES, 1945– . Historian. Born on May 19, 1945 and educated in the Universities of Bordeaux and Paris in History, Essakomba returned to Brazzaville in 1977 to teach at Marien Ngouabi University. He has written a number of works on Congolese history and is currently head of his department.

ETA-ONKA, EMMANUEL (General). Chief of Staff of the armed forces since July 1993, replacing General Jean-Marie Mokoko when the latter indicated he could not recognize the government of President Pascal Lissouba. Eta-Onka, a Batéké, is also somewhat unusual among the Congolese military since he is an aspiring poet, though his work has only been intermittently published within Congo.

ETSOU, THEOPHILE see ITSOUMOU, ELIE THEOPHILE

ETUMBA. Press organ, and party newspaper of the MNR and later of the PCT.

EUCALYPTUS PROJECT. In the 1980's this was Congo's single major priority State project. Embarked upon at the end of the 1970's, the project involved the planting of 20,000 hectares of eucalyptus trees in the sandy areas of Pointe Noire, to serve as the raw material for a projected costly $600 million paper pulp mill, the largest industrial project in Congo. A fast-growing eucalyptus hybrid was used, assuring a mature tree in 6–8 years, with the plantation scheduled to produce forty cubic meters of tree-stock per hectare, twice the yield elsewhere. This anticipated yield was supposed to provide the mill with raw material to reach a production of 200,000 tons a year. Though the plant was small by global standards, the cost of its erection would have equalled Congo's annual budget, and was the country's most prestigious project during the 1980's. Though neighboring countries (e.g. Gabon and Cameroun) had developed similar integrated plants in the past that proved white elephants (with Gabon's actually closed down in 1984), the Congolese regime was convinced that its lower cost of production (by 30%) compared to European plants, proximity to the port of Pointe Noire (further minimizing local costs), adequate supplies of water and salt for the necessary bleaching process, would make it viable.

Cautionary advice was ignored. This included the high cost of amortizing the large loan needed to construct the mill; the high wage bill of the 100 expatriates needed to man it; that the high cost of transport of the pulp to European ports might erode any profitability of the production of the raw material itself; that supply-demand factors might affect market-prices and that the global demand might not be as high as Congo's projected steady annual increase of 5%. However, not to be trapped in the project alone, the Congolese government mounted the eucalyptus planting project, and then sought other global partners for the mill on which the State's financial role was limited to 30%. Neither France, that had been heavily counted upon, nor other financial entrepreneurs, were found for the project, so that when the eucalyptus forests that had been planted matured in the late 1980's, they initially remained untouched, and later, rather than being used to produce pulp, they were either exported to Europe, at relatively unprofitable terms, or used (by new state company that was set up) as the raw material for creating telephone poles.

EVEIL CONGOLAIS. Publication of the Young Lari opposition party, PDC, which in the 1980's was headed by Dr. Seraphin Bakouma.

EYENI, RICHARD, 1939– . Former radical PCT member of the national assembly. Born in Ngouangala (in the Sangha) on February 19, 1939, he served with the foreign ministry before becoming propaganda secretary of the central committee of the PCT's youth branch, the UJSC. He was also concurrently director of the Congolese TV station and political commissar of Niari. In 1980 he was appointed ambassador to East Germany and Poland; on his return to Congo in 1984 he was elected to the national assembly, serving until 1989.

-F-

FABRIQUE DE PEINTURE EN AFRIQUE. Enterprise, with two plants in Pointe Noire and Brazzaville (at Mpila) producing declining amounts of paint products despite the installation of new machinery in 1982.

FEDERATION DES ETUDIANTS DE L'AFRIQUE NOIRE EN FRANCE (FEANF). Militant union of Francophone Africa's students in France, with branches in most university cities.

FILA-NDZIENDOLO, MARCELINE, 1939– . Educator and diplomat. Born in 1939, and educated in the Sorbonne where she obtained a Master's degree in English, Fila-Ndziendolo returned to Congo to head a girls' school and be in charge of English language programs in the educational system. In the mid-1970's she joined the ministry of foreign affairs as head of its United Nations division, attending also the General Assembly's meetings in New York. Since 1985 she has been head of multilateral cooperation services in the same ministry.

FINANCES. Throughout the 1960s, the Congo's budgets varied little in their structure from those of the colonial era. Revenues continued to depend largely on foreign aid and trade, and the public debt grew apace, as did the budget and trade deficits, the former due principally to the growth of the civil service. The main innovations of that period were the introduction of a separate investment budget in 1964, a diversification in the sources of foreign aid, large expenditures for the new state monopolies (including recently nationalized private enterprises), and an increase in those taxes that affected principally the European business community.

With the consolidation of permanent military rule in the 1970s, the volume of the Congo's budgets increased rapidly, doubling between 1972 and 1974 (from 25 to 50 billion CFAF), and jumping an additional sixfold between 1979 and 1982 (from 60.8 billion to 388 billion CFAF) where they stabilized. The sudden rise in revenues from oil was responsible for these upsurges, just as the equally unexpected drop in its output and sale caused the subsequent shrinkage in budgetary resources. The first such decline, in 1975, caused the PCT leadership to mount austerity measures, to partially revise the tax system so as to tap more local resources, and to pull back on cherished scheduled projects. Yet in that same year, the cost of the Congolese civil service was 4.5 percent higher than it had been in 1973, due to recruitments by the ministries of education, defense, and health. In fiscal year 1975–76 expenditures continued to increase at the rate of 10 to 20 percent a year, owing in part to a rise of five billion CFAF in the cost of civil service that by then numbered 30,000, whose salaries had been raised and their perquisites restored.

The regime's effort to counterbalance its growing budgetary deficits by practicing austerity was a conspicuous failure, and its more positive approach to offsetting them by increasing revenues proved to be equally futile. Inasmuch as customs duties on imports and exports have long been more remunerative to the Congo government (providing 41 percent of its revenues) than the proceeds from direct taxes, it was decided to improve the latter's yield, and introduce higher fees for registrations and issuance of licenses. Still, even an increase in taxes on foreign companies' profits in 1977 brought in less than had been expected (13.5 billion CFA francs), disappointing PCT leaders, already demoralized by Ngouabi's assassination in March 1977, and by the closing of the Holle potash mine three months later. Moreover, galloping inflation and continuing declines in oil production and royalties augured poorly for the future.

When Sassou-Nguesso took power early in 1979, he expressed concern over the plight of the state enterprises, the rapid escalation of the country's budget and deficit, and the fiscal burden of Congo's public debt, then estimated at 150–250 billion CFAF. But he was no more able than his predecessors to compress public expenditures, and already by September 1979 he was in Paris to solicit further French investment and aid. It was Sassou-Nguesso's good fortune that his reign coincided with the discovery of more offshore oil deposits ushering in unprecedented State revenues and investments. The budget's volume soared from about 60 billion CFAF in 1979 to 163.5 billion in 1982, when for the first time ever Congo's revenues exceeded expenditures, and the balance of trade (positive since 1976, showed substantial surpluses). Per capita income, one of the highest in subsaharan Africa, zoomed from $540 in 1978 to $900 in 1983 before the oil-bust came, and the excesses of the past came home to roost leading Congo to virtual bankruptcy. In 1983, the awesome amount of 241 billion CFAF went for Congo's operating expenses, and 147 billion for investments, of which only 46 percent came from Congo's own resources. Fully 100 billion CFAF of the "investment" funds were spent to rehabilitate the public sector whose massive debts the regime took over 1980: a few years later, even more deficitory and mismanaged, the regime, at the verge of fiscal collapse, had to begin the process of closing down, privatizing, or restructuring the State sector—a process still not completed in 1995 due to vociferous resistance of the country's powerful unions. All along the security forces continued to receive a disproportionate share of the budgetary resources: throughout the 1980's education and the armed forces vied (as they had for several years) for first place, with allocations for health and social affairs in third rank, followed by public works and communications.

With the deterioration in Congo's public finances in the early-1980's Sassou Nguesso turned to France for additional aid but found Paris adamant that until Congo curtailed its runaway public expenditures, accepted and implemented in full a structural adjustment program, no additional grants would be forthcoming. Resisting being shackled to the World Bank/IMF the country attempted an "internal SAP" but failed because the relative political stability in Brazzaville had literally been bought by heavy doses of patronage and civil service appointments. Opposition by hard-line Marxist elements and unionists prevented even the closure of heavily deficitory state enterprises, and an IMF-imposed program was inevitable in 1985. French assistance to Congo has been parsimonious even after the end of

Marxism and the emergence of multipartyism in the 1990's, partly because all economies implemented in Congo have been half-hearted and minimal, and the SAP was not implemented.

An analysis of Congo's budgets during 1974–1984 (before the country's economic slide began in earnest) reveals the mixed role played by oil revenues in the country's economy and foreign relations. Oil liberated the country from its pre-1974 fiscal morass and the debts accumulated during the first years of military rule. Yet in so doing it created a misplaced spending euphoria that inexorably led, within a few years, to Congo's renewed, but more serious fiscal collapse. In 1974, the regime, optimistically assuming an indefinite source of oil revenues, incurred large debts that could not be repaid when oil revenues declined. The sobering-up period of fiscal shortfalls that followed (1975–1977) did not teach the PCT any lessons. The next, and bigger, oil boom in the early 1980's, and the formulation of the 1982–86 development plan, indicated the regime was unable to resist the temptation to incur further foreign obligations, while at the same time failing to discharge earlier ones. By July 1983, the Congolese treasury was again empty, and the regime was once again forced to seek now loans in order to pay off its excesses. (See PETROLEUM.) The tragedy of Congo's fiscal policy throughout the country's history, has been that revenues from petroleum have primarily been used to pay off debts incurred by an ill-conceived of, mismanaged non-productive public sector, and bloated non-productive civil service, rather than to shore up the economy on a lasting basis. The availability of heightened revenues from oil have thus in fact actually increased the country's need for external subsidies and loans, further shackling the country to a dependency on foreign sources of capital. The foreign debt rose in one year (1981–82) from 290 billion to 470 billion CFAF, when servicing it absorbed 40.2 percent of the 1983 budget, and it further spurted in subsequent years. The fact that Congo's credit abroad remained strong until the mid-1980's, allowed the regime to further dig its fiscal grave by securing debts that eventually could not be repaid given the leadership's inability to impose prudent and ideological fiscally-neutral management and self-discipline. Since the debt and economic paralysis inherited by the new Lissouba regime boggle the imagination, and a semblance of order can only be imposed by massive economic restructuring and personnel lay-offs (that unionists and ideological hold-outs still resist), both the political and economic stability of the country remains under serious doubt.

FISHERIES. Fish are a basic source of animal protein for many Congolese, but like the country's meat production, the local fish catch must be supplemented by imports (which amount to around 6,000 tons of salted and frozen fish). Despite abundant resources of both fresh-water and sea fish, industrial fishing has been left to foreigners (African and European), though individual Congolese do fish, mainly in the country's rivers and on tributaries of the Congo and in the Cuvette. Such fishing is unregulated and unorganized, and much of the catch is consumed by the riverine groups, and is not marketed elsewhere. Deep-sea fishing, mainly for tuna and, in smaller amounts, for shrimp, has been of little benefit to Congolese, since only around 3,500 tons a year were sold for a decade after independence. Beginning in 1967, the government has periodically announced plans to modernize Congolese fishing techniques and equipment, build a fishing fleet at Pointe Noire, lower the cost of fish in the urban markets, and to Congolize the industry—but with few concrete results until the 1980's when an effort was indeed mounted, only to be cut short by declining oil revenues.

In 1971 Congo's territorial waters were extended to thirty nautical miles, and the next year an announced formation of Pecheries Congolaises promised to increase the national share in maritime fishing. In 1975, the industrial fish catch totaled 15,480 tons rising to 19,000 tons in 1980, but this increase was due not to the zeal of indigenous fishermen, but to an enlargement of the foreign fishing fleets operating off the Congolese coast. The principal foreign fishing firms based at Pointe Noire are Cotonnec, Faucan, Sicap, and Socimex. They provide tuna to the Socofroid's refrigerated facility there. An elaborate fishing complex was constructed at Pointe Noire by the Coongolaise des Peches Maritimes (COPEMAR), which, besides owning a sizable fleet, manufactures fish meal and manages ten entrepots of fish in the hinterland. See also SICAP.

FONDS D'AIDE ET DE COOPERATION (FAC). Successor, following the independence of Francophone Africa of the FONDS D'INVESTISSEMENT POUR LE DEVELOPPEMENT ECONOMIQUE ET SOCIAL (FIDES) which see.

FONDS D'INVESTISSEMENT POUR LE DEVELOPPEMENT ECONOMIQUE ET SOCIAL (FIDES). A law passed by the French Parliament on April 30, 1946, authorized creation of this fund to systematically finance the economic and social development of France's overseas dependencies. It was to receive annual subsidies from the metropolitan budget and contributions from the territories concerned. In 1959 its name was changed to Fonds d'Aide et de Cooperation (FAC) so as to make it conform to the territories' political evolution and changing relations with France.

FONDS EUROPEAN DE DEVELOPPMENT (FED). The European development fund is an agency of the European Economic Community with which most of Africa is linked via the Yaoundé treaties (1963 and subsequent). It dispenses economic and technical assistance to all member and associate states, and since 1959 Congo has received annual grants from the Fund to finance the study or execution of development projects.

FORCE OUVRIERE. Labor unions affiliated with the French socialist party (SFIO). See LABOR—ORGANIZATION AND GOVERNMENT POLICY.

FOREIGN RELATIONS. (1) FRANCE AND THE WEST. From every standpoint, Congo's relations with France have been by far more important than those with any other nation. The close ties forged during 75 years of French colonial rule, similar institutions, a common official language, and, above all, self-interest account for the continued cooperation between the two governments. To maintain its image as a Marxist African nation, Congo, especially under Massamba-Debat and in the first years of Ngouabi's regime, tried to assert its independence from France in all fields, but without jeopardizing the considerable technical and financial benefits its received from France. In 1971, to indicate its displeasure with the hardening Marxist regime in Brazzaville, France demanded the repayment of the large debt owed it by Congo; the cash-strapped Ngouabi regime retaliated by withdrawing from OCAM, nationalizing an increasing number of French enterprises, placing rigorous restrictions on French business operations, and denouncing French policies in exceptionally strong terms. Subsequently France endeavored not to provide the extreme-Left in Congo an excuse for a further deterioration in relations, and indeed, in January 1974 a new cooperation agreement was signed between the two countries.

Thereafter, relations improved markedly, with exchanges of high level visits and France's favorable response to the Congo's frequent requests for ever more financial and technical aid. During the rest of that decade, Franco-Congolese economic relations depended on the rise and fall of Congo's revenues from its oil deposits, discovered and exploited by the French company Elf-Aquitaine. In 1979, oil revenues rose rapidly and with them French investments and influence in Brazzaville. France continued to be Congo's main trade partner and also the latter's principal source of foreign aid. In 1980, for example, 230 million French francs were granted by Paris to Brazzaville, to be used to finance over sixty projects in the fields of communications, research, agro-industry, mineral prospecting, health, to expand Marien Ngouabi University, as well as to pay for the services of 448 technicians and cooperants in the country. The 1980's briefly saw a spectacular growth in Franco-Congolese trade, which in 1981 more than doubled to 2.89 billion CFAF from 1.21 billion the previous year, with Conglese exports to France amounting to 711.7 million CFAF, of which 556 million represented oil, reversing the trade balance that traditionally had been unfavorable to Congo and a cause of chronic complaints by Brazzaville.

An exceptionally warm welcome was given to the French delegation that attended the centenary of Brazzaville (where the number of French residents had increased by 50 percent, to 2,903), but even greater enthusiasm greeted the socialist leader François Mitterand when, in October 1982, he became the first French president to ever visit Congo. That same year, Congo sent 160 officers and NCOs to French military schools for training. Later, in September 1983, as Brazzaville began to feel the budgetrary pinch due to the spending excesses of the previous few years, Sassou-Nguesso made an urgent plea in Paris for supplementary subsidies to help meet Congo's operating expenditures, and to train Congolese to replace French technicians working for the petroleum companies that Congo alleged were pursuing minimalist exploitation policies detrimental to Congo interests.

As for Western countries other than France, the European Economic Community (of which Congo is an associate member) has made the most important and varied contributions. Between 1970 and 1982, the EEC granted Congo nearly 16 billion CFAF in aid, mainly for improving communications and transport. On an individual basis, West Germany, Canada, and to a lesser extent Italy have been outstanding, with, in the early 1980's Great Britain, the United States, and Spain offering Brazzaville aid. Western assistance has been motivated by the desire to keep Congo from over-dependence on the communist countries, to participate in its oil boom, and to help it prepare for a future with declining petroleum revenues. Since the political liberalizations of the 1990's U.S. investments have gone up markedly, both on the part of American oil companies that have secured concessions, and individual entrepreneurs who have been interested in some of Congo's bankrupt state companies.

Congo's first president, Youlou, beginning in 1961, established Congo's diplomatic relations with countries such as Israel, Taiwan and South Korea. The more radical policies of Youlou's successor, Massamba-Debat, and escalating contacts with the Eastern Bloc alienated the conservative Far Eastern nations to the point where they closed their embassies in Brazzaville in 1964, followed the next year by Great Britain and the United States. Congo's diplomatic rupture with Israel in 1972 was more serious, for that country's substantial aid in agrarian technology and training was not matched, as originally promised, by subsequent Arab assistance to Congo. By the mid-1980's however, the Sassou Nguesso regime had made overtures to

Israel, and a few years later diplomatic relations were restored. Indeed by the 1990's an Israeli military program in the country (invited by president Lissouba, uneasy with his unreliable northern army) had, just as in the 1970's, brought about a knee-jerk reaction from a hitherto reluctant Paris, that reversed itself and decided to send Congo military aid.

In the 1970s radical PCT leaders, due to ideological blinkers rejecting the role of supply-demand in international trade, declared their belief that the West aimed to make central Africa the scene of their confrontation with the Eastern bloc. Specifically, they found it hard to believe that technical difficulties and declining world-market prices, and not the malevolence of the Western mining companies, were responsible for the closing of the Holle potash company and the diminished flow of oil revenues to Congo from 1975 to 1977. Only the rising value of the dollar, in which Congo's oil sales were paid, succeeded in reconciling PCT leaders to friendly contacts with the American government, which in November 1982 sent a cabinet member to inaugurate a cultural center in Brazzaville. At about the same time, missions and ministerial visits were exchanged with Great Britain, where in February 1983 rolling stock for the CFCO was ordered. Concurrently, business contacts with Spain and Italy were renewed, those with Brazil were initiated, and relations with Portugal became friendly after its African empire was liberated in 1974. The new openings for mining investments in the Congo and a mellower attitude toward the West on the part of the Congolese hard-liners in the late 1970s persuaded Washington and London to overcome their aversion to dealing with a government so aggressively Marxist as that of Brazzaville and to offer it substantial aid for the first time. In regard to certain African issues with broader international implications, such as the Western Sahara, Chad, and South Africa, Congo remained militantly hostile (verbally) to "Western imperialism." On the other hand, Brazzaville did not view the international agencies, notably those of the UN and the OAU, in that light, and gratefully received the funds and technological expertise proffered by the UN Development Fund, the FAO, the World Bank, and other such agencies.

Notwithstanding this, as the fiscal crisis of the mid-1980's became more serious, Congo found itself in an increasingly untenable situation. The very size of its new fiscal needs began to deter traditional Western sources of aid, while private investors had become disenchanted by Congo's prospects and were pulling out, or reining in their investments; at the same time whatever little non-Western aid Congo had been receiving began to dry to a trickle as Eastern Europe began to unravel. The option of a structural adjustment loan from the World Bank had been explored already, but was for long resisted because at its core was a major revision of the underpinnings of the country's Marxist commitment to a State economy. Ultimately, of course, by the late 1980's Congo had no choice but to knuckle down, both to the World Bank and to conditionalities from Paris. The 1990's also saw a diplomatic rapprochement with several countries not present in Brazzaville during the heights of the Marxist era, most notably with Israel, that in 1993 was invited to train selected units of President Lissouba's personal bodyguard, and provide specialized manpower to monitor the loyalty of the mostly northern (and hence suspect) armed forces.

(2) THE FORMER COMMUNIST STATES. Reversing Youlou's obsession with the Communist menace, Massamba-Debat rapidly initiated relations with the Marxist countries of Europe and Asia. His move immediately produced aid in various forms from both continents. This reaction was due in part to Sino-Soviet rivalry in the Third World, but more to Congo's strategic geographical position. In January 1964, Congo became the first UAM state to recognize the People's Republic of China, after which, diplomatic relations with other Communist countries were established and trade and cultural agreements entered into. By January 1965, the U.S.S.R. had pledged a large loan to Congo, and in that year air service between the two countries began with Massamba-Debat making the first of two state visits to Moscow. Soviet-Congolese trade soon boomed, and by August 1968 (when Massamba-Debat was overthrown) Moscow had loaned Congo the equivalent of three billion CFAF, 60 Soviet professors were teaching in the country, and 300 Congolese were studying in the U.S.S.R. During the same five-year period, ties with Peking developed even more rapidly and more advantageously to Congo in terms of cash and goods than with the Soviet Union. Congo's fear of alienating the U.S.S.R., and its worsening relations with its neighbors, induced Ngouabi, as had been the case with Massamba-Debat, to cultivate contacts with the smaller communist countries, such as North Korea, North Vietnam, Rumania, and especially Cuba, as a means of counterbalancing relations with the major communist powers. However, by 1968 China had far outdistanced the U.S.S.R. with respect to the volume and variety of its aid and the number of its nationals working in Congo, but by 1975 their roles had been reversed, owing to the greater Soviet involvement in Angola and in the development of Congo's material and manpower resources. During the 1970s, Sino-Congolese relations marked time, not as a result of any change in Congo's attitude, but because of China's greater preoccupations elsewhere. Indeed, the Congolese military and civilian leaders alike treated both communist giants with great and evenhanded consideration, while at the same time they went to great pains not to overly alienate the West. In the early 1980s, Brazzaville persevered in its pol-

icy of diversifying its international contacts by cultivating relations with affluent Latin American nations such as Brazil and Argentina, partly with a view to offset Congo's closer working partnership with Cuba since 1975.

In their overriding concern to promote Congo's economy, its Marxist leaders found Soviet aid more effective than China's despite the existence, especially under Ngouabi, of powerful Maoist cliques espousing (as did **Ange Diawara**) a strong pro-China preference. Still, under Sassou-Nguesso, a better balance was struck since 1979 between the two major communist powers, and Chinese-sponsored projects that had stagnated for years were revitalized. Nevertheless, with respects to military equipment and training, and also in the mining industry, the Soviet Union became preeminent, whereas Chinese activities have been mostly in fields such as public works and improvements of the rural economy. Still, in terms of culture and influence on policy, the Soviets were more effective than the Chinese, thanks to their programs of student and professorial exchange and, more important, the military training that many Congolese officers underwent in the U.S.S.R., as well as the guidance given by Soviet officers to the Congolese army. No accurate figures have been available as to the number of Soviet and Chinese citizens who lived in Congo, but the number of 500 or so of each has been estimated in the press. Among the concrete attainments credited to aid from these powers are: the Soviet-built maternity hospital and Hotel Cosmos in Brazzaville and aid in gold and phosphate mining; and China has assisted with a crushing plant at Madingou, SOTEXCO's textile plant at Kinsoundi, a shipyard at Brazzaville, and the above-mentioned Bouenza hydro-electric station. Relations with East Europe have been of lesser importance, though East Germany had provided valuable aid. In 1985 Sassou-Nguesso visited the latter country, as well as Romania and Bulgaria, signing five agreements of cooperation, under which several mining projects were initiated in 1989. Brazzaville has, however been adamant in not agreeing to allow Soviet ships to use Pointe Noire as a naval base, and the friendship treaty that Sassou-Nguesso did sign with the U.S.S.R. on May 13, 1981, contained no military provisions. The Congolese did, however, make some concessions, such as publicly reversing their stand against the Soviet occupation of Afghanistan and denouncing Western support for Solidarity in Poland as a capitalist plot.

Of all the other Communist states, the role of Cuba stands out. Until 1979, direct relations between Congo and Cuba were confined to official visits and the execution of a few public-health and education programs in rural areas. They involved the presence of only about a couple hundred Cubans, of whom twenty served in the Congolese presidential bodyguard. Indirect relations, however, included the stationing of a few thousand Cuban troops in the Pointe Noire region, used as a rear base to support Angola's MPLA. The latter were fighting against Portuguese colonial domination and also against the FNLA, a rival faction of conservative Angolan rebels whose opposition to the Portuguese administration was favored by Zaire and some Western governments.

Portugal's withdrawal from its African colonies after the April 1974 revolution removed the unifying force among the rebels in Angola, as well as in the Cabinda enclave wedged between Congo and Zaire. This split among the guerrillas posed a problem for all African governments which, in principle, backed any anticolonial liberation movement. The Congo government, however, never wavered in its support of the MPLA. In Cabinda, on the other hand, the issues were not so clear-cut between radicals and conservatives, both of whom founded rival subsidiary groups in Zaire and Congo. Brazzaville initially supported Cabinda's indigenous anti-Portuguese separatists, the Front de Liberation pour l'Enclave de Cabinda (FLEC), but later shifted to help its rival, the MPLA, although not for the same ideological reasons as those for its backing of the MPLA in Angola. The rivalry between the FLEC and the MPLA's subsidiaries (and between the leaders of both of those groups) stemmed from their shared determination to control Cabinda's extensive oil resources (discovered and mined by the Gulf Oil Co. of the U.S.). As regards Cabinda, the main mission of the Cubans who had been brought to the Congo by the U.S.S.R. was to help the MPLA prevent FLEC (backed by Zaire) from establishing a separate state in Cabinda that would deprive the MPLA Angolans of the enclave's oil revenues. In that rivalry, Congo's interests were peripheral, but in the attempt made by some FLEC followers early in 1977 to kidnap a group of French technicians and Congolese working on the CFCO, the Brazzaville authorities were directly concerned. More strongly than before, therefore, they supported the claims made successfully in 1979 by the MPLA leaders at Luanda to sovereignty over Cabinda and its oil deposits.

Studiously inconspicuous as was the Cuban presence in Congo, cordial relations soon developed between the two governments that extended beyond their common support of the MPLA. More and more high-ranking Congolese and Cuban leaders exchanged visits. Brazzaville often expressed admiration for the Cuba's "successful revolution," but the extent and orientation of Cuba's interest in Congo did not become apparent until October 1979. Then the Dutch press reported the dispatch of some 1,000 youthful Congolese for military and civil training in Cuba—a report that aroused strongly adverse reactions in Western countries. Cuba's motives in this case may have been simply to establish a foothold in central Africa by exerting its influence over the rising generation of Congolese. In accepting Cuba's offer, Congolese leaders and also parents seized the opportunity to have their children reared and trained for future desirable posts, without any expense or effort on their part. Cubans were reportedly the most popular foreign group among the Congo's rural inhabitants, with whom they have merged easily and for whom they have carried out many small-scale but useful projects.

(3) THE ARAB COUNTRIES. Except for Egypt, with which the Congo's early ties disappeared with Nasser, Congolese contacts with the Arab world multiplied after Brazzaville broke off relations with Israel in 1972, renouncing valuable Israeli cooperation, especially in the field of agrarian development. Two years later, Congo began to exchange high-level visits with both radical and conservative Arab governments, and expressed its "militant solidarity with the Palestine martyrs," though little of the anticipated Arab fiscal largess was to ensue as a result of this action. This anti-Israel stand changed as Congo's public finances dramatically deteriorated in the mid-1980's, and under the influence of **Saidou Badian** informal relations with Israel were re-opened (full diplomatic relations were restored in August 1991) and in 1987 the services of an Israeli team of experts in anti-terrorism was secured. After the eclipse of Sassou-Nguesso in 1991, the subsequent rise of the Lissouba government, and the establishment of full relations with Israel, Lissouba's insecurity vis-a-vis a hostile and unreliable northern army beholden to Sassou-Nguesso multiplied military relations with Israel. In 1992 it was reported that an unspecified number of former Israeli security officers had taken over as the backbone of Lissouba's bodyguard, with the approval of Jerusalem.

Among the Gulf states, Iraq was the most responsive to Congo's overtures, but the most financially productive contacts were those with Saudi Arabia, which granted the Congo a loan of 4.4 billion CFAF. In north Africa, Algeria became the closest and ideologically most congenial collaborator, and many cooperation agreements with Algiers were signed, beginning in 1972. They moved from culture and information to trade and the equivalence of academic diplomas, and were capped a decade later by the formation of a joint timber company. In the process, Algeria became the Congo's informal adviser on oil policy, and Congo reciprocated by applauding the military successes of Algeria's protege, the Polisario Front, and supporting RASD's candidacy for membership in the OAU.

Elsewhere in the Maghreb, except belatedly, with Morocco, Congo made little effort and slight headway. In 1974, Qadhafi alienated Christian Congolese leaders by urging black Africans to adopt Islam and the Arabic language, and by marrying Marx with Islam in his peculiar State ideology. Congolese Marxists have reproached Libya with diverting Africans from the fight against imperialism, their common enemy. Nevertheless, in June 1977, Yhomby Opango visited Tripoli, where he pledged cooperation with Qadhafi and agreed to form with Libya, a joint agricultural venture to develop Congo's rural economy. In an effort to secure additional aid from Libya in 1977 Yhomby Opango moved to support Qadhafi's ally, Goukouni Oueddei, against the anti-Libyan Hissene Habre. The next year, Congo voted against the dispatch of an OAU peace-keeping force to Chad, but in 1979, Yhomby Opango's successor, Sassou-Nguesso, sent a few Congolese troops to supervise the application there of decisions taken at the Lagos conference of August 21 of that year. Within a few months, those troops were withdrawn from Ndjamena without having done more than a neighborly gesture on behalf of central African peace and the government of national union (GUNT) installed at Ndjamena in 1979.

Congo's attitude toward Libya has all along been complicated by Brazzaville's far-longer-standing relations with France and Chad. Like other pro-Soviet African countries, such as Benin and Ethiopia, Congo actively supported Goukouni and the GUNT against the strongly anti-Libyan Hissene Habre. (This caused Congo additional complications when Habre finally ousted Goukouni in Ndjamena.) In mid-August 1983, Nguesso utilized the presence of ten heads of African states attending the twentieth anniversary of the Congo's "Les Trois Glorieuses" at Brazzaville to explore the means of achieving a negotiated peace in Chad. While Sassou-Nguesso was providing an impetus to the peace process in Chad, he was at the same time permitting Libya to disembark soldiers secretly at Pointe Noire to be flown to Bangui, and allowing the pro-GUNT elements in southern Chad to cross Congolese territory into the Central African Republic. Although Congo, like all of Chad's other immediate neighbors, wanted peace in that country and fears Libya's aggression, Nguesso remained so strongly opposed to Habre that he refused to attend the UDEAC meeting at Yaounde in December 1982 if the head of the FANT was also invited there. In August 1991 Libyan security elements were finally implicated in arranging the placing of a bomb in Brazzaville on board the UTA DC-10 plane that exploded over the Sahara in September 1989, causing considerable antagonism to Libya in Brazzaville

Relations with Morocco, minimal at outset, became much closer as Sassou-Nguesso came under the influence of his new security adviser, the marabout **Saidou Badian**. It was the latter who introduced the two state leaders, paving the road for the dispatch in 1987 of an originally small complement (later several hundred) of Moroccan security and internal intelligence officers who progressively replaced Congo's Cuban military contingent. But apart from close diplomatic relations arising from this exchange, the two countries have had few common interests.

(4) AFRICAN STATES. Of all the inter-African organizations to which Congo has belonged, the Union Douaniere et Economique de l'Afrique Centrale (UDEAC) has been the most useful to it and is consequently the one to which it has been the most loyal. Of the four French Equatorial African states that founded the UDE in 1960, only Congo and Gabon have remained steadfast and mutually cooperative members, largely because of an expanding community of economic interests. In 1961, Cameroon joined the UDE, which four years later became the UDEAC. That organization was threatened with erosion because of Zaire's partially successful attempt in 1968 to lure the Central African Republic and Chad into joining (temporarily) still another central African group under Mobutu's leadership. The 1964 treaty that gave birth to the UDEAC embodied the UDE's decision to establish a common tariff, tax structure, investment code, and industrial program, leading eventually to closer economic integration. To varying degrees, all the UDEAC members have benefited by an organization that has lessened competition between them, provided a market for their processing industries, and strengthened their bargaining position vis-à-vis other international organizations. Ironically, it was the Congo—the nation with the most to gain from a strong UDEAC—that almost destroyed it. In 1969, the Ngouabi government unilaterally expropriated the port and railroad, which, albeit situated in the Congo, had been the French Equatorial Federation's common property. By forcing those of its partners who used Congo's transport facilities to pay more for their use, Brazzaville especially angered the RCA, which depended on them for its foreign trade. In retaliation for Bangui's failure to pay the new rates in 1978, Congo banned the transport of the RCA's vital imports. The ill feeling thus aroused between the two countries was not dissipated until after Yhomby Opango and Bokassa were succeeded as heads of state by Nguesso and Dacko. (See also UNION DOUANIERE DES ETATS DE L'AFRIQUE CENTRALE.) Congo's overall unpopularity with its neighbors stemmed in part from the privileged position it had held in the FEA. With Zaire and Cameroon, resentment flared up when those countries believed that Congo was serving as a place of refuge and plotting for adversaries of their regimes. The frequent quarrels between Kinshasa and Brazzaville were rooted to varying degrees in the disparities between their colonial heritages, the size of their territory, populations, and natural resources, and their governments' ideological orientation and partisanship in the Angolan civil war. Conspicuous by its absence was any

dispute over the demarcation of frontiers. By the mid-1970s, the very proximity of the two capitals, along with Portugal's withdrawal from Africa, induced the presidents of Zaire and Congo to move toward improving their relations. However, despite some later cooperation between the two countries in deporting to each other subversive elements that have sought refuge in the neighboring country, tensions have periodically erupted by the mass expulsions of each state of non-nationals. The most recent example of this took place in mid-April 1989 when Congo expelled Zairiens for "irregular conduct" leading to Zaire's retaliation by expelling 40 Congolese, that in turn brought another round of expulsions, notably 5,000 more Zairiens from Congo. These mutual expulsions continued with Brazzaville's November 20, 1991 expulsion of 40,000 non-nationals working in Brazzaville, among them over 30,000 Zairiens.

As to the ill will between Yaoundé and Brazzaville in the first years of their independence, it was soon replaced by indifference. With its far stronger economy and independent transport system, Cameroon was largely aloof from the disputes over the means of communication and the division of tariff revenues that were bones of contention among its fellow members. In fact, it was not until 1981 that a joint Congo-Cameroon commission was formed and January 1982 that Sassou-Nguesso paid a state visit to Yaounde and the first ambassadors were appointed. That the UDEAC as an entity has survived the dissensions caused by internal rifts and international competition is a tribute to the useful service it has performed for its member states. This has been well illustrated by the understanding reached between Gabon and the Congo, despite incompatible ideologies, joint use of the CFCO's tracks, and a potentially competitive lumber industry. Moreover, the return of the RCA and Chad to the UDEAC fold, after interludes of infidelity, is another endorsement of its utility. However Congo-Gabonese relations have not been free of tensions since Gabon has intermittently given refuge to Congolese opposition elements, and in the late 1980's the completion of Gabon's Transgabonaise railroad led to a diversion of Gabon's massive manganese ore exports away from the fiscally hard-strapped Conglese CFCO railway. Congo's retaliation by confiscating 60 billion CFAF worth of COMILOG rail assets in Congo, now idle, caused further friction only partly alleviated by Gabon's President Bongo's marriage to Sassou-Nguesso's daughter.

Congo's indifference to African countries other than members of the UDEAC and those that can promote its economic evolution is striking. Even countries such as Guinea and Mali, whose governments were similarly Marxist-oriented, aroused no special enthusiasm in Brazzaville. And the country in September 1977, without warning expelled some 5,000 alien Africans on the ground that they had entered the country illegally. Nearly half of those driven out were Malians (2,234), the rest being various other west African nationals. So great was Congo's self-absorption and determination to regain control of its retail trade that the chorus of angry protests from the countries to which the refugees returned caught the Brazzaville authorities by surprise. They quickly sent conciliatory missions to the countries concerned and promised to set up a center for aid to departing refugees. At the same time, however, stricter measures of control were imposed on the 3,000 West Africans allowed to remain.

FORESTRY. Forests cover 60 percent of Congo's surface—20 million hectares, of which nearly 13 million are considered suitable for logging. The three areas into which the forests are divided vary greatly as to their dimensions and their composition. To what degree they are productive of revenues depends principally on their accessibility and on their proximity to shipping ports, and also on world-market conditions. Between 1972 and 1982, wood exports alone yielded revenues of more than 47 billion CFAF. As of 1982, forests directly and indirectly accounted for 10 percent of the Congo's GNP. Together the forests of Kouilou-Mayombe (12 million hectares) and those of northern Niari and Lekouzou (3.3 million hectares) occupy an area of about 4.5 million hectares. They are the domain of the valuable okoume and limba trees and account for 80 percent of the Congo's total production of logs (averaging some 500,000 cu. meters in a normal year). Congo's far larger northern, or third, zone consists of the Sangha and Likouala forests (15.5 million hectares), whose vast potential has scarcely been touched because of the region's lack of roads, swampy ground, and general inaccessibility. Without altering the zone's basic production potential, some 250,000 cu. meters could be produced from trees grown on eight to nine million hectares there, consisting mainly of red woods (sipo, sapelli, and iroko), as well as 300,000 cu. meters of white woods. Even as late as 1993 only eight logging companies were operating in the north, exploiting the most accessible timber areas near Ouesso, on the Sangha tributary and near Betou just south of the Central African Republic. Of the more than 3,000 varieties of trees found in the heterogeneous Congolese forests, comparatively few of the most valuable and accessible trees are cut each year for local industrial uses or for export. (See INDUSTRY—(5) WOOD.)

For many years, and especially between 1955 and 1974, lumber was Congo's principal source of revenue, far outdistancing the returns from agriculture. Aside from the lumber produced in Gabon, the RCA, and southeastern Cameroon, which was also shipped from the port of Pointe Noire, Congo itself produced annually between 500,000 and 800,000 cu. meters (at the maximum) of logs. In the period 1955–74, all of the Congo's wood exports came from its southern forests, and consisted exclusively of their most valuable varieties. Owing to the rise in oil exports from the Congo in the early 1970s, and also to the concurrent economic depression in those countries that had been the best clients for Congo's lumber (West Germany, France, Italy, and Spain), exports of wood declined rapidly. After 1975 they began to increase, reaching in 1980 603,000, and in 1988 750,000 cubic meters. Throughout, however, lumber's standing among the country's total exports has been only around 4.5 percent, as compared with 53.6 percent in 1957. In the mid-1970s, the sharp decline in lumber exports prompted the government to revise its forest policy and to assert greater control over wood production, processing, and exports. Its major objectives, as expressed in the Forestry Code of 1974, were the encouragement of production from the northern forests, mainly by reducing duties on exports from that region; a prolongation of the southern forests' productivity by the reforestation of the most valuable varieties; and development of the wooded savannah areas so as to provide the local inhabitants with firewood and building material, the railroad with fuel, and a cellulose industry with abundant raw material.

Foreigners have long dominated the felling, processing, transportation, and exportation of Congo's woods, and a major objective of the PCT leaders had been to transfer control of those remunerative activities to Congolese hands. They attribute the relatively poor showing of the local companies and individual foresters to their lack of organization, capital resources, and skill, not to mention their insufficient experience and knowledge of the conditions prevailing in the highly specialized world wood markets. In keeping with their convictions, the military government believed that by further regulations, by creating more official organizations, and by expanding the state sector of the economy, it could increase and stabilize the production of wood, monopolize its sale, encourage the export of locally processed lumber, and, generally speaking, transform Congolese forestry into a truly national and socialist enterprise. Among the regulations prompted by this conviction were those setting quotas for felling by foreigners, curbing the extension of agricultural land by the age-old custom of burning off forest areas in the Kouilou and Mayombe, and devising programs with the aid of the FAO and the UN Development Fund for better utilization of the country's forest resources. (See forestry and related enterprises listed in ACRONYMS as follows: CIB, OCB, OCF, PLACONGO, SIDETRA, SNEB, SOCOBOIS, UAIC, UEB.)

The government's success in attaining its objectives has been uneven. As regards the state sector in lumber production, the government's share has never exceeded 5 percent of the total. Although the number of individual foreign foresters and traders declined since the government monopolized all wood sales, that move adversely affected

Congolese individuals as well as firms. Private interests, consisting of 12 foreign firms and 50 Congolese companies, were responsible for virtually all of the 603,138 cu. meters of logs produced in 1980, and of that total, the French, German, and Belgian concerns accounted for 349,817 cu. meters, the Congolese for 120,000, and the state sector for 47,022. By 1990 the figures had not changed appreciably: in that year expatriate companies logged 76 percent of the timber produced in the country, private Congolese concerns 20 percent, and the state only 4 percent, though production had inched upwards in the 1980's to reach the figure of 750,000 cubic meters.

With respect to sizable capital investments, needed primarily for equipment and labor, and as to access to foreign markets, Congo is still dependent on outsiders. In most other domains, the military government was in control, notably with regard to the areas and location of the forests to be worked, the selection of recipients for permits to fell trees and process wood, the decision whether to export logs or sell sawn planks, and the wages and organization of the labor force. Export of timber is controlled by the Office Congolaise du Bois, a state company.

In 1964, four cutting permits covering 340,000 hectares of southern forest that had been recently opened up thanks to construction of the Congo-Ocean railroad were auctioned off, mainly to large foreign companies. The policy changes initiated in 1974–75 and the goals embodied in the 1982–86 development plan eliminated any possible resumption of such concessions to the private foreign firms still operating in the Congo. A large proportion of the 194,826 million CFAF spent on forestry under the development plan was earmarked for encouraging production of the less valuable woods from the northern forests by state and mixed companies and for the reforestation of the southern forest areas, not only to offset their depletion but also to supply the new paper-pulp industry from new eucalyptus plantations created for that project. (See EUCALYPTUS PROJECT.)

In view of the ten million hectares of virgin forest remaining in Congo, and of the forest's capacity for self-renewal, there is little likelihood of any serious depletion of the country's lumber resources through overcutting. For its surest revenues in the inevitable post-petroleum future, the government is relying upon those resources—in conjunction with greater agricultural production—as a more stable and longer-lasting national asset. However, as if to underscore that nothing can be taken for granted in Congo, a major cloud of uncercertainty began to loom over Congolese timber exploitation. With one of the largest private logging companies suspending operations in 1990 because of financial uncertainties having to do with currency fluctuations in southern Europe, its prime market, with three of the other eight companies doing so due to logistics problems, in January 1993 Prime Minister Da Costa was advised that the evacuation of timber from Congo's large northern forestry zones was at a standstill. With 200,000 cubic meters of northern logs already awaiting for over two years in Brazzaville for transportation on CFCO to the coast, the poor organization of traffic on the waterways leading to Brazzaville, and rail transport to the Atlantic Ocean, was threatening most companies with bankruptcy due to failing cash-flows. The problem was also unlikely to abate since the CFCO itself was in decrepit condition, and despite improvements made on its rail in the early 1980's, did not have adequate locomotives to maintain an adequate service.

As to local processing of timber logged in Congo, the country has fifteen sawmills, four peeled veneers plants and one plywood mill, many state-owned. As a whole all are losing money due to inefficiency and mismanagement, as well as due to systematic large-scale looting of their output for sale to private contractors. Notwithstanding timber's low export role in the Congolese economy, in terms of manpower, the sector employs fully 25 percent of workers employed in the modern economy. In 1990, with oil exports still in the doldrums, the government issued a new Economic and Social Action plan, that included a development strategy for the forestry sector. It included a plan to rent out selected timber zones of between 50,000 and one million hectares for periods of a maximum of 20 years to timber companies, that were to be restricted (with hefty fines for violations) to selective logging operations, not to be repeated in that zone for a subsequent period of 20 years to allow the forests to regenerate. The plan later met with World Bank approval and in March 1993 the latter granted Congo a gift of three billion CFAF aimed at preservation and reafforestation of the country's forests, and also for promoting tourism in the northern regions.

FORT ROUSSET see OWANDO.

FORUM POUR LA DEMOCRATIE SOCIALE (FDS) Small political party set up by Andely Beeve in 1992. In mid-1994 it merged with the Parti Nationale (PN).

FOUNDOU, PAUL. Former Secretary-general of Congo's UNESCO commission, and director of primary studies in the ministry of education in Brazzaville. Foundou is the author of several works on oral literature in Congo.

FOUNGUI, ALPHONSE, 1946— . Former PCT organizer and member of the party Central Committee. Born in 1946 in Bouenza, as an early radical militant he has been Political Commissar of Bouenza, and in 1984 was elected to the national assembly.

FOUTOU, ANTOINE, 1945– . Regional trade union leader. Born in 1945 in Bounou (Mouyoundzi), and entering the civil service as an administrative secretary, Foutou's trade union activities made him general secretary of the Confédération syndicale Congolaise in the Kouilou region. In that capacity he was elected in 1984 to the country's national assembly where he served as second secretary of the assembly.

FOUTOU, GOMA (Captain). Military officer and PCT member who served briefly as Foreign minister of Congo before succeeding Ange Diawara in November 1973 as first political commissar of the armed forces after the latter's attempted putsch.

FRENCH EQUATORIAL AFRICA, GOVERNORS OF (1886–1960).

1886–1898	Savorgnan de Brazza
1898–1901	H. F. de la Mothe
1901–1904	L. A. Grodet
1904–1908	E. Gentil
1908–1917	M. H. Merlin
1918–1919	G. L. Angoulvant
1920–1924	J. V. Augagneur
1924–1934	R. V. Antonetti
1935–1939	D. F. Reste
1939–1940	F. P. Boisson
1940	L. Husson
1940–1944	F. A. Eboué
1944–1947	A. M. Bayardelle
1947	C. J. Luizet
1947–1951	B. Cornut-Gentille
1951–1958	P. L. Chauvet
1958	P. A. Messmer
1958–1960	Y. Bourges

FRONT DE LIBERATION DES MBOCHI ET DES MAKOUTAS (FROBOMA). A clandestine organization set up in the early 1980's by Mbochi to counter the **FROLIBABA**, with the aim to promote regional Mbochi interests, and to support their leader Sassou-Nguesso.

FRONT DE LIBERATION DES BATEKES ET DES BAGAN-GOULOUS (FROLIBABA). A clandestine organization set up as early as 1978 to advance the political interests of the Batéké disillusioned by the monopoly of power exercised by the northern populations under Ngouabi and Sassou Nguesso. FROLIBABA was behind the wave of mysterious bombings in Brazzaville in 1981 and 1982.

FRONT POUR LE DEFENCE DE LA DEMOCRATIE (FDD). An alliance of 13 political parties in opposition to Milongo's interim leadership in Congo in the early 1990's. Its coordinator was Jean-Marie Tassoua.

FRONT UNI DE L'OPPOSITION. An opposition newsletter, disseminated abroad in the early 1980's by the **MPC** that first led the call in 1984 for a restoration of multiparty elections, and tried to undermine the M22-Sassou Nguesso link by supporting Yhomby Opango's return to power.

-G-

GABOU, ALEXIS, 1936– . Jurist. A Lari, born on November 14, 1936 in Brazzaville, Gabou was educated at the Chaminade Seminary (1950–57) following which he proceeded to France to study law at the University of Nancy (1957–62) and Nantes (1962–63). On his return to Brazzaville he joined the Congolese judicial system as a judge, moving up the hierarchy to become president of Congo's Court of Appeal (1965–69), and then Attorney General and in November 1969, judge on the Supreme Court. Between 1966 and 1978 he also taught constitutional law and politics at Marien Ngouabi University. A PCT member, Gabou played an equivocal role during the liberalizations of the 1990's, supporting the emergence of the interim administration of Milongo, but remaining a PCT leader. He was named minister of interior in the 1991 interim Milongo government: while in that role he was involved in a conspiracy to discredit chief of staff General Mokoko.

GAKOSSO, GILBERT-FRANCOIS, 1944– . Journalist. Born in Pointe Noire on October 4, 1944, Gakosso attended schools at home and later secured training in France as a journalist. The author of a couple of books on Congo, he was for long (1966–1979) the Reuters agency representative in Brazzaville for whom he wrote numerous articles.

GALIBA, DR. BERNARD. Former cabinet minister. A medical doctor trained abroad, Galiba was appointed minister of health and labor in Massamba-Debat's first government in 1963. In the reshuffle of October 1964, he retained the health portfolio but lost that of labor. In February 1965 he was briefly imprisoned in connection with the murder of three high officials, and after his release he retired from politics. In October 1971, he became head of the National Laboratory of Public Health in Brazzaville, where he still works.

GALIBALI, BERNARD, 1927– . Former cabinet minister. Born in Brazzaville on November 2, 1927, and with a medical degree from the

University of Bordeaux, Galibali served as director of public health between January 1962 and August 1963, deputy to the national assembly (1963), and after the ouster of president Youlou minister of health (1963–1965). He then left the government for medical practice. Between 1971 and his retirement he was also director of the national public health laboratory.

GALIBALI, LAMBERT. Former Mayor of Brazzaville. After serving as a civil servant and deputy to the national assembly, Galibali became mayor of Brazzaville in 1968, and joined the central committee of the PCT. In 1971 he was dropped from the PCT Central Committee on the grounds of "ideological deficiencies" but continued in his mayoral duties until 1973.

GANAO, DAVID-CHARLES, 1928– . Former foreign minister. Born on July 20, 1928, at Djambala, and of Bateke origins, Ganao studied at a teachers' training college, following which he became a teacher and then inspector of primary schools at Brazzaville. After brief specialized training in France, he joined the Congolese foreign ministry as head of its political division (1960–63). After President Youlou's overthrow he joined Massamba-Debat's government as foreign minister (also of tourism and cooperation, 1966–68), serving until January 1968, when he was re-assigned the portfolio of planning. In September 1969, President Ngouabi named him permanent representative of Congo to the UN in Geneva, a post he occupied until 1973, serving also as ambassador to Switzerland (1970–73). He was recalled from there to become once again foreign minister on January 7, 1973, serving until 1976. He was then appointed deputy executive secretary of the United Nations Economic Commission for Africa (based in Addis Ababa) where he served until 1980 when he was reassigned to Vienna, Austria. With the political liberalizations in Congo Ganao returned to Congo and set up a political party, the Union des forces démocratiques (UFD), that secured some support in Batéké areas.

GANDOULOU, JUSTIN-DANIEL. Anthropologist. Originating from the Bacongo quarter of Brazzaville, and educated in the Sorbonne where he obtained a PhD in social anthropology, Gandoulou currently teaches in Rennes. He has published three highly acclaimed books assessing the attitudes, behavior, and values, of modern urban Congolese youth, in Brazzaville and in Paris.

GANDZION, PROSPER, 1927– . Former cabinet minister. Born in 1927 at Ombina, a nephew of the historic **Batéké king Makoko**, Gandzion completed his schooling locally to become a teacher in 1949 and an inspector of primary schools in 1958. After joining the

UDDIA party he was elected to the territorial assembly from Djoué in 1957, and became its first vice-president in May 1958. A few months later, Fulbert Youlou named him minister of education. Arrested after Youlou's overthrow for corruption, he was sentenced to 10 years' imprisonment in June 1965. Subsequently released and exiled, he lived in Chad until returning to Congo in January 1974, amnestied by President Ngouabi.

GANGA ZANDZOU, JEAN. Former president of the national assembly. A lawyer by training, Ganga Zandzou served as Congo's attorney general until 1973 when he was integrated into highest echelons of the PCT as one of its few Lari. In 1974 he was appointed president of the PCT committee on control, and a member of the politburo as well as of the PCT central committee. On January 9, 1975 he was named minister of waterways and forests and tourism. In January 1976 he was reappointed attorney general to Congo's Supreme Court. In July 1979 the PCT put him up as candidate for the national assembly, where he was elected president of that organ, to be re-elected five years later. In that capacity he has been one of the most influential people in Congo.

GANGOUO, MICHEL (Colonel). An army officer, who was arrested in July 1990 for a plot against Sassou-Nguesso, Gangouo was expelled from the army before being integrated back into it by the new multiparty government to emerge in Brazzaville. He was then appointed minister of defence by interim Prime Minister Milongo on January 2, 1991. However, Milongo had no choice but to drop him from the cabinet three weeks later because of strenuous opposition to this appointment by the northern military hierarchy.

GANONGO, GEORGES, 1945– . Secretary general of Scientific Research. Born on December 6, 1945, and educated in biology at the University of Rennes (1968) and obtaining a doctorate in Agronomy from the University of Toulouse (1971), Ganongo taught Animal Physiology at Marien Ngouabi University in Brazzaville before his appointment.

GAP GROUP. An American company operating in Zaire since the 1960's, the political and economic liberalizations in Brazzaville in the 1990's brought its entry into Congo. In 1992 the company erected a 200 million CFAF metal seal manufacturing plant to produce crown-corks for both the country's and the entire region's breweries and soft-drinks companies. The company has also been negotiating with the Congolese government for the purchase of the defunct (since 1990) SOVERCO glassworks at Pointe Noire, as well as SIDETRA for $3 million. Trade union insistence on re-employment of the entire original manpower complement has been rejected (slowing negotiations) since GAP felt only 40% of the manpower (or 400 workers) were needed.

GARDE PRESIDENTIELLE (GP). An elite corps of armed personnel specifically charged with protecting the Presidency and the head of state. Apart from the GP, primarily a heavily-armed bodyguard, there have been a multiplicity of other specialized intelligence-gathering police units, reporting via their commanders to the head of the presidential guard. Under Sassou Nguesso the GP was a large (600-man) unit of hand-picked northerners, many from his own home-village, under the command of presidential relatives responsible to **Colonel Oba.** With the rise of the civilian government of President Pascal Lissouba, the "old" Garde Présidentielle became (minus its name) Sassou Nguesso's personal bodyguard, headquartered normally at Oyo in the Cuvette, and accompanying the former president whenever he travelled, usually to Brazzaville. A new Garde Présidentielle was formed, largely from **Nibolek** personnel, headed by Colonel Yves Ibala, a Bembe officer from Bouenza, with the GP Inspector General Major Emmanuel Massala, liasing with the Presidential Office where he is on Lissouba's military staff. Since France declined several times to provide additional military assistance to Congo, 65 decommissioned Israeli officers (including a former General and a Colonel) were recruited to train the force. They arrived in Brazzaville early in 1994. Until then a French former commissioner of France's Diréction de la Surveillance Territoriale (DST) and former head of the Elysée Palace anti-terrorist unit, served as technical advisor. The Israeli presence disturbed France, that felt its influence in Brazzaville was waning, and a military training mission was then also dispatched.

GATSONO YOKA ICCOULLAH, PLACIDE, 1948– . Born in 1948 in Mouétchou (Owando region) and a high civil administrator by profession, he has been mayor of Loubomo and deputy to the national assembly between 1980 and 1991.

GENDARMERIE. Originally this was a largely southern-staffed part of the defence forces, that was dismantled after the March 1970 Pierre Kikanga armed assault from across the Congo river against the regime of Ngouabi. The gendarmerie's constant support for such Youlouist assaults, or lack of alacrity in reporting, or blocking them, led to the decision to replace it with a People's Militia, ideologically committed force shackled to the military. Paradoxically, the People's Militia was later to support the dangerous leftist attempted coup by **Ange Diawara.**

A new gendarmerie nationale, a rural police, was set up in 1992, re-cruited largely from Bembe and other **Nibolek** elements, and under the command of the Bembe General Mankoumba N'Zambi. The structure, and other small specialized political police and intelligence units, was set up in order to develop some armed forces outside the reach of the predominantly northern and intrinsically suspect regular armed forces. Israeli military training specialists, invited to retrain a new re-structured **Garde Présidentielle** participated in some of the training of the gendarmerie, but in 1992 France—previously rejecting a role—stepped in with a training program, allegedly worried of losing influ-ence to Israel, and indirectly the U.S.

GOMA, ETIENNE (Colonel). Director-general of the national police.

GOMA, LOUIS-SYLVAIN (General), 1941– . Former Prime Minis-ter. A Vili of Cabinda origin, born on June 28, 1941, at Pointe Noire, Goma joined the armed forces, studied mathematics in Versailles, and attended (1961) the elite St. Cyr officers' staff college. He completed his training in 1963, graduating as Lieutenant, and proceeded to Anger for administrative studies, to return to Brazzaville where he joined the army engineering corps, being named its commander in 1966. He en-joyed a meteoric rise under Ngouabi, being appointed army chief of staff in August 1968 for his role in helping topple the Massamba-Debat regime. A year later, he was named secretary for defense after being reconfirmed commander-in-chief of the people's army in Feb-ruary 1969. He held the defense portfolio until April 1970, when he was assigned that of public works and transport. In December 1971, he also became minister of civil aviation and a member of the PCT central committee. He remained loyal to Ngouabi during the danger-ous **Ange Diawara** attempted putsch of February 1972, and in Janu-ary 1973 was promoted in rank from captain to major. He was brought into the PCT Politburo in January 1975, and on December 2, 1975 was named Congo's prime minister and chairman of the planning com-mission. After Ngouabi's assassination, he remained as premier and minister of the plan in the government formed April 5, 1977, and sec-ond vice-president of the new ruling military committee that was es-tablished. On February 8, 1979, he was retained as prime minister, and was ranked third in the regime after Nguesso and Thystère-Tchicaya. He continued as premier in the governments of April 3, 1979, and De-cember 28, 1980, but in due course fell afoul of Sassou Nguesso. Dis-missed from the government, Sassou-Nguesso tried to appease him by an offer of the post of president of Air Afrique, but Goma rejected the offer. In 1984 he was appointed president of the country's Constitu-tional Council, set up after the 1979 constitutional modifications, as the final arbiter of the legality of state legislation. Goma came back to prominence in December 1990 when Sassou Nguesso appointed him interim prime minister until the **national conference** elected Milongo on June 8,1991, to replace him. He then returned to his prior post.

GOMA-FOUTOU, CELESTIN (Colonel). Military officer and powerful regional boss of the Niari region, politically active for over 25 years. Until 1990 Goma-Foutou served on the PCT secretariat charged with ideological indoctrination, and was the only one who dared question Sassou-Nguesso's actions. In 1984 he joined the Poungui government as minister of territorial administration, avoiding the problems that tripped, and brought about the arrest of his colleague Thystère-Tchicaya to whom he had been close. In December 1990, during the transitional era between military and civilian rule, Goma-Foutou was appointed interim minister of interior, information and sports in the government of General Goma.

GONDOU, LOUIS. Trade union leader. Gondou had been the deputy-head of the unified **Confédération Syndicale Congolaise** by virtue of his presidency of the latter's largest affiliate that groups government workers, the Fédération des Travailleurs de l'Administration Générale et Municipale. Originally a PCT member, Gondou disengaged his union from the CSC, setting up a separate federation in 1990, followed by six former CSC affiliates.

GOURA, PIERRE, 1917– . Early political leader, former cabinet minister and mayor of Loubomou. Born on January 2, 1917, in the Sibiti district, after attending a Catholic primary school Goura worked briefly as a forester. As a PPC militant he was elected as a deputy and represented Niari in the territorial assembly from 1946 until 1957, when he was defeated for re-election by Kikhounga-Ngot. In 1957, he joined the UDDIA while serving as senator from Congo (1955–59). In 1959 he was elected mayor of Dolisie, and from 1959 to 1963 he was Fulbert Youlou's minister of finance. Arrested after Youlou's overthrow, he was given a suspended sentence of two years in prison in June 1965. He has been in retirement since 1970.

GOVERNMENT OF CONGO, 1994.

Prime Minister & Chair, Priorities Committee	Joachim Yhomby Opango
Chairman, Development Committee	Claude Antoine Da Costa
Chairman, Socio-Cultural Committee	Stepháne Bongho-Nouarra
Chairman, Defence Committee	Gen. Raymond Damase Ngollo
Chairman, Legislation, Judiciary, Reform	Aimé Matsika
Minister of Interior	Martin M'Beri

Minister of Foreign Affairs & Cooperation	Benjamin Bounkoulou
Minister of the Economy & Finance	N'Guila Moungounga Nkombo
Minister of Planning	Clement Mouamba
Minister of Communications	Albertin Lipou Massala
Minister of Industrial Development, Mines	Jean Itadi
Minister of Equipment and Public Works	Lambert Galibali
Minister of Animal Husbandry	Gregoire Lefouoba
Minister of the civil service	Jean Prosper Koyo
Minister of Transportation & Aviation	Maurice Niaty Mouamba
Minister of Commerce, Small & Medium firms	Marius Mouambenga
Minister of Health & Social Welfare	Jean-Roger Ekoundzola
Minister of Labor, Social Security	Anaclet Tsomambet
Minister of Hydraulic resources	Benoit Koukebéné
Minister of Tourism & Environment	François-Auguste Tchichéllé
Minister of Culture	Dandou Abel Dibindou
Minister of Water, Forestry, Fisheries	Rigobert Ngouolall
Minister of National Education	Noutété Nabone Tangui
Minister of Human Rights	Gabriel Matsiola

GRAILLE, CLAUDE NDALLA see NDALLA, CLAUDE.

GROUPEMENT POUR LE PROGRES SOCIAL AU MOYEN-CONGO. This short-lived party was founded in 1956 in the Niari region by Kikhounga-Ngot.

-H-

HAUT CONSEIL DE LA REPUBLIQUE (HCR). Congo's interim 153-member legislature, elected by the 1991 **national conference** out of its 1,200-odd membership, under an executive leadership of André Milongo, charged with preparing for local, parliamentary and presidential elections. After the elections the HCR was replaced by the new assemblée national.

HAUT CONSEIL REGIONAL DE TAI LANGAI. A group of northern traditional chiefs based in the Brazzaville suburbs, to whom Sassou Nguesso paid particular attention during his period in office.

HAVEACONGO. New parastatal company erected in 1986 to cultivate and process, among others, a 5,000 hectare rubber plantation and a self-contained industrial and social complex. Roughly half of the funds for the $38 million project was lent from the African Industrial Bank.

HEALTH. Congo's public-health service retains the centralized organization given it by French military doctors at the turn of the century. In the 1920s it acquired mobile medical units that tracked down and treated epidemic and endemic diseases in the rural areas. Initially, the territory's medical personnel concentrated on the elimination of trypanomiasis and smallpox, and after World War II extended its activities to include leprosy, yaws, malaria, and tuberculosis. The Brazzaville branch of the Pasteur Institute through its research and supply of drugs contributed to a marked reduction in the incidence of Congo's major maladies. But tuberculosis has been spreading among town-dwellers and malaria is still the scourge of the rural populations, which continue to seek aid from fetishists and sorcerers. The concentration of public health services and a paying clientele for private practitioners in the towns stems from the country's shortage of qualified medical personnel. In 1964 this shortage was made more acute by the withdrawal of French military doctors, when France repatriated most of its troops in central Africa.

By central African standards, Congo's medical installations and personnel are relatively good. The country has two major and three minor hospitals, totaling about 6000 beds, including 1500 in the maternity clinics; 32 medical centers; 82 infirmaries; 371 dispensaries, which sell medicines at discount rates; and 17 health education units. In 1981 nearly two thirds of the 266 medical doctors serving in Congo were expatriates or had been trained abroad (a ratio that has not changed since though the number of doctors has nearly doubled), whereas all paramedical personnel were locally trained Congolese. Among their upper echelons were 244 midwives, 953 trained nurses, and 179 sanitary assistants. To offset the increasing operating costs of the public health services and to combat the rising tide of epidemics, especially of trypanomiasis, as well as to modernize and restock some Congolese hospitals, France made a special contribution in 1982. From time to time, the European Development Fund, China, and Sweden have also contributed funds and specialists to supplement and improve the local medical facilities. In December 1982, the Soviet Union, that had already provided a maternity clinic in Brazzaville, pledged to build the largest hospital in the Congo at Loubomo. Considerable funds were slotted for health improvements under the 1982–1986 development plan, but the country's deteriorating finances aborted many projects.

HOMBESSA, ANDRE, 1935– . Former radical youth leader. A Lari born in Brazzaville in 1935, Hombessa received his secondary degree from a Protestant lycee before being sent in 1956 by Canadian missionaries to study at an evangelical institute in Cameroon, destined for a teaching career. After his return to Brazzaville in 1959, he was elected president of the Congolese youth council and to the executive committee of the World Assembly of Youth. As a committed radical and a JMNR leader, he was invited in October 1964 to join Massamba-Debat's cabinet as secretary of state for youth, and six months later replaced Bicoumat as minister of interior. His strongly anti-Western and anti-Catholic views were reflected in the articles he regularly contributed to the JMNR organ, *Dipanda,* and they earned for him the name of "wild man of the Congolese revolution." In January 1968, Massamba-Debat demoted him by leaving him only the portfolio of information, precipitating a cabinet crisis. Popular with youth, and especially within the JMNR that he cultivated as a stepping stone to power, after the Ngouabi coup d'etat he mobilized his Lari JMNR armed youth to resist Ngouabi, holding out at Camp Biafra in September 1968. Sentenced to three years in prison for his role, he was amnestied a year later. In February 1978 he was implicated in the assassination of Ngouabi, and, having fled abroad, was sentenced to death in absentia at the subsequent trials of Ngouabi's assassins.

HOUA-NGAPARO, ASSOURI, 1944– . Physician. Born on July 22, 1944, and educated at home and at the university of Lille in France, where he earned a degree in tropical medicine, Houa-Ngaporo returned to Brazzaville to join Marien Ngouabi university. Since 1978 has been head of the department of medicine and chief medical doctor of gastro-enterology.

HUILERIE DE NKAYI (HUILKA). Formerly one of Congo's money-losing state companies based in Nkayi, Huilka was privatized in 1989 and purchased by a Lebanese consortium that had also just purchased **Savcongo**.

HYDRO-CONGO. State oil marketing monopoly set up in 1973 with, in 1988, a 60 billion CFAF turnover, and including several subsidiaries such as the Pointe Noire refinery (see CORAF). In 1981 Maurice Sassou Nguesso, the president's brother, was its Political Commissar. With 1,483 workers and a huge payroll, Hydro-Congo has been one of Congo's most deficitory companies, and was scheduled (since 1988) to be broken down into several components, restructured or privatized, at the insistence of the IMF. Despite an announced policy in 1988 to indeed do so, vicious trade union strikes have erupted whenever any change in the company's status was mentioned. Unable to impose his will, Sassou Nguesso in 1990 loosened Hydro-Congo's marketing monopoly, allowing other foreign oil companies to enter fields formerly held by Hydro-Congo. This led to Amoco, British petroleum, Chevron, Anglo-Dutch Shell to petition for licenses. Under the agreement Hydro-Congo was to engage in exploration for oil alone or jointly with foreign companies, with Amoco sharing in the oil-refining operations hithero undertaken by Hydro-Congo and Elf-Congo. Hydro-Congo's director in 1993 was Aimé Portella, who was being opposed by workers for fiscal mismanagement and favoritism. In that year, also, the Lissouba regime stopped paying it subsidies since its financial accounts were four years in arrears. Hydro-Congo's privatization is one prime demand of global donor-agents, who do not wish new funds channeled into the latter's bloated payroll (46 billion CFAF, which is half its annual turnover) that assures continued massive operating losses. In 1993 the company owed the Congolese treasury 16 billion CFAF and to the Congolaise de Raffinage refinery 24 billion CFAF.

-I-

IBALA, YVES (Colonel). Commander of the newly restructured Presidential Guard of President Lissouba. A Bembe from the Bouenza province, Ibala's Guard is completely different from the Presidential Guard of Sassou Nguesso, that was heavily dominated by Mbochi from Sassou Nguesso's home-town.

IBALICO, MARCEL, 1924–1964. Early political leader. A Bateke (of the Fumu branch) born at Itatolo 6 kms. north of Brazzaville on September 30, 1924, Ibalico studied for the priesthood but in 1953 entered the educational service as a teacher. His oratorical skills gained him access to Radio-AEF and opened to him a journalistic career as well, contributing to the literary periodical *Liaison*. In 1956 Ibalico joined Fubert Youlou's political camp, becoming one of the latter's closest municipal advisors after Youlou became mayor of Brazzaville. As a member of the UDDIA he was elected, in 1957, to represent Djoué in the territorial assembly; the same year he was elected vice-president of the AEF Grand Council. He traveled widely in Europe after being elected a senator of the Franco-African Community. In 1961 he was given charge of Radio Brazzaville, and in 1962 succeeded Massamba-Debat as president of the legislature. After Youlou's overthrow Ibalico fled to Kinshasa where he tried to organize an anti-Massamba-Debat movement to reverse the latter's rise to power. He was killed in an automobile accident in March 1964, in full view of Zairien police to whom he was at the time showing his ID, leading to speculation that his death was the work of the Congolese secret service.

IBATA, DR. RAYMOND, 1942– . Economist. Born on June 12, 1942 at Makoua, and educated at Makoua and Pointe Noire, Ibata first attended Marien Ngouabi University and he then proceeded to France for additional studies. He attended University of Caen, University of Bordeaux and the University of Paris studying, inter alia insurance, and a year after his return to Brazzaville in 1973 was already director-general of Société Assurances et Réassurances, a post he still holds.

ICKENGA, AUXENCE, 1937– . Senior Vili administrator and diplomat. A nephew of **Charles Assemekang** Ickenga was born in July 1937 in Makoua, and after studies at home proceeded to Paris where he studied at the IHEOM. Returning home he was first appointed prefect of Sangha, then director-general of administration in the foreign ministry, and director of the cabinet of the minister of foreign affairs. In November 1966 he was named ambassador to the UAR by Massamba-Debat, returning to Brazzaville in 1969 to join Ngouabi's cabinet as minister of agriculture, and, six months later, also that of foreign affairs. A PCT member, he was elected to the latter's central committee as well. Dropped from the cabinet and the PCT central committee in December 1971, he became the director of Ngouabi's presidential cabinet the next month. In October 1972, he was named ambassador to France and representative to UNESCO. Briefly under suspicion of plotting with his counterpart in Belgium against the Ngouabi regime, he was reappointed to a new ambassadorship, this time to England. On his return to Brazzaville in 1977 he was first appointed director-general of the national electricity company, and then director of the newly established state company Hydro-Congo. A good friend of Sassou Nguesso, in 1985 Ickenga was nominated by him for the post of president and director-general of Air Afrique, and secured the appointment, serving in that capacity until dismissed in August 1989, precipitating calls in the M-22 for Congo's pullout from Air Afrique. On his return to Brazzaville he assumed the post of controller-general of state companies, working out of the Presidential office, holding that post until 1991.

IKONGA, AUXENCE. See ICKENGA, AUXENCE.

IKOUEBE, BASILE, 1946– . Senior aide to Sassou-Nguesso. Born in 1945 and studying Political Science at the University of Bordeaux and Public Administration in Paris, he graduated in 1972. Ikouebé then returned to Brazzaville and with Sassou Nguesso's rise to power became one of his senior aides, working out of the presidential office. Between 1982–87 he was the latter's diplomatic advisor, and between 1987 and 1991 he was the director of the presidential office.

ICKOUNGA, MARTIAL DE PAUL. An engineer by profession, Ickounga currently serves as the head of President Lissouba's presidential office staff.

IMPFONDO. Congo's northernmost town, administrative headquarters of the distant, isolated and relatively neglected Likouala region. Because of its regional role, and the paucity of any other modern facilities in Likouala, Impfondo has had the highest annual demographic growth rate among Congo's urban towns (8.34 percent in the 1980's). By 1992 it had passed some other towns to assume, with a population of around 16,000, ninth rank, hard-behind **Ouesso** in the Sangha region, that by 1995 it is projected to pass in size. Impfondo is on the Oubangui affluent of the Congo river, and seasonal river travel to Bangui (in the Central African Republic) is possible when the Oubangui is at its height, usually between September and December when very heavy rains (2,060 mm.) fall in the district. At times, however, the river is so shallow that all barge traffic is at a standstill for months on end, and logs floating south to Brazzaville clog the river. The town is also connected with Brazzaville by twice-weekly air service of Lina-Congo. The district of Impfondo, comprising 12,000 sq. kms., is situated on the Oubangui river and is comprised of dense forests and swamps with occasional cleared savanna area.

IMPFONDO GROUP. Former informal clique, including some members of the M-22 (which see), many personally loyal to **Major François-Xavier Katali** until his death. The clique encompasses northern Impfondo and Sangha leaders, united to press for the development of their neglected distant regions, and especially to assure that after the era of the Cuvette political leadership in Congo (i.e. Ngouabi, Yhomby Opango, Sassou Nguesso) ends, Impfondo's "turn" at the helm of the nation should come. One of their most prominent leaders has been former foreign minister Pierre Nze Mba, who had to be purged due to his overly vocal hard-line stands. Katali himself was demoted from his headship of the security services in 1984 (where he had been much feared) to the ministry of agriculture, and his death gave Sassou-Nguesso comfort. The Impfondo group had significant influence among the security and armed forces, and during the Ngouabi and Sassou-Nguesso era were discreetly supported by advisers (and funding) from Algeria, East Germany, and Cuba. Since the group moved from its "Maoist" positions in the 1970's the regime has not seen it as a major threat, but has tried to assuage it with top appointments in the State sector. Among their leaders was also **Ambroise Noumazalaye** whom Sassou Nguesso counted as his friend, and who has been used to keep the group under control. With the move to multipartyism in the 1990's (that the group strenuously opposed) there have been persistent, though unconfirmed reports, that the group is biding its time until the Lissouba regime stumbles and "Impfondo's time" comes.

IMPRESSION DE TEXTILES DE LA REPUBLIQUE DU CONGO (IMPRECO). See SOCIETE D'IMPRESSIONS DE TEXTILES DU CONGO (IMPRECO).

INDUSTRIES. Moyen-Congo owed the remarkable variety of its industrial output to its transport facilities, urban development, and Brazzaville's status as a federal and territorial capital. By 1960, Congo had two tanneries, a shoe factory, a brewery, 15 sawmills, a plywood factory, a sugarmill, a sugar refinery, three industrial ricemills, 28 semi-industrialized oilmills, a cigarette factory, a textile and clothing enterprise, two soap factories, and a fish cannery. Power for the Brazzaville area (and for Kinshasa) was supplied by a hydroelectric dam at Djoué, with Pointe Noire's electricity coming from a thermal generating plant (see ELECTRIC POWER). Production of consumer-goods was limited because of the small local market and limited resources.

Despite many advances in the 1980's and 1990's industry still, petroleum apart, occupies a comparatively modest place. It is concentrated at Brazzaville, Pointe Noire, and Nkayi, consisting at its heyday (before many enterprises were closed bankrupt in 1987–1992) of about 120 companies employing some 19,000 workers, and with a turnover of around 24.7 billion CFAF. The great majority of Congo's industries fall into the category of agro-industries, processing the output of the rural economy and producing sugar, textiles, edible oils, beer, and soap. (See also MINING and PETROLEUM.) Next in importance are the building industries, notably those relating to public works. Among these are such enterprises as the rolling mill at Loubomo, a foundry at Mossendjo, and a plant making hand tools and agricultural equipment. As regards consumer industries, the most notable are those producing textiles, clothing, shoes, cigarettes, and furniture, some recently privatized or closed down. They are the smallest and most heterogeneous of all, being handicapped by the lack of capital, aged and poorly maintained equipment, irregularity and insufficiency of basic supplies, inefficient and often corrupt management, and the small size of the domestic market (one million consumers). Certain categories of industrial enterprises deserve special mention, either because of the scope of their operations and the nationality and character of their ownership (foreign or domestic, public or private), or because of the role they play in Congo's finances. Among the food industries, which accounted in the 1980's for 10 billion CFAF of the total industrial turnover, one could note the former state-owned Sucreries de Congo (SUCO), Huilerie d'Arachide de Nkayi (HUILKA), and the Minuterie-Aliments de Betail (MAB), currently rehabilitated with private foreign funds and experts. The privately owned French Société Congolaise des Brasseries de Kronenbourg (SCBK) at Pointe Noire and the Belgian-Dutch Brasserie de Brazzaville are flourishing, as are two private charged-water firms, the Boissons Africaines de Brazzaville (BAB) and a subsidiary of the Société Nationale de Distribution des Eaux (SNDE). The most productive of the textile industries (which total 7 billion CFAF in business turnover) has been the former stated-owned Société des Textiles du Congo (SOTEXCO) at Kinsoundi and the mixed state (30 percent) and foreign-owned Société d'Impressions de Textiles de la République Populaire du Congo (IMPRECO). As for the chemical industries, two of the most important — the oil refinery of HYDRO-CONGO and the Société des Verreries du Congo (SOVERCO), both in Pointe Noire — required reorganization and additional financing before they finally were able to get under way in the early 1980's, only to founder financially in 1987 when efforts to either close, restructure or privatize them were fiercely resisted by the trade unions until fairly recently.

Under the 1982–1986 five-year plan, the country's industrialization was scheduled for unprecedented development, with approximately half of the total investment funds (546 billion of the 1105 billion CFAF) allotted for the public works program, two thirds for infrastructure, including extension and improvement of roads and bridges and dams, many in the northern part of the country. However, though much (costly, and according to some experts, unnecessary) paving of roads took place, the Plan had to be curtailed and then terminated as Congo's oil-bonanza came to an end. The scheduled massive infusions of capital into the financially ailing state enterprises was one part of the development plan that could not be completed, with the result that most state companies found themselves bankrupt by the late 1980's. Some have in the past few years been privatized.

(1) FOOD AND TOBACCO. Among the processing industries, those producing food are by far the most important, inasmuch as their business turnover accounts for more than half of the total. Within that category, the output of beer and charged water has increased considerably, doubling between 1973 and 1978, and again since, to a volume considered exceptionally large for a country with two million inhabitants. Congo's beverage companies, in the order of importance, are the SCBK, the Brasserie de Brazzaville, and the BAB.

Société Congolaise des Brasseries Kronenbourg (SCBK). Its capital, amounting to 920 million CFAF, is divided chiefly between two French companies, Gervais (38 percent) and CFAC (37.5 percent). At Pointe Noire, it operates a plant producing beer and charged water, which began functioning in 1965, and it installed a second plant at Brazzaville in 1980, increasing beer-production capacity to 350,000 hl.

Brasserie de Brazzaville. This firm's capital is divided evenly between Heineken and the Belgian firm Lambert. It began production in 1952, and by 1979 had reached its capacity output of 263,726 hl. of beer. It has since increased production to 360,000 hl. with a new bottling plant and investments of 1.2 billion CFAF.

Boissons Africaines de Brazzaville (BAB). Private Belgian and Congolese interests have provided most of this plant's capital, amounting to 140 million CFAF. It began operating in 1964, and reached its productive capacity of 150,000 hl. in 1980 when a modernization of the plant took place.

Société Industrielle et Agricole du Tabac Tropical (SIAT). This company, capitalized at 600 million CFAF and owned by a subsidiary of JOB, Unipar, and the Société Nouvelle des Cigarettes Nationales, produces from its Brazzaville factory some 35 million packs of cigarettes. It began operating in 1947, has a capacity of 60 million packs annually, and supplements local tobacco supplies by imports.

Sucrerie du Congo (SUCO). Formerly a state company formed in 1978, to replace two successive sugar companies, the Société Industrielle et Agricole du Niari (SIAN) and SIACONGO, also a state company. SIAN was founded in 1929, with a grant of 20,000 hectares in the Niari valley. It tried growing cassava, peanuts, sisal, corn, bananas, and sugarcane without marked success, and in 1949 the enterprise was bought by the Vilgrain interests, which controlled the Grands Moulins de Paris. Under its new management, SIAN made progress by concentrating on the cultivation of sugarcane. In 1956, it was granted funds to build a sugarmill capable of crushing 10,000 tons of cane annually, on condition that it would sell its output exclusively in the AEF. In the late 1950s SIAN acquired more capital and began processing peanuts, wheat, cassava, and fiber crops. It formed a subsidiary, SOSUNIARI, which created new cane plantations and built a sugar refinery at Nkayi in 1964. Encouraged by the 1966 OCAM sugar agreement which guaranteed a market for about 52,000 tons of Congolese sugar each year, SIAN-SOSUNIARI tripled its production. But between 1966 and 1970 world prices for sugar declined by about 35 percent and the cost of the company's labor rose by about the same percentage, so that it paid no dividends to its shareholders for three years. In 1970, the company's board of directors threatened to cease operations and to dismiss its workers who were then on strike for higher pay and better working conditions. Because this would have caused great hardship to the SIAN-SOSUNIARI's 3,000 to 10,000 workers, the company, viewed by the Congolese government as a symbol of neocolonialism, was nationalized in 1970. To replace it, a state company, SIACONGO was formed, and negotiations were undertaken to reimburse SIAN's shareholders and purchase its equipment and installations. As a result of this move SIACONGO was faced with so many technical, labor, and, above all, marketing difficulties that it could not survive. SUCO, after taking over with the help of the government and with foreign experts and funds, was eventually able to cope with the problems of its predecessor, to become briefly the outstanding agroindustry in the Congo. Like its predecessors, SUCO cultivated cane in the Niari valley and processed its output at a plant in Moutela until 1979. In that year, the government took it over, reduced its debt to the state (notably the cost of its personnel), and entrusted its management to Somediaa. The latter was a specialized sector of the far-flung Grands Moulins de Paris, which had helped to create SIAN 41 years before its nationalization. Somediaa, in turn, formed a Société d'Ingenierie, de Gestion et de Service en Afrique (SIGAS) in conjunction with the Banque de Paris et des Pays-Bas (Paribas) and a Dutch company, HVA. Between 1980 and 1982, SUCO produced annually 12,000 tons of raw sugar, setting up as its target for the 1980's about 70,000 tons, to be milled from the 700,000 tons of cane grown on 13,000 hectares. However, despite several good years the company once again started to suffer from declining productivity and output and had to once again be restructured.

Minoterie-Aliments de Betail (MAB). Situated in Nkayi, this state company produced throughout the 1970's and 1980's only around 4–5,000 tons of flour, some 3,000 tons of fodder, and 600 tons of bran. Despite poor productivity, MAB has retained its monopoly of imported flour and wheat.

Huilerie d'Arachide de Nkayi (HUILKA). Still another poor-performance state company, in Nkayi, its output of unrefined peanut oil in 1981 amounted to only 1,321 tons. It has since been bought by foreign private interests.

(2) TEXTILES AND LEATHER. Société des Textiles du Congo (SOTEXCO). The various services of this company, capitalized at 1.7 billion CFAF, were put into operation between 1968 and 1975. It is equipped to spin, weave, dye, and print cloth, as well as to manufacture knitwear, and has a capacity of 3.5 million meters of cloth a year. In 1976 a combination of worn-out machinery (of Chinese origin), poor management, and insufficient supplies forced SOTEXCO to suspend operations; when they were resumed three years later it was on a partial and irregular basis, and deficitory. The company has since been privatized.

Société d'Impressions de Textiles de la République Populaire du Congo (IMPRECO). This mixed economy (30 percent State owned) is considered to be one of the Congo's most important processing industries and an example of successful Franco-Congolese economic cooperation. Capitalized initially at 720 million CFAF, raised to 1.3 billion in 1981, IMPRECO began production in January 1975, and by 1980 was working to capacity. It turned out 15.3 million meters of printed cloth that year, and its business turnover was 4.8 billion CFAF. Two years later it began carrying out its third expansion plan.

Bata S. A. Congolaise. The well-known Czech shoe manufacturing company BATA established a factory at Pointe Noire in 1965, with a capital of 200 million CFAF and an annual capacity of 1.5 million pairs of shoes. By 1979 it was producing nearly 700,000 pairs of shoes a year and realizing a business turnover of 1.4 million CFAF. By early 1982, successive additions had increased its capital to 522 million CFAF and its network of sales outlets had grown to 30.

(3) CHEMICALS. This category of industries includes the manufacturers of paint, the Fabrique de Peintures en Afrique (FPA); industrial gas, Société Congolaise des Gaz Industriels (SCGI); soap, Savonnerie du Congo (SAVCONGO); arms and ammunition, Manufacture d'Armes et de Cartouches (MACC); plastics, Industrie Africaine des Plastiques (AFRICAPLAST); perfumes and cosmetics, Société Congolaise de Parfumerie et de Cosmetiques (COPARCO); and lubricants, Usine de Formulation de Librifiants (HYDRO-CONGO). All of the foregoing were financed by private French capital. Two of the most important enterprises—the Raffinerie de Petrole, and the Société des Verreries du Congo—are based in Pointe Noire.

Raffinerie de Petrole. This plant, HYDRO-CONGO's oil refinery, with a capacity of refining one million tons of crude oil a year, was installed in 1978 by three West European companies, but never began operating because of technical difficulties and the extraordinarily-high cost of processing Congolese crude. International arbitration was required to settle the suit brought by Congo against its builders. In 1980, Brazzaville signed an agreement with the French technological firm TECHNIP to put the plant into operation by the end of 1982 at a cost of 33 billion CFAF, but it remained into the 1990's very much a white elephant.

Société des Verreries du Congo (SOVERCO). This former state company, whose plant at Pointe Noire was built in 1967–68 by British firms and, like that of the Raffinerie de Petrole, was judged to be inoperable, was able to begin production after being completely rebuilt by the French firms Saint-Gobain Emballages and TECHNIP in 1981. It was then expected to work to capacity, which meant producing 12,000 tons of glass a year. The company constantly lost money and was finally privatized in 1991.

(4) METALS AND MISCELLANEOUS. Société pour la Transformation de l'Aluminum et Autres Metaux au Congo (ALUCONGO). The outstanding metal industry in the Congo, it was established at Pointe Noire in 1959 by the Alucam company. Its production of nails and tacks, household articles, and casks accounts for about half of its capacity. In 1980 an additional sum of 86 million CFAF was invested in its plant.

Chantiers et Ateliers du Congo. In both 1977 and 1978, this company worked to half its capacity in producing 500 tons of steel, and its business turnover amounted to 300 million CFAF. The company ultimately had to close down.

Cimenterie Domaniale de Luutété. This former state company was at one time the sole industry making building materials in Congo. Capitalized at 900 million CFAF, and with a capacity of 90,000 tons, it began production in 1968 with 350 employees, all Congolese. By 1979, its output amounted to only 47,800 tons. A project was launched in 1980 with a loan of 1.7 billion CFAF, to restore its production of cement to the original 80,000 tons by 1983 and, by increasing its capacity, to attain 130,000 tons by 1986. The plans were not successful and after closing down for a while the company was privatized.

(5) WOOD. The Congolese wood industry is so little developed that as yet its potential importance to the country's socioeconomic advancement has not been fully realized. Faced with the alternatives of selling their output to the few Congolese enterprises making lumber or veneer, or of shipping it abroad in the form of logs, the big foreign private foresters have preferred to export the logs, especially to European markets where they have clients and contacts (see FORESTRY). Consequently demand from abroad has shaped the local wood industry, which is limited to sawmills and plants making veneers and, in very limited quantity, plywood, which is made exclusively by the PLACONGO company. It is further limited to topography, the scarcity of skilled labor, and the high cost of installing and operating modern machinery.

Until 1974, only 41 percent of the logs produced in Congo were processed there, and in 1982 not more than 45 percent, whereas under the aborted 1982–86 plan it was expected that by 1984 at least half of the total production would be so utilized. In the government's penetration and development of the nascent Congolese wood industry, the PCT leaders saw an opportunity not only to tighten the state's grip on the national economy but also to increase the employment opportunities open to Congolese labor, for there are fewer than 8,000 loggers. Although the state companies and the mixed-economy sector were unable to compete successfully with private foreign foresters in selling logs abroad, it was hoped that they might be able to dominate the local market. Furthermore, in determining how and where the internal means of communication were to be developed, the government selected areas that it wanted industrialized, in addition to the Kouilou-Pointe Noire region, where most of the existing industries are concentrated. Inasmuch as the country's industrialization has not advanced beyond the early processing stages, private investors have not felt justified in launching more advanced industries, such as those making furniture on a large scale or wood derivatives like formica.

The difficulties encountered by Congo's few wood industries have discouraged a direct state role in this area. Of greater importance was the mixed-economic sector, represented only by PLACONGO, SIDETRA, and in 1982 the **eucalyptus project** or Société d'Etudes de la Cellulose du Congo (SECC) that, however, was completely abandoned in 1988. Sawmilling continues to be dominated by the privately owned timber firms, although many of the twenty or so sawmills in the country combine several operations related to wood processing. They are of very disparate capacity, some function only seasonally, and together they are capable of handling about 120,000 cu. meters of logs a year, and a total output of 70,000 cu. meters of veneer.

With few exceptions, Congo's wood industries are in a precarious financial position for various reasons, including labor troubles, the cost of applying advanced technology, and the irregular supply of electricity and raw materials, because of delays in transportation. Of the major industrial firms, only SNEB showed a profit from its sale of logs. The short history of the country's wood industry suggests that a company's survival in Congo depends on multiple operations since the market is too limited to permit any marked degree of specialization. The most important industrial project in the 1980's was the plan to manufacture white paper pulp from newly planted hybrid eucalyptus groves in the Kouilou region. The initiative for that venture came from Congo, but it was based on two previous projects proposed by an English and a Bulgarian company in 1965 and 1970 respectively. Experiments conducted over a 25-year period by the CTFT on fast-growing eucalyptus and pine trees culminated in the production of a hybrid tree capable of yielding 28 cu. meters of wood per hectare annually on the poor and sandy soil of the Pointe Noire region. The site of the experiment was chosen for its accessibility, its proximity to a port, and abundant supplies of fresh water and labor. But though the forests were planted, and matured, the paper-pulp mill never materialized so that the logs are now merely stripped and prepared as telephone poles, a very uneconomical operation.

Pointe-Noire is economically unproductive because it is unsuited to agricultural crops. Construction of the paper-pulp plant began in the early 1980s, with the expectation that it would be finished within five years; reforestation with hybrid eucalyptus proceeded in three stages, of which the first (9,000 hectares) was completed in 1981. The labor force employed on the plantation and in construction at that time numbered 4–5,000. It had been anticipated that the permanent staff would number 300 in the forest and 1,200 in the plant itself, with a concomitant 40% increase in the traffic of Pointe Noire creating even more new jobs.

Of the total cost of the paper-pulp project, estimated between 150 and 210 billion CFAF, the government was expected to supply only 6 percent. Technical aid was provided by Swedish and French experts. In 1982 a Société d'Etudes de la Cellulose du Congo (SECC) was formed, capitalized at 550 billion CFAF, 20 percent of which was supplied by Congo and 20 percent by Sweden. The roster of other shareholders—Elf-Aquitaine, Banque Europeenne d'Investissement, and the Société Financiere Internationale—indicated the original confidence inspired by the project. The most important potential investor, France, however, viewed the costs involved prohibitive in light of uncertainties about the price-competitiveness of the eventual paper-pulp produced. For lack of assured funds, work on building the plant came to a halt by August 1983. Shortly later France's reservations were vindicated when new projections indicated that even if all had proceeded smoothly marketing of the paper-pulp would have been uneconomical. The matured eucalyptus trees since the late 1980's are now either shipped abroad at low prices or converted into telephone poles.

Office Congolais des Bois (OCB). Born of a merger of the Office Congolais de l'Okoume and the Bureau Congolais des Bois, both emanations of the Office des Bois de l'Afrique Equatoriale Française, OCB was created on April 15, 1975, capitalized at 580 million CFAF, its staff numbered 98 and it had a monopoly of the sale of all Congolese logs and semifinished woods. Its founding marked the first step in the state's assumption of partnership in the wood industry and in the sale of its output. A rapid, severe drop in the volume of wood sales, from 800,000 cu. meters in 1973 to about 300,000 the next year, was attributed chiefly to the organization's inexperienced management and to unsuccessful attempts to push sales in European markets of wood species little known there. However, thanks to the large-scale resumption of shipments of the so-called "noble" woods (okoume and limba logs), Congo's wood exports rose regularly and strongly from 1975 to 1980, when the business turnover of the OCB amounted to nearly ten billion CFAF. At the same time it has continued its efforts to popularize lesser wood species abroad, by means of fairs and advertising campaigns.

Office Congolaise des Forets (OCF). Created at Pointe Noire in 1974, OCF was made responsible to the Ministry of Rural Economy. It was charged with "reconstituting the national-forest patrimony" by the reforestation of the depleted forest and savannah zones of the south. It was also authorized to experiment in developing fast-growing eucalyptus and pine trees, with a view to creating plantations that would supply the wood required by the projected paper-pulp factory. Operating with subsidies from the Forestry Fund, financed by taxes on the wood industry and exports, and from State funds OCF's budget in the 1980's was around 450 million CFAF, and it had a staff of about

300, of whom 10 were engineers and technicians, dispersed among seven forest stations, of which two were in the forest zone and five in the savannah. In collaboration with other official agencies in Congo, the OCF has won renown for its pioneering work in developing the eucalyptus and limba species.

Société Congolaise de Bois (SOCOBOIS). This enterprise was created at Pointe Noire in 1964 by two West German companies, which provided 80 percent and 20 percent respectively of its capital of 214 million CFAF. Initially it turned out about 10,000 cu. meters a year of okoume and limba veneers. In 1968 it built another plant, doubling capacity, and ten years later it again increased its output with a third factory at Loubomo. Thanks to the large investments by SOCOBOIS in modern machinery, its production of veneers reached 20,000 cu. meters in the 1980's, when it had a business turnover of around 3 billion CFAF. About 120 of its 500 or so employees, of whom only 15 are foreign experts, work in the forest. This company is noteworthy not only for its relatively high technology but also for the large percentage of Congolese on its staff.

Société Congolaise Industrielle des Bois (CIB). Established in 1968, CIB merged in 1972 with the Société Forestiere de La Sangha (SFS) and also absorbed the Société Industrielle de Bois Congolais (IBOCO). Owned by the German firm of Heinrich Feldmeyer, it maintained a strong position among Congo's sawmill companies. Its capital, originally 163 million CFAF, later raised to 420 million, allowed it to intensify felling operations in the Ouesso region near Pokola. Its modern sawmill, situated at Brazzaville, is equipped to process 30,000 cu. meters of logs a year, and it employs 350 workers. In July 1980 it signed an agreement with Congo to open up a new area of 420,000 hectares in the north, creating 250 new jobs. The CIB produces both for the domestic market and for export.

Société des Placages du Congo (PLACONGO). A company of mixed economy, formed in 1965 with 400 million CFAF capital, of which the state holds 25 percent and foreign interests the balance. When PLACONGO's capital was increased to 1.1 billion CFAF, the state retained the same percentage as before. This company operates a large sawmill, is responsible for about 46 percent of the country's production of veneers (about 30,000 cu. meters), and produces 8,000 cu. meters of plywood a year. In early 1981, PLACONGO was heavily in debt, from which it was rescued later that year by a loan of $3.5 million from the Société Financiere Internationale. The irregularity of its wood supplies, which are carried by the CFCO, is a major cause of its difficulties that have intermittently continued.

Société Industrielle de Deroulage et Tranchage (SIDETRA). Sawmilling has been an important part of this mixed company's operations since its founding in 1966 at Pointe Noire by German sponsors, with 400 million CFAF in capital. SIDETRA is the most versatile of the Congolese wood companies, producing planks, veneers, and plywood. Although its supply of logs has increased, as did its capital (to 950 million CFAF), labor troubles caused SIDETRA to suspend veneer production altogether in 1980 and to reduce its other operations. It has experienced additional problems since.

Société Nationale d'Exploitation des Bois (SNEB). Created by the Congolese government in 1976 at Monsendjo, for technical supervision of the national forest domain, it is in charge of all the felling operations in the forests belonging directly to the state.

Société Nationale de Transformation de Bois (SONATRAB). Initially this was a state company whose plant at Pointe Noire produced veneers. In 1975 its losses were so heavy that it had to reduce the salaries of its managerial staff, as well as its number. In 1978 the company was taken over and revived by AFRI-BOIS, an Israeli company. Two years later, when it produced 12,000 cu. meters, it was reportedly working to capacity, and was exporting three fourths of its veneers to France. The company later was nationalized by the state, but in 1990 was privatized.

Union d'Exploitation de Bois (UEB). In 1973, the eleven Roumanian experts then studying Congo's wood resources were asked by the Brazzaville government to help in developing 110,000 hectares in the forest of Betou. An agreement was signed, providing that Roumania would supply the equipment and expertise and Congo the services of 280 laborers. Three years later, access roads had been built and work began on the felling of iroko, tisma, sipo, and sapelli trees. From outset, the enterprise has been handicapped by an overcentralized administration, irregular and insufficient supplies of wood and also of spare parts, and an unskilled labor force which inadvertently damaged the machinery.

Unite d'Afforestation Industrielle du Congo (UAIC). Launched for a three-year period as a mixed Franco-Congolese enterprise on May 10, 1978, the UAIC resulted from an informal successful collaboration between a French government agency (the CTFT) and the OCF. The UAIC's French predecessor, the Centre Technique Forestier Tropical (CTFT), had been founded in 1958 as a research center for the development of two tree varieties. One was a fast-growing eucalyptus suited to the needs of a paper-pulp industry and the other a slower-growing tree whose timber was becoming an increasingly valuable resource of the wood industry. The CTFT's annual budget of 96 million CFAF was provided on an equal basis by the French and Congolese governments, and its staff of 37 included five French and three Congolese engineers. In 1978 CTFT was superseded by the UAIC, whose specific task was to provide the raw material needed for the production of paper pulp at a plant to be built about 15 klm. from Pointe Noire. To that end, more than 9,000 hectares at Kissoko and Livuiti, and also near Pointe Noire, were planted between 1978 and 1981 with fast-growing species of eucalyptus developed by UAIC's agronomists, the goal being the production of 240,000 cu. meters of wood a year.

UAIC had an impressive annual budget of 2.1 billion CFAF (of which France provided one third and Congo two thirds) and a staff of 250, of whom three were Congolese engineers and two were French. Nothing ultimately came out of the pulp-paper mill project, while timber from the maturing eucalyptus forests were either exported, rather uneconomically, to Europe, or processed as telephone poles at a new plant in Pointe Noire.

INSTITUT DE RECHERCHES POUR LES HUILES ET LES OLEAGINEUX (IRHO). Created during World War II by the Free French authorities to study ways of increasing the production of vegetable fats and reducing their cost to the consumer. In tropical Africa, IRHO came to specialize in oil-palm culture and processing.

INSTITUT DE RECHERCHES SCIENTIFIQUES AU CONGO (IRSC). During World War II, the French government created the Office de la Recherche Scientifique des Territoires d'Outre-Mer (ORSTOM) to direct and coordinate scientific work on socioeconomic problems in its overseas dependencies. ORSTOM opened an institute of central African studies in 1946 at Brazzaville, with branches in the other AEF territories. After 1960, the territorial branches became autonomous, though still very largely dependent financially and technically on the ORSTOM. The Brazzaville institute, which in 1961 was renamed the Institut de Recherches Scientifiques au Congo, has a permanent staff of about 30 French scientists and technicians who have been working on problems of local hydrology, pedology, agriculture, botany, philology, and the social sciences. The IRSC publishes memoranda, notes, bulletins and monographs, many of which have been extremely valuable, and some of which have been co-published by the parent organ in Paris. IRSC has a library of more than 15,000 volumes, and its facilities are open to qualified scholars of all nationalities.

INSTITUT SUPERIEUR DES SCIENCES D'EDUCATION (ISSE). Pedagogical school, established in Brazzaville in 1962 with UN funds to train students from the AEF countries.

ISLAM. Islam, "introduced" in Congo only in 1916, has few adherents in the country, in 1991 estimated at only 25,000. (Though some estimates put the number to double that.) Most of these 25,000 (or 75%), are, moreover, foreign nationals, either from upcountry states or from West Africa. The religion was formally recognized by Ngouabi as an acceptable "sect," something reconfirmed in 1988 by Sassou-Nguesso regime when only seven faiths were permitted to practice in the country. The country's Islamic community held its first General Assembly of Congolese Muslims on November 26–27, 1988, during which a 101-member Islamic Council (Comité Islamique du Congo) was set up with an executive arm of ten officials including one woman. Its leaders are Habibou Soumaré, Bachir Gatsongo, Bouilla Guibidanesi. See also RELIGION.

ISLAMIC COUNCIL. See ISLAM.

ISRAEL. Congo's relations with Israel have vacillated over the years. Under the Youlou administration the country had a number of valuable agrarian projects on which Israel was assisting with technical assistance, and a couple of Israeli companies were involved in the timber sector. These were terminated as the Massamba-Debat and Ngouabi regimes became radicalized, and Congo ruptured diplomatic relations, as did most African states, prior to the 1973 Middle East war. As the successor Sassou Nguesso regime began to mend its fences with the West in the mid-1980's informal relations with Israel were resumed (they were in reality never completely broken, since many Bakongo were pro-Israel) notwithstanding a pro-Palestinian speech made by Foreign Minister **Oba**, Sassou Nguesso's uncle, at the U.N. Long before diplomatic relations were re-established by interim prime minister Milongo in 1991 (and a Congolese embassy established in East Jerusalem) informal trade and military cooperation had been reestablished. With the phasing out of **Cuban** personnel in the late 1980's, a number of Israeli officers took their place as advisors in the army and gendarmerie, and in 1993–1994, a training mission of 65 former Israeli officers arrived in Brazzaville to train Lissouba's newly erected **Garde Présidentielle**. See also FOREIGN RELATIONS.

ISSOMBO, ROGER. Diplomat. Serving in various capacities abroad during the 1980's, in 1991 Issombo was appointed Ambassador to the United States.

ITADI, JEAN, 1949– . Economist. Born in Komono on March 24, 1949, and educated as an agronomist at the Agronomic Institute in Algiers, Itadi returned to Brazzaville where after a stint as a lecturer he joined in 1975 the ministry of rural economy as director of studies and planning. He was promoted in 1976 to director-general of the department of agriculture and animal husbandry, and in 1977 to secretary-general of the ministry of rural economy, before joining the cabinet of Sassou-Nguesso in 1979 as minister of rural economy. In January 1980 he exchanged portfolios with Marius Moua-Mbenga and became minister of industry and tourism, and December 28, 1980, he became minister of industry and fisheries.

ITOUA, DIEUDONNE. Former cabinet minister. An administrator under the French regime, Itoua became commissar of the Likouala region in 1960. President Ngouabi named him secretary of state in August 1968, and in January 1970 member of the PCT central committee and minister of territorial administration. He held both posts until December 1971, when he was given the portfolio of health and social affairs. In early 1973 he was dropped from the government, and shortly later dispatched to Peking as ambassador to China. In the government formed November 18, 1978, he became minister of industry and tourism, but was replaced in that post in April 4, 1979 when he was moved to the state sector.

ITSOUMOU, ELIE THEOPHILE, 1936–1972. Radical supporter of **Ange Diawara**. Named director of people's education in May 1968, director of the PCT party school, and member of its politburo in March 1970, Itsoumou was appointed in February 1971 secretary of state of the newly created secretariat for health and labor in Ngouabi's government. He was one of the three key leaders of the Diawara attempted putsch of February 22, 1972, and was killed during its repression.

-J-

JACOB. Former name of NKAYI, which see.

JAYLE, CHRISTIAN, 1905– . Early Youlou aide. Born on August 6, 1905, in Paris, Jayle obtained a legal training and became a lawyer for the Conseil d'Etat. He then embarked on a journalistic career, editing and publishing two papers in Brazzaville and in Douala, Cameroun. Joining the UDDIA party in Congo he was elected to the municipal council of Brazzaville and to Congo's territorial assembly as deputy from the Pool. He served as president of the assembly from 1957 to 1959, becoming one of Fulbert Youlou's most influential advisers. In July 1959 he joined Youlou's cabinet as secretary of state for information, but was dropped from it together with other Europeans in February 1960. On his return to France, he became director-general of the Agence Parisienne de Presse.

JEUNESSE DU MOUVEMENT NATIONAL DE LA REVOLUTION (JMNR) Youth organization of the MNR party set up by the

Massamba-Debat presidency. At inception the JMNR was little more than a structural umbrella for the incredibly fast-spreading, spontaneous, highly rowdy and autonomous unemployed youth gangs that clamped their reign of terror over the entire country to "protect the revolution" of 1963. They set up their own vigilante groups (Comités de Vigilance), erected road checkpoints (including at the outskirts of Brazzaville), unseated and beat up village chiefs, destroyed fetish sites, caught and killed witches, taunted with jeers the "reactionary neo-colonial" police and armed forces, harassed strangers (including diplomatic vehicles), and were virtually a law unto themselves throughout the country especially between December 1964 and March 1965. Very anti-chiefly and biased against old-age, receiving support and funding from the Chinese embassy in Brazzaville, the JMNR was described by one scholar as an "age-class." Wearing paramilitary khaki uniforms (later blue ones donated by North Vietnam), the youth groups (estimated at over 35,000) continued their autonomous definition of their revolutionary "role" even when encompassed under the JMNR hierarchy in the summer of 1964 and more tightly in February 1965. (2,000 of their members were recruited to form a People's Militia, trained by Cuban instructors in Congo.) Their unruliness was one of the reasons for the withdrawal of the U.S. embassy in Brazzaville, whose vehicles had numerous times been stopped and searched by them. A number of ambitious politicians (e.g. Michel Bindi and Minister of Youth and Sports André Hombessa) capitalized on this revolutionary ardor, using it as a steppingstone to power. Inevitably the JMNR's bravado brought them into conflict with the armed forces, and in a shootout at camp Biafra over 300 of them died, marking the end of their "independence." Later in December 1969, following the rise of Ngouabi, the JMNR was tightly integrated as an ancillary organization of the PCT under the name of the Union des Jeunesses Socialistes Congolaise, which though occasionally restless, never played a destabilizing role as during 1964–65.

JUDICIARY. Successive changes in the Congo's judicial system as inherited from the French administration have been affected by Congo's various constitutions. Under that of July 8, 1979, Congo's judiciary included a court of appeals, a criminal court, and tribunals of first and second instance. In addition, there were labor courts and traditional courts, in which African assessors were empowered to apply the customary law of litigants until such point when these courts were to be replaced by modern magistrates' courts. On July 11, 1983 the minister of justice announced such a reform would take place later in the year, following the election of nonprofessional judges chosen to work in close association with career magistrates. The new constitution of 1991 made a number of important innovations to entrench human and civil rights, but did not change most of the actual legal structures of the country.

Between independence and 1991 the Congolese judiciary had been progressively politicized, subsequent to successful coups, or in the aftermath of attempted putsches or revolts. On those occasions, temporary revolutionary courts or courts martial have been created by the leadership, for the purpose of punishing enemies, warning potential adversaries, and (in case of a change in leadership) to discredit the previous regime. A comparatively large number of death sentences have been pronounced at these trials, but apart from the aftermath of Ngouabi's assassination, most of these sentences have not been executed. Indeed, whenever leaders of aborted rebellions have been judged as particularly dangerous (e.g. Diawara in 1972; Anga in 1987) they tended to be "killed" during shootouts with the security forces. External public opinion became an important factor in the military authorities' adopting internationally accepted legal procedures in the second (as opposed to the first, where summary executions took place) trial of Ngouabi's alleged assassins, when non-Congolese lawyers appeared for the defense and the proceedings were televised. Similarly, because of its adverse effect on opinion in the West, whose aid was vital for the execution of Congo's development projects, Amnesty International's strong criticism of the harsh treatment of political prisoners in Congolese prisons was both resented and denied. Practical considerations have also played a role in the Congolese legal system. Such was the case in 1976, when embezzlement was made a criminal offense, less to punish embezzlers, who were found at all levels, and more in order to save the state enterprises that were facing bankruptcy. However, throughout the 1970's and 1980's only those individuals already at odds with the military regime, or not too vital to bolster its claims to be ethnically "representative" have been brought to dock. Moreover, since the top posts in the state sector have always gone to influential power-brokers, even then the sentences have been light, or commuted within a short period, with the offenders allocated other appointments where they continued their disruptive activities. This has continued in the 1990's, when only two of the former era's major embezzlers were imprisoned.

-K-

KAINE, ANTOINE. Early cabinet minister. Between 1963 and 1973, Kaine served successively as the cabinet director of the minister of national economy, later of the minister of finance, and finally of the vice-president of the state council. In 1973 Kaine was appointed minister of electric power, and in January 1975 minister of justice, before being shifted exactly a year later to become director-general of the country's administration.

KAKISM (or N'GOUNZISM). Indigenous religious sect in the Congo basin. The name "Kakism" was given to the cult of the followers of Simon-Pierre M'Padi because of the khaki color of the uniforms they wore. M'Padi was a Belgian Congolese, who claimed to be Kimbangou's heir and founded his protest movement on the right bank of the Congo River as N'Gounzism. To escape arrest in 1938, M'Padi fled to Moyen-Congo, where he built up a following among the local Bakongo. In 1949, he was arrested by the French police on charges of swindling, and was turned over to the Belgian authorities. See also KIMBANGOUISM; RELIGION.

KATALI, FRANCOIS-XAVIER (Major), 1941–1986. Until his death one of the main leaders of the pro-Soviet M-22 clique, with a powerbase in the northern Impfondo-Sangha region, and a thorn in the side of Sassou-Nguesso. Born in 1941 of the northern Bondjo ethnic group, Katali (also referred to as Kitali) became a member of the PCT central committee on December 31, 1972, and stayed on that organ until his death. On January 7, 1973, he was named minister of agriculture, animal husbandry, water, and forests, and in the Lopes cabinet of August 30, 1973, he became minister of water and forests.

He was political commissioner for the Kouilou region with its capital in Pointe Noire, and commander of the Pointe Noire military zone when, in May 1975, he was named delegate of the central committee to that region, with the aim of strengthening the PCT's hold over the port. During the Yhomby Opango regime (1977–79), he was both a member of the CMP and minister of the interior, retaining that post in the governments formed April 4, 1979, and December 28, 1980. Widely feared and detested in the country during this time, Sassou Nguesso shunted him aside in 1984, utilizing the **Lassy Zepherin affair,** to head the ministry of agriculture, and in 1986 to minister of rural development. He died shortly later, in May 1986 of a heart attack.

KAYA, PAUL, 1933– . Diplomat. A Bakamba born on October 17, 1933, at Madingou, Kaya was educated at Brazzaville's Chaminade seminary, following which he went to France to study economics and engineering, graduating from the University of Paris in 1959. He then joined the staff of the Congolese embassy in Paris as an economic counselor, and on his return to Brazzaville was named director of economic and social affairs. In 1962, after joining the UDDIA party he was appointed to the analogous post in the Union Africaine et Malgache de

Cooperation Economique. After Youlou was overthrown in 1963, Kaya joined Massamba-Debat's cabinet as minister of economics. He was dropped from the cabinet in October 1964 when the president of the national assembly warned a censure motion against the cabinet was being prepared unless he was dismissed. Fearing arrest because of his moderate political views, Kaya fled to Abidjan, where he became administrative secretary of the Council of the Entente's Guaranty Fund. He remained in that post, ignoring the amnesty offered by Ngouabi to Congolese political exiles in 1974. He returned to Congo to run as an independent in the 1992 presidential elections.

KELLE. District covering 24,000 sq. kms in the Cuvette region bordering Gabon, with administrative headquarters in the village with the same name. At the border of savanna and forest zones, and geographically also transitional between Congo and Gabon, Kellé receives torrential rains (1,900 mm. per year). It is in this district that significant alluvial gold deposits were discovered in the late-1980's, leading to the formation of an American consortium to exploit a concession granted it.

KERHERVE, ANDRE, 1911– . Former minister. Born in Brittany (France) on August 14, 1911, Kerherve went to Africa soon after finishing secondary school. He became a merchant and small-scale entrepreneur in Moyen-Congo, and after World War II entered local politics. He represented Likouala-Mossaka in the territorial assembly from 1957 to 1959, and for most of that period he was also Fulbert Youlou's minister of industry and mines.

KIAKOLO, AMBROISE. One of former president Youlou's closest associates. A perennial fixture of Youlou's government, Kiakolo was briefly imprisoned after the 1963 coup, and then joined Youlou in exile in Madrid. He was several times implicated in sponsoring plots to reverse the 1963 coup and bring Youlou back, and was sentenced to death in absentia in 1969 by the Congolese judiciary for these plots. After Youlou's death Kiakolo relocated to Zaire where he was granted immunity.

KIBAHT, CHARLES, 1910– . Early political leader. Born September 17, 1910, at Boundji, Kibaht worked in a clerical position with the forestry service when he founded the Front Démocratique Congolais in 1955. Two years later, he joined the UDDIA and was elected to the territorial assembly as deputy from Djoué. He was a subprefect of Gomboma in 1959, and moved into the higher reaches of the territorial administration after independence.

KIKADIDI, BARTHELEMY (Captain), 1944–1978. Allegedly head of the suicide squad that assassinated president Ngouabi in 1977. A

Bakongo officer, and for five years heading the second bureau of the armed-forces general staff in charge of military intelligence under president Massamba-Debat, Kikadidi was retained by Ngouabi as a member of his personal military cabinet. After Ngouabi's assassination, Kikadidi was immediately accused of the act, but escaped. Later that month he was sentenced to death in absentia for the murder. He was allegedly cornered in Brazzaville and shot on February 13, 1978. Mystery still surrounds the entire issue of who was behind the 1977 assassination of Ngouabi, and the reasons for the alacrity with which most of the key conspirators were either shot down (e.g. Kikadidi) or condemned to death and executed with undue haste (e.g. Massamba-Debat).

KIKANGA, PIERRE (Lieutenant), 1944–1970. A pro-Youlou Lari lieutenant stationed at Brazzaville, Kikanga served as a contact man in preparation for the so-called "mercenaries' coup" of May 1968. Implicated in another plot, allegedly directed by **Mouzabakany**, Kikanga fled to Kinshasa in December 1968. He was sentenced to death in absentia by the Brazzaville revolutionary court in July 1969. He was involved in another plot in March 1970 when he was killed at the head of a band of commandos that assaulted Brazzaville.

KIKHOUNGA-NGOT, SIMON-PIERRE, 1920– . Former cabinet minister. A Bakongo born in 1920 near Dolisie, Kikhounga-Ngot attended primary school in that region and briefly studied medicine in the Belgian Congo. He worked in a variety of vocations, established links with Congo's trade unions, and with left-wing groups during a trip to France and East Europe in 1954. Earlier, in 1952 he was elected deputy from Niari to the territorial assembly. By 1957, when he was re-elected to the assembly he became regional (Niari) secretary for the CGAT unions. With the rise to power of Fulbert Youlou, Kikhounga-Ngot was appointed to various ministerial portfolios. He was briefly arrested for anti-government activities in May 1960, but released four months later; he assumed his former post as minister of economic affairs in January 1961, and in May 1963 became minister of labor. After Youlou's downfall he was arrested, but was acquitted of various charges by a people's court in June 1965. With the rise to power of Marien Ngouabi, Kikhounga-Ngot briefly emerged as a key 1st Vice Chairman of the CNR, but was dropped from that body in February 1969, and faded into obscurity.

KIMBANGOU, SIMON see KIMBANGOUISM.

KIMBANGOUISM. A large important messianic sect found in Zaire and Congo, named after its founder Simon Kimbangou (1889–1951), a Belgian Congolese who had been a catechist of the British Protestant mission at Thysville. In 1918 he proclaimed himself to be a prophet and the Son of God, and his cult spread among the Bakongo like wildfire through religious tracts and hymns written in the Kikongo vernacular. Kimbangou borrowed from Christian practices the ritual of baptism and the confessional, and from African tradition the cult of ancestors. Because he also stressed those biblical passages that endorsed the right of the oppressed to revolt, he was arrested by the Belgian police in 1921 and died, in detention, in Katanga prison in 1951. His teachings were brought to Moyen-Congo by Simon-Pierre M'Padi, whose sect was known there as Kakism or N'Goundzism (see KAKISM). In 1969, Kimbangouism was admitted to membership in the World Council of Churches, the church, known as L'Eglise de Jésus-Christ sur la Terre par son Prophète Simon Kimbangou (E.J.C.S.K) having a very large following in Zaire. See also RELIGION.

KIMBEMBE, DR. DIEUDONNE, 1944– . Former minister. Born on March 19, 1944 in Brazzaville, and educated in law at the University of Paris, Kimbembe returned to Congo, joined the PCT party and became a legal adviser in the ministry of interior. In 1980 he was integrated into the cabinet as minister of justice, a ministry expanded in December 1985 to include also labor and social security. He served in that capacity until 1989.

KIMBOUALA, N'KAYA (Major), 1938–1977. Former head of Congo's armed forces. As a Captain commanding the armored car division, Kimbouala was in 1966 Chief of general staff, and after Ngouabi the army's second ranking officer. After Ngouabi's rise to power, Kimbouala, regarded as a radical, joined the PCT and was named to the central committee, commissar of the army in charge of economic activities, and commander of the Pointe Noire military zone. During the **Diawara** 1972 attempted putsch Kimbouala was tricked to join the rebels and was sentenced to death, a sentence commuted to life imprisonment next month. Later released, he was assassinated in his home on March 18, 1977, the same day Ngouabi was assassinated.

KINDOKI. Sorcery, the practitioner being a *koundou,* whose evil effects are detected and treated by *nganga* doctors. See also WITCH-CRAFT.

KINGAMBA NGOYA, GILBERT, 1942– . Born in 1942 and trained as a teacher, Kingamba Ngoya has been deputy-mayor of Poto-Poto, former PCT militant, and deputy to the national assembly.

KINKALA. District encompassing 2,100 sq. kms. in the Pool region with administrative headquarters in the town with the same name. It is 70 kms. from Brazzaville on the road to Pointe Noire, and is an important Lari settlement. Kinkala is also the administrative capital of the Pool region.

KINZONZI. The act of effective public speaking (from "zanza" to speak, argue, discuss in Kongo) widely admired in Bakongo society. It has been argued by some that much of the ideological rhetoric-reality in Congo's revolutionary era was due to youth having been convinced by their own rhetoric of the actualization of Marxism in the country.

KITALI, FRANCOIS-XAVIER see KATALI, FRANCOIS-XAVIER.

KODIA-RAMATA, NOEL. Poet and dramatologist. Trained as a teacher, Kodia-Ramata teaches French at the Lumumba lycée in Brazzaville, while writing plays and poetry.

KOLELAS, BERNARD. Powerful Lari politician and current mayor of Brazzaville. Born in Brazzaville and general secretary of **Youlou's** UDDIA, Kolelas took refuge in Leopoldville after Youlou's overthrow. After the death there of Ibalico in 1964, he assumed leadership of the Congolese anti-Massamba-Debat dissidents, and mounted an assault across the river at Brazzaville. For this he was sentenced to death in absentia in June 1965. Ngouabi invited him to return from exile in August 1968, which he did, resuming his former post in the foreign ministry in June 1969. As the alleged mastermind behind the November 1969 attempted coup against Ngouabi, he was for the second time, sentenced to death, but was freed on January 1, 1972. In mid-August 1978, he was again accused of plotting against the state, but was again released. Kolelas finally reemerged in the limelight with the liberalizations of the 1990's. He set up the MCDDI party, that won the second-highest number of seats (29) in the 1992 elections. He also competed in the presidential elections the same year, coming second in the first round with 22.89% of the vote, but was defeated in the second round by Lissouba, gaining only 38.6%. During the campaigns Kolelas made a strong effort to project himself as the heir to the **Matsouanist** mantle, and obtained some support from remaining elements from that group. In the legislative elections Kolelas' party won 29 seats, becoming the second largest formation in Congo after Lissouba's UPADS that won 39 seats. He realigned his MCDDI with the PCT, forcing Lissouba to integrate a large number of their key members into the latter's cabinet.

KOLOLO, JEAN-BLAISE. An academic from Marien Ngouabi university, and an important member of Bernard Kolelas' MCDDI party. On June 14, 1992 Kololo was brought into the interim Milongo cabinet as minister of foreign affairs, serving until the elections of 1992.

KOMBO, ERNEST. Bishop of Owando. A southerner serving in his northern diocese, Kombo, one of the delegates to the national conference, was elected by the membership as the president of the conference, and his balanced leadership facilitated what turned out to be a lengthy and troubled transition to civilian rule.

KOMBO, NGUILA MOUNGOUNGA. Current minister of commerce, fisheries and industrial development, appointed in September 1992.

KONDO, ANATOLE, 1942– . Former union leader. Born in 1942 at Makoua, Kondo worked as a clerk in Brazzaville and was active in the trade-unions. In October 1969, he became general secretary of the Confédération Syndicale Congolaise, and in January 1971 was appointed to the central committee of the PCT. In 1976 he was drummed out of all his party and union positions because of his role in the abortive general strike of March 24, 1976, and he was also forbidden to seek elective office in any trade union. Because of his residual clout with unionists he was partly rehabilitated and given an array of government positions, including in December 1982 the ambassadorship to Angola.

KONGO. Major ethnic group, estimated at over 4 million people, living in Congo, Zaire and northwest Angola, founders of the ancient **Kongo kingdom** whose center of gravity was in contemporary Zaire and Angola. In Congo the Bakongo (people of Kongo) are estimated at up to fifty percent of the population. They are composed of several important, historically competitive clans, the main ones being the: Bakongo, Vili, Lari, Yombe, Bembe, Kougni, Kamba, Sundi, Dondo, Bahangala and Manianga. In the 1950's and early 1960's there was talk of "resurrecting" the historic unity of the Kongo on both sides of the river.

KONGO, KINGDOM OF. Historic, large (300,000 sq. kms.), decentralized kingdom, spanning both sides of the Congo river, controlling diverse populations from Gabon to Angola. Kongo coalesced in the 14th century, and began disintegrating around 1665. According to legend the Bakongo originated at Mbanza Kongo (baptized by the Portuguese as Sao Salvador, in Angola) which became their capital.The nucleus of the kingdom was south of the Congo river, and east of the Atlantic. In 1491 they came in contact with the Portuguese who baptized their king, established diplomatic relations and took some Bakongo back to Portugal. (The introduction of Christianity created serious internal dissension.) Expectations of Kongo-Portugal cooperation did not materialize. King Afonso I (1506–1545) requested military and technical aid, but received little, since the Portuguese were more interested in plunder. A century later even the pretense of cooperation ended when denied by Antonio I the right to prospect in Kongo, the Portuguese invaded Kongo and killed him in the ensuing battle. Though the Portuguese were to leave shortly later, Kongo never fully recovered and regional hegemony passed to groups to their south. The final disintegration of the kingdom commenced in 1702 with the appearance of the syncretic religious movement of St. Anthony, in some ways similar to 20th century **Kimbangouism**. Vassal regions seceded, including the Loango kingdom and the Batéké kingdom or Nzikou, both in Congo.

KONGO, MICHEL, 1944– . Geographer. Born on September 29, 1944 in the Pool region, and trained in France in geography, Kongo has conducted research and published on conditions in the Niari valley. He teaches at Marien Ngouabi University, and was a founder of the African Association of geographers.

KOTA. Ethnic group, numbering around 150,000, residing in southwestern Congo along the border with Gabon where they are also found. The Kota (also Bakota) are subdivided into a number of clans, the most important of which are the Tsangui, Bamba, Voumbou, Nzabi and Ndassa. They migrated south from the Upper Ogooué region in Gabon after conflicts with new ethnic arrivals. They are well-known for their highly distinctive funerary statues of inlaid copper.

KOUILOU. Coastal region of Congo, stretching from Gabon to Cabinda, with a dense population of 665,502. In the interior a low plateau (of 150 m.) until the Mayombé mountains, the region has an area of 10,285 sq. kms. and is divided into the districts of Madingou-Kayes, Mvouti and Loandulu, and containing Congo's second largest city, Pointe Noire. The region is settled predominantly by the Vili, whose kingdom of Loango had its capital just north of today's Pointe Noire. The lower portion of the Kouilou river, spilling into the Bay of Loango, can be used for floating goods south. A paved road, the Congo-Ocean railway, and several flights daily connect Pointe Noire with the capital.

KOUKA-BEMBA, DANIEL, 1941– . Former cabinet minister. Born on August 22, 1941 and securing his medical degrees in France, specializing in surgery, Kouka-Bemba has taught at the Institute of Health Sciences of Marien Ngouabi University, and has also been minister of health and social services under Sassou-Nguesso. He is currently director of maternity services at the Brazzaville hospital.

KOUKOUYA. A **Batéké** sub-group, inhabiting the Koukouya plateau in the district of Lekana in the Plateaux region of Congo.

KOUMA, PAUL (Colonel), 1934– . Key military commander. Born on April 21, 1934 in Ouesso, northern Congo, Kouma, a member of the PCT and its central committee, was appointed Commander of the Brazzaville Military Zone, and was elected in 1984 a member of the national assembly representing the armed forces.

KOUNKOU, FRANCOISE VALENTINE ROSE, 1948– . Lawyer and militant women's leader in the Niari region. Born in Port Francqui, Zaire, and married to **Timothée Kounkou,** Mrs. Kounkou was first educated in Kinshasa, then acquired a degree in private law in Paris in 1975. On her return to Congo that year she was appointed examining magistrate, juvenile magistrate, and attorney to the Loubomo high court, positions she still holds. During the PCT era she was also a member of the coordinating bureau of the Niari region of the Union Révolutionnaire des Femmes du Congo.

KOUNKOU, TIMOTHEE, (Major) 1941– . Military officer. Born on August 13, 1941, at Brazzaville, Kounkou, head of the central services of the Brazzaville court of appeals, was named to the PCT central committee in December 1969, to be appointed political commissar of Likouala in January 1971. In October 1972 he was named commander of the Congo's air force.

KOUNKOU-LOUYA, GUILLAME-JOSEPH, 1932– . Administrator. Born in the Central African Republic on August 5, 1932, and educated in Congo at Ouesso, Mossaka, Owando and at Brazzaville's Chaminade seminary. Between 1955 and 1958 he was head of personnel services of the Congolese Customs department, and then for a year (1959) head of Brazzaville's postal customs office, following which he was dispatched to France to obtain specialized training in customs inspection and administration (1960–1963). On his return to Brazzaville he was appointed assistant director of the central customs office (1963–1964), and in 1964 joined the ministry of trade and industry as the cabinet director of the minister. He subsequently held a variety of similar high administrative posts, including in the **UDEAC.** Since 1966 he has been attached to the Economic Commission for

Africa, most recently as president of the latter's promotions and recruitment office.

KOUYOU. Major component of the Mbochi ethnic group, found in the Cuvette, including in Owando. Arriving from the north in the middle of the 18th century (a date, however, still contested), and establishing suzerainty over riverain trade, their further expansion south was resisted by the Batéké. Many Kouyou secured important political positions with the advent of the rise to power of Ngouabi (who was a Kouyou), but with the latter's assassination and the advent of the Sassou Nguesso (Mbochi) regime, a split developed between them and the Mbochi. This was reflected in the revolt of **Captain Anga** in 1987. Currently the Kouyou are supportive of General Yhomby Opango, one of their kinsmen, and the leader of the RDD political party.

KOUYOU RIVER. River in the Cuvette region, intermittently navigable for 300 kms. between Mossaka and Owando.

KYEBE-KYEBE. Celebrations, accompanied by spirited dances in honor of a serpent-spirit, practiced by initiates of the Mbochi and Kouyou ethnic groups in the Cuvette, especially in Owando. The dances, that included a large (5-meter) wooden sculpture of a head (*afia*), no longer have the religious significance they had in the 19th century.

-L-

LABOR. Already prior to independence Congo had the most developed industries and vocational-training facilities, the highest percentage of government employees, and the strongest organized labor movement. At the same time Congo had the greatest dearth of rural laborers and the highest levels of urban unemployment. Independence heightened these characteristics and gave rise to fresh problems. New industries created thousands of additional jobs, but never enough to absorb a large enough proportion of the burgeoning urban populations. The number of government employees grew even faster than that of other wage earners. Wages were periodically increased, but did not keep pace with the faster rising cost of living. Trade unions were rapidly radicalized and played an important political role during the 1960's before being reduced to that of executors of party policies by the PCT government, and especially by Sassou-Nguesso.

Legislation. Labor legislation in Congo dates from the interwar period. The first laws passed by Paris aimed to protect Congolese workers against the abuses practiced by the concessionary companies and against forced labor. Employers were required to sign a written contract specifying the wages and living conditions of laborers they hired. The abolition of forced labor in 1946 was followed by the Overseas Labor Code of 1952, which marked a big advance in labor legislation and, above all, its enforcement. A Labor Inspectorate and Labor Advisory Committees were established, to enforce the new laws and to advise the government on how to implement them. Minimum wages, maximum working hours, and family allowances were introduced, restrictions were placed on the number of foreigners who could be hired by private employers; collective agreements, vocational training, and unionization were encouraged; and the machinery for settling labor disputes was installed.

The 1952 code proved so satisfactory in operation that it was not amended until 1964. The Massamba-Debat government then added regulations anticipating a complete Congolization of the labor force. It also gave more protection to workers against "abusive dismissals" and to female and child labor, improved the conditions of pay and promotion of wage earners, and altered the procedure for handling labor disputes. The first labor laws enacted under the military regime aimed at filling the gaps in the code of June 25, 1964, tightening the government's control over labor, and above all, forced the pace of Congolization of the labor force, ending the disparity between the pay of Europeans and Congolese. Some petty regulations of this period, such as the requirement for State employees to wear Mao-type uniforms, soon went by the board. A new labor code of 263 articles was adopted on January 1, 1975, stressing acceptance of collective agreements to be negotiated between labor and management, in which both the rights and the duties of wage earners would be incorporated. Those rights included longer paid vacations and maternity leaves, monthly payment of wages, and training in vocational skills and Marxist-Leninist doctrine. Penalties were specified for failure to respect legal working hours, and the authority of labor inspectors was reinforced.

The new emphasis on training skills reflected the difficulties that the administration had encountered in applying the very popular ruling of December 21, 1967, issued by the Massamba-Debat government for the purpose of widening the MNR's base of popular support. This was the requirement for all employers to hire only Congolese workers by the end of 1974. Long before that deadline, however, it had become clear that for many of the posts then held by Europeans there were no Congolese qualified to replace them. Virtually the only exceptions were those given on-the-job training by foreign-owned enterprises that employed them. Furthermore, by the late 1970s, the military authorities realized that many of their national economic goals could not be attained by legislation but only by enlisting the good will of the labor force.

Employment. Even after forced labor was abolished in 1946 Congolese showed reluctance to earn wages by working regular hours, especially in the employ of Europeans. Of a total population of 690,000 in 1949, only 52,000 were wage earners. About half of these were employed on agricultural plantations and in mining and forest industries, the other half in miscellaneous occupations, especially government service. By 1958, the population had grown to 765,000 and wage earners numbered 63,400, of whom 46,200 were in the private and 17,200 in the public sector. Thus in less than a decade, wage earners had increased faster than the total population, but they still formed only a small segment of the working population (then estimated at 360,000) and their occupations did not accurately represent Congo's overall economy. Of the working population, 76 percent were engaged in agriculture, animal husbandry, and fishing, but only 12,000 wage earners were so employed. The analogous proportions and numbers for mining and industry were 9.5 percent and 10,000, and for trade, transport, and administration, 14.5 percent and 36,000. These percentages and figures reflected the growing Congolese disaffection for farming, the continuing importance of trade and transport in the economy, and the expansion of the bureaucracy, industries, and towns. After World War II, unskilled rural youths flooded into southern towns to escape the dullness of life in the countryside, and sought jobs as day laborers under the big urban public works programs. With that program's completion in the late 1950s, unemployment became rife, especially in Brazzaville, which continued to attract numbers of unskilled newcomers. In 1962, it was estimated that barely 31 percent of that town's male population had regular employment.

Since independence, the unemployment problem became more acute because of the urban population's phenomenal growth. It was hardly arrested by successive desperate official measures, including crash vocational-training courses, the offer of free transportation back to one's native village, the development of regional village centers, obligatory civic service, and/or tens of thousands of new jobs in the State sector. Under the Youlou and Massamba-Debat regimes, admission to the bureaucracy became even more the goal of young Congolese than it had been during the colonial years, because of its prestige, higher salaries, and perquisites. By 1968, the number of state employees (21,000) was rapidly overtaking the number in private employment. Since then, the expansion of state enterprises and, above all, the tight rein that the military regime tried to keep on its employees caused some educated Congolese to prefer private to public employment, but the numbers in government employ continued to zoom up, especially in the early 1980's when booming oil revenues allowed the regime to expand the State sector. By 1990 over 25% of Congo's potential work force was in one way or another a State employee: some 80,000 in the civil service, 40,000 (figure to decline shortly) in State enterprises and 25,000 in the security forces.

The basic dilemma remains the same today, even though the Lissouba regime faces political conditionalities that insist on trimming the government payroll. The country's population is increasing at a faster rate than jobs are created, and the rapid expansion of the State sector during the Marxist era (that provided thousands of jobs) is virtually over with many enterprises either closed down due to inefficiency or privatized with retrenched numbers of workers. At the same time the rural exodus simply refuses to abate, aggravating agricultural underemployment and lack of productivity.

The unemployment situation in Congo is extremely serious, and because of its obvious political ramifications has been a prime concern to successive regimes in Brazzaville. A year after independence, 26 percent of the total population was unemployed, compared to 19 percent in 1955. By 1980 between 40 and 50 percent was without regular work in a population of around 1.9 million, and by 1990 the estimated percentage had grown to an incredible 55 percent in a population of over 2.5 million. Since 1974 unemployment has risen at twice the rate of the population growth (2.5 percent). Since Congolese under 20 years of age account for more than 60 percent of the total population, this means that over 12,000 youths with school diplomas, as well as 20,000 others of that age group, are joining those already unemployed to seek jobs on the labor market. In 1980, wage earners numbered approximately 100,000 among a total urban population of some 700,000, underscoring the degree to which unemployment is most acute among the educated urban youth, the most politically volatile element in society. Efforts to stem the rural exodus, increase the number of government jobs by lowering the mandatory retirement age (currently 55), and require employers to fill job vacancies from among the youngest candidates for employment have not been successful.

Wages: For many years wages were exceptionally low in Congo, both in absolute terms and in comparison with European earnings. Almost all employers, including the colonial-government officials, were Europeans, who justified the disparate wage scale for native laborers on the ground of their lack of skills. In 1946 three pay-scales were established in Congo, for which a minimum wage (Salaire Minimum Interprofessionnel Garanti, or SMIG) was decided on annually by the government upon advice from a labor advisory committee. In principle, the SMIG was based on a worker's "incompressible needs" and the local cost of living, but everywhere it was markedly lower for agricultural laborers than for other wage earners. Under the Youlou administration, the minimum wage was increased by 18–42 percent, but this was largely offset by the imposition of a tax on wages in 1962 and 1966. Massamba-Debat did raise wages for the lowest-paid category of workers and reduced discrepancies among the wage-scales, and between pay in the major towns and elsewhere.

In the first years of the military regime, the cost of living rose to levels where the lowest-paid Congolese were unable to maintain decent living standards. Europeans, then fewer than 10 percent of all those employed in Congo, received salaries that were eight times more than the aggregate of the entire Congolese labor force. In December 1974 the government changed its course by increasing the SMIG, reducing taxes on monthly incomes of 15,000 CFAF and less, and freezing rents and the prices of certain foodstuffs. This change in policy was due to the sudden increase in oil revenues, which made possible a pay raise for both state and private employees. The new policy persisted even after oil revenues declined suddenly. Later the SMIG was raised in April 1976 by as much as 70 percent, and the second wage category was eliminated. The collective agreements authorized in January 1977 increased the hourly minimum wage from 78 CFAF to 320, and higher salaries for employees earning from 21,000 to 166,000 CFA francs a month. A sharp decline of oil revenues in 1978 once again disrupted the upward trend in the Congolese pay scale, at a time when it was estimated that not even a fourth of the state employees were receiving their pay regularly. By 1980, when oil revenues had resumed their rise, the government had become more cautious, and it postponed additional wage increases until it had provided for the financing of certain development projects. Nevertheless, it did enter into negotiations with the CSC that culminated in an agreement in 1982 to raise wages across the board from 7 to 25 percent. Such an increase was more than justified by the accelerated rise of the cost of living, which between 1980 and 1982 had climbed by 13 percent (as compared with a 10.6 percent rise between 1974 and 1980), with further increases annually. However the rapid fall in state revenues in the mid-1980's put an end to such efforts to cautiously augment salaries, and by the late 1980's decompression of salaries, inflation, and the government's virtual bankruptcy resulted in non-payment of salaries for months on end. At the same time the trade unions resisted efforts to reorganize, privatize or retrench money-losing state enterprises, leaving the entire mess to the new civilian regime, that to date had not been able to cope better.

Labor disputes: Labor disputes have intermittently flared in Congo. After the abolition of forced labor in 1946, a series of work stoppages induced the government to form labor-advisory committees, representing employers, wage earners, and the administration, and to strengthen the labor inspectorate. Application of the 1952 Overseas Labor Code necessitated the establishment of ten labor courts to help labor inspectors settle disputes between employers and employees. Most of the cases they dealt with were brought by workers against their employers, for alleged arbitrary dismissals and failure to respect the eight-hour working day and pay wages promptly. Although the number of workers on strike doubled between 1950 and 1960, in the latter year they involved fewer than 2,000 wage earners. The generally peaceful labor situation throughout the 1950's could be attributed to reinforcement of the arbitration machinery, the growing number of urban youths seeking jobs, and the weakness of the labor unions. Nor did labor disputes seriously trouble the administration of either Youlou or Massamba-Debat, despite the rapid increase in urban unemployment and the politicization of the unions, though the political radicalization of society was another matter.

Under the military regime, however, labor conflicts, came to the fore. This was largely due to the contradictory policies of Ngouabi and later Sassou-Nguesso in dealings with wage earners in the public and private sectors. In 1969, for example, Ngouabi denounced striking civil servants as unpatriotic and bourgeois, dismissed their ringleaders, and reorganized their trade union. On the other hand, he generally supported strikes against private European employers, notably the strike against SIAN in early 1970. (Later, Ngouabi rejected the very same demands after SIAN was nationalized!) Wage earners beset by soaring living costs found it difficult to grasp the distinction drawn by the government between strikes that would force concessions from alien capitalist employers and those against a Marxist state. Nevertheless, the wide scope of the March 1976 strike, and its support by radical politicians, combined with the evidence of the spiraling cost of living, wrested concessions from Ngouabi. Subsequently, however, organized labor suffered so severe a setback under Yhomby Opango's regime (1977–79) that under the latter's more liberal successor, Sassou-Nguesso, the CSC remained too wary to strike. By an adroit combination of moderate wages and other concessions, Sassou-Nguesso induced the government employees to be content, and not to strike for more. The military regime's hard-won victory over the CSC came under pressure in the mid-1980's as the virtually bankrupt regime was unable to pay salaries for months on end, and its plans to close down or privatize (with great losses in jobs) much of the State sector set the CSC on confrontational courses. Moreover, it was ultimately the CSC's 1989 disengagement from the PCT, and the threat of an unlimited general strike unless a national conference were convened, that set into sequence the return to civilian rule and multiparty elections.

Trade Unions: Labor in Moyen-Congo was first organized after World War II by French union leaders. Initially the labor movement was confined to the towns, but under Congolese leadership, unions were organized in all enterprises employing numerous wage earners. With the rapid industrialization of Congo in the 1970's and 1980's, union membership grew, but no figures exist as to how many of the country's 140,000 wage earners actually pay union dues. Organized labor remains weak at the base, and its leadership has been dominated by whatever government is in power. Such improvements in labor's status as took place during the colonial regime came from laws passed by the French Parliament. Those made since Congo became independent were the result of the movement's political role rather than of spontaneous action by organized wage earners themselves. After WW II, the three big French labor federations—the Force Ouvriere (Socialist), the Confédération Générale du Travail (Communist) and the Confédération Française des Travailleurs Chretiens (Catholic)—established branches in Moyen-Congo, where small autonomous unions were also being formed. The funds and tutelage supplied by the parent federations encouraged competition among Congolese union leaders, whose strength depended on the political fortunes of their respective sponsoring parties in France. The FO, being the first in Congo, acquired control over the railroad workers, who comprised the largest single category of wage earners. It lost its early lead with the ebbing political fortunes of the socialist party in France. Membership in the autonomous unions also soon declined, for lack of external funds and a strong local political base. In 1958, the Congolese unions emulated the local political parties in severing their ties with foreign organizations.

At first their autonomy was simply nominal, but gradually it took on substance. The Socialist unions now called themselves the Confédération Congolaise des Syndicats Libres (CGSL), the Communist unions the Confédération Générale Africaine des Travailleurs (CGAT), and the Catholics, the Confédération Africaine des Travailleurs Croyants (CATC), but all continued to receive funds and guidance from abroad. By 1960, the CATC emerged the strongest local labor organization, thanks to competent Congolese leaders and to the support of the local Catholic mission. It then comprised 40 percent of all unionized Congolese workers, compared with 33 percent for CGAT and 15 percent for CCSL, and its most important component was the civil-servants union. In May 1960, the CGAT suffered a setback when its leaders were arrested following their abortive attempt to organize a revolutionary party. Youlou's authoritarian regime, rather than his labor policy, united Congo's mutually antagonistic unions against him. His overthrow in August 1963 was spearheaded by the whole-hearted joint action of CATC and CGAT. Within two years, however, Massamba-Debat's left wing government deprived CATC's leaders of any role in public life, dissolved their federation, and formed under the MNR's aegis a single union, the Confédération Syndicale Congolaise (CSC). Its membership came exclusively from the CGAT and CCSL unions, whose leaders were given high posts in the government and in the party. Progressively, the CSC extended its organization to include wage earners in the European planting, forestry, and mining enterprises, but lost its separate identity as a labor movement. In 1968, its leaders echoed the dissatisfaction expressed by MNR's radicals with Massamba-Debat's government. They deplored its conservative foreign policy, failure to cope with urban unemployment and the high cost of living, and refusal to nationalize the economy. Yet it was the army, not the unions, that overthrew Massamba-Debat, and the military regime showed its determination to exert control over organized labor.

Soon after he came to power in 1968, Ngouabi reorganized the CSC under handpicked leaders, and the next year he forcibly broke a strike by the civil-servants union. Concurrently, however, he raised wages, opened up more jobs by increasing the number of state companies and promoting Congolization of all employees, and appeased the radical labor leaders by Marxist-oriented foreign and economic policies. A testimonial to Ngouabi's skill in handling labor leaders came in 1971–72, when they refused to join student, regional, and ethnic forces opposed to his regime. His carrot-and-stick policy, however, was less successful with the rank and file of wage earners, whose dissatisfaction was shown by sporadic strikes, often led by the state employees in the CSC. For their own convenience, Ngouabi and his two military successors insisted on dealing with a single labor organization, in which the subordinate unions were divided according to occupation, rather than dealing with smaller groups designed to express their members' aspirations and grievances. Ngouabi, Yhomby Opango, and Sassou Nguesso have all viewed organized labor as being the same as other categories of Congolese, notably the soldiers and farmers, whose main function in official eyes was simply to cooperate with the government and the party in carrying out the latter's policies. In short, labor was compelled to reverse the role it had played during the "Trois Glorieuses," when it triggered the mass uprising that overthrew Youlou, and was required to become the revolutionary government's handmaiden. Under such circumstances, mutual misunderstandings and conflicts were inevitable.

The CSC, organized as Congo's single labor union in 1964, at once tried to assert its domination over other labor groups and also to pursue a policy independent of the MNR government. It rapidly disposed of opposition from the Christian trade unions (CATC) by forcing the CATC's formerly powerful leader, Gilbert Pongault, out of the government and into exile. It was far less successful in its relations with Massamba-Debat, whose principal supporters were highly educated radicals not associated with the labor movement.

Theoretically, labor unions and student organizations should have provided the revolution's driving force. This was in fact what brought about Youlou's overthrow, but the very spontaneity of the mass uprising that brought the MNR government to power could not be maintained because of lack of organization and shared motivation. It was to put an end to specific abuses attributed to Youlou's government that he was overthrown, and not to carry out a long-term reform program. Such civilian radicals as Hombessa, Ndalla, and Noumazalaye were not, and did not aspire to be, union leaders, and their aim was to build a socialist society. Labor, for its part, simply wanted better living and working conditions and a certain degree of autonomy. Although Brazzaville had the largest population and concentration of intellectuals in Congo, its only "industry" was government service, and its greatest problems were related to employment. Indeed, organized labor's greatest weakness lay in the paucity and dispersal of the Congo's industries. By their nature, the agroindustries, forestry, and mining were scattered throughout the southern region, and only in the neighborhood of Pointe Noire was there any industrial aggregation. The single employer against which grievances could be formulated by labor was the government. It was only natural, therefore, that the most effective resistance to governmental directives was shown by the civil service, and that the bureaucracy would become the principal target of official reproaches and repression. Idrissa Diallo, the CSC's first secretary-general (1964–66), was a minor civil servant, soon dismissed from both posts on charges of embezzlement. His successor, Paul Banthoud (1966–68), was known for his admiration of the Russian revolution and, after his official visit to the U.S.S.R. in 1967, for his advocacy of mass nationalization in Congo. He, too, was soon accused of mismanagement and for inciting the JMNR to revolt, and was later arrested for opposing the army takeover of the Biafra camp in August 1968. With Anatole Kondo, the CSC's third secretary-general (1969–79), the military government had better luck. Although his long incumbency was interrupted by his role in the general strike of March 1976, Kondo was soon released, along with other union strikers, but he and his CSC colleagues were forbidden to run for elective office in that organization. It was not until Sassou-Nguesso succeeded Yhomby Opango in February 1979 that a new secretary-general was appointed: a union leader satisfactory to the military authorities (Jean-Michel Boukamba-Yangouma), who was to outlast those who elevated him to office. Perhaps because Sassou Nguesso raised him from relative obscurity to membership on the committee preparing for the PCT's third extraordinary congress, Boukamba-Yangouma followed PCT directives. Thanks to his docility and cooperation, he was appointed to the PCT's politburo and central committee, and eventually joined Sassou Nguesso and Thystère-Tchicaya as Congo's ruling triumvirate. Notwithstanding this, when the living standards of unionists started to seriously deteriorate in the 1980's, it was the CSC that provided the nail in Sassou Nguesso's coffin by, on the one hand refusing to consider any restructuring of privatization of the State sector (that would have meant loss of jobs) while threatening, in 1989, an unlimited, general strike unless a national conference were convened. Trade unity was then partly shattered as several separate unions seceded from the CSC to set up their own separate federation. But, the fact that the post-1992 Lissouba government, just as Sassou Nguesso's antecedent one, is also regarded as 'the enemy' (out to cut jobs and restrict unionist powers), has resulted in continued trade union unity in Congo.

LABOU TANSI, SONY, 1947– . One of Congo's most famous and well-published authors and playwrights. Born on June 5, 1947 in Kimwanza, Zaire, to a Zairien father and Congolese mother, Labou Tansi (whose real name is Marcel Sony) studied in Brazzaville and trained for a teaching career. He taught English and French for several years, and worked in various government ministries. In 1979 he founded the Rocado Zulu Theater in Brazzaville, one of the most exciting and novel groups in Africa, that he has directed ever since. Labou Tansi has won worldwide recognition for his plays and literature, and is one of Congo's towering literary personalities.

LAC TELE. Small (5 km. in diameter) lake midway between Ouesso and Impfondo, that can only be found on small-scale maps. It acquired notoriety in the 1970's when pygmies from the region claimed it contained within it a live dinosaur. Originally greeted very sceptically in the West (there have been other very bizarre "sightings" reported in the barely populated northern regions of Congo), a re-reading of old missionary reports revealed a series of similar accounts. A number of scientific expeditions were mounted, but with no results. Swamps guard the lake that only pygmies can reach. It is 30 kms. west of Epéna in the Likouala region, and some 130 kms. east of Ouesso.

LANGUAGE. French is the official language of Congo and the vehicle of instruction in the educational system. Because each ethnic group has its own language, two of them, Lingala among the Batéké in the north and Koutouba (Kikongo) of the Bakongo in the south, that are closely related, have become the lingua franca in trading. Sangho is also used by riverain groups right through the Central African Republic. More radical Congolese nationalists have intermittently suggested replacing French by an indigenous language, but ethnic jealousies and the rudimentary written nature of both languages, make such a prospect remote.

LASSY ZEPHERIN, 1908–1984. Founder and head of a messianic sect. Born around 1908 in Pointe Noire to a prominent Vili family. During the interwar period he traveled widely as a sailor and lived for some years in Europe, allegedly as a professional boxer and acrobatic dancer. In 1946 he deserted the Belgian army, in which he had served during World War II, and returned to Moyen-Congo. In 1951 he joined the Salvation Army at Dolisie, but left it after two years to found a messianic sect which he called N'Zambie-Bougie. He became a protege of Tchicaya, who helped him to build a chapel near Holle, where he preached an updated form of Kimbangouism (see KIMBANGOUISM). By combining magic, prophecy and oratorical talent, Lassy Zepherin gained thousands of converts, grew wealthy, and delivered his followers' votes to the PPC party in the 1957 elections. At its height the N'Zambie-Bougie sect was estimated to have over 50,000 members in the area from Dolisie to Cabinda. In an effort to gain official recognition for his sect, Lassy Zepherin cultivated good relations with the French colonial administration. His rapacity and fraudulent cures, however, incurred the displeasure of the Ma Loango. With the disappearance of the PPC in 1960, Lassy Zepherin faded somewhat from the Congolese political scene, though he continued preaching and had a significant following, especially in Pointe Noire. When he died in 1984 there was a major succession dispute as his son, returning from Zaire to take over the leadership mantle, was rejected in favor of Zepherin's cousin. The radical **Major Katali** sided with the son leading to riots in which the army intervened, killing at least 13 faithful. The incident greatly tarnished the PCT regime among the Vili, and marked the beginning of Katali's eclipse; more importantly, the fact that the PCT's number two leader, **Thystère-Tchicaya,** threatened to resign over the imbroglio, also brought his eventual downfall.

LEFINI. Congo affluent that serves as the border between the Pool and Plateaux regions.

LEFOUABA, GREGOIRE. Minister of Tourism and Leisure. A northerner and former PCT militant and Sassou Nguesso supporter, Lefoauba bolted the party in September 1992 to form his own Parti Congolais de Rénouveau when the PCT joined the opposition to Lissouba. In a December 1992 cabinet shuffle he was appointed to the cabinet.

LEGISLATURE. The parliamentary regime installed in the late 1950s was replaced, after Congo became independent, by a presidential system of government. Under it there was no change in the five-year mandate of deputies, who, as before, were elected by direct universal suffrage. But in 1961, for the first time, they were chosen from a single list approved by the president, their powers were limited to certain domains, and their resolutions could be subjected to a public referendum if the president so decreed. After the overthrow of Fulbert Youlou in 1963, the MNR government tried to devise a compromise between the parliamentary and presidential systems of government. As before, a single list of candidates to serve for five years in a unicameral national assembly was drawn up by the government, but under certain circumstances the president could dismiss the assembly and rule temporarily by decree. An important change occurred in 1970, when all electoral bodies were eliminated. Then, under the June 24, 1973 constitution, an elected national assembly with a five-year mandate was revived, its membership was increased from 45 (in 1960) to 115, regular sessions were held in May and November, and legislation—which could be initiated by deputies as well as by the president—required their approval, as did the national budget. Officers of the assembly elected by the deputies became ex-officio members of the new state council, and the cabinet was charged with applying the laws as voted by the national assembly. The constitution of July 8, 1979, once again enlarged the size of the legislature, from 115 to 153 members. To all appearances, the electorate's authority was increased by a provision permitting voters to recall a deputy if they so desired, and to refuse approval of a constitutional amendment proposed by the PCT. However, as before, each increase in the size of the national assembly was accompanied by a diminution of its powers. Inasmuch as the authorized division of seats in the legislature assured the PCT, together with its mass organizations, 68 percent of the membership, any differences of opinion between them would be automatically settled in favor of the single party.

The national conference that Sassou Nguesso was forced to convene brought an end to single-party rule and the sycophantic national assembly. In the new multiparty elections that were held in 1992, under a new constitution, a large number of parties participated. Though Pascal Lissouba's UPADS party secured the largest number of seats, the creation of an unexpected anti-Lissouba alliance by two former enemies—the Bakongo under Kolelas, and the Mbochi under Sassou Nguesso—created a parliamentary balance of power forcing Lissouba to expand his cabinet, and giving the legislature considerable autonomy. (The Senate, created by the new constitution, was less a legislative body as an effort to assure all ethnic regions some autonomy.) See also CONSTITUTIONS.

LEKANA. District in the Plateaux region with headquarters in the village of the same name. It includes the Koukouya plateau inhabited by a Batéké subgroup of the same name.

LEKOUMOU. One of Congo's regions, northwest of the Pool, covering an area of 25,500 sq. kms. and a population of 74,420 (third-smallest in the country) with administrative headquarters in Sibiti, and comprising the districts of Komono, Bambama, Zananga and Sibiti. One quarter of the arable land is planted with rice: coffee, peanuts and palm oil are also produced in the region. The population includes some pygmies, Lari, Batéké, Bakota, Bayaka and Babamba.

LEKOUNDZOU, JUSTIN ITIHI-OSSETOUMBA. Economist, banker and one of Sassou Nguesso's key lieutenants. Of Mbochi ethnicity, Lekoundzou was director-general of the BCCO, chairman of the Banque Commerciale Congolaise, as well as of the CNR committee for organization when named to the PCT politburo in January 1970. Three months later he was appointed head of Congo's state enterprises. In December 1971, he was shifted to become minister of industry but was eliminated from the party politburo, and he was also dropped from the cabinet in August 1973, when he resumed duties as president of the BCC, and later of Pointe Noire's refinery. After the rise of Sassou-Nguesso Lekoundzou returned to the summit of power: he rejoined the PCT politburo in March 1980, and in December the same year he was appointed minister of finance and the budget, remaining in that post until 1987. In that year he was shifted to head the ministry of rural development, remaining in the cabinet until July 1989. He was then assigned head of the PCT organizational department, a post he held until 1991. After the demise of Sassou-Nguesso's administration Lekoundzou was arrested in August 1991 on multiple charges of embezzlement of 13 billion CFAF from the Banque du Commerce et Credit International. Sentenced to 15 years in prison, due to ill-health he was released from prison in June 1992.

LETEMBET-AMBILY, ANTOINE, 1929– . Playwright. Born in December 1929 near Boundji in the Cuvette, Létembet-Ambily arrived in Brazzaville in 1936 and attended Catholic schools before working for the administration in a variety of minor posts. He wrote for a number of local cultural journals, and in 1969 finally received recognition for his theatrical works by winning the inter-African grand prize for theater with his *L'Europe*. He is the author of several other plays. In June 1991 he was appointed minister of culture and arts in the interim government of Milongo, remaining until the 1992 elections.

LEYET-GABOKA, MAURICE, 1926– . Early parliamentarian. A Kouyou born on November 25, 1926 in Owando, Leyet-Gaboka was working as a teacher when he was elected deputy to the territorial assembly from Djoué on the socialist ticket in 1957. Reelected in 1959, he continued to represent Likouala-Mossaka in the legislature until the coup d'etat of 1963. He then left political activities, resuming his educational career, becoming an inspector of schools.

LHONI, PATRICE, 1929– . Author and cultural administrator. Born in 1929 at Nzunghi (Boko) some hundred kms. south of Brazzaville to a village chief, after his education in Congo he obtained a scholarship from the director of Brazzaville's Chaminade seminary to study in France. On his return to Brazzaville he taught at Chaminade between 1950 and 1958. He then renounced teaching and turned to journalism, editing *Liaison* until 1960 when he joined the municipality of Poto Poto, later joining the ministry of interior and serving in Congo's radio and cultural services. A man of many initiatives, he was the co-founder of the Institut d'Etudes Congolais (1960), the Centre Congolais du Theatre (1964), and he also set up a review in the vernacular. He is the author of several plays and works of fiction.

LIGNES NATIONALES AERIENNES CONGOLAISE. See LINA-CONGO. Congo's national air carrier.

LIKOUALA. (a) Congo's isolated, northernmost region, bordering the Central African Republic, through which the Oubangui affluent of the Congo river runs. The region, that covers 60,000 sq. kms. and has a population of 70,675 (second-lowest in Congo) has its administrative headquarters in Impfondo, on the Likouala river. The region, that is Congo's least significant agriculturally, has three districts: Impfondo, Epéna and Dongou, whose district headquarters (also of the same name, and close together) are connected by the only roads in the entire region, contact and trade otherwise conducted by dugout canoe. The extremely sparse region includes some pygmies, but most of the people are Banza and Bomitala. The region produces some palm products, ivory and kola. Large and important forest resources are not exploited. Using the Oubangui and Likouala rivers is the most convenient way to travel south, but at times of very shallow water it is either impassable or completely clogged with timber on its way to Brazzaville. The region is ideal for big game hunting, and the rivers are full of numerous fish species. Hippos and crocodiles abound in all the region's rivers. (b) Likouala is also the name of a Congo affluent that joins the latter just north of Mokassa, and runs through the Sangha region. It is intermittently navigable for 445 kms. between Mossaka, Makoua and Etoumbi.

LINA-CONGO (LIGNES NATIONALES AERIENNES CONGO-LAISE). Congo's deficit-ridden national airline, linking Brazzaville with Pointe Noire (several times daily) and Ouesso, Owando, Impfondo, Nkayi, Loubomo, Sibiti and other secondary centers. It also flies once-weekly to Bangui, in the C.A.R. Established in 1965 and at its height operating two Antonov 24 planes, and one each DC 6, DC 4, DC 3, and Fokker F27 plane. During the 1970's the airline transported around 50,000 passengers a year and over 1,100 tons of cargo and mail, the most popular lines being those connecting Brazzaville with Pointe Noire, and the north. A perennial money-loser, the airline was several times a candidate for liquidation but survived all such attempts. In February 1990 it was forced to reveal its balance sheet for the past three years, and its cumulative $20 million loss once again raised talk of liquidating the airline. By then Lina Congo owned only one plane, a Fokker 28, leasing from France a 737 jet for its only (once-weekly) international flight to Bangui in the Central African Republic. All other flights are domestic. See also TRANSPORTATION.

LINGALA. A local dialect widely used in northern Congo, and among northerners in Brazzaville as a lingua franca. See LANGUAGE.

LISSOUBA, PASCAL, 1931– . President of Congo. Born on November 10, 1931, at Mossendjo in the Niari region close to Gabon, and of Bandjambi ethnicity, Lissouba attended school at Dolisie and Brazzaville. From 1947 to 1952, he studied at a lycée in Nice and then proceeded for higher education in agriculture in Tunis (1953–56) and at the Sorbonne where he studied agricultural engineering (1958–61) to become the first Congolese to obtain a doctorate in Science. On his return to Congo he was appointed head of the country's agricultural service. He was a member of the interim 8-man committee appointed to govern Congo right after the August 1963 coup that toppled Youlou, and was named minister of agriculture in Massamba-Debat's provisional government, and in December 1963 became the latter's Prime Minister, and right-hand man. Though more outspoken against France than Massamba-Debat, Lissouba was in essence a moderate Marxist. He increasingly became irrelevant and a liability in the rapidly radicalized Congo and in April 1966, he was replaced as Premier by Noumazalaye. Between 1966 and 1968 professor of genetics at the local university, Lissouba returned to the political scene from August 1968 to June 1969 as minister of planning, and then of agriculture in Ngouabi's government. He then again returned to teach at the university, where he was also appointed Dean, reemerging into politics in January 1973, when he was named a member of the PCT central committee and of its new planning commission. He was arrested for alleged contacts with **Ange Diawara's** partisans in February 1973, but when tried two months later he was acquitted. He was forced, however, to resign from the PCT in 1974. In March 1976, he was again accused of plotting and in March 1977 he was given a life sentence for being an accomplice in Ngouabi's assassination, allegedly by demanding the latter's resignation, warning him that otherwise his life was in jeopardy. Spared from the death sentence by the intercession of neighboring president Omar Bongo of Gabon, Lissouba was kept in a special prison compound that was built in a remote forest area at Epéna in the north. He was freed in August 1979 and went abroad for medical treatment, his health having been impaired by the harsh prison conditions. He then joined UNESCO serving between 1980 and 1990 as head of its Africa Bureau for science and technology based in Nairobi.

With the advent of multipartyism Lissouba returned to Brazzaville on February 8, 1992 to be greeted by thousands of supporters at the airport, immediately becoming Congo's most serious political contender, at the head of the **Union Panafricaine pour la Démocratie Sociale**. Since he had not yet organized his **Nibolek** support, Lissouba was defeated in his bid to become prime minister of the interim **Haut Conseil de la République** that was elected by the national conference. In the final of four ballots, Lissouba lost to André Milongo by a vote of 454 to 419. However, organizing a strong coalition of political groups behind him, he was successful in the subsequent presidential elections, scoring the highest number of votes in the first round, and in the second run-off ballot he beat Bernard Kolelas to become Congo's new President. His party also won nearly half the local government seats, 40% of the senate seats, and a third of the legislative seats in the elections in 1992.

LOANDULU. Southern district in **Kouilou** region, 1,900 sq. kms. in area, with headquarters in the village of the same name.

LOANGO. Strong kingdom of the Vili (a Bakongo subgroup) with its capital at Buali (15,000 people in the 1780's, a small village today) and its core stretching inland along 120 miles of the coastal plain between the Chiloango river to Banda Point in the north, with the Mayombé mountains in the hinterland a natural boundary. There are contradictory legends about the ancient history of Loango, some traditions referring to the common origins of the Kongo, Vili, Batéké and Woyo from an earlier Nguunu kingdom in the interior, with the Vili peacefully migrating to the coastal plains. Until the 15th century

Loango was one of the vice-royalties owing fealty to the **Kongo kingdom**. With the latter's decay, Loango became independent under semi-divine kings, the Ma Loango. Hierarchically organized, Loango engaged in trade with (originally) Dutch and Portuguese merchants (selling ivory, copper, and acting as middlemen for slaves obtained from the interior), and sent caravans inland (with salt and European goods) as far as the Pool region trade entrepot. Disintegrating by 1870, Loango signed a treaty with Brazza in 1883 ceding hegemony to France. Descendants of the royal family have occupied important political positions during the colonial and the post-colonial eras, since they still retain considerable respect in society.

LOCAL ADMINISTRATION. For many years, French local-government officials struggled to increase their own authority at the expense of their superiors. Decentralization of the administration's authority, however, did not reach down to the local-government level until 1955. That year, the French Parliament passed a municipal-reorganization bill which transformed Brazzaville and Pointe Noire (and Dolisie in 1959) into full communes, administered by elected councils and mayors. Elsewhere, in Congo's 12 prefectures and 36 subprefectures, the highly centralized authority of French officials remained intact. To fill the vacuum in local-government institutions, the Youlou administration passed a law in 1961 creating six pilot rural communes. Councilors of those communes, elected by their fellow-villagers, were to manage communal affairs. This law, like the French administration's project in 1954 to transform the appointed Councils of Notables into genuine district and regional councils, remained a dead letter, and for the same reasons. Neither the Congolese deputies nor the first Congo government were willing to share their powers, or to impose the taxation that was indispensable for the success of their proposed institutions.

The traditional chieftaincy in Congo constituted no challenge to the central government, for the Vili Ma Loango and the Bateke Makoko retained only limited authority over their kinsmen. Although the chiefs were organized into customary councils, the majority of them in practice acted as agents of the central administration under both the French and the Congolese government. It was only during election campaigns that Youlou showed special honor to the Makoko and the PPC candidates sought the support of the Ma Loango, these moves being in both cases of little significance. In the larger settlements, the inhabitants belonging to different ethnic groups lived in separate districts, each electing its oldest male member as "mayor." Soon after he came to power Massamba-Debat decided to eliminate this practice by dismissing the "mayors" and replacing them with elected officials. But faced by the debacle of many former office-holders being democratically elected in February 1964, he annulled the elections and passed the management of communal affairs to special delegations composed of MNR militants.

Massamba-Debat experienced another setback when the strong opposition of the Vili and Bateke forced him to desist from his attempt to undermine the authority of their paramount chiefs. After he changed from a frontal attack on the chieftaincy to indirect tactics, Massamba-Debat was more successful. By reorganizing the administration into nine economic regions, each headed by a political commissar, Massamba-Debat sapped chiefly and ethnic influences and, at the same time, strengthened the authority of his government and party. On August 23, 1967, Congo was reorganized into nine regions: Kouilou, Niari, Lekoumou, Bouenza, Pool, Cuvette, Plateaux, Sangha, and Likouala. Representation in the National Assembly elected on June 24, 1973, reflected the comparative political importance assigned to those regions and their communes by the PCT leaders. Brazzaville, considered a separate constituency, was allotted twenty-four seats, Kouilou and the Pool seventeen each, Bouenza thirteen, Pointe Noire and Niari twelve each, the Plateaux and Cuvette ten each, Lekoumou five, and Sangha three. In the regional councils elected at the same time, that of Kouilou had forty-one members, those of the Niari, Plateaux, Bouenza, and the Cuvette thirty-six each, and Sangha and Lekoumou thirty-two each. On June 28, 1973, the residents of four of the Congo's five full communes were to choose councilors to replace their appointed mayor-administrators. Brazzaville's municipal council was allotted forty-one seats, as was that of Pointe Noire, but those of Jacob (Nkayi) and Dolisie (Loboumo) were rejected by a majority of their respective populations. The three last-mentioned towns, along with Ouesso, remained for the time being under the regime of government appointed administrators. The election on January 12, 1974, of Okyemba Moriende, first vice-president of the national assembly, as president of the executive committee for the new municipal council of Brazzaville, was the first such election for Congo's regional, district, and municipal councils (except for the five full communes). Early in February 1974, new elections were held for the municipal councils of Loubomo, Nkayi, and Bouenza, which this time inevitably gave them ample PCT majorities. In preparation for the second regular PCT congress, ten political commissars (all members of the PCT central committee) were sent out from Brazzaville in October 1974 to establish new party bases in the regions, inform themselves of the population's political desiderata, and promote the election of more peasants to the local councils. To encourage expansion of the PCT outside the main towns, a PCT committee was to be formed in every arrondissement where there were already five party members. These measures marked the first effective steps toward a rapid increase of party membership outside the towns and toward administrative decentralization, but their primary goal was not so much to give rural Congolese new channels for self-expression as to undermine the power and influence of the bureaucracy. In June 1975, the regional councils of Bouenza, Niari, and Cuvette voted to "Congolize" the French names of Dolisie (to Loubomo), Jacob (to Nkayi), and Fort Rousset (to Owando). Elsewhere it was hard to learn to what degree the Congolese used the new councils, inasmuch as government appointees replaced mayors and all elective bodies were in a state of suspended animation during Yhomby Opango's military reign (1977–79). In any case, the councils were closely supervised by party delegates and lacked the financial means to give practical application to their resolutions. Under the constitution of July 8, 1979, the people's regional, district, and communal councils were confirmed as corporate entities, and provision for their financial autonomy was made under the 1982–86 development plan. The elections to those councils scheduled for July 1982 were postponed for two years, however, after the bombing incident that month at Brazzaville airport.

After the demise of PCT rule the first competitive local elections in Congolese history took place, and decentralization (largely for political purposes) was given new teeth by the creation of a second house, the Senate. The results of the 1992 elections reflected both the changed political balance of power in the country, and the ethnic distribution in the regions. For the results see ELECTIONS (LOCAL) OF 1992.

LOMBOLOU, EDOUARD, 1939– . Aviation engineer. Born in 1939 and educated in France, Lomboulou served as special advisor to the minister of transport and later was appointed deputy director-general of civil aviation. In 1980 he was named secretary-general of CAFAC, the Francophone African civil aviation commission, and relocated to Dakar, Senegal, to take up his post.

LOPES, HENRI, 1937– . Author and former Prime Minister of Congo. Born in September 12, 1937, at Kinshasa, Zaire, Lopes studied in primary schools at Brazzaville and Bangui, following which he earned a master's degree in France, where for some years he taught history in the Paris region. On returning to Brazzaville in 1965, he became a school principal and then minister of education in 1968. Late in 1969 he briefly held the portfolio of information and in January 1970, he was named minister of justice at the same time as he was appointed to the PCT central committee. In December 1971, he succeeded Ikonga as foreign minister, serving until 1973. In 1973 he was also appointed Chairman of the Revolutionary Court charged with trying enemies of the state. That same year his book of short stories, satirizing African political and social life, was published under the title of *Tribaliques*: the book has been widely praised internationally, and in 1972 it was awarded the Black Africa's Prize for Literature. Lopes was also the author of the Congolese national anthem.

On August 31, 1973 he became Congo's first prime minister under the 1973 constitution, serving in that capacity until he resigned two years later on December 2, 1975. In January 1976, he was named director of the PCT newspaper, *Etumba*, but was replaced the following May by Eugene Sama. He became minister of finance in the Goma government of April 5, 1977 until dropped from the government in the cabinet change of December 28, 1980. In January 1982, he became deputy director-general of UNESCO. Besides *Tribaliques,* he has published several other works of fiction.

LOS FORESTEROS. Name of the Cuban foreign expeditionary brigade stationed in Congo near Pointe Noire and Loubomo until 1990. See also CUBA.

LOUBOMO. District, originally known as Dolisie, in the Niari region of Congo, with administrative headquarters in the town with the same name. The district lies east of the Mayombé mountains, and is the land route connecting Cabinda and Zaire on the one hand and Gabon on the other. The district is a series of plateaux (average height 300–400 meters) dissected by valleys, through one of which flows the Niari river, with savanna lands in the south and heavy forests in the north. The attractive town of Loubomo, originally named Dolisie (after Brazza's lieutenant, Albert Dolisie), owes its foundation and growth to the Congo-Ocean railroad. Between 1958 and 1972 its population doubled, and in the latter year, it had 20,000 inhabitants, of whom 350 to 400 were Europeans. By 1982, the town's population was estimated at 30,000, and in 1992 at over 52,000, being then for some time Congo's third-largest. Dolisie's name was changed in 1975 to Loubomo. In addition to its role as a major rail center, Loubomo has some cultural importance as the "capital" of the messianic sect of **Lassy Zépherin**.

LOUDIMA. District in the Bouénza region with administrative headquarters in the town of the same name. The town has a population of 18,000, and was an important stop in the caravan trails from Loango to the Pool region. The district has sugar plantations and a SUC-CONGO plant.

LOUEMBE, DELPHINE, 1947– . Academic. Born on November 29, 1947 and educated in biochemistry (Bordeaux, 1971) and in biophysics (Orleans, Paris, 1976), Louembé returned to Brazzaville where he currently is the head of the department of cellular and molecular biology at Marien Ngouabi University.

-M-

M-22 see MOUVEMENT DU 22 FEVRIER.

MA LOANGO. Title of the paramount chief of the Vili. In 1883 the Ma Loango signed a treaty with naval Lt. Cordier granting France rights over his dominions.

MABALLO, ALPHONSE (Captain). Former deputy-chief of staff, demoted to the rank of Captain after the November 1969 plot for "lack of courage." He was then himself involved in another conspiracy and dismissed from the armed forces.

MABASSI, ENOCH. One of Congo's most prolific poets, having published some 100 poems by 1980 alone.

MACOSSO, FRANCOIS-LUC, 1938– . Early cabinet minister. Born in Madingou-Kayes in the Kouilou region on October 18, 1938, Macosso was trained locally as a banker and at the time of the 1963 coup was manager of the Pointe Noire branch of the national development bank. Elected to the national assembly in 1963, he was brought into the Massamba-Debat cabinet in April 1965 as minister of justice and civil service, performing so efficiently that he was later also assigned the portfolio of labor. However he lost influence and authority in the rapidly radicalized cabinet, and was replaced by more militant members, reverting to his banking duties.

MADINGOU. District, encompassing 5,000 sq. kms. in the region of Bouénza with administrative headquarters in the town of the same name.

MADINGOU, EDOUARD, 1940– . Civil administrator. Originally appointed director of the cabinet of the minister of posts and communications, Madingou then became its chief inspector during 1969–1970, and member of the central committee of the PCT. In January 1970 he was named secretary of state for trade, industry and mines, and three months later director-general of the Office National de Commercialisation (ONACOM). In March 1970, he was dropped from the central committee of the PCT, and in 1972 he was shunted to lesser duties within the ministry of trade and industry.

MADINGOU-KAYES. District in the Kouilou region with an area of 8,000 sq. kms. stretching from the Atlantic Ocean to the Mayombé forests in the interior.

MAGANGA-BOUMBA, A. Foreign ministry division head. Educated in Political Science at the Sorbonne where he earned a PhD, Maganga-Boumba returned to Brazzaville to assume a variety of positions within the Congolese foreign ministry. He has been head of the OAU division in the ministry, and more recently head of its Africa division. In 1986 he also served as acting head of the OAU itself.

MAHE, RENE, 1926– . Early Youlou minister. Born on June 24, 1926, in Marseilles, Mahe grew up on Reunion Island where his father served as an administrator. In the 1940s, he went to Brazzaville where, after several unsuccessful business ventures, he took up journalism and became editor of *Le Progrès*. He was an early member of the UDDIA party and represented Fulbert Youlou at several international conferences. In November 1956, he was elected to the Brazzaville municipal council and to the territorial assembly from the Pool region. Youlou named him minister of economic affairs in December, 1958, and after independence he was secretary-general of the national assembly. He lost all his positions after the 1963 coup d'etat, and reentered private affairs.

MAHOUNGOU, DIEUDONNE MANOU, 1936– . Former cabinet minister. Successively appointed economic counselor at the Congolese embassy in Paris, and later director of regional planning of Congo (1969–71), Mahoungou joined the cabinet as minister of trade on December 16, 1971, to be replaced in August 1973. He has since been working in the state sector as an administrator.

MAHOUNGOU, SEGOLO DIA. Dramatologist. Mahoungou has been one of the pioneers of contemporary Congolese theatre, and secretary-general of the Union Congolaise des Arts Scéniques (UCAS).

MAKA (also MAKAA). Small ethnic group comprising 4 percent of Congo's population, subdivided into several clans including the Njem, Bakwélé, Mabéza, Bamouali and Pomo. They are very recent arrivals (from the 20th century) from Cameroun in the northeast, where the rump of the group is found. They are primarily found in the Sangha region, at Souanké, Ouesso and Sembé.

MAKAMBILA, PASCAL, 1944– . Chief conservator of the National Museum. Makambila was born on August 6, 1944, and was educated in Bordeaux and Paris in ethnology, musicology and political science. He also teaches these fields at the Marien Ngouabi University in Brazzaville.

MAKANY, LEVY, 1931– . Botanist, international administrator and former cabinet minister. A Lari, born on September 30, 1931 in Mossendjo, Makany received his doctorate in science from the University of Montpellier where he studied (with absences in Congo) between 1961 and 1973. Between 1963 and 1964 he was assistant director of education, and president of the Alliance Française in Brazzaville. He was promoted to director of education in 1964, the same year he joined the **JMNR**. In 1966 he was appointed minister of education, retaining the portfolio until January 1969, when he was shifted to become permanent secretary of the National Council of Scientific Research. Later that year he was appointed professor at Marien Ngouabi University, and in 1973 became the rector of the university. Since the mid-1970's he has been in Paris with UNESCO. He is the author of numerous works on Congo's vegetation.

MAKAYA, ETIENNE, 1939– . Born on June 19, 1939 in Pointe Noire, Makaya graduated in 1962 from the Ecole Nationale des Services Exterieurs du Tresor in Paris and became a treasury inspector. Between 1963 and 1965 he was financial comptroller of AOMPI in Yaoundé. In 1965, he was attached as first counselor in the Congolese embassy in Moscow, and was transferred in the same capacity to Paris later that year, staying there until 1969. Returning to Brazzaville he was integrated in ministry of finance as Treasurer-General of Congo.

MAKHELE, CAYA, 1952– . Born on August 3, 1952 in Pointe Noire, and trained as a teacher, Makhele has been very active in cultural affairs and was the founding member of a number of organizations including the Cercle Litteraire de Brazzaville and the Centre Cultural Congolais.

MAKOKO. Title of the paramount chief of the Batéké, resident at Mbé, with whom **Brazza** signed in 1880 a treaty that gave France entry to the Congo basin. The Batéké were by that time a spent power, under pressure from other groups, especially the Mbochi.

MAKON, MARCEL. Secretary general of the right-wing *Parti Liberale Congolaise* that was set up in November 1990.

MAKOSSO, FRANCOIS-LUC, 1938– . Former minister of justice. A Vili born on October 19, 1938 in Madingou-Kayès, Makosso was the manager of the Pointe Noire branch of the National Development Bank and an ardent critic of the Youlou regime. After the latter's overthrow Makosso was elected to the legislature and in April 1965 he was named minister of justice and civil service. He was also given the labor portfolio in 1966. Ngouabi appointed him to succeed Bindi in August 1968 as head of the security police. In February 1970 he was shifted to diplomatic duties and named ambassador to Belgium, and a year later he was also accredited to the Netherlands. In May 1983 he returned to Brazzaville where he was appointed rector of Marien Ngouabi University, a post he held for three years.

MAKOSSO, JEAN-AIME. Early union leader. Son of a chief from the Mayombé region, Makosso was employed in the postal service and became an active member of the CATC union. He was defeated when he ran on the PPC ticket for a seat in the territorial assembly in 1957. He joined the UDDIA the next year, and was elected to the legislature in 1963. As a Catholic trade-union leader and outspoken critic of Massamba-Debat's plans to unify the trade union movement, his parliamentary immunity was lifted in November 1964 and he was subsequently expelled from the legislature in 1965. He then reverted to his civil service post.

MAKOUA. A district covering 10,000 sq. kms. in the Cuvette region with administrative headquarters in the town of the same name. The district is dependent on the Likouala river, a Congo affluent, that runs through it and provides communications with the capital. The town is exactly on the equator, and receives heavy rains.

MAKOUANGOU, ANTOINE. Diplomat and former head of national security. Makouangou, a police officer, was originally commissioner general of Brazzaville. With Ngouabi's rise to power he was shunted to a diplomatic career, being named in 1969 charge d'affaires in Israel. In 1970 he was moved to become ambassador to Ethiopia, and he also served as ambassador to the Central African Republic from July 1971 to April 1973. He then returned to Brazzaville, and was appointed head of a new national security corps that replaced the former police force.

MAKOUNDOU, DOMINIQUE. Physician. Makoundou has been head of the antituberculosis center at Brazzaville, and also head of the public health service's national laboratory before being appointed, in October 1971, director of epidemiology services in the ministry of health in Brazzaville.

MAKOUTA MBOUKOU, JEAN-PIERRE, 1929– . Highly published author and educator. Born on July 17, 1929 in Kindamba in the Pool region, after studies in Cameroun and Brazzaville he earned a Ph.D. in Linguistics from the universities of Grenoble and the Sorbonne, Makouta Mboukou taught at several universities including in Dakar, Brazzaville (1963–1970), the Sorbonne (1971–1978), and then went to head the French department at an Abidjan lycée. He was also a deputy to the national assembly between 1963 and 1968. He is the author of several studies on linguistics and numerous acclaimed works of fiction and poetry. With the political liberalizations of the 1990's he joined the MCDDI party, and in 1992 was elected to Congo's Senate, and to the latter's political bureau.

MALALOU, ALPHONSE, 1930– . Diplomat. Born July 13, 1930, at Saras, and an agricultural technician by profession, between 1951 and 1961 Malalou was in charge of the export standardization services, and then was appointed first as attache (1963–1967), then director of the cabinet of the minister of agriculture (1967–1969). In 1970, he was named economic counselor and permanent delegate of Congo to the Food and Agriculture Organization at Rome, returning in 1972 to his old administrative post in the ministry of agriculture in Brazzaville.

MALEKAT, FELIX. Diplomat. A civil servant under the French administration, Malekat became first counselor of the Congo embassy in Algeria after the latter's independence. In January 1970, he was placed in charge of the Office National du Tourisme. In 1973 he was shifted to head a division in the ministry of interior and recently was retired.

MALONGA, JEAN, 1907–1985. Early politician and author. A Lari born in Miwé-Ngoyi in the Pool region, Malonga's early career was as an interpreter for the colonial administration, teacher, male-nurse, and bank clerk. He only completed his primary schooling at age 35. With the political liberalization in Congo after the end of WWII Malonga joined the PPC party and in 1947 was elected deputy to the territorial assembly, and in 1949 to the AEF Grand Council. Between 1949 and 1955 he was also Senator in Paris, following which he returned to Brazzaville as head of personnel at the Brazzaville Hospital. In 1958, however, he began a new career as director of Radio Congo, a post he held until his retirement in 1965. Malonga is the author of three books written in the 1950's and is considered the dean of Congolese authors. In 1984 Congo awarded him the presidential prize for his lifelong literary output.

MAMBEKE-BOUCHER, AUGUSTE, 1919– . Early politician. Born on February 2, 1919 in Brazzaville, where he became a teacher and was naturalized as a French Citizen, Mambéké-Boucher served as a sociologist in the local office of the World Health Organization before joining the MSA party to be selected by Opangault as his minister of education and youth in 1957. In 1959 he was elected deputy to the territorial assembly from Likouala-Mossaka, but retired from public life in 1963.

MAMONSONO, LEOPOLD-PINDY, 1952– . Author and poet. Born on November 10, 1952 in Bko-Songho, and trained as a teacher of English, Mamonsono has also been involved in journalism and television. He is the author of a seminal survey of Congolese poetry, several other works, including two collections of his own poetry.

MAMPOUYA, CONSTANT, 1944– . President of the Congolese commission of zootechnical and veterinary research, and director of the institute of rural development at Marien Ngouabi University. Mampouya was born in April 22, 1944 and has a doctorate in agronomy and animal physiology.

MAMPOUYA, DOMINIQUE, 1940– . Economist. Born in 1940 and earning a doctorate in economics in France, Mampouya has been serving with the Congolese Mission to the United Nations.

MAMPOUYA, JOSEPH, 1951– . Academic. Born in 1951 and educated in philosophy at Marien Ngouabi University, Mampouya then proceeded to Patrice Lumumba University and the Academy of Social Sciences in Moscow where he continued his studies between 1977 and 1981. He currently teaches at Marien Ngouabi University, and has written several academic texts.

MANGBENZA, RAYMOND. Diplomat. An inspector of primary education before becoming director of the cabinet of the foreign minister, Mangbenza was named Congo's permanent representative to UNESCO in Paris in June 1970. He has since held several other similar appointments with international organizations.

MANKASA, COME, 1936– . Born on April 28, 1936 in Brazzaville, Mankasa received his doctorate in literature, and trained also as a journalist at the University of Lille. On returning to Congo, he was placed in charge of the Centre National de Documentation Economique.

MANN, LAURENT, 1938– . Former cabinet minister. Born in 1938 in Souanké, and trained as a teacher, after several years in the public-school system, Mann entered the diplomatic service and held several posts in Congo's embassies at Bruxelles and Berlin. He then joined the Lopes government of 1973 as minister of information, and on January 8, 1975 he was named minister of arts, culture, and sports. The following year he was dropped from the cabinet and appointed head of a division in the latter ministry.

MARIEN NGOUABI UNIVERSITY. See UNIVERSITY OF BRAZZAVILLE.

MASSALA, GILBERT SALLADIN. Artist. Of Bembe origins, Massala's talents are multi-faceted, having at one time or another been artist, author, painter, musician and actor. He has been Cultural director of the Voice of the Congolese Revolution, and in 1983 was elected secretary of the Congolese Union of Fine Arts. Since 1985 he has been in residence in Paris.

MASSAMBA-DEBAT, ALPHONSE, 1921–1977. Second President of Congo. A Bakongo born at Nkolo in the Pool area in 1921, after graduating from a Protestant secondary school, Massamba-Debat became a teacher in Chad and in Congo, and then a school principal in Brazzaville (1957–59). In the latter year, he was elected on the UDDIA ticket to the territorial assembly and became head of the cabinet of the minister of education. He was president of the assembly from June 1959 to May 1961, when he joined Fulbert Youlou's cabinet as minister of planning. Disagreeing with some of Youlou's archconservative policies, he was forced to resign from the latter's cabinet two years later. This was greatly in his favor, together with his personal utter honesty and integrity, since after Youlou's overthrow he was appointed to head a provisional government from August to December 1963. In the subsequent elections he was elected president of the republic. A moderate and pragmatic Socialist Massamba-Debat was constantly on the defensive from both leftist elements and from Youlouists, and progressively lost control of the reins of power until he was ousted in August 1968 by Marien Ngouabi. He was publicly tried but acquitted in October 1969, and was pensioned and retired to his native village. In March 1977 he was allegedly implicated in Ngouabi's assassination, and rushed to secret trial by court martial, sentenced to death and executed on March 25,1977. The nature of trial, its secrecy, and the immediate execution of its sentence has always been cause for speculation about his guilt.

MASSIF DE CHAILLU. An area northwest of the **Pool** that comprises of heavily-forested hills with a multitude of streams and cataracts.

MATHEY, ALBERT, 1939– . Director of Posts. Born in Brazzaville on August 27, 1939, Mathey was trained in postal administration and started off as a postal inspector, rapidly becoming head postal inspector of Congo. Between 1965 and 1968 he was attached to the AEF postal system, returning to join the cabinet of the minister of posts and telecommunications in Brazzaville. In January 1969 he was appointed director of Posts and of the postal national savings fund.

MATINGOU, BONIFACE. Former cabinet minister. Trained in France in economics, and briefly a professor at the university of Brazzaville, Matingou joined the ministry of the Economy and Finance as a technical advisor and in August 1969 became secretary of state for financial and economic affairs. In April 1970 he served in the cabinet as minister of finance, leaving it in June 1972. After serving as director-general of the Société Nationale d'Energie, he was named minister of trade in the Lopes cabinet of August 30, 1973.

In the cabinet formed January 9, 1975, he became minister of public works and transport, and in the Goma cabinet of December 28, 1980, minister of tourism and environment, serving until 1984. He has been retired from public life since then.

MATINGOU, SEBASTIEN. Well known musician, poet and Secretary General of Congo's Office of Cultural Activities. He has published five collections of poetry.

MATOUMBA-MPOLO, PROSPER (Lieutenant), 1940–1972. Ringleader of the 1972 attempted coup. Born in 1940, and trained as a teacher, Matoumba-Mpolo became first a teacher and then an administrator in the education service. A radical militant, he was active in organizing youth, and became President of the JMNR. In August 1968 he was named minister of youth and information. Two months later, he became a member of the CNR, and in January 1970 of the PCT central committee. He was then also appointed commissar of the Office du Kouilou. A ringleader of the **Ange Diawara** attempted putsch of February 22, 1972, he was killed five days later near Pointe Noire by government troops.

MATSECOTA, LAZARE, 1931–1965. Former attorney general and cousin of Fulbert Youlou. A Lari born August 12, 1931 in Brazzaville, and a cousin of Youlou, after graduating from primary school in 1945, he entered the M'Bamou seminary but was expelled from it two years later for lack of discipline. He then joined the army, but in 1948 left it having received a scholarship to the Ecole des Cadres through family influence. After receiving his BA he studied law in Paris and joined the anticolonial student movement there. On his return to Brazzaville in 1957, he joined the UDDIA. Another scholarship enabled him to continue his studies in Paris, where he acquired a doctorate of law in 1959. Back again in Congo, he was named attorney general, a post he held even after Youlou's ouster, when he was kidnapped and murdered, along with two other prominent Lari civil servants, in February 1965.

MATSIKA, AIME. Former radical cabinet minister, and one of the founders of Congolese trade unionism. A Lari born in Yetela in the Kinkala district, Matsika was a student at the Vocational School in Brazzaville until expelled for lack of discipline in 1951. He then worked as an industrial designer in the public works department, but was dismissed for his failure to respect regulations. He moved to Dolisie, where he remained unemployed except for a brief job with a local architect. He then joined the CGAT trade union secretariat and became a popular orator for Congolese independence at trade-union meetings. He led the CGAT campaign for a negative vote in the referendum of September 1958, earning a reputation with the police as being the most active Communist agent in Brazzaville. After traveling extensively in East Europe, he was briefly arrested upon his return to Brazzaville in April 1960 for smuggling in Communist propaganda. After his release, he became secretary of the Union of Congolese Youth (UJC), editor of its organ, *L'Eveil,* and active in cultivating contacts with students. He played a role in inciting unionists against the regime of Fulbert Youlou, and after the latter's ouster he was brought into Massamba-Debat's cabinet as minister of trade and industry in December 1963, and eight months later was assigned the portfolio of civil aviation. He was subsequently shifted to head the ministry of public works. In November 1969 he was charged with plotting against the Ngouabi military regime, and was sentenced to death in absentia. Making his peace with the regime Matsika assumed middle-rank administrative work, and was appointed manager of the Loutété cement plant. By 1982 he was living in France in exile.

MATSIONA, BERNARD COMBO. Former cabinet minister and hard-line member of **M-22** group. A Bakongo, Matsiona was appointed minister of labor in Sassou-Nguesso's cabinet on December 28, 1980, and in 1984 was reassigned the health portfolio that he held until 1991.

MATSOUA, ANDRE GRENARD, 1899–1942. Founder of a mutual-help society, whose persecution by the French triggered a xenophobic, anti-French, religious movement among the Lari. A Lari born on

January 17, 1899 in Mandzala-Kinkala in the Pool region, after training in the Mbamou mission for a priestly career Matsoua resigned in 1919 to join the Customs service in Brazzaville. He then went to France, and later joined the colonial armies and saw action in North Africa in 1924. In 1926 he established himself in Paris, became involved in union affairs, and in 1926 founded an *Amicale,* a socio-cultural mutual-help society. The success of the movement, its spread to Congo where it sought recruits and contributions, and Matsoua's anti-indigenat pronouncements, brought the hounding of his agents in Congo. In 1929 he was arrested and returned to Congo, where despite being a French citizen he was sentenced by a traditional court to three years in jail and ten years exile in desolate Chad. Escaping to Nigeria in 1935, and from there to Oubangui Chari where he was caught, he again escaped, ending in Paris under a false name. He again volunteered for military service in World War II, was wounded in action, and arrested in the hospital where he was recovering. Repatriated to Congo, strong European pressure for his incarceration brought about a life-sentence of hard labor. He died in prison (allegedly murdered) and was buried secretly. Not accepting the fact that he was dead, Matsoua became the symbol of Lari resentment against colonial rule, and the subject of religious adulation. Large numbers of Lari withdrew into their own affairs, refused to participate in any civic projects or pay taxes, and with the political liberalizations of the 1940's twice entered Matsoua on the ballot, massively "electing" the dead Matsoua as their deputy to the French National Assembly in Paris. The Lari political withdrawal allowed other ethnic groups (Vili, Mbochi) to advance politically at their expense, until the defrocked Lari priest Fulbert Youlou succeeded to project himself as the heir to Matsoua, gaining their vote. Even so, Youlou had to harshly crack down on die-hard Matsouanists who continued their campaign of civil disobedience against any government. Since the 1970's Matsouanism has been eclipsed somewhat among the Lari, even though tapping Matsouanist sentiments can result in strong political paybacks, as was visible in 1992 when **Bernard Kolelas's** campaigns included appeals to Matsouanists, who flocked to his banner. A statue honoring Matsoua stands prominently in downtown Kinkala, the administrative headquarters of the Pool region.

MATSOUANISM. See MATSOUA, ANDRE GRENARD.

MAVOUNGOU, FRANCOIS, 1926– . Administrator. Born in Diosso on March 4, 1926 and a teacher who studied at Ecole William Ponty in Dakar, Mavoungou was president Massamba-Debat's chef de cabinet (1963–1968). He was then sent to Congo's embassy in the U.S.

as economic councillor. Between 1970 and his retirement he was director of the Office National de Kouilou.

MAYA-MAYA. Congo's international airport, in the western outskirts of Brazzaville. Expanded several times, it has Francophone Africa's longest runway (3,300 meters) and was used in the 1980's by some carriers as a refueling stop on long-distance Europe-South Africa flights.

MAYANZA, AUGUSTE. A medical doctor, Mayanza is the leader of the Parti du Travail (PT) that he set up in 1991.

MAYINGUIDI, ETIENNE, 1933– . Magistrate. Born in Brazzaville on August 19, 1933 and trained in law, Mayinguidi served between 1964 and 1970 as president of the labor court, during the last year also as attorney general of Congo. Since 1971 he has been with Congo's court of appeals.

MAYOMBE MOUNTAINS. Series of mountainous plateaus separating the plains of Niari from the coastal plains, historically loosely controlled by the **Loango kingdom** though inhabited by a number of small Bakongo chiefdoms. From 30–60 kms. in width and reaching a height of 930 meters at Mt. Bamba, the rough terrain of the Mayombé has caused problems to the Congo-Ocean railroad that crosses them.

M'BAMOU. Large island in **Stanley Pool** where houses are built on piles as protection against occasional rises in the Congo's water level. Since 1992 there have been negotiations to create a tourist resort on the island.

MBANGUI, BEMAB-DEBERT WA, 1946– . Civil administrator and poet. Born in 1946 in Kéouya in the Lokouala-Mossaka region of Mbangui-Opoo ethnic origins, after studies in the Chaminade seminary in Brazzaville, he started working as a teacher. In 1973 he was elected deputy and vice-president of the executive committee of the popular council for the district of Ewo. In 1972 he had won first prize for his poetry, in 1979 third prize, and in 1980 first prize again. Since 1982 he has been head of a department in the ministry of education.

M'BE. Ancient village 150 kms. from Brazzaville, historic capital of the Batéké kingdom where the treaty between their king, Makoko, and Brazza was signed. A plaque exists there commemorating this event: once encompassing 15,000 people, M'bé currently has only 300 people. See BATEKE.

M'BEMBA, FRANCOIS, 1935– . Director general of taxes. Born in Brazzaville on July 13, 1935, and originally an inspector of taxes, in July 1965 he served for a year as head of a division in the ministry of finances dealing with taxation. In 1967 he was moved to head verification of tax revenues, and since 1968 he has been director general of taxes.

M'BEMBA, JEAN-MARTIN. Former minister of justice. A Batéké from the Pool region, with the political liberalization of the 1990's M'bemba was appointed minister of justice in Milongo's interim government of June 1991. He was then named chairman of CONOSEL, the commission charged in December 1992 with organizing the forthcoming elections. He himself is leader of the *Union pour le Progrès* (UP), allied with the URD.

M'BEMBA, THEOPHILE, 1917–1971. First Congolese archbishop of Brazzaville. Born in 1917 in Mpiala near Brazzaville, M'Bemba attended school in Brazzaville, and in Cameroun, following which he entered the Yaoundé seminary in 1936, Libreville's (Gabon) seminary, completing his theological training in Brazzaville between 1939 and 1946 when he was ordained a priest. After a series of lower church appointments, he was consecrated archbishop of Brazzaville in June 24, 1969. That year he strongly criticized nationalization of the mission schools and led the Catholic opposition to Massamba-Debat's government. When the Ngouabi military regime came to power, however, M'Bemba came to terms with it, since much more was at stake than in his clashes with Massamba-Debat. When he died in June 1971, he was praised by Ngouabi for having rid the Congolese Catholic church of all colonial vestiges.

M'BENI-M'BONGO. See MOUMBEMBA, JEAN-PAUL.

MBERI, MARTIN. Powerful minister of interior. A Bembe teacher from Bouenza in the National School of Administration, and deputy from Niari in the national assembly, Mberi was elected president of the JMNR in February 1965. After Ngouabi succeeded Massamba-Debat, Mberi was named secretary of state for propaganda and a member of the CNR directorate. He was dismissed from the CNR in December 1968, but was named director of the National School of Administration in September 1969, a post he held until May 1971. He was then charged with writing and distributing subversive tracts against the military government, the tracts being in effect complaints about the increasingly northern-bias of the regime, and its eliminating all southern cadres from the administration. He was tried and sentenced to five years in prison; amnestied after 18 months, he was surprisingly named secretary for education of the PCT central committee in January 1973. In January 1976, he was named attorney general to the High Court at Brazzaville, but lost that post in April 1977. He was in self-exile in Paris during the 1980's, not joining any of the political formations there. With the liberalizations in Brazzaville Mberi returned home, joined Lissouba's UPADS, and in 1992 was named minister of the interior. He has become one of the most powerful men surrounding the beleaguered Lissouba regime, especially during the violence in Brazzaville during 1993–94. Aware that the bulk of security forces are not ethnically loyal to the regime, he has pursued a policy of weeding out, in particular, Lari (who tend to support **Bernard Kolelas**), from the police, replacing them with Bembe personnel. Lissouba himself is a bit uneasy with his powerful interior minister, and the growing Bembe clan's predominance in the new security services.

MBETI. Small ethnic group, comprising 3 percent of Congo's population, originating from Gabon where they are found in larger numbers.

M'BIA, MARTIN (Major). M'Bia was commander of the Pointe Noire military zone before being named on October 2, 1975 head of the military cabinet of Ngouabi. He was military commander of the Place de Brazzaville when appointed a member of the PCT military committee formed after Ngouabi's assassination in March 1977. The next month he was brought into Goma's government as minister of transport and public works, but was dropped in April 4, 1979, reverting back to military duties.

M'BINDA. Village near the Gabon border, linked to Mont-Belo near Nyaki by the 286 kms. COMILOG railway spur, through which Gabon's manganese was shipped until 1990.

MBOCHI. The dominant ethnic group in the Cuvette region in northern Congo. The Mbochi call themselves Ombosi (singular) and Ambosi (plural). Oral history suggests common descent from an ancestor called Ndinga. They are subdivided into several clans, the most important of which are the Mbochi proper, the Kouyou, Makoua, Likouala, Bangala and Bonga. Not much is definitively known about the early origins of the Mbochi, but they were relatively recent arrivals to their current habitat (arriving in the middle of the 18th century, this date being disputed), from the east. Settling in relatively empty territory along the confluence of the Sangha, Likouala and Congo rivers around Mossaka, they established hereditary fishing rights and controlled riverine traffic, eventually pressing further south to encounter the Batéké. The Mbochi are Congo's third-largest group, with around 13 percent of the population. During the colonial era many Mbochi moved to Brazzaville, and even more with the rise in 1968 of northern-dominated military rule, though their natural habitat remains the Cuvette region. With the rise of the Ngouabi military regime northern influence and appointees rose dramatically in Brazzaville, though there was friction between the Mbochi and the **Kouyou**, which though lumped together as "northerners" have as often as not been in competition for supremacy. In the early 1980's a secret society FROBOMA was set up to support Sassou-Nguesso (a Mbochi) against remnants of Ngouabi's supporters (Kouyou) and their counterpart southern FROLIBABA secret society. By 1985 Mbochi influence in Congo's corridors of power was immense: fully one-third of the PCT politburo and central committee were Mbochi, specifically from Edou/Oyo, Sassou Nguesso's home village. In the 1950's supportive of Opangault and his MSA party, their political leader currently is Sassou Nguesso. In the 1992 multiparty elections the latter's PCT secured most of its vote from Mbochi communities. See also POPULATION.

MBONGO, PIERRE OTTO. Powerful businessman and power-baron. A leading member of the Mbochi surrounding Sassou Nguesso before the liberalizations of the 1990's, and member of the radical **M-22** clique (though he had powerful enemies there), Mbongo grew extremely rich through his official contacts. A multi-millionaire in a Marxist society, whose business enterprises were neither nationalized nor taxed, Mbongo's wealth and influence stemmed from ownership of the Transafrica regional airline which he used to import items efficiently and at short notice for the elites of the region. (His planes, for example, were at the instant beck and call of the presidents of Zaire and the Central African Republic.) He was the region's major sanctions' buster vis-a-vis South Africa, since many of his dealings were with that country. He handled a large percentage of the diamonds sold by the Central African Republic to South Africa; imported fresh meat from the latter to equatorial Africa, and specialized equipment urgently needed from that country. In the late 1980's he strongly urged Sassou Nguesso and the M-22 to pull Congo out of Air-Afrique over the latter's dismissal of its Congolese head, Auxence Ickenga—an event that would have aided his own airline immeasurably. Mbongo was also involved in the **Mistral affair fiasco**. After the liberalizations of the 1990's his influence did not wane. Being a close relative of the new finance minister, Ngakosso, he became a broker for Congo's oil, and bought or acted as middleman for foreign interests interested in several of Congo's state companies then being privatized.

MBOUNGOU-MAYENGUE, DANIEL, 1950– . Linguist. Born in 1950 and with higher degrees in English, Mboungou-Mayengue was attached to the ministry of education before assuming his current post as program officer for translation and information of the Association of African Universities based in Accra.

MENGA, GUY, 1935– . Minister of information and one of Congo's leading authors and radio-TV administrators. A Bakongo born in 1935 in Mankonango, south of Brazzaville, after secondary studies Menga became a teacher, and then a school director. In 1961 he quit his job and went to Paris to study journalism, and on his return to Congo was given the post of program-director of Radio Brazzaville, before his 1967 appointment as director general of Congo's radio and television network. Purged from the civil service in 1971 Menga relocated to Paris, where he worked for Radio-France Internationale. A very productive literary figure, known for his collections of fables and legends, and his plays and novels, with the political liberalization in Congo in 1990 Menga returned to Congo. He was appointed minister of communications in the interim 1991 cabinet of André Milongo. He promptly fell afoul of the country's journalists with some of his policies that were seen as reintroduction of censorship, and was shifted to head the health ministry, serving until the 1992 elections that produced a new government.

MFOULOU, RAPHAEL, 1948– . Statistician and international administrator. Born in 1948 and trained in Abidjan, Yaoundé and Munich in statistics and demographics, Mfoulou was between 1971 and 1981 director of social and demographic statistics with the Congolese ministry of the plan. An international consultant since then, in 1987 Mfoulou joined the Institut de formation et de recherche démographique in Cameroun, where he still serves.

MIAKASSIBA, DIEUDONNE. Trade union leader and former President of the national assembly. A trade-union leader and manager of the Caisse Nationale de Prevoyance Sociale, Miakassiba was appointed to Congo's Economic and Social Council by Massamba-Debat in 1965. He was elected deputy to the national assembly and, becoming its president on July 20, 1973, thereby became also ex-officio member of the PCT politburo, and technically the number two person in Congo according to the constitution. He was not, however, a member of the PCT, and perhaps for that reason he received a no-confidence vote in December 1974 and lost his post as assembly president. In mid-August 1978, he was accused of plotting against the

Congo's revolutionary institutions and arrested. He was amnestied and reassigned middle-echelon duties in the state sector.

MIEAKANDA, DR. JOSEPH M'BADI. Physician. A Lari born on October 7, 1932 in Brazzaville, after attending the Catholic Chaminade mission school in Poto-Poto, he received a scholarship to study medicine in France. There he joined the PPC and contributed anti-colonialist articles to its press organ. He earned his medical degree from the University of Paris, and on returning to Congo, he became the third political secretary of the MNR (1964–68). In 1965–68, he was director of the Brazzaville general hospital, and in 1968 was named head of the Joseph Loubakou Medical School. With the rise of the northern Ngouabi regime Mieakanda was progressively closed out of political appointments, and concentrated on his medical work.

MIERASSA, CLEMENT. Minister of industrial development, fishing and crafts. A statistician by profession, and formerly a PCT militant from the Plateaux region, during the military era Mierassa had been a member of the PCT central committee where he was secretary for management and economic activity. He was dropped from the central committee in November 1984, and in 1989 was one of the first ex-PCT members to move into the opposition. In June 1991 he was appointed minister of trade and small and medium enterprises in the interim government of André Milongo, serving until the 1992 elections. The leader of a small party, the Parti Social-Démocrate Congolais, Mierassa was a candidate at the 1992 presidential elections but received only a very small vote. In a cabinet reshuffle in December 1992 he rejoined the cabinet.

MILANDOU, FULGENCE. Lari long-time mayor of Pointe Noire during the Sassou Nguesso era.

MILONGO, ANDRE, 1935– . Former interim Prime Minister of Congo. A Bakongo born on October 20, 1935 in Mankondi, after secondary education Milongo proceeded to the University of Nancy where he studied law (1957–1961) and at the Ecole nationale d'Administration in Paris (1961–1964). On his return to Brazzaville in 1964 he was appointed general treasurer of Congo. In 1969 he was shifted to director of the ministry of the plan's investments, and in 1975 he was attached to the Prime Minister's office as economic counsellor. In 1976 Milongo commenced his international career joining the African Development Bank in Abidjan, later also serving with the World Bank. Returning to Congo, Milongo got caught up in the drive for multipartyism and played a prominent role in the National Conference that brought about the eclipse of Sassou Nguesso and PCT rule. On June 8, 1991, at the end of the National Conference, he was elected interim Prime Minister of Congo, defeating Pascal Lissouba (the future President of Congo) on the fourth ballot by 454–419 votes. Charged with governing Congo until competitive elections were held, Milongo was not electorally strong enough in the subsequent presidential elections in which he presented his candidacy, being forced to drop out after the first round obtaining only 10.18% of the vote. He was, however, elected to the national assembly in 1993, and became speaker of the house. Milongo's party, the Union pour la Démocratie et la république (UDR), has only one seat (his own) in the assembly.

MINDOULI. District in the Pool region with administrative headquarters in the town of the same name.

MINING. Before French occupation, indigenous mining took place in Congo of iron, copper, and lead. Copper was the first to be mined on an industrial scale, but during the interwar period the focus shifted to lead and zinc. For many years, Moyen-Congo was known to be rich in various minerals, but most were thought to exist in too small quantities to justify mining. In 1957, a petroleum find at Pointe Indienne changed this picture, and although that deposit was soon exhausted, offshore drilling led to the discovery in 1969 and 1972 of far larger oil resources (see PETROLEUM). In 1959, petroleum prospectors came upon a vast potash deposit near Hollé. Because reserves of potash, iron, phosphates, and petroleum, as well as hydroelectrical resources, existed near Pointe Noire, industrialization of that region has been the most advanced.

Congo's mining code of 1962 was supplemented in 1965 by legislation that made mines the exclusive property of the state, with mining restricted to state companies, except for artisanal-type enterprises, and mixed-economy companies receiving special authorization to operate, in which case the state was to receive free at least 20 percent of the company's equity.

The history of Congo's mining sector has been of exaggerated expectations followed by disappointments. Initially, the great variety of minerals found in the country misled both the colonial and Congolese governments, as well as some foreign entrepreneurs to invest heavily in developing the two most promising resources, petroleum and potash. In the case of petroleum, the high hopes raised by the 1972 oil finds were soon dashed, only to be raised again with the newer ones in 1978. Then, for the second time disillusionment followed euphoria, but with a difference, since it was largely due to the global decline in prices, while in 1975–77 it was a result of assessments of imminent exhaustion of Congo's known oil resources. This has carried over into the 1990's since oil-prices have not recovered. No such recovery was experienced with respect to Congo's potash, that began to be exploited after inadequate geological studies, vast expenditures, and a failure to develop the proper techniques, leading to large initial losses and eventual closure of the mines after their flooding in 1977.

Mining (except for oil) received relatively small allocations in Congo's large 1982–86 development plan (curtailed when oil-royalties fell dramatically). The main projects supported were creation of a school of mines; development of lead, zinc and copper deposits at Yanga-Koubenza (near where a million tons of iron ore were discovered in 1986), and more quarries for building materials; feasibility studies of a chemical industry based on potash and phosphates, and prospecting in the Mayombe area.

(1) COPPER, LEAD, AND ZINC. Traces of copper in the Niari valley were first noted in 1877–78. Beginning in 1905, the deposit at Mindouli was worked by a Franco-Belgian concern, the Compagnie Miniere du Congo Français (CMCF). Between 1911 and 1914, that company shipped 47,000 tons of ore to Brazzaville. When the company ceased operations at Mindouli in 1936, a total of 9,100 tons of the metal had been exported from Congo. After World War II, prospecting in the same region was resumed. Although reserves amounting to 850,000 tons of ore, containing about 42,000 tons of metal, have been located in that area, copper output has been small, slow, and irregular. Briefly reopened after the war, the mine was closed again in 1971, after having produced only 2,000 tons. In 1980, the newly formed Société Congolaise de Recherches et d'Exploitation Minieres (SOCOREM), in association with a Swiss company, made still another attempt to mine copper, always in the same area. However, that mixed company, like its predecessors, was soon forced to cease operations.

The existence of lead and zinc in Congo has long been known, with indigenous mining taking place in the 19th century. In 1936, the CMCF transferred its activities from copper to those minerals, deposits of which had been discovered in the Mfouati area in 1931. From 1936 until it ceased operations in 1961, CMCF produced 115,000 tons of ore of 52 percent metal content, and 25,000 tons of over 40 percent metal content, mining the ore only when global prices for the metals were high. Because lead prices were usually higher than for zinc, production of the former was more regular, reaching a peak of 8,889 tons in 1959. Zinc production, on the other hand, ceased completely for long periods at a time, notably between 1946 and 1948 and from 1951 to 1962. In that year all the Mfouati mines were closed down, with prospecting and limited production resuming under a new company, the Société Miniere de M'Passa (SMM). In 1969, exhaustion of the richest deposits required SMM to buy new machinery, but by 1971 it had mined a total of only 3,000 tons of copper, lead, and zinc.

In 1965, a new impetus was given to mining in Niari by Soviet geologists, who estimated 350,000 tons of lead at Djenguile and 1.2 million tons at Yanga-Koutanza, at an average of 20 percent metal content. Within seven years, the Djenguile reserves were exhausted, and those at Yanga-Koutanza could not be mined by SOCOREM even though it had been formed in July 1979 to mine all deposits at Mfouati, including a plant to be built by the U.S.S.R. for experimentation in the enrichment of locally mined ores. Long delays in the arrival of Soviet machinery for the plant, and then its unsuitability for the task, retarded production, and in 1981 the USSR drafted a new project for both mining and processing the Yanga-Koutanza deposits. Under the 1982–86 development plan, output was to reach 30,000 tons of lead a year, almost twice the tonnage of that mineral produced in 1982. However, this project also suffered from the massive cuts in the expenditures originally scheduled under the 1982–86 Plan. No lead or zinc was exported in 1987, though starting in 1988 exports (at the level of 5,000–6,000 tons) recommenced. A large deposit of bitumen was also discovered in Mayombé in 1983, with at least 10% ore content, but no exploitation has commenced.

(2) GOLD. Gold mining was also mined in pre-colonial days Congo, and in 1935 it was organized along modern lines in Mayombe, and also at Sembe, Souanké, and Mayoko near the Gabonese frontier. The 504 kg. of gold exported in 1946 represented an accumulation during the war years. Annual production from that year until independence peaked at 435 kg. in 1950. With the exhaustion of the richest deposits and the abandonment of the poorest ones, production sank to 81 kg. in 1961 and 2.5 kg. in 1980. The last company to mine gold in Congo by modern methods was the Société Miniere Ogooué-Lobaye, that closed down in 1965. The 1982–86 plan called for continuing gold prospecting, but only a small deposit in the Kouilou region was added to the 4,500 to 5,000 kg. estimated as Congo's gold reserves.

(3) IRON. The discovery of Congo's iron resources date from 1962, when a BRGM mission found deposits in the Sangha, Zanaga, and Makoyo regions. Subsequently, millions of tons of iron ore, ranging from 50 percent to a very high 70 percent metal content, have been located, some not far from the tracks of the Comilog railroad. Mining of these deposits have not begun, nor did the ambitious 1982–86 plan envisage developing this sector, since the Congolese government preferred to devote available funds to higher-value minerals.

(4) TIN. Cassiterite (in association with wolfram and colombo-tantalite) was discovered in 1956 in Kayes district, 40 km. from the

Atlantic Ocean. Low metal content tin has also been mined in the Mayombé area, where production came to 44 tons in 1959. Since 1969, tin has not been listed among the Congo's exports. In mid-1972, the Bureau Minier Congolais completed prospecting for cassiterite at Moufoumbi, near the Gabon frontier, with reserves identified there in scattered deposits, estimated at 1,400 tons of low metal content.

(5) POTASH. Prospecting for oil by the Société des Petroles de l'Afrique Equatoriale (SPAFE) in the Pointe Indienne region in 1959 led to the discovery of potash near the Congo-Ocean railroad, 35 km. from Pointe Noire. Studies conducted (1960–1962) by the BRGM and the Mines de Potasses d'Alsace indicated the deposits extended over 4,000 sq. km. and contained 40 million tons of potassium oxide, as well as comparatively rare potash derivatives of carnallite and sylvanite. A concession was granted in 1964 by the Compagnie des Potasses du Congo (CPC), capitalized at 2.5 billion CFAF exclusively by French and Congolese funds. Plans were made to build a rail spur from Congo-Ocean's main line to Hollé, where a new city for some 1,200 workers was to be built, and to create a chemical industry for processing potash.

Additional capital totaling 25 billion CFAF were received from the BRGM, SPAFE, and the two local oil companies, as well as a loan from the World Bank. In 1969, when the CPC began mining potash, its output was 66,622 tons, leading to optimism that Congo would become Africa's leading potash producer. During the nine years of CPC's operations production totaled 3.11 million tons. By 1975, however so many technical difficulties had arisen that mining for sylvanite ceased, and by 1977, CPC ceased operations altogether because of a disastrous flood; its debt amounted to nine billion CFAF. Already by 1975, when CPC threatened to close down, Congo denounced the move as an "imperialist" effort to undermine the revolution, and proposals to recompense dismissed mine employees as a "poisoned gift from France," but two years later, after several attempts to salvage the CPC, the unexpected flooding of the mine settled the issue. In 1985 the CPC (with 51% Congolese funding) was revived to prospect and exploit other potash sites. New deposits were discovered but cost considerations have prevented any actual mining.

(6) DIAMONDS. Diamonds are found in Divenié, Komono, Sibiti, and in a few other sites in Congo, but in small amounts and of poor quality. From 1951 through 1959, 3,200 carats were produced, but since then production has ceased. Smuggled stones from neighboring countries have sometimes been mistaken for indigenous stones.

(7) MARBLE. Marble is mined in quarries at Yanga, Ouesso, and Malélé for building purposes in towns. Reserves at Lake Kitina are estimated at four to five million tons.

(8) URANIUM. Prospecting for uranium is a relatively recent de-

velopment. A concession in 1980 to Agip Recherches Congo for a 36,000 sq. km. area in the southwest was followed the next year by a similar prospecting permit to Elf-Aquitaine in all areas not covered by Agip's permit. France was offered aid to Congo in the search for uranium in the Mayombe range, but in the mid-1980's the global uranium glut made uranium production economically not viable.

(9) PHOSPHATES. Since 1938 phosphate has been found along a band of 100 km. parallel to the west flank of the Mayombé range. Smaller deposits have also been found in an area running from the Gabonese frontier to Cabinda, the most important of which are at Tchivoula (4.4 million tons), which is under water, and at Loufika, in swampy ground. Studies of these deposits have been going on since 1946, and successive companies have been formed to mine them, but no production has occurred. The most promising of these companies is a mixed Bulgaro-Congolese concern, SOPHOSCO. Congo possesses large resources of phosphates, but their low metal content and dispersal over difficult terrain are deterrents to their development, unless high global prices can be assumed, an unlikely eventuality.

MINOTERIE-ALIMENTS DU BETAIL (MAB). State enterprise set up in 1978 with 2,650 million CFAF in Nyaki with a checkered production history. MAB took over the non-sugar activities of the deficit-ridden SIA-CONGO, and has a monopoly over the import of cereals, the production of flour, farina and cattle-feed. Perennially deficitory, it has intermittently been bankrupt.

MISTRAL AFFAIR. A convoluted 1988 attempt by high state individuals to purchase 50 highly sophisticated French Mistral surface-to-air missiles (comparable to the U.S. Stinger missiles) allegedly for the use of the Congolese armed forces, and ship them onwards to a third party for profit, the third party variously identified as either South Africa or Angola. The plot was unravelled when defence officials in Paris questioned the need of the Congolese armed forces for such sophisticated weaponry, that had never before been exported to Africa. In querying the purchase order, Congolese defence officials whose signatures were on the documents, and from whom large deposits had been received, alleged they were unaware of the deal, and claimed their signatures had been forged. In France a trial took place of several French middlemen, though in Congo the matter was brushed under the carpet, since it involved the activities of high PCT and cabinet members.

MITAKO. A brass rod, of differing diameter/length, used as a currency from the Loango coast through Batéké areas until the first two decades of the twentieth century. See also CURRENCY.

MKOUKOUELE, CHRISTOPHE. Secretary general of the **UPADS** political party alliance backing current President Pascal Lissouba. He had previously been a political commissioner in the Sangha region until 1989 when he was accused of being involved in ivory smuggling.

MOKOKO, JEAN-MARIE MICHEL (General), 1947– . Congo's senior-ranking military officer and former chief of staff. Born in Mossaka on March 19, 1947 of Batéké origins, and a cousin of the then-powerful **Major Katali**, Mokoko in 1983, then a Captain, headed the Direction de Renseignements Militaires (DRM). Originally a protege of Colonel Yhomby Opango, he shifted loyalties to Sassou Nguesso and progressed through the officer ranks. Rapidly promoted to Colonel in July 1985, he then became chief of staff of Congo's ground forces and commander of the Brazzaville autonomous military zone. In July 1987 he was appointed chief of general staff of the Congolese armed forces. He was personally involved in the operation sent out to quell the rebellion in Owando of **Captain Anga**, that was done with many deaths. Promoted to the rank of General in 1990, he was not regarded as intrinsically loyal by the new civilian regime in Brazzaville, and was reassigned to other duties by Lissouba who chose another chief of staff.

MONDJO, NICOLAS, 1933– . Former foreign minister. Born on June 24, 1933, in Owando, Mondjo served as a clerk at various courts in Congo and Chad following which he attended IHEOM in Paris. He was then named prefect of the Sangha district, moved later to be prefect of Djoué. In 1963 he was appointed director of the ministry of interior and in 1964 was appointed by Massamba-Debat ambassador to France. In January 1968 he returned to Brazzaville to join the cabinet as foreign minister. He retained that portfolio under the military regime of Ngouabi until June 1970, when, regarded as too moderate, he was appointed Congo's permanent representative to the United Nations, as well as ambassador to Canada. At the end of his appointment he remained overseas.

MONKA, ERNEST, 1941– . Civil engineer. Born in 1941, and educated as a civil engineer in Bamako, Mali, Monka worked with the ministry of public works between 1960 and 1980 when he was attached to work on the Mombasa-Lagos transafrican road project, periodically shifted to sites of construction, most recently to Bangui, Central African Republic.

MONMONDJO, LECAS ATONDI, 1940– . Journalist. Educated in both Congo and France and possessing an MA in Linguistics, in 1971 he was appointed director of the Ecole Nationale d'Administration. Shortly later, in 1972 he was arrested in connection with the **Ange Diawara** ultra-Left attempted putsch. Sentenced to death, he was soon released. He then went overseas into self-exile and taught in a school in Pontoise, France. After Sassou Nguesso's rise to power he returned to Brazzaville to teach at Marien Ngouabi University (1980–1984) and in 1985 was appointed director of the People's Bookshops network. He was again arrested in 1987 for complicity in the **Anga** rebellion, sentenced to death, and was only released in 1992.

MONOKOTUBA. A local dialect widely used by southern Congolese as a lingua franca. See LANGUAGE.

MOSSAKA. District in the Cuvette region, with headquarters in the town with the same name. The district is dissected by numerous rivers (Sangha, Likouala, Likouala-aux-Herbes, Kouyou, N'Deko), and for most people communication is by dugout canoes. There is forestry exploitation in the district, as well as palm, coffee and cacao plantations.

MOSSENDJO. Congo's seventh-largest town, in the Niari region. The town has been growing very slowly, losing population to other regional centers, and especially to Pointe Noire. In 1992 its population was estimated at around 15,000, and it had just lost sixth rank to Sibiti. Mossendjo is also a district in the region of Niari, with administrative headquarters in the town with the same name.

MOUA-MBENGA, MARIUS. Former cabinet minister. Moua-Mbenga joined the cabinet on December 18, 1975, as minister of rural economy and retained that post till April 1979 when he was shifted to become minister of industry and tourism. In January 1980 he was shifted back to his old post as minister of rural economy, and in the cabinet reshuffle of December 28, 1980, his portfolio was changed to minister of agriculture and animal husbandry. He was retired from the cabinet in 1984 and assigned director of a division in the ministry of agriculture.

MOUAMBA, CLEMENT. Minister of finance, the economy and planning. A former PCT member, with the political liberalizations in Congo Mouamba changed loyalties, supporting Lissouba, and joined the cabinet on September 8, 1992.

MOUANGASSA, FERDINAND, 1934–1974. Civil administrator and playwright. Born in the Bacongo quarter of Brazzaville on December

18, 1934 to a family of petty civil servants, Mouangassa attended the Chaminade seminary in Brazzaville, and in 1952, at the age of 18, formed his first theatrical group. Having to fend for a living he enrolled in 1955 in a course for infirmary workers, and by 1965 was administrator at a Pointe Noire hospital. There he again put together a theatrical group that was very successful. In 1967 he published his first play, followed next year by another. In 1968 he also assumed the post of director of statistical services at the ministry of health and social services. In 1974 he was dispatched to France for further studies prior to promotion but died in a traffic accident.

MOUDILENO-MASSENGO, ALOYSE, 1933– . Former vice-president of Congo. A Lari born on March 11, 1933 in Vinza in the Pool region, Moudileno-Massengo earned a law degree in France. He remained there for 17 years and was an active member of **FEANF**. With the rise of the Ngouabi regime he was named minister of justice and labor, and he also acquired the information portfolio in February 1971. As a result of the major purge of the PCT in December 1971, he succeeded Raoul as vice-president of Congo while remaining minister of justice. In August 1972, he too was expelled from the PCT because he refused to return to the Congo following an official trip to France. He briefly returned to Congo in February 1974 under a broad amnesty but eventually returned to France. There he wrote the book *Ideological Imposture,* denouncing Ngouabi and the latter's Marxist pretensions. In the mid-1980's he set up a moderate Marxist opposition movement in exile, the *Mouvement Patriotique Congolaise* (MPC), calling for Yhomby Opango's reinstatement as President. The MPC, however, became immobilized due to leadership splits between him and co-leader Ekondi Akola, and was largely moribund. After the liberalizations of 1990 in Congo he returned to Congo and set up a small political party.

MOUKOUEKE, CHRISTOPHE. Former minister. A teacher by profession, Moukouéké was named in December 1971 minister of primary and secondary education, and was co-opted into the central committee of the PCT. He served on the revolutionary court of justice where he was elected its vice-president. He was dropped from the government in January 1973, but was then named a secretary for the PCT central committee's commission on propaganda. On January 9, 1975 Moukouéké rejoined the cabinet as minister of information, and in January 1976 was named secretary general of the University of Brazzaville.

MOUNKOUNGOUNA. An anti-sorcery movement that began sweeping through Bakongo areas in 1951, promising relief from witchcraft-related diseases and malfunctune.

MOULOUNDA-MALONGA, OMER, 1946– . Former Sassou Nguesso cultural attache. Born on September 8, 1946 and educated in Algeria in Physical Education (1975), he served until 1977 as director of studies at the national institute of sports in Brazzaville. He was then brought into the Presidential Office as cultural attache with particular duties over coordinating sport activities in Congo, on secondment from the higher institute of physical education. In 1985 he rejoined the latter institute where he coordinates all sports activities in the country.

MOUMBEMBE, JEAN-PAUL. Better known under his literary pseudonym, M'Beni-M'Bongo, Moumbembe is a published author who studied economics at Marien Ngouabi University and works in the ministry of the plan.

MOUNGALLA, JEROME, 1943– . Educationist. A Vili born on June 18, 1943 in Pointe Noire, Moungalla was educated in Sibiti and Loubomo following which he went to France for studies at the University of Caen. In 1965 he was appointed director of technical education in Congo, and in 1969 was named inspector-general of technical education serving in that post until 1973. He was then named secretary-general of higher education, and in 1974 head of a variety of senior educational bodies including of INRAP and of the department of teacher training for technical education at Marien Ngouabi University.

MOUNTHAULT, HILAIRE, 1931– . Former cabinet minister. A Vili born in Pointe Noire on June 27, 1931, Mounthault was educated as an engineer and then secured additional training in economics at Washington's International Development Institute. A public works engineer in Brazzaville, and later director general of public works (1962–1970), Mounthault was also a member of the MNR politburo and director of its bimonthly, *Etumba.* After the rise of the Ngouabi regime he was elected to the national assembly, serving between 1973 and 1977. In 1977 he was appointed director-general of the Agence Transcongolaise de Communications, serving in this post until 1979. He was then integrated into the cabinet as minister of transport and civil aviation serving until 1985 when he was shifted to head a state corporation.

MOUNTOU, BAYONNE. Vili PCT militant from the Pointe Noire area, and until 1989 president of the Congo women's movement.

MOUNTSAKA, DAVID (Colonel). Former commander in chief of the Congolese armed forces. A Bakongo, Mountsaka was one of the very few indigenous officers at the time of the 1963 upheavals against President Fulbert Youlou. Unwilling to give the order to fire at the demonstrators calling for Youlou's demise, Mountsaka, together with Major Mouzabakany, led the delegation that persuaded Youlou to resign peacefully on August 15, 1963. Named by his cousin, President Massamba-Debat, commander-in-chief of the armed forces, he was sent to Peking in September 1964 on a good-will mission. Mountsaka was very unpopular with the armed forces troops, most northerners, and was twice kidnapped by mutineers, in 1963, and again in 1966 at the time when Massamba-Debat ordered Ngouabi arrested. After the second episode, he was not reinstated in his command, but in August 1967 was named ambassador to Algeria. In December 1970, he was appointed head of the Société de Transformation du Bois, then technical adviser to the presidency, and still later, director of Congo's publishing services. Assumed to be implicated in Ngouabi's assassination in 1977, he was sentenced, but later freed. In 1980 he went into self-exile, to form an opposition party, the *Conseil National de l'Opposition Congolaise.*

MOUSSA, PIERRE. Important Cuvette leader, Sassou Nguesso ally, and former foreign minister. Moussa joined the government of April 4, 1979 as minister of planning, and remained in the inner circles of power virtually until Sassou Nguesso's eclipse, most recently as foreign minister. Leader of a faction of the M-22, Moussa has been at loggerheads with the latter's Mbochi segment, and especially with **Pierre Otto Mbongo**. Moussa was strongly under M-22 attack in 1989 over his alleged role in the **Mistral affair**. He retained his party post, however, being elected in the July 1989 PCT congress as president of the planning and economic committee.

MOUVEMENT CONGOLAIS POUR LE DEMOCRATIE ET LE DEVELOPPEMENT INTEGRAL (MCDDI). Bernard Kolelas' largely Bakongo political party that is in opposition to Pascal Lissouba's UPADS and in a parliamentary alliance with the PCT of Sassou Nguesso, Set up in 1990, in the subsequent series of competitive elections it garnered much of the Lari-Bakongo vote, especially in the Pool region and in Brazzaville, secured Kolelas Brazzaville's mayoralty, won 297 of the 1,000-odd local government seats, 29 of the legislature's and 13 of the Senate seats.

MOUVEMENT DU 22 FEVRIER (M-22). Radical inter-ethnic pressure group in the Congo of the 1970's and 1980's. Created in the early 1970s by those who escaped after the **Ange Diawara** leftist attempted putsch of 1972. The M-22 was underground for some time, and many of its leaders were arrested or went into exile. Later resurrected as a hard-line pro-Soviet (rather than pro-Chinese) movement, and casually referred to also as the *Parti Communiste du Congo,* Sassou Nguesso rehabilitated a number of its top leaders in order to counterbalance **Colonel Katali's Impfondo group** subclique's influence, by sustaining a second Marxist pole. The leader, and most influential member of the M-22 was **Camille Bongou**, who as PCT secretary-general was also technically Sassou Nguesso's regime's number two man. Other leading politicians included Joseph Elenga-Ngaporo; Bernard Combo Matsiona; Atondi Monmondjo; Ambroise Noumazalaye and Florent Tsiba. Until the movement was eclipsed with the fall of global Marxism and, of course the PCT military regime, their support was mainly in the armed forces, among northern students and the trade unions. M-22's strategy was to constantly exert pressure upon the regime for greater radicalization, and eventually gain supreme power. Though the movement was inter-ethnic, it had sharp inter-personal, inter-ethnic (Kouyou vs. Mbochi) and regional cleavages. Within it, in particular, the Impfondo group was very vocal about the need to assure that region "also" had a turn at the presidency, since all other regions had had "their turn."

MOUVEMENT NATIONAL DE LA REVOLUTION (MNR). This was the single party under the Massamba-Debat reign. Constituted in July 1964, it later served as the prototype for Marien Ngouabi's *Parti Congolais du Travail* (PCT), created in December 1969, though their ethnic base was different, and the PCT was (until 1989) a vanguard party of (mostly) dedicated Marxists. In the countrywide network of party cells, supplemented by women's and youth mass movements, were the base for a pyramidal structure. At its apex was the national party congress, to which the constituent units sent delegates every five years. A central committee chosen by that congress met four times each year; in the intervals between quarterly meetings, the central committee in turn delegated its authority to the politburo (initially called the *Conseil National de la Révolution,* or CNR), whose chairman was also the head of state. Attaining Scientific Socialism was the goal of the MNR.

The MNR's membership was a mix of UDDIA holdovers, trade-union leaders, and intellectuals trained in France, more or less agreed on a policy embracing (1) the elimination of neocolonialism in the government and bureaucracy, armed forces, and support for the struggle against imperialism throughout the world, (2) a diplomatic opening and commercial relations with the Eastern bloc, completely precluded from Brazzaville under the antecedent government of Youlou, (3) establishment of a secular state in which public education would be nationalized, (4) an emphasis on state enterprises in the country's economy, and (5) unification under MNR's aegis of mass organizations of women, youth, and labor, in which the **JMNR** would be the radical standard-bearer.

The coexistence of parallel executive bodies in the government and in the MNR enabled Massamba-Debat as head of state and president of the party's central committee, to play their members off against each other, but with decreasing effectiveness. His insistence on technical expertise as the yardstick for holding office disappointed many ethnic leaders, especially the Lari, and the mild form of socialism he practiced disenchanted the increasingly radical youth. Their plottings caused Massamba-Debat to dismiss his left-wing premier, Ambroise Noumazalaye in January 1968, and himself take over the government. During the next months, Massamba-Debat's increasing authoritarian and conservative stances alienated former supporters, including the army officers who in August joined forces with his ethnic and ideological opponents. On September 4, 1968, Massamba-Debat resigned as president of the republic and of the MNR, and Major Marien Ngouabi assumed power.

MOUVEMENT PATRIOTIQUE CONGOLAIS. During the latter part of the reign of General Sassou Nguesso, the MPC was one of two main opposition groups in exile in France, headed by the lawyer **Moudileno-Massengo** and by **Ekondi Akola**. The fact that the two were at loggerheads with each other robbed the party of both unity and vitality. Moreover, the MPC's mild Marxist leanings meant it was isolated from the broad spectrum of more moderate Congolese opinion in France and at home. The MPC supported the return to power of colonel Yhomby Opango, and became irrelevant with the onset of multipartyism. See also POLITICAL PARTIES.

MOUVEMENT SOCIALISTE AFRICAIN (MSA). Early political party. Founded in 1946 by **Jacques Opangault** and affiliated with the French SFIO, this party was the main rival of **Félix Tchicaya's** PPC until 1956 when Fulbert Youlou's UDDIA began to rise in strength, dislodging the hitherto apolitical Lari rivetted to Matsouanism. The party grouped more militant members in Congo, had close relations with the 'progressive' leader of neighboring Oubangui Chari (Barthelemy Boganda) but was essentially a party of the country's northern ethnic groups, especially the Mbochi. The MSA was outmaneuvered in the territorial assembly, allowing the formation of a government under Youlou that led the country to independence. See also POLITICAL PARTIES.

MOUYABI, ANDRE-GEORGES, 1935–. Minister of the Civil Service and former president of the national assembly. Born in 1935 in Madingou, after attending school in Gabon, he became a teacher and school principal in Congo. In 1960, he went to France for further training. Upon his return, President Youlou placed him in charge of the Centre National de Documentation Pedagogique. He was elected to the legislature in December 1963 and to its presidency in May 1966, after the assembly expelled Leon Angor. With the rise of the Ngouabi regime he was appointed, in September 1968, secretary of the CNR directorate. Dropped from that post a few months later, he was named ambassador to Cuba. He joined the government of Lopes in August 1973 as minister of industry and mines, leaving the government two years later to assume a position in the state sector. Later in self-exile for several years, he returned to Brazzaville with the onset of the political liberalizations and was appointed minister of the civil service on September 8, 1992.

MOUYELO KATOULA, MICHEL, 1951–. Mathematician. Born in 1951 and educated in mathematics and statistics, on his return to Brazzaville in 1977 Mouyelo Katoula was appointed director of statistics and economic accounts in the ministry of the plan, before assuming the post, later that year, of director of economic coordination and research at the same ministry. In 1980 he was reassigned to the national accountancy division of the Union Douanière et economique de l'Afrique Centrale, based in Bangui, Central African Republic.

MOUZABAKANY, FELIX (Colonel). Former deputy chief of staff of the Congolese armed forces. A Bakongo, and one of the few indigenous officers at the time, in 1963 Mouzabakany refused to order his troops to fire against the demonstrators calling for Fulbert Youlou's overthrow (during Les Trois Glorieuses), and together with **Captain Mountsaka** convinced Youlou to resign peacefully. Promoted to Major and deputy chief of staff serving under Mountsaka by the successor President Massamba-Debat, Mouzabakany was arrested in 1966 for a plot to restore Youlou to power. He was released by the army mutineers in August 1968 (who released all military prisoners). Mouzabakany was brought into the subsequent Ngouabi government as minister of interior but was dropped from the cabinet a few months later. He was re-arrested again in February 1969 and sentenced to life imprisonment in July that year for anti-revolutionary activities. Amnestied in 1973, he was in 1978 implicated in Ngouabi's earlier assassination, at which time he slipped away to Zaire and eventually to France.

MOYAMBE MOUNTAINS. A chain of hills of 800 meters-height, stretching for 60 kms. southwest of Brazzaville, at the midst of which is found the city of Loubonou, Congo's third-largest. The region is ethnically mixed, includes a number of smaller Bakongo clans, and historically demarcated the divide between the zones of influence of the Vili of Loango and the Batéké.

MPAN, OKANA. Politician aspirant, leader of a political party, the Union du Centre (UC), set up in 1992.

MUSLIMS. See ISLAM; RELIGION.

M'VOUAMA, PIERRE, 1934– . Former cabinet minister. A Bakongo born in Kamon in the Kinkala district on May 24, 1934, M'Vouama was trained locally and then went to France to study physics at the universities of Bordeaux, Grenoble and Paris, becoming a telecommunications engineer. He was active in student politics in France, and was elected president of the Congolese students' association there, and after the 1963 coup as vice-president of the MNR students' section in Paris. On his return to Brazzaville in July 1965 he was appointed head of the telecommunications section of the ministry of posts, and in May 1966 he was brought into Massamba-Debat's government as minister of information, popular education, culture and arts. He was not cut out, however, for the rough and tumble of the radicalization of Congolese politics, and by 1968 he was dropped, reassigned back as head of telecommunications.

M'VOUTI. District in the Kouilou region with administrative headquarters in the village of the same name. It has an area of 385 sq. kms. and includes the core of the **Mayombé** mountains.

MWETI. A national French-language newspaper that began publication in Brazzaville on September 1, 1977. It gradually evolved from a twice-weekly publication schedule (1977–79) to publication four times a week (August 1982). Its director is Emmanuel Kiala-Matouba, and its chief editor is Hubert Madouaba. Of the 8,000 copies of each tabloid-form issue (12–16 pages) printed, 7,500 are distributed; it also prints special issues in larger runs.

-N-

NABEMBA. Congo's highest peak at 1,000 meters, found in the northern Sangha region.

NATIONAL CONFERENCE. See CONFERENCE NATIONALE.

NATIONAL PARKS. Congo, a country of considerable beauty, nevertheless does not have any particular sites of such outstanding tourist potential to merit investment in easily-accessible national parks, nor does the high cost of visiting the country bring in many visitors in any case. (Only 40,000 a year.) Thus the parks that exist are essentially nature and wildlife reserves more protected by the relative absence of human predators (due to the sparse population) than by legislation. The country has one park (the Parc National d'Odzala, 126,000 hectares), in the Congo river basin, where one can find elephants, hippos, large antelopes, buffalo, leopards, gorillas, and aquatic muskdeer; and five reserves: Lefini (630,000 hectares), 300 kms from Brazzaville via a paved road where one can see monkeys, bushbucks and buffalo; Lekoli-Pandaka (54,000), contiguous to the Odzala park, with the same wildlife and also lions; Mont Fouari (16,000), Nuanga-Nord (18,000), and the Domaine de Mboko (2,800). In 1994 the World Bank granted Congo funds for, *inter alia,* promoting tourism and tourist facilities in the northern forests, an area still little explored, and the natural habitat of pygmies, gorillas, and the alleged 'pre-historic monster' that was sighted in the 1970's and resulted in several scientific expeditions being mounted.

NBIHOULA, ALPHONSE. Secretary general of the 1991 party, the Union pour le progrès du peuple congolais (UPPC).

NDALLA, CLAUDE-ERNEST 1943– . Radical politician, former cabinet minister, and one of the "wild men" of Congo. Born on May 25, 1937 in Brazzaville, where he attended secondary school, Ndalla then studied mathematics at the University of Toulouse from which, without receiving a degree, he went on to study chemistry in Moscow (also not obtaining a degree); he also visited Peking. Returning to Brazzaville after Fulbert Youlou's overthrow, he utilized the youth movement in Niari, his political fiefdom, to ride to power, adopting a suffix to his name "Graille" (Ndalla-Graille). He was elected to the JMNR executive committee and became editor of its organ, *Dipanda* (1964–68). Later, in April 1965 he was appointed secretary of state for youth. He was charged with embezzlement early in 1966 and was dropped from the cabinet. He soon returned to public life, however, as director of Brazzaville radio, and held that post until appointed ambassador to China, North Korea and North Vietnam in February 1969. On his return to Brazzaville later that same year, with a reputation as the leading Maoist, he helped found the PCT party, served as its first secretary (thus becoming the regime's number two man) and was its politburo secretary in charge of propaganda. He was nevertheless dropped from the party in the major purge of December 1971 for "ideological insufficiency." Arrested as a leader of the **Ange Diawara** February 1972 revolt, he was first given a death sentence, but later this was commuted to life imprisonment. In 1976 he was pardoned by Ngouabi, but was again arrested after Ngouabi's assassination in March 1977 on suspicion of participating in the plot. Sentenced to a life sentence with forced labor, he was banished to a camp in the Far North. He was amnestied after Sassou Nguesso's rise to power, and rehabilitated joined the cabinet in 1979 as minister of youth and sports, remaining in that capacity until 1981. In 1986 he was arrested for conspiracy in a 1982 coup plot and for the third time was sentenced to death. Commuted to life imprisonment, Ndalla was only released from prison on August 15, 1990, in time to join the national conference.

NDALLA-GRAILLE. See NDALLA, CLAUDE-ERNEST.

N'DEBEKA, MAXIME, 1944– . Former radical army officer, poet and dramatologist. Born in Brazzaville on March 10, 1944, and educated at the College Chaminade, N'Débéka specialized in electronics, studying in both French and Soviet military colleges. After additional training with artillery in China he was integrated in the Congolese army and returned to Brazzaville, becoming a JMNR leader, and in 1968 was appointed director-general of cultural affairs, and later was brought into the PCT Politburo. Regarded as the "poet of the Congolese revolution" some of his early poems reflected his impressions from China. Involved in the **Ange Diawara** leftist attempted putsch, N'Débéka was purged from the party and army and condemned to death for his role. Kept in Brazzaville and Ouesso, he was amnestied two years later and retired to Mbamou (in the Pool region) where, under strict house surveillance, he continued writing poetry. In 1976 he started working in the library of Marien Ngouabi University for a living, and in 1982 relocated to France where he has coordinated cultural affairs. N'Débéka is the author of several books and collections of poetry, and since the 1980's he has branched off into writing plays. He is regarded as one of Congo's greatest authors.

NDINGA-OBA, ANTOINE, 1941– . Former foreign minister. A Mbochi born in 1941 in Biala, Ndinga-Oba earned a doctorate in linguistics in France, following which he was appointed in 1971 director of the Institut National des Recherches et d'Action Pédagogique, moving in 1973 to head the Institut Supérieur des Sciences et de l'Education. In 1976 he was appointed rector of the University of Brazzaville, until 1977 when he entered the cabinet as minister of education. He remained in that position for the lengthy period of seven years, until 1984, being also a member of the PCT Politburo. In 1984 he replaced Nze as foreign minister. His tenure in that post was short. In November 1986 he caused a diplomatic flap with the US by comparing Israel and South Africa to Nazi Germany, that necessitated an official apology from president Sassou Nguesso and his replacement as foreign minister and PCT Politburo member. He has since returned to the academic world.

NDJOBI. One of Congo's many syncretic religious cults. Spreading in the 1940's from the Obamba living in the vicinity of Franceville in neighboring Gabon, among whom it was first established, Ndjobi is currently found in many parts of Congo. It requires adherents to dispose of any prior fetishes acquired (that it regards as false) and medals (viewed as "European fetishes"). It recruits males, provides magic and herbal cures against sorcery, illnesses and spells (for a fee), and is so influential in some districts, having integrated village chiefs and influentials, or undermined the influence of those who have refused to join, that local authorities, and during the revolutionary era PCT hierarchies, have co-opted some of its leaders into consultative and decision-making structures. Indeed, even residents of Brazzaville and Pointe Noire travel to Ndjobi centers to obtain occult protection from its practitioners.

NEWSPAPERS. See PRESS.

NGAA-PFUNA. Among the **Kukuya**, a Batéké clan, the Ngaa-pfuna is the possessor of witchcraft powers, that is passed on within each family. Witchcraft is called *pfuna*.

NGAKOSSO, EDOUARD, 1941– . Former cabinet minister. Born in Brazzaville, and a member of the PCT Ngakosso worked up the administration, serving as director of taxation until July 1989 when he was appointed minister of finance and the budget. He served in that post until 1991.

NGANGA, APOLLINAIRE, 1941– . Educationist and deputy to the national assembly. Born on November 21, 1941 and educated at the University of Paris in Literature, Nganga returned to Brazzaville to teach at the Higher Institute of Education of Marien Ngouabi University. Elected to the national assembly in 1984 he also served as its secretary-general.

NGANGA, BERNARD, 1945– . Vice-rector of Marien Ngouabi University. Born on August 6, 1945, and earning a doctorate in English at the University of Bordeaux in 1972, Nganga was head of the department of languages (and former Dean of the Faculty of Humanities) before his appointment as vice-rector.

NGOIE-NGALLA, DOMINIQUE, 1943– . Educationist and poet. Born in 1943 in Kivembe in the Bouenza region, he obtained a PhD in history at the university of Poitiers (1967) and Bordeaux (1970). Introduced at an early age to organ music and 15th-16th century Flemish painting, Ngoie-Ngalla, a former head of department, teaches ancient history at Marien Ngouabi university, and is the author of five collections of poetry and an autobiography.

NGOLLO, RAYMOND-DAMAS (General). Minister of Defence. A Batéké from Gomboma (Plateaux region) trained in St. Cyr, Ngollo was a member of the PCT central committee when, in December 1975, he was appointed chief of general staff, and, after Ngouabi's assassination, a member of the ruling PCT military committee. On December 28, 1980 he was named minister of defense. In 1984 he was shifted to head the ministry of local government, and later the ministry of forestry. Ngollo returned back to his defence ministry in December 1990, ceding it at the outset of the interim civilian government of Milongo, but was invited back to assume the ministry when Milongo's choice was unacceptable to the army. Authoritative, loyal to civilian rule, he has played a major stabilizing role in civil-military relations in contemporary Congo, by bridging the inter-ethnic chasm.

NGOLONDELE, EMMANUEL MONGO (General). Former director-general of Congo's security forces. Specializing in internal security, Ngolondélé headed Congo's security services between 1978 and May 1988 when he was re-assigned to other duties. Though deeply implicated in the **Mistral affair**, Ngolondélé, a Batéké from the Plateaux region, was in 1992 appointed head of President Lissouba's military staff, being regarded as reliable.

NGOT, SIMON-PIERRE KINGOUGA. Early politician. Ngot was a close collaborator of former president Fulbert Youlou, and mayor of Dolisie (currently Loubomo.)

NGOUABI, MARIEN, 1938–1977. Former President of Congo. A Kouyou, born in Ombélé, near Owando (ex-Fort Rousset) in northeast Congo, to a chiefly branch of his village on December 31, 1938. Ngouabi attended the Général Leclerc school for children of veterans in Brazzaville, and, joining the army served in Bouar (CAR) where he became a Sergeant, saw action against the Bamiliké rebellion in Cameroun in 1958–1960, and then was dispatched for military training in France, first at Strasbourg (where he obtained his paratrooper wings), and then to St. Cyr, graduating in 1962 with the rank of second lieutenant. His impetuous temperament was already twice evident in those early years: in 1960 in Douala, where he was arrested for 30 days and then shipped back to Congo, for commenting aloud about the injustice in suppressing the Bamiliké, and in Brazzaville immediately after that when he joined in the Poto Poto ethnic riots and was imprisoned for 60 days. A telex from St. Cyr accepting his officer's candidacy saved him on the latter occasion.

He was trained in St. Cyr together with Yhomby Opango, and also met there Raoul, the three later becoming key allies in the army and in the regime Ngouabi was to establish after he seized power. On his return to the Congo, he was named second in command of the Pointe Noire garrison. In 1963, he was given charge of the newly created paratroop corps at Brazzaville with the rank of captain. During this period he allegedly began reading Marxist literature. In 1965 he was integrated into the ruling MNR party as representative of the armed forces. Friction with the **JMNR**, the latter's taunts against the "reactionary" army, and attempts to ideologically retrain the army by individuals outside the military hierarchy polarized the army, that progressively became disenchanted with Massamba-Debat. The latter twice tried to ward off the military threat posed by Ngouabi: by demoting him in June 1966 for insubordination, and having him arrested in July 1968. However, Ngouabi, a charismatic officer fully in control of the armed forces, could not be shunted aside, and in the second instance his arrest led to the army mutiny that released him from prison and led to the military takeover of power.

After his takeover Ngouabi became commander-in-chief of the armed forces. He founded the new Marxist-Leninist PCT party, and was president of Congo until 1977. His reign was punctuated by a variety of armed assaults and/or conspiracies from both the left and the right, the most serious of which was the 1972 attempted putsch by

Ange Diawara that nearly succeeded. A sincere, honest, and popular leader, ideologically he was very much a moderate middle-man, constantly forced to balance competing ideological party factions, civilian and military political barons, periodically purging them in his quest for personal loyalty, and ultimately threatening all groups. He was assassinated by a suicide squad on March 18, 1977 under still-mysterious circumstances, allegedly on the orders of a coalition of northern military leaders (Sassou-Nguesso's name has been constantly linked to the plot) and PCT political barons worried about a possible opening of political space for former Bakongo civilian leaders. After his assassination (in which all those involved were inexplicably shot to death) a number of important Bakongo leaders were summarily executed (notably Massamba-Debat) or murdered (Cardinal Biayenda). In what has been referred to as the "trial of revolution" televised and broadcast directly by TV and radio, another group of accused, 95% of them southerners, were denied basic defense rights in a trial that became a settling of old scores, spilling over into a campaign against magic and traditional religion, with no real charges against the accused really proven. Most of those sentenced by the court for their role in the murder were in due course released by Sassou-Nguesso. Rumors about who ordered Ngouabi's assassination continue: in 1984 Sassou Nguesso was accused by Congolese Marxists in exile in France; the 1987 rebellion of **Captain Anga** was over a similar accusation; during the 1991 national conference the charge was voiced publicly. In March 1972, Ngouabi married a Congolese of Bakongo ethnicity, after having been separated for two years from his French wife. His son, Marien Ngouabi Jr. (born in 1964) committed suicide in Brazzaville on September 14, 1992.

NGOUNZISM. See KAKISM.

NGOUONIMBA, NZARI HENRI PIERRE. Educator and former diplomat. Trained as a teacher, Ngounimba worked as an instructor in public primary schools until he was appointed director of the People's College at Brazzaville in July 1969. In that year he was also appointed president of the Congo's revolutionary court of justice. He was briefly a member of the PCT central committee, but was dropped from that body when he was named secretary of state in charge of development (1970–1971). In August 1971, he succeeded Boukambou as ambassador to the USSR, following which he returned to Brazzaville to join the ministry of education as head of one of its divisions.

NGOUOTO MOUKOLO, CHARLES, 1938– . Former cabinet minister and civil administrator. Born December 7, 1938 in Mouyali,

Ngouoto studied tropical geography in France, and graduated from the Institut International d'Administration Publique of Paris. Returning to Congo, he taught there from October 1961 to January 1963 and served with the administration from January 1963 until December 1967. He was then appointed director of the National School of Administration serving until March 1969, when he was named political commissar for the Kouilou region. In March 1970 he became minister of health, labor and social affairs and also a member of the PCT central committee. In December 1971 he was dropped from the cabinet and made head of the new PCT commission for information and organization. In December 1972, he became a member of the PCT politburo and state council and four months later headed a Congolese delegation visiting Moscow. He was named minister of agriculture and livestock in the government of August 31, 1973, and minister of agriculture as well as vice-premier in the government of January 9, 1975. In January 1976, he became director-general of the ATC.

N'GUILA, KOMBO MOUNGOUNGA. Minister of the economy and planning, appointed in early 1993.

NIANGOULA, ALPHONSE. Current ambassador to France, appointed in December 1992 to replace Jean-Marie Elengué, Sassou Nguesso's uncle.

NIARI. Key agricultural (the richest in Congo) and industrial region in western Congo, with a population of 220,075 (third largest), and administrative headquarters in Loubomo (ex-Dolisie), divided into the districts of Divinié, Mayoko, Kibangou, Mossendjo, Loubomo and Kimongo. The region produces some gold (at Mayoko), palm oil, coffee, timber, rice and manioc. There are good roads linking it with both Pointe Noire and Brazzaville, and the Congo-Ocean railway also crosses Niari. At M'Binda is found the terminal of the COMILOG rail spur connecting the Gabonese aerial cableway with the CFCO, through which, until 1993, Gabon evacuated some 2 million tons of her Moanda mine's manganese to Pointe Noire. The Niari river, with multiple rapids, is of no use for purposes of communications. There is still some big wildlife in the region, including elephants, buffalo and panthers, especially in the Mount Fouari reserve in the Divinié district. The vast majority of Congo's stockbreeding takes place in Niari valley that lies beyond the Mayombé escarpment and is covered with wooded land and savannas.

Historically the Niari valley was a no-man's land between the interior Batéké and the coastal Vili kingdom of Loango, and the scene of their battles. Though Niari has produced many political leaders, and some of them have attained high position, most fell afoul of the Sassou Nguesso regime, leading to growing dissatisfaction in Niari. Among Niari's leaders have been Claude Ndalla, once Ngouabi's number two man, purged and arrested by Sassou Nguesso in 1984 for plotting; Poungai, former Prime Minister in 1984, who however, was not very powerful, and unable to secure Niari's allegiance for the Sassou Nguesso regime was also in due course dropped; Celéstin Goma-Foutou, the former PCT secretary in charge of ideology; Martin Mberi, in self-exile during the 1980's, but currently the powerful minister of interior who is ethnically cleansing the security forces and packing them with Bembe loyalists for Lissouba.

NIARI RIVER. See NIARI.

NIBOLEK. Acronym, that began to crop up in 1990, referring to the regions and peoples of the Niari, Bouénza and Lekoumou regions, that are the main supporters of the current regime of president Pascal Lissouba.

NINJAS. Self-styled name of Brazzaville's newest Lari/Bakongo spontaneously-formed youth formations, joining ranks to protect the cause of **Bernard Kolelas** the undisputed political boss of the capital, and harass ethnic members of President Lissouba's coalition. Forming a private militia, in 1992–94 they fought pitched battles in Brazzaville with the "Zoulous" their equivalent formations protective of **Lissouba** drawn from the Niari, Bouénza and Lekoumou peoples. Some members of the armed forces (heavily northern) have supported the Ninjas, since politically the PCT and Kolelas' MCDDI are allied in the URD. Up to 1,000 people may have died in the 1993–94 fighting in Brazzaville until peace slowly descended on the capital.

NITHOUD, JEAN-DE-DIEU. International administrator. An accountant by profession, Nithoud was integrated as minister of trade and industry in September 1968 in the first government formed by the military regime. Six months later, he renegotiated cooperation agreements with the U.S.S.R. in Moscow. He was replaced from the cabinet post in June 1969 and a year later was appointed head of the accountancy department of the UDEAC, a post he still holds.

NJIKINI. A **Téké** subgroup, heavily intermixed with Mbochi, with whom they live in proximity.

NKAYI. Congo's fourth largest town, formerly called Jacob, and district in the region of Bouénza with administrative headquarters in the same town. The town's original name honored the French engineer who, in 1887, headed the first of many missions sent to select the best route for the Congo-Ocean railroad. Nkayi's growth was due to the rapid development of SIAN's cane plantations in the Niari valley, and it later became the site of important agroindustries, such as SUCO, MAP, and HUILKA. Jacob's population grew from 10,000 in 1962 to 25,000 in 1975, when its name was changed to the traditional one of Nkayi. By 1982, its population numbered 35,000 and it already ranked as the fourth largest town in Congo. By 1992 Nkayi was estimated to have a population of 48,000 people.

N'KISI. Indigenous medicines, charms, as well wooden sculpture containing medicines and charms within them, aimed at warding off evil spirits, especially at childbirth.

NKOUA, CELESTIN. Secretary general of the 1991 political party, Union patriotique pour la démocratie et le progrès (UPDP).

NKOUA, PIERRE-FELICIEN, 1936– . Civil administrator and former cabinet minister. Born on May 18, 1936 in Anguiémé, Nkoua was educated in France, attending IHEOM in Paris, later proceeding to obtain a law degree. On his return to Brazzaville he first assumed duties as controller of finance, then director-general of the national agricultural marketing board. In 1975 he was appointed ambassador to France, but was recalled after Ngouabi's assassination, and reassigned as director-general of one of the country's parastatal companies.

NKOUKA, ALPHONSE, 1946– . Administrator and development expert. Born in 1946 and earning a PhD in development studies in France, Nkouka served as councillor at Congo's embassy in France between 1975 and 1982, following which he was director of the ministry of foreign affairs in Brazzaville until 1985. Since 1985 Nkouka has been head of the U.N.D.P. office in Brazzaville.

NKOUKA, LAZAIRE, 1945– . Agricultural engineer. Born in 1945 and obtaining a PhD degree in France in parasitology, Nkouka was appointed on his return to Brazzaville scientific head of the research program of the local branch of ORSTOM. He was later named concurrently deputy-director of scientific research in Congo's department of scientific and technical affairs. In 1981 he was appointed head of the agricultural program but in 1982 went for a year to teach at the University of Montreal in Canada, following which he relocated to France. Nkouka has written a number of monographs on Congo's agriculture.

NONAULT, JEAN-PIERRE, 1937– . Born in 1937, Nonault was appointed government commissar of Kouilou in 1971, then ambassador to the Soviet Union in 1974. In 1978 he returned to Brazzaville and was integrated into the PCT central committee. He was dispatched overseas again as ambassador to France in 1979. In 1984 he returned to the foreign ministry where he was named head of a department.

NOUMAZALAYE, AMBROISE, 1933– . Former prime minister of Congo, and one of the country's foremost radical Maoist leaders. Born on September 23, 1933 in Brazzaville, Noumazalaye attended the Salvation Army's primary school in that town following which he obtained his secondary education at Dolisie and Brazzaville, and an M.A. in mathematics at the University of Toulouse. While in France, he married a Frenchwoman and joined the French Communist Party and **FEANF**. Interrupting his advanced studies at the Institut National de Statistiques, he returned to Brazzaville to become general secretary of the MNR in July 1964, and also its director of economic affairs. In April 1966, he succeeded Lissouba as Massamba-Debat's prime minister and minister of planning, after returning from Moscow, where he attended the Soviet Communist Party congress. In the mutiny of the armed forces a few months later, he and his government were chased to the protection of the local stadium, where they were protected by the Cuban troops then in Brazzaville. He rejected an ultimatum that the government dispose of these troops, though he reinstated Captain Ngouabi, whose dismissal had been the cause of the mutiny. Later, in January 1968 Massamba-Debat dismissed him from the government, since Noumazalaye was becoming a threat to his own authority. After Ngouabi took over the power, Noumazalaye served for two months as secretary of state for information. In November 1969 he was assigned a comparatively minor post in the planning ministry. He did not again become politically prominent until after the abortive Kikanga raid in March 1970, when he was reintegrated into the PCT politburo as head of its planning committee. Soon after replacing Raoul as second secretary of the PCT, he was arrested and condemned to death—later commuted to life imprisonment—for his alleged participation in the **Ange Diawara** attempted putsch of February 22, 1972. In 1973 he was pardoned and reintegrated into the civil service, by 1980 becoming a special adviser to the minister of planning. A leading member of the **Impfondo pro-Soviet M-22** faction, Noumazalaye was increasingly used by Sassou Nguesso to keep the more radical members in M-22 in line, since the former had become over time more malleable than in his earlier days. In 1984 he rejoined the cabinet as minister of industry, fishing and crafts, serving until 1987 when he was reassigned as head of one of the state timber companies. With the political liberalization of 1990 Noumazalaye briefly set up his own party, but returned to the PCT fold as its secretary general.

NTIMA, BIZOL. See VALETTE, ALICE .

N'ZABA, PHILIPE, 1947– . Educator. Born on April 27, 1947 and obtaining a PhD in sociology and demography from the University of Paris, N'Zaba has been teaching at the higher institute of education at Marien Ngouabi university, assisting also in the research and reports prepared by the ministry of the plan.

N'ZALA-BACKA, PLACIDE, 1932– . Civil administrator and author. Born in Brazzaville in 1932 and educated in Bangui and Brazzaville, he continued with higher studies at what was to become the university of Brazzaville. Prior to Congo's independence N'zala-Backa served with the educational inspection service of the A.E.F. and then served as the personal cabinet secretary of High Commissioners Pierre Messmer and Yvon Bourges. With independence N'zala-Backa, who had been involved in the **Matsouanist** movement, was appointed by president Youlou as administrative head of the district of Gamaba (Brazzaville). Between 1961 and 1964 he went for higher studies at IHEOM in Paris, and after his return he occupied a variety of middle echelon posts in the administration, being dispatched abroad on a number of missions. In 1970 he was appointed secretary-general of Pointe Noire's chamber of commerce, a post he held until his retirement. N'zala-Backa has also been involved in journalism, writing for the cultural review *Liaison,* and published his first book in 1968, followed by additional ones later.

NZALAKANDA, BLAISE (Colonel). During the Sassou-Nguesso era Nzalakanda was one of the very few senior Bakongo officers in the armed forces. Serving as head of the Congo's forces in Chad, and later military attache to Moscow, Nzalakanda was on two occasions (during the 1982 bombings in Brazzaville; and at the time of the 1984 conspiracy) accused of involvement in plots against the regime, but was each time vindicated. Since the rise of the civilian regime of President Lissouba, Nzalakanda has been Bernard Kolelas' liaison with the **Ninja** armed youth formations in Brazzaville.

NZALAKANDA, DOMINIQUE, 1917– . Former minister of interior. A Lari, born in 1917 in the Pool region, Nzalakanda received secondary schooling, and became a teacher in 1939 and an inspector of primary schools in 1958. Between 1961 and 1963 he was minister of interior in the government of his cousin, president Fulbert Youlou, but was so unpopular with the trade unions that they demanded his dismissal. After the coup that ousted Youlou, Nzalakanda was arrested and sentenced in June 1965 to 15 years in prison at hard labor. He was amnestied in August 1967, when he retired from public life.

N'ZAMBI, MANKOUMBA (Colonel). Since 1992 commander of the 400-man restructured rural gendarmerie nationale. A Bembe from the Bouenza region, N'zambi's appointment was part of a conscious policy, by minister of interior **Mberi** to develop several ethnically loyal security services as a bulwark against the northern-dominated army that could not be easily restructured.

N'ZAMBIE-BOUGIE. See LASSY ZEPHERIN.

NZE, PIERRE, 1939– . Former minister of foreign affairs and long-term Congolese politician. Born and raised in the northern Impfondo and Sangha regions, and trained as a teacher, Nze was an instructor at the Brazzaville Lycée Savorgnan de Brazza when he was appointed secretary for foreign relations and education in the CNR directorate of August 1968. Six months later, his rank was raised to that of minister. In January 1969 Ngouabi, Raoul and himself were the only members of the government who were also members of the CNR executive committee, underscoring his influence in the regime. In June 1969, he lost his cabinet post but in January 1970 was reintegrated into the government as minister of justice. Three months later he was also placed in charge of organizing the PCT, and became vice-president of its Politburo. Originally viewed as a radical "Stalinist," Nze was nevertheless expelled from the PCT politburo in December 1975 when a program of ideological radicalization began in earnest in Congo, and his brand of radicality clashed with Ngouabi's. He was also arrested after Ngouabi's assassination in 1977 on suspicion of complicity in the affair. He was later exonerated and readmitted to the PCT politburo in March 1979 to become in April minister of foreign affairs and cooperation, holding that post until 1984. In November 1986 he also lost his Politburo seat together with his successor in the foreign ministry, Ndinga-Oba, who caused a diplomatic flap with the US by comparing Israel and South Africa with Nazi Germany. Nze has been a leading member of the **Impfondo** and **M-22** faction in the PCT. With the onset of multipartyism Nze set up his own party, the Union national pour la démocratie et le progrès (UNDP), and aligned it with the FDC.

NZE-MBA, PIERRE. See NZE, PIERRE.

NZIKA KABALA (or TSIKA KABALA), VICTOR (Major), 1940– . Born in 1940, Nzika was appointed in July 1966 head of the land forces stationed at Brazzaville, replacing Captain Mathias Ferre. Later arrested by Massamba-Debat (in July 1968, together with Ngouabi), he was freed by mutineering paratroopers. In January 1970, he was appointed deputy chief of staff of the Congolese armed forces, and in September 1973 replaced his superior, Colonel Yhomby Opango as chief of staff. A few years later he was assigned to administrative duties in the state sector.

NZIKOU. Batéké vice-royalty, historically part of the decentralized **Kongo kingdom** until the latter began to fall apart in the 17th century when Nzikou attained autonomy. See also BATEKE.

NZINGOULA, SAMUEL, 1941– . Physician. Born on 1941 and trained in Tours, France (1976) in medicine, specializing in pediatrics, Nzingoula returned to Brazzaville to head one of the departments in the School of Health at Marien Ngouabi university, and later was appointed head medical officer at the Brazzaville General Hospital.

NZOALLA, PATRICE. Currently Congo's attorney-general.

N'ZOUNGOU, ALPHONSE. Former minister of interior. N'Zoungou, formerly a PCT central committee member, joined the Milongo interim government in May 1992 after the local elections.

-O-

OBA, ANTOINE NDINGA. Former cabinet minister. Oba, an uncle of Sassou-Nguesso, served as minister of education until August 1984 when he was promoted to become foreign minister. He remained in that post until 1991.

OBA, PIERRE (Colonel), 1950– . Key security aide to Sassou-Nguesso, to whom he is related. Until September 1987 director of Presidential security, and commander of the Presidential Guard, in the aftermath of the **Anga** revolt in 1987 Oba became also director-general of public security. He held that post until the advent of multi-partyism when he became Sassou-Nguesso's aide de camp. Though no longer a presidential guard, the roughly 600 members of that armed formation, still under the command of Colonel Oba, serve as Sassou-Nguesso's private armed force. They accompany Sassou-Nguesso wherever he goes, and normally are based in his home-village in Oyo. Oba himself is known for his integrity.

OBA APOUNOU, GABRIEL. Former cabinet minister and member of the PCT central committee. Sassou-Nguesso's nephew, Oba Apounou was appointed minister of youth and sports in the cabinet formed December 28, 1980, a key ministry in light of the role played by youth in Congo's history. He had also headed the UJSC youth movement that gave Sassou-Nguesso important support when he took over power from Yhomby Opango. Oba Apounou left the cabinet in December 1985 when Sassou-Nguesso had to assuage Camille Bongou, leader of the M-22 and the important PCT secretary-general with whom Oba Apounou was on very bad terms. However, he returned to the cabinet as minister of youth and rural development in the new government of August 1989, remaining until 1991.

OBEMBE, JEAN-FRANCOIS. PCT ideologue. A teacher by training, Obembe was for long director of the PCT Party Training School. In November 1985 he was appointed PCT central committee secretary in charge of propaganda, press and ideology.

OBENGA, THEOPHILE, 1936– . Minister of communications, posts and telecommunications, and former foreign minister and scholar. Born on February 3, 1936 in Brazzaville, Obenga studied paleontology and prehistory at several universities including the Ecole Pratique des Hautes Etudes and the College de France, the Sorbonne, and the University of Pittsburgh, obtaining a PhD and developing linguistic skills as well. After heading a secondary school in Brazzaville (1972–73), he was awarded the chair of Egyptology at the University of Brazzaville. On December 18, 1975 he was appointed minister of foreign affairs, continuing to teach twice weekly. He was replaced as foreign minister by Pierre Nze in April 4, 1979. Obenga has published a number of books, including *La Cuvette Congolaise* (1977), for which he was awarded the Prix Georges Bruel. In 1982 he left for neighboring Gabon to become the director of the Centre International de la Civilisation Bantou. He returned to Congo in 1991 to participate in the national conference. On September 8, 1992 he joined the cabinet again.

OFFICE CONGOLAIS DES BOIS (OCB). State marketing monopoly over the export of timber, established in 1973 and capitalized at 1.5 billion CFAF. The company, that employs 116 workers, purchases logs from concessionaries at prices largely dictated by global market prices. In 1986 business turnover was 13.65 billion CFAF with 322,000 cubic meters of logs sold. Its managing director is Alexandre Denguet-Attiki. See also FORESTRY.

OFFICE CONGOLAIS DES FORETS (OCF). State reafforestation agency, established in 1974 with seven forestry stations, three in Niari, two in Kouilou and one each in Bouénza and in the Pool regions.

OFFICE CONGOLAIS DU TABAC (OCT). State organ charged with collection of tobacco manufactured by farmers, and its marketing.

OFFICE DE CACAO ET DE CAFE (OCC). Parastatal marketing organ, responsible for buying and marketing farmers' cacao and coffee produce. Set up in 1978 with 1.5 billion CFAF in capitalization. While the OCC has been generally profitable, this was attained through paying of low producer prices to farmers, something that depressed the growing of the two crops in Congo. Its managing director is Paul Yora. In 1992 it was announced OCC's marketing monopoly would be ended, with the company having to compete with private traders.

OFFICE DES CULTURES VIVRIERES (OCV). State organ established in 1978 with responsibility over the marketing of all food crops, and managing several state farms. Notwithstanding its broad mandate OCV only handled a few products such as maize, peanuts and rice. The company has been riddled with management and financial problems, hampered by the small number of vehicles in operational state for evacuation of produce and marketing the commodities, and has been mostly deficitory. Since the mid-1980's the World Bank has urged the State should withdraw from managing farms and marketing schemes. In 1992 the government withdrew OCV's marketing monopoly, and the company now has to compete with private traders. It is headed by Gilbert Pana. See also AGRICULTURE.

OFFICE DU GROS BETAIL (OGB). State organ that took over most of the flagging stockbreeding and ranching activities of **SONEL** in 1984. Despite the reorganization OGB only slowly increased fresh meat production that covers one-sixth of Congo's domestic needs. The creation of a new ranch at Diessé, and other farms elsewhere were responsible for most of the increase, but both the IMF and the World Bank have been pressing for the State's withdrawal as much as possible from agrarian and stockbreeding activities.

OFFICE NATIONAL DE COMMERCE (OFNACOM). This commercial State agency was formed in June 1964, at the same time as **ONCPA,** representing the state's entry into the field of wholesale and retail trade, showing the government's determination to exercise greater control over road and river transport. OFNACOM was an importer and distributor of general merchandise. Within a year OFNACOM had opened 123 sales outlets, and within two years was doing business valued at 990 million CFAF. Yet, between 1965 and 1967 its losses were estimated at 480 million CFAF and it had incurred a debt of 240 million to the private sector. Its deficiencies were due to inefficient and cumbersome administration, over-rapid growth of its retail trading activities, the lack of coordination in its transport services, and, finally, competition from the private sector, which bought OFNACOM's most profitable merchandise for resale at marked up prices. To meet these problems, OFNACOM liquidated most of its retail business, concentrated on the wholesale trade in a few imported commodities, and coordinated its transport system with that of ONCPA. Although OFNACOM continued to operate at a loss, the government in July 1972 entrusted to it a monopoly of the importation of certain foodstuffs (including rice, salt and salted fish, textiles, and enamelware). Throughout its entire period of operations the firm was deficitory and unable to fulfill the needs of the population. As part of the PCT's privatization efforts in the mid-1980's OFNACOM was transformed into a mixed-economy society.

OFFICE NATIONAL DE COMMERCIALISATION DES PRO-DUITS AGRICOLES (ONCPA). With the aim of monopolizing trade in northern agricultural products, Congo formed ONCPA in June 1964 (at the same time as OFNACOM) to market all agricultural products except for sugar. It took over the agricultural activities of CFHBC, but was even less able than its predecessor to make them profitable. ONCPA agents lacked technical skill and business experience. They made purchases from producers too late in the season, paid middlemen too little or not at all, and the movement of crops to the market was slow and costly. Dissatisfied with their performance, the government reorganized ONCPA several times. Eventually its operations were merged with those of OFNACOM.

OFFICE NATIONAL D'IMPORTATION ET DE VENTE ET VIANDE EN GROS (ONIVEG). Formed in 1975 with 177 million CFAF in capital, this state agency has a monopoly over the import and distribution of wholesale meat. Its director is Robert Paul Mangouta.

OKABANDO, JEAN-JULES. PCT militant. A northerner, Okabando was appointed in 1972 secretary-general of the PCT's youth branch, the UJSC. He was involved in a March 24, 1976 plot against Ngouabi and was subsequently purged. Exiled to Mossundjo, Okabando was rehabilitated after Yhomby Opango's assumption of power, and was named political commissar of Lekoumou. Later, in 1984 he was appointed mayor of Brazzaville, serving until 1991 when he vacated the post though continuing for another two years as deputy-mayor. In July 1994 he was arrested for the embezzlement of 64 million CFAF during his tenure of office.

OKABE, SATURNIN, 1936– . Former cabinet minister. Born on November 6, 1936 in Makoua, after graduating from the Ecole Nationale des Douanes in France, he entered the customs service in Congo and became its chief inspector in April 1964. On January 7, 1973, he succeeded Poungui as minister of finance, and in December 18, 1975 he was again shifted to head the ministry of commerce, industry, and tourism. Okabe was dropped from the government in the reshuffle of November 1978, and was appointed head of one of the country's state industries.

OKANDZA, JACOB. One of Congo's ideological hard-liners. Educated at Brazzaville's Chaminade lycée and later abroad, Okandza was one of the hard-line pro-Soviet leaders of the M-22 faction of the PCT party. In 1982 he was appointed ambassador to the Soviet Union, and in 1986 ambassador to Mozambique.

OKIEMBA-MORLENDE, PASCAL. Cabinet minister and trade union leader. As the president of the CATC trade union, Okiemba-Morlende played a prominent part in helping overthrow the regime of president Fulbert Youlou. After the 1963 coup he was appointed minister of justice by Massamba-Debat in December 1963. Along with other CATC leaders, he was dismissed from his post in October 1964. He reverted to union duties until he was appointed ambassador to Peking in July 1970. On his return he was appointed political commissar and deputy mayor of Brazzaville.

OKO, CAMILLE. Mbochi Security officer. Formerly head of Congo's counter-espionage services, in 1988 he replaced Colonel Ngolondélé as director-general of Congo's security services. After the emergence of a southern civilian regime in Brazzaville in 1991 he was removed from that post since he was not regarded as loyal to the regime, and assumed duties in Sassou-Nguesso's personal retinue. He is the latter's cousin.

OKOKO, JACQUES. Kouyou lawyer, former state prosecutor and cabinet minister. Okoko, a former legal advisor to Massamba-Debat in 1963, was the government prosecutor who condemned Massamba-Debat to death in March 1977 and later led the government legal team at the public trial of those others charged with Ngouabi's assassination. Okoko later entered private practice, but in June 1991 he was appointed interim minister of transport in the Milongo government. In that post he antagonized Gabon by remarks he made at the time of a **COMILOG** rail accident, and was shifted to head the ministry of civil service, holding the post until the 1992 elections led to a new government. He then reentered private practice. On March 8, 1993 he acquired notoriety when he filed a petition in Congo's courts, on behalf of the family of slain **Captain Anga**, against former president Sassou-Nguesso, challenging the latter's personal immunity from future prosecution that was granted by the national conference as part of the deal that brought about civilian multipartyism to Congo.

OKOKO-BAHENGUE, LOUIS. Teacher and poet. A teacher by profession, but best known for his mystico-religious messages and the fervor in his poetry that has been published mostly within Congo.

OKOMBA, FAUSTIN, 1929– . Early cabinet minister. A Mbochi born at Kelle on June 5, 1929, Okomba only attended primary school, entering the administration as a simple clerk. In 1957 he joined the MSA party and was elected deputy (1957–1959) from Likouala-Mossaka in the territorial assembly. Arrested and held briefly for alleged participation in the Brazzaville riots of February 1959, he was appointed minister of labor five months later. In December 1962, his portfolio was shifted to that of public works and transport. Arrested again after President Fulbert Youlou's overthrow, he was acquitted by the People's Court in June 1965, and resumed his administrative career.

OKOUME. The most valuable of Congo's indigenous wood species. See also FORESTRY.

ONDONGO, GEORGES. Editor in chief of Radio Brazzaville. A former PCT member, Ondongo replaced Antoine Gangoye, a UPADS supporter, in 1993.

OPANGAULT, JACQUES, 1907–1978. Former Vice-president of Congo and early Mbochi political leader. Born on December 13, 1907 in Ikagna (Likouala-Mossaka) and educated in a Catholic mission school, in 1938 Opangault became a clerk in the judicial service. After the liberalizations following World War II, he entered politics, founding Congo's branch of the French socialist party (SFIO). Beginning in 1946, he was elected regularly to the territorial assembly and was as regularly defeated when he ran as candidate for the French National Assembly, his political career being marked by extremes. An undisputed leader of the northern Mbochi and of the MSA, he was consistently loyal to France and to the SFIO. He was arrested after the Brazzaville ethnic riots of February 1959, but was released after six months in prison and a year later became a minister of state in Fulbert Youlou's government. In 1961, he was named vice-president of the republic, only to be demoted to the post of minister of public works the next year. After Youlou's overthrow, he was again arrested, and upon his release, he returned to private life in Brazzaville, where he died on August 20, 1978.

ORGANISATION COMMUNE AFRICAINE ET MALGACHE (OCAM). An outgrowth of the earlier African and Malagasy Union, OCAM was founded in 1965 as an organization of moderate francophone African states. Although formed with president Fulbert Youlou's active participation, and despite marked changes in the group, OCAM survived almost a decade with its original membership largely intact. The partially economic orientation of this body, as well as France's sponsorship, furthered Congo's interests and impelled its Marxist leaders to overlook for many years the political conservatism of its partners. Specifically, OCAM's common sugar market and airline offered the Congo advantageous guarantees and services. By 1972, however, the threatened disintegration of OCAM precipitated Ngouabi's withdrawal from all but the organization's technical commissions. Moreover, UDEAC, had developed into an alternative organization more appealing to Congo, being also more geographically compact. See UDEAC.

OUESSO. Administrative headquarters of the northern Sangha region. With an estimated 14,750 people in 1988, Ouesso is Congo's eighth-largest urban center, having tripled in size since 1965, with an astonishing 79% of them below the age of twenty. (Projections indicate, however, that Ouesso is about to cede rank to Impfondo.) At the juncture of the Sangha and the Ngoko (or Dja) rivers, Ouesso is accessible by river transport from Brazzaville with its 62-meter river wharf, built in 1970, that handles up to 10,000 tons of traffic. In appearance and facilities the town remains a disorderly oversized village. Near the Cameroun border, across which many supplies reach the town, and with which Sangha has historical contacts, the town has an oil palm mill that processes Sangha's palm products, and nearby cocoa plantations, Sangha producing the vast majority of the country's cocoa on its fertile soils. In the vicinity there are unexploited gold, uranium and iron deposits. Despite these prospects, the town languishes, youth try to move on to Brazzaville, and the plantations and other state enterprises have been ill-managed and poorly tended-to. In the last years of the Sassou-Nguesso regime a new airport was inaugurated, capable of receiving jet aircraft, with the town hitherto serviced four times weekly by turbo-prop planes of Lina-Congo. There are pygmy groups in the Sangha region.

OWANDO. Congo's fifth-largest town, formerly known as Fort Rousset, found on the right bank of the Alima river. Rapidly growing due to an influx of rural population from the Cuvette region of which it is regional headquarters, Owando (and the Cuvette as a whole) has also benefitted from being the home of many of the northern military leadership in office during 1968–1990. In 1992 the town, only recently connected by a paved road south, was estimated to have a population of over 18,000 people. It is connected to Brazzaville by Lina-Congo turbo-prop service three times weekly. Owando is also the administrative headquarters of a district in Cuvette with the same name. The district, covering 13,000 sq. kms. and dissected by the Kouyou river, is monotonously flat, with sandy soil, savannalands and heavy forests along the rivers. At M'Bémbé there is a Protestant church and school that trained many of the Cuvette's leaders. The town and region are the current political fief of Yhomby Opango.

OWI-OKANZA, 1939– . Playwright and former minister. Born in Makoua, after higher studies at the University of Bordeaux (completed in 1966) he taught literature at several local schools before joining the Marien Ngouabi University to teach. Active in trade union activities, he has been secretary general of the union of Congolese teachers. In 1972 Owi-Okanza was Ngouabi's cultural advisor, and the following year he was appointed director of Ngouabi's presidential cabinet. He is the author of five acclaimed plays.

OYO. Town in the Cuvette region best known as the home-town of former president Sassou-Nguesso, who was born in its vicinity. During the latter's period in office large numbers of its youth were recruited into the Presidential Guard, and the security forces in general.

-P-

PALM OIL. See AGRICULTURE.

PARASTATAL SECTOR. Starting with the overthrow of president Youlou, accelerating during the Ngouabi era and especially during the brief but huge spurt in oil-revenues in 1979–82, a large number of state enterprises were erected in Congo. The vast majority of these have been deficitory: in 1985 only two of Congo's 87 state enterprises turned a profit—a bookshop chain and the national pharmaceutical company. Eschewing cost-benefit criteria, viewed during the revolutionary era as inappropriate "capitalist" considerations, the regime continued pumping new funds into the state enterprises in an effort to "rehabilitate" them. This was impossible, since at the root of the problem (and there were many other problems, including mismanagement and embezzlement) was the fact that most companies were grotesquely over-staffed and hence simply could not turn a profit. In 1985 some 38,000 Congolese worked in state enterprises that were piling up an annual 28 billion CFAF deficit, and a total of 75 billion for the period 1980–1984. In 1985 the PCT central committee re-examined all state enterprises in light of Congo's extremely tight fiscal straits and the horrendous debt-load the state sector was posing (amounting to 40% of the national budget) but reached the conclusion nothing could be done. Contracting the state sector was judged ideologically "incorrect," as was the concept of dismissing workers in a Socialist economy (apart from its likely negative political repercussions), so the constant drain on the state treasury went unabated. Even companies in inherently profitable areas piled up running deficits and contracted unmanageable debts, while productivity also plummeted. As the drop in oil-revenues continued and the state was simply unable to continue to cover the deficits, plans were announced for the restructuring and privatizing of some state enterprises. This inevitably brought vociferous opposition from the CSC trade union, and in the stalemate that ensued in the last years of the Sassou Nguesso regime some companies were simply allowed to close down bankrupt.

Both the interim Milongo and the succeeding Lissouba governments were committed to reducing the state role in the economy, but encountered the same problems with the unions. Efforts at privatization have thus been exceedingly slow in Congo. Workers at Hydro-Congo, ATC, and Congolaise de Raffinage, for example, blocked for several years scheduled restructuring and/or privatization plans; even Congo's national bank, that the **national conference** itself recommended in 1991 be closed down, remained open until mid-1994 due to pressures by the trade unions worried about the 168 jobs that would be lost. Progressively, however, some twenty of the state enterprises have been privatized as French, American, Scandinavian and Lebanese groups moved in, especially into those companies already closed down. Even then trade union pressures for the hiring by the new owners of the entire original labor-complement has stalled negotiations. In most cases, however, the new enterprises opened with 50–60% less manpower than originally. In 1993 the Lissouba government announced plans to privatize another fifteen enterprises, though the process has remained inordinately slow. See also ECONOMY.

PARTI CONGOLAISE DE RENOUVEAU (PCR). Small party set up by a former PCT militant, Gregoire Lefouaba, who bolted when the PCT joined the URD opposition in 1992.

PARTI CONGOLAIS DU TRAVAIL (PCT). See POLITICAL PARTIES.

PARTI DEMOCRATIQUE CONGOLAIS (PDC). Opposition party set up in exile in the mid-1980's against the Sassou Nguesso regime. Headed by Dr. Séraphin Bakouma, and supporting free enterprise, its organ was *Eveil Congolais*.

PARTI DU RENOUVELLEMENT ET DU PROGRES (PRP). Political party set up in 1991 by Henri Marcel Doumanguelé.

PARTI DU TRAVAIL (PT). Political party, set up in 1991 by Dr. Auguste Mayanza.

PARTI LIBERAL CONGOLAIS (PLC). Small conservative party set up in November 1990, headed by Marcel Makon.

PARTI NATIONALE (PN) Small party set up in 1992 by Yvon Norbert Gamberg. In mid-1994 it merged with the *Forum pour la démocratie et la solidarité* (FDS).

PARTI POPULAIRE POUR LA DEMOCRATIE SOCIALE ET LA DEFENSE DE LA REPUBLIQUE (PPDSDR). Small party that was set up in 1991 by Stanislas Bathéus-Mollomb.

PARTI PROGRESSISTE CONGOLAIS (PPC). Early political party. Founded in 1946 by **Félix Tchicaya** and encompassing mostly civil servants, teachers and Vili influentials. The party, until 1958 affiliated with the interterritorial RDA, later merged with Fulbert Youlou's **UDDIA**. See also POLITICAL PARTIES.

PARTI SOCIALE-DEMOCRATE CONGOLAIS (PSDC). Political party, set up in 1990 and headed by Clement Mierassa.

PEANUTS. See AGRICULTURE.

PELEKA, WILFRED JEROME. Civil administrator. Peleka served as prefect of Mossaka during the colonial administration. From 1964 to 1965, he was second counselor at Congo's Embassy in Paris and between October 1967 to June 1969 he held the same post in the embassy at Moscow. He then served as cabinet director of the minister of finance from June 1969 to March 1971, when he was appointed manager of the Société Nationale d'Elevage (SONEL).

PEOPLES' MILITIA. Originally a 2,000-man force that was recruited in 1965 from among the more militant **JMNR** youth, and trained by Cuban military instructors in Congo. The unruliness of the JMNR (and their arrogating for themselves the role of defending "the revolution" of 1963), and the creation of the Peoples' Militia as an armed force outside the control of the military, were factors that caused unrest among the armed forces and ushered in Ngouabi's coup d'etat. A shootout between the military and the JMNR (at the meteorological station, dubbed Camp Biafra) crushed the militant youth with 100–300 dying in the clash and led to the restructuring of both Congo's youth formations and the Peoples' Militia, the latter more tightly shackled to the armed forces. In March 1970, after a Youlouist armed assault from across the Congo river led by Pierre Kikanga, the **gendarmerie**, that had not shown alacrity in reporting, blocking or tracking the armed group (with some elements actually joining it) was dismantled, and replaced in its functions by an expanded Peoples' Militia, now ideologically trained and controlled by Political Commissars. Paradoxically two years later elements of the Peoples' Militia were used by **Ange Diawara**, their Political Commissar, in his dangerous leftist putsch.

PETROLEUM. Although traces of petroleum had been found along the coast of Congo since the late nineteenth century, systematic prospecting did not begin until 1928. In that year, the first of three exploratory missions was sent by the French government to Congo, but not one was successful. After World War II, prospecting was resumed in both Gabon and Congo by the newly formed Société des Petroles de l'Afrique Equatoriale (SPAFE), which finally struck oil in 1957 at Pointe Indienne. During the next ten years, that small deposit produced 700,000 tons of crude, after which its flow lessened to the point where it could only fuel the potash mine at Holle. When the CPC closed down in 1977, the Pointe Indienne deposit was virtually abandoned in favor of richer deposits that had been found offshore.

In 1969, SPAFE ceded the few productive deposits it had located on the Congolese mainland to the Société Nationale Elf-Aquitaine, which three years earlier formed a subsidiary, Elf-Congo, with a capital of one billion CFAF. At the same time, the Italian national company, ENI, founded its own subsidiary, Agip Recherches Congo, capitalized at 600 million CFAF. Those two companies, working together in Congo, have financed, prospected, and developed the country's oil resources. Under permits granted by Brazzaville, Elf-Congo prospects mainly in the Grands Fonds area offshore from Pointe Noire; Agip Congo's area lay to the north. Almost immediately, Elf found the vast Emeraude deposit; it was not until later that Agip discovered oil at Loanda. Between 1969 and 1980, Elf sank fifty holes and invested 170 billion CFAF in Congo, by 1982 increasing its investment to 238 billion francs. During that same period, Agip-Congo raised its investments from 130 to 198 billion CFAF, extracting correspondingly less oil than did its senior partner. Initially, the two foreign firms shared their earnings on a 65–35 basis, and the Congolese government, that had neither invested funds nor discovered deposits, took 20 percent of their joint earnings, later announcing its intention of raising that percentage to 35. Together royalties from Elf and Agip covered at least half of Congo's budget.

In an effort to gain greater control over the country's petroleum resources, Congo in 1974 created a national company, Hydrocongo, and granted additional prospecting and operating permits to American, Canadian, Swiss, and Brazilian oil companies. Because of lack of capital, technological expertise, and experience, Hydrocongo has been unable to compete with the international French and Italian companies' subsidiaries. In conformity with conditions stipulated for their operations by Brazzaville, Elf and Agip have conceded to Hydrocongo an ever-larger share of their earnings (e.g. 35 percent in 1981), and three American oil companies, to obtain prospecting licenses, agreed to grant Hydrocongo eventually half (as against an original 15-22.5 percent) of the net earnings from their production after amortizing their prospecting costs. Late in 1979, the IDA granted Hydrocongo a $5 million loan to train its Congolese employees in the administration of an oil company and for use in "secondary participation."

During the first decade of its existence (1974–83), Hydrocongo participated in marketing all oil produced for export by the foreign companies operating in Congo, but its concurrent attempts to wrest from Elf and Agip the control of the refining and marketing of the country's oil output were unsuccessful. Starting in the early 1980s, friction developed between Sassou-Nguesso and Elf-Aquitaine's president at that time, Albin Chalandon. The former tried to pressure the latter into making larger investments in prospecting for more oil and gas deposits, and in financing Brazzaville's major development projects. Congo felt that Elf should involve itself in projects in Brazzaville, and not only in Pointe Noire, where Elf had improved the latter's port facilities because of the latter's proximity to the offshore oil deposits of Angola and Congo. With the subsequent rapid decline of global oil prices, and concomitantly Congo's revenues from oil royalties, Brazzaville's friction with Elf increased, with grievances also voiced at Chalandon's over-optimistic forecasts of Congo's oil production and revenues, on which its ambitious 1982–86 development plan had been based, which soon had to be scrapped. Elf-Aquitaine, on the other hand, aware that the majority of its oil operations in 1985 were in Black Africa (88 percent of 28.3 million tons) had decided to diversify, necessitating cutting down the costly explorations in the Gulf of Guinea, a policy directly contradictory to Congo's desires. Indeed Elf had invested in exploration for new deposits in Africa only one-third of its exploration funds, and roughly the same amount (30 percent) of its development budget, despite obtaining the bulk of its oil from wells in that continent.

Twice during the 1970s, revenues from oil exports followed classical boom-bust sequences. The country's sudden prosperity, in contrast to its chronic poverty, gave rise to exaggerated expectations on the part of the Congolese and foreign investors alike. The disillusionment that ensued was bitter each time, and in Brazzaville's highly charged ideological climate and very poor understanding of the vacillations of a market economy, charges of 'global conspiracies' (by the capitalist world; by the 'global petroleum monopoly') were rife, just as they re-emerged when again, in the mid- and late-1980's declining revenues from oil similarly dashed original high expectations. Unfortunately, Congo's leaders have always pinned their hopes of development on oil, the most easily exploitable resource, failing to regard it as a temporary and wasting asset allowing them the time needed to bring under exploitation other resources, which though pursued, were done so in a very lackadaisical and inefficient manner. Moreover, revenues from oil-royalties were spread widely over a wide array of development and social projects, including in raising public salaries and standards of living, which while otherwise admirable, meant that no particular large revenue-producing sector was successfully pursued to conclusion.

The collapse of the global price of oil in 1981 heightened Congo's dependence on foreign oil companies' funds and expertise and intensified resentments at Hydrocongo's inability to replace them. (Indeed, the latter not only had not even become a factor in the petroleum sector, but had also made no profits from local sales of Congo's 200,000 tons of domestic oil needs, and as most other state companies had incurred massive debts, in this case of over seven billion CFAF.) By 1983 policy-conflicts between Elf and Congo were bitter with Sassou-Nguesso accusing the former of consciously trying to torpedo Congo's 'Revolution' by pumping out of Congo's oil-fields lesser amounts and selling this oil at lower prices. (There was some truth in these allegations though market conditions and global marketing considerations and projections were at the root of this and not a conscious political policy.) During the foregoing period, Elf-Congo had more than held its own financially, despite its large contributions to the construction (and management) of Djeno port and the Pointe Noire refinery, participation in the search for uranium and gold, a detailed study of the feasibility of a gas-liquefaction unit, and the development of a new technique to make the old Emeraude deposit more productive. Indeed in 1982, Elf-Congo was still pumping 66 percent of all oil extracted in Congo, offshore and on land, and was widening the range of its prospecting to areas not preempted by other oil companies.

Because Congo had over the years become completely dependent on revenues from oil to meet budgetary expenditures, spread patronage—very important to the northern military regime with multiple sources of opposition—and carry out the country's development plan, the PCT was adamant to sell as much oil and as fast as possible, irrespective of global quantity and price restrictions set by OPEC, of which Congo was not a member. Elf-Aquitaine, on the other hand, for which Congo was a minor oil producer—compared to Gabon, for example, whose resources were larger and whose free-enterprise economy was not hampered by the many restrictions and regulations imposed by the Marxist regime in Brazzaville—was opposed to all-out oil production and to sales at less than the world-market price, apart from not desiring a major confrontation with OPEC. Indeed in February 1983 the chairman of Elf-Aquitaine warned President Sassou-Nguesso that if he persisted with such pressures and demands the company would not underwrite any losses incurred by Elf-Congo, a fact that would not only not boost, but actually undermine existing Congolese oil-revenues. Fear of alienating such a big investor as Elf-Congo, at the time extracting oil from five deposits, prospecting for additional oil deposits as well as for other minerals and gas, and employing a labor force in which there were 700 Congolese among its 1,000 employees, defused the crisis, but the regime remounted efforts to open up its oil-potentials to other companies, something that was especially successful as the Marxist era drew to a close. In 1983, also, the government, operating through Hydrocongo, formed with Agip and Elf a mixed company to inventory the Congo's natural-gas resources, then estimated at 50 billion cu. meters, and in January opened at long last the Pointe Noire refinery, with an annual capacity for processing one million tons of crude oil. By midyear, however, the refinery proved too expensive to operate, yet another disillusionment. On the other hand other oil-fields came on line, such as Elf-Congo's Tchibouela well that was inaugurated in December 1987, followed in 1988 by Amoco's Yombo-marine, and Elf-Congo's Sendji and Likouela, and others in 1989–91.

During the transitional run-up to civilianization in the 1990's Elf-Aquitaine supported Sassou-Nguesso, and indeed supported the PCT and Sassou-Nguesso's own presidential candidacy. This because the company was aware that a new regime in Brazzaville would adopt a policy of diversifying the oil companies operating in the country, something that would intrude into what Elf had regarded as its own private preserve. (By the late-1980's the US was a main purchaser of Congolese oil—nearly $100 million—and Congo had became the US's third most important African trading partner.) This indeed transpired as the new Lissouba regime parcelled out new exploration zones and aggressively invited an array of foreign companies, particularly American, to enter the country.

The issues involved in Congo's constant oil-policy dilemma, including the budgetary and economic crises created by wildly fluctuating oil revenues in the 1970's and 1980's were not due to overestimates of the country's oil resources (believed to total some two billion tons) but to (a) an underestimate of the technical difficulties involved in extracting them from small and widely dispersed deposits, and the practical handicaps of selling so viscous an oil, especially at a time when there was a world glut of more easily salable petroleum, (b) the acute dependence of the regime on oil-revenues that made any sustained drop in global-prices into a major budget-balancing crisis, as in 1986 when the budget had to be cut to 46% of its 1985 size, (c) the massive wastage of those oil-resources through corruption and an ostentatious consumerism that spread throughout society and the parastatal sector and (d) that only 50 million of Congo's estimated 800 million tons of reserves are exploitable with currently known technologies. The oil boom also disguised the weakness of all other aspects of the country's economy—the rural exodus, overurbanization, and rudimentary communications system, and the abysmally poor performance of the public sector.

The civilian regime that followed political liberalization in 1991 inherited the economic morass and bankruptcy of the preceding era, compounded by various additional last-minute increases in the civil-service. Aware that trimming the latter and undertaking a major program of privatization of the state sector was political suicide, the interim Milongo regime and Lissouba's dragged its heels on both. Isolated from standby credits from an adamant IMF demanding major structural adjustments, and faced by a threat by American creditors of the confiscation of Congolese assets abroad unless debts incurred were paid promptly, prime minister Milongo was forced in 1991 to engage in forward-selling of oil from the Yombo-marine well (operated by an AMOCO-Kuwaiti combine with a 50% Hydro-Congo role)—a policy assuring immediate funds but risking future revenue shortfalls unless oil royalties increased substantially.

Currently, Congolese petroleum exports (just over 8 million tons in 1993) are projected to steadily rise to 13 million of crude by the year 2000 as Elf-Congo's N'Kossa offshore fields came on stream in 1996, and Agip's Kitina fields in 1997. The production imbalance between these two companies remains, with Elf-Congo's production of 6 million tons in 1993 anticipated to rise to 11 million by the turn of the century. By the end of 1994 over a dozen new petroleum companies had been granted oil concessions off the shores of Congo, with hopes of future strikes once again high. However, any new oil royalties that may reach the Congolese treasury are already heavily mortgaged for the repaying of the country's recently (1994) rescheduled national debt.

PFUNA. Among the Kukuya, a Batéké clan, *pfuna* is the term used for witchcraft, still widely practiced.

PLANNING. French public funds financed Moyen-Congo's infrastructure, met its budgetary deficits, and, after World War II, were channeled successively through two state organizations—the Fonds d'Investissements pour le Developpement Economique et Social (FIDES) and the Fonds d'Aide et de Cooperation (FAC)—to carry out a ten-year development plan. Since independence, France maintained this policy, both for political reasons and to protect its nationals' appreciable interests in Congo.

Private capital investments—formerly concentrated in the trading, lumber, and transport enterprises—turned more in the 1970's to the mining and oil sectors, while public investments, principally from foreign government loans and subsidies but during the late 1970's increasingly from national revenues, favored transport and industry. Moyen-Congo's first plan (1947–52) allotted about 60 percent of the 1,545 million CFAF from France to improvement in communications. This spurred urban expansion at the expense of rural production, which was allotted only 1.23 percent of the funds. The second plan (1952–56) increased the allocation for the rural economy (32.4 percent of about two billion CFAF), but still favored the infrastructure

(52.1 percent) and, to a much lesser degree, social equipment (15.5 percent). When Congo launched its own plan in 1958, president Fulbert Youlou asked French experts to make a detailed inventory of the country's resources and to schedule priorities for utilizing them. They advised abandoning grandiose schemes that would require international financing, favoring instead small-scale pilot projects to be carried out by the local population. Youlou eventually adopted a laissez-faire policy based on increasing Congo's transit trade, and industrialization to be powered by the proposed Kouilou hydroelectric dam. Since no start had yet been made on executing this plan when Youlou was overthrown in 1963, his successor was free to chart a new course.

The Massamba-Debat government rejected economic liberalism, and stressed the state's role in controlling the economy, heavily relying on foreign aid. Furthermore, its 1964–66 plan (extended to 1968) introduced the principle of decentralization by creating nine economic regions, each of which was to be developed according to its particular resources. In practice, however, little was done to promote decentralization, and the development plan thus marked no fundamental change in priorities. Of the plan's estimated cost of 54.27 billion CFAF, 20 percent was allotted to transport, trade, and telecommunications; 19.9 percent to industry, mines,and energy; 11.9 percent to agriculture and forestry; 8.2 percent to urbanization and housing; 5.5 percent to education and health; and 0.6 percent to administration. The major innovations in Massamba-Debat's plan were the allocation of about one third of total expenditures to the state's buying shares in mining companies, nationalizing selected private enterprises, and launching some industries, and it was he who instituted an investment budget from the Congo's own resources. The government still relied on private capital to furnish 40 percent of the funds required to carry out the plan, and actual investments came to 46.05 billion CFAF. This permitted attaining the plan's ambitious goals in industry (wood and food processing) and in transport, but only 60 percent of those for agriculture, fishing, and urbanization.

Completion of the 1964–68 plan coincided with rise of military rule. Ngouabi drew up his own plan for 1970–74, which again subordinated the development of agriculture to that of industry and transportation and further reinforced the state's role throughout the economy. This policy attracted large investments from the East without decreasing funds arriving from the West. Between 1964 and 1970 the regime allocated 6.5 billion CFAF to investments in industrial projects, and also spent 3.1 billion in buying out or nationalizing six private enterprises. Ngouabi's clampdown on private enterprises, either by outright nationalization or by creating competitive or monopolistic state companies, increasingly deterred from the country foreign risk-capital, that Congo still desperately needed, creating a dualism between official rhetoric and economic reality that dogged the Marxist regime until the liberalizations at the end of the 1980's.

In 1963, there were 62 companies of all kinds operating in Congo, with a total capital of some 10 billion CFAF. Almost all were small-scale firms, and only SIAN had a capital exceeding one billion CFAF. In 1964, the CPC became the country's largest single industrial enterprise, with a capital of 2.5 billion CFAF, of which 15 percent was held by the state. Later in the same year, the state acquired a 40 percent interest in the newly formed SOSUNIARI subsidiary of SIAN. This growing participation of the state in private enterprises gave substance to Massamba-Debat's announced policy of favoring companies of "mixed economy." At the same time the first of many vain appeals was made to local foreign businessmen to invest their profits in enterprises to which priority had been given in the national development plan.

Progressively, state enterprises encroached on originally private sectors, culminating in the nationalization of urban transport and utilities, of Air Congo and SIAN. Many small businesses were forced to the wall by the withdrawal of French troops from Congo, and the big companies' confidence was further shaken by the regime's instability. During the post-independence decade, total investments in Congo amounted to 98 billion CFAF, to which private capital contributed nearly ten billion. Of these combined funds, 40 percent were allotted to transport, telecommunications, and trade; 36 percent to industry, mines and energy; 10 percent to agriculture, forestry, and fishing; 13 percent to social-welfare activities; and one percent to general administration. Thus the orientation of investments only changed a little, despite the big increase in the amount available and in the proportion of public funds to private capital. In the consumer-goods and trading enterprises, public funds were taking up the slack left by the growing concentration of large-scale private investments in the potash and petroleum industries. Aside from the continued control by private European capitalists of the most dynamic sector of the economy, and mounting budget deficits, the Congolese leaders generally considered the expansion of the economy as satisfactory. So accustomed were the Congolese in the late 1960s to the general economic situation, and so addicted were their leaders to professing a Marxist ideology little related to Congolese realities, that the economic factor did not seriously influence their planning until the 1970s.

It was the prospect of a rapid economic expansion raised by the expanded oil revenues in the early years of that decade, and a belated awareness of the negative repercussions of the growing rural exodus and urbanization of Congo, that were the basis for the drafting of the 1975–77 plan. Regarded as a prelude to Congo's first real development plan, to be launched in 1978, the 1975–77 plan was endorsed by the PCT congress in December 1974. Although anticipated oil revenues failed to materialize in 1975, prime minister Goma stated in January 1976 that the government's first task was to carry out the plan as drafted notwithstanding, and that it was imperative for the state industries to control and mold all the other sectors.

Foremost among the plan's allocations were projects related to the rural economy: agrarian reform was to be launched by forming cooperatives, and 5.5 billion CFAF were to go on improving cocoa, oil palm, and manioc production, as well as on pig and poultry farms and on ranching. In order to acquire a monopoly over the development and sale of woods from the northern forests, to create a wood-processing industry, and to reforest 4,000 hectares so as to supply the Ouesso paper-pulp plant, 118.7 billion CFAF were allocated. To rescue Congo's industrial plants (notably those producing sugar, textiles, vegetable oils, cement, and potash) 6.1 billion CFAF were earmarked. The sum of 6.9 billion CFAF was allocated to increasing energy production. Among other projects were improved transportation (the building and repairing of certain roads, realignment of the CFCO, and air and river transport services), telecommunications, urbanization, and housing. Still other projects included building more schools and vocational-training centers and hiring 6,000 teachers. This program and a supplementary list of projects costing another 40 billion CFAF, for which no attempt was made to raise funds abroad, were simply shelved. The investment budget, based exclusively on national resources, was reduced from 23 billion to 3 billion CFAF in 1976; no work was started on any project outlined in the 1975–77 plan.

The continuing decline in oil revenues (to 37.9 percent of the amount anticipated) coincided with Ngouabi's assassination and the rise to power of the conservative Yhomby Opango as head of state in 1977. Any further execution of the 1975–77 program was constrained by the availability of only a third of the investment funds required. In 1978, therefore, it was decided to "restructure the country's economy as a whole," using the defunct 1975–77 plan as the basis for a new one, with priority to the rural sector, the economy to rely not on the expansion of trade, but on agriculture and forestry, associated with agroindustry and mining.

On May Day 1978 Yhomby Opango announced 60 state enterprises were "sick," owing the national treasury 11 billion CFAF for taxes and customs duties. A few days later, his minister of planning blamed the overstaffed and overpaid bureaucracy—as well as the shortage of private investments—for the economy's sorry plight. Such criticisms were heretical from a Marxist viewpoint, and it was Sassou-Nguesso, who came to power in 1979, who put Congo back on the Marxist path of "socialist planning as the only way to guide and promote economic progress"—a path in due course to lead to total insolvency.

Still, at the time a spurt of oil revenues, as well as aid from the IMF, allowed planning to recommence. The 1982–86 development plan, adopted in December 1981, was even more ambitious than its predecessors, though a gamble based on sustained oil production and continued high prices: when these proved false, the plan had to be trimmed in 1983, and abandoned in 1985, with the country by then in a severe liquidity crisis and virtually at the mercy of the World Bank.

That plan's two objectives were officially described as the physical integration of the country (via roads), and a better utilization of its human and material resources. The main stress was placed on a stronger infrastructure and improved means of production. Of the plan's total 1,105 billion CFAF, the state was to supply 780 billion and the public together with the private sector, 32.5 billion, with additional funds hopefully forthcoming from abroad. The infrastructure and equipment programs were supposed to absorb 48 percent of investments; production, 36 percent; social and cultural activities, 8 percent; and the state apparatus, 8 percent. The wide-ranging projects in infrastructure and equipment related to the CFCO railroad, river transport, port facilities, postal service and telecommunications, distribution of electricity, and warehousing for stocking crops. The programs related to increasing production were allocated 400 billion CFAF, to be applied to increasing the output of both peasant and state farms for local consumption, for the processing industries, and for export, as well as for forestry, fishing, and mining.

The Plan's earmarking of huge funds for the infrastructure did not pass unchallenged, but Congo's military rulers, coming from the north, preferred to reduce their region's isolation in anticipation of future major developmental thrusts that could not take place without a comprehensive road-paving program of the mud-tracks of the north. (Not paradoxically, this part of the Plan was completed, the funding shortfalls that developed notwithstanding; in the absence of maintenance funds, however, the torrential northern climate eroded much of the costly northern artery by 1992.) Such a policy also was assumed likely to stem the rural exodus by improving living conditions in a series of new urban centers in the north for which 157 billion CFAF were allocated to building the first of these village centers. A novel feature of the 1982–86 plan was a category of expenditures earmarked for specific regions, and another was the creation of permanent committees to supervise implementation of the regional projects and to correct deficiencies as they became evident.

The 160 billion CFAF allocated for execution of the Plan's 1982 tranche was based on the assumption the economy would grow at the rate of 10 percent annually. Not all revenues materialized that year because of the continued deficits of the state sector (30 billion CFAF in 1982 alone) and the collapse of the price of oil, on whose earnings the plan depended for 70 percent of its funds. Before the end of 1982, it was the Plan had to be trimmed, but the regime decided to continue with the core projects (oil, gas, uranium prospecting, communications, promotion of forest and food production) costing 700 billion CFAF, postponing others. As for the state enterprises, the government exhibited a similar unwillingness as all preceding regimes to bite the bullet and terminate those with the biggest deficits or those perennially deficitory: the PCT committee simply recommended that Sassou-Nguesso "require them to appoint a more rigorous management, hire more honest and competent personnel, and pressure private companies to become mixed companies so that the state could exercise more control over them." Nothing along these lines was done until the late 1980's when part of the state sector simply had to close down due to lack of funds. By then the state was also bankrupt, salaries were paid in arrears, and the CSC was demanding the convening of a national conference, all of which brought about the downfall of the military regime. Today there is not even a semblance of planning in Congo, with the country living from hand-to-mouth, attempting to privatize as much as possible of the former state sector.

PLATEAUX. Central Congolese region, with administrative capital in the town of Djambala and a population of 119,722, Congo's seventh largest. The region is composed of a series of four plateaus of between 600–860 meters in altitude with typical savanna vegetation. It is administratively divided into the districts of Abala, Lekana, Gamboma and Djambala. It produces tobacco, palm products, peanuts, coffee and a variety of staple produces. Communications within the region improved significantly in the mid-1980's when several paving projects were concluded. A number of Congo affluents are used to float logs to the Congo and on to Brazzaville, as is the Alima river that is navigable. The region has within it the Léfini nature reserve with elephants, panthers, lions, buffalo and crocodiles. The Plateaux is the original habitat of the **Batéké** ethnic group, one of whose kings, the Makoko at Mbé, signed the famous treaty with Brazza that opened up the Congo basin to French control, and granted land for the construction of what was to became Brazzaville.

POATY-SOUCHLATY, ALPHONSE, 1940– . Former prime minister of Congo. Born in 1940, and a former civil administrator, Poaty-Souchlaty was appointed minister of trade and small business in 1986 serving until July 1989. Integrated into the PCT Politburo on that date, he was appointed Congo's prime minister next month in the transitional phase before the liberalizations in Congo commenced. He resigned on December 3, 1990 shortly before the 4th extraordinary PCT congress, and three months before the **national conference** was convened, when he set up his own political party, the Union Républicaine pour le progrès (URPP) that in the subsequent legislative elections won three seats.

POIGNET, AUGUSTIN, 1928– . Briefly Acting President of Congo and currently president of its Senate. Of mixed Franco-Congolese (Bayaka) parentage, Poignet was born on April 28, 1928 in Sibiti. He joined the aviation corps of the French army and returned to Congo after independence with the rank of lieutenant. Massamba-Debat sent him on a mission to Peking in 1964, and in January 1968 named him secretary of state for defense—the first time that cabinet post had been occupied by a professional, French-trained officer. During the August 1968 crisis, he was acting head of state for a short time after Massamba-Debat's resignation. Within a few weeks, he was eliminated from the military government and, in compensation, promoted to the rank of captain. Arrested in February 1969 on charges of trafficking in firearms, he was given a suspended sentence of eight years in jail. He was implicated in the abortive Kikanga raid of March 1970 and fled the country before being sentenced to death by a court-martial. He did not return to Congo after the amnesties of 1973–74 but only in 1991 when he joined the political bloc supporting Lissouba, UPADS. On October 1, 1992 he was elected president of Congo's new upper house, the Senate.

POINTE NOIRE. Congo's second-largest city, its main ocean port, one-time capital, entrepot for considerable amount of the imports and exports for neighboring landlocked countries such as the Central African Republic, and to a lesser extent Chad, and until the 1990's for large tonnages (up to 2 million tons a year) of Gabonese manganese using the **COMILOG** rail spur. Called after the headland's black rocks seen on the coast (called Punta Negra by sixteenth century Portuguese traders)—currently behind the Hotel Zamba PLM Azue—that offered shelter to the slave ships of many nations. In nearby Buali, where European traders were installed, was the capital of the Ma Loango, paramount chief of the Vili ethnic group. In 1893 a treaty negotiated with the Ma Loango gave the French suzerainty over Pointe Noire. That settlement remained a small fishing village until 1923, when it was chosen as the terminus for the Congo-Ocean railroad, and became the seaport of all of AEF's foreign trade. Among Francophone Africa's seaports, Pointe Noire ranks third in importance, after Dakar and Abidjan. Improvements in its port and in the railroad after World

War II and its promotion to the status of territorial capital in 1950 increased its population, as did president Fulbert Youlou's project to build the Kouilou hydroelectric dam nearby and to create an industrial center and free-trade zone at Pointe Noire. Although this project failed to materialize and the territorial capital was transferred back to Brazzaville by Youlou in 1958 (Pointe Noire being controlled by his political opposition), the town's population continued to grow—from 30,000 in 1958 to 55,000 in 1962. This created serious unemployment in a town whose economy was stagnant and whose only new industries, installed in the mid-1960's, were a brewery and a plywood factory. By 1970, however, the foreign trade handled by the port and railroad had appreciably increased, and the anticipated expansion of the petroleum, potash, and fishing industries brightened Pointe Noire's future prospects.

When Congo became independent, Pointe Noire was the country's most modern and cosmopolitan city. It was the site of a bishopric, had wide paved streets, a large airport, and two hotels. Nowadays its population and appearance reflects the fluctuating fortunes of oil pumped from its offshore deposits. By 1982, its population was 200,000 (doubling since 1972), half of Brazzaville's, and it increased to nearly 300,000 by 1985, and an estimated 360,000 in 1994. It has a sizeable resident European community working in the oil industry, and their high salaries and material needs have galvanized a service sector rivalling Brazzaville's. Port facilities have been expanded several times, both with overseas funds and through contributions from Congo's main oil companies. Apart from the separate petroleum and manganese loading facilities the port has 1,300 meters of quais. The port has always handled, including after the phasing off of manganese exports, up to four times as many exports as imports, and recent exports amount to ten million tons, one half of this of oil.

On the other hand municipal services by the 1980's were in an acute state of disrepair. Thus though the contrast between Pointe Noire's businesslike bustle and the atmosphere of political tension in Brazzaville (both during and after Congo's Marxist phase) is very pronounced, Pointe Noire's has suffered urban deterioration. Sand has made many streets impassable; housing was so decrepit and in such demand that oil companies at times have booked entire hotels as lodging for employees. Breakdowns occur frequently in the electrical and water supply, and recurrent shortages of basic staples are frequent. There is excellent fishing in the region, with the record being 124 kgs.

POLITICAL PARTIES.

(a) *The colonial and Youlou years*: Moyen-Congo's first three parties—the *Parti Progressiste Congolais* (PPC), *Mouvement Socialiste*

Africain (MSA), and *Rassemblement du Peuple* Français (RPF)—all formed in 1946, were either branches of French parties (RPF, *Section Française de l'Internationale Ouvriere,* or SFIO) or of the interterritorial *Rassemblement Démocratique Africain* (RDA). After the Congolese branch of the RPF had become almost wholly a European party, it faded from the local political scene. The MSA, which was an offshoot of the SFIO, languished for the same reason until it found an indigenous leader in Jacques Opangault who transformed it into a largely northern Mbochi party. The PPC, on the other hand, was from the outset a wholly Vili party, localized in the Pointe Noire region and affiliated with the West African RDA. Under **Felix Tchicaya,** Moyen-Congo's perennial deputy to the French National Assembly, the PPC gained an early lead over the MSA, but gradually lost ascendancy as other Vili leaders arose to dispute Tchicaya's authority. The last and most successful of Moyen-Congo's regionally based ethnic parties was the *Union Démocratique pour la Défense des Interets Africains* (UDDIA), whose prime clientele were the Lari (and Kongo) from the Pool and Brazzaville area. The UDDIA was founded in 1956 by Fulbert Youlou as his vehicle for the territorial elections. Patiently, skillfully, and as a rule peacefully, Youlou worked for seven years through the established parliamentary system to win over or neutralize Tchicaya and Opangault and their parties. His efforts were crowned with success when on April 13, 1963, he pressured the legislature into declaring his UDDIA Congo's sole legal party. But barely four months later, he was overthrown by a combination of forces of which he seemed almost unaware, largely because they had assumed no politically recognizable form. Youlou's concept of a single party controlling the government and embracing all the country's "vital forces," including the opposition, was adopted and given an ideological and organizational foundation by his successor, Alphonse Massamba-Debat.

(b) *The Massamba-Debat presidency.* Massamba-Debat's *Mouvement National de la Révolution* (MNR), constituted in July 1964, served as the prototype for Marien Ngouabi's later *Parti Congolais du Travail* (PCT), created in December 1969, though their ethnic base was quite different. In both the MNR and PCT, a countrywide network of party cells, supplemented by women's and youth mass movements, were the base for a pyramidal structure. At its apex was the national party congress, to which the constituent units sent delegates every five years. A central committee chosen by that congress met four times each year; in the intervals between quarterly meetings, the central committee in turn delegated its authority to the politburo (initially called the *Conseil National de la Révolution,* or CNR), whose chairman was also the head of state. Scientific Socialism was the goal proclaimed by both the MNR and PCT.

The MNR's membership was a mix of UDDIA holdovers, trade-union leaders, and intellectuals trained in France, who were more or less agreed on a policy embracing a commitment to (1) elimination of neocolonialism in government, the civil service and army, and support for the struggle against imperialism throughout the world, (2) a diplomatic opening and commercial relations with the Eastern bloc, completely precluded from Brazzaville under Youlou, (3) establishing a secular state in which public education would be nationalized, (4) organization of a network of state enterprises covering the country's economy, and (5) unification under MNR's aegis of mass organizations of women, youth, and labor, in which the JMNR would be the radical standard-bearer.

The coexistence of parallel executive bodies in the government and in the MNR enabled Massamba-Debat as head of state and president of the party's central committee, to play their members off against each other, but with decreasing effectiveness. His insistence on technical expertise as the yardstick for holding office disappointed many ethnic leaders, especially the Lari, and the mild form of socialism that he practiced did not satisfy the increasingly radical youth. Their alleged plotting made Massamba-Debat dismiss his left-wing premier, Ambroise Noumazalaye in 1968, and himself take over the government. During the next months, Massamba-Debat's increasing authoritarian conservatism alienated his former supporters, including army officers who in August joined forces with his ethnic and ideological opponents. On September 4, 1968, Massamba-Debat resigned as president of the republic and of the MNR, and his place was taken by Major Marien Ngouabi.

(c) *The PCT*: From his analysis of the cause of Massamba-Debat's loss of authority, Ngouabi believed only an avant-garde Marxist-Leninist party could bridge the inter-ethnic and inter-generational divisions in the country while building a truly socialist state. Structurally, his PCT, constituted on December 31, 1969, was a replica of the MNR, but differed from its predecessor in style, in expressions of revolutionary fervor, and above all in assuming all the functions of the government. Yet within two years of its founding, the PCT itself came under heavy attack from youthful radicals, and was deeply split between moderates and "Maoists." Like Massamba-Debat four years before, Ngouabi convinced himself that no compromise was possible with the PCT's intransigent revolutionaries, and he purged them from the party organs in December 1971. An armed attempt by the hardliners led by **Ange Diawara** to overthrow the government failed in February 1972 because the army, led by Yhomby Opango, rallied behind Ngouabi. Nevertheless, Diawara's ability to escape capture for more than a year thereafter in the Pool region showed that opposition to the government was not confined to Ngouabi's party opponents. To win wider support from the population and left-wingers alike, in 1972 Ngouabi began to implement some of the nationalist rhetoric he had until then only preached. Extraordinary sessions of the PCT congress in July and December resulted in a new constitution, in which the distinction between party and government was restored but the PCT was left in control of policy-making and of membership in the elective assembly and local councils.

By 1973, the abortive coups d'etat led by Lt. Kikanga (in 1970) and by Lt. Diawara (in 1972) had disclosed such deep divisions between the right and left wings of the armed forces that Ngouabi had to seek another instrument through which to attain his goals. The civilian intellectuals, who had been the backbone of Massamba-Debat's MNR, proved too radical to accept Ngouabi's relatively moderate program, and also too disorganized following his purge of their leadership in 1971. He turned to the PCT as the only effective alternative. He was unanimously elected chairman of the PCT central committee, becoming consequently head of state; a party school was set up in which PCT cadres would receive indoctrination under the ideological guidance of Pierre Nze; and the CSC and the UJSC, whose radicalism had been getting out of hand, were reined in sharply.

By 1975, total membership of the formerly severely purged PCT had increased from 227 to 1427; its politburo had expanded by acquiring new members in addition to the incumbents (Ngouabi, Lopes, Nze, Poungui, and Ngouoto); and its central committee had grown from forty to fifty, and included several army officers and the president of the UFRC, its first woman member. The most spectacular development of this period was the party's extension into the regions, where ten political commissars, all of them members of the central committee, were posted to reorganize and guide its development.

In the process of this enlargement and reorganization the PCT lost much of its homogeneity and revolutionary zest. By reducing members of the CSC and the UJSC to the status of functionaries, their dynamism was not—as was intended—channeled into executing the party program but was dissipated, and the purge of "irrecuperable" cadres concentrated the left-wing extremists in Brazzaville and in Paris, among Congolese students and exiles. The PCT, by creating seven committees and new party units throughout the country in an effort to create widespread consensus, weighed down the governing apparatus and so diluted its sense of purpose that it reached an impasse that was aptly described as "a revolution in search of revolutionaries." By 1976, the much-heralded "radicalization of the party" had become such an abysmal failure that Ngouabi himself was seeking allies among the civilian radicals, who had been Massamba-Debat's partisans and whom he had harassed in the early 1970's. Fear of a "re-civilianization," and a Lari-Bakongo one to boot, reiteration of a plan to convene a third extraordinary PCT congress in 1977 to effectuate yet another reorganization and purification of the party, aroused widespread alarm, added to the number of his enemies and led to the coalescence of forces even now not fully identified that led to Ngouabi's assassination in 1977. To the end, Ngouabi remained a devout Marxist, never doubting the universality of Marxism's basic principles or his own abilities as to apply them, if only he could find the proper instrument through which to operate.

Yhomby Opango's interregnum (1977–79) marked a pause rather than a retrogression in the PCT's revolutionary process that had been so ardently promoted by Ngouabi. Owing largely to Yhomby Opango's senior rank and Sassou-Nguesso's self-abnegation (and, alleged complicity in Ngouabi's murder) the PCT on April 5, 1977 elected Yhomby Opango head of its central committee and of the eleven-member *Conseil Militaire du Parti* (CMP). The latter included a triumvirate composed of Yhomby Opango, Sassou-Nguesso, and Goma, who were the government of Congo for the next two years. The Fundamental Act which Yhomby Opango decreed after his elevation abrogated the 1973 constitution and all elective bodies, confirmed the CMP's dependence on the PCT central committee, and placed under the CMP, in the new hierarchy, the sixteen-member government promptly formed by prime minister Goma. On this occasion, and subsequently, Yhomby Opango, an acknowledged conservative hedonist, swore fidelity to Marxism-Leninism, proclaimed the overall supremacy of the PCT, and sought to legitimize his regime by claiming to be Ngouabi's heir. Taking advantage of the shock caused by the murder of Ngouabi, Yhomby Opango and his allies lost no time in settling old accounts with civilian politicians, as well as with subordinates among their colleagues.

By calling back to office competent and moderate politicians as Henri Lopes and Justin Lekoundzou, and by stressing law and order, Yhomby Opango and the CMP won some popularity with Congo's Western supporters and local conservatives. In time, however, the rigorous disciplinary and punitive measures, and the vengeful aftermath of the trial of Ngouabi's alleged assassins, alienated many Congolese. Moreover, Yhomby Opango's autocratic military regime, his suppression of the militia, his flouting of Marxist principles in his private life, reliance on a Cuban bodyguard rather than support from the PCT central committee, and the increasingly depressed condition of the economy and the regime's inability to pay government employees combined to bring about his downfall, that occurred under surprisingly peaceable conditions.

Sassou-Nguesso, like Yhomby Opango, came to power according to the principle of military and party seniority, but unlike his predecessor, Sassou-Nguesso adopted moderation vis-a-vis his political opposition, including the deposed Yhomby Opango. He invited Congolese exiles to return home, and in August 1979, amnestied all political prisoners in Congolese jails. His policy of continuity, as well as his clemency, soothed Congolese, who needed some stability after eleven tumultuous zig-zag "revolutionary" years. Congolese radicals and intellectuals generally came to applaud the sincerity of Sassou-Nguesso's Marxist convictions, his concern for legality, his prompt convening of the third extraordinary PCT congress according to Ngouabi's agenda, and his support for the constitution it drafted and submitted to a popular referendum. Partisans of the single party, both civilian and military, especially commended his restoration of primacy to the PCT central committee, which had not met for two years. Not only did Sassou-Nguesso carry out his pledge to widen and reinforce that committee's authority in the regions, but he ensured that it would dominate the elective national assembly and people's councils revived under the 1979 constitution.

Although Sassou-Nguesso, like Yhomby Opango, worked through a triumvirate, he altered its membership, as he did that of the central committee. The radical ideologue Thystere-Tchicaya replaced Yhomby Opango (though he was later progressively displaced), and the pliable CSC secretary-general, Bokamba-Yangouma, succeeded Goma. Unlike Yhomby Opango, who was aloof and authoritarian in his dealings with the rank and file, Sassou-Nguesso kept in touch with public opinion and tried to be close to union members. Though emulating Ngouabi consciously, Sassou-Nguesso was more of a pragmatic realist where Ngouabi had been doctrinaire, and resilient where Ngouabi had been intransigent, a great master at retaining the form but subtly altering the substance. At the same time membership in the summit of the PCT, the central committee and the smaller Politburo, became very sought after remunerative posts, enforcing greater docility on the part of party militants. In 1988, for example, Politburo members were entitled (apart from various perks) to a salary of 800,000 CFAF per month, central committee members to 600,000 CFAF, both higher than cabinet ministers whose salary was 500,000 CFAF per month. That these salaries were powerful inducements on more independent-minded militants, may be seen from the fact that the highest salaries in the civil service were at the time between 85,000–150,000 CFAF per month, while the minimum wage in Congo stood at 13,000 CFAF.

For all Sassou-Nguesso's political skills, it was the fortuitous revival of Congo's oil revenues that consolidated his reign. Prosperity, combined with continuity and stability, eased long-standing tensions, causing the glaring inconsistencies between Sassou-Nguesso's rhetoric and actions to be overlooked. Frequent denunciations of Western imperialism by Sassou-Nguesso did not prevent a marked improvement in Franco-Congolese relations, and a constitutional ban on capitalism did not hinder foreign domination of what had long been Congo's most flourishing industries—those of oil and wood. So long as oil exports enabled the majority of Congolese to enjoy a higher living standard than in the past, popular unrest was generally restricted to sporadic street violence in Brazzaville and Pointe Noire. But with the decline of government revenues in 1982–83, unemployment grew apace, as did divisiveness between the military and civilians, between ethnic groups and also regions, and between power-seeking individuals, which was to cause the recurrence of the Congo's political instability as austerity began to bite deep in the mid-1980's. The austerity was much more destabilizing than previous such recurrences because that many more individuals were affected in the much larger state sector of the 1980's.

The PCT's decision to liberalize the political scene was a direct result of the fact that an "internal" adjustment plan in the mid-1980's, aimed at avoiding stiffer IMF conditionalities, failed. Trimming the State's finances was incredibly difficult in light of the tenacious resistance of the trade unions, aware that large layoffs and closures in the state sector would be inevitable. Bankrupt and unable to meet debts or payrolls, an IMF structural adjustment program was signed, and the PCT party was made more representative, by restructuring the PCT's top hierarchy, and dropping the hardline M-22 permanent secretary, **Colonel Camille Bongou**. The PCT resisted pressures, however, for a national conference, even when the CSC in its 1990 congress declared its independence and urged convening a national conference. However, when the CSC declared an unlimited strike unless one was convened, the government capitulated, since with no funds in its coffers only massive brute force could have enforced its authority, possibly igniting a truly revolutionary situation in "enemy" territory, Brazzaville. To adjust to the new realities in its December 1990 4th extraordinary congress the PCT disassociated itself from Marxism-Leninism, and transformed itself from a vanguard to a mass party, as attested to by the much larger central committee that was elected.

When the **national conference** convened in 1991 the PCT's political monopoly was shattered as the conference declared its corporate sovereignty. Dozens of new political formations emerged, some created by former PCT militants, and others by self-exiled or banned individuals who returned to Brazzaville to set up their own political parties.

(d) *Opposition parties abroad during the PCT era.* Until 1990 a number of opposition movements were formed abroad, mostly in

France. All were moribund, intermittently issuing newsletters, at times falling prey to internecine splits. Among the most notable one can note: *Le Mouvement Patriotique Congolais* (MPC). This was one of the two main opposition groups to the PCT in France. The party was headed in the 1980's by the southern Pool area lawyer Moudileno-Massengo, and by Ekondi Akola, both at loggerheads with each other. The MPC's moderate Marxist leanings alienated it from other parties in Paris, and especially from the *Parti Démocratique Congolais,* as was its choice of future leadership, Yhomby Opango.

Parti Démocratique Congolais (PDC). The PDC was the other main group in Paris, pro-West, pro-free enterprise, and to a significant extent supported by a Bakongo membership. It was headed by Dr. Seraphin Bakouma, and published a newsletter called *L'Eveil Congolais.*

Union Démocratique Congolais (UDC). Opposition group set up in Abidjan at the end of 1989 by Sylvain Bemba, a former associate of Fulbert Youlou, calling for free enterprise and multipartyism. The party "relocated" to Brazzaville in 1990 and competed in the legislative elections.

Conseil Nationale de l'Opposition Congolaise (CNOC). Moribund opposition group set up in Paris in 1980 by self-exiled former Colonel David Mountsaka.

(e) *The post Marxist era.* With the political liberalization of the 1990's and the eclipse of PCT paramountcy, a large number of new political parties emerged. Like in other parts of Francophone Africa where similar developments occurred, many were ephemeral, small, personal power vehicles, or ethnically/regionally based. Moreover, through the process of internal fractioning or fusion with other formations, the formation of temporary electoral alliances and/or coalitions supporting one or another of the presidential candidates to emerge in 1992, a great deal of epistemological confusion reigns in the field of contemporary Congolese political parties. Already by the end of 1991 fully 72 political formations were officially registered as parties in Brazzaville, and over 115 at one point or another announced their creation. Despite considerable consolidation since 1992 when the Lissouba presidency came to power, at last count some forty-five political parties still existed in Congo, the rest being largely inactive. New ones, are, however, continuously being formed.

Some possible confusion about contemporary Congolese politics may be averted if one conceptualizes the political situation as a dynamic tug-of-war between two large alliances, Pascal Lissouba's UPADS party (itself a relatively tight coalition of regional power-wielders, especially from the southwest of the country) and Bernard Kolelas' URD alliance in which his own largely Bakongo/Lari MCDDI party is by far the strongest component. The badly truncated

PCT (today largely a Cuvette and Mbochi party), that briefly flirted with the UPADS in 1992, bolted to the URD in order to secure greater representation in the government. (A third, very small alliance, hoping to control the balance-of-power between the two larger groupings, the CDC, was formed in January 1993, but as of now is basically irrelevant.) Since Lissouba's UPADS does not control the national assembly, and wishes to avert a vote of no-confidence such as the one that toppled prime minister Bongho-Nouarra in 1992, UPADS can only govern by allotting to the "opposition" (the URD-PCT) a large number of cabinet posts, so that a de facto wall-to-wall coalition has emerged in Brazzaville. While the latter could be relatively stable, and given the disastrous state of the economy, may be the best political solution for Congo, the diverse personalities, ethnicities and ideologies compressed in it, and their ambitions, may not be easily constrained.

As to the political parties themselves, as noted before most are clearly ethnic or regional formations, strongly beholden to some powerful political baron, or structural creations by individuals left out of the spoils of the game to acquire a measure of influence, whose real strength will not be tested until the next elections.

AD HOC ALLIANCES.

Forces de Changement (FDC): A highly fluid Lari-Kongo-Batéké alliance of political groups that emerged in 1991 under the coordination of Lecas Atondi Monmondjo, supportive of Yhomby Opango, based on his Kouyou regional strength. Within it were also found Bernard Kolelas and his MCDDI. The FDC changed its name in 1992 adding the word 'Progrès' to its title, but by that time the alliance had fallen apart, with most of its powerful leaders running in the elections under their own party labels. By 1992 the FDC remained solely Milongo's political vehicle.

Front pour la defence de la démocratie (FDD). A temporary alliance of thirteen different parties that coalesced under Jean-Marie Tassoua's leadership, in opposition to the transitional government of André Milongo.

Alliance nationale pour la Démocratie (AND). This was the first broad anti-PCT and pro-UPADS electoral alliance to emerge in 1991. It included a large number of former PCT members who deserted the latter party with the onset of multi-partyism. Coordinated by Stephane Bongho-Nouarra, later briefly prime minister of Congo, at its height it groups 43 political formations. In the local elections of 1992 the party was especially successful in Kouilou where it denied a victory to Thystère-Tchicaya's RDPS, obtaining 12 of the region's 31 seats.

Union pour le renouveau démocratique (URD). A coalition of seven political parties that formed in 1991 in opposition to Pascal

Lissouba's **UPADS**. The largest of the URD components was Bernard Kolelas' largely Bakongo party, the **MCDDI**, and included also the RDPS of Thystère-Tchicaya. The URD was joined by the PCT that bolted a temporary UPADS coalition, transforming it into the largest bloc of votes in the national assembly. As such it passed a vote of no-confidence against Prime Minister Bongho-Nouarra, forcing Lissouba to change his premiers (Da Costa was appointed temporarily) and allot the URD-PCT alliance a greater number of ministries. The governmental deadlock triggered riots and demonstrations in downtown Brazzaville.

Centre Démocratique Congolaise (CDC). Very small January 1993 coalition of six political parties attempting to play a balancing role between UPADS and URD. Its component parts are the MPC, URD, RNDP, RAD, MOLIDE and RDC.

POLITICAL PARTIES

Union pan-Africaine pour la démocratie sociale (UPADS). Congo's largest party, set up and headed by Pascal Lissouba in 1991, and sustaining his presidency. UPADS, itself a coalition of regional power-wielders, scored heavily in the 1992 local, municipal, legislative and senate elections, emerging the strongest party in the country, limiting the strength of the MCDDI of Bernard Kolelas to the Pool region. The party is especially strong in the southwest, Lissouba's political base, in the Niari, Bouenza and Lekoumou regions. As UPADS did not secure a majority of the seats in the national assembly, it was forced to enter into alliances with other parties, including early on with the PCT, and the URD. UPADS is supported by a variety of other parties in the country such as Yhomby Opango's RDD, but is opposed by most of the Bakongo/Vili parties.

Mouvement Congolais pour la Démocratie et le développement Intégral (MCDDI). Political party set up in 1990 by Bernard Kolelas. A predominantly Bakongo party, very strong in Brazzaville in particular, and in the Pool region, this was the political vehicle of Bernard Kolelas, at various times allied with one or another of the coalitions that emerged in Congo. It won roughly 30% of the seats in the local government elections, and 13 seats in the Senate elections of 1992. Kolelas, defeated in several bids for senior office, is currently mayor of Brazzaville. The MCDDI was the building block for the anti-UPADS opposition, URD, and especially when joined by the PCT (formerly allied with UPADS) was able to force Lissouba to grant the opposition a large share of the cabinet seats.

Parti Congolais de Travail (PCT). The party remained in the post-1991 civilian era, truncated of most of its former (though not all) southern leaders/members, with Sassou Nguesso as the chairman of its general committee and Ambroise Noumazalay as its secretary general, until the latter resigned to set up his own party. Still, it is solidly a northerner party, and especially of the Mbochi, since the Kouyou have strongly flocked to the party set up in the Cuvette by Yhomby Opango (the RDD). It includes mostly Mbochi leaders and some civilian and military members not reconciled with the eclipse of Socialism, northern political hegemony, or military rule, and is still controlled by Sassou Nguesso, who contested the 1993 presidential elections though he failed to reach the second round. The PCT only gained three of the senate seats in 1992, and a small number of seats in the local elections the same year. The fact that the still largely northern army (that engaged in the civil-strife in Brazzaville in 1992–94) is beholden to Sassou Nguesso, made a measure of accommodation with the PCT necessary on the part of Lissouba regime, especially during the transition period. The PCT briefly joined the UPADS in a coalition government, but bolted it to join the opposition URD, of which Kolelas' MCDDI is the major component.

Rassemblement pour la démocratie et le progrès social (RDPS). A largely Vili party set up with Thystère-Tchicaya as its secretary general. In the local, municipal, legislative and senate elections of 1992 it was not as successful as expected, being strongly challenged and conceding many seats in Kouilou, where an alliance close to Lissouba garnered the largest number of seats. Its weakness presaged the poor performance (5.78%) of Thystère-Tchicaya when he ran for the presidential elections in 1993. The RDPS has been a member of the URD anti-UPADS alliance headed by Bernard Kolelas.

Rassemblement pour la démocratie et le développement (RDD). Moderate political party set up in 1990 by Yhomby Opango to tap his support among the Kouyou. In the 1992 Senate elections it won 8 seats in the Cuvette, and it also gained 15 of the 31 seats of the Cuvette in the local elections that year, essentially confirming the independence of the region from the Mbochi PCT party that did poorly in the Cuvette. The party could not sustain Yhomby Opango's bid for the presidency, however, as he obtained only 3.49% of the total vote. The RDD joined in supporting the UPADS party of Lissouba, and Yhomby Opango was subsequently appointed prime minister of Congo.

Union pour le progrès social et la démocratie (UPSD). Political party set up in 1991 by the trade union leaders Jean Ganga-Zandzou, Ange-Edouard Poungui, and Jean-Michel Bokamba-Yangouma. The party's platform was strongly in favor of private enterprise and personal freedoms.

Union pour le Progrès (UP). Small largely regional (Batéké) party set up in 1992 by Jean-Martin M'Bemba to tap the Batéké vote in the Pool region.

Parti Libérale Congolais (PLC). Small conservative party set up in November 1990 by its leader, Marcel Makon.

Union de Forces Démocratiques (UFD). Political party set up in 1992 with a number of former PCT members. Infighting within its leadership, lethargy and its conservative positions brought it to disintegration in 1993 when nine of its founding members resigned, some, like Christophe Bouramoué, rejoining the PCT.

Forces de Changement (FDC). Originally a broad alliance of parties, by 1992 this was only André Milongo's small political party. The party won only one seat in the 1992 Senate elections, and was unable to garner Milongo many votes in his bid for the presidency in 1993.

Parti populaire pour la démocratie sociale et la défence de la république (PPDS). Small party set up in 1991 by Stanislav Batheals-Mollomb, former PCT central committee member and ambassador to Roumania.

Union National pour la démocratie et le développement (UNDD). Party created in1990 in opposition to Milongo's interim leadership in Congo. Its president was **Pierre Nze**, who in aligning the party with the FDC in 1991 alienated a segment of its membership, including secretary general Antoine Malonga who consequently resigned.

Parti Social-Démocrate Congolais (PSDC). Small political party set up in 1991 by Clement Miérassa and Celestin Nkoua. The party was not successful in garnering the former many votes when he contested the presidential elections, and in the 1992 local elections it only obtained three seats.

Parti Congolais de Renouveau (PCR). Formed by a number of former PCT militants (originally considered moderates) that bolted that party when the PCT joined in 1992 in a tactical alliance with the URD, headed by Bernard Kolelas. The PCR is headed by Gregoire Lafouaba, who had been one of Sassou Nguesso strongest supporters during the 1992 presidential elections.

Mouvement patriotique du Congo (MPC). Political party, set up in France, that in January 1992 joined a few others to form the **CDC** alliance.

Rassemblement démocratique et populaire du Congo (RDPC). Political party, set up in 1991 by Jean-Marie Tassoua.

Rassemblement pour la défense des pauvres et des chomeurs au Congo (RDPCC). Populist party set up in 1991 by Angéle Bandou.

Mouvement africain pour la réconstruction sociale (MARS). Political party set up in 1991 headed by Jean Itadi.

Union pour la Démocratie et la République (UDR). Small political party that in January 1992 joined a few others to form the **CDC** alliance.

Union des forces démocratiques (UFD). Political party, set up in 1991 by **David-Charles Ganao.**

Union du Centre (UC). Political party, set up in 1992 and headed by Okana Mpan.

Ralliement Nationale pour le développement et Progrès (RNDP). Small political party that in January 1992 joined a few others to form the **CDC** alliance.

Union écologigue du Congo (UEC). Political party stressing ecological and environmental issue set up in 1991 by Mandzengue Younous.

Union Républicaine pour le progrès (URP). Political party set up in September 1990 by Souchlaty-Poaty, former prime minister.

Union nationale pour la démocratie et le progrès (UNDP). Political party set up in 1990 by Pierre Nze.

Ralliement pour une alternative démocratie (RAD). Small political party that in January 1992 joined a few others to form the **CDC** alliance.

Union Patriotique pour la démocratie et le progrès (UPDP). Political party set up in 1990 and headed by Célestin Nkoua.

Mouvement pour la liberté et le Démocratie (MOLIDE). Small political party that in January 1992 joined a few others to form the **CDC** alliance.

Union patriotique pour la réconstruction nationale (UPRN). Political party, set up in 1991.

Ralliement Démocratique Congolais (RDC). Small political party that in January 1992 joined a few others to form the **CDC** alliance.

Union pour la démocratie congolaise (UDC). See previous sections about parties in exile.

Parti Nationale (PN). Small political party formed in 1992 and headed by Yvon Norbert Gamberg. The party merged with the *Forum pour la Démocratie et la Solidarité* in mid-1994.

Forum pour la Démocratie et la Solidarité (FDS). Small political party formed in 1991 and headed by Andely Beev. The party merged with the *Parti Nationale* in mid-1994.

Parti de renouvellement et du progrès (PRP). Political party set up in 1991 by Henri Marcel Doumanguele.

Parti du Travail (PT). Political party set up in 1991 by Dr. Auguste Mayanza.

Union pour la démocratie et la république (UDR). Political party, set up in 1992 by André Milongo.

Union pour le développement et le progrès social (UDPS). Political party, set up in 1991 by a breakaway faction of the UPSD. The party is headed by Jean-Michel Boukamba-Yangouma.

Union pour le progrès du peuple congolais (UPPC). Political party set up in 1991 and seeking national reconciliation. Its leader is Alphonse Nbihoula.

Union pour le progrès social et al démocratie (UPSD). Political party, set up in 1991 and headed by Ange-Edouard Poungui.

PONGAULT, GILBERT, 1925– . A Mbochi born at Mossaka in 1925, Pongault attended Catholic mission schools. After World War II, he worked for Radio Brazzaville and then wrote for *La Semaine de l'A.E.F.* Active in trade unions, by the mid-1950s, he had become head of all the CATC unions throughout AEF, frequently attended labor congresses in Europe, and was a member of the French Economic and Social Council. In January 1959, the Christian labor unions of many African countries met at Brazzaville under his aegis and formed the Union Pan-Africaine des Travailleurs Chretiens. The next year he was elected secretary of the International Confederation of Free Trade Unions for AEF-Cameroun and, in 1961, vice-president of that organization. Subsequent to president Fulbert Youlou's fall, in which he played an active part, Pongault joined the MNR, but he was excluded from that party after the CATC was dissolved in November 1964. Accused of plotting to restore Youlou, he was condemned to death in absentia in 1966 having fled first to Lagos and then to Geneva. There he became prominent in international labor movements. After nine years in exile, he returned to the Congo under an amnesty in January 1974.

POOL REGION. Key heavily-populated and most developed region in Congo, with administrative headquarters in Kinkala, and including the districts of Kinkala, Boko, Kindamba, Mayama, Mindouli, N'Gamba, and the capital, Brazzaville. In terms of population the Pool region is Congo's fifth largest, with 195,792 people, not including Brazzaville's estimated population of 909,542. The Pool is the political center of gravity of Congo and is heavily peopled by Bakongo and Lari, though there have been many other ethnic arrivals from other regions. It has good road, rail and air communications with the Atlantic coast. The Djoué and N'Douo rivers allow logs to be floated to the Congo river. In the pre-colonial era the Pool was a major commercial entrepot, with caravans reaching it from the Loango kingdom with European goods and salt, and goods from upriver by canoes.

The region takes its name from Stanley Pool, a lake on the Congo River on which Brazzaville (and across it Kinshasa) is located. Also called the Plateau de Cataractes, the Pool region is a series of bare hills (600–800 meters high) cleared for farming, that rise, in the northwest, to the Massif de Chaillu.

POPULATION. Congo's population at the time of the Presidential elections in 1992 was officially estimated to be 2,679,000, with the urban component over 1.5 million, with just over 900,000 in Brazzaville and 400,000 in Pointe Noire. All of these figures are some 20% higher than estimates published in 1990. Projections for the year

2000 indicate a population of 3 million. The demographic distribution is uneven, as is the population's rate of growth, that has increased from the 1.7% annual rate in the 1950's, 2.7% in the 1980's, to 3.4% in the 1990's. Almost 81 percent of the people live in the southern regions, especially in the vicinity of Brazzaville and on the coastal plain, where communications are relatively easy. In the north, the inaccessibility of the area, its dense forests and swampy terrain account for the small size of its population and its concentration along the waterways. Traditionally the northern ethnic groups have migrated to the southwest, whereas southerners, under the pressure of population, have tended to move into the Batéké plateaux. None of these internal migrations, however, have eliminated regional and ancient antagonisms, for the immigrants tend to segregate themselves geographically and socially, especially in towns. The interethnic riots that occurred at Brazzaville and Pointe Noire during the first years after World War II have ceased as such, but have sometimes resurfaced in a less belligerent form when partly disguised by political-party labels.

The last country-wide census was conducted in 1985: current estimates are based on projections from that census. The earlier 1974 census had already confirmed the trend towards regional imbalance and the rapid growth of the two main towns, in striking contrast to the decline in the growth rate of the secondary settlements and in the nine regions, which is why the 1982–84 Plan tried to reverse this trend by stipulating the building up of regional centers. However, the cuts in the Plan occasioned by Congo's dire fiscal straits in the early-1980's eliminated most of such anticipated expenditures, and rural exodus and urban overconcentration have not abated.

In the populous south, inhabited by the related but mutually suspicious Bakongo, subgroups are larger and more competitive than those among the Mbochi-Kouyou in the sparsely settled north. Thus the Vili and Bakongo in particular were deeply divided during much of the 1968–1991 Kouyou-Mbochi military reign. The central Kongo have held the presidency only briefly (1963–68), following the longer tenure of the Lari in that office. The armed forces, composed in large majority of Mbochi-Kouyou, seized control of the government successively under Ngouabi, Yhomby Opango, and Sassou Nguesso. Currently, with Lissouba as president, political power passed to the southwest groups in Congo, the **Nibolek** that he represents. Nevertheless the Batéké and Bakongo continue to dominate the administration through the bureaucracy, owing to their superior cultural attainments.

A numerical ethnic breakdown of the population is not available, but the main ethnic groups, their subgroups and estimated percentages in the country in 1992 are:

Ethnic group	Subgroups	% of total
Kongo	Vili	53
	Bakongo	
	Lari	
	Yombe	
	Bembe	
	Kamba	
	Kougni	
	Sundi	
	Dondo	
	Bahangala	
	Manianga	
Téké	Koukouya	13
	Téké	
	Téké-Lari	
	Gangoulou	
	Nzikou	
	Aboma	
	Njikini	
	Tegue	
Mbochi	Mbochi	12
	Makoua	
	Kouyou	
	Likouala	
	Bangala	
	Bonga	
Kota	Tsangui	10
	Bamba	
	Voumbou	
	Nzabi	
	Ndassa	
Boubangui	Boubangui	4
	Bondjo	
	Mondjombo	
	Bondongo	
	Bomitaba	
	Bandza	
	Babolé	
Maka	Njem	4
	Bakwélé	
	Mabéza	
	Bamouali	
	Pomo	
Mbéti	Mbéti	3

Percentages rounded up.

When Congo became independent, Europeans (largely French) living there numbered 10,212. Soon after independence, their number declined, and after Congo declared for Marxism-Leninism, it was halved. By 1990, however, their numbers have gone up to some 6,000, concentrated in Pointe Noire and Brazzaville.

The 1992 figures for the population of the country's regions and capital city were: Brazzaville 909,542; Kouilou 665,502; Niari 220,075; Bouénza 219,822; Pool 195,792; Cuvette 151,539; Plateaux 119,722; Lokoumou 74,420; Likouala 70,675; Sangha 52,135. Some 50 languages or dialects are in use in Congo but there are two lingua franca: Lingala, in the north and central Congo, the Koutouba (or Kikongo) in the south.

PORTELLA, AIME (Major). Director general of Hydro-Congo. Trained in France, Portella, then a Lieutenant, first came to public notice in May 1968 when he was wounded in the skirmish known as the "mercenaries' plot." After Massamba-Debat's downfall, he was named second vice-president of the CNR directorate. Promoted to captain by Ngouabi, he was for a brief period the third most important military leader in the CNR. In December 1968, he was dropped from the CNR, and placed in command of the important Pointe Noire garrison. In April 1970, he was shifted into the civil administration and appointed director of civil aeronautics, and in June 1971, of LINA-CONGO. He then served on several other state companies, and in 1988 was named director-general of Hydro-Congo. The workers of that company called for his dismissal in 1993, on the grounds of fiscal mismanagement and ethnic favoritism.

POTASSIUM. Congo has large known potassium reserves, estimated at over one billion tons. Their exploitation could catapult the country into a globally-ranked exporter. However, the first effort to exploit the mineral (under a joint French-Congo enterprise) at Hollé not far from Pointe Noire, ended in 1977 in disaster, as cost-escalations made exploitation uneconomical, and later an undetected geological fault brought about the flooding of the mines and their closure. In 1985 the CPC was revived (with Congo holding majority, 51%, control) to prospect and exploit at other sites. Though new reserves were discovered the cost of exploitation was estimated so high, and Congo's financial straits were so tight, that little effort has been made in this direction. See also MINING.

POTO-POTO. One of Brazzaville's two main African quarters (the other being Bacongo), in the northern part of the town, spreading west from the CFCO station, and its most culturally vibrant. The name is descriptive of the heterogeneous building materials used there. Poto Poto hosts the world-famous Ecole peinture du Poto Poto, that has trained numerous highly talented artists, an original theater group, lively night-clubs, and in its markets a wealth of arts and crafts, sculpture, jewelry, traditional medicines, magic potions and fetish goods.

POUNGUI, ANGE-EDOUARD, 1943– . Banker, and former vice-president and prime minister of Congo. Born in 1943 and with a degree in economics, during his years in France Poungui was president of the union of Congolese students in that country. A prominent Marxist in his early years, Poungui rose to prominence via leadership over Congo's youth and student organizations, building a political base in the Niari region. In 1967 he was elected to the five-man executive committee of the **JMNR**, and a year later, as president of the students union, the Union Générale des Elèves et Etudiants Congolais (UGEEC) he presided over the latter's crucial July 1968 congress at Brazzaville that harshly criticized Massamba-Debat's presidency, contributing to his downfall. With the rise of the Ngouabi regime Poungui was integrated (mid-August 1968) into the CNR, and made president of its extremely influential economic, financial and social commission. In 1969 he was appointed secretary of state for foreign affairs. When the PCT was formed in December 1969, Poungui became a member of its politburo and, a few days later, was placed in charge of the party's finances. In June 1971, Ngouabi named him minister of finance, and in August 1972, vice-president of the republic, when Moudileno-Massengo did not return back from overseas. Although he lost the vice-presidency in August 30, 1973, Poungui remained a member of the PCT politburo and the state council. He then joined the IMF, and was for three years (1976–79) assistant director-general of the African Development Bank. In 1980, after the rise to power of Sassou Nguesso, his brother-in-law, Poungui was appointed president, and later director-general, of the Banque Commerciale Congolaise, serving at that post until 1984. By now purged of some of his early militancy, and regarded more of a technocrat, in the summer of 1984 he was brought back into the political center-stage by Sassou Nguesso as prime minister of Congo. He served in that post until August 1989, his longevity in office ascribed to Sassou Nguesso's need to appease Congo's foreign creditors during the country's difficult negotiations with the IMF/World Bank, and in order to bring the regime some support from Niari, Poungui's home region, that saw one of their popular leaders, Claude Ndalla arrested in 1984. (Poungui's appointment did not assuage Niari, since he was opposed by Celéstin Goma-Foutou, the Niari-originating PCT ideology head.) In August 1989

Poungui resigned as prime minister and was appointed president of the economic and social council. As multipartyism dawned on Congo Poungui resigned from the PCT to set up his own party, the UPSD.

PREFECTURES. Name of administrative divisions that prior to independence were named regions. There were 15 prefectures, internally subdivided into 44 sous-prefectures (formerly districts). In 1967 an administrative re-organization changed the name back to regions, with the sous-prefectures becoming districts. The administration of the prefectures/sous-prefectures and regions/districts has been entrusted to an array of advisory councils, with greater or lesser autonomy, whose nomenclature has changed over the years. See ADMINISTRATION.

PRESIDENTS OF CONGO. Apart from interim presidents (such as Lt. Augustin Poignet, briefly in August 1968, Captain Alfred Raoul in September-December 1968, etc.), Congo has had six heads of state: Fulbert Youlou (1959–1963); Alphonse Massamba-Debat (1963–1968); Marien Ngouabi (1968–1977); Joachim Yhomby Opango (1977–1979); Denis Sassou Nguesso (1979–1993) and Pascal Lissouba (1993–   ).

PRESS. Brazzaville's highly literate population, superior communications services, and position as capital city made it the most lively center for journalism in AEF. However, the ephemeral nature of its publications, their frequent changes of name and ownership, their small circulation, and the controls over the press increasingly exercised by the various governments between independence and 1991 eliminated all but official and heavily censored publications.

Under the colonial regime, journalism was the virtual monopoly of a few Frenchmen, and of socio-cultural organizations. Outstanding among the latter were the Catholic mission's *La Semaine de l'A.E.F.* (later called *La Semaine*) and the education service's *Liaison*. The main handicaps of the local press were insufficient funds and competition from France's and neighboring Kinshasa's publications. With the awakening of Congolese political consciousness in the 1950s, new and equally short-lived publications were founded to publicize the policies of parties, labor unions, and youth associations. Privately owned journals disappeared, except those that identified themselves with such groups. In turn, these publications foundered because of lack of funds or of sufficient local news or as a result of the disappearance of the groups for which they were the spokesmen. Such was the fate of the Force Ouvriere unions' *Conscience Ouvriere,* the MSA's *L'Essor,* the PPC's *L'AEF Nouvelle,* the UJC's *L'Eveil,* and the successive organs of the UDDIA—*France Equateur, Cette Semaine*

AEF, Le Progrès, and *L'Homme Nouveau.* Official censorship of the press was instituted by president Youlou, who banned the local sale of French papers critical of his regime and forbade the publication of opposition papers except for the influential weekly *La Semaine.*

Massamba-Debat in 1963 proclaimed a policy of press freedom and promised journalists regular briefings by his government, but two years later he arrested the chief editor of *La Semaine* for writing editorials critical of MNR's policy toward the Catholic church. In 1966, he announced that the role of the press was that of an instrument of the government and the party, and he revived Youlou's practice of seizing issues of the foreign press that contained criticism of his policy. Repressive measures in this sphere have been intensified by the military regime. The PTC took over the MNR press organ, *Etumba* (Combat) to express its own views; the JMNR bulletin, *Dipanda,* disappeared after that group's extreme left wing was purged; and in 1970 the Congo's only two provincial papers—*L'Eveil de Pointe Noire* and *L'Eveil de la Sangha*—were ordered to cease publication. In 1971, the official Agence Congolaise d'Information, founded by Youlou, was given a monopoly of all the news about Congo that Congolese and foreign journalists were allowed to print.

During the era of the Ngouabi and Sassou Nguesso military regimes, relations with writers and journalists were ambiguous. Brazzaville was widely recognized as one of francophone Africa's intellectual capitals, with the country producing an extremely large number of talented and internationally-published writers, journalists, poets and intellectuals in general. It also had a people's library, a National Association of Congolese Authors and Artists, and a book fair. Since the mid-1970s, censorship was far more to foreign publications that circulated in Congo than to indigenous output. A wide range of mainly French-language publications were banned after Ngouabi's assassination and during Yhomby Opango's regime. Although that ban was formally lifted in April 1980, the military government under Sassou-Nguesso kept correspondents of these publications (and especially their local stringers) under surveillance. Nevertheless, the disappearance of some local newspapers such as *La Voix de la Révolution* and the opposition's *L'Eveil Congolais* was due more to lack of vitality than official censorship. Longevity has not been a characteristic of the Congolese press, and ephemeral publications have come and gone fairly frequently. Indeed, the mortality rate among Congo's publications has always been high. By 1982, the two daily papers (*Le Courrier d'Afrique* and *Le Petit Journal de Brazzaville*) and two of the monthly periodicals published a decade before had disappeared, and only two of the weeklies (*Etumba* and *La Semaine*) still existed, as did one triweekly (*Mweti*) founded during that period. Of the two weeklies, *La Semaine* was the older and stronger, for its Christian sponsors had been able to survive the closing of their church missions and schools. Only *Etumba,* as the party organ, remained unperturbed, though it too had a swift rotation of its chief editors in 1976–77.

The three news publications that survived into the 1990's (when they were joined by new ones, as press censorship was lifted) were *La Semaine Africaine,* the Catholic weekly, dating from the colonial era, and with a circulation of 8,000; the daily news bulletin (circulation 1,000) of the Agence Congolaise d'Information, launched in 1961; *Mweti* (Star), that first appeared as the national paper in 1977. Some of the influential new ones to appear are *La Stade,* set up in 1985 with a circulation of 12,000 and *Le Soleil,* organ of the **MCDDI**. In 1994 faced with the necessity for austerity the Lissouba regime announced that with immediate effect all newspapers, and social, economic and cultural publications published under its aegis, except for the daily newsletter issued by the ACI (that earlier was supposed to be closed down) would cease to be issued.

PROPHETIC MISSION. One of Congo's many religious sects, currently established especially in Brazzaville, and headed by Prophet Lassy Zepherin.

PUNU. Small Eshira ethnic sliver of several thousand, found in greater numbers in neighboring Gabon.

PYGMIES. Properly known as Babinga or Aka, most of Congo's pygmy population lives in the forests of the north, as hunter-gatherers, trading their surpluses for agrarian products with neighboring sedentary groups with which they have a symbiotic relationship. Among the first indigenous populations of Congo, they have a low demographic growth, estimates of their numbers differ, and only in the last few decades have there been attempts to study them and their language systematically.

-R-

RADIO CONGO. Post-1990 name of Congo's radio station, replacing La Voix de la Révolution Congolaise, with two stations, in Brazzaville and Pointe Noire. It transmits 133 hours a week, with 80% of its programs in French, the rest in Lingala and Kikongo. The radio also broadcasts to Namibia in English and vernacular languages. Its director is Lucil Oba.

RADIO DE L'ALLIANCE. Illegal radio station operating in Brazzaville in 1993 and broadcasting political messages supportive of **Bernard Kolelas** and his **MCDDI** alliance, and against the government of president Pascal Lissouba. A major attempt to find and close the station in November 1993 brought about its relocation to Kinshasa, across the Congo river in Zaire.

RADIODIFFUSION-TELEVISION CONGOLAISE (RDC). Congo's radio and television service. For radio see RADIO CONGO. Congo also has a color TV station in Brazzaville, broadcasting 46 hours a week, with 90% of the programs in French, the rest in Lingala and Kikongo. There were 250,000 radio sets in Congo and 13,000 TV sets in 1991. Its director is Jean-François Sylvestre Souka.

RAOUL, ALFRED, (Major) 1938– . Former prime minister and vice-president of Congo. Born on December 13, 1938 in Pointe Noire of mixed ethnicity and Cabinda origin, and receiving his secondary education in Brazzaville and France, in 1960 Raoul was admitted to the St. Cyr military academy, where he met and became friends with Ngouabi, and from which he graduated as an army engineer, and then continued his studies at Angers. On his return to the Congo, Raoul was promoted to the rank of captain and named adjutant to the commander-in-chief of the armed forces, a post that he held when Ngouabi came to power in August 1968. In 1965 he was also appointed head of the army's engineering corps. After Ngouabi became president, Raoul was named secretary for defense in the CNR, prime minister and was also, briefly, acting head of state. After 1969, he was appointed minister of trade, and integrated into the PCT Politburo, and spent much time abroad as Ngouabi's roving ambassador. In December 1971 he sided with Ngouabi's opponents in the PCT, and for that lost the vice-presidency and his portfolio of trade. He was subsequently arrested and sentenced to twenty years imprisonment for allegedly participating in the February 1972 **Ange Diawara** aborted putsch, but was freed six months later. He served as ambassador to the EEC at Brussels (accredited also to Norway) from March 1976 until November 1977, when he was named ambassador to Egypt. Since falling from grace in 1971, however, he has been outside the public limelight. He was the most pro-French and pro-Western officer in the Ngouabi entourage.

RASSEMBLEMENT DEMOCRATIQUE AFRICAIN (RDA). An interterritorial movement founded at Bamako, French Soudan (later, Mali), in 1946, and with which many political parties throughout Francophone Africa were affiliated, as territorial branches. The RDA's manifesto demanded the constitutional confirmation of the rights of the French overseas populations and the elimination of colonialism throughout the world by legal means.

RASSEMBLEMENT DEMOCRATIQUE ET POPULAIRE DU CONGO (RDPC). Political party set up in 1991 by Jean-Marie Tassoua.

RASSEMBLEMENT DU PEUPLE FRANCAIS (RPF). See POLITICAL PARTIES.

RASSEMBLEMENT POUR LA DEFENSE DES PAUVRES ET DES CHOMEURS AU CONGO (RDPCC). Populist party, appealing to the large numbers of urban unemployed in Congo. Set up in 1991, it is headed by Angele Bandou.

RASSEMBLEMENT POUR LA DEMOCRATIE ET LE DEVELOPPEMENT (RDD). Political party set up in 1990 by Joachim Yhomby Opango. The party, grouping primarily Kouyou of the Cuvette, was very successful in that region, winning, in the local elections of 1992, 15 of the 31 seats, and in particular containing the Mbochi PCT party that had hoped to score inroads there.

RASSEMBLEMENT POUR LA DEMOCRATIE ET LE PROGRES SOCIAL (RDPS). New political party, set up in 1990 with Jean-Pierre Thystère-Tchicaya as its secretary general. The party was not as successful as expected in the local and senate elections that were held in 1992, especially in the Kouilou region where it won only a few seats compared to **AND**, close to Lissouba's **UPADS**, that won 12 of the region's 31 seats.

REFERENDUM OF MARCH 15, 1992. Referendum that approved Congo's new constitution by a 96.32% vote of a 70.93% turnout. See CONSTITUTIONS.

REGIE NATIONALE DES PALMERAIES DU CONGO (RNPC). State organ created in June 1966 with a monopoly over the palm-oil sector, and to administer the former palm-tree plantations of the private CFHBC in the Sangha and Cuvette (2,900 exploitable hectares) and operated the five oil-mills at Ouesso, Etoumbi, Kunda, Sibiti and Komono. Later, in the 1970's the RNPC expanded, and with EDF funds planted new groves, modernized the mills at Etoumbi and Kunda, and built a new one in Etoumi. Many of Congo's palm-tree plantations are aged, and weak producers. Despite serious infusions of capital (though projected funding under the 1982–86 plan was trimmed) Congo only produced around 2,000 tons of palm oil a year.

RELIGION. Religious breakdowns of Congo's populations have always been difficult to ascertain, and have been rough estimates. In 1991 it was estimated that about half the population is Christian, the rest following indigenous religions. Catholics were estimated to number 925,450 (up from 530,000 in 1981), Protestants were estimated at 110,461; Muslims, 25,000, though some estimates put their numbers at twice this; and adherents of various Messianic cults and animists, over one million. In that year the Catholic ecclesiastical hierarchy consisted of an archbishop (Barthélémy Batantu, archbishop of Brazzaville) and two bishops, 128 priests, 17 lay religious leaders, and 101 nuns, in one archdiocese and five dioceses. All three bishops were Congolese, as were 50 of the priests and 60 of the nuns. The main Protestant Church was the Eglise Evangélique du Congo in the Bacongo quarter of Brazzaville, founded in 1909, autonomous since 1961, and headed by Jean Mboungou.

Most of Congo's 25,000 Muslims are urban non-Congolese, found largely in Brazzaville and Pointe Noire where they have 49 mosques. Their number has been particularly susceptible to major change in light of periodic expulsion from Congo of "aliens" among whom have been a large number of Muslims from West Africa. (Some estimates put their number at around 50,000.)

The various Congolese regimes have, in general, been tolerant towards different religious practices, despite periodic "banning" of various sects (mostly for involvement in political activities) and early friction with the Church following the 1963 Revolution and the nationalization of private schools (mostly Catholic) under Massamba-Debat. Still, the very close intertwining, especially in equatorial Africa, of religion and politics, has caused several sects to be banned or persecuted. This happened at the outset of the Revolution, when JMNR gangs went on a violent rampage during 1965 to stamp out various animist practices inconsistent with Scientific Socialism, and also against **Matsouanists** some of whom had assisted Fulbert Youlou rise to power. Later, in 1976, the PCT central committee recommended that all Jehovah's Witnesses be banned from admittance to the Congo, and in 1977, in connection with Cardinal Biayenda's and Ngouabi's assassination, there was an interdiction against a small Messianic sect. All of the sects continued operating however. The strongest clampdown against religious unorthodoxy came late in 1985. Angered over the fact that every urban demonstration (in this case the Brazzaville student riots of November) brought out also large numbers of Congo's various religious sects, Sassou Nguesso announced only seven religions would henceforth be allowed to publicly hold services. (Like many edicts, this was only intermittently enforced.) The seven "recognized" religions were: the Catholic Church; the Congolese Protestant Evangelical Church; the Salvation Army; Simon Kimbangou's Church of Christ on Earth; the Congolese Islamic Committee; Tenrykio; and the Prophetic Mission of Prophet Lassy Zepherin. The rest, over 80 sects, were officially banned. Among them were, significantly, the IAM sect of which Sassou Nguesso himself had been a chief prophet, and Anzimbo, the sect of which Yhomby Opango was a main prophet.

(1) CATHOLICS. The first Catholic mission, founded by the Portuguese in 1663 at Loango, gradually declined. Catholicism did not revive in Congo until the 1880s, when French missionaries began establishing stations in the hinterland. By 1910 there were ten mission stations, including Loango; the most important of them were at Boundji, Linzolo, and M'Bamou. Their influence spread mainly through education, and the Mbochi, Vili, and, above all, Lari, who attended mission schools became the clerks and interpreters of the colonial administration and business firms. Only at the two Catholic seminaries was secondary schooling available in Moyen-Congo until the mid-1950s. Consequently young, ambitious Congolese, such as Fulbert Youlou, were among the 150-odd students trained as priests during the interwar years. French officials at first regarded Catholic missionaries as rivals to their authority over the Congolese, more of whom were educated at mission than at state schools until after World War II. Gradually, however, they cooperated in resisting the massive spread of Messianic cults in the region, many arriving across the Congo River from Belgian Congo, and in increasing local educational and health facilities. Beginning in 1946, all mission schools that conformed to official standards were granted substantial subsidies and were also allowed to give religious instruction in vernacular languages. The French nationality of almost all the Catholic missionaries, the zeal and competence with which they ran their schools and organized Catholic labor and youth groups, and the strict discipline they imposed on church members became assets in the eyes of the colonial administration. After 1960, however, they were handicaps in the mission's relations with independent Congo. The rift between Church and State began even under Abbe Fulbert Youlou,when the missionaries so strongly disapproved of his political activities that they forbade him to say the mass. The Catholic labor-union confederation, that spearheaded Youlou's overthrow for a variety of reasons, including his attempt to merge them into a single trade union, was promptly dissolved by the subsequent MNR government, and outstanding Catholic leaders were jailed or forced underground or into exile. In 1965, mission schools were nationalized, with almost all the teaching missionaries leaving the country except those in the seminaries, and an indigenous Congolese priest was consecrated archbishop of Brazzaville. Relations

between the government and the Congolese Catholic Church became less tense after Massamba-Debat's overthrow, and were actually cordial under the military interregnum. Perhaps indicative of that attitude was the fact that *La Semaine,* the Catholic weekly published in Brazzaville since pre-independence (and considered one of Congo's best periodicals) continued to appear regularly at all times.

In May 1980, Congolese Catholicism received a fresh impetus from the visit to Brazzaville of Pope John Paul. He said mass in French before a gathering estimated at 400,000, many of whom had arrived from neighboring countries. He was warmly acclaimed by thousands of Congolese when he addressed them briefly in Lingala and Koutouba. Both then and two years later, when a delegation of Congolese Catholic clergy was received by the Pope at the Vatican, he urged them to further Africanize the Congolese church, encourage vocations among Congolese Catholic youth, and form more Christian lay preachers, promising assistance in the form of guidance for the Congolese church, and priests to help in the effort.

(2) PROTESTANTS. Swedish evangelical missionaries founded the first Protestant mission in 1909 near Kinkala, where they made converts among the Bakongo. Within 20 years, the 30 pastors of the Swedish mission had established 12 stations, converted 47,000 Congolese, and had 11,000 Congolese children attending their schools. The success of Protestantism in Moyen-Congo was the more remarkable in that, for political reasons, its activities aroused more opposition among colonial officials than did those of the Catholics. The great majority of Protestant missionaries were Swedes and Norwegians, who used local dialects instead of French as the linguistic vehicle in their schools, and who trained from the start an indigenous clergy, all regarded suspiciously by the French. There was also the fear that the denominational divisions in the Protestant faith would polarize or reinforce existing local African interethnic antagonisms, while the Protestant doctrine of individual responsibility to God would encourage nonobedience to the secular authorities. After World War II, however, Church-government relations improved markedly for the same reasons as those that reconciled the administration with the Catholic missions, and subsidies were granted to Protestant schools on the same basis as to Catholic schools. Since Congo's independence, Protestant missionaries, unlike their Catholic counterparts, have had no difficulty cooperating fully with the government of the day, and among their converts have been many of the Congo's political leaders.

Provisions for freedom of religion in the international treaties of 1885 and 1919 opened the door for the installation of the Salvation Army and Jehovah's Witnesses in Moyen-Congo. The former arrived in the 1930's and had an immediate success in the Niari region. Its hymns, ceremonials, ranks and uniforms were adapted by many of its converts to the indigenous African culture and inspired some of the Messianic cults. Because the Salvation Army remained apolitical, the Congolese government allowed it to continue operating three schools for training its officers and soldiers after the Catholic mission schools were nationalized. Jehovah's Witnesses, locally called Kinsinga, did not reach Moyen-Congo until after World War II. They gained only a limited following in Brazzaville, Pointe Noire, and Dolisie because every Congolese government opposed their doctrine as hostile to secular authority and because the Witnesses' aggressive type of propaganda antagonized many Congolese. Among the resolutions passed at the PCT congress in November 1976 was one forbidding Jehovah's Witnesses to reside in the Congo. They were accused of a wide range of anticivic acts, such as failing to sing the national anthem and disobeying the party's directives. The sect was, as previously noted, banned from conducting public services by Sassou-Nguesso in 1985.

(3)MESSIANIC CULTS. Inspired by both Protestant and Catholic missionary activity, Messianic cults took root in Moyen-Congo during the interwar period. Kimbangouism and one of its derivatives, Kakism, arrived from nearby Belgian Congo in 1921. (See KIMBANGOUISM; KAKISM.) Their success among the Bakongo gave rise to other indigenous local sects, which were similarly movements of socio-religious protest against an alien government and religion and a return to African sources. Among these the first and most important was Matsouanism, whose appeal was largely to the Lari of the Brazzaville region. After World War II, another regionally based sect was the N'Zambie-Bougie, which flourished among the Vili of the Pointe Noire area. (See LASSY ZEPHERIN.) Some cults, such as Ngol and Labi, are confined to specific regions, in this case northern Congo, but with some 80 different cults in Congo today, many have spread beyond their original "home region" with the rural-urban drift itself.

All these Messianic cults adopted the monotheism and ecclesiastical hierarchy of the Christian churches, and the latter's hostility to sorcery and fetishism. Yet they also retained many traditional customs, such as polygamy, and some developed xenophobic tendencies. Matsoua gave his Lari followers a nationalistic orientation and organization that soon transcended his movement's religious aspect. Matsoua's death in prison during World War II, did not abate his following. On the contrary, his death was not accepted by his Lari followers, who on two successive occasions "voted" for his election to the national assembly. He then came to be venerated as a martyred divinity, in whose name the Lari actively and passively opposed the colonial administration, being in turn distrusted by the latter. (At Kinkala, the Lari "capital" and administrative headquarters of the Pool region, Matsoua's statue dominates the town.) Since the Lari were among Congo's most developed groups, this inward withdrawal placed them at a major political disadvantage at a time of major colonial devolution of power. Both the Vili, and the northern Mbochi and Kouyou benefitted from this and made serious inroads at the expense of the Lari. Politically weak until 1956, Matsouanists finally came into the limelight when they gave massive electoral support to their fellow-Lari, Fulbert Youlou, who—cultivating Matsoua's mannerism and rhetoric—came to be believed as Matsoua's heir. After Youlou became head of the Congolese government and tried to enforce his laws, however, Matsouanists turned against him, as against all prior established authority. In 1959 Youlou forcibly put down a Matsouanist riot at Brazzaville, and he was forced to break up that movement by deporting some of its leaders. Matsouanist resistance to established authority continued, however, even after his ouster, and Matsouanism was repressed in the aftermath of Massamba-Debat's rise to power, especially by autonomous youth (later JMNR) groups "cleansing" the countryside of "backward" practices. Though still very much alive, by the 1990's the Matsouanist movement was no longer prominent, at least in public life as before. However, the strong neo-Matsouanist postures of **Bernard Kolelas** in the various recent elections (1992–1993) underscore the residual political importance of this sect. Among the Vili, the less entrenched and weaker N'Zambie-Bougie sect backed the PPC at the polls. But its members were never so partisan or violent as the Matsouanists, though that sect refused to fade away from the political arena, and in 1992–93 was courted by Vili political contenders.

Although many leaders of the Messianic cults have retained sufficient influence to be courted by aspiring politicians, of the major sects (many are small or localized) only the Kimbangouists and Lassy Zepherinists have been actually growing in influence. The Kimbangouists, in particular, are now estimated to number eight million in central African countries, though the majority are in Zaire. They were considered sufficiently important to be admitted to the Ecumenical Council of Churches in 1969. The Lassy Zepherinists, in southern Congo, have been sufficiently numerous and motivated, to bring out crowds of 20,000 on important occasions, and they have been an important political factor in Kouilou and Niari regions among others.

RESERVE DE FAUNE DE LA LEFINI. One of Congo's more popular nature reserves. See also NATIONAL PARKS. It is reached via Ngo midway on the Brazzaville-Owando recently-tarred road.

-S-

SAMA, EUGENE. Militant Marxist poet, best-known for a collection of revolutionary poems published under the title *Poemes Diplomatiques*.

SAMBA, ANDRE BERNARD, 1933– . Journalist. A Bassoundi born on July 6, 1933 in Mindouli, where his father had been mayor, Samba was educated mostly in mission schools and at Brazzaville's institute of general administration (1954–56). After four years studying theology and philosophy at the Grand Seminary in Brazzaville, Samba joined the Congolese broadcasting authority in 1960 as assistant editor. In 1961 he joined the French broadcasting corporation for specialized training and in 1962 rejoined Radio Congo as editor, becoming in 1964 editor-in-chief of the renamed Voice of the Revolution. After several brief appointments in the ministry of information in 1972 he was appointed director of the Congolese information agency.

SAMBA, ZACHARIA, 1939– . Director of the School of economics, judicial and public administration at Marien Ngouabi university in Brazzaville. Born on October 9, 1939, Samba in 1971 acquired a law degree at the university of Bordeaux.

SAM'OVHEY-PANQUIMA, GUY-NOEL, 1945– . Journalist and statistician. Born on December 25, 1945 in Embouma-Lékana, after secondary studies he attended a variety of universities (including the University of Brazzaville; Morocco's Rabat Ecole des cadres supérieurs d'entreprise; Strasbourg's Centre universitaire de journalisme, and the Louis Pasteur institute of geography) obtaining two M.A. degrees in journalism and in economic geography, and diplomas in public administration. Returning to Brazzaville he first lectured at Marien Ngouabi university (1975–77) before moving into journalism and broadcasting. He held a series of progressively more important appointments with Radio Congo, including as editor-in-chief in 1976 and director of research, documentation and production during 1976–77, before being appointed in 1977 director of the Presidential Office's information and press bureau.

SANGHA. Congo's sparsely populated (52,135 people) northwestern region, with its administrative capital in Ouesso (870 kms from Brazzaville), and composed of the districts of Ouesso, Souanké and Sembé. Including a territory of 55,000 sq. kms., the region for long has been isolated from the rest of Congo, and has economic and trade links with Cameroun. Plans to link Ouesso by paved road to Owando (315 kms.) in the mid-1980's had to be scrapped due to the severe trimming of the 1982–86 development plan. Communications are thus still only possible during the dry season, since at other times the tracks become unpassable. On the other hand during the dry season (February-May) river traffic on the Sangha (a main artery for the supply of goods to Ouesso and evacuating the region's produce) and N'Goko rivers is as often as not impossible since the water is too shallow, and some river courses disappear altogether. The Sangha region has an elevation of between 400–900 meters, and within it is found Congo's highest peak, Nabemba, at 1,000 meters. Cocoa is widely planted in the Sangha region, even though most of the processed cocoa reaches the region from Cameroun. There are also some palm plantations, coffee, tobacco and rice, but most are neglected as rural youth gravitate to Ouesso and further south. The Sangha river, an affluent of the Congo, allows riverine access from Brazzaville to Ouesso and Salo, but not further upstream. Ouesso is connected by air to Brazzaville. There is an abundance of big game in the Sangha (including elephants) but the difficult terrain and complete absence of facilities make a tourist industry impossible.

SARIS-CONGO. See SOCIETE AGRICOLE POUR LA RAFFINAGE DU SUCRE.

SASSOU NGUESSO, DENIS (General), 1943– . Former military President of Congo. A Mbochi born at Edou in the Owando district of the Cuvette in 1943, Sassou-Nguesso attended a secondary school at Loubomo (1956–61) following which he joined the armed forces and was sent to attend military schools in France (including Saint-Maixent) graduating as a second lieutenant in 1962. He returned to Congo to assume command, in 1963, of the airborne infantry company, later of the airborne infantry battalion, being promoted to Captain. He then assumed command of the key Brazzaville Military Zone. With the rise to power of Ngouabi, Sassou Nguesso became a member of the CNR, and later was elected a member of the PCT's central committee, with duties as secretary of the permanent commission to the armed forces. He was briefly purged from the PCT in December 1971, but bounced back shortly later. In 1975 Sassou Nguesso was appointed minister of defense. He was re-confirmed in that post after the 1977 suicide squad assassination of Ngouabi, a conspiracy in which persistent though unsubstantiated rumors have linked Sassou Nguesso's name.

In 1977 Sassou Nguesso also became part of the military troika governing Congo under the leadership of President Yhomby Opango, and was named first vice-president of the PCT military committee that was then set up. On February 8, 1979 he peacefully engineered Yhomby Opango's ouster from power, and was elected by the PCT president of its central committee and president of Congo, being subsequently re-elected twice, in 1984 and 1989. The early years of the Sassou Nguesso era coincided with a major influx of oil royalties that greatly helped stabilize his regime by increased salaries, urban standards of living, and the period of relative tranquility in Congo's turbulent po-litical life. (The civil service payroll doubled between 1980 and 1985.) A very ambitious 1982–86 development plan was also initiated under his aegis, based on the assumption of continued high oil prices and in-creased production of Congolese crude. Sassou Nguesso also made his grip over the military forces virtually unassailable by heavily recruit-ing military personnel, and a bodyguard, from among relatives and kinsmen at his home-village of Edou, while packing the PCT central committee and its Politburo with Mbochi and personal loyalists.

However, by the early 1980's a downswing in global oil-prices cut short Sassou Nguesso's policies of political stabilization via patron-age and the execution of most of the development plan. Also, the con-tinued massive deficits piled up by Congo's state corporations ushered progressive austerity policies, cash-flow crises and eventual bank-ruptcy. Despite forewarnings of doom, and Sassou-Nguesso's at-tempts to reorganize and trim both the bloated civil service and defici-tory state enterprises, he was opposed at every turn by PCT hard-liners, unionists and students, with the result that most of the state sector lan-guished untouched. At the same time student unrest erupted as a civil service hiring freeze no longer assured automatic entry into it by uni-versity graduates. Graffiti criticizing Sassou Nguesso began to appear in downtown Brazzaville, and unrest proliferated. Unable to imple-ment restructuring, nor able to force Congo's oil-companies to in-crease production of crude, Sassou Nguesso was eventually forced to accept stringent IMF guidelines for an adjustment loan.

In 1987 came a revolt by **Captain Anga** in the northern Owando, reflecting a dangerous split among the northern officer corps, as many Kouyou were implicated, charging Sassou Nguesso with a role in the 1977 assassination of Ngouabi. The revolt was crushed with many deaths, alienating new segments of the army. Later, on May 19, 1989 Sassou-Nguesso escaped an assassination attempt by a Kouyou offi-cer linked to Ngouabi's mother, after the previous night saw a kidnap attempt on his son-in-law and director of the Presidential military staff, Colonel Angom. Cuban intelligence officers in the security ser-vices had warned Sassou Nguesso of a multiplicity of plots against him. The Ngouabi issue did not disappear, and in 1991 Yhomby Opango and others publicly called for an inquiry into the matter. And, after Sassou Nguesso was forced to convene a **national conference** a civil lawsuit was lodged against him (in 1993) on behalf of 14 families of military personnel killed in the 1987 revolt, alleging he had ordered them killed rather than captured, to squash allegations of his involvement in Ngouabi's murder.

By 1989 domestic pressures, Congo's parlous economic situation, and the changed international scene forced Sassou Nguesso to liberalize the political system, abandon Marxism-Leninism, invite home all foreign-based opposition movements, and convene a **National Conference** that inevitably declared itself sovereign and ushered in a competitive multiparty system. Though the PCT had already in July 1989 restructured itself for the new era, dropped its former hard-line elements, and in particular the Stalinist PCT permanent secretary, **Colonel Camille Bongou**, large numbers of key members deserted it. On April 26, 1991 in a televised speech Sassou-Nguesso publicly begged for understanding, forgiveness and indulgence for his regime's wastage of public resources and serious abuses of power. (This was not the first time an ousted military leader cleansed his slate in such a manner; the speech triggered the comment of one opposition leader that forgiveness was not in the cards since "we are not the Catholic Church.") Despite resistance from elements in the heavily-northern military officer corps, die-hard radicals, and members of the Impfondo group (who had banked on producing the next leader of Congo) that resulted in a prolonged, and violent transitional phase, interspersed with multiple shootouts in downtown Brazzaville, Sassou Nguesso's eclipse was secured after the parliamentary and presidential elections of 1992. He was eliminated in the first round of the latter, securing only 16.87% of the vote, the majority coming from northerners. Sassou Nguesso still remains an important factor in politics, and in the armed forces, if only because he remains the rallying point of the Mbochi vote that his "new" (non-Marxist, mass rather than elite) PCT party has been able to garner. In the new parliament he has aligned the PCT (that elected 19 deputies) with the Bakongo opposition (MCDDI) to President Lissouba.

SASSOU NGUESSO, MARIE-ANTOINETTE. Wife of former President Sassou Nguesso. A Vili born in Kinshasa (Zaire), her mother is an important businesswoman there, with access to President Mobutu. Marie-Antoinette's younger sister married in 1985 a cousin of Mobutu, and in January 1990, Sassou Nguesso's daughter Edith, then 28, married the divorced Gabon's President Bongo, sparking gossip of a dynastic rearrangement of central Africa. Marie-Antoinette Sassou Nguesso has acted as the personal diplomatic representative of her husband, making an increasing number of trips abroad, cementing in particular relations with Zaire, and bringing the regime some support from Pointe Noire's Vili population.

SASSOU NGUESSO, MAURICE. A brother of former president Sassou Nguesso placed in 1981 as political commissar of **Hydrocongo**. In 1985 he was the subject of investigations for massive embezzlement, and was removed to a more inconspicuous post in the state sector. He was arrested in August 1991 by the new civilian regime and tried for fraudulently obtaining insurance bonuses amounting to 9 million CFAF.

SAVONNERIE DU CONGO (SAVCONGO). Deficitory soap producing state company, with capacity to produce 6,000 tons of soap products. Savcongo was privatized in 1989, being bought by a Lebanese syndicate that also purchased the Huileries de Nkayi (Huilka).

SENATE. One of the innovations of the 1992 constitution was the creation of an upper house of 60 members, none of whom could be less than 50 years of age. In the July 26, 1992 elections, Lissouba's UPADS gained 23 seats, Kolelas' MCDDI 13, Yhomby Opango's RDD 8, Sassou Nguesso's PCT 3, Milongo's FDC 1 and the rest were won by independents.

SIANARD, CHARLES, 1927– . Former cabinet minister and civil administrator. Born on October 12, 1927 in Boko-Sangha, after graduating from the Ecole des Cadres at Brazzaville, Sianard entered the administration. From 1961 to 1963, he served as president Fulbert Youlou's cabinet director, and under Massamba-Debat was promoted to the post of director of economic affairs. After Massamba-Debat's ouster Sianard was appointed by Ngouabi as minister of finance, then of trade, a post he held from June 1969 to April 1970. In the latter month, he was dropped from the state council following an attempted coup, but was named general director of the administration of Congo.

Later he was transferred to head SIACONGO, and was reintegrated into president Ngouabi's cabinet as minister of interior in January 1973. In August of the same year he was also given the posts and telecommunications portfolio. In March 1975, he was named secretary-general of the state council, an administrative post, an appointment reconfirmed in April 1977. In 1989 he was reassigned to administrative duties in the public sector, and shortly after that went into retirement.

SIBITI. Congo's sixth-largest town and administrative headquarters of the Lékoumou region northwest of Brazzaville. Growing strongly, by

1992 the town had passed in size Moussendjo, and had a population of over 16,000. Sibiti is also the name of one of the districts in the Lékoumou region with headquarters in the town of the same name. The district (8,000 sq. kms.) is mostly a forested plateau at an altitude of 500 meters, and a partly hilly terrain interspersed with plains paralleling the Niari river.

SILOU, THOMAS, 1951– . Scientist. Born in Brazzaville on February 14, 1951, and securing a first degree from the University of Brazzaville in 1971 before proceeding to the universities of Orleans and Montpellier where he earned a Science doctorate in Chemistry and biochemistry, Silou returned in 1976 to a teaching career at Marien Ngouabi University. Between 1979 and 1982 head of the chemistry department, Silou has headed other departments/divisions in the university and was appointed to a variety of governmental bodies, including since 1986 as councilor on the Council for research in science and technology.

SINDA, MARTIAL, 1935– . Author and poet. Born in M'Bamou-Kinkala in the Pool region, he went for his higher education in Chartres and Paris, completing his PhD degree there. His dissertation on Congo's messianic movements, published in 1973 is a classic. He has also published a number of collections of poems.

SMIG. See LABOR.

SOCIETE AGRICOLE POUR LA RAFFINAGE DU SUCRE (SARI-CONGO). Industrial sugar-processing and refining company, that finally replaced the former state-owned **Sucrerie du Congo** after privatization in 1991, following fierce resistance from its labor force. The company is capitalized at 2 billion CFAF and is now owned by a private French group with Congo retaining a 15% equity. It currently employs 1,200 workers, a much-reduced complement from its 2,577 workers in 1989. Since privatization sugar production has gone up from 25,961 tons in 1991 to 36,000 in 1993, with a planned target of 50,000 by 1995.

SOCIETE CIMENTIERE DU CONGO (SOCICO). Mixed economy enterprise, with 50% Norwegian ownership, successor since 1987 of CIDOULOU. Since it was restructured the company has expanded its plant and now has a capacity to produce 300,000 tons a year, adequate for all of Congo's domestic needs.

SOCIETE CONGOLAISE ARABO-LIBYENNE (SOCALIB). Joint Congo-Libyan forestry company, set up in 1982 and logging 10,000 cubic meters of wood in 1987.

SOCIETE CONGOLAISE DE CONSERVERIE ET DE CONGE-LATION (SOCOFROID). Formed in 1964 to process tuna caught by all the companies operating in Congolese waters. Its capacity is 1500 tons, its capital 35.5 million CFAF, and its main shareholders are the Société de Développement de l'Afrique Equatoriale and the Sovetco company of Dakar.

SOCIETE CONGOLAISE DE RECHERCHES ET D'EXPLOITA-TION MINIERES (SOCOREM). State enterprise created in 1980 to engage in systematic exploration in Congo. See MINING.

SOCIETE CONGOLAISE DES BOIS D'OUESSO. Timber company set up in 1983 to exploit forest resources in northern Congo. Congo has a 51% equity in the company.

SOCIETE CONGOLAISE DES BRASSERIES KRONENBOURG (SCBK). Beer-brewing company and producer of an array of fruit juices. The company has several plants with its headquarters in Pointe Noire. The SCBK is capitalized at 1,872 million CFAF, employs nearly 700 people and moved into new premises in 1984.

SOCIETE CONGOLAISE D'IMPORT ET EXPORT (SOCIM-PEX). State company involved in industrial fishing and the import of fish for the local market. By 1986 SOCIMPEX had become the prime Congolese fish producer with 5,540 tons.

SOCIETE CONGOLAISE DU BOIS (SOCOBOIS). See INDUS-TRIES.

SOCIETE DES TEXTILES DU CONGO (SOTEXCO). Originally a state enterprise set up in 1982 at Kinsoundi, producing cotton goods and with confectionary outlets. In 1983 SOTEXCO absorbed **UTS**, and in a few years it was transformed into a mixed-economy company.

SOCIETE DES VERRERIES DU CONGO (SOVERCO). Former state glassworks in Pointe Noire, established in 1977, capitalized at 500 million CFAF and with a productive capacity of 12,000 tons. Employing 253 workers, the company piled up large deficits during the 1980's. In 1985 it was restructured and benefitted from foreign technical assistance, but to no avail. In 1990 the government could no longer pick up its annual deficits, and SOVERCO closed down. The American GAP Group, established in Zaire, entered negotiations for the purchase of the plant in 1992, encountering resistance from the trade union (of the laid off workers) that insisted the entire original complement be hired, rather than only the 40% GAP felt were needed.

SOCIETE D'IMPRESSIONS DE TEXTILES DU CONGO (IM-PRECO). Mixed economy company with 750 million CFAF in capital, 30% of it state money, the rest from private foreign origin, and employing 252 workers. Set up in 1975 in Brazzaville with a productive capacity of over 21 million meters of finished products, the company encountered a variety of problems in the mid-1980's with production plummetting in 1985 to 12.5 million meters.

SOCIETE INDUSTRIELLE D'ARTICLES EN PAPIER (SIAP-CONGO). State company, producing paper products. During the 1980's its production slipped by 50%. In 1993 the government announced privatization of the company.

SOCIETE INDUSTRIELLE DE DEROULAGE ET DE TRANS-FORMATION DU BOIS (SIDETRA). Wood processing state company, based in Pointe Noire. The company closed down bankrupt in 1990. The American GAP Group expressed interest in buying the company late in 1992, but its plans to re-open it with a drastically reduced manpower encountered resistance from the unions (insisting the entire original complement should be rehired) and negotiations stalled.

SOCIETE INDUSTRIELLE ET AGRICOLE DU CONGO (SIA-CONGO). State enterprise that in 1970 took over a variety of recently nationalized private agricultural assets, including the sugar plantations and facilities of **SIAN** and **SOSUNIARI**. At the time Congo's largest agricultural employer, by 1978 the company was bankrupt, owed huge amounts to the treasury, and had brought about an 80% decline in sugar production (from 60,000 to 12,000 tons.) In 1978 it was broken into three parts, with **SUCO** taking over the sugar section.

SOCIETE INDUSTRIELLE ET AGRICOLE DU NIARI (SIAN). Former mixed-economy company operating sugar plantations and a sugar refinery in the Niari region. The company encountered serious labor unrest and was nationalized in 1970. Mismanagement promptly brought it to economic collapse and it was restructured and taken over by SIA-CONGO which see.

SOCIETE INDUSTRIELLE ET AGRICOLE DU TABAC (SIAT). Cigarette-producer, established in 1942 and capitalized at 900 million CFAF. Employing around 200 workers, its turnover has been around 4 billion CFAF. SIAT's cigarettes are sold also in neighboring states. In 1984 the company was licensed to produce a number of American brands.

SOCIETE INTERNATIONALE DES BRASSERIES DU CONGO (SIBC). Mixed-economy beer-bottling enterprise with 51% state capital and 49% private (the majority by **Pierre Otto Bongo**) with two plants, in Brazzaville and Oyo in the north.

SOCIETE ITALIENNE-CONGOLAISE D'ARMEMENT ET DE PECHE (SICAPE). Joint Italian-Congolese fishing company, in which Congo holds a majority interest. Formed in 1974, SICAPE's charter was to undertake coastal and deep-sea fishing, establish a fish canning factory, construct a deep-freeze plant in Pointe Noire and a network of cold-storage stores throughout the country, and to produce fish-meal. Notwithstanding this mandate the company has only engaged in fishing, with its entire catch destined for overseas buyers.

SOCIETE MINIERE DE M'PASSA (SMM). State company exploiting mineral ores in the Pool region. Despite assistance from the Soviet Union the company, that produced only 7,310 tons in 1985, closed down bankrupt. See MINING.

SOCIETE MIXTE BULGARO-CONGOLAISE DE RECHERCHE ET D'EXPLOITATION DES PHOSPHATES (SOPHOSCO). Joint Bulgarian-Congolese enterprise set up in Pointe Noire in January 1976 with 250 million CFAF in capital (51% from Congo). Though several important mineral deposits were discovered in its concessions, no exploitation has taken place.

SOCIETE NATIONALE DE DISTRIBUTION D'EAU (SNDE). State waterworks, with an additional monopoly over the import of mineral water. SNDE was in the process of being privatized in 1994.

SOCIETE NATIONALE D'ELEVAGE (SONEL). State enterprise based in Loutété, and established in 1964 with 80 million CFAF to manage state farms and cattle ranches, mostly in the Niari region. Deficit-ridden, SONEL was replaced in 1984 by the Office du Gros Betail.

SOCIETE NATIONALE D'EXPLOITATION DU BOIS (SNEB). State company with headquarters in Pointe Noire, set up in 1974 to process timber. It has recorded deficits throughout most years of its operation.

SOCIETE NATIONALE DE RECHERCHE ET D'EXPLOITATION PETROLLIERES. See HYDRO-CONGO.

SOCIETE NATIONALE DE TRANSFORMATION DU BOIS (SONATRAB). State timber-processing company established in 1970 taking over the operations of the Israeli company Afri-Bois. The company encountered various difficulties, including lack of assured supplies of logs, and had needed constant state subsidies.

LE SOLEIL. Weekly newspaper, founded in 1991, and organ of Bernard Kolelas' MCDDI political party.

SONY, MARCEL. See LABOU TANSI, SONY.

SOUANKE. District in the extreme northwest of Congo with administrative headquarters in the town with the same name near the Cameroun border. Souanké is in the region of Sangha, entirely covered by untapped primeval forests, mountaineous towards the east, flat towards the north and west. The district covers an area of 21,000 sq. kms., and has coffee and cacao plantations, many not fully exploited due to the desertion of young people to the regional headquarters (Ouesso) and further south. Communications in the district are difficult, and there is as much contact with nearby Cameroun as with the distant Brazzaville.

LE STADE. Mass-circulation weekly, founded in Brazzaville in 1985 and with Hubert-Trésor Madouaba-Ntoualani as director and Bertin Ebinda as chief editor. In 1991 the paper had a circulation of 12,000.

STANLEY POOL. A lake 28 kms. long and 24 kms. wide on the Congo River, on opposite sides of which are found Brazzaville and Kinshasa, the capital of Zaire. Below the Pool stretch a number of rapids that make river navigation to the coast impossible.

SUCRERIE DU CONGO (SUCO). Former state-owned sugar company, capitalized at 500 million CFAF and at its height employing 4,300 workers. In 1978, under a Franco-Dutch management team, SUCO took over the sugar processing unit of **SIA-CONGO** that itself had taken over **SIAN**, that had been run to the ground after nationalization. Supplied by sugar plantations that in 1988 covered 22,000 hectares, the company has been deficitory due to an excessively large manpower. In 1989 the government decided to dismiss 777 workers and in 1991 privatized the company that became SARI-CONGO which see.

SUGAR. See AGRICULTURE.

-T-

TAMBA-TAMBA, VICTOR. Secretary of state or minister in all Congolese governments between June 1969 and August 1973, Tamba-Tamba alternately headed public works and transportation, or urbanization and housing. A meteorological technician by profession, Tamba-Tamba was also in the mid-1970's a member of the PCT central committee, and its secretary in charge of organization. Later Political Commissar of the Cuvette region, he rejoined the cabinet on April 4, 1979, as minister of labor and justice, but lost his post in the reshuffle of December 28, 1980. With the onset of multipartyism he joined the UPADS party and is on its steering committee.

TASSOUA, JEAN-MARIE. Political leader who in 1992 set up the Rassemblement démocratique et populaire du Congo (RDPC).

TATI-LOUTARD, JEAN-BAPTISTE, 1938– . One of Francophone Africa's best-known and most-published poets. A Vili born on December 15, 1938 at Ngoyo, near Pointe Noire, where he completed primary schooling. He then studied in Brazzaville's Chaminade seminary (1953–1959) and taught for two years before proceeding to the University of Bordeaux for higher studies, earning a degree in literature in 1963, and two additional diplomas in 1964 and 1965. Returning to Congo in 1966 he taught literature at the University of Brazzaville while working on his PhD specializing in poetry. Successively promoted at the university to head of department, and dean, by 1975 Tati-Loutard was director of higher studies and scientific research. His literary output has been voluminous, starting with his first work in 1968, and he is Congo's best known author abroad, his work translated into English and a variety of other languages. On December 18, 1975 he commenced a political career, joining the Goma cabinet as minister of higher education in charge of culture and arts, being shifted on April 5, 1977, to minister of arts, culture, and sports. He remained in the cabinet for over a decade until 1989.

TCHIBOUELA. One of Congo's richest oil-deposits. Discovered by Elf-Aquitaine in 1984, it entered production in 1986.

TCHICAYA, FELIX, 1903–1961. Congo's early dominant politician. The leader of the Vili in the Pointe Noire region, Tchicaya was born in Libreville, Gabon, on November 9, 1903. After graduating from the William Ponty School at Dakar, he became an accountant and journalist in Moyen-Congo. During World War II, he fought with the Free

French (becoming a Sergeant), and in 1945 was elected Congo's representative to the French Constituent Assembly. The next year, 1946, he founded the Parti Progressiste Congolaise party, that grouped Vili and some Batéké, and was successively elected Congo's deputy to the French National Assembly. The PPC was affiliated to the interterritorial RDA party, until the link was revoked in favor of Fulbert Youlou's UDDIA. In 1952 Tchicaya was also elected grand councilor of the AEF. In that year, and again in 1956, he was reelected to the French National Assembly. Politically dominant so long as the more numerous Lari were withdrawn from political activity as a result of their **Matsouanist** affiliations, once Fulbert Youlou succeeded to tap that source of support in 1956 Tchicaya's political hold over Congo declined. He also lost local support by not keeping in touch with his political machine in Pointe Noire, preferring to stay in Paris for prolonged periods. Tchicaya won no seats in the 1957 elections and the PPC disappeared, its membership merging with Youlou's UDDIA. His son, **Gérard-Felix Tchicaya U'Tamsi**, attained global distinction as a poet and novelist.

TCHICAYA U'TAMSI, GERARD-FELIX, 1931–1988. One of Africa's greatest poets and playrights. Born in 1931 in Mpiti, son of **Felix Tchicaya** the early Moyen-Congo deputy and politician, he did most of his secondary studies in France. Adding "U'Tamsi" ("'little pen that speaks for his country") to his surname, Tchicaya's first work, a collection of poems, was published in 1955. With his second collection he won, in 1957, the AEF Grand Prix Litteraire, continuing on with a string of works as well as radio-scripts. He was then briefly editor-in-chief of the MNC organ *Congo* in Belgian Congo, appointed by Patrice Lumumba. After the latter's assassination he returned to Paris to pursue a career as an administrator with UNESCO, continuing with a steady string of much acclaimed plays and collections of rich and difficult poems. In 1966 he won the Grand Prix for poetry at the Dakar Festival of African Arts. He died on April 21, 1988 of a heart attack.

TCHICHELLE, FRANCOIS AUGUSTE. See TCHICHELLE, TCHIVELLE.

TCHICHELLE, STEPHANE, 1915–1984. Early Vili political leader, former foreign minister and vice-president of Congo. Born January 12, 1915 in N'Gaya-Binda in the Kouilou region, Tchichéllé was educated in the Loango mission school. In 1930, he was employed by the Congo-Ocean railroad and six years later became Pointe Noire's station-master. Becoming a union leader, after the post World War II political reforms, he joined the Vili-based PPC party and was elected representative of Kouilou in the Moyen-Congo territorial assembly, serving consecutively there from 1946 to 1959. He was also territorial councillor for Kouilou between 1952 and 1957, grand councilor of the AEF from Congo between 1947–57 (where he served one year as its vice-president) and mayor of Pointe Noire in 1956. In 1957 he switched allegiances from the PPC to the UDDIA and entered Fulbert Youlou's government, where he was successively minister of labor and health (1957), of interior (1959), of foreign affairs (1960–63), and vice-president of the republic (1961–63). After Youlou's overthrow, he was arrested and sentenced to 15 years in prison with hard labor. He was amnestied three years later, in August 1967, returning to private life. In 1970, in an effort to secure Vili support Ngouabi appointed him director of the Congo-Ocean railroad, a post he occupied until his death in November 1984.

TCHICHELLE, TCHIVELLE, 1940– . Minister of Environment, Tourism and Leisure, former armed forces medical doctor, and novelist. A Vili born on October 22, 1940 in Pointe Noire, after studies in Congo he earned a medical degree at the university of Bordeaux (1961–1969) during which period he changed his first name (François) to Tchivéllé. He then continued his specialization at the university of Toulouse (1969–1975) in pediatrics and sports medicine, obtaining also a public health diploma at the university of Rennes in 1978. He finally returned to Congo in 1980 and was immediately appointed head of pediatrics at the Army Central Hospital. Between 1981–83 he was also director of the hospital. Since 1983 he has been director of health services in the autonomous military zone of Brazzaville, with, in 1985, a rank of Colonel. He combined a literary career with his medical one, being also a novelist, his first work published in Paris in 1986, and his second three years later. On September 8, 1992 he was named to the new civilian cabinet.

TCHIOUFOU, AUGUSTE-CASIMIR, 1933– . Civil administrator. Born on May 5, 1993 in Pointe Noire, though of Cabinda origin, after studying at Catholic seminaries in Mbamou and in Cameroon, he earned his BA in 1954 in preparation for being ordained as a priest. In 1955, however, he joined the civil service instead, in the posts and telecommunications department. Originally a member of the PPC, then dominant politically in Pointe-Noire, he changed his membership to the UDDIA and also joined the CGAT trade union in 1956. After independence he was named chief inspector of the postal and telecommunications service, a position he held until his early retirement in 1976.

TEKE see BATEKE.

TELECOMMUNICATIONS. In 1943, the Free French authorities added to the small facilities owned by Brazzaville's radio a powerful 50-kw. station. Radio Brazzaville then broadcast in the major European languages and in Arabic, with its post-war operations financed and controlled from Paris. A smaller Brazzaville station, Radio AEF, was also under French management, and its broadcasts were beamed to all AEF territories until it came under Congolese control in 1959. After independence, radio programs were rapidly expanded to include more local news and broadcasts in Congolese dialects. Beginning in 1965, the Massamba-Debat government asserted more control over both radio and TV transmissions, which it used to publicize party politics and accomplishments. In 1966 there were approximately 5,000 radio and 400 TV sets in Congo, the great majority of which were owned by Europeans and urban Congolese. In 1970, the French Radio and Television Organization (ORTF) ceased to relay its African programs through Radio Brazzaville, which by then had been renamed "The Voice of the Congolese Revolution." The next year, the Congolese government took over from ORTF ownership the latter's two short-wave and three medium- and long-wave transmitters in Brazzaville and Pointe Noire, as well as the television station that had begun operating in 1963 in Brazzaville. In the early 1970s, the Chinese built a new transmitter for the Ngouabi government that formed a "revolutionary committee" to coordinate and control all broadcasts from Congolese stations, as well as an Office des Telecommunications Internationales du Congo. The number of radio and TV programs, which were beamed to both domestic and foreign audiences and included educational telecasts, steadily increased. The most important development in telecommunications during the rest of the 1970's was the inauguration by Brazzaville in May 1978 of a land satellite station built by a French company financed by a loan from Paris. During the 1980's The Voice of the Congolese Revolution broadcast from its stations in Brazzaville and Pointe Noire during 133 hours a week, mostly in French (80 percent of broadcast time) and in Lingala and Koutouba. Although Pointe Noire was promised a color television station, the only one operating in Congo was the one at Brazzaville, which telecast every week for 46 hours, in French (90 percent) and also in Lingala and Koutouba (Kikongo).

The history of telecommunications in Congo during the revolutionary era, like that of the cinema and other media, has been one of rapid nationalization and the extension of governmental controls. In the case of the postal and telecommunications organization (ONPT), founded in 1964, there was an important increase in infrastructure throughout the country in 1970, and another starting in 1976. A central post office and regional branches were built, but the volume of written communications they handled declined rapidly because of frequent breakdowns in the postal service and heavy debts the postal service incurred. The means of telecommunication, on the other hand, grew in volume and radius. In the 1980's the ONPT telecommunications network consisted of seventeen automatic telephone exchanges, of which only six were in the vast northern region, something partly corrected in the mid-1980's as part of the (truncated) 1982–86 development plan. In addition to international telecommunications effected through the Brazzaville satellite station, Congo had sixty-five transmission centers. Under the 1982–86 plan, 23.5 million CFAF were allocated to improvements in telecommunications, but only a segment of that amount was actually spent.

TELEVISION NATIONALE CONGOLAISE. Congo started TV transmissions in 1963, with color programs commencing in 1983. There were 13,000 TV sets in the country in 1991. Programming amounted to 46 hours per week, most programs in French, but including a few hours in Lingala and Kikongo. Its director is Jean-Gilbert Foutou.

TENRYKIO. A religious sect in Congo.

THAULAY-GANGA, ABEL, 1920– . Early political militant. Born on September 20, 1920 in Kinkala, of Lari origins, after secondary studies Thaulay-Ganga became a teacher in the Brazzaville Catholic mission school which he had attended. Leaving the teaching profession in 1939, he held successive jobs as accountant in the private sector, and in 1953 became treasurer of the CGAT trade union. Several years later he took the labor-training course offered by the CGT in France, after which he attended labor conferences in Peking, Prague, and Sofia. He returned to Brazzaville in December 1957 and became an active member of the UJC. Massamba-Debat named him secretary of the CNR in August 1963 and Congo's first ambassador to the U.S.S.R. in April 1965. He was a member of the MNR politburo when he was appointed, in March 1968, the first political commissar of the people's army. Arrested by the military on August 31, 1968, but freed by the courts on September 5, he was re-arrested soon afterward, when a cache of arms was discovered in his native village. In November 1968, he was sentenced to five years in prison. Though rehabilitated soon later, Thaulay-Ganga faded into obscurity.

THYSTERE-TCHICAYA, JEAN-PIERRE, 1936– . Deputy-mayor of Pointe Noire, former PCT party Marxist ideologue and second-ranking leader of the PCT, and currently minister of mines, energy and hydrocarbons. Born in Pointe Noire on January 7, 1936 a member of the former royal family of the Vili Loango kingdom, and married to a French wife, after higher education in France he was successively director of the Lycée Chaminade (1965–67) and the Ecole Normale Superieure (1967–1971). After Ngouabi's rise to power Thystère-Tchicaya was appointed minister of technical and higher education (December 1971), and in February 1973 he was given the information portfolio. In December 1974 he was appointed president of the PCT central committee, in which capacity he cemented relations with the French Communist Party in Paris the next year. Political Commissar of the Pool region, he also became a member of the special revolutionary general staff formed December 12, 1975, and a member of the state council created January 6, 1976. After Ngouabi's assassination Thystère-Tchicaya played a key role in helping displace the latter's successor, Yhomby Opango, and bringing to power Sassou-Nguesso, for which he was rewarded by being integrated into the ruling troika that emerged out of the extraordinary congress of March 1979. Guardian of Marxist purity, official ideologue of the politburo, secretary in charge of party propaganda and information, he was technically Congo's second-ranking politician, though a major thorn in Sassou-Nguesso's side and in poor relations with other important leaders of the PCT. In February 1983 he was named president of the Banque Commerciale Congolaise, and was further shunted aside when accused by **Claude Ndalla** of treason, and plotting against the regime. Removed from his posts and placed under house arrest for two years in 1984 for an alleged role in a plot that had resulted in 1982's two bombings (at Maya Maya international airport and at the popular Star Cinema in Poto Poto), in his much-awaited trial Thystère-Tchicaya merely received a five-year suspended sentence, in essence being exonerated of all charges. He was later (1988) amnestied. Throughout this period there was growing unhappiness among the Vili in the Pointe Noire region over his purge, complicating Sassou-Nguesso's efforts to balance ethnic representation in the cabinet. Eclipsed until the era of multipartyism dawned, Thystère-Tchicaya retained support among a broad segment of the Vili in his home-region. With the dawn of multi-partyism his continued regional importance was confirmed by the seats captured in the legislative elections by his new political party, the *Rassamblement pour la Démocratie et le Progrès Social,* though Thystère-Tchicaya himself was not successful in moving into the second round in his presidential bid since he only secured 5% of the popular vote. He was, however, integrated into President Lissouba's government, most recently as minister of petroleum. He was then also deputy-mayor of Pointe Noire. Later, the PCT in parliament suggested his appointment as prime minister of a government of national salvation, on the grounds that the June/July 1993 elections had been fraudulent.

TIO. See BATEKE.

TOBACCO. Grown on plantations in the Niari (70%) and Pool (30%) regions, and destined partly for local cigarette manufacture by **SIAT** and for export, the old age of the plantations and the rural-urban exodus have caused production to plummet to only 80 tons by 1990. See also AGRICULTURE.

TOUASSILENOHO, MICHEL, 1949– . Administrator and poet. Born in 1949 in Brazzaville, Touassilenoho has for long been the administrative assistant to the secretary general for Culture and Arts, himself both an author and artist in his spare time.

TOURISM. Congo has only a small number of spectacular natural sites and unusual attractions that might draw tourists, and many of these are inaccessible by road or even by plane. Furthermore, those that can be reached are poorly distributed throughout the country, and roads are in such a bad shape, that it is virtually impossible to organize tourist circuits. In 1989 only 40,000 tourists visited Congo, with revenue from tourism a bare six million dollars. An additional 20,000 foreign arrivals a year are either established residents, or businessmen. Congo's tourist clientele is limited to the most adventurous and/or prosperous travelers since facilities are very limited. Indeed there are only 1,000 hotel rooms in all categories in the entire country, over half of these in Brazzaville alone. Of 522 hotel rooms of international quality, 171 are in the Meridien Hotel in Brazzaville and 120 in Pointe Noire's Novotel. Four other hotels, divided between these towns, were renovated and modernized in the late-1970's, offering lodging for an additional 221 persons. The other towns in the Congo possess together only four hotels, two each in Loubomo and Nyaki. Both hotel accommodations and rental cars are inordinately expensive in Congo, as elsewhere in equatorial Africa, further discouraging genuine tourism, as do the sparse communications in the country especially in Congo's northern reaches. There were plans in the early 1990's to develop M'Bamou island in Stanley Pool into a tourist resort and, also, to establish a new regional chain of hotels for tourists, but nothing has yet come out of this.

TRADE. France's dominant trading position in Congo to this day has been assured by the fact that the first entrepreneurs and enterprises in the colony were French, by the large import-export houses established in Congo, by the various agreements signed at independence by the two countries and by France's indirect control of the CFA monetary reserves. Since independence, and especially after Youlou's overthrow in 1963, this dominance has been slowly eroded by the more nationalist regimes that came to office.

In the first decade since independence the volume of Congo's trade increased by leaps and bounds (from 376,000 to 794,000 tons, and in terms of value from 13.6 billion to 31.9 billion CFAF) but so did Congo's trading deficit that amounted to 8.9 billion CFAF in 1970. Among Congo's exports in 1971 (10.9 billion CFAF) wood was still first in value (7.3 billion CFAF) as well as in volume. Competition with Gabon's timber industry was crucial since Congo withdrew from the Office des Bois de l'A.E.F. (OBAEF) in 1971. That office had been organized jointly by the two countries in 1944 and reinforced by an agreement in 1963. The Congolese government proceeded to form two national companies under the ministry of agriculture—the Office National de l'Okoume (ONO) and the Bureau Congolaise du Bois (BCB)—which were given monopolies over all the country's wood sales. Agricultural exports, which had long been declining or had remained stationary, earned nearly three billion CFA francs in 1971. This marked improvement was due almost entirely to the spectacular increase in sugar production, which doubled between 1967 and 1969, but after 1970, the output and sales of sugar declined. The relative importance of both wood and sugar in Congo's foreign trade decreased with the rapid development of the mining industry. The most valuable minerals shipped from Congo during the first postindependence decade were reexports, both licit and contraband, from neighboring countries. Small tonnages of copper from Zaire were carried by the Congo-Ocean railroad to Pointe Noire, but far more important were the diamonds smuggled out from South Kasai and, later, much smaller legitimate diamond reexports from the Central African Republic. Congo's petroleum shipments were, similarly, reexports (from Gabon) until 1960, when it exported its first locally produced oil (51,850 tons). Two years later, sales of oil from the Pointe Indienne deposit reached 123,393 tons, but after 1969, when 24,000 tons were exported, they ceased entirely. Oil did not figure again among Congo's exports until March 1972, when the Emeraude deposit came on line. The value of Congo's traditional mineral exports rose from 273 million CFAF in 1968 to more than two billion in 1971. In the latter year, however, earnings (1.5 billion CFAF) from potash, a newcomer to Congo's mineral exports, were fast catching up, but they ceased entirely in 1977 when the potash mine closed down. It was only with neighboring countries that Congo enjoyed a favorable trade balance until 1979. Contraband trade between Zaire and Congo has long flourished, whereas their legitimate commercial exchanges have fluctuated with the varying political relations between Brazzaville and Kinshasa. In normal years, about one quarter of the traffic handled by the port of Brazzaville has consisted of goods in transit from Kinshasa to Pointe Noire via the Congo-Ocean railroad. Periodically traders from across the river visit Brazzaville for commodities unavailable in Kinshasa.

More consistently favorable is Congo's balance of trade with its northern neighbors. Although Chad withdrew from the UDEAC customs union and Congo nationalized the transport facilities situated in its own territory, Congo has benefited handsomely from transit trade to/from the UDEAC countries. In 1968 consumer-goods exports (beer, sugar, and cigarettes) to these countries amounted to 2.6 billion CFAF, and its imports from them (almost exclusively meat) totaled only 460 million. Since then, Congolese exports have encountered more competition from new industries in the UDEAC states, and they have shrunk further when most developed alternate means of transport for their foreign-trade. (Particularly hurting was Gabon's construction of her Transgabonaise railway, eliminating completely millions of tons of manganese ore that had been transported by the Congo-Ocean railway to Pointe Noire, greatly assisting both the railroad's and the port's finances.

In 16 of the 21 years between 1960–1980 Congo experienced trade deficits, and only during 1974–1976 was its trade balance favorable. Following a serious deficit recurrence in 1978, foreign trade once again picked up, and during the oil-boom years since 1979 provided increasing surpluses that amounted to 77 billion CFAF in 1980. Among Congo's exports in that extraordinary year, those of crude oil (worth 181.5 billion CFAF) far exceeded those of wood (19.2 billion CFAF), its nearest competitor, followed by diamonds, coffee, cocoa, and other rural products. Congo's two prime imports then consisted of foodstuffs (17.2 billion CFAF) followed by machinery (16.3 billion). With regard to trading partners, France accounted for 41.4 billion CFAF of all Congo's imports in 1980, but was only Congo's eighth-ranking customer, behind Italy and Brazil. Europe accounted for 50.9 percent of Congo's trade, with trade with China and the U.S.S.R. largely composed of import of war materiel, and very few exports to them. By the late 1980's the U.S. became a main importer of Congolese oil, and hence an important trading partner: around $100 million of imports reached the US from Congo (mostly oil) with $12.2 million of exports to Congo, mostly tools and spare parts for the petroleum industry. By 1988 Congo was the third most important African trading partner for the US.

Insofar as internal trade is concerned domestic trade in Congo has always been little more than the distribution of imported goods. Despite appearances, most locally produced consumer items, including staples such as bread, have been made with imported ingredients. When Moyen-Congo became independent, there were more than 400 European trading firms in the country, about half with headquarters abroad, controlling exports and imports, as well as marketing. With the withdrawal of the French garrisons in Congo, and the rise of the Massamba-Debat regime, many of the smaller French traders disappeared and marketing of food and consumer goods was taken over by state companies and/or by local and alien African merchants. Still, the larger European companies remained in the country, unaffected, while the state companies, incurring growing deficits, were unable to compete with them. The cost of living dramatically went up and product shortages became frequent, exacerbated by declines in local agricultural production and the increased rural-urban drift. The regime laid the blame for this on traders for raising prices, not stocking adequate supplies, repatriating their profits, and being reluctant to sell state industries' products. The traders, in turn, laid the blame on high customs duties on imports (fully 90 percent on foodstuffs and 46 percent on other consumer goods), the high wage increases legislated by Brazzaville that increased inflationary trends, and the delays of the State on paying of debts to the private sector. In 1971, following a sharp rise in the cost of imported consumer goods, a sales tax was imposed on all local and imported goods, and in 1972 the price of 51 basic necessities was frozen by the government at November 1971 levels. Unable to affectuate either prices, or to control inflation (averaging 6.54 per year between 1970 and 1973, escalating to over 13 percent a year in 1980, and more since) in 1972 Ngouabi's government announced new measures to Congolize trade. A monopoly for the sale of certain commodities, and a reduction of the number of foreign merchants allowed to trade in the Congo was announced. Only traders resident in the country for five consecutive years would be accorded a trading license, at an annual cost of 5,000 CFAF, that would be made available as loans to nationals lacking capital to enter trading. Other measures undertaken on an assumption that the galloping cost of living could be reduced by nationalizing trade were taxation of capital and profits repatriated by foreign companies, a requirement that they hire only Congolese employees, and the limitation of high-priced imports from the EEC. None of these measures, modified over the years by Sassou-Nguesso, had much effect beyond inclining some foreign companies and individual traders to leave the country, with the high cost of living remaining untouched.

Internal Congolese trade can be divided into kinds: that controlled by the foreign trading houses, by the state monopolies, and by the private sector. The first two are well developed, whereas the third is largely made up of craft products and suffers from competition with contraband that crosses Congo's long river frontier with Zaire. The expatriate trading sector, composed of large, established companies such as CCSO, SCKN, and CFAO-Congo (in order of importance) have a monopoly of working capital and expertise, experienced staff, efficient management, close ties with international companies, especially in France, participate in Congo's industrial development, and dominate the sectors of foodstuffs, textiles, building materials, and industrial equipment. Ngouabi's determination to nationalize the major sectors of the economy led to the creation of six state trading monopolies in the mid-1970's. Among the oldest such organizations were OFNACOM for the distribution and sale of basic foodstuffs, ONLP (for paper), ONIVEG (meat), OCC (coffee and cocoa), OCT (tobacco), and OCMC (building materials). Their impact on the Congolese market has varied with the zeal, efficiency, and honesty of their personnel, which has usually been minor, and more importantly their operations had nearly always resulted in large deficits in comparison to the healthy profits of expatriate companies. Notwithstanding this, in part for doctrinal reasons, in 1981 Sassou-Nguesso extended even more the monopolies enjoyed by companies in the state sector, aiming at bringing most of the country's foreign and domestic trade under Congolese control. Towards that end, with uninterrupted state revenues from oil royalties envisaged in the 1980's, the 1982–86 development plan allocated 17 billion CFAF to improving the country's infrastructure and warehousing facilities, encouraging cooperative societies, granting loans to small and medium-size enterprises, and establishing a bank to promote foreign trade. In the mid-1980's, with much of the development plan truncated by a fall in state revenues attending the decline in global market prices of oil, and state companies piling ever-larger operating deficits that could not be covered, Sassou-Nguesso tried to backtrack on his earlier policies. However his push for a restructuring of the state monopolies, and even the privatization of some, was met with fierce resistance from various quarters. Aware that notwithstanding all past efforts nearly three-quarters of Congo's foreign and internal trade remained directly or indirectly under foreign control, PCT Marxist hard-liners blocked such moves. The country's trade-union likewise, aware that restructuring or privatization were synonyms for, or would inevitably lead to, closures or massive layoffs went on vicious strikes forcing the government to place the entire issue on the back-burner. Eventually some companies simply closed doors, while the fate of the others was left to the new civilian regime of Lissouba in 1992. The latter, despite some important trade liberalization and state company privatization initiatives, the effect of which cannot yet be assessed accurately, has not proceeded as fast on these issues as was originally expected, largely because of the same massive opposition on the part of organized labor.

TRADE UNIONS. See LABOR.

TRANSPORTATION.
(1) AIR SERVICES. Among Congo's companies nationalized in 1964 was Air Congo. At that time the latter's fleet consisted of six planes, the company was in debt, and it greatly needed reorganization and more efficient management. Lignes Aeriennes du Congo (Lina-Congo), its successor, was given a monopoly of civil aviation in Congo, in association with another small firm, Aero-Service, and was placed under the authority of the Agence Nationale de l'Aviation Civile (ANAC). Lina-Congo was assigned the task of exclusively serving the "masses," for whom its services, however, proved to be too limited and expensive. Moreover, most of the funds and effort expended on air services in the 1970's went on improvement on the two main airfields: Maya-Maya at Brazzaville (enlarged three times, beginning in the 1950's, eventually able to accommodate large jet planes and with the longest runway in francophone Africa), and Pointe Noire's, progressively enlarged and modernized due to the town's importance as the oil-capital of Congo. Under both the 1970–75 and 1982–86 plans, secondary airports were built or enlarged, and with them the operations of Lina-Congo, thanks to financial and technical aid provided by the EEC, Canada, and Arab banks. Following the dismissal of Lina-Congo's director in 1977 for political reasons, that company was entrusted to SODETRAF for reorganization, and new French funds were loaned to it by the French ministry of cooperation. Its new function was both to encourage tourism and to make accessible those parts of the Congo that were served neither by road nor by rail. By 1981, twenty-four airfields had been built or enlarged, the most important of which were at Ouesso, Impfondo, Loubomo, Djambala, Nkayi, Mossendjo, and Owando. At the secondary airfields, traffic—though small—has been increasing, the number of passengers ranging between 35,000 and 45,000 a year and the volume of freight between 250 and 270 tons. Still, it has been the Brazzaville-Pointe Noire service that has grown fastest, especially between 1980 and 1981 when it jumped by more than 32 percent. In the latter year,

131,327 passengers and 10,947 tons of freight were handled at Brazzaville; the corresponding figures for Pointe Noire were 94,384 and 1,115. Although most of the 32.5 billion CFAF allotted to air transportation under the 1982–86 plan was slated for Maya-Maya, a larger proportion than before was earmarked for the enlargement and modernization of Pointe Noire's airport. These projects were actually completed, despite the truncation of the plan as anticipated revenues failed to materialize. Still, insofar as Lina-Congo itself is concerned, the airline remains grossly deficitory, a function of inefficient, and at times corrupt management, and the non-payment to it of debts for flights incurred by virtually every state office or corporation using its services. Insofar as airplanes in Congo, of the 49 registered in the country in 1990, 25 belonged to individuals or companies, 6 to air-clubs, 3 to the administration, and only 15 to Lina-Congo. As many as one-third of the latter, however, were since the late 1980's inoperative due to lack of funds for repairs or maintenance.

(2) PORTS. As the railhead of the CFCO and terminus of the navigable portion of the Oubangui and Congo rivers, Brazzaville's river port serves as the entrepot for all of northern Congo's foreign trade, most of that of the RCA, and a part of Cameroun's and Chad's imports and exports. It is also the site of the Chacona shipyards, which since 1972 have built many of the barges and boats that ply Congo's numerous rivers. Of Congo's nine other river ports—at Boundji, Impfondo, Etoumbi, Batoua, Okoyo, Obouya, Makoua, Loukouala, and Ouesso—the last has developed most rapidly, serving an agricultural district targeted as a priority for further development.

Congo's sole seaport, Pointe Noire, consists of a public port on the Atlantic coast and another deepwater port at Djeno, 9.5 km. to the southeast, which handles only oil shipments. Pointe Noire is the terminus of the CFCO (which is also under the authority of the ATC) and is thus of major importance to much of equatorial Africa. Between 1970 and 1980, the ATC invested nearly seven billion CFAF in dredging, enlarging, and building special facilities for loading lumber and minerals at the port of Pointe Noire. Despite all these improvements, the port was barely able to cope with its traffic by 1980, which averaged between 3.35 and 3.45 million tons a year, being visited in 1980 by 1,047 ships. Imports (principally fuel, machinery, and foodstuffs) remained fairly constant, but exports (mainly lumber, manganese, and agricultural products) fluctuated. An upsurge in the port's activities, expected in the 1990's, and for which various additional improvements had been planned, did not materialize, largely due to Gabon's diverting its heavy manganese mineral ore exports away from the CFCO and Pointe Noire to its own ports via the newly completed Transgabonaise railway.

(3) RAILROAD. Until Gabon completed its railroad in the late 1980's the only one in all of the AEF was the Congo-Ocean (CFCO), connecting Brazzaville and Pointe Noire. It took twelve years to build (1922–34), at great cost of money (231 million gold francs) and manpower (120,000 laborers, tens of thousands forcibly brought down from as far away as Chad, of whom some 20,000 died during its construction). To its 515 km. of meter-gauge tracks was added in 1962 a branch line, 286 km. long, from P. K. 200 to M'Binda on the Gabon frontier, where it received shipments of Gabonese manganese ore for export through Pointe Noire. By 1970, a year after the ATC had taken over the Pointe Noire port as well as the CFCO, the railroad was carrying 3.1 million tons annually, of which more than half consisted of manganese ore, compared to only 655,000 tons in 1958, when shipments consisted mostly of lumber. To enable the CFCO to cope with this increased tonnage, the ATC drafted an investment plan for the period 1971–75, while the government negotiated an agreement with Gabon to assure that the CFCO continued to carry up to two million tons a year of Gabonese manganese, despite Libreville's plans to build the Transgabonais railroad, that Congo did not give credence to until construction actually commenced.

By 1975 CFCO's anticipated prospects for transporting 10 million tons of freight annually led to Ngouabi's appeal for foreign capital, and in January 1976 a meeting took place with ten potential investment groups in Brussels that led to funds that allowed CFCO's replacing its ancient steam engines with diesels, building or expanding 25 stations, training local engineers and technicians, and replacing 88 km. of tracks where they crossed the Mayombe mountain range. That steep and winding section limited CFCO's train speeds and carrying capacity, caused frequent derailments, bottlenecks and large stockpiles in both Brazzaville and Pointe Noire, and was to prove much more technically difficult and enormously more costly to build. Moreover, in January 1977 an attack on the workers re-laying the tracks by rebels from Cabinda (see FOREIGN RELATIONS) further delayed its completion and it was only in 1988 the track was completed, with additional improvements necessary into the 1990's.

In 1985, when Sassou Nguesso attempted to introduce cost-reductions in all the state corporations, CFCO personnel had grown to over 6,000, constituting Congo's largest pool of organized labor, and their payroll was the biggest drain in the Congolese manpower budget. They strenuously resisted various austerity policies decreed by Brazzaville, including a projected restructuring of the ATC (by breaking it up into its three components, rail, ports, air) that would have affected economies and made dealing with resistance to redundancies more easily enforceable. Rather than striking, that would have brought upon them the wrath of the military regime, the CFCO undertook a policy of slow, poor and dilatory performance, compounding ATC's difficulties throughout the system, with major negative effects on other segments of the economy. The resulting cargo bottlenecks created shortages of vital supplies throughout the country, leading *inter alia* to the discharge of some workers in the oil refinery that worked well below capacity, and shortages of basic staples in Brazzaville itself. Though some restructuring has taken place since, a serious trimming of CFCO's manpower—more pressing after the phasing out of two million tons of Gabonese manganese ore in the late 1980's—has evaded the government to this day.

CFCO has always suffered from relatively low numbers of passengers carried (due to the length of the voyage by train, though with the Mayombe improvements a pick-up has taken place) and an imbalance between imports and exports, incurring periodic deficits in its revenues compounded by its high operating costs. Since up to 80 percent of the ATC's revenues (when manganese ore moved on its tracks) came from the CFCO, and the railroad is of paramount importance to Congo's communications, placing it on a fiscally healthy basis has always been of crucial importance to the government. Currently a far-ranging process of economizing on its costs is under way, despite unionist resistance, if only because Congo literally has no funds to meet its payroll.

(4) ROADS. The dense forest that covers most of northern Congo and the north-south orientation of the country's main waterways hamper surface transportation. Other handicaps are the difficulty and expense of road building and maintenance in such terrain and under tropical climatic conditions, the small scale and slight value of many of the country's inland products, and the sparseness of its population. With a total area of 342,000 sq. km., Congo has 11,000 km. of officially classified roads, of which only 547 km. were in the late-1970's paved. These paved roads linked the south's principal towns and settlements, with Route Nationale No. 1 (the Brazzaville Pointe Noire highway) being its largest paved component. Until the late 1970's whatever funds were available for road-improvements were invested (where not embezzled), including by the northern Ngouabi, Yhomby Opango and Sassou Nguesso regimes, in southern Congo, where human, economic, and topographical conditions resulted in immediate and concrete rewards. Under the impetus of the BCEOM in 1972 and with funds provided by the FED, IDA, Italy, and Yugoslavia, together with small contributions from the national budget, upkeep of the Congo's main roads was assigned to the RNTTP, with the minor roads—2,730 km. of tracks—the responsibility of local authorities. Since road-maintenance was never accorded priority in Congo's

budget, and even potholes and other problems on the Brazzaville-Pointe Noire road were only patched up in desultory fashion, Congo's road system rapidly deteriorated, some segments to the point of no longer being repairable.

The rise of Sassou Nguesso to power, coinciding with an unanticipated flow of oil royalties, made major road improvements suddenly possible. The regime, heavily packed with northerners, decided to undertake a vast road-building and maintenance program, including in the hitherto untouched north, that commenced even before it was formally spelled out in the 1982–86 development plan. The main thrust was to open up the north by a system of interconnecting roads, fanning out north and west from Brazzaville and ultimately linking the latter with Ouesso by a highway that was designated Route Nationale No. 2. Access roads were also planned to allow trucks to distribute imported goods to the domestic market, and gather local produce for export. The latter, it was assumed, together with the project of developing new village centers, would stem the heavy ongoing rural-urban influx by making life in the stagnant north more bearable and rural agriculture more profitable. At the same time improvements in the south were also projected, with the paving of 552 kms. of existing tracks in the Pool Bend.

By mid-1982, 25 sectors of the northern road system had been started, some contracted with a Brazilian firm, expected to take four years at a cost of about $85 million. Control and maintenance of the road system was placed under a Centre National d'Administration Routiere (CENAR). The most important segments begun were roads connecting Etsouali and Obouya (256 km.); Ngo, Djambala, and Lekana (168 km.); and, particularly of import to the leadership, Owando and Ouesso, (311 km.); as well as in the Cuvette (370 km.). Despite a major shortfall in anticipated oil revenues that were supposed to finance the 1982–86 development plan and the paving program, Sassou-Nguesso proceeded with the northern paving projects. Indeed between 1979 and 1984 most public spending was on road-paving, that linked, until money literally ran out, the Cuvette with Brazzaville. Major cost over-runs and abuses took places. The most notorious case was with the 74.5 km. Bihoua road, built by an Italian company (since banned from Congo) whose cost mushroomed 900% from the original $2.95 million, with the paved road beginning to fall apart only months after being completed. With Congo hard-strapped for funds already by 1982, and progressively bankrupt since, few funds have been available for maintenance, especially important in the north, a region where lush tropical growth and torrential rainfall rapidly undermine roads. Already by 1990 the northern roads, that saw only marginally increased export-oriented traffic, were in an acute state of neglect and disrepair, pocked by potholes.

(5) WATERWAYS. For many years Congo was dependent on the country's 4,500 km. of navigable rivers as the population's sole means of surface communication between the northern and southern regions. Even today, after the construction in the 1980's of part of the North-South road artery, these waterways still provide the most extensive, cheapest, and easiest form of transportation for many people living in two thirds of the country. Rivers were especially important for areas that produced Congo's logs, veneers, and sawn wood, and agricultural produce for export (such as cotton, coffee, peanuts, and palm products), though the current paved roads in the north have reached prime cocoa/coffee regions.

The three most heavily utilized waterways are the Oubangui-Congo (through which flow, on barges, the foreign trade of the Central African Republic and part of Chad's), the Ngoko-Sangha (for Cameroun), and the Pool (for Zaire). In the 1980's only 23.6 percent of the river traffic reaching Brazzaville port came from Congolese sources, the Central African Republic accounting for 35.7 percent and Cameroun 40.5 percent. There are, however, large variations in the volume of the riverine traffic, including important seasonal (occasionally prolonged) changes in the depth of the rivers that may completely prevent traffic, for example, through the Ougangui to/from the Central African Republic. In recent years, moreover, most of Congo's neighbors have explored, or developed, alternate means of evacuating their produce and importing necessities to the Atlantic Ocean (by plane, truck, or train), bypassing the slow, and at times bottlenecked riverine transport option of the past. The record of riverine freight carried over Congo's waterways was attained in 1977 when a total of 218,000 tons were moved, more downstream than upstream, while the number of passengers carried has declined.

TSIBA, FLORENT (Lt. Colonel). Senior Batéké military officer with a checkered career. A member of the PCT central committee, Tsiba was appointed to the party military committee after Ngouabi's 1977 assassination as spokesman and first vice-president. Two years later he became minister of information and telecommunications and in 1982 he was appointed Rector of Marien Ngouabi university. He lost all posts, and PCT central committee membership, and was dismissed from the army in April 1983, for "ideological irrelevancy." Tsiba was nevertheless rehabilitated later as his Bateke kinsmen, disgruntled by his purge that eclipsed the last kinsman at the summit of the power, organized behind a "front"—FROLIBABA—to protect their interests. In a subsequent cabinet shuffle Sassou-Nguesso appointed four Bateke to ministerial posts and Tsiba himself was appointed (in 1984) director-general of the Ciment du Congo state company. In 1989 he was back in the cabinet as minister of the environment, remaining until the civilian government in 1991.

TSIBINDA, MARIE-LEONTINE, 1957– . Poet and actress. Born in the Kouilou region, after completing her MA in English at Marien Ngouabi university in 1983, she joined the American Cultural Center in Brazzaville as a librarian. She published two collections of poems in 1980, and the next year won the national Prix de Poésie. She has also been an actress with Sony Labou Tansi's Rocado Zulu theater.

TSIKA KABALA. See NZIKA KABALA.

TSIKA, NORBERT (Captain). Former head of the gendarmerie with a checkered career. Ordered arrested in August 1963 by Massamba-Debat, for offences during the preceding Youlou era, he was released five years later with the rise of the Ngouabi's military regime, and reinstated in his old command. Only two years later, however, he was demoted to the rank of private for failing to warn Ngouabi about the plot of November 8, 1969, and then prosecuted for criminal negligence before the revolutionary court. Drummed out of the gendarmerie, he entered commerce.

TSIKA-KABALA, VICTOR (Colonel), 1940– . Former Kouyou general chief of staff. Tsika-Kabala's career advanced together with Ngouabi's whom he replaced in 1966 as commander of the Paratroopers Battalion. After Ngouabi's rise to power Tsika-Kabala was appointed (in 1970) assistant chief of staff. After the **Ange Diawara** attempted putsch of 1972 he advanced once again becoming head of the ground armed forces under the overall command of Yhomby Opango, whom he replaced in 1974. Shunted to administrative postings after Sassou-Nguesso's rise to power, in July 1987 he was arrested for complicity in the Captain Anga rebellion.

-U-

UNEMPLOYMENT. See LABOR.

UNION CONGOLAISE DE BANQUES (UCB). Formed on October 1, 1974, the fusion of the Société générale de banques au Congo and of the BICI, the UCB was capitalized at 2 billion CFAF. The Banque

Nationale de Paris held 24.5% of equity. With five branches in Brazzaville, 3 in Pointe Noire, and others in Loubomo, Madingou, Djambala and Impfondo, the UCB was a strong competitor of the BCC.

UNION DES FORCES DEMOCRATIQUES (UFD). Conservative political party set up in 1992 by a number of former PCT members and headed by **David-Charles Ganao**. By 1993 the party was in disarray due to ideological and leadership splits, leading to the mass resignation of nine of its founding members, some of whom (e.g. Christophe Bouramoué) returned to the PCT.

UNION DE LA JEUNESSE CONGOLAISE (UJC). A Marxist organization of young Congolese, mainly Lari from the Brazzaville area, which in the 1950's cooperated with, but was not dependent on the CGAT. The UJC was a forerunner of the JMNR and the UJSC, and had close ties with the French Communist party and world Communist youth groups.

UNION DE LA JEUNESSE SOCIALISTE CONGOLAISE (UJSC). A reconstitution of the Massamba-Debat era **JMNR** by Ngouabi, that in August 1969 became the youth branch of the new PCT political party. The UJSC supported the regime in its trials of strength with student strikers in November 1971 and January 1974, though some of its more radical elements had supported the 1972 **Ange Diawara** leftist attempted putsch. After the **UGEEC** was suppressed the UJSC's authority over all Congolese youth, from adolescents to university students, was confirmed by the PCT central committee. The UJSC not only took over the earlier UGEEC's proposal to found a People's School but was given the task of propagating the PCT's revolutionary principles in the country's lycées and the university. In mid-1975, it was placed in charge of the Chantiers de Vacances, which were agricultural work brigades disarmingly named the Ecole Agréable. In coercing several thousand students to perform hard manual labor and to share Congolese peasants' life for a month during their vacations, the PCT hoped to foster their acceptance of party discipline and eliminate students' zest for ideological extremism. But instead of damping down "avant-gardism," as it had been ordered to do, the UJSC itself, in mid-1975, began to demand "truly revolutionary" changes in the government's structure, claiming that it was up to the country's youthful majority to purify the state and to purge it of its bourgeois bureaucracy. By January 1976, however, the UJSC again toed the line, and helped the PCT to "unmask youthful saboteurs of the revolution" and provide the example for young people to contribute by their labor to the country's economic development. In February 1977, the UJSC expressed its renewed confidence in Ngouabi's leadership, and later, after his assassination balked at the rise to power of the conservative Yhomby Opango. Indeed UJSC's increasingly vocal snipings at the latter played an important role in helping Sassou-Nguesso replace him in 1979. At its fourth congress in August 1981 it accepted Sassou Nguesso's proposal for a period of civic service preliminary to the performance by Congolese youths of their military duties. Aware of the critical role of youth in Congo, Sassou Nguesso subordinated the UJSC through his own cousin, **Gabriel Oba-Opounou**, who was also minister of youth. Increasingly restless as renewed austerity began to afflict Congo in the mid-1980's, students went on a riot in Brazzaville in 1984 in protest over the regime's announcement on a clampdown on scholarships for higher studies, and the hitherto automatic assurance of a senior civil service appointment on graduation. Later, in 1985 Sassou Nguesso himself was heckled when he addressed them, arguing for the need for self-sacrifice to save the revolution. As the austerity measures bit harder during the late-1980's, more and more unrest began to afflict Congolese youth. When political liberalization finally arrived in 1991, the regime had lost much of its support among students that split politically among the various main political contenders.

UNION DE MOYEN-CONGO (UMC). Early colonial era party grouping nearly all French settlers in the colony. As the colonial era began to draw to an end, the UMC swung its support behind **Fulbert Youlou** and his UDDIA, regarded as the most pro-French political leader in the colony.

UNION DEMOCRATIQUE POUR LA DEFENSE DES INTER-ETS AFRICAINS (UDDIA). Early largely Bakongo political party, that ushered in independence under the leadership of **Fulbert Youlou**. Formed in 1946, the party had difficulty combatting the PPC and MSA electoral dominance in Congo, partly because numerous Lari were withdrawn from political life. (See MATSOUANISM.) Supported by French settlers and their **UMC**, by traditional Bakongo chiefs, and eventually by a segment of the Lari when Youlou was able to project himself as the successor of Matsoua, 1956 was the party's turning point. Though Youlou was defeated again by the Vili **Félix Tchicaya** in his quest for a seat in the assembly, electorally the UDDIA drew to near parity with the MSA, and Youlou was elected mayor of Brazzaville. In 1957 the UDDIA weaned (or bribed) away from the MSA one deputy, giving the UDDIA a one-man majority (23 vis. 22) allowing it to form a government under Youlou's leadership. Youlou's government was opposed, however, by hard-core Matsouanist elements and bitter fighting took place with them during the elections of June 1959. The UDDIA was Congo's ruling party between independence and Youlou's overthrow in 1963, when it was banned, and Youlou himself was arrested (to eventually escape to asylum in Spain). Several Youlouist conspiracies and armed assaults took place in subsequent years. The political successor to the UDDIA, in the post-1990 era in the MCDDI of Bernard Kolelas, who himself was a senior Youlou aide. See also POLITICAL PARTIES.

UNION DEMOCRATIQUE CONGOLAIS (UDC). Small political party in exile, set up in Abidjan at the end of 1989, supporting capitalism, free-enterprise and multipartyism.

UNION DOUANIERE ET ECONOMIQUE DE L'AFRIQUE CENTRALE (UDEAC). On the eve of AEF's independence in 1960, the leaders of the four territories formed a Conference of Equatorial Heads of State. It was a purely advisory body concerned with the management of existing economic and cultural agencies such as the Agence Transequatoriale des Communications (ATEC), the Export Standardization Service, and the Federation de l'Enseignement Superieur en Afrique Centrale (FESAC). Some progress was made when the Conference decided to form a customs union (Union Douaniere Equatoriale, or UDE) as the first step toward creating a central African common market. In June 1961, an even bigger step forward was taken when Cameroun was admitted to the UDE as an observer and a permanent secretariat was established, in part to coordinate their fiscal and industrial regulations. A treaty embodying its decision to establish a common tariff, tax structure, investment code, and industrial program was signed in December 1964 between the four AEF states and Cameroon. This treaty brought into being on January 1, 1966 the Union Douaniere et Economique de l'Afrique Centrale (UDEAC), an organization that has had to contend with serious obstacles. Among these was the partly successful attempt by Zaire in 1968 to replace the UDEAC by the Union des Etats de l'Afrique Centrale (UEAC), a similarly oriented organization but one under its control. Then in 1969, unilaterally and without prior consultation of his partners, Ngouabi nationalized the ports, riverine transport system and CFCO railroad that had been their common property, and replaced the ATEC by a national agency. In so doing, Ngouabi revived his partners' old grievance against Congo's privileged position in the AEF, but nevertheless they had to acquiesce to renegotiate new bilateral agreements enabling them to use Congo's transport facilities on terms less advantageous than before. Only Cameroun, that had an independent transport system, was not adversely affected by Ngouabi's action, and later Gabon that developed its Transgabonese railroad. Ngouabi's further abrogation of stipulated UDEAC assumptions by promoting Congolese industries competitive to those of other UDEAC partners (though every country did the same), his grant of special tariff privileges to Chinese and Soviet imports in violation of the UDEAC charter, and his attempt to spread abroad radical doctrines revived resentment and awakened fears among Congo's neighbors.

During 1970 UDEAC's erosion gained momentum with the dissolution of the Conference of Equatorial Heads of State, and of FESAC, under the centrifugal forces unleashed by nationalism. By 1971, however, the partners began to draw closer together again, because of mutual dissatisfaction with OCAM and OAU and the need to take a common stand distinct from that of West Africa in forthcoming negotiations with the EEC and GATT. In 1972, Ngouabi, acting as president of UDEAC, secured in Paris increased representation for the central African states on the board of management of their common central bank. Of all the member states, Congo had most to gain from a strong UDEAC, for the latter to some degree curtails trade competition among them, provides a market for Congo's processing industries, and strengthens Brazzaville's bargaining position in its frequent confrontations with Zaire. See also FOREIGN RELATIONS.

UNION ECOLOGIQUE DU CONGO. Political party, stressing ecological and environmental issues, set up in 1991 and headed by Mandzengue Younous.

UNION GENERALE DES ELEVES ET ETUDIANTS CONGO-LAIS (UGEEC). Students' organization founded by the JMNR in 1965 to mobilize Congolese students above the primary grades behind radical political programs. That same year, joint UGEEC-JMNR pressure forced Massamba-Debat's government into nationalizing mission schools in the country. The UGEEC's fourth congress in 1968 touched off the army coup that ousted Massamba-Debat, and it organized and politicized the student strike of November 1971. Ngouabi likewise had to yield to many UGEEC demands for the Congolization of the economy and the school system, but like Massamba-Debat he frequently criticized its leadership for their intemperate language, indiscipline, lack of realism of "infantile Marxism." In 1969, Ngouabi refused to give the UGEEC representation in the PCT politburo, and in 1971, he put down a public demonstration by the UGEEC of support for the Lovanium University student rebels in Kinshasa. Subsequently he reconciled the UGEEC leadership by his more radical foreign policy, notably Congo's rupture with Israel, denunciations of American activities in the Far and Near East, withdrawal from OCAM, and negotiations with France for revision of the cooperation agreements.

Increasingly dominated by more radical members, many from the Cuvette region (southern and/or more conservative elements were unofficially aggregated under a rival organization, the AEC), on January 10, 1974, soon after Brazzaville's university reopened, UGEEC members demanded the institution's "democratization," denouncing the government's "neocolonialist" policy in general and Ngouabi's recent warning that a university degree would no longer automatically assure graduates of civil service posts. A UGEEC strike was followed by a turbulent demonstration against the university authorities. Ngouabi retaliated January 12th by banning the UGEEC, and the police liberated university buildings occupied by the UGEEC, arresting over 100 students. In Paris some fifty UGEEC members seized the Congolese embassy, phoning their grievances to Ngouabi, an act that was deeply embarrassing to the regime. Though the police withdrew from Brazzaville university buildings and released some ninety students within a week, twenty UGEEC leaders were forcibly inducted into the army and 111 others remained under military surveillance. The regime reaffirmed the UGEEC was a banned organization and anyone claiming membership in it would have his scholarship suspended, and if abroad, would be repatriated; indeed in January 1978, when seven Congolese students in Moscow tried to revive the organization they were promptly extradited. In March 1974, the PCT central committee reaffirmed the authority of the UJSC over all Congolese youth, including those previously in the UGEEC, and the following month appointed a Conseil Superieur de l'Université as the ultimate authority over Congolese students above the secondary-school level.

UNION NATIONALE DES ECRIVAINS, ARTISTES ET ARTISANS DU CONGO (UNEAC). Important organization headquartered in Brazzaville but with a branch in Pointe Noire, linking Congo's many authors, poets, playrights, musicians and actors, for cultural activities, but also as a pressure group vis-a-vis the government. Congo's outstanding reputation as a literary and cultural center in Africa has led all regimes in Brazzaville, even when fiscally hard-strapped, to subsidize the arts (especially since the sums demanded were generally modest) assisting many a budding author (through publication of his work in the State presses), or cultural events.

UNION NATIONALE DES TRADIPRATICIENS CONGOLAIS (UNTC). National association of Congo's traditional herbalists and traditional healers, established in 1974.

UNION NATIONALE POUR LA DEMOCRATIE ET LE PROGRES (UNDP). Political party, founded in September 1990 by some former hard-line PCT militants, and headed by **Pierre Nze**. See POLITICAL PARTIES.

UNION PANAFRICAINE POUR LA DEMOCRATIE SOCIALE (UPADS). Congo's largest political party, set up in 1990 and headed by **Pascal Lissouba**. Very strong in the southwest regions of Bouenza, Niari and Lekoumou regions, and the core of the government in Brazzaville today, the UPADS is currently pitched against an opposition comprising the Bakongo MCDDI party of Bernard Kolelas and the smaller northern PCT of Sassou Nguesso, that moved from a brief early alliance with UPADS to the MCDDI opposition. In the Senate elections UPADS won the largest number of seats, 23, and in the local and municipal elections it won the largest number of seats (39) of all the parties. The party was, at least at outset, a tight alliance of a number of regional parties and power-barons coalescing behind Lissouba's political leadership.

UNION PATRIOTIQUE POUR LA DEMOCRATIE ET LE PROGRES (UPDP). Political party set up in 1991 and headed by Celéstin Nkoua.

UNION PATRIOTIQUE POUR LA RECONSTRUCTION NATIONALE (UPRN). Political party, set up in 1991, with a platform of ethnic reconciliation.

UNION PATRONALE ET INTERPROFESSIONELLE DU CONGO (UNICONGO). Established in 1960 in Brazzaville, and currently under the presidency of Bernard Fraud and secretary general Michel Gérard, UNICONGO is the country's employers' union.

UNION POUR LA DEMOCRATIE CONGOLAISE (UDC). Political party advocating a liberal economy, set up in 1989 and headed by **Sylvain Bemba**.

UNION POUR LA DEMOCRATIE ET LA REPUBLIQUE (UDR). Political party, set up in 1992 by **André Milongo** the former interim prime minister chosen by the national conference. The party has been singularly unable to carve itself a constituency against the overwhelming strength among the Lari-Bakongo of Kolelas' **MCDDI**.

UNION POUR LA DEVELOPPEMENT ET LE PROGRES SOCIALE (UDPS). Political party set up in 1991 by **Jean-Michel Boukamba-Yangouma**. The UDPS was a breakaway faction from the **UPSD**.

UNION POUR LE PROGRES (UP). Political party set up in 1991 and headed by **Jean-Martin M'Bemba** tapping Batéké support in the Pool region.

UNION POUR LE PROGRES DU PEUPLE CONGOLAIS (UPPC). Political party, founded in 1991 with a platform of national unity. It is headed by Alphonse Nbihoula.

UNION POUR LE PROGRES SOCIAL ET LA DEMOCRATIE (UPSD). Political party set up in 1991 by the trade union leaders Jean Ganga-Zandzou, Jean-Michel Boukamba-Yangouma, and Ange-Edouard Poungui who is its president. The party's platform was strongly in favor of private enterprise and personal freedoms. A segment of the party broke away later in 1991 to set up the **UDPS**.

UNION POUR LE RENOUVEAU DEMOCRATIQUE (URD). A coalition of seven political parties in opposition to the Lissouba government, of which Bernard Kolelas' **MCDDI** Bakongo party is the largest component. The URD was joined by the PCT in 1991 (the latter bolting the UPADS ruling political grouping after a very brief alliance with it) leading to riots and demonstrations in downtown Brazzaville, Kolelas' stronghold. Another party in the alliance is the RDPS.

UNION REPUBLICAINE POUR LE PROGRES (URPP). Political party set up in September 1990 by former PCT prime minister **Alphonse Poaty-Souchlaty**. See POLITICAL PARTIES.

UNION REVOLUTIONNAIRE DES FEMMES DU CONGO (URFC). PCT women's ancillary organization, aimed at organizing women behind the Marxist regime. Headquartered in Brazzaville but with sections in all large towns and regions as well, in 1986 the URFC was restructured along occupational lines with specific sections set up, for example, for tradeswomen, craftswomen, peasants, housewives etc. This took place because leadership of the URFC in many regional centers had fallen into professional women's hands, whose style had brought declines in active membership.

UNIONS. See LABOR.

UNITE D'AFFORESTATION INDUSTRIELLE DU CONGO (UAIC). State agency, cooperating with the **Office Congolais des Bois** in planting new eucalyptus forests primarily in southern Congo. See EUCALYPTUS FORESTS.

UNIVERSITE DE BRAZZAVILLE. Created in December 1971 to replace the Centre d'enseignement supérieur de Brazzaville, that had served the AEF, the university started off with faculties of law and social sciences, of humanities, of science, and a school of education. A large number of its instructors were originally French nationals. The university rapidly expanded and its faculty Congolized. After the assassination of president Ngouabi in 1977 the university was named after him as Université Marien Ngouabi. Student figures rapidly progressively mushroomed from the original 2,000 in 1971 reaching a high in 1986 at just over 11,000, at which level they stabilized. Part of the stabilization in numbers (that is expected to move higher shortly) was that graduation increasingly did not assure, as in previous decades, automatic entry into the higher echelons of the civil service, a function of the bloated civil service and the bankruptcy of the Congolese government.

UNIVERSITE DE MARIEN NGOUABI. Name, after president Ngouabi's assassination, of the **Université de Brazzaville**.

URBAN AREAS. The historically strong rural-urban migration rates in Congo, that show no indication of slowing down, have made the country one of the most urbanized in Africa. It has been estimated that in 1992 fully 65 percent of the population lives in urban centers of over 10,000 people. The different growth rates of Congo's towns also make any size rankings (as those that follow) highly temporary. In 1985, for example, the highest demographic growth rate (15.92 percent) was recorded for Bouanza (then with 6,319 people) followed by Impfondo at 8.34 percent (11,142) and Kinkala at 7.41 percent (9,492), while the lowest being recorded by Loudima (0.51 percent, 9,034) and Mindouli (0.56, 7,859). In 1992 the estimated populations and rankings of Congo's ten largest towns were: 1) Brazzaville, just over 900,000; 2) Pointe Noire, 350,000; 3) Loubomo, 58,000; 4) NKayi, 48,000; 5) Owando, 20,000; 6) Sibiti, 19,000; 7) Mossendjo, 18,000; 8) Ouesso, 16,750; 9) Impfondo, 16,000; 10) Makabana, 15,000. Three other urban centers were closely clustered around the 14,000 population level: Gamboma, Makoua, Kinkala.

USINE DE TEXTILES SYNTHETIQUES (UTS). State enterprise,set up in 1982 with Roumanian technical assistance, to produce synthetic fibres, with a productive capacity of 2.8 million meters. In 1983 the company was absorbed by SOTEXCO.

USSR. See FOREIGN RELATIONS.

-V-

VALETTE, ALICE. Authoress, poet and playwright, writing under the pseudonym of Bizol Ntima.

VIAL, JOSEPH, 1908– . Early French minister in Youlou's government. Born in southern France on January 5, 1908, after completing his university studies there, Vial went to Moyen-Congo where he became manager of several companies. After World War II, he became active in local politics, representing Djou between 1947 and 1960 in the territorial assembly. In November 1956 he also assumed the post of assistant mayor of Brazzaville. He was appointed to Youlou's cabinet as minister of finance in May 1957, serving until February 1960. His appointment was a stumbling block for a reconciliation of the MSA with Youlou, since one of their insistences was that Vial be dropped from the cabinet. Vial's contacts with French capital in the country, and his personal contributions to the UDDIA kept him, however, at Youlou's side until early 1960, when he returned to France.

VILI. See POPULATION.

VOUAMA, PIERRE, 1934– . Former cabinet minister. Born on May 24, 1934 to a prominent chiefly family in the Kinkala district, Vouama received his early schooling at Brazzaville and his higher education at French universities. In Paris, he acquired a doctorate in engineering and was elected president of the Congolese students' association. On returning to Brazzaville in July 1965 he was employed in the telecommunications service and served as minister of telecommunications between 1966 and 1969, following which he was appointed head of a division in the same ministry.

-W-

WA MBANGUI, BEMBA-DEBERT. Until 1990 Wa Mbangui, who is a poet, headed the division in the ministry of education responsible for literary and press censorship in the country. He attended schools in Kébouya and Brazzaville.

WITCHCRAFT. Witchcraft, sorcery, and belief in magic and ghosts abound throughout the Congo basin, despite the country's high literacy and scholarization rates, and repeated, at times violent, attempts to eradicate these manifestations, especially during the JMNR campaigns in 1964–66. While there are many varieties, witchcraft among the Bakongo specifically is a negative cult of the dead. Witches go about at night assuming the bodies of other people, fierce animals or even mosquitoes, to attack members of their own clan or relatives, stealing their souls and either imprisoning them in a jar, or in a wild animal, or by using their spirit's energy for their own purposes. Ghosts, on the other hand, are dead witches denied admission to their ancestors' village. Individuals who take too long to die, are seen as being interrogated at the threshold of death about the witchcraft they practiced, before being allowed to enter the world of spirits. Suspected witches, following an accusation, are forced to undertake a ritual involving poison that proves or disproves his/her guilt. There are numerous religious cults throughout the country that promise protection against witchcraft, either for a hefty payment or as part of mutual-aid societies with complex rites and rituals.

There have been many explanations for the prevalence of such beliefs in Congo: some stress its universality in Africa, and in particular in equatorial Africa, that has produced myriads of syncretic cults. Others refer to the basic intertwining of political power with indigenous religious beliefs; and yet others argue that the colonial power's destruction of the institution of chiefdom in Congo opened the door for the assumption of former chiefly religious powers by "commoner" prophets, sorcerers, diviners and healers. However that may be, apart from periodic references in the Congolese press about sorcery practiced in the countryside, and in Brazzaville's Poto Poto quarter, there have been numerous instances of PCT officials being dismissed from office for involvement in occult practices: in 1972 the mayor of Brazzaville himself, and the president of the Congolese youth movement, were purged for witchcraft, though it has been suggested that in a society where witchcraft is a common occurrence, this was the excuse used for the purge rather than their sole sin.

WOMEN. Women play an increasingly important role in modern Congo, but are still subservient in traditional society. Efforts by Christian missionaries during the colonial era, and later by the independent Congolese government, political parties, and women themselves to improve their status have been only moderately successful in the countryside. The missions provided their first schooling for girls, but in vain attacked polygamy. After World War II, the French government gave women the right to vote and encouraged girls to attend public cschools, but took no stand on polygamy or divorce. In 1951–52, however, laws were passed raising the age of consent to marriage, regulating the bride-price, and limiting working hours and the type of labor for women wage-earners. French social legislation remained a dead letter because it was not supported by Congolese public opinion, and the labor regulations (expanded by Massamba-Debat) affected only the small segment of women who worked for wages. It was in girls' education that the greatest progress was made though it was not until 1959 that the first Congolese women teachers graduated from the Mouyondzi school (later transferred to Brazzaville). By 1972, however 62 percent of Congolese girls of school age were attending primary schools, though females accounted for only 23 percent of students in secondary school and 6 percent of those in higher educational institutions. In southern towns, Congolese women occupy a position very different from that of those up-country. A far larger proportion of urban girls attend and remain longer in school than do their rural counterparts. The latter are married off earlier by their parents so as to collect their bride-price, and with the increasing exodus of young rural men to the towns, country women have been bearing a larger share of hard agricultural work. Furthermore, it has been among urban women that the political parties have organized their parallel women's sectors. The PPC created the Union des Femmes Africaines in 1946; the UDDIA, the Femmes Caimans ten years later; and the MNR, the Union Revolutionnaire des Femmes du Congo in 1965. For a brief period, the MSA and the UJC had analogous branches. Members of such groups were in most cases wives of male party militants, whose political objectives they echoed. They had no authentic activity of their own, except perhaps in the case of the MNR Union, which at its constituent congress passed a few resolutions of direct interest to women. These included demands for equal rights for women, limitation of the bride-price to 10,000 CFA francs, and an end to forced marriages and arbitrary divorces. The PCT, which took over the MNR Union, became the first Congolese party to discuss family problems fully at its congress in mid-1972. At that time, the PCT agreed in principle to abolish the bride-price, but its delegates could reach no unanimity as to the respective merits of monogamy and polygamy, and the bride-price remained despite the consensus for its abolition. (Indeed, when Sassou Nguesso married off his daughter to neighboring Gabon's president Bongo in 1990, the local press noted how he had conformed to traditional practice about bride-price, and stressed he had not asked for more than the maximum 50,000 CFAF allowed by law.)

According to the 1985 census, women outnumber men in Congo by roughly 53 percent to 47 percent. The disparity between the sexes differs markedly in the north and in the south, in each of the nine regions and the communes, and between a region's main town and the region itself. For example, males predominate in Pointe Noire (52 percent), whereas women are more numerous than men in the Kouilou region. A similar situation exists in Nkayi and wherever there is a seaport or a concentration of industries requiring a large male labor force. In the regions, the outstanding example of female predominance is to be found in rural Lekoumou (55 percent) and an even higher percentage in its Ewo district (57 percent). Obviously this sex differential relates to the prevalence of polygamy (which is higher in the rural districts than in the towns), just as the birth rate is linked to the greater availability in Brazzaville and Pointe Noire of sanitary facilities and medical care for women, as well as the practice of contraception. The census indicated, moreover that over 21 percent of Congolese households were polygamous, but they are less numerous in the main towns (Brazzaville 10 percent, Pointe Noire 13 percent) and are most widespread in the northern regions of the Cuvette (29 percent), Lekoumou (31 percent), and the Plateaux (45 percent), where women are numerically predominant. As to longevity, the respective percentages of life expectancy to the age of 60 and over are 43.1 percent for males and 50.3 percent for females, but this disparity becomes less accentuated in the towns, where there is a better numerical balance between the sexes. There, too, are to be found more facilities for maintaining good health, as well as greater professional opportunities for women to be trained and employed as midwives (236) and as registered nurses (923) in the national health service.

There has been little particular concern to women in PCT organs. The URFC, one of the three mass organizations taken over by the PCT from the MNR, has held only five congresses in its eighteen years of existence, and has reelected the same president (Mme. Elise Therese Gamassa). In chairing the March 1982 URFC congress Sassou-Nguesso urged Congolese women to work through the URFC and the cooperative societies to promote the productivity of the rural economy, while the minister of health, who was chairman of the family-planning seminar held in October 1982, merely took a stand against abortion and in favor of greater medical care for mothers and young children, but led no debate on polygamy, the bride-price, professional training, and other subjects of direct concern to women.

-Y-

YEKA, EMMANUEL (General). Northern officer who between 1982 and 1984 served as minister of cooperation. In 1984 he was shifted to head the ministry of mines and power, and in 1986 he was reassigned back to military duties.

YHOMBY OPANGO, JOACHIM (General), 1939– . Prime minister of Congo, and former President of Congo. Born in Owando in 1939, Yhomby Opango, a Kouyou and Marien Ngouabi's cousin, enlisted in the French colonial army in July 1957, and on attaining NCO rank was sent for officer's training at the Strasbourg military school and at St. Cyr (1960–1962), following which he was transferred to the Congolese armed forces as a second lieutenant and commander of the First Congolese company. Promoted to the rank of lieutenant in April 1963, he served as military aide and head of the military cabinet to president Massamba-Debat after the latter rose to power in 1965. He was later posted as military attache at the Congolese embassy in Moscow between 1965 and 1968. Promoted to captain in July 1967, he assumed command of the paratroop battalion in September 1968, and in 1969 became Ngouabi's army chief of staff, serving in that post until 1973. In 1972 he was the prime officer instrumental in blocking the dangerous **Ange Diawara** attempted putsch, of which he also was a key target. Promoted for his decisive action to colonel (at the time the highest rank in the armed forces), he was later also brought into the PCT politburo (January 1973), though he was to be dropped from the politburo later that year for his overly conservative stances. He was then named inspector-general of the armed forces and secretary-general of the council of state with ministerial rank. After Ngouabi's assassination in 1977, as the army's most senior officer he became president of the PCT's military committee and head of state. Opposition against his hedonistic life, pro-West and pro-French orientations on the part of PCT hardliners and youth, led to his easy replacement at the summit of power by Sassou-Nguesso on February 8, 1979. The following month he was arrested, expelled from the PCT and his property was confiscated. He was released in 1984, though watched carefully in his home in Owando, for he retained influence over some of the officers from the Cuvette, had links with many exiled opposition groups in France, and was popular among the Kouyou. For some time he was used by Sassou Nguesso as counter-weight against the left-wing in the PCT; indeed, during the November 1985 student riots in Brazzaville some placards called for Yhomby Opango to return to power. Yhomby Opango was again arrested in July 1987 in connection with the **Anga** rebellion. Since he was found not to be involved in that affair, he was released later.

As the era of political liberalization commenced in Congo Yhomby Opango set up a political party to further his interests, the Rassemblement pour la Démocratie et le développement. Popular in the Cuvette among the Kouyou who resented Sassou Nguesso's antecedent pro-Mbochi policies, his RDD party won 8 of the Senate seats, 15 of the 31 regions' seats, and five seats in the legislative elections, in which the RDD was pitched in particular against the PCT. As a northern moderate pro-Westerner he seemed an ideal candidate for Lissouba's broadly-based cabinet, and in 1992 Yhomby Opango was appointed prime minister of Congo.

YOKA, AIME-EMMANUEL. Former minister-delegate, in charge of cooperation, appointed on December 28, 1980. Yoka, who is Sassou-Nguesso's uncle, retained his post until December 1985, and was also director of Sassou Nguesso's presidential cabinet. He was one of the prime movers behind Congo's slow improvement of relations with France in the 1980's. He returned to the cabinet in August 1989 as minister of mines and energy serving until the liberalizations of 1991. With the fall of the Sassou Nguesso regime Yoka remained one of the latter's personal advisors.

YOULOU, FULBERT, 1917–1972. Congo's first president. Born to a small Lari merchant in Madibou near Brazzaville on June 17, 1917, Youlou was baptized a Catholic in 1926 and entered the seminary three years later. He completed secondary education in mission schools in Cameroon and Gabon, meeting there the Gabonese leader, Jean-Hilaire Aubame, and the future president of Oubangui-Chari, Barthelemy Boganda, who became his friends. On his return to Brazzaville he taught at mission schools, and was ordained a priest in 1946. Reproached by his superiors for lack of zeal and indiscipline, he was forbidden to exercise his priestly vocation when, despite their disapproval, he decided to campaign for public office. He nevertheless continued to wear his ecclesiastical robes, emphasized the Lari meaning of his name (Youlou = "heaven") and adopting mannerisms reminiscent of **Matsoua** whose leadership mantle he claimed, appealed to the Lari, at the time alienated from politics. Youlou rapidly acquired a political stranglehold over the Lari-Matsouanist vote and was elected mayor of Brazzaville in November 1956 and vice-president of Moyen-Congo's government council in May 1957 at the head of the UDDIA party that he founded. President of the Congo after it became independent in 1960, his rule was arch-conservative and venal. Though he succeeded in bringing about single-party unity, his efforts to unite all the trade unions, then smarting over unemployment and the stagnant Congolese economy, led to three days in August 1963 of urban strikes (Les Trois Glorieuses) at the end of which the armed forces called for his resignation. Arrested and imprisoned, in April 1965 his supporters succeeded to spirit him away to Kinshasa. Flying to Europe, the French government refused to give him sanctuary, and he finally settled in exile in Madrid. Several armed assaults were mounted on his behalf by supporters from Kinshasa, against both the

Massamba-Debat and the successor Ngouabi regime, and as late as 1970 funds were being collected both in France and in Congo to support his comeback. He died in Madrid on May 6, 1972, and his body was returned for burial in Congo in 1973. Youlou was the author of a study on Matsouanism, and of a book in which he accused China of responsibility for central Africa's troubled post-independence history.

YOUNOUS, MANDZENGUE. Political aspirant who in 1991 set up an ecological/environmental political party, the Union écologique du Congo (EUC).

-Z-

ZANAGA. District covering an area of 11,000 sq. kms. in the Lékoumou region that borders Gabon in the southwest of the country. Its capital is in the town with the same name. Half of the district is within the Ogooué river basin (of Gabon) and half within the Niari river basin. The average altitude is 500–600 meters, and parts of the district are heavily wooded.

ZEPHERIN see LASSY ZEPHERIN

ZOULOUS. Self-styled name of Brazzaville's newest manifestation of spontaneously formed youthful private militias. The Zoulous, composed mostly of youth from **Nibolek** ethnicity, have acted as the private guard of President Lissouba, fighting pitched battles in 1992–94 against their "Ninjas" counterpart, drawn from the Lari and Bakongo, supporting **Bernard Kolelas**. Up to 1,000 people may have died in the violence, with some elements of the northern armed forces joining the Ninjas, in light of the PCT's political alliance with Kolelas' MCDDI party.

Introduction to the Bibliography

Like with most other Francophone countries, there is a voluminous literature on Congo, though most is in French. While in a few fields (e.g. on contemporary developments) material in English has slowly accumulated, in most little exists, or is uneven in its coverage.

The bibliography that follows cannot, for reasons of space, be completely comprehensive. It presents to the serious reader most of the literature in English, and a cross-section of the most valuable material in French, with particular stress on the humanities and social sciences. Even then, in some fields the material has had to be selectively curtailed as, for example, with respect to the Bakongo kingdom, more directly relating to Zaire where the core of the kingdom was, and where significant fieldwork has been conducted.

The material is alphabetically organized under several broad topics, and as a further guide to some of the more useful studies the following comments may be of use. Under GENERAL WORKS the recent book by Noel is a useful introduction, just as the quarterly reports and annual profile of The Economist Intelligence Unit are invaluable for snapshots of Congolese developments. SCIENTIFIC STUDIES are totally dominated by French scholarship, and any specialists interested in these fields would need no guidance here. Under HISTORY the works of Balandier, Brunschwig, Coquery-Vidrovitch and the two Dupré's are seminal. Gide's accounts of his travels through French Congo helped change history, and are still of interest. Laman's controversial book on the Kongo is still much cited today. Mazenot's accounts of the penetration of northern Congo are without rival as is Martin's work in English on the Loango Vili. Obenga's (1977) survey of the history and the peoples of the Cuvette is also useful. Finally one can note the many outstanding works of Vansina on the Bateke.

ANTHROPOLOGY/SOCIOLOGY is suffused with fine studies on Congo's heavy rural-urban drift and urban unemployment. Balandier's work is seminal as is Bonnafé's, whose 1968 study of the JMNR links up with Congolese politics. Croce Spinelli's book is a classic. Gandoulou's studies of contemporary Congolese youth (in Paris and in Brazzaville) have been widely acclaimed. Jacobsen-Widding's book is also very perceptive. Finally, the seminal works by Sautter, Soret and Vennetier need no introduction.

Under POLITICS, apart from the studies in English attention should be drawn to the important books by Bertrand, Gabou (1984), the collected speeches of Ngouabi (1975), and Wagret's 1966 book that is the best single-volume study of the country. There are too many good studies on ECONOMICS to be individually isolated, especially since some of the works already mentioned previously (e.g. Bertrand's book) cover Congo's economy as well.

Under RELIGION one can note the books by Andersson, Mac-Gaffey (that deal more with Zaire), and Sinda. Students of LITERATURE need no introduction to Congo's literary outpouring, only a segment of which has been translated into English. One should also note Jacquot's remarkable scholarship in the field of LINGUISTICS. With respect to primary sources the monthly twin series of *Africa Research Bulletin,* the weekly *West Africa,* and the fortnightly *Africa Confidential* are indispensable, especially for those with only a command of English.

General Works

Badian, Seydou. *Congo: terre généreuse, forêt féconde,* Paris, Editions Jeune Afrique, 1983.

Ballard, John A. "Four equatorial states," in Gwendolyn Carter (ed.), *National Unity and Regionalism in Eight African States,* Ithaca, Cornell University Press, 1966, p. 244–253.

Ballif, Noel. *Le Congo,* Paris, Karthala, 1993.

Delaye, T. J. "Pointe-Noire, port océane," *Revue maritime,* no. 174, Feb. 1961, 169–190.

Denis, Jacques. "Pointe-Noire," *Cahiers d'Outre-Mer,* no. 32, Oct.–Dec. 1955, p. 350–368.

Economist Intelligence Unit. *Congo: Country Profile,* London, EIU, annual.

————. *Congo: Quarterly report,* London, EIU, quarterly.

Francheschi, Patrice. *Au Congo jusqu'au cou, chez les pygmées,* Paris, Fernand Nathan, 1977.

Frey, R. *Brazzaville,* Paris, Encyclopédie mensuelle d'Outre-Mer, no. 48/49, Aug.–Sept. 1955.

Gakosso, Gilbert-François. *Le realité congolaise,* Paris, La Pensée Universelle, 1983.

Klotchkoff, Jean-Claude. *Le Congo aujourd'hui,* Paris, Jeune Afrique, 1987.

Pellerin, Pierre. *Une enfance en brousse congolaise,* Paris, Arthaud, 1990.

Putorac, Jean de. *Makambo: une vie au Congo,* Caidelhan, Zulma, 1992.

Soret, Marcel. *République du Congo,* Paris, Larousse, 1964.

La Zone franc et l'Afrique, Paris, Ediafric, 1981.

Scientific Studies: Geography/Soils/Medicine/Health

Aimé, J. and L. Roche. *Monographie hydrologique du Kouilou-Niari,* Paris: ORSTOM, 1960.

Babet, V. "Exploration de la parti méridionale des plateaux batékés," *Bulletin du Service des mines de l'A.E.F.,* no. 3, 1957, p. 21–56.

Barrilly, A., B. Pouyaud. *Le bassin de la Sangha,* Brazzaville, ORSTOM, 1971.

Bascoulergue, P. *Enquete nutritutionelle de Brazzaville-Ouenzé,* Brazzaville, ORSTOM, 1957.

Billon, B., F. Chaperon et al. *Hydrologie du bassin supérieur du Niari,* Brazzaville, ORSTOM, 1965.

Bjerhagen, Torbjorn, Ingemar Savfors. *L'Habitat traditionnel dans la République populaire du Congo,* Uppsala, Scandinavian Institute of African Studies, 1972.

Blache, J. et al. *Travaux du Centre océonographique de Pointe-Noire,* Paris, ORSTOM, 1962.

Bocquier, G. and R. Guillemin. *Aperçu sur les principales formations pédologiques de la République du Congo-Brazzaville,* Brazzaville, ORSTOM, 1959.

Boissezon, P. de. *Contribution á l'étude de la microflore de quelques sols typiques du Congo,* Brazzaville, IEC, 1961.

————. *Les sols des plateaux de Djambala et koukouya,* Brazzaville, ORSTOM, 1963.

————, and G. Martin. *Les sols de la vallée du Niari,* Paris, ORTOM, 1975.

Bouboutou, M, Petit, M. *Géographie de la République populaire du Congo,* Paris, Hatier, 1976.

Bouquet, A. *Inventaire des Plantes médicinales et toxiques du Congo-Brazzaville.* Paris, ORSTOM, 1965–1967, 2 vol.

————. "Notes sur la préparation du poison de flêches dans le Nord-Congo," *Journal d'Agriculture Tropicale et de Botanique appliquée.* vol. 14 no. 8–9, Aug–Sept. 1967.

————. *Plantes médicinales du Congo-Brazzaville,* Paris, ORSTOM, 1972.

————, and A. Jacquot. "Essai de géographie linguistique sur quelques plantes médicinales du Congo-Brazzaville," *Cahiers d'ORSTOM,* vol. 4 no. 3/4, 1967, p. 4–35.

Bruel, Georges. "Les basses vallées de l'Oubangui et de la Sangha," *La Géographie,* vol. 19, 1909, p. 353–366.

————. "L'inventaire scientifique et économique du Moyen Niari," *Bulletin du Comité d'Afrique française,* no. 4/5, 1925, p. 91–120, 149–161.

Bugieres, J. M. *La connaissance des sols dans le Mayombé, la vallée du Niari et le massif du Chaillu,* Brazzaville, ORSTOM, 1962.

Bultot, Franz. *Atlas climatique du bassin congolais,* Bruxelles, INEAC, 1971–77, 4 vol.

Carlotti, V. *Projet d'implantation cacaoyére pilote à Loukoléla: étude pédologique,* Brazzaville, ORSTOM, 1967.

Cavalan, P. "Les essais d'introduction et de culture de plantes fourragères dans la vallée du Niari," *Bulletin de l'Institut Centrafricaine,* no. 17/18, 1959, p. 43–70.

————. "Etudes spéciales faites à la Station agronomique de Loudima," *Bulletin trimestriel ORSTOM,* no. 34, 1958, p. 1–75.

————. "Experimentation sur les plantes et cultures fourragères," *Agronomie Tropicale,* no. 2/3 Feb.–March, 1962, p. 158–165.

————. "The problem of farming techniques in the Niari valley," *Agricultural mechanization,* no. 1 June 1960, p. 30–34.

————. "Le problème de la conservation de la fertilité du sol dans le Niari," *Bulletin trimestriel du C.T.A.T* no. 2, 1956, p. 2–17.

————. "Technique aratoire et conservation du sol dans la vallée du Niari," *Bulletin de la Chambre de Commerce du Kouilou Niari,* Aug. 1957, p. 9–12.

Chaar, A. et al. "Approche de l'allaitement maternel: étude de 112 cas à l'hospital Général de Brazzaville," In: D. Lemonnier and Y. Ingenbleck, *Les malnutritions dans les pays du tiers monde,* Paris, INSERM, 1986, p. 115–120.

Chabi-Gonni, D. *Inventaire des ressources en eau de surface en République populaire du Congo,* Ouagadougou, Comité interafricaine d'études hydrauliques, 1987.

Chevalier, Auguste. "Les essais de cultures nouvelles et de mécanisation de l'agriculture au Moyen-Congo," *Revue internationale de botanique appliquée,* vol. 3 no. 347–8, 1951, p. 507–12.

De Champ, G., B. Denis. *Le sols de la région de Brazzaville,* Brazzaville, ORSTOM, 1970.

Denis, J. "Pointe Noire," *Les Cahiers d'Outre-Mer,* no. 32, 1955, p. 350–368.

————, and J. M. Rieffel. *Carte pédologique Madingou,* Paris, ORSTOM, 1975.

Devauges, R. *Atlas de Brazzaville,* Paris, ORSTOM, 1984.

Duboz, P. "Mortalitié et morbidité infantile et juvenile en République Populaire du Congo," *Cahiers ORSTOM,* vol. 20 no. 2, 1984, p. 157–169.

Evrard, C. *Recherches écologiques sur les peuplement forestièr des sols hydromorphes de la Cuvette centrale Congolais,* Paris, INEAC, 1968.

————. *Les recherches géophisiques et géologiques et les travaux de sondage dans la Cuvette congolaise,* Bruxelles, 1957.

Fontana, André. *Milieu marin et ressources halieutiques de la République populaire du Congo,* Paris, ORSTOM, 1981.

Franzini, F. "Les boissements artificiels dans les savanes de la région Pointe-Noire," *Bois et Forets des Tropiques,* May–June 1957, p. 25–52.

Froment, E. "Trois affluents français du Congo. Rivières Alima, Likouala, Sanga," *Bulletin de la Société de Géographie de Lille,* vol. 7, no. 1, 1887, p. 458–474.

Galessamy, J. "Les problèmes de la santé publique en République Populaire du Congo-Brazzaville," PhD thesis, University of Toulouse, 1975.

Géographie de la République Populaire du Congo, Paris, EDICEF, 1976.

Gilbert, G., J. Lebrun. *Une classification écologique des forets du Congo,* Paris, INEAC, 1954.

Giresse, P., R. Lanfranchi, S. Peyrot. "Les terasses alluviales en République Populaire du Congo," *Bulletin ASEQUA,* no. 63, 1981, p. 43–66.

————., A. Massengo. "Introduction à une étude géologique du fleuve Congo," *Annales de l'Université de Brazzaville,* no. 7, 1971, p. 77–95.

Groulez, J. "Essais d'acclimation de coniféres tropicaux au Congo-Brazzaville," *Bois et Forets des tropiques,* no. 96 July–Aug. 1964, p. 19–25.

Gruenais, M. E., D. Mayala. "Revaloriser la médicine traditionnelle ou comment de débarasser de son 'efficacité symbolique': l'exemple de la République Populaire du Congo," *Politique Africaine,* no. 28, 1987.

Guillemin, Rene. *Les facteurs physiques du milieu conditionnant la production agricole dans la république du Congo,* Brazzaville, Haut Commissariat general, 1962, 2 vol.

Guillot, Bernard. "Analyse systematique du milieu de mosaique foret-savane à Mouyoundzi," *Espace Géographique,* vol. 2, 1987, p. 85–99.

————. "Problèmes de développement de la production cacaoyère dans le district de Sembé et Souanké," *Cahiers ORSTOM,* vol. 14, 1977, p. 151–169.

————. *Recherches sur les structures agraires dans le district de Mouyondzi,* Brazzaville, ORSTOM, 1977.

————. *La Terre Enkou (Congo),* The Hague, Mouton, 1973.

Hiez, G. et al. *Hydrologie du bassin supérieur du Niari* Paris, ORSTOM, 1965.

Kivouvou, D. *Le chemin de fer Congo-océan,* Heidelberg, Editions Bantoues, 1985.

————. "Les types d'habitat dans l'agglomération de Brazzaville," PhD thesis, University of Rennes, 1987.

Knaebel, G. "Les problèmes d'assainement d'une ville du Tiers-Monde: Pointe-Noire," PhD thesis, University of Paris, 1978.

Koechlin, Jean. "Sur quelques usages de plantes apontanées de la région de Brazzaville," *Bulletin de l'Institut d'Etudes Centrafricaines*, no. 2, 1951, p. 103–109.

————. *La végétation des savanes dans les pays du Niari*, Paris, ORSTOM, 1961.

————. *La végétation des savanes dans le sud de la République du Congo*. Montpellier, ORSTOM, 1961.

————, and P. Cavalan. "Les essais d'introduction et de culture de plantes fourragères dans la vallée du Niari," *Bulletin de l'Institut d'Etudes Centrafricaines*, no. 17/18, 1959, p. 43–70.

————, and Jean-Louis Trochain. "Sur l'existence d'un post-climax forestièr au Moyen-Congo," *Comptes-rendu hebdomadaire de l'Academie des sciences de Paris*, vol. 241 no. 3, July 1955, p. 329–331.

La Maréchal, A. *Contribution à l'étude des plateaux Batéké*, Brazzaville, ORSTOM, 1966.

Lanfranchi, Raymond, and Dominique Schwartz. "Paléogeographie du site de Brazzaville," In: *Journées d'études sur Brazzaville*, Brazzaville, ORSTOM, 1986, p. 23–36.

Laporte, G. *Reconnaissance pédologique le long de la voie ferreé COMILOG*, Brazzaville, ORSTOM, 1962.

La Souchère, P. de. *Etude Pedologique de trois terrains*, Brazzaville, ORSTOM, 1974, 2 vol.

Loembé, Dieudonné, "Problème de drainage des eaux pluviales sur la site urbain de Brazzaville," In: *Journées d'etudes sur Brazzaville*, Brazzaville, ORSTOM, 1986, p. 111–136.

Louis, Jean and Joseph Fouarge. *Essences forestières et bois du Congo*, Bruxelles, INEAC, 1943.

Luc, M. et al. "Enquete sur les nématodes parasites des culture de la république centrafricaine et du Congo Brazzaville," *Agronomie tropicale*, no. 8/9 Aug.–Sept. 1964, p. 723–46.

Mackal, Roy P. *A living dinosaur?: in search of Mokele-mbembe*, Leiden, E. J. Brill, 1987.

Makambila, C. "Une nouvelle maladie de la baselle au Congo," *Agronomie Tropicale*, vol. 41 no. 1, 1986, p. 69–74.

Makita, D. "Climat et habitation dans l'agglomeration de Brazzaville," PhD thesis, University of Paris, 1987.

Maumon, Michel. *Rapport provisoire de la mission d'études dans la cuvette congolaise*, Brazzaville, Commissariat au plan, 1961, 2 vol.

Mayindou, F. "Le role de Brazzaville dans l'organisation de l'éspace national congolais," PhD thesis, University of Paris, 1976.

Mengho, Bonaventure M. "L'habitat rural au Congo: reflet du milieu naturel, expression culturelle," *Cahiers d'Outre-mer,* vol. 33, no. 129, 1980, p. 65–86.

———. "Ouesso: quelques aspects géographiques d'une centre semi-urbain au Congo," *Cahiers d'Outre-mer,* vol. 37, no. 147, 1984 p. 235–255.

———. "Quelques aspects de la ruralité des 'petits villes' au Congo," *Cahiers d'Outre-mer,* vol. 38 no. 151, 1985, p. 263–276.

———. "L'utilisation de l'energie domestique et l'approvisionnement d'eau potable dans les petits villes au Congo," *Cahiers d'Outre Mer,* no, 162, 1988, p. 159–178.

———, and M. Sautter. *La mise en valeur de la cuvette congolaise,* Paris, Ministère de la coopération, 1962, 3 vol.

Michel, M. T. *Nutrition et alimentationdes ménages à Pointe-Noire,* Paris, Secretariat d'Etat aux Affaires Etrangeres-Cooperation, 1971.

Mingole, A. "Les problèmes d'aménagement portuaire à Pointe-Noire en République Populaire du Congo," PhD thesis, University of Nantes, 1981.

Moukolo, Noel. "Ressources en eau souterraine et approvionnement. Données hydrogéologiques de la region de Brazzaville,' In: *Journees d'études sur Brazzaville,* Brazzaville, ORSTOM, 1986, p. 97–110.

Mounsambotte, A. "L'évolution économique et demographique le long des routes dans l'arrière-pays de Brazzaville," PhD thesis, 1987.

Muller, Hans-Peter, *Volksrepublik Kongo.* Hamburg, Institut fur Afrika-Kunde, 1990.

Nzingoulé, S., M. Lallemant, G. Jourdain. "Epidémiologie urbaine: l'exemple de la santé maternelle et infantile à Brazzaville," In: *Journees d'études sur Brazzaville,* Brazzaville, ORSTOM, 1986, p. 467–477.

Piettre, M. "Elevage extensif, premiere étape de la mise en valeur des sols pauvres," *Revue internationales de botanique appliquées et d'agriculture tropicale,* no. 347/48, 1951, p. 512–16.

"La Production des fibres jutiéres au Congo: Bilan de 10 années de recherches," *Coton et fibres tropicales,* no. 2 Aug. 1963, p. 361–67.

Rapport de mission sur la mise en valeur de la vallée du Niari, Paris, CGOT, 1951.

Reste, J. F. "Note sur la Likouala-Mossaka. Constitution géologique, faune et flore de régions de Makoua, Mondzéli, Abolo et Odzala," *Bulletin de la Société de recherches congolaises,* no. 3, 1923, p. 23–52.

Riou-Chartier, A. "Etude du bilan d'énergie à Brazzaville," *Cahiers ORSTOM,* no. 4, 1968, p. 25–42.

Rogier, M. and A. Lyon-Caen. "La culture mécanique de l'arachide et la conservation des sols dans la région schisto-calcaire du Moyen-Congo," *Bulletin agricole du Congo belge,* no. 3–4, Sept.–Dec. 1949, p. 2010–28.

Samba Kimbata, M. J. "Le climat du Bas Congo," PhD thesis, University of Dijon, 1978.

Sautter, Gilles. *De l'Atlantique au fleuve Congo, une géographie de sous-peuplement, République du Congo, République Gabonaise.* Paris, Mouton, 1966, 2 vol.

————. *Essai sur les formes d'érosion en 'cirques' dans la région de Brazzaville,* Paris, CNRS, 1979.

————. "Esquisse d'une géographie régionale du Moyen-Congo," *Cahiers de l'Information géographique,* no. 1–3, 1954, p. 33–44.

————. *Essai sur les formes d'erosion en "cirques" dan la région de Brazzaville,* Paris, CNRS, 1970.

————. *La cuvette congolaise: monographie régionale des bassins de la Likouala-Mossaka,* Paris, Ministère de Coopération, 1962.

————. "Notes sur la construction du chemin de fer Congo-océan (1921–1934)," *Cahiers d'études Africaines,* vol. 7 no. 26, 1967, p. 219–299.

————. "Notes sur l'érosion en cirque des sables au nord de Brazzaville," *Bulletin de l'Institut d'Etudes Centrafricianes,* vol. 2, 1951, p. 49–61.

————. "Le plateau Congolais de Mbé," *Cahiers d'Etudes Africaines,* no. 2, 1960, p. 5–48.

————. *Les villages des Plateaux Batéké et le problème de l'eau,* Brazzaville, Institut d'Etudes Centrafricaines, 1953.

Schwartz, Dominique. *Histoire d'un paysage: le lousséké, paleoénvironnement quaternaires et podzoloiation sur sables Batéké,* Paris, ORSTOM, 1988.

————. "Les sols des environs de Brazzaville et leurs utilisation," In: *Journées d'études sur Brazzaville,* Brazzaville, ORSTOM, 1986, p. 37–56.

Scolari, Georges. *Etude géologique du Bassin du Niari et de les mineralisations,* Paris, BRGM, 1965.

Tchivelé-Tchichéllé. "La mortalité des enfants en République Populaire du Congo," *Peuples Noire-Peuples Africaines,* vol. 3 no. 15, 1980, p. 10–22.

Trape, J. F. "Malaria and urbanization in central Africa: the example of Brazzaville," *Transactions of the Royal Society of Tropical medicine,* 1987, p. 1–9.

Vennetier, Pierre. "Aspects pratiques de la recherche géographique en Afrique francophone et plus particulièrement au Congo," *ORSTOM: Bulletin de liaison des Sciences Humaines.* no. 9 Dec. 1967, p. 21–8.

————. *Géographie du Congo-Brazzaville.* Paris: Gauthier-Villars, 1966.

————. "La Navigation intérieure en Afrique Noire: le réseau français

Congo-Oubangui," *Les Cahiers d'Outre-Mer,* vol. 12 no. 48 (1959) p. 321–48.

————. "Note au sujet d'une étude foret-savane," *ORSTOM: Bulletin de liaison Sciences Humaines,* no. 8 April 1967, 207–16.

————. *Pointe-Noire et la façade maritime du Congo-Brazzaville,* Paris: ORSTOM, 1968.

————. "Les ports du Gabon et du Congo-Brazzaville," *Les Cahiers d'Outre-Mer,* vol. 22 no. 88, 1969, p. 337–355.

————. *Les transports en République du Congo, au Nord de Brazzaville,* Brazzaville, ORSTOM, 1962.

————. "Les transports dans le Nord du Congo," *Cahiers d'Outre-mer,* no. 61 Jan.–March 1963, p. 126–32.

————. et al. *Atlas de la République Populaire du Congo,* Paris, Jeune Afrique, 1977.

Yetela, J. M. "Les contacts forets-savanes dans la région de Brazzaville, sur les sables Batékés," PhD thesis, University of Bordeaux, 1988.

History

Ackermann-Athanassiades, Blanche. *France-Libre, capitale Brazzaville,* Paris, Editions La Bruyere, 1989.

Aissi, Antoine. "Le justice indigène et la vie congolaise 1886–1936," Thesis, University of Toulouse, 1978.

————. "Le tournant des années 30: les Blancs du Congo face à l'eveil politique congolaise," *Cahiers Congolais d'Anthropologie,* vol. 7 1982, p. 39–50.

Autin, Jean. *Pierre Savorgnan de Brazza, une prophète du Tiers Monde,* Paris, Perrin, 1985.

Azevedo, M. "The human price of development: the Brazzaville railroad and the Sara of Chad," *African Studies Review,* vol. 24 no. 1, 1981, p. 1–19.

Balandier, Georges. *Daily life in the Kingdom of the Kongo from the sixteenth century to the eighteenth century,* New York, Pantheon, 1968.

Banzouzi, Jean-Pierre. "Le représentation de l'histoire du Congo à travers les noms des rues de Brazzaville," In: *Journées d'etudes sur Brazzaville,* Brazzaville, ORSTOM, 1986, p. 75–86.

Bastian, A. *Die deutsche expedition an die Loango kuste,* Paris, Iena, 1874, 2 vol.

Bonnafé, P. "Les formes d'asservissement chez les Kukuya de l'Afrique Centrale," In: C. Meillassoux (ed.), *L'esclavage en Afrique précoloniale,* Paris, Maspero, 1975, p. 529–556.

Boussoukou-Boumba, A. "L'organisation de la chefferie indigène à Ntima et à Divinié, 1923–1941" *Présence Africaine,* no. 107, 1978, p. i–iii.

Breard, C., D. Neuville. *Les voyages de Savorgnan de Brazza. Ogooué et Congo (1875–1882)*, Paris, Berger-Levrault, 1884.

Brunschwig, Henri. "Brazza et les scandales du Congo Français (1904–06), *Academie Royale des Sciences d'Outre-mer*, no. 2, 1977, p. 112–129.

———. *Brazza explorateur: les traités Makoko 1880–1882*. Paris, Mouton, 1972.

———. Les cahiers de Brazza, 1880–1882" *Cahiers d'Etudes Africaines*, vol. 6 no. 22, 1966, p. 157–227.

———. "Le Congo," *La Revue Historique*, no. 485, Jan.–March 1968, p. 133–158.

———. "La négociation du traité Makoko," *Cahiers d'Etudes Africaines*, vol. 5 no. 17, 1965, p. 5–56.

———. "Note sur les technocrates de l'imperialisme français en Afrique noire," *Revue Française d'Histoire d'Outre-mer*, no. 194–7, 1967, p. 171–187.

———. "La troque du traité Makoko," *Cahiers d'Etudes Africaines*, vol. 5 no. 18, 1965, p. 2–55.

Coquery-Vidrovitch, C. De Brazza à Gentil: la politique Française en Haute-Sangha à la fin du XIX siècle," *Revue Française d'Histoire d'Outre-mer*, vol. 52 no. 186, 1965, p. 22–40.

———. *Brazza et la prise de possession du Congo, 1883–1885*, The Hague, Mouton, 1969.

———. *Le Congo au temps des grandes compagnies concessionaires 1898–1930*, Paris, Mouton, 1972.

———. "L'échec d'une tentative économique l'impot de capitation au service des compagnies consessionaires," *Cahiers d'Etudes Africaines*, vol. 8, 1968, p. 96–109.

———. "L'idées économiques de Brazzaville et les premières tentatives des compagnies de colonisation au Congo Français 1885–1898," *Cahiers d'Etudes Africaines*, no. 17, 1965, p. 57–95.

Cornevin, R. "La fondation de Brazzaville," *Europe Outre-mer*, May 1980, p. 5–9.

Cuvelier, J. *L'ancien Royaume de Congo*, Bruges, Desclée de Brouwer, 1946.

Droux, G. "Gisement préhistorique de la Pointe hollandaise (Brazzaville)," *Bulletin de la Societe de Recherches Congolaises*, no. 27, June 1939, p. 137–145.

———. "Nouvelles stations préhistoriques au Congo français," *Bulletin de la Societe de Recherches Congolaises*, vol. 23, 1937, p. 171–178.

———. "Préhistoire africaine. De la présence d'outils en pierre taillée dans la terrasse de vingt métres du Stanley Pool," *Bulletin de la Société de Recherches Congolaises*, no. 28, 1941, p. 137–142.

———. "Recherches préhistoriques dans la région de Boko-Songho et à Pointe Noire," *Journal de la Société des Africanistes,* vol. 9 no. 1, 1939, p. 71–84.

Dufeil, M. M., R. Lanfranchi. "Note sur la préhistorie du Congo: inventaire de restitution au musée national," *Annales de l'Université de Brazzaville,* vol. ii, 1975, p. 69–89.

Dupré, Georges. "Le commerce entre sociétés lignagères. Les Nzabi de la traite à la fin du XIX siècle," *Cahiers d'Etudes Africaines,* vol. ii, 1972, p. 378–399.

————. "Creation et développement des marchés chez les Beembé 1870–1911," *Annales: Economies, Sociétés, Civilisations,* 1975, p. 1447–1476.

————. *Les naissances d'une société, espace et historicité chez les Beembé du Congo,* Paris, ORSTOM, 1985.

————. *Un ordre et sa destruction. Economie, politique et historie chez les Nzabi de la République Populaire du Congo,* Paris, ORSTOM, 1982.

Dupré, Marie-Claude. "Contribution à l'histoire de la République Populaire du Congo. Les Téké-tsaayi des origines á 1898," *Annales de l'Université de Brazzaville,* vol. 9, 1973, p. 55–82.

————. "La dualité politique chez les Téké de l'Ouest. Pouvoir tsaayi et pouvoir nzineké," Ph.D. thesis, University of Lyon, 1972.

————. "Génealogies de heros chez les Téké Tsaayi au Congo," *History in Africa,* vol. 16, 1989, p. 137–165.

————. "Pour une histoire des productions. La métallurgie du fer chez les Téké Ngungulu, Tio, Tsaayi, République Populaire du Congo," *Cahiers d'ORSTOM,* vol. 18, 1982, p. 195–223.

Emphoux, Jean-Pierre. "Un site de proto et pré-histoire au Congo-Brazzaville: Mafamba," *Cahiers ORSTOM,* vol. 2 no. 4, 1965.

Froidevaux, H. "La politique indigène au Congo Français" *Questions Diplomatiques et Coloniales,* no. 21, 1906, p. 385–99.

Gbagbo, L. *Reflexions sur la Conference de Brazzaville,* Paris, 1979.

Gide, André. *Souvenirs de la Cour d'Assises, voyages au Congo,* Paris, Gallimard, 1924.

————. *Voyages au Congo, carnets de route,* Paris, Gallimard, 1927.

Glénisson, M. "Les royaumes de la cote congolaise avant l'arrivée de Brazza," *Liaison,* no. 37/8 August 1953, p. 33–40.

Goma-Foutou, Celestin. *Histoire des civilisations au Congo,* Paris, Anthropos, 1981.

————. "Le Moyen Age dans le bassin congolais: la naissance des premiers états," *Revue des Sciences Sociales,* no. 7, Aug.–Sept. 1986.

Guillot, Bernard. "Notes sur les anciennes mines de fer du pays Nzabi dans la région de Mayoko," *Cahiers d'ORSTOM,* vol. 6 no. 2, 1969, p. 93–99.

———, and A. Massala. "Histoire de pays Beembé," *Cahiers d'ORSTOM,* vol. 7 no. 3, 1970, p. 41–74.

Hagenbucher-Sacripanti, Frank. *Les fondements spirituels du pouvoir au royaume de Loango,* Paris, ORSTOM, 1973.

Heiser, Eugene. *Emile Gentil: 1866–1914,* Sarreguemines, Heiser, 1976.

Heusch, Luc de "Le roi, le forgeron et les premières hommes dans l'ancienne société kongo," *Systèmes de pensée en Afrique Noire,* 1975, p. 165–179.

Janzen, John M. "Laman's Kongo ethnography: observations on sources, methodology, and theory," *Africa* vol. 42 no. 4, Oct. 1972, p. 316–333.

Joly, V. "A Dolisie et les débuts de la présence française au Congo," PhD thesis, University of the Sorbonne, 1980, 2 vol.

Laman, K. E. *The Kongo,* Stockholm, Studia Ethnographica Uppsalensia, 1953–1962, 3 vol.

Lanfranchi, Raymond. "Le gisement de la Pointe Hollandaise," *Cahiers Congolais d'Anthropologie et d'histoire,* vol. 1, 1976, p. 13–19.

———. "Préhistoire du site de Brazzaville," In: *Journées d'études sur Brazzaville,* Brazzaville, ORSTOM, 1986, p. 57–74.

———. "Recherches préhistoire dans la moyenne vallée du Niari," PhD thesis, University of Paris, 1979.

Leroy, M. "La préhistoire à Brazzaville et dans le Moyen-Congo," *Liaison,* no. 31, Jan. 1953, p. 39–49.

Lethur, R. "Etudes sur le royaume du Loango et le peuple Vili," *Cahiers Ngonge* no. 4, 1960.

Lombard, J. "Materiaux préhistoriques du Congo français," *Journal de la Société des Africanistes,* vol. i no. i, 1931, p. 50–56.

Malonga, Jean. *La legende de M'foumou Ma Mazondo,* Paris, Présence Africaine, 1973.

Maran, R. *Brazzaville et la fondation de l'A.E.F,* Paris, Gallimard, 1941.

Martin, Phyllis M. *External trade of the Loango coast,* Oxford, Clarendon Press, 1972.

———. "The trade of Loango in the seventeenth and eighteenth centuries," In: R. Gray, D. Birmingham (eds.), *Precolonial African Trade,* London, Oxford University Press, 1970, p. 39–74.

Matumba Makombo. *Makoko, roi des Batéké, 1880–1892,* Kinshasa, Centres de recherches pédagogiques, 1987.

Mazenot, Georges. *La Likouala-Mossaka: Histoire de la penetration du Haut-Congo 1878–1929,* Paris, Mouton, 1970.

———. "L'occupation du bassin de la Likouala-Mossaka, 1909–1914" *Cahiers d'Etudes Africaines,* vol. 6 no. 22, 1966, p. 33–56.

———. "La problème de la Likona-Nkundja et la délimitation du Congo Français et de l'Etat indépendant (Congo Belge)" *Cahiers d'Etudes Africaines,* vol. 7 no. 25, 1967, p. 127–151.

Mazoyer, L. "Monographie du cercle de Koundé au Congo," *Revue des troupes coloniales,* 1907, p. 218–229, 346–354, 446–457.

Mutumba Makombo. *Makoko, roi des Batéké, 1880–1892,* Kinshasa, Centre de recherches pedagogiques, 1987.

Ndinga-Mbo, Abraham. "Histoire de cuivre au Congo des origines à 1935," PhD thesis, University of Paris, 1979.

―――. *Introduction à l'histoire des migrations au Congo: hommes et cuivre dans le Pool et la Bouenza avant le xxe siècle,* Heidelberg, Editions Bantoues, 1984.

―――. "Quelques réflexions sur la civilisation du cuivre au Congo," *Cahiers Congolaise d'Anthropologie,* no. 1, May 1977, p. 31–44.

Ndomo Deo, Bynafashe. "Etablissement de la souverainete français et vie administrative au Congo-Brazzaville des origines à 1920," Thesis, University of Provence, 1981.

N'goie-N'galla, D. *Les Kondo de la vallée du Niari. Origines et migrations, XIIe-XIXe siècle. Bakamba, Badondo, Bakunyi, Basundi, Babeemba,* Brazzaville, Presses Universitaires de Brazzaville, 1981.

Nwoye, Rosaline Eredapa. *The public image of Pierre Savorgnan de Brazza and the establishment of French imperialism in the Congo, 1875–1885,* Aberdeen, University of Aberdeen African Studies Group, 1974.

Obenga, Théophile. *La Cuvette Congolaise: Les Hommes et les Structures,* Paris, Présence Africaine, 1977.

―――. *Introduction à la connaissance du peuple de la République du Congo,* Brazzaville, Librairie Populaire, 1973.

―――. Le rois-dieux au royaume Loango," *Revue des Sciences Sociales,* no. 3, July-Sept. 1985, p. 21–47.

―――. "Le royaume de Makoko," *Présence Africaine,* no. 70, 1969, p. 28–45.

Ollandet, J. "Les contacts téké-mbosi. Essai sur les civilisations du bassin du Congo," PhD thesis, University of Montpellier, 1981.

Phillis, M. *The external trade of the Lwangu coast (1576–1870),* Oxford, Oxford University Press, 1972.

Préclin, Louis. *Pointe-Noire sous la Croix de Lorraine,* Paris, Promotion, 1967.

Rabut, Elisabeth, *Brazza, commissaire général,* Paris, EHESS, 1989.

Randles, W. G. L. *L'ancienne royaume du Congo des origines à la fin du xixe siècle,* Paris, Mouton, 1968.

Robineau, Claude. "Contribution à l'histoire du Congo: la domination européenne et l'exemple de Souanké (1900–1960)," *Cahiers d'Etudes africaines,* no. 26, 1967, p. 300–344.

Rouget, F. *L'expansion coloniale au Congo Français,* Paris, Larose, 1906.

Samarin, William J. *The Black Man's burden: African colonial labor on the Congo and Ubangi rivers, 1880–1900,* Boulder, Westview Press, 1989.

————. "The state's Bakongo burden-bearers," In: C. Coquery-Vidrovitch and Paul E. Lovejoy (eds.) *The workers of African Trade,* Beverly Hills, Sage, 1985, p. 269–292.

Soret, M. *Histoire du Congo (Capitale Brazzaville),* Paris.

Thornton, John K. *The Kingdom of Kongo: civil war and transition, 1641–1718,* Madison, University of Wisconsin Press, 1983.

Ulriche, Sophie. *Le Gouverneure Général Felix Eboué,* Paris, Larose, 1950.

Vansina, Jan. "Comment reconstituer la société Batéké de la fin du XIXe siècle," *Revue Française d'Histoire d'Outre-Mer,* vol. 57 no. 1970, p. 253–267.

————. "The Kingdom of the Great Mokoko," In: Daniel McCall et al. *Western African History,* New York, Praeger, 1969, p. 20–44.

————. "Notes sur l'origine du royaume du Congo," *Journal of African History,* vol. 4 no. 1, 1963, p. 33–38.

————. *The Tio kingdom of the Middle Congo 1880–1892,* Oxford, Oxford University Press, 1973.

Vincent, Jean-Françoise. "Traditions historiques chez les Djem de Souanké," *Revue Française d'Histoire d'Outre-Monde* no. 178, 1963, p. 64–73.

West, Richard. *Congo,* New York, Holt, Rinehart & Winston, 1972.

Anthropology/Sociology/Demography

Althabe, Gérard. *Le Chomage à Brazzaville.* Paris: Cahiers d'ORSTOM vol. 1 no. 4, 1963.

————. *Le chomage à Brazzaville, étude psychologique,* Paris, ORSTOM, 1959.

————. "Problèmes socio-économique du Nord-Congo," *Cahiers de l'ISEA,* no. 131, Nov. 1962, p. 189–382.

Amega, Louis Koffi. "Etude sociologique des facteurs de la délinquance juvenile au Congo Brazzaville," *Bulletin d'IFAN,* no. 2, May 1964, p. 214–220.

Andersson, Efraim. *Contribution à l'éthnographie des Luta.* Uppsala, Almquist & Wiksell, 1953.

Anglade, F. "L'Attraction démographique des centres urbains de Congo," *Cahiers d'Outre Mer,* vol. 41 Jan.–Mar. 1988, p. 41–59.

Auger, Alai. *L'Arriére-pays brazzavillois,* Brazzaville: ORSTOM, 1971.

————. *Kinkala. Etude d'un centre urbain secondaire au Congo.* Paris, ORSTOM, 1973.

————. *Kinkala: centre urbain secondaire et sa vie de relations,* Brazzaville, ORSTOM, 1965.

————. "Notes sur les centres urbaines secondaires au Congo Brazzaville," *Les Cahiers d'Outre-Mer,* no. 81, Jan.–March 1968, p. 29–55.

————, and P. Vennetier. "La croissance periphérique des villes: naissance et développement d'une banlieue brazzavilloise," *Travaux et documents de géographie tropicale,* 1976.

Badier, M. "Monographie de la tribu des Batéké," *Recherches Congolaise,* no. 10, 1929, p. 37–45.

Balandier, Georges. "Approche psychologique des jeunes évolués de Brazzaville," *Proceedings of the 3rd International West African Conference,* Lagos, Nigerian Museum, 1956, p. 337–355.

————. "Approche sociologique des Brazzavilless-Noire," *Africa,* vol. 22 no. 1, Jan. 1952, p. 22–34.

————. "Enquete sociologique sur la cité africaine de Brazzaville," *Aspects sociaux,* 1956, p. 119–123.

————. "Les problèmes du travailleur africain au Congo et au Gabon," *Bulletin international des sciences sociales,* March 1954, p. 208–18.

————. *Sociologie de Brazzavilles Noires.* Paris: Armand Collin, 1955.

————. "Le travail non-salarié dans les Brazzaville noires," *Zaire,* July–Aug. 1952, p. 675–690.

————. "Le travailleur africain dans les Brazzaville noires," *Présence Africaine,* Special Issue 1952, p. 315–330.

Ballif, Noel. *Les pygmées de la grande foret,* Paris, Harmattan, 1992.

"Banlieue noire de Brazzaville," *Cahiers d'Outre-Mer,* Apr.–June 1957, p. 131–157.

Bayle des Hermes, R., Lanfranchi, D. "L'Abri tshitolien de Ntadi Yomba," *L'Anthropologie,* vol. 82 no. 4, 1978, p. 539–564.

Biniakounou, P. *Chomeur à Brazzaville,* Dakar, Nouvelles editions Africaines, 1977.

Bjerhagen, Torbjorn. *L'habitat traditionnel dans la république populaire du Congo,* Uppsala, Scandinavian Institute of African Studies, 1972.

Bockie, Simon. *Death and Invisible powers. The world of Kongo beliefs,* Bloomington, Indiana University Press, 1993.

Bonnafé, Pierre. "L'apparation d'une nouvelle 'classe' à l'interieur du champ politique dans la République du Congo-Brazzaville," *Revue de l'Institut de Sociologie,* vol. 2–3, 1967, p. 321–335.

————. "Un aspect religieux de l'idéologie lignagere. Le Nkira des Kukuya du Congo-Brazzaville," *Cahiers d'Etudes Africaines,* no. 6 (July 1969), p. 209–297.

————. "Une cérémonie de découverte du sorcier," PhD thesis, University of Paris, 1967.

——. "Une classe d'age politique: la JMNR de la République du Congo-Brazzaville," *Cahiers d'Etudes Africaines,* vol. 8 no. 31, 1968, p. 327–67.

——. "Une grande fete de la vie et de la mort, Le mayili, cérémonie funeraire d'un seigneur du ciel Kukuya," *L'Homme,* vol. 13 no. 1–2, Jan.–June 1973, p. 97–166.

——. *Histoire sociale d'un peuple congolais,* Paris, ORSTOM, 1988, 2 vol.

Bonnefond, P. and Jean Lombard. "Notes sur les coutumes Lari," *Bulletin de l'Institut d'Etudes Centrafricaines,* no. i, 1950, p. 141–177.

Bouboutou, M. "Le Niari oriental: tradition et modernisme," Thesis, University of Lyon, 1973.

Boudimbou, Guy. *Habitat et mode de vie des immigrés africains en France,* Paris, Harmattan, 1991.

Bouquet, A. *Féticheurs: médicines traditionnelles du Congo-Brazzaville,* Paris: ORSTOM, 1969.

——. *Pharmacopée des Kota et des Téké.* Brazzaville: ORSTOM, 1966.

——., A, Jacquot. "Essai de géographie linguistique sur quelques plantes médicinales du Congo-Brazzaville," *Cahiers ORSTOM,* vol. 4 no. 3–4, 1967, p. 3–35.

Boussoukou-Bouma. "L'évolution politique et économique des Boukougnis du Congo, 1910–1941," Ph.D. thesis, University of Paris, 1977.

——. "L'organisation de la chefferie indigène à Ntima et à Divinié, Congo (1923–1941)" *Présence Africaine,* no. 107, 1978, p. 111–134.

Bouveignes, Olivier de. *Entendu dans la brousse. Contes congolais,* Paris, Paul Gauthier, 1938.

Brazzaville 1880–1980. Mission d'urbanise et d'habitat au Congo, Paris, Urbanor, 1980.

Bruel, Georges. "Les populations de la moyenne Sangha: les Babinga," *Revue d'ethnographie et de sociologie,* no. 5–7, 1910, p. 111–126.

Les budgets des ménages africains a Pointe-Noire, Paris, INSEE, 1962.

Cabanac, P. "Les tribus Ballali et Bassoundi de la subdivision de Mayama," *Recherches Congolaises,* no. 7, 1925, p. 77–94.

Centres sécondaires: etude socio-urbaine, Paris, Urbanor, 1980.

Chaumeton, Josette. "Note préliminaire sur les niveau de vie dans les villes indigènes de Poto-Poto, Wenzé et Bacongo," Brazzaville, Institut d'Etudes Centrafricaines, 1947.

Cleemput, J. "Proverbes de Bakongo. Essai d'Etudes," *Mouvement des Missions catholiques au Congo,* March 1914, p. 29–36.

Cleene, N. de. "Les chefs indigènes au Mayombé," *Africa,* vol. 8 no. 1, 1935.

————. "La famille au Mayombé," *Africa*, vol. 10 no. 1, 1937.

————. "La famille dans l'organisation sociale du Mayombé," *Africa*, vol. 10, no. 1, 1937.

Clement, P. *Contribution à l'étude démographique des population du M'Boumou*, Paris, ORSTOM, 1957.

Congo. Ministère du Plan. *Operation villages-centres. Exode rural des jeunes.* Brazzaville, 1983.

————. ————. *La population du Congo, perspectives 1980–2000*, Brazzaville, 1980.

————. ————. *Recencement général de la population de Brazzaville*, Brazzaville, 1961.

————. ————. *Recencement général de la population de 1974.* Brazzaville, 1975.

————. ————. *Recencement général de la population de la population et de l'habitat, 1984*, Brazzaville, 1985, 2 vol.

Crapuchet, S. "Femmes Villageoises des Plateaux du Congo," *Le Mois en Afrique*, Mar.–Apr. 1982, p. 79–112.

Creth, A. *Enquete socio-urbaine de 12 centres sécondaires*, Paris: URBANOR, 1980.

Croce Spinelli, M. *Les Enfants de Poto-Poto*, Paris, 1967.

Crocquevieille, A. "Etude démographique de quelques villages likouéla du Moyen Congo," *Population*, no. 3, July–Sept. 1953, p. 491–510.

Dacyelo, A., A. Kouvouama. "Conscience éthnique et conscience de classe au Congo," *Annales de la Faculté de Lettres* (Brazzaville), vol. i, 1985, p. 277–293.

Daho, E. "La compensation matrimoniale chez les Mbosi au Congo," thesis, University of Paris, 1983.

Darre, E. "La tribu Bondjo: ses moeurs, ses coutumes," *Bulletin de la société de recherches Congolaises*, vol. 3, 1923, p. 53–73.

Debikat, M. "L'urbanisation et la question des transports à Brazzaville," Ph.D. thesis, University of Paris, 1987.

Decapmaker, J. "Les funerailles chez les Bakongo," *Aequatoria*, vol. 14, 1951, p. 81–84, 125–128.

Delobeau, J. M. "Les pygmées dans la colonisation," *Afrika-Zamani* (Yaounde), no. 14, 1984, p. 115–133.

Demesse, Lucien. *A la recherche des premiers ages: les Babinga*, Paris, P. Amiot, 1957.

Dennet, Richard E. *Notes on the folklore of the Fjort, French Congo*, London, Nutt, 1898.

Desjeaux, D. "Conscience lignagère et alliances de classe au Congo-Brazzaville," *Tiers Monde*, Oct.–Dec. 1977, p. 881–889.

————. "L'acces à la terre chez les paysans basundi, Congo," In: Emile Le Bris et al (eds.), *Enjeux fonciers en Afrique Noire*, Paris, Karthala, 1982, p. 126–132.

Devauges, Roland. *Les chomeurs de Brazzaville et les perspectives du barrage du Kouilou,* Paris, ORSTOM, 1959.

———. *Les Conditions Sociologiques d'une Politique d'Urbanisme à Brazzaville,* 2 vols., Paris, 1959.

———. "Croyances et vérification: les pratiques magico-religeuses en milieu urbain africain," *Cahiers d'Etudes Africaines,* no. 66/67, 1970, p. 299–305.

———. *Etude du chomage à Brazzaville: Etude sociologique.* Paris: ORSTOM, 1959.

———. "Les grandes circonstances de la vie de l'individu," *Cahiers ORSTOM,* vol. i, no. 3, 1963.

———. *Les marchés africains de Pointe Noire. Note sur quelques aspects socio-économiques,* Brazzaville, IRSC, 1963.

———. *L'Oncle, le ndoki et l'entrepreneur. La petite entreprise congolaise à Brazzaville.* Paris: ORSTOM, 1977.

———. "La population urbaine au regard de ses conditions de survie: dépéndants et producteurs," In: *Journées d'etudes sur Brazzaville,* Brazzaville, ORSTOM, 1986, p. 275–296.

Dhont, Yves. *Les budgets familiaux dans les villages du Niari,* Brazzaville, ORSTOM, 1965.

———. *Notes sur l'alimentation dans la vallée du Niari,* Brazzaville, ORSTOM, 1966.

———. *La peche à Pointe-Noire et ses possibilités de développement,* Paris: Brazzaville, 1963.

Dolisie, A. "Notice sur les chefs Batékés avant 1898," *Bulletin de la Société des Recherches congolaises,* no. 6, 1927, p. 44–49.

Dorier, Elisabeth. "Une traversée des quartiers est de Brazzaville," In: *Journées d'études sur Brazzaville,* Brazzaville, ORSTOM, 1986, p. 199–212.

Dresch, J. "Villes congolaises," *Revue de géographie humaine et d'éthnologie,* no. 3 July–Sept. 1946, p. 3–24.

Duboz, P. "Aspects démographiques de la région de la Lékoumou," *Cahiers ORSTOM* vol. 12 no. 4 (1975), p. 287–316.

———. *Etude démographique de la ville de Brazzaville 1974–77* Bangui, ORSTOM, 1979.

Dupré, Marie-Claude. "Comment etre femme. Un aspect du rituel Mukisi chez les Téké de la République Populaire du Congo," *Archives de Sciences Sociales des Religions* (Paris), no. 461, 1978, p. 57–84.

———. "Les femmes Mukisi chez Téké-tsaayi. Rituel de possession et culte anti-sorcier," *Joural de la Société des Africanistes,* vol. 44 no. i, 1974, p. 53–69.

———. "Histoire et rituels. L'observations du Siku en pays beembé, République Populaire du Congo," *Cahiers ORSTOM,* vol. 18 no. 2, 1981, p. 171–194.

Durand-Lasserve, A. *Croissance péripherique des villes: cas de Bangkok et Brazzaville*, Bordeaux, CNRS, 1976.

Dusselte, Elsa. *Les Tégués de l'Alima, Congo Français*, Antwerp, Imprimerie de Cauwer, 1910.

Ekondy, Akala. *Le Congo-Brazzaville: essai d'analyse et explication sociologique selon la methode pluraliste*, Berne, P. Lang, 1983.

Enquete socio-démographique dans la région du Niari, Brazzaville, Service de la Statistique générale, 1955.

Even, A. "Le caractére sacré des chefs chez les Babambas," *Journal de la Société des Africanistes*, no. 2, 1936, p. 187–195.

———. "La circonsission chez les Babambas, Mindassas d'Okondja," *Recherches congolaises*, no. 18, 1933, p. 97–194.

———. "Le feu et ses légendes au Moyen-Congo," *Recherches Congolaises*, Nov. 1937, p. 79–82.

———. "La grossesse, la naissance et la prime enfance chez les Bakota du Haut Ogué et du Nord de Mossendjo," *Recherches Congolaises*, Nov. 1938, p. 5–22.

———. "Quelques coutumes des populations de la Haute-Sangha," *Bulletin de la Société des Recherches Congolaises* no. ii, 1930, p. 23–33.

———. "Quelques coutumes des tribus Badondos et Bassoundis," *Recherches Congolaises*, no. 13, 1931, p. 17–31.

Faivre, S. and A., "Les Bondogos," *Recherches Congolaises*, no. 9, 1928, p. 21–26.

Fortems, G. *La densité de population dans le bas-fleuve et le Mayombé*, Bruxelles, Mémoires de l'Academie Royale de Sciences Coloniales, vol. ii no. 4, 1960.

Fourneau, L. "De Libreville au fleuve Congo par la Likouala-Mossaka. Notes ethnographiques," *Bulletin du Comité de l'Afrique Française*, no. i, 1907, p. 3–ii.

France. Ministere de la Coopération. *Enquete Démographique, 1960–1961, République du Congo-Brazzaville*, 1965.

Francheschi, P. *Au Congo jusqu'au cou: chez les Pygmées de la foret équatorial*, Paris, Hatier, 1977.

Gabou, Alexis. *Le mariage congolaise ladi et koukouya*, Brazzaville, Imprimerie St. Paul, 1979.

Galland, Henri. "Les Babi," *Revue d'éthnologie et des traditions populaires*, 1921, p. 16–21.

Gamandzori, J. "Le chemin de fer et l'urbanisation au Congo," In: C. Coquery-Vidrovitch (ed.) *Processus d'urbanisation en Afrique*, Paris, Harmattan, 1988, p. 98–108.

Gandoulou, Justin-Daniel. *Au coeur de la sape: moers et aventures du Congolais à Paris*, Paris, Harmattan, 1989.

———. *Dandies à Bacongo: la culte d'elegance dans la société congolais contemporaine*, Paris, Harmattan, 1989.

————. *Entre Paris et Bacongo*, Paris, Centre de création industrielle, 1984.

Ganon, F. *Enquete démographique et agricole dans la region du Kouilou, 1958–1959*, Paris, INSEE, 1960.

————. *Recensement démographique de Pointe-Noire 1958. Résultats definitifs*, Paris, INSEE, 1958.

Gassombo, B. *Otwere: la judicature ancestrale chez les Mbochis*, Brazzaville, Editions les Lianes, 1979.

Gaud, Fernand. *Les Mandjo, Congo Français*, Bruxelles, Albert de Witt, 1911.

Gomah, E. "'Minjioula Wroumbi', une coterie d'étranges gangsters au Moyen-Congo," *Liaison*, no. 52, 1956, p. 23–25.

Gruénais, M. E. "Une approche sociologique de malnutritions graves à Brazzaville," In: D. Lemonnier and Y. Ingenbleck, *Les malnutritions dans les pays tiers-monde*, Paris, INSERM, 1986, p. 53–60.

————. and Dominique Mayala. "Comment se débarrasser de 'l'efficacité symbolique' de la médicine traditionnelle?" *Politique Africaine*, October 1988, p. 51–65.

Guena, A. "La circonsission chez les Bakouelés, subdivision de Sembé Souanke," *Recherches Congolaises*, no. 25, 1938, p. 164–174.

Guillot, Bernard. "Le pays Bandzabi au nord de Mayoko et les déplacements récents de population provoquées par l'axe COMILOG," *Cahiers ORSTOM*, vol. 4 no. 3/4 1967, p. 37–56.

————. "Réflections sur les problèmes démographiques à propos du Plateau Koukouya," *Cahiers ORSTOM*, vol. 4 no. 1, 1967, p. 53–63.

————. *La terre Enkou—recherches sur les structures agraires du plateau Koukouyoa*, Brazzaville, ORSTOM, 1968, 2 vol.

————. and A. Massala. *Histoire du pays Beembé*, Paris, Cahiers ORSTOM, 1970.

Guiral, Leon. *Les Batéké*, Paris, Leroux, 1886.

Haeringer, Philippe. *L'Economie rurale dans la région de Mouyondzi*, Brazzaville, ORSTOM, 1965.

————. "L'éxode rural. Notes méthodologiques," *Bulletin ORSTOM de liaison Sciences Humaines*, no. 4 Feb. 1966, p. 63–67.

————. *La phenoméne suburbain à Brazzaville*, Brazzaville: ORSTOM, 1965.

————. *La recherches urbaine à ORSTOM: bibliographie analytique 1950–1980*, Paris, ORSTOM, 1983.

Harms, Robert W. *Games against nature: an eco-cultural history of the Nuna of Equatorial Africa*, Cambridge, Cambridge University Press, 1987.

Hauser, André. "Les Babinga," *Zaire*, vol. 7 no. 2, Feb. 1953, p. 146–179.

————. *Rapport de mission chez les Babinga de la Likouala,* Brazza-ville, Institut d'Etudes Centrafricaines, 1952.

Hochegger, H. "La mort et le culte des morts chez les populations d'expression téké," *Cahiers des Religions Africaines* (Kinshasa), vol. 4, 1970, p. 75–87.

Hubschwerlin, A. "Le régime foncier indigène dans la region de Boko: coutumes Balali, Basoundi, Bacongo et Bacongo Ntséllé," *Bulletin de la Société de Recherches Congolaises,* no. 24, 1937, p. 125–135.

Ibalico, M. "L'origine des Batékés d'Imfita," *Liaison,* no. 46, 1955, p. 37–39.

————. "Origines et sens des noms Batékés," *Liaison,* no. 52, 1956, p. 29–32; vol. 53, 1956, p. 41–44.

Ingarao, E. et al. *Etude typologique de l'habitat du plus grand nombre à Brazzaville,* Paris, Urbanor, 1985.

INSEE. *Recensement de Brazzaville, 1961.* Paris: INSEE, 1965.

Jacobsen, Anita. *Marriage and money,* Lund, Berlingsta Boktr, 1967.

Jacobsen-Widding, Anita. *Red-white-black as a mode of thought,* Uppsala, Almqvist & Wiksell, 1979.

Jonghe, E. de., C. van Overbergh. *Les Mayombé, sociologie descriptive,* Bruxelles. Institut Internationale, 1907.

Jung, Renee. "Notes sur les cases des Bambis," *Journal de la Société des Africanistes,* vol. 15 (1946), p. 9–21.

Labrouhe, O. de. *Chez les pygmées,* Paris, Berger-Levrault, 1933.

Laisne, P. "Chez les Dandos," *Recherches congolaises,* no. 23, 1937, p. 157–162.

Lallemant, Marc. "Malnutrition et problematique urbaine," In: D. Lemmonier and Y. Ingenbleck, *Les malnutritions dans les pays du tiers-monde,* Paris, INSERM, 1986, p. 53–60.

Lalouel, D. "Les forgerons Mondjombo," *Bulletin de l'Institut d'Etudes Centrafricaines* vol. 2 no. 3, 1947, p. 106–114.

Le Bourhis, A. "Coutumes Bomitaba de la Likouala aux herbes," *Bulletin de la Société de Recherches Congolaises,* no. 22, 1936, p. 63–116.

Legrand, J. M. "L'Urbanisme des agglomérations africaines au Moyen Congo," *Industries et Travaux d'Outre-Mer,* Mar. 1956, p. 141–148.

————. "L'urbanisme de Brazzaville," *Industries et Travaux d'Outre-Mer,* vol. 8 no. 74 (Jan. 1970), p. 27–35.

Lheyet-Gaboka, M. "Les jumeaux chez les Kouyous," *Liaison,* no. 42, 1954, p. 55–61.

Liedermann, Jean-Louis. *Analyses socio-démographiques de la population africaine de Pointe-Noire,* Brazzaville, ORSTOM, 1962–65, 2 vol.

————. *La modéle de croissance démographique de Pointe-Noire, 1920–1970.* Abidjan: ORSTOM, 1972.

————. "Recherches socio-démographiques en milieu urbain: orientation et moyens nécessaires," *Bulletin de liaison des Sciences Humaines,* no. 6, Aug. 1966, p. 87–97.

————. "Structures et évolution de la population Africaine de Pointe-Noire," *Nouvelles ORSTOM de l'IRSC* (Brazzaville), no. 7 Nov. 1962, p. 5–15.

Loemba, F. X. *Essai d'anthropologie sur les peuples de la cote congolaise,* Brazzaville, ORSTOM, 1972.

Loukombo Sengha, A. "Les problèmes du logement à Brazzaville: Etude socio-économique," PhD thesis, University of Bordeaux, 1985.

Loyre, E. "Les populations de la moyenne Sangha," *Questions Diplomatiques et Colonailes,* vol. 27, 1909, p. 406–420.

Makisa, Pierre, "Fiançailles et mariage Lari," *Liaison,* Sept. 1951, p. ii–16.

Malonga, J. "Contribution à la connaissance de l'ethnie Lari," *Liaison,* no. 55, 1957, p. 26–29; no. 56, p. 17–20; no. 57, p. 18–22.

————. "La famille chez les Makoua," *Liaison,* no. 47, 1955, p. 23–25.

Mampoya, Joseph. *Le Tribalisme au Congo,* Paris, La Pensée Universelle, 1983.

Mangomo, Norbert. "Quelques traits de vie chez les Babembé," *Liaison,* no. 39, 1953, p. 32–35.

Mankassa, C. "La société Bakongo et ses dynamismes politiques," PhD thesis, University of Paris, 1968.

Migrations rurales et urbanization en République populaire du Congo, Addis Ababa, ILO, 1984.

Monnier, L. *Ethnie et intégration régionale du Congo: Le Kongo central, 1962–1965,* Paris, ECEF, 1962.

"Naissance d'une ville: Dolisie," *Bulletin d'information et de documentation du Gouvernement Générale,* Brazzaville, no. 37, 1949.

Ndombi, Christian. "Les regroupements et restructurations des villages au Congo," Thesis, University of Laval, Quebec, 1971.

N'kaloulou, Bernard. *Dynamique paysanne et développement rural au Congo,* Paris, Harmattan, 1984.

Nsika-Nikaya, Henri. "Statut sexuel et statut socio-professionel dans la construction de l'identité psycho-sociale chez la jeune Brazzavilloise: la double aliénation," In: *Journées d'études sur Brazzaville,* Brazzaville, ORSTOM, 1986, p. 567–580.

Nzacakanda, Dominique. "Essai d'étude sur le mariage des Ballali et leurs frères de race," *Liaison,* no. 8, 1951, p. 23–25; no. 9, 1951, p. 28–29.

Obenga, Theophile. *La Cuvette Congolaise, les hommes et les structures,* Paris, Presence Africaine, 1976.

Ossebi, Henri. "Questions a la 'Sociologie congolaise,'" *Annales de la Faculté de Lettres et Sciences Humaines,* vol. 1, 1985, p. 237–242.

————. "Un quotidien en trompe-l'oeil. Bars et 'bganda' à Brazzaville," *Politique Africaine,* October 1988, p. 67–72.

Palmer, G. "Les conditions sociales des Basundi du Bas-Congo," *Congo,* 1926, p. 537–550; 1927, p. 23–44.

Papy, L. "Les populations Batéké," *Cahiers d'Outre-Mer,* vol. 2 no. 6 1948, p. 112–134.

Pargoire, J. "Brazzaville, capitale de l'A.E.F.," *Tropiques,* no. 383, p. 3–12.

Pechuel-Loesch, Eduard. *Volksunde von Loango.* Stuttgart, Strocker & Schroder, 1907, 2 vol.

Poaty, Jean-Pierre. "De la survie en milieu urbain," *Politique Africaine,* October 1988, p. 30–38.

Pouabou, T. "Les peuples Vili ou Loango," *Liaison,* no. 58, 1957, p. 50–53, no. 59, p. 57–59.

Poupon, A. "Etude éthnographique de la tribu Kouyou," *Anthropologie,* vol. 29, 1918–19, p. 178–209.

Prevost, M. P. *Barabane, récit congolais,* Paris, A. Redier, 1928.

Raoul-Matingou, Emilienne. "L'emploi des femmes à Brazzaville," In: *Journées d'études sur Brazzaville,* Brazzaville, ORSTOM, 1986, p. 403–410.

"Recensement de la population de Brazzaville en 1961," *Bulletin Mensuel de statistique,* no. 2, 1962, p. 31–36.

Regnault, P. "Les Babinga," *Anthropologie,* no. 22, 1911, p. 261–288.

Roberdeau, A. "Etude sur la race Sangha," *Recherches Congolaises,* no. 12, 1932, p. 37–45.

Robineau, Claude. "Anthropologie économique," *Bulletin de Liaison Sciences Humaines,* no. 3, Jan. 1966, p. 71–71.

————. "Culture matérielle des Djem de Souanké," *Objets et Mondes,* vol. 7 no. i, 1967, p. 35–50.

————. "L'étude des phénomènes économiques traditionnel et ses problèmes," *Bulletin de Liaison Sciences Humaines,* no. 4, Feb. 1966, p. 1–21.

Romaniuk, A. "Aspects démographiques de la sterilité des femmes congolaises," *Studie Universitatis Lovanium,* no. 3, 1961.

————. "Evolution et perspectives démographiques de la population du Congo," *Zaire,* vol. 13 no. 6, 1959, p. 563–626.

Sautter, Gilles. "Aperçu sur les villes 'Africaines' du Moyen-Congo,' *L'Afrique et l'Asie,* no. 14, 1951, p. 35–53.

————. *De l'Atlantique au fleuve Congo. Une géographie du souspeuplement, République du Congo, Republique du Gabon.* Paris, Mouton, 1966, 2 vol.

————. "Economie du pays Bacongo," *Encyclopedie coloniale et maritime mensuelle,* vol. i, May 1951.

————. *Note sur la peche dans le région de Mossaka,* Brazzaville, Institut d'Etudes Centrafricaines, 1952.

————. "Les pecheurs de l'ile Abamou," *Institut d'Etudes Centrafricaines,* 1951.

————. "Les pecheurs du Stanley-Pool," *Geographia,* vol. 83, 1958, p. 21–28.

————. "Le plateau congolais de Mbé," *Cahiers d'Etudes Africaines,* vol. 2, 1961, p. 123–166.

————. *La système de culture des villageois dans le district de Boko,* Brazzaville, Institut d'Etudes Centrafricaines, 1953.

Sénéchal, J. "Notes sur le dépeuplement des villages au Congo," In: *Maitrise de l'Espace et développement des villages au Congo.* Paris: ORSTOM, 1979.

Soret, Marcel. "Aperçu sur la République du Congo," Brazzaville, Institut d'Etudes Centrafricaines, 1959.

————. *Aspects démographiques de Poto-Poto,* Brazzaville, Institut d'Etudes Centrafricaines, 1950.

————. *La Cuvette Congolaise. Monographie régionale des Bassins de la Likouala-Mossaka, de l'Alima et de la N'Kéni.* Paris, Ministère de la Coopération, 1962.

————. *Démographie et Problèmes Urbains en AEF: Poto-Poto, Bacongo, Dolisie,* Brazzaville, Institut d'Etudes Centrafricaines, 1954.

————. *Dolosie, étude démographique.* Brazzaville: ORSTOM, 1952.

————. *Enquete démographique de Pointe-Noire. Directives générales pour la formation d'enqueteurs démographes,* Brazzaville, Institut d'Etudes Centrafricaines, 1962.

————. *Enquete démographique de Pointe-Noire. Plan d'exploitation de la documentation,* Brazzaville, 1962.

————. *Essai de nomenclature des structures sociale,* Brazzaville, Institut d'Etudes Centrafricaines, 1957.

————. *Ethno-sociologie Africaine,* Paris, CCTA, 1960.

————. *Etude de la population de Bacongo.* Brazzaville, Institut d'Etudes Centrafricaines, 1952.

————. *Etude sur la main-d'oeuvre sans emploi dans les agglomérations Africaines de Brazzaville et les possibilités de son utilisation,* Brazzaville, Institut d'Etudes Centrafricaines, 1954.

————. *L'Evolution démographique de la zone du chemin de fer Congo-Ocean,* Brazzaville, IRSC, 1964.

————. *L'Homme Africain et son comportement,* Brazzaville, Institut d'Etudes Centrafricaines, 1957.

————. *Les Kongo Nord-occidentaux,* Paris, Presses Universitaires de France, 1959.

————. "Mariage coutumier au Moyen-Congo," *Résonnances,* Special issue no. 2, 1954, p. 87–89.

————. "La population et l'économie du Congo," *Cahiers d'Outre-mer,* no. 60 Oct.–Dec. 1962, 360–380.

————. *Problèmes de démographie urbaine.* Brazzaville: ORSTOM, 1952.

————. "Problèmes fonciers chez les Kongo du Nord-Quest. Problèmes de terres ou problèmes démographiques?" *Cahiers de l'Institut de Sciences Economiques Appliquées* (Paris), vol. 5, October 1965, p. 141–167.

————. "La propriété foncière chez les Kongo du Nord-Ouest. Caracteristiques générales et évolution," *African agrarian systems,* London, International African Institute, 1963, p. 281–296.

————. *Rapports sur l'énquete démographique par sondage dans la République du Congo,* Brazzaville, IRSC, 1962.

————. "Répartition géographique et numérique des ethnies de la République du Congo," *Bulletin mesuelle de Statistique,* vol. 13 no. 129, 1959.

————. "République du Congo: la propriété," Brazzaville, Institut d'Etudes Centrafricaines, 1962.

————. "Les Sciences Humaines en République du Congo de 1948 à 1960," *Bulletin de l'Institut d'Etudes Centrafricaines,* no. 19/20, 1960, p. 169–182.

————. *Structures sociales et leur évolution en milieu rural,* Brazzaville, Institut d'Etudes Centrafricaines, 1957.

————. "Le Téké de l'est. Essai sur l'adaptation d'une population à son milieu," PhD thesis, University of Lyon, 1970.

Tastevin, C. "Les antilopes revenants, fables des Ba-Kanba," *Recherches Congolaises,* no. 25, 1938, p. 54–74.

Tchibinda, J. F. "Le conflit entre fils et neveu au Congo-Brazzaville," PhD. thesis, University of Paris, 1971.

Thomas, Jacqueline M. C. and Serge Bahuchet. *Encyclopedie des Pygmées Aka,* Paris, SELAF, 1981.

Trezenem, Edouard. "Contribution à l'étude des négres africains: le Batéké-Balali," *Journal de la Société des Africanistes,* vol. 10, 1940, p. 1–63.

Trilles, R. *L'ame du Pygmée d'Afrique,* Paris, CERF, 1979.

Van Roy, H. *Proverbes Kongo,* Bruxelles, Musée royal de l'Afrique centrale, 1963.

Van Wing, Joseph. *Etudes Bakongo. Sociologie, religion et magie.* Bruxelles, Desclee de Brouwers, 1959.

————. "Une évolution de la coutume Bakongo," *Congo,* vol. 2 no. 3, 1920, p. 353–359.

————. "Nzolongo ou les rites de la puberté chez les Bakongo," *Congo,* vol. 2 no. 6, 1920, p. 229–246; vol. 3, no. 1, 1921, p. 48–60; vol. 3 no. 3, 1921, p. 365–389.

Vennetier, Pierre. "Banlieue Noire de Brazzaville: la vie rurale et les rapports entre la ville et la campagne Bacongo," *Cahiers d'Outre-Mer* no. 38, April—June 1957, p. 131-57.

————. "Documents démographiques sur le Congo Brazzaville," *Les Cahiers d'Outre-mer*, vol. 14 no. 56, 1961, p. 431-34.

————. *Les hommes et leurs activités dans le nord du Congo-Brazzaville*, Paris, ORSTOM, 1965.

————. "Mvuti, une agglomération semi-urbaine dans la République du Congo," *Revue de géographie de Lyon*. vol. 36 no. i 1961, p. 51-81.

————. *Nature et aspects de la croissance urbaine péripherique à Loubomo*. Bordeaux, CEGET, 1978.

————. *Pointe-Noire et la façade maritime du Congo-Brazzaville*, Paris, ORSTOM, 1968.

————. "La population de Pointe Noire," *Cahiers d'Outre-Mer*, no. 66, 1964.

————. "Un quartier suburbain de Brazzaville: Moukondji-Ngouaka," *Bulletin Institut d'Etudes Centrafricaines* no. 19/20, 1960, p. 91-124.

————. *Rapport sur le village des pecheurs de la cote mondaine à Pointe-Noire*, Pointe-Noire, ORIK, 1959.

————. *Rapport sur les activités urbaines et suburbaines à Pointe-Noire*, Pointe-Noire, ORIK, 1959.

————. "Un quartier suburbain de Brazzaville: Moukondji-Ngouaka," *Bulletin de l'Institut Centrafricaine*, no. 19/20, 1960, p. 91-124.

————. "Rapport sur le village des pecheurs de la Cote Mondaine à Pointe-Noire," Pointe-Noire, ORIK, 1958.

————. "L'Urbanisation et ses Consequences au Congo-Brazzaville," *Cahiers d'Outre-Mer*, vol. 16, 1963, p. 263-289.

————. "La vie agricole et urbaine à Pointe-Noire," *Cahiers d'Outremer*, no. 53, 1961, p. 60-84.

————. "Un village de pecheurs sur la Cote Congolaise," Brazzaville, ORSTOM, 1961.

————. *Les villes d'Afrique tropicale*. Paris: Masson, 1976.

Villien Rossi, M. L. "Jacob, ville champignon," *Annales du Centre d'Enseignement Supérieur de Brazzaville*, vol. 6, 1970, p. 43-53.

Vincent, Jean-Françoise. *La culture du cacao et son retentissement social dans la region de Souanké*. Brazzaville: ORSTOM, 1962.

————. "Dot et monnaie de fer chez les Bakwélé et les Djém," *Objets et Mondes*, vol. 3 no. 4 1964, p. 273-92.

————. "L'évolution féminine dans les villes," *Afrique-Documents*, no. 70-71, 1963, p. 191-97.

————. *Femmes Africaines en Milieu Urbain*, Paris, ORSTOM, 1966.

————. *Influence du milieu sur la vie traditionnelle des femmes de Bacongo-Brazzaville*, Brazzaville: ORSTOM, 1963.

————. *Perles et objets de dot Kota Mbamba et Ndasa de la région de Sibiti-Komono.* Brazzaville: ORSTOM, 1964.

Wannyn, R. *L'art ancienne du métal au Bas-Congo,* Bruxelles, Champles, 1961.

Wickers, Serge. *Contributions à l'étude du droit privé de Bakongo,* Bordeaux, Taffard, 1954.

————. "La propriété immobiliére au Moyen-Congo. Observations relatives au tribus Batéké et Ballali-Bassoundi," *Revue Juridique et Politique de l'Union Française,* no. 3, July–Sept. 1955, p. 549–576.

Wolfe, Alvin W. *In the Ngomba tradition: continuity and change in the Congo.* Evanston, Northwestern University Press, 1961.

Ziavoula, Robert Edmond. "La course a l'éspace urbain: les conflits fonciers à Brazzaville," *Politique Africaine,* October 1988, p. 22–29.

Politics/Law

Adouki, D. "Les ordonnances de l'article 49 de la constitution Congolaise," *Revue Congolaise du Droit,* no. 7/8, 1990, p. 46–57.

Antoine, P., P. Cantrelle, F. Sodter. "L'état civil urbain en Afrique: exemples de Libreville et Brazzaville," *Cahiers ORSTOM,* vol. 13 no. 3, 1976, p. 267–282.

Arsac, A. *Ville de Pointe Noire: quartier Saint-Pierre,* Paris, SCET, 1962.

————., M. Serpette. "L'amenagement de Pointe Noire et de sa région," *Industries et Travaux d'Outre Mer,* no. 58, 1958, p. 534–544.

Assemekang, C. "Le parlement congolaise dans la constitution du 24 Juin 1973," *Penant,* vol. 85 no. 753, 1976, p. 335–350.

Astrow, Andre. "Denis Sassou-Nguesso, President People's Republic of Congo, Chairman, Organization of African Unity," *Africa Report* Nov.–Dec. 1986, p. 55–57.

Ballard, J. "Four Equatorial States," in Carter, G. M. (ed.), *National Unity and Regionalism in Eight African States,* Cornell University Press, 1963.

Bambi, Jean-Guy. *Chronologie des principaux événements au Congo 1482–1979,* Kinshasa, Centre de commerce du Zaire, 1980.

Bankounda, F. "Circonstances exceptionnelles et libertés publiques au Congo," *Revue Congolaise du Droit,* no. 4, July–Oct. 1988, 73–90.

Banthoud, Paul. *Congo: naissance d'une république populaire en Afrique centrale,* Brazzaville, ABM, 1979.

Bertrand, Hugues. *Le Congo.* Paris: Maspero, 1975.

Biarnes, Pierre. "Congo-Brazzaville: Un Coup de Barre à Droite," *Le Mois en Afrique,* Feb. 1968.

Bigemi, F. "La Commune au Congo-Brazzaville," *Revue Juridique et Politique,* April–May–June 1968.

Bonnaié, P. "Une Classe d'Age Politique, la JMNR du Congo-Brazza-ville," *Cahiers d'Etudes Africaines,* vol. 8, 1968.

Bouboutou, J. B. "Contribution à un debat: nouvelles reflexions sur le pre-mariage en droit congolaise de la famille," *Revue Congolaise du Droit,* no. 6, July–Dec. 1990, p. 26–38.

Boumakani, B. "Droit de propriété: droit de l'Homme. Quel droit au Congo," *Revue Congolaise du Droit,* no. 4, July–Oct. 1988, p. 104–111.

Boutet, Remy. *Les 'Trois Glorieuses' ou la chute de Fulbert Youlou,* Dakar, Editions Chaka, 1990.

"Brazzaville: Sept Ans apres les 'Trois Glorieuses,'" *Afric-Asia,* Aug. 30, 1970, p. 31–46.

"Brazzaville: Ten Years of Revolution," *West Africa,* Aug. 13, 20, 1973.

Breton, Jean-Marie. "Les bases formelles de l'ordonnancement juridique congolais: évolution et réformes," *Revue juridique et politique,* vol. 38 no. 3, Sept. 1984, p. 743–755.

———. "Le Congo apres 20 ans de régime socialiste," *Penant,* vol. 95, no. 786-7, Jan.–June 1985, p. 89–106.

———. "Les contentieux administratif et la réorganisation de la justice en République Populaire du Congo," *Revue Juridique et Politique,* vol. 37 no. 4, 1983, p. 762–794.

———. "Le cour supreme et le régime contentieux congolais," *Penant,* vol. 96, no. 790–91, p. 48–76.

———. *Droit publique congolais,* Paris, Economica, 1987.

———. "Les entreprises publiques et la reonte de la réglementation des marchés publics en droit congolais," *Penant,* vol. 93 no. 780, 1983, p. 176–199.

———. "L'évolution des institutions de la RPC," *Revue de Droit Publique,* October 1986, p. 1327–1352.

———. "La réforme domaniale et foncière en République Populaire du Congo," *Penant,* vol. 94 no. 783, p. 41–82.

Clark, John F. "Socio-political change in the Republic of Congo: political dilemmas of economic reform," *Journal of Third World Studies,* vol. 10 no. i (1993), . 52–78.

Combo, B. "Au Congo Brazzaville," *La Nouvelle Revue Internationale,* Nov. 1967.

Comte, G. "Echec aux 'Conservateurs,'" *Revue Française d'Etudes Politiques Africaines,* April 1970.

———. "L'Embarras Français," *Revue Française d'Etudes Politiques Africaines,* June 1970.

Conac, Gerard (ed.), *Les institutions administratives des etats Francophones d'Afrique Noire,* Paris, Economica, 1979.

"Le Congo aux deux visages," *Afrique Contemporaine,* Sept.–Oct. 1982, p. ii–13.

"Congo: the barons mind the shop," *Africa Confidential,* Jan. 22, 1993, p. 5–6.

"Congo: characteristic ambiguity," *Africa Confidential,* March 6, 1992, p. 5–6.

"Congo: embattled," *Africa Confidential,* Jan. 15, 1986, p. 4–6.

"Congo: ideology is out," *Africa Confidential,* 17 Oct. 1984, p. 1–4.

"Congo: of petrol and perestroika," *Africa Confidential,* Jan. 1, 1990.

"Congo: price of patronage," *Africa Confidential,* July 3, 1985, p. 5–6.

"Congo: radicalization and Angola," *Africa Confidential* Jan. 23, 1976, p. 3–6.

"Congo: the revolution goes West," *Africa Confidential,* 7 Sept. 1983, p. 1–3.

"Congo: the state of Ngouabi's nation," *Africa Confidential,* April 7, 1972, p. 5–7.

"Congo: testing the waters of democracy," *Africa Confidential,* 19 June 1992, p. 6–7.

"Congo: the triumvirate in transition," *Africa Confidential,* Dec. 6, 1991, p. 6–7.

"Congo: what kind of Marxism?" *Africa Confidential,* Jan. 16, 1980, p. 6–8.

"Congo-Brazzaville: discovering Yhombi," *Africa Confidential,* Feb. 3, 1978, p. 3–4.

"Congo-Brazzaville: East or West," *Africa Confidential,* Jan. 1, 1981, p. 5–7.

"Congo-Brazzaville: enigma with variations," *Africa Confidential,* Nov. 18, 1977, p. 3–5.

"Congo-Brazzaville: 15 Mois de Révolution," *Europe-France-Outremer,* Nov. 1964.

"Congo-Brazzaville: pupil power and politics," *Africa Confidential,* Jan. 21, 1972, p. 2–3.

Constantin, F. "Fulbert Youlou, 1917–1972," *Le Mois en Afrique,* June 1972.

"La constitution congolaise," *Afrique Contemporaine,* Jan.–Feb. 1980, p. 24–30.

"Constitution de la République du Congo," *Afrique Contemporaine,* May 1992, p. 35–59.

Debreton, Jacques. *Coup d'état à Brazzaville,* Bruxelles, Espace, 1976.

Decalo, Samuel. "Congo: Revolutionary rhetoric and Army cliques in Congo/Brazzaville," *Coups and Army Rule in Africa: Studies in Military Style,* New Haven, Yale University Press, 1976, p. 122–172.

———. "Congo: Revolutionary rhetoric and the overdeveloped state," In: *Coups and Army Rule in Africa: Motivations and Constraints,* New Haven, Yale University Press, 1990, p. 39–88.

———. "Ideological rhetoric and scientific socialism in Benin and Congo," In: Carl Rosberg and Thomas Callaghy (eds.), *Socialism in sub-Saharan Africa,* Berkeley, University of California Institute of International Studies, 1979.

———. "The morphology of radical military rule in Africa," *Journal of Communist Studies,* vol. 1 no. 3/4, Sept.–Dec. 1986, p. 69–93.

———. "People's Republic of Congo," In: B. Szajkowski (ed.), *Marxist Governments: a world survey,* London, Macmillan, 1985, vol. i, p. 212–235.

———. "Socio-economic constraints on radical action in the People's Republic of Congo," *Journal of Communist Studies,* vol. i, no. 3/4, Sept.–Dec. 1986, p. 38–57.

Decheix, P. "La constitution de la République Populaire du Congo," *Revue Juridique et Politique,* vol. 1, 1970, p. 111–126.

Decraene, P. "Huit Années d'Histoire Congolaise," *Revue Française d'Etudes Politiques Africaines,* Dec. 1974, p. 61–79.

Denis, J. "Les institutions juridiques congolaises," *Penant,* no. 766, 1979.

Desjeux, D. "Le Congo Est-il Situationiste?—Vingt Ans d'Histoire Politiquede la Classe Dirigeante Congolaise," *Le Mois en Afrique,* Oct.–Nov. 1980.

Doumat, A. "Le mouvement national pour la révolution," Ph.D. thesis, University of Paris, 1978.

Dreux-Breze, J. de. *Le Problème du Regroupement en Afrique Equatoriale,* Paris, 1968.

Drouin, Jeanne and Michel Voisin. "Aperçu de la législation actuelle de sécurité sociale dans quelques pays d'Afrique," *Bulletin de l'Association internationale de la sécurité sociale,* no. 718, July–Aug. 1961, p. 394–422.

Dubula, Sol. "The Congo on the road to Socialism," *African Communist,* no. 64, 1976, p. 43–51.

Ekani-Onambele, M. "Le Congo-Brazzaville Face à Son Evolution Sociale," *Communauté France-Eurafrique,* Jan. 1963.

Eliou, Marie. *La formation de la conscience nationale en République Populaire du Congo,* Paris, Anthropos, 1977.

Etonokani, J. R. *Génése et évolution du mouvement syndical congolais,* Brazzaville, SPCSC, 1985.

"Fluctuations Politiques au Congo-Brazzaville," *Revue Africaine,* Aug. 1968.

France. La Documentation Française. *La République du Congo.* Notes et Etudes Documentaires no. 2732, 1960.

Gabou, Alexis. "L'administration centrale congolaise" Ph.D. thesis, University of Nantes, 1973.

————. *Les constitutions congolaises,* Paris, Librairie générale de droit de jurisprudence, 1984.

————. "Les sucessions coutumières au Congo," *Revue Juridique et Politique,* vol. 38 no. 2, 1984, p. 64–75.

————. "Le juge controleur de la legalité administrative au Congo," *Revue Juridique et Politique,* vol. 37 no. 3/4, 1983, p. 699–705.

Gakosso, G. F. *La réalité congolais,* Paris, La pensée universelle, 1983.

Ganga-Zandzou, J. "La condition politique de la femme au Congo," *Revue juridique et politique,* no. 4, 1974, p. 623–630.

————. "La droit du travail au Congo-Brazzaville," PhD thesis, University of Paris, 1969.

————. "Responsabilité des Chefs de Groupements Coutumiers au Congo," *Revue Juridique et Politique,* Oct.–Dec. 1973.

Gaulme, F. "Le Congo et l'Equilibre," *Marches Tropicaux,* Aug. 5, 1983.

Gauze, R. *The Politics of Congo-Brazzaville.* Stanford: Hoover Institution Press, 1973.

Hodges, Tony. "Congo: the IMF logjam," *Africa Report,* vol. 30 no. 6 Nov.–Dec. 1985, p. 58–63.

House, A. H. "Brazzaville: Revolution or Rhetoric?" *Africa Report,* April 1971, p. 18–21.

IFES. *Petit guide des élections démocratiques au Congo,* Brazzaville, CSR, 1992.

Iloki, A. "Le conseil constitutionnel: une nouvelle institution en République populaire du Congo," *Penant* vol. 96 no. 790–91, Jan.–June 1986, p. 9–12.

————. "L'evaluation du prejudice corporal par le juge congolaise," *Revue Congolaise du Droit,* no. 6, July–Dec. 1990, p. 39–53.

————. "Une jurisdiction d'exception en République Populaire du Congo," *Penant,* vol. 95, no. 788/9, July–Dec. 1985, p. 255–261.

————. "La justice au Congo: pouvoir au service public," *Penant* vol. 98 no. 796, Jan.–May 1988, p. 113–142.

————. Les tribunaux populaires au Congo," *Penant,* vol. 95 no. 786–7, Jan.–June 1985, p. 108–114.

Kauppi, Mark V. "Moscow and Congo," *Problems of Communism,* vol. 39 March–April 1990, p. 42–60.

Kelley, R. "Problems to socialist transformation in Africa: the Congolese experience," *Ufahamu,* vol. 12 no. 2/3, 1984, p. 259–282.

Kiese, Mboka. "La faillité du monopartisme au Congo," *Peuples Noires,* no. 63–66, May–December 1988, p. 160–188.

Lee, J. M. "Clan loyalties and Socialist doctrine in the People's Republic of Congo," *The World Today,* Jan. 1971.

Le Vine, Victor T. "Military rule in the People's Repulic of Congo," In: John Harbeson (ed.), *The Military in African Politics,* New York, Praeger, 1987, p. 123–140.

Lissouba, P. *Conscience du Développement et Démocratie,* Dakar, 1975.

Mabounda, M. "Le Congo et la Commission de Droits du l'Homme des Nations Unis: le bilan d'un participation," *Revue Congolaise du Droit,* no. 4, July–Oct. 1988, p. 91–104.

Marchat, P. "D'une Révolution a l'Autre au Congo-Brazzaville," *Revue Militaire Générale,* Sept. 1969.

Massengo, Moudileno. *Proces de Brazzaville,* Paris, Harmattan, 1982.

Matthews, Ronald. "The Congo," In: *African Powder Keg,* London, Bodley Head, 1966, p. 88–114.

Mavoungou, Valentin. "Le syndicalisme dans les pays d'Afrique à ideologie Marxiste-Léniniste," *Penant,* no. 803, June–Sept. 1990, p. 268–98.

Mayetele, Narcisse, "Aperçu de l'histoire constitutionnelle congolaise, 1958–1988," Thesis, Université Marien Ngouabi, Brazzaville, 1989.

Mberuba, J. M. "La phase révolutionnaire au Congo-Brazzaville après la chute de Youlou," thesis, University of Paris, 1973.

Mboukou, Alexandre. "An African triangle," *Africa Report,* Sept.–Oct. 1982, p. 39–44.

―――. "Pragmatic relations," *Africa Report,* Nov.–Dec. 1981, p. 12–18.

―――. "US-Congo pragmatic relations," *Africa Report,* Nov.–Dec. 1981, p. 12–18.

Miserez, Marc-André. "La réalité africaine: éclarage par l'analyse politicio-économique ou par le roman?" *Cahiers du CEDAF,* no. 1–3, 1987, p. 159–179.

"Missiles and clan warfare," *Africa Confidential,* April 14, 1989.

Molongya, Antoine Justin. *Etude sur le problème de l'assistance technique étrangère à l'Armée Nationale Congolaise,* Brazzaville, Ecole de administrateurs militaires, 1967.

Moudileno-Massengo, M. *République Populaire du Congo: Une Escroquerie Ideologique,* Maisonneuve et Larose, 1975.

Mouguengue, F. "Les croits de la personne humain en République Populaire du Congo," *Revue Congolaise du Droit,* no. 4, July–Oct. 1988, p. 61–72.

―――. "Le droit internationale privé de la famille en République Populaire du Congo," *Revue Congolaise du Droit,* no. 6, July–Dec. 1990, p. 11–25; vol. 7/8, 1990, p. 36–45.

"Le Mystere s'Epaissait," *Le Mois en Afrique,* Sept. 1966.

Nagy, L. "L'apport tribal dans la création et l'évolution des partis politiques congolais," *Génève-Afrique,* vol. 1, 1962, p. 36–50.

Ngolongolo, Appolinaire. *L'Assassinat de Marien Ngouabi, ou, l'histoire d'un pays ensanglante,* Paris, Autoédition, 1988.

Ngouabi, Marien. *Les Paroles du President Marien Ngouabi,* Brazzaville, Editions du Comité Centrale du PCT, 1978.

————. *Rectifions Notre Style de Travail,* Brazzaville, Editions du
Comité Centrale du PCT, 1974.

————. *Vers la Construction d'une Société Socialiste en Afrique,* Paris,
Presénce Africaine, 1975.

Ngouilou-Mpemba, Moussoungou. "L'administration congolaise dans
son environnement socio-économique," PhD thesis, University of
Grenoble, 1983.

————. "Garanties et protection des droits fondamentaux au Congo,"
Revue Congolaise du Droit, no. 4, July–Oct. 1988, p. 183–194.

Nkouka, A. "La coopération franco-congolaise," PhD thesis, University
of Paris, 1976.

Ntsikabaka-Babela, Augustin. "L'évolution des parties politiques au
Congo, de 1946 à 1981: du multipartisme au parti unique," In: Catherine Coquery-Vidrovitch (ed.), *Histoire démographique,* Paris, Harmattan, 1985, p. 147–156.

Obembé, Jean-François. *Principaux problèmes liés à l'édification du
Parti Congolais du travail, première parti marxiste-léniniste en pouvoir en Afrique,* Brazzaville, Parti Congolaise du Travail, 1987.

Odicky Eyenga Ekoto, I. "Coexistence des droits coutumiers et du droit
moderne dans la République Populaire du Congo, et conflits person-
nelles" PhD thesis, University of Aix—Marseille, 1977.

Ondimba-Yepigat, G. Les mouvements syndicaux et les mouvements
politiques du Congo et du Gabon, 1940–1964," PhD thesis, University of Paris, 1978.

Opangault, Jacques. *Discours et écrits politiques,* Paris, Présence Africaine, 1987.

Owana, J. "La consolidation de l'ordre économique et social marxiste,"
Le Mois en Afrique, Jan.–Feb. 1974, p. 56–73.

————. "Un droit administratif de transition vers le socialisme: l'exemple de la République Populaire," *Penant* vol. 87 no. 760, 1978, p.
155–174.

————. "La nouvelle constitution de la République Populaire du Congo:
un présidentialisme monopartisan d'assemblées?" *Penant,* vol. 88, no.
769, 1980, p. 239–253.

————. "La nouvelle organisation des pouvoirs publics en République
Populaire du Congo," *Penant,* vol. 88, no. 770, 1980, p. 440–452.

————. "La République populaire du Congo après l'assassinat du President Ngouabi," *Revue Française d'Etudes Politiques Africaines* Feb.
1978, p. 54–66.

Parti Congolais du Travail. *Congrès extraordinaire: congrès de radi-
calisation,* Brazzaville, Editions Graphic Africa, 1979.

———. *3e Congrès extraordinaire du Parti Congolais du travail,* Brazzaville, Editions du Comité central, 1980, 2 vol.

Pereira, Claude C. *L'Administration Congolaise,* Paris, Berger-Levrault, 1979.

———. "L'administration régionale congolaise," *Bulletin de l'Institut Internationale d'Administration,* vol. 31, July–Sept. 1974, p. 83–124.

———. "Conseils populaires et structures administratives régionales en République Populaire du Congo," *Revue Jurdique et Politique,* vol. 36 no. 3, 1982, p. 759–775.

———. "Les délégations spéciales de région et de district dans l'organisation administrative du Congo," *Revue Juridique et Politique,* vol. 33 no. 2, 1979, p. 169–184.

———. "Evolution constitutionnelle et politique du Congo: le pouvoir exécutif dans la constitution du 8 Juillet 1979," *Revue Juridique et Politique,* vol. 34 no. 1, 1984, p. 53–67.

———. "Les grands pouvoirs politiques congolais. Contribution à la théorie generale de l'état africain," *Revue Juridique et Politique,* vol. 32 no. 4, 1978, p. 991–1024.

Philippe, C. "Congo: l'experience de la conference nationale," *Défence Nationale,* November 1991, p. 115–126.

———. "Démocratie au Congo: la transition difficile," *Défence Nationale,* May 1992, p. 43–56.

Poungui, A. E. "Le cadre institutionnel des enterprises d'état," *Revue des Sciences Sociales,* no. 2, Apr.–June 1985, p. 119–132.

Racine, A. "The People's Republic of Congo," In: P. Wiles, *The new Communist Third World,* New York, St. Martin's, 1982.

Radu, Michael S. and Keith Somerville. "The Congo," In: Chris Allen et al. *Benin, the Congo, Burkina Faso,* London, Pinter, 1989, p. 145–233.

"Le Regime de l'Abbé Fulbert Youlou," *Révolution Africaine,* Aug. 24, 1963.

"La République Populaire du Congo," *Afrique Contemporaine,* no. 47, Jan.–Feb. 1970.

"La République Populaire du Congo," *Europe Outremer,* Special issue, no. 604, May 1980.

"Une Révolution Inquiete et Permanente," *Revue Française d'Etudes Politiques Africaines,* Dec. 1969.

Sassou-Nguesso, Denis. *Pour l'Afrique,* Paris, Groupe Media International, 1987.

———. *Poursuivons le combat de Marien Ngouabi,* Brazzaville, Publi-Congo, 1980.

Schissel, Howard. Congo: Parties and presidents," *West Africa,* Aug. 8, 1983, p. 1813–15.

———. "Congo: trading in a hostile world," *West Africa,* Aug. 22, 1983. p. 1936–38.

———. "Pragmatists and partisans in Brazzaville," *Africa Report,* Jan.–Feb. 1984, p. 55–57.

"Les Successeurs de Youlou" *Revue Africaine* May 1964.

Tchicaya, B. "L'évolution du droit foncier en République Populaire du Congo," PhD thesis, University of Paris, 1983.

Terray, Emannuel. "Les Révolutions Congolaise et Dahoméenne," *Revue Française de Science Politique,* Oct. 1964, p. 917–43.

Thomas. L. V. "Le Socialisme Congolais," *Le Mois en Afrique,* Nov. 1966.

Torres, P. *L'administration congolaise,* Brazzaville, ENA, 1969.

Trugnan, Roger. "Repéres pour une approche du Congo Populaire," *Cahiers du Communisme,* vol. 22 no. 3, March 1984, p. 88–95.

Viellard, J. L. "Mythes et Realités Congolaises," *France-Eurafrique,* June 1966.

Yhombi-Opango, Joachim. *L'arme théoretique du militant de la révolution Congolaise,* Brazzaville, Parti Congolais du Travail, 1977.

———. *Message à la nation du colonel Joachim Yhombi-Opango, president du Comité militaire du parti,* Brazzaville, Parti Congolais du Travail, 1977.

Youlou, Fulbert. *Comment sauver l'Afrique,* Troyes, Paton, 1968.

Wagret, J. M. "L'ascension politique de l'UDDIA (Congo) et sa prise de pouvoir 1956–1959," *Revue Juridique et Politique,* no. 2, 1963, p. 334–344.

———. *Histoire et Sociologie Politiques de la République du Congo-Brazzaville,* Paris, Librairie Générale de Droit et de Jurisprudence, 1966.

Wamba-dia-Wamba, E. "The experience of struggle in the P. R. of Congo," in Peter A. Nyong'o, *Popular struggles for democracy in Africa,* London, Zed Press, 1987, p. 96–111.

Wickers, F. *Contribution à l'étude du droit privée des Bakongo,* Bordeaux, Taffard, 1954.

Woungly-Massaga, A. *La révolution au Congo, contribution à l'étude des problèmes politique d'Afrique centrale.* Paris, Maspero, 1974.

Youlou, F. *J'Accuse la Chine,* Paris, 1966.

Economics

"L'Activité des travaux publics au Congo," *Industries et Travaux d'Outre-mer,* March 1963, 219–230.

Agriculture au Moyen Congo. Paris, Comité de coordination des recherches agronomiques et productions agricoles, 1955.

Alibert, Jacques. *Le guide Bancaire du Congo.* Paris, EDITH, 1987.

Aménagement d'une zone de culture maraicheres dans la zone de Pointe-Noire, Pairs, BDPA, 1964, 5 vol.

Amin, Samir and C. Coquery-Vidrovitch. *Histoire Economique du Congo, 1880–1968,* Paris, Anthropos, 1969.

Andrieux, J. F. *Afrique centrale: guide juridique et fiscal,* Paris, Editions Lefebre, 1987.

Anheier, Helmut. "Private voluntary organizations, networks and development in Africa: Nigeria, Senegal and Togo," Ph.D. dissertation, Yale University, 1986.

Apertet, M. "Le projet d'aménagement hydroélectrique du Kouilou," *Industries et Travaux d'Outre-Mer,* Sept. 1958, p. 505–515.

Arnoux, M. "Bilan de 10 années de recherches sur les fibres jutiéres à la station de l'IRCT de Madingou," Paris, IRCT, 1959.

Aubry, M. J. "Industrialisation dans la region de Brazzaville," *Tropiques* vol. 58, 1960, 29–32.

Ayessa, A. "Congo: un rendement fiscal dépendant des facteurs exterieurs," *Le Mois en Afrique,* vol. 22, no. 249/50, 1986, p. 76–96.

Bafouetela, R. "Le travail sous la période coloniale Congo (1897–1945)," *Cahiers Congolais d'Anthropologie,* vol. 6, 1981, p. 77–94.

Balandier, G. "Le travail non salarié dans les Brazzaville noires," *Zaire,* vol. 6 no. 7, June–August 1952, p. 675–690.

Becheret, T. *Analyse statistique de la structure de la Fonction publique,* Brazzaville, 1985.

Belotteau, Jacques. "Situation économique du Congo," *Afrique Contemporaine,* Dec. 1984, p. 23–43.

Biniakounou, P. *Chomeur à Brazzaville,* Dakar, 1977.

Bologna, L. M. "Appunti sulla vallata del Niari," *Rivista de Agricultura tropicale e subtropicale,* 1956, p. 496–520.

Boungou, Jean-Claude. "L'activité des étrangèrs à Brazzaville," In: *Journées d'etudes sur Brazzaville,* Brazzaville, ORSTOM, 1986, p. 427–432.

Boutiller, Jean-Louis. "Les effets économiques por le Moyen Congo de l'installation de l'ensemble industriel," *Industries et travaux d'Outre Mer,* Sept. 1958, p. 543–548.

Bruel, Georges. *Le Congo français au point de vue économique.* Melun, Imprimerie Administratif, 1909.

Bye, Maurice. *Note sur la planification pour la République du Congo,* Paris, Ministère de la Cooperation, 1962.

Chantran, Pierre et al. *Encadrement agricole et modernisation rurale en A.E.F., doctrine et bilan,* Paris, Inspection Générale de l'Agriculture, 1956, 1956.

Chatenay, J. N. "L'économie générale du Moyen-Congo," *Industries et Travaux d'Outre-Mer,* Sept. 1958, p. 495–505.

Chauvet, P. "Le Realisme de la Politique Economique," *Europe-France-Outremer,* Dec. 1967.

Chemin de fer Congo-Océan et les ports de Pointe-Noire et de Brazzaville, Monaco, Editions Paul Bory, 1959.

Congo. Ministère de l'Agriculture. *Evaluation des ressources humaines.* Brazzaville, 1982.

————. ————. *Plan quinquennal 1982–1986. Esquisse sur l'organisation du monde rural.* Brazzaville, 1981.

————. ————. *Propositions pour la mise en place d'un système national de vulgarisation agricole.* Brazzaville, 1982.

————. ————. *Situation agricole de l'axe Komono-Kingani (Lekoumou) et propositions d'intervention.* Brazzaville, 1982.

————. Ministère de l'Education Nationale. *Situation de la main-d'ouevre au Congo, 1974–1990.* Brazzaville, 1980.

————. Ministère du Plan. *Avant-projet du ier plan quinquennal de développement économique et social 1964–1968,* 1964.

————. ————. *Evaluation emploi et niveau de vie en 1982.* Brazzaville, 1983.

————. ————. *Operation Villages-centres.* Brazzaville, 1983, 3 vol.

————. ————. *Plan intérmaire de développement économique et social 1964–1968,* 1964.

————. ————. *Plan Quinquennal 1982–86. Esquisse de développement régional,* Brazzaville, 9 vol. 1982.

————. ————. *Plan Quinquennal 1982–86. Identification des besoins et ressources en main-d'oeuvre en 1982–1986,* Brazzaville, 1982.

————. ————. *Projet du ier plan quinquennal de développement économique et social, 1964–1968,* Brazzaville, 1963.

————. Service de la Statistique. *Etudes socio-économique du plateau de Koukouya,* Brazzaville, 1957.

"Congo 1982," *Marchés Tropicaux,* special issue July 2, 1982.

"Congo: L'Economie en Expansion Rapide," *Europe-Outremer,* Dec. 1982.

————. *Les Depenses Exceptionnelles dans les Budgets de Menage à Pointe-Noire,* Paris, 1963.

Courcier, A. *Données de base sur l'économie,* Paris, Ministère d'état charge de l'aide et de la cooperation, 1959.

Couvert, C. *Secteur informel et emploi en République Populaire du Congo: une vue d'ensemble,* Addis Ababa: ILO, 1982.

Dampierre, E. de. "Coton noir et cafe blanc. Deux cultures de Haut Oubangui à la veille de la loi cadre," *Cahiers d'études africaines,* no. 2 May 1960, p. 128–147.

Descoings, B. *Les possibilités pastorales de la cuvette congolaise au sud de la Mambili,* Brazzaville, Commissariat au Plan, 1961.

Desjeux, Dominique. *Rapport préliminaire d'évaluation du projet de développement rural,* Brazzaville, I.D.R., 1979.

————. *Stratégies paysannes en Afrique noire, Le Congo,* Paris, Harmattan, 1987.

Destruhaut, Georges. *Les principales cultures du Pool et du Djoué,* Paris, BDPA, 1964, 2 vol.

————. *Les principales cultures du Niari forestier,* Paris, BDPA, 1963, 2 vol.

Devauges, Roland. "Le chomeurs de Brazzaville et les perspectives du Barrage de Kouilou," *Cahiers ORSTOM,* vol. 1 no. 2, 1963.

————. "Etude du chomage Brazzaville en 1957. Etude sociologique." *Cahiers ORSTOM,* vol. 1 no. 4 (1963).

————. *L'Oncle, le ndoki et l'entrepreneur: le petit entreprise congolaise,* Paris, ORSTOM, 1977.

————. and L. Biffot. "Les dépenses exceptionnelles dans les budgets de ménage a Pointe-Noire," *Cahiers ORSTOM,* vol. i, no. 3, 1963.

Dhont, Yves. *Les budgets familiaux dans les villages du Niari,* Brazzaville, ORSTOM, 1965.

————. "Les dépenses dans la population rurale du Niari," In: *Problèmes socio-économiques de la région du Niari,* Brazzaville, ORSTOM, 1963, p. 14–60.

————. *Les marchés Africains de Pointe-Noire,* Brazzaville, ORSTOM, 1963.

————. *Le peche à Pointe-Noire et ses possibilités de développement,* Brazzaville, ORSTOM, 1963.

Diallo, Y., B. Guillot. *Systèmes agraires et cultures commerciales: l'exemple du village de Boutrab, région de Sangha,* Paris: ORSTOM, 1984.

"Disparités de revenus entre les villes et les campagnes en République Populaire du Congo," Geneva, International Labor Office, 1982.

"Economie Congo 1964," *Bulletin de l'Afrique Noire,* no. 328, 3 June 1964, p. 6656–6671.

L'Economie Congolaise, Paris, La Documentation Française, 1983.

L'Economie Congolaise, Paris, Ediafric, 1983.

L'Economie forestière et ses prolongements industriels, Paris, SFED, 1963.

Enquete sur les oléagineaux au Congo, zone sud, Paris, IRHO, 1962, 2 vol.

Faure, H. M. "Notes sur l'éxploitation de la Haute Sangha," *Bulletin de la Société des Recherches Congolaises,* no. 24, 1937, p. 113–123.

Flamigni, A., A. F. M. Hacquart. "Une ferme de métayage au Mayombe," *Bulletin agricole du Congo Belge* (Bruxelles), vol. 46, no. 5, 1955, p. 1065–1074.

France. Ministère de la Cooperation. *Economie et Plan de Développement: République du Congo-Brazzaville,* 1965.

————. ————. *Quinze ans de travaux et de recherches dans les pays du Niari.* Paris, 1967.

Francou, J. "L'aménagement hydro-électrique de Souanda sur le fleuve Kouilou-Niari au Moyen-Congo," *Houille blanche,* vol. 14 no. 4, 1959, p. 426–438.

Galland, P., G. Martin. "Culture mécanise de l'arachide et sélection au Moyen Congo," *Oléagineux,* no. 11 Nov. 1954, p. 759–765.

Ganon, F. *Enquete d'inventaire statistique dans le district de Kibangou (region du Niari),* Brazzaville, Organisation de la Région Industrielle du Kouilou, 1958.

Godard, X., J. Kama. "Quel modèle de transports collectifs pour les villes africaines?" *Politique Africaine,* no. 17, Mar. 1985, p. 41–57.

Goma, P. M. "Fiscalité indirecte et logique budgétaire au Congo," *Le Mois en Afrique,* no. 11, 1987, p. 45–61.

Goma-Foutou, Celestin. "La formation socio-économique de la République Populaire du Congo," *Revue des Sciences Sociales,* no. 3, July–Sept. 1985, p. 3–20.

————. "Le Parti Congolais du travail," *Revue des Sciences Sociales,* no.2, Apr.–June 1985, p. 9–57.

Gomez, R. "Le statut juridique des sociétés étrangères au Congo," PhD. thesis, University of Montpellier, 1980.

Gonidec, P. F. "Le Droit et la Pratique des Conventions Collectives du Travail au Congo-Brazzaville," *Penant,* July–Sept. 1969.

Goujon, J. "Les Sociétés mutuelles de développement rural au Moyen-Congo," *Bulletin de l'Association des études et problèmes de l'Union Française,* no. 132, 1959, p. 6–10.

Groulez, J. "Le reboisement des savanes pauvres de la ceinture brazzavilloise, "*Bois et Forets des tropiques,*" no. 50, Nov.–Dec. 1956, p. 9–15.

Guegan, J. C. and P. Judet. *Le développement de l'industrie en République Populaire du Congo,* Grenoble, Université de Grenoble, Centre de recherches sur l'Industrie, 1980.

Guet, R. "L'Industrie minière au Congo," *Industries et Travaux d'Outremer,* no. 87, Feb. 1961, p. 159–163.

Guerrini, Paul. *L'économie rurale de la cuvette congolaise, situation actuelle, possibilités de développement et de modernisation,* Brazzaville, Commissariat au Plan, 1961.

Guichaoua, Andre. *Destins paysans et politiques agraires en Afrique centrale,* Paris, Harmattan, 1987.

————. "Développement rural et décentralisation régionale au Congo: le Plan quinquennal 1982–86 à mi-parcours," *Le Mois en Afrique,* Feb.–Mar. 1985, p. 71–80, 97–103.

Guichard, J. *Etude de l'infrastructure routière dans le bassin du Niari,* Brazzaville, 1959, 2 vol.

356 • Bibliography

Guillaume, M. "La mise en valeur de la vallée du Niari," *Agronomie Tropicale,* no. 3, May–June 1954, p. 324–62.

Guillemin, Rene. *La mise en valeur de la vallée du Niari,* Brazzaville, Comite de coordination A.E.F., 1956.

Guillot, Bernard and Yveline Diallo. *Systèmes agraires et cultures commerciales: l'exemple du village de Boutzab, Sangha,* Paris, ORSTOM, 1984.

Haeringer, Philippe. "L'économie rurale dans la région de Mouyondzi," In: *Quinze ans de travaux et de recherches dans le pays du Niari,* Paris, ORSTOM, 1967, p. 245–293.

Hauser, André. "Les exploitation mécanisées du Moyen Congo," *Africa,* vol. 24 no. 2, Apr. 1954, p. 114–129.

Hung, G. Nguyen Tien. *Agriculture and rural development in the People's Republic of Congo,* Boulder, Westview Press, 1987.

Jeannin, M. "La société sucrière du Niari," *Annales du Centre d'Enseignement Supérieur du Brazzaville,* vol. 5, 1969, p. 29–46.

Judet, P. and Gueguen, J. C *Le développement de l'industrie en République Populaire du Congo,* Grenoble, IREP, 1980.

Julia, H. *Le palmier à huile dans la cuvette congolaise,* Brazzaville, Commissariat au Plan, 1961.

Kongo, Michel. "Le petit métiers crées a Partir du traffic entre le Zaire et le Congo," In: *Journées d'études sur Brazzaville,* Brazzaville, ORSTOM, 1986, p. 411–426.

———. "Petits métiers et commerce de l'artisanat à Brazzaville," PhD Thesis, University of Bordeaux, 1975.

"Le Kouilou," *Industries et Travaux d'Outre-Mer,* Sept. 1958.

Laigroz, Jacques. "Le complexe industriel du Kouilou-Pointe Noire," *Hommes et Commerce,* vol. 8 1959, p. 83–87.

Lapierre, J. *Projet de création dans le port de Pointe-Noire d'une zone commerciale franche et d'une zone industrielle priviligiée,* Paris, Ministère de la cooperation, 1961.

Leplaideur, A. and Sylvain Berton. *Programme conjoint CIRAD-IRAT/ AGRICONGO sur la filiere maraichere à Brazzaville,* Brazzaville AGRICONGO, 1989.

———. and Paule Moustier. *Dynamique du vivrier à Brazzaville: les mythes de l'anarchie et de l'inefficace,* Montpellier, DCV/Labo agro-économie, 1990.

Le Ray, J. "La mise en valeur des forets du Nord-Congo," *Bois et Forets des Tropiques,* no. 84 July–Aug. 1962, p. 27–44.

Martin, G. "La station de Loudima, IRHO au Congo," *Oléagineaux* no. 4 Apr. 1962, p. 361–68.

Martinenq, L. "Les caractéristiques et l'avenir de l'éxploitation forestière au Moyen-Congo," *Etudes d'Outre-mer,* no. 1, 1959, p. 1–10.

M'Buetani, M. "Le port et le ville de Pointe-Noire dans l'économie congolaise," PhD thesis, University of Grenoble, 1985.

Mengho, B. "L'agriculture traditionnelle chez les Bakouélé et les Djém du Congo," *Les Cahiers d'Outre-Mer,* vol. 31 no. 121, Jan.–March 1978, p. 48–84.

Millet, C. "Le projet hydro-électrique et industriel du Kouilou dans la république du Congo et les problèmes humains posés par sa réalisation," *International African Labour Institute,* vol. 6 no. 5, Sept. 1959, p. 9–28.

"La Mise en Valeur des Pays du Niari," *Industries et Travaux d'Outre-Mer,* Aug. 1968.

Moal, Roland and Jacques Le Noan. *Creation d'une complexe industriel de peche à Pointe-Noire,* Paris, SCET, 1968.

"Modalités du plan quinquennal, 1964–1968," *Bulletin de l'Afrique Noire,* 25 Mar. 1964, p. 6477–79; 8 Apr. 1964, p. 6497–99; 22 Apr. 1964, p. 6539–6541.

Moreuil, C. "La manguier au Congo," *Fruits,* no. 6 June 1963, p. 295–301.

Muller, Hans-Peter. *Volksrepublik Kongo: soziookonomische analyse als grundlage fur die energieplannung,* Hamburg, Institut fur Afrika-Kunde, 1990.

Nagorski, Bodan. *Le port de Pointe-Noire,* Pointe-Noire, ONUC, 1964, 3 vol.

Ngassaki, Athanase. *Congo, gestion publique,* Paris, Messidor, 1991.

———. *Les entreprises d'Etat au Congo,* Paris, Messidor, 1989.

Nicault, J. "Les ressources minérales du Moyen-Congo," *Industries et Travaux d'Outre-mer,* Sept. 1958, p. 522–27.

N'Kaloulou, B. *Dynamique paysanne et développement rural au Congo,* Paris, Harmattan, 1984.

"A Novel Experiment in Africa: the Kinsoundi Textile Mill," *Africa Today,* July 1971.

Ondo Ossa, Albert. "Changes flottants et développement dans les pays de l'Afrique centrale," Upper Montclair, N.J., Montclair State College Department of Economics, 1989.

Pargoire, J. "La Vallée du Niari," *Encyclopedie Mensuelle d'Outre-Mer,* Jan. 1955.

Platon, P. "Congo 1982," Special Issue *Marchés Tropicaux,* July 1982, p. 1739–1875.

"Le port de Pointe-Noire et ses projets d'extension," *Industries et travaux d'Outre Mer,* Sept. 1958, p. 527–34.

Pouzet, P. "Les recherches de pétrole au Moyen Congo," *Industries et Travaux d'Outre-mer,* Sept. 1958, p. 567–72.

Prevost, P. L. "L'Union Douaniere et Economique de l'Afrique Centrale (UDEAC)," *Revue Française d'Etudes Politiques Africaines,* Oct. 1968.

"Principales modalités de l'avant-projet du plan quinquennal de développement du Congo," *Bulletin de l'Afrique Noire*, no. 290, Sept. 1963.

Le projet d'ensemble hydro-électrique et industriel du Kouilou-Pointe Noire, Pointe-Noire, 1958.

"Les projets industriels du Kouilou et de Pointe-Noire," *Industries et Travaux d'Outre mer*, Special no. 58, 1958, p. 478–593.

Renaud, D. "Difficultés Economiques et Tensions Politiques," *Revue Française d'Etudes Politiques Africaines*, Feb. 1970.

Répertoire des entreprises congolaises de commerce éxterièure, Brazzaville, Centre congolais du commerce exterieur, 1988.

Rey, P. P. *Colonialisme, neo-colonialisme et transition au capitalisme*, Paris: Maspero, 1976.

————. "Articulation des modes de dépendence et des modes de production dans deux sociétés lignagères," *Cahiers d'Etudes Africaines*, vol. 9 1969, p. 415–440.

Robineau, Claude. "Contribution à l'histoire du Congo. La domination européenne et l'exemple de Souanké 1900–1960," *Cahiers d'Etudes Africaines*, no. 26 (1967), p. 300–344.

————. *L'évolution économique et sociale en Afrique Centrale: l'exemple de Souanké, République du Congo-Brazzaville*. Brazzaville, ORSTOM, 1966.

————. "L'Histoire au Congo: un éclairage des processus et perspectives du développement," *Tiers-Monde*, no. 90, 1982, p. 320–325.

Rouzaud, H. "La canne à sucre au Congo," *Agronomie tropicale*, no. 7/8 Aug–Sept. 1962, p. 531–542.

Sautter, Gilles. "Une économie indigène progréssive: les Bacongo du district de Boko (Moyen-Congo)," *Bulletin de l'Association des Géographes Française*, no. 216–217, 1951, p. 64–72.

————. "Notes sur l'agriculture des Bakamba de la vallée du Niari," *Bulletin de l'Institut d'Etudes Centrafricaines*, no. 9, 1955, p. 67–105.

————. "Notes sur la construction du chemin de fer Congo-Ocean 1921–1934," *Cahiers d'Etudes Africaines*, no. 26, 1967, 219–299.

————. "Le plateau congolais de Mbé. Les problèmes que posent une trés faible densité de population," *Cahiers d'Etudes Africaines*, vol. 1 no. 2, 1960, p. 5–48.

————. "Le régime des terres et ses modifications récentes aux environs de Brazzaville et au Woleu Ntem," *Bulletin de l'Institut d'Etudes Cantrafricaines*, no. 7/8, 1954, p. 201–209.

Sirven, P. "Les industries de Brazzaville," *Cahiers d'Outre-Mer*, no. 99, 1972, p. 277–92.

"Situation de l'exploitation forestière au Congo," *Bulletin de l'Afrique Noire*, no. 244, 25 July 1962, p. 4976–4978; no. 342, 7 Oct. 1964, p. 6945–6947.

Société d'Aménagement de la Vallé du Niari (SAVN) et la production arachidière au Congo. Brazzaville, Ministère de l'Agriculture, 1963.

"La société industrielle et agricole du Niari," Banque Centrale d'Etats d'Afrique Equatoriale, no. 88, March 1964, p. 139–147.

S.O.F.R.E.D. *Situation et problèmes de l'économie congolaise,* Paris, 1962, 7 vol.

Soret, M. "Etude sur la main-d'oeuvre sans emploi dans les agglomérations africaines," ORSTOM, July 1954.

Stauch, A. *Contribution à l'etude de la peche dans la cuvette congolaise,* Brazzaville, Commissariat au Plan, 1961.

Tariel, J. and J. Groulez, "Les plantations de Limba au Moyen-Congo," *Bois et Forêts des Tropiques* no. 61, 1958, p. 9–25.

Textes relatifs au développement rural: République du Congo, Paris, BDPA, 1963.

Thornston, John K. "The Kingdom of Kongo ca. 1390–1678: the development of an African social formation," *Cahiers d'Etudes Africaines,* vol. 22 no. 3/4, 1982, p. 325–342.

Timar, J. and J. Kutas. *Situation de la main-d'oeuvre au Congo 1974–1980,* Brazzaville: Ministère de l'Education Nationale, 1980.

Vennetier, Pierre. *Les activités agricoles urbaines et suburbaines a Pointe-Noire,* Brazzaville, ORSTOM, 1959.

———. "Au Congo-Brazzaville: le SIAN en 1964," *Les Cahiers d'Outre-Mer* vol. 18 no. 69, 1965, p. 87–90.

———. "Une entreprise agricole et industrielle au Congo-Brazzaville," *Les Cahiers d'Outre-Mer,* vol. 16 no. 61, p. 43–80.

———. "Les hommes et leurs activités dans le Nord du Congo-Brazzaville," *Cahiers d'ORSTOM,* vol. 2 no. 1 1965, 296p.

———. "Note sur l'économie du Congo," Brazzaville, ORSTOM, 1962.

———. "La population et l'économie du Congo," *Les Cahiers d'Outre Mer* vol. 15, no. 60, 1962, p. 360–380.

———. "A propos du théme: relations villes-campaign," *Bulletin d'ORSTOM,* no. 8 Apr. 1967, p. 173–87.

———. *Rapport sur les cultures maraichères à Pointe-Noire,* Pointe-Noire, ORIK, 1959.

———. "La société Industrielle et Agricole du Niari (SIAN)," *Cahiers d'Outre-Mer,* Jan.–Feb.–March 1963, p. 43–80.

———. *Les transports en république du Congo au Nord de Brazzaville,* Brazzaville, Commissariat au Plan, 1962.

———. "La vie agricole urbaine à Pointe-Noire," *Les Cahiers d'Outre-Mer,* vol. 14 no. 53, 1961, p. 60–84.

———. "La vie rurale et les rapports entre la ville et la campagne à Bacongo," *Cahiers d'Outre-Mer,* vol. 10, 1959, p. 131–157.

Villele, G. de. "Le port de Pointe-Noire et le chemin de fer Congo-Océan," *Communautés et Continents,* no. 8, Oct.–Dec. 1960, p. 35–38.

360 • Bibliography

Villeneuve, M. "La République du Congo: le plan triennal de développement," *Europe-France-Outremer,* vol. 34 no. 366, May 1960, p.
34–40.
Vincent, Jean-Française. "Le Travail des femmes à Tonkama, village
Lari," *Annales du Centre d'Enseignement Supérièur de Brazzaville,*
vol. 2 1966, p. 17–31.

Education

Assama, Philippe. *Pour une contribution au redressement du système
scolaire congolais,* Brazzaville, Imprimerie des armées, 1987.
Babassana, H. *La productivité technologique du système éducatif au
Congo.* Paris, IIPE, 1983.
Bouya, A. "Contribution à l'élaboration de la notion d'intelligence au
Congo," *Présence Africaine,* no. 136, 1985, p. 85–123.
Colloque bilan sur l'énseignement en République populaire du Congo,
Brazzaville, P.C.T., 1988.
Congo, Commission du Plan. *Esquisse d'un Plan de Développement de
l'Université dans le cadre du Plan Quinquennal 1982–86.* Brazza-
ville, 1981.
———. Ministère de l'Education Nationale. *La révolution congolaise et
l'éducation 1963–1983.* Brazzaville, 1983.
———. ———. Service de la Planification Universitaire chargé de la
Documentation Rectorale. *Annuaire Statistique de l'Université Mari-
en Ngouabi 1980–81.* 1981.
———. Ministère d'énseignement secondaire et supérièur. *Programmes
de l'énseignement fondamental 2e degree,* Brazzaville, 1987.
———. Service des statistiques et de la carte scolaire. *Statistiques sco-
laires,* Brazzaville, annual.
Didillon, H. "Modèles d'identification des collègions brazzavillois:
quelles personnes admirent-ils le plus?" *Annales de la Faculté de Let-
tres,* vol. 1, 1985, p. 19–32.
Dumont, M. "A propos d'une experience fétichiste de l'échec scolaire à
Brazzaville," *Actes de la Recherche en Sciences Sociales,* no. 43 June
1982, p. 47–52.
Eliou, M. *Enseignants Africains: Enquetes au Congo et au Mali,* Paris,
University of Paris Institut de l'étude du développement, 1975.
———. *La Formation de la Conscience Nationale en République Pop-
ulaire du Congo,* Paris, 1977.
———. "La fuite en avant dans l'énseignement supérièur. Les boursiers
Congolais," *Tiers Monde,* July–Dec. 1974, no. 59–60, p. 567–82.
Erny, P. "Choix professionnels à Brazzaville," *L'enfant en Milieu trop-
icale,* no. 37, 1967, p. 11–19.

————. "L'explosion de la jeunesse à Brazzaville," *Terre entière*, no. 16, 1966, p. 15–27.

"From mass literacy to functional literacy: the Congolese experience," *Eduafrica*, no. 9, June 1983, p. 145–169.

Grange, A. *Republique du Congo. Problème de formation profession-nelle dans le cadre du service civique de la jeunesse*, Paris, Secrétàriat d'Etat aux relations avec les etats de la Communauté, 1961.

"Institut de Recherches Scientifiques au Congo," *Journal of Modern African Studies*, Nov. 1964.

Jullien, M. *Problèmes psychologiques de l'énseignement secondaire au Congo*, Brazzaville, ORSTOM, 1965.

Klimes, B. "Formation de professeurs de l'enseignement moyen général et polytechnique," Brazzaville, UNESCO, 1981.

Kuama, Felix. "A study of problems faced by teachers in the Congo, and some practical solutions," Nairobi, African Curriculum Organization, 1981.

Louembert, E. "Le Centre de formation professionnel rapide de Brazza-ville," *Cance*, no. 3 July 1963, p. 22–23.

Lucas, Gerard, "Formal Education in the Congo-Brazzaville," PhD thesis, Stanford University, 1965.

Magnen, Andre and Joseph Grelier. *Etude sur harmonisation de l'en-seignement et de la formation professionnelle agricoles dans les pays francophones d'Afrique tropicale et à Madagascar*, Paris, BDPA, 1963.

Makonda, Antoine. "Une Ecole pour le peuple?" *Politique Africaine*, October 1988, p. 39–50.

Mombod, Jesephine Ntinou. "Developing models/techniques in the teaching of English as a foreign language in secondary schools in the Congo," Nairobi, African Curriculum Organization, 1983.

Ndinga Oba, Antoine. *L'enseignement en Afrique*, Paris, Presence Afri-caine, 1989.

Pellerin, Pierre. *Une enfance en brousse congolaise*, Paris, Arthaud, 1990.

Le Révolution Congolaise et l'éducation 1963–1983, les progrès, les problèmes et les perspectives, Brazzaville, Ministère de l'Education, 1983.

Sita, Julien. "A study of the problems of teaching business and technical English in secondary technical colleges in the Congo," Nairobi, African Curriculum Organization, 1982.

Tchicaya, Adolphe. *La question nationale et la prise de conscience des jeunes au Congo*, Paris, La pensée universelle, 1988.

Tchikaya, Joseph, and Marc Lallemant. "Brazzaville, ville d'écoliers et d'étudiants," In: *Journées d'etudes sur Brazzaville*, Brazzaville, ORSTOM, 1986, p. 367–374.

Vincent, Jeanne-Françoise. "Les citadins Africaines et le problème de la scolarisation des filles à Bacongo-Brazzaville," *L'enfant en milieu tropical* (Paris), no. 23, 1965, p. 24–36.

Religion

Alden, Karl. "The Prophet movement in Congo," *International Review of Missions,* vol. 25, 1936, 347–53.

Allys, A. "La secte secréte des Koulas," *Recherches Congolaises,* no. 22, 1936, p. 155–159.

Andersson, E. *Churches at the grass-roots: a study in the Congo-Brazzaville,* New York, Friendship Press, 1968.

————. *Messianic popular movements in the Lower Congo.* Uppsala, Almquist & Wiksell, 1958.

Balandier, Georges. "Brèves remarques sur les 'messianismes' de l'Afrique congolaise," *Archives de la Sociologie des Religions,* vol. 3 no. 5, 1958, p. 91–95.

————. "Messianisme des Bakongo," *Encyclopedie Mensuelle d'Outre-Mer,* Aug. 1951, p. 216–220.

————. "Messianismes et nationalismes en Afrique Noire," *Cahiers de l'Institut de Sociologie,* 1953, p. 41–65.

Bernard, G. "Diversité des nouvelles eglises congolaises," *Cahiers d'Etudes Africaines,* vol. 10, 1970, p. 203–227.

Beslier, C. G. *L'Apotre du Congo. Monseigneur Augouard,* Paris, Editions de la Vraie France, 1946.

Boucher, A. *Au Congo français, les missions catholiques,* Paris, Librairie Pierre Tequi, 1928.

Bouquet, A. *Féticheurs et médicines traditionnelles du Congo,* Paris, ORSTOM, 1969.

Charbonnier, F. "La société secréte d'hommes panthères de la terre des Bokyalas," *Afrique Equatoriale Française,* 1934, p. 20–24.

Chome, T. *La passion de Simon Kimbangu,* Paris, Présence Africaine, 1959.

Commauche, F. *Le Père Edouard Epinette,* Paris, Procure Générale des Pères du St. Esprit, 1919.

Devanges, H. "Croyances et vérification: les pratiques magico-religieuse en milieu urbain africain," *Cahiers d'Etudes Africaines,* vol. 17 1977, p. 299–306.

Domont, J. M. *Un territorial au pays des sectes politico-religieuses pendant les années 1939–1945,* Bruxelles, Academie royale des sciences d'Outre-Mer, 1988.

Dupré, M. C. "Les femmes musiki de Téké Tsaayi, rituel de possession et culte anti-sorcier en République Populaire du Congo," *Journal de la société des Africanistes,* vol. 44 no. 1, 1974, p. 53–69.

Even, A. "Les confrèries secrétes chez les Babambas et les Mindassas d'Okonja," *Recherches congolaises,* no. 23, Aug. 1937, p. 31–114; no. 24, Nov. 1937, p. 233–237.

———. "Les propriétés maléfiques du sexe de la femme selon les croyances des Bambabas et des Mindassas," *Bulletin de la Société d'Anthropologie,* 1937, p. 51–73.

Goyau, Georges. *Monseigneur Augouard,* Paris, Plon, 1926.

Kiener, A. "Note sur les fétiches des populations Bassoundis, habitant la subdivision de Pangala," *Recherches Congolaises,* no. 1 (1922), p. 21–27.

Kimbembo, D. *Fétichisme et croyance de l'au-dela chez les Bacongo du Congo,* Brazzaville, College Saint-Pierre-Apotre, 1964.

Konga, Romain. "Les debuts de la mission catholique de Landana," *Cahiers d'études africaines,* vol. 2 no. 7 (1962), p. 362–372.

Lacombe, Bernard. *Congo-Océan, ou recits de la vie sorcière,* Paris, Publisud, 1989.

Lebeuf, Jean-Paul and Bernard Mambeke-Bouchek. *Un mythe de la creation,* Rome, Edizioni Dell'Ateneo, 1964.

Le Roy, M. "Le Congo français," *Annales de la Propagation de la Foi,* 1896, p. 200–220.

Le Testu, G. "Etudes sur le fétiche N'Gwema," *Recherches Congolaises,* no. 12 p. 73–76.

Loukou, T. "Quelques croyances et superstitions du Bas-Congo," *Liaison,* no. 67, 1959, p. 71–74.

MacGaffey, Wyatt. "Bakongo cosmology," *The World and I,* Sept. 1988, p. 229–235.

———. *Modern Kongo prophets. Religion in a plural society"* Bloomington, Indiana University Press, 1983.

———. *Religion and Society in Central Africa: the Bakongo of Lower Zaire,* Chicago, University of Chicago Press, 1987.

———. "The Religious commissions of the Bakongo," *Man,* March 1970, p. 27–37.

Makambila, P. "Croyances et pratiques magiques des Kongo-Lari de la République Populaire du Congo," Ph.D. thesis, University of Bordeaux, 1976.

Makosso, S. M. "L'Eglise Catholique et l'Etat au Congo de 1960 à Nos Jours," *Afrique Contemporaine,* Nov.–Dec. 1976, p. 6–11.

Malonga, J. "La sorcellerie et l'ordre de 'Lemba'" *Liaison,* no. 63, 1958, p. 51–61.

Marchielle, Christophe. "Tablette d'un Congolais: Notice historique sur la mission et les indigènes de Loango," *Missions Catholiques,* 1910, p. 178–179, 190–191, 201–204, 213–215, 225–228, 237–240, 244–245, 258–261, 269–272, 285–286.

Marthey, J. "L'oeuvre missionaire pour la population féminine au Congo," *Revue d'histoire des Colonies,* no. 1, 1957, p. 79–101.

"Matswa," *Monde non-chretien,* no. 26, June 1935, p. 202–210.

N'Deko, G. *Le kundu ou kindoki dans la société Lari,* Brazzaville, IN-SEED, 1976.

Okum, A. "Nzambi-Mjanja. Dieu unique etre supreme, invoqué par les montagnards de Kibenza," *Annales de Pères du St. Esprit,* Apr. 1938, p. 106–109.

Pedron, Marc. *Itineraire d'un missionaire: le Père Marc Pedron,* Bangui, Maison St. Charles, 1989.

"Problèmes d'Eglise au Congo," *Evangeliser,* Sep.–Oct. 1956, p. 175–180.

Raymaekers, P. "L'eglise de Jésus-Christ sur la terre par le prophète Simon Kibangou," *Zaire* (Bruxelles), vol. 13 no. 7, 1959, p. 675–756.

Renouard, G. *L'Ouest africain et les missions catholiques Congo et Oubangui,* Paris, H. Oudin, 1956.

Roelandt, Robert. "Ou en est l'église au Congo," *Etudes,* Dec. 1960, p. 352–360.

Sinda, Martial. *André Matsoua: fondateur du mouvement de liberation du Congo,* Paris, ABC, 1977.

———. *Le Messianisme Congolais,* Paris, Payot, 1972.

Siroto, Leon. "Masks and their uses among the Bakwete people of the Dja and Ivindo River basins, Republic of Congo-Brazzaville," Ph.D. dissertation, Columbia University, 1962.

Stercky, A. "Problèmes d'Eglise au Congo," *Evangeliser,* Sept.–Oct. 1956, p. 176–180.

———. and Van Wing, Joseph. "L'etre supreme des Bakongo," *Recherches des sciences religieuses,* May–June 1920, p. 70–81.

Tonda, Joseph. "Marx et l'ombre des fétiches. Pouvoir local contre *ndjobi* dans le Nord-Congo" *Politique Africaine,* October 1988, p. 73–83.

Van Wing, Joseph. "Bakongo magic," *Journal of the Royal Anthropological Society,* vol. 71, no. 1–2, 1941, p. 85–95.

———. "Les mouvements messianiques populaires dans le Bas Congo," *Zaire* (Bruxelles), no. 2/3, 1960, p. 225–237.

Vincent, Jean-Françoise. "Le mouvement Croix-kama: une nouvelle forme de lutte contre la sorcellerie en pays Kongo," *Cahiers d'Etudes Africaines,* vol. 6 no. 2, 1966, p. 527–563.

———. "Sorcellerie en pays Kongo," *Cahiers d'Etudes Africaines,* vol. 1 no. 6, 1960, p. 527–563.

Witte, Baron Jehan de. *Les deux Congo. 25 ans d'apostolat au Congo français.* Paris, Plon et Nourrit, 1913.

————. *Monseigneur Augouard archeveque titulaire de Cassiopée, vicaire apostolique du Congo français,* Paris, Emiles Paul Freres, 1924.

Woodall, Ann. *Congo encounter: pages from the diary of Ann Woodall in Congo,* London, Salvationist publishers, 1974.

Literature

L'Afrique de Sony: une voix du Congo, Milan, Agip, 1987.

Anyinefa, Koffi. "Bibliographie de la littérature congolaise d'expression française," *Research in African Literatures,* vol. 20 no. 3, Fall 1989, p. 481–507.

————. *Littérature et politique en Afrique Noire: socialisme et dictature comme themes du roman congolais,* Bayreuth, Bayreuth University, 1990.

Balandier, Georges. "La littérature noire de langue française," *Présence Africaine,* no. 8/9, 1950, p. 393–403.

Bamana, Alphonse. *Coeur sur la braise,* Paris, St. Germain-des-Près, 1982.

Banos-Robles, Bernard. "Huits années de coopération theatrale au Congo," *Notre Librairie,* July–Aug. 1990, p. 134–139.

Batambica, Maurice. *Le maitre d'école a tué sa femme.* Brazzaville, Editions du Théatre Congolais, 1965.

Bemba, Sylvain. *Le dernier des cargonautes,* Paris, Harmattan, 1984.

————. *L'Enfer, c'est Orfeo,* Paris, ORTF, 1970.

————. *Eroshima,* Yaoundé, CLE, 1980.

————. *Une Eau dormante,* Paris, RFI, 1975.

————. *L'Homme Qui Tua le Crocodile,* Yaoundé, CLE, 1972.

————. *Un foutou monde pour un blanchisseur trop honnette,* Yaoundé, CLE, 1979.

————. *Léopolis,* Paris, Hatier, 1986.

————. *Reves portatifs,* Dakar, NEA, 1979.

————. *Le soleil est parti a M'Pemba,* Paris, Présence Africaine, 1982.

————. *Tarantelle noire et diable blanc,* Paris, Oswald. 1976.

————. *Theater and politics: an international anthology,* New York, Abu Repertory Theater, 1990.

————. and Léopold Mamonsono-Pindy. *Bio-bibliographie des écrivains congolais,* Brazzaville, Editions Littéraires Congolaises, 1979.

Bemba-Debert, A. *Essaim d'abeilles,* Brazzaville, Editions Littéraires Congolaise, 1982.

Bignacounou, Pierre. *Une Chomeur à Brazzaville,* Dakar, NEA, 1977.

Bilombo-Samba, Blaise. *Témoignages,* Paris, Oswald, 1976.

B'Kune, Tchicaya Unti. *Les poèmes à la gorge, la mise au monde,* Paris, Debresse, 1981.

————. *Soleil sans lendemains,* Paris, Harmattan, 1981.

Boundzeki-Dongala, E. *Un fusil dans la nuit,* Paris, Albin Michel, 1973.

Brench, A. C. *The Novelists inheritance in French Africa,* London, Oxford University Press, 1967.

Brezault, Alain and Gerard Clavreuil. *Conversations Congolaises,* Paris, Harmattan, 1989.

Cantot, Cecile. *Dans la foret du Mayombe.* Paris, Les Presses Universelles, 1971.

Chemain, Arlette. "De l'oralité à l'écriture en République Populaire du Congo," *Présence Africaine,* no. 132, 1984, p. 62–70.

———. "Image féminine et révolte dans l'oeuvre poétique de Tchicaya U Tamsi," *Annales de l'Ecole des Lettres* (Lomé), vol. 1, 1972, p. 97–128.

———. "Poésie et affleurement du mythe: introduction a l'oeuvre lyrique de Jean-Baptiste Tati-Loutard," *Présence Africaine,* no. 145, 1988, p. 115–140.

———. "Tchicaya U Tamsi par lui meme," *Cahiers de l'auditeur* (Paris), no. 2, 1978, p. 2–4.

Clair, Andrée. *Bemba,* Abidjan, Nouvelles Editiones Africaines, 1981.

Cornevin, Robert. "Ecrivains et littératures de langue française au Zaire et au Congo," *Civilisations* vol. 29 no. 1/2, 1979, p. 137–56.

Croce-Spinelli, Michel. *Macbeth negre,* Paris, Edition spéciale, 1972.

Daninos, G. "L'Image de la Femme dans la Littérature Congolaise," *Le Mois en Afrique,* Aug.–Sept. 1981, p. 132–142.

———. "L'Importance de la littérature orale en Afrique noire, et en particulier au Congo," *L'Afrique littéraire et artistique* no. 48, 1978, p. 2–19.

———. "La Notion d'Identité dans la Littérature Congolaise," *Le Mois en Afrique,* April–May 1983, p. 132–36.

———. "La Prise de Conscience du Racisme Colonial a Travers la Littérature Congolaise d'Expression Française," *Le Mois en Afrique,* Apr.–May 1981.

Dongala, Emmanuel B. *Le feu des origines,* Paris, Albin Michel, 1987.

———. *Une fusil dans la main,* Paris, Albin Michel, 1973.

———. *Jazz et vin de palme,* Paris, Hatier, 1982.

Ebaka, Jean Michel Paul. *Fruits interdits,* Brazzaville, Editions Littéraires congolaise, 1981.

Ecrivains d'Afrique noire, ecrivains meconnus?, Bruxelles, Cooperation par l'éducation et la culture, 1986.

Etoumba, Paul. *Un mot fracasse un avenir,* Paris, Oswald, 1971.

Foundou, Paul. *Un des aspects de la culture congolaise,* Brazzaville, Foundou, 1980.

Gaimpio, Edouard. *Les crudités,* Brazzaville, ABC, 1976.

Gauhy-Zingou, Medard. *Lamentations nocturnes,* Brazzaville, Editions Gaudard, 1982.

Godard, Roger. *Trois poétes congolais,* Paris, Harmattan, 1985.

Ibitokun, B. M. "The hemorrhage of time in Tchicaya's 'Le Mauvais Sang'," *Ufahamu,* vol. 10 no. 3, Spring 1981, p. 29–41.

Kambi-Bitchene, Albert. *Les faméliques,* Paris, Debresse, 1981.

Kegni, Alphonse-Diob. *La voix du matin,* Brazzaville, Editions Littéraires Congolaises, 1980.

Kuenemann-Pelletier, Claudette, *Sorciers père et fils,* Mulhouse, Pelletier, 1968.

Labou Tansi, Sony. *L'ante peuple,* Paris, Seuil, 1982.

————. "Antoine m'a vendu son destin," *Equateur,* no. 1, 1986, p. 66–104.

————. *Conscience de tracteur,* Dakar, NEA, 1979.

————. *L'Etat honteaux,* Paris, Seuil, 1981.

————. *La parenthése de sang,* Paris, Hatier, 1981.

————. *Une vie et demie,* Paris, Editions du Seuil, 1979.

————. *Les yeaux du volcan,* Paris, Editions du Seuil, 1985.

Letembet-Ambily, Antoine. *Les Aryens,* Yaoundé, CLE, 1977.

————. *L'Europe inculpée,* Yaoundé, CLE, 1970.

————. *La femme infidèle,* Brazzaville, Imprimerie Nationale, 1975.

Lhony, Patrice. *Matricule 22,* Brazzaville, Imprimerie Nationale, 1975.

————. *Les trois francs,* Brazzaville, Imprimerie Nationale, 1977.

Loango, Dominique. *La cité flamboyante,* Paris, Editions du Scorpion, 1959.

Lombalé-Bare, Gilbert. "Foret genereuse, littérature feconde," *Notre Librairie,* vol. 92/93, 1988, p. 16–25.

Lopes, Henri. *The laughing cry,* New York, Readers International/ Persea Press, 1987.

————. *La nouvelle romance,* Yaoundé, CLE, 1976.

————. *Le Pleurer-rire,* Paris, Présence Africaine, 1982.

————. *Sans tam-tam,* Yaoundé, CLE, 1977.

————. *Tribaliques,* Yaoundé, CLE, 1971.

Luce, Louise Fiber. "The women of Sony Labou Tansi," *The French Review,* vol. 64 no. 5 April 1991, p. 739–746.

Mabassi, Enoch. *Balbutiements,* Brazzaville, Editions Heros dans l'Ombre, 1977.

Mabounga, Daniel Kani. *In-dehors-anywhere,* Paris, La Pensée Universelle, 1981.

Mackitha, Raymond Timothee. *Les clairons de Cain,* Paris, Le Quatre fils, 1983.

Macouba, Augustin. *Bantou grand soir,* Paris, St. Germain-des-Près, 1978.

Magel, Emil A. "Theme and imagery in Tchicaya U Tam'si's A Triche-Coeur," *Studies in 20th century literature,* vol. 4 no. 2, Spring 1980, p. 189–212.

Mahoungou, Dina. *Le mémorial juvénile*, Paris, Saint-Germain-des Près, 1980.

————. *La superbe de l'emotion*, Paris, La Pensée Universelle, 1982.

Makhele, Caya. *Une vie d'élephante*, Dakar, NEA, 1987.

Makita, Philippe. *Sandales retournée*, Paris, Saint-Germain-des Près, 1978.

Makouta-Mboukou, Jean-Pierre. *L'Ame bleue*. Yaoundé, CLE, 1971.

————. *Cantat de l'Ouvrier*, Paris, Oswald, 1974.

————. *Le Contestant*, Paris, Pensée Universelle, 1973.

————. *Les dents du destin*, Abidjan, Nouvelles Editions Africaines, 1984.

————. *En quete de la liberté*, Yaoundé, CLE, 1970.

————. *Les exilés de la foret vierge ou le grand complot*, Paris, Harmattan, 1981.

————. *Les initiés*. Yaoundé, CLE, 1970.

————. "La littérature congolaise d'expression française. Bilan et perspective," *Comptes rendus trimestriels de l'Académie des Sciences d'Outre-Mer*, vol. 34 no. 4, 1974, p. 793–809.

Malanda, Ange-Severin. "L'Oeuvre de Sylvain Bemba," *Présence Africaine*, no. 130, 1984, p. 93–117.

————. "Le projet littéraire de Sony Labou Tamsi," *Le Mois en Afrique*, no. 205/6 Feb.–March 1983, p. 145–55.

Malonga, Jean. "Coeur d'Aryenne," *Présence Africaine*, no. 16, 1953, p. 161–285.

————. *Fleurs écarlates*, Paris, Saint-Germain-des Près, 1983.

————. *Legende de M'Foumou ma Mazono*, Paris, Présence Africaine, 1954, 1973.

Mamonsono-Pindy, Léopold. *Bio-bibliographie des écrivains congolais*, Brazzaville, Editions litteraires congolaise, 1979.

————. *Chronologie des oeuvres des ecrivains congolais, 1953–1983*, Brazzaville, Union des ecrivains congolais, 1983.

————. *Equinoxes*, Heidelberg, Kivouvou verlag, 1983.

————. *Heros dans l'Ombre*, Brazzaville, Editions Littéraires congolaises, 1979.

————. *Light-houses: poems*, Brazzaville, Editions Littéraires congolaises, 1978.

————. *Lizingu-Lua-Liadi: une vie d'enfer*, Brazzaville, Editions Héros dans l'Ombre, 1976.

————. *Mutantu*, Brazzaville, Editions Héros dans l'Ombre, 1976.

———— (ed.) *La nouvelle génération de poétes congolais*, Brazzaville, Editions Bantoues, 1984.

————. *La petit histoire d'Autopsie*, Kinshasa, Editions Ilutch-Ceco, 1983.

————. and Sylvain Bemba. *Bio-Bibliographique des écrivains congolais,* Brazzaville, Editions Littéraires congolais, 1979.

Manki, Manseke. *Echo,* Paris, Oswald, 1978.

Martial, Sinda. *Premier chant du depart,* Paris, Seghers, 1955.

Matondo, Kubu Ture. *Les visages noirs du pays qui tue,* Paris, Saint Germain-des Près, 2 vol., 1978.

Mbangui, B. Wa. *Essaim d'abeilles,* Brazzaville, Editions Littéraires Congolaises, 1981.

Menga, Guy. *L'affaire du silure,* Dakar, NEA, 1985.

————. *Les aventures de Moni-Mambou.* Yaoundé, CLE, 1971.

————. *Case de Gaulle.* Paris, Karthala, 1984.

————. *Le Dieu du clan,* Paris, ORTF, 1973.

————. "Expérience d'un dramaturge: L'essor d'un théatre moderne au Congo," *Ethnopsychologie,* vol. 35 no. 2/3, 1980, p. 81–86.

————. *Les indiscrétions du vagabond,* Sherbrooke, Naaman, 1974.

————. *Kotawali,* Dakar, NEA, 1977.

————. *Le Marmite de Koka-Mbala,* Yaoundé, CLE, 1976.

————. *Nouvelles aventures de Moni-Mambou.* Yaoundé, CLE, 1971.

————. *L'Oracle,* Yaoundé, CLE, 1976.

————. *La palabre stérile,* Yaoundé, CLE, 1968.

————. "Quel avenir pour le théatre en langue française au Congo?" *Culture Française,* no. 3/4, 1982/3, p. 45–48.

Mfouillou, Dominique. *Les corbeaux,* Paris, Akpagnon, 1980.

————. *La soumission,* Paris, Harmattan, 1977.

————. *Vent d'espoir sur Brazzaville,* Paris, Harmattan, 1991.

Mfuou-Tsially, Gilbert. *Case-tete congolais pour Berto* Paris, Jean Oswald, 1970.

Misere-Konka, Raphael. *Poémes liturgiques,* Paris, Editions Henri Pinson, 1985.

Mouangassa, Ferdinand. *Les Apprivoisés,* Brazzaville, Imprimerie Nationale, 1975.

————. *N'Ganga Mayala,* Yaoundé, CLE, 1976.

Moumbembe-Mbenimbongo, A. *Bruits de Mars,* Paris, La Pensée Universelle, 1980, 2 vol.

Mperet, Ngampika. *Flamme de sang,* Paris, St. Germain-des-Près, 1981.

Navarre, Pierre. *Olo, roman de brousse,* Paris, Editions du Dauphin, 1949.

Ndamba, Josue. "Entretien avec Maxime N'Débéka," *Melanges* (Brazzaville), no. 3, October 1980.

N'Débéka, Maxime. *Equatorium,* Paris, Présence Africaine, 1987.

————. *Les lendemains qui chantent,* Paris, Présence Africaines, 1983.

————. *L'Oseille, les citrons,* Paris, Oswald, 1975.

————. *Le President,* Paris, Oswald, 1970.

————. *Les signes du silence,* Paris, Editions Saint-Germain-des Près, 1978.

————. *Soleils neufs,* Yaoundé, CLE, 1969.

Ndzanga-Konga, Alphonse. *Flamme de la huitiéme lune,* Paris, Silex, 1984.

Ngampika-M'Peret, Jean-Pierre. *Flamme de sang,* Brazzaville, Editions Littéraires Congolaises, 1981.

Ngoie-Galla, Dominique. *Les Mandouanes,* Brazzaville, Imprimerie St. Paul 1977.

————. *Nocturnes,* Brazzaville, Imprimerie St. Paul, 1978.

Ngoma, Eugene. *Primitives,* Paris, Paris, Oswald, 1972.

————. "La Saison des Pluies," Brazzaville, *Revue Littéraire et Scientifique,* 1978.

Nkouka, Alphonse. *Chemins croises,* Paris, St. Germain-des-Près, 1981.

————. *Deuxieme bureau,* Yaoundé, CLE, 1980.

Nkounkou-Moundele, Dominique. *Zola,* Paris, St. Germain-des Près, 1981.

————. *L'hirondelle des riviéres,* Montereau, Imprimerie artisanale, 1983.

N'tsoulamba, Kiyila. *Prémices,* Paris, St. Germain-des-Près, 1980.

Nzala Baka, Placide. *Le Tipoye dore,* Paris, Oswald, 1968.

Nziengué, Bonard. *La carte postale,* Sherbrooke, Naaman, 1982.

Obenga, Theophile. *Astres si longtemps: poémes en sept chants,* Paris, Présence Africaine, 1988.

————. *La littérature traditionnelle des Mbochi,* Paris, Présence Africaine, 1984.

————. *Stéles pour l'avenir,* Paris, Présence Africaine, 1978.

Owi-Okanza. *Cha l'instituteur,* Bucharest, Ilexim, 1975.

————. *Le fou demoniaque,* Bucharest, Ilexim, 1975.

————. *Sélé-Sélé, le mauvais cadre agricole,* Bucharest, Ilexim, 1977.

————. *La trilogie déterminante,* Bucharest, Temoignage de l'Afrique contemporaine, 1977.

Quintec, L. "Djembu Tchicaya U Tamsi," *Liaison* (Brazzaville), no. 54, July–Aug. 1956.

Rouch, Alain and Gérard Clavreuil. *Littératures nationales d'écriture française,* Paris, Bandas, 1986.

Safoux, Daniel. *Morceaux de brise,* Paris, St. Germain-des-Près, 1980.

Sama, Eugéne. *Poémes diplomatiques,* Paris, Oswald, 1976.

Samba-Kifwani, Lucien. *L'intérimaire noir,* Paris, Présence Africaines, 1986.

Sédar-Ndinga, Christian. *Chroniques de l'ombre,* Paris, Silex, 1983.

Sianard, Yves. *Le dialogue des anges,* Heidelberg, Kivouvou Verlag, 1985.

————. *La fille de M'Vouti,* Heidelberg, Kivouvou Verlag, 1985.

————. *La calvaire de Kwazulu,* Heidelberg, Kivouvou Verlag, 1984.
Sinda, Martial. *Premier chant du depart,* Paris, Seghers, 1955.
Souamouhnoux-dia-Siassia. *Les Aurorales,* Paris, Editions Saint-Germain-des Près, 1982.
Tati-Loutard, Jean Baptiste (ed.) *Anthologie de la Littérature Congolaise d'Expression Française,* Yaoundé, CLE, 1976.
————. *Chroniques congolaises,* Paris, Oswald, 1974.
————. *Le dialogue des plateaux,* Paris, Présence Africaine, 1982.
————. *L'envers du Soleil,* Paris, Oswald, 1970.
————. *Les feux de la planéte,* Dakar, NEA, 1977.
————. *Les Normes du temps,* Paris, Editions du Mont-Noir, 1974.
————. *Nouvelles Chroniques congolaises,* Paris, Présence Africaines, 1980.
————. *Poémes de la mer/Poems of the Sea* (trans. by Gerald Moore), Ibadan, New Horn, 1991.
————. *Le poéte africain,* Lumumbashi, Mont-Noir, 1975.
————. *Les racines Congolaises,* Paris, Oswald, 1968.
————. *Le récit de la mort,* Paris, Présence Africaine, 1987.
————. *La tradition du songe,* Paris, Présence Africaine, 1986.
Tchicaya, U Tamsi. *Arc Musical,* Paris, Oswald, 1970.
————. *Brush fire,* Ibadan, Mberi press, 1964.
————. *Les cancrelats,* Paris, Albin Michel, 1980.
————. *Le Destin glorieux du Maréchal Nnikon Nniko,* Paris, Présence Africaine, 1979.
————. *Ces fruits si doux de l'arbre a pain,* Paris, Seghers, 1987.
————. *Epitome,* Paris, Oswald, 1970.
————. *Feu de brousse,* Paris, Oswald, 1970.
————. *Légendes africaines,* Paris, Seghers, 1987.
————. *The madman and the Medusa,* Charlotteville, University Press of Virginia, 1989.
————. *La main séche.* Paris, Robert Laffont, 1980.
————. *Le mauvais sang,* Paris, Oswald, 1957, 1970.
————. *Les méduses,* Paris, Albin Michel, 1982.
————. *Les phalènes.* Paris, Albin Michel, 1984.
————. *Selected Poems,* London, Heinemann, 1970, 1972.
———— "Tchicaya, poéte congolais," *Afrique,* no. 29, Dec. 1963, p. 42–45.
————. *Soleil sans lendemain,* Paris, Harmattan, 1981.
————. *A triche-Coeur,* Paris, Oswald, 1970.
————. *La Ventre, le pain ou la cendre,* Paris, Présence Africaine, 1978.
————. *La Veste d'interieur,* Paris, Nubia, 1977.
————. *Le Zulu,* Paris, Nubia, 1977.
Tchivela, Tchivelle. *Longue est la nuit,* Paris, Hatier, 1980.
————. *L'exil ou la tombe,* Paris, Présence Africaine, 1986.

Touassilenoho, Michel. *L'oeil,* Parris, St. Germain-des-Près, 1980.

Tsibinda, Marie-Léontine. *Conversations congolaises,* Paris, Harmattan, 1989.

———. *Mayombé,* Paris, St. Germain-des-Près, 1980.

———. *Poémes de la terre,* Brazzaville, Editions Littéraires congolaises, 1980.

———. *Une lévre naissant d'une autre,* Heidelberg, Kivouvou Verlag, 1985.

———. et al. *Conversations congolaises,* Paris, Harmattan, 1989.

Valdi, Française. *La femme antilope,* Paris, A. Delpauch, 1928.

Valette, Alice. *Un coeur de femme,* Sherbrooke, Naaman, 1982.

Viau, Sarah. *La foret sous la pluie,* Paris, Scorpion, 1960.

Linguistics

Baumer, Seigmund. "Problèmes actuels du développement des langues nationales en République Populaire du Congo," In: S. Baumer and N.V. Ochotina (eds.), *Studien zur nationalsprachlichen Entwicklung in Afrika,* Berlin, Akademie-Verlag, 1982, p. 99–126.

Bendor-Samuel, John et al. (eds.) *The Niger-Congo languages,* Lanham, University Press of America, 1989.

Bentley, William Holman. *Dictionary and grammar of the Kongo language,* London, Baptist Missionary Society, 1887.

Boyi, Jean. "Description phonologique du Munzombo," Thesis, Brazzaville, Marien Ngouabi University, 1977.

Butaye, R. *Dictionnaire Kikongo-Française,* Paris, Roulers, 1910.

Carter, Hazel. *Syntax and tone in Kongo,* London, School of Oriental and African Studies, 1973.

Creissels, Denis. *Aperçu sur les structures phonologiques des langues negro-africaines,* Grenoble, Editions littéraires et linguistiques, 1986.

———. *Description des langues negro-africaines et théorie syntaxique,* Grenoble, Editions littéraires et linguistiques, 1991.

Eliet, E. *Les langues spontanées dites commerciales du Congo. Le Monokutaba comparée au Lingala et au Lari de la région du Pool,* Brazzaville, Simarro, 1953.

Goody-Karady, Veronika. "Vili genesis stories: texts and analysis," *Research in African Literatures,* vol. 15 no. 2, Summer 1984, p. 238–261.

Hauser, André. "A propos de langues et d'enseignement en Afrique Noire," *Notes Africaines,* no. 60, Oct. 1953, p. 120–24.

———. "La frontière linguistique Bantoue-Oubanguienne entre le Bas-Oubangui et ses affluents de droite," *Zaire,* vol. 8 no. 1, 1954, p. 21–26.

Jacquot, André. "La classification nominale comme système de dérivation en Laadi (Congo)," In: *Colloque Internationaux de Centre National de la Recherche Scientifique,* Paris, CNRS, 1967, p. 117–132.

———. "Données linguistiques," In: Marcel Soret and André Jacquot (eds.), *Les Kongo Nord-Occidentaux*, Paris, Presses Universitaires de France, 1959, p. 26–31.

———. *Enquetes socio-linguistiques concernant la langue Sango*, Brazzaville, ORSTOM, 1959.

———. "Essai de systèmatisation de la graphie pratique des ethnonymes du Congo," Brazzaville, ORSTOM, 1966.

———. *Etudes Beembé (Congo)*, Paris, ORSTOM, 1981.

———. "Forme du pronom objet de 2ème personne de singulier en Kikongo," *Journal of African Languages*, vol. 6 no. 1, 1967, p. 58–60.

———. "La langue des Pygmées de la Sangha: Essai d'identification," *Bulletin de l'Institut d'Etudes Centrafricaines*, no. 17/18, 1959, p. 35–42.

———. "Les langues bantoues du Nord-Ouest. Etat des connaissance. Perspectives de la recherches," *Recherches et Etudes Camerounaises* (Yaoundé), vol. 2, 1960, p. 3–39.

———. "Les Langues du Congo-Brazzaville," *Cahiers ORSTOM*, vol. 8, no. 4, 1971, p. 349–359.

———. "Lari ou Laadi? Une problème de transcription," *Nouvelles de l'IRSC*, Brazzaville, ORSTOM, May 1964, p. 39–44.

———. *Le nom personnel chez les laadi*, Paris, CNRS, 1974.

———. "Notes sur la phonologie du Beembe," *Journal of African Languages*, vol. 1 no. 3, 1962, p. 232–242.

———. "L'Orthograph française et la transcription des langues vernaculaires," *Education Africaine* (Dakar), no. 39, 1957, p. 55–60.

———. "Précisions sur l'inventaire des langues téké du Congo," *Cahiers d'Etudes Africaines*, vol. 5 no. 2, 1965, p. 335–340.

———. "A propos d'une langue Téké," *Nouvelles ORSTOM del'IRSC* (Brazzaville), no. 6, 1962, p. 23–25.

———. "Remarques sur le Française parle à Brazzaville," Brazzaville, ORSTOM, 1963, 12p.

———. *République du Congo. Carte linguistique*, Brazzaville, Institut d'Etudes Centrafricaines, 1960.

———. *Textes laadi (Koongo)*, Paris, ORSTOM, 1978.

———. "La transcription des toponymes Africaines," Brazzaville, ORSTOM, 1956, 24p.

———. et al. *Etudes bantoues (Myene et laadi)*, Paris, SELAF, 1976.

Laman, K.E. *Dictionnaire kongo-française*, Bruxelles, Institut royal colonial belge, 1936.

Lumwamu, Française, *Essai de morphosyntaxe systematique des parlers Kongo*, Paris, Klinsieck, 1973.

———. "Quelques aspects de la linguistique congolaise," *Bulletin de l'Association d'Etudes Linguistiques interculturelles Africaines*, March 1984, p. 19–23.

————. *Situation linguistique en Afrique Centrale: inventaire preliminaire, le Congo*, Paris, Agence de cooperation culturelle et technique, 1987.

Makonda, Antoine. *Quatre-vingt-un congolismes*, Brazzaville, INRAP, 1987.

Makouta-Mboukou, S. "La particule 'nga' et la notion de la propriété dans certains langues bantu du Congo-Brazzaville: étude psycholinguistique," *Annales du Centre d'Enseignement Supérieur du Brazzaville*, vol. 4, 1968, p. 37–42.

Marichelle, C. *Dictionnaire vili-française*, Loango, Imprimerie de la mission, 1902.

Miehe, Gudrun. *Die prafixnasals im Benue-Congo und im Kwa*, Berlin, Reimer, 1991.

Nikouka, Marie-Thérèse. "La langue francophone Kongo d'aujourd'hui," Thesis, Brazzaville, Marien Ngouabi University, 1976.

Obenga, Théophile. "Le Kikongo, fondement de l'unité culturelle," *Africa*, vol. 25, 1970, p. 131–156.

Paullian, Christiane. *Le Kukuya*, Paris, SELAF, 1975.

Pepper, Herbert. "Un spécimen de la langue des Pygmées Bangombé, Moyen-Congo," *Bulletin de la Société de Linguistique*, vol. 51 no. 1, 1955, p. 106–20.

Prat, J. *Grammaire M'bochie et dictionnaire. Rivière Alima, Congo Française*, Brazzaville, Mission Catholique, 1917.

Queffelec, Ambroise. *Le française au Congo*, Aix-en-Provence, University of Aix-en-Provence, Marseilles, 1990.

Soderberg, Bertil and Ragnar Widman. *Publications en Kikingo*, Uppsala, Scandinavian Institute of African Studies, 1978.

Art/Music

Arts bakongo et Batéké, approches formes-fonctions en Afrique Equatoriale, Les Sables-d'Olonne, Musée de l'Abbaya, 1972.

Bemba, Sylvain. *50 ans de musique du Congo, Zaire*, Paris, Présence Africaines, 1984.

Bonnefond, P. and Jean Lombard. "Notes de folklore Lari," *Journal de la Société des Africanistes*, vol. 4, 1934, p. 81–109.

Brandel, R. "Types of melody movement in Central Africa," *Ethnomusicology*, vol. 6 no. 2, 1962, 75–87.

Chillon, B. "Le sculpteur Massengo et son buste de la reine N'-Galiourou," *Liaison*, no. 60, 1957, p. 37–38.

Demetz, H. "Les Poterries des peuplades Batéké du Moyen-Congo," *Comtes-rendus de la lére conférence internationale des Africanistes de l'Ouest*, Dakar, IFAN, 1958, p. 260–271.

Duponcheel, C. "Masterpieces of the People's Republic of Congo," New York, African-American Institute, 1980.

Dupré, M. C. "Le masque Kidumu maitre de l'histoire tsaayi," *Canadian Journal of African Studies,* vol. 22, 1988, p. 42–72.

———. "Naissance et renaissance du masque Kidumu. Art, politique et histoire chez les Téké tsaayi, République Populaire du Congo" PhD dissertation, University of Paris, 1984.

Grimaud, Yvette. *Notes sur la musique des Bochiman comparée à celle des Pygmées Babinga,* Paris, Musee de l'Homme, 1957.

Italiaander, Rolf. "Les artistes graveurs de Poto-Poto" Legon (Ghana), University of Ghana Occasional Paper, 1962.

Kamba, Sebastien. *Production cinematographique et parti unique: l'exemple du Congo,* Paris, Harmattan, 1992.

Kamer, Henri. *Arts du Congo,* Paris, Galerie Kamer, 1967.

Kobo Ture, Matondo. "Théatralisation de l'univers urbain dans la chanson contemporaine des orchestres congolo-zairois," In: *Journées d'études sur Brazzaville,* Brazzaville, ORSTOM, 1986, p. 533–546.

Kouvousama, Abel. *Les représentations sur la ville dans la chansone congolaise," In:* Journées d'études sur Brazzaville, *Brazzaville, ORSTOM, 1986, p. 519–532.*

Lebeuf, Jean-Paul. "L'école des peintres de Poto-Poto," *Africa,* vol. 26 no. 3, 1962, p. 277–280.

Lehuard, Raoul. *Les Phemba du Mayombé: les figures sculptés dites 'phemba' du Mayombe,* Arnouville, Arts d'Afrique Noire, 1977.

———. *Statuaire du Stanley-Pool,* Villiers-le-Bal, Arts d'Afrique Noire, 1972.

———. "Un voyage au Congo," *Arts d'Afrique Noire,* vol. 46, 1983, p. 17–22.

Masson-Detourbet, A. "Le tissage du raphia chez les Batéké," *Journal de la Société des Africanistes,* vol. 28 no. 1, 1957, p. 67–79.

Nourrit, Chantal and Bill Pruitt. *Musique traditionnelle de l'Afrique Noire: Congo 1985,* Paris, RFI, 1985.

Pepper, Herbert. "L'enregistrement du son et l'art musicale ethnique," *Bulletin de l'institut d'Etudes Centrafricaines,* no. 4, 1952, p. 143–149.

———. "Essai de définition d'une grammaire musicale Noire d'aprés les notations empruntées à une inventaire Babembé," *Problèmes d'Afrique Centrale,* no. 26, 1954.

———. "Histoire contée sur un vieux tambour de bois," *Jeune Afrique* (Elizabethville), June 1949, p. 13–15.

———. "Images musicales equatoriales," *Tropiques,* no. 1, Dec. 1950, p. 47–51.

———. "A la recherche des traditions musicales en pays Vili," *Bulletin d'Information et de documentation du gouvernement générale,* Brazzaville, no. 69, 1950.

———. "Trois danses chantées avec accomagnement de Linga," *Etudes Camerounaises,* no. 21/22, June–September 1948.

Robineau, Claude. "Culture materielle des Djém de Souanké," *Objets et Mondes,* vol. 7 no. 1, 1967, p. 37–70.

Siroto, Leon. "A mask style from French Congo," *Man,* no. 232, Oct. 1954, p. 149–150.

Soderberg, Bertil. "Les figures d'ancestres chez les Babambé," *Arts d'Afrique Noire,* no. 13, 1975, p. 21–32.

———. *Les instruments de musique au Bas-Congo et dans les régions avoisinantes,* Stockholm, Ethnograficka, 1956.

Stout, Renee. *Astonishment and power. The art of Kongo Minkisi.* Blue Ridge Summit, Smithsonian Institution Press, 1993.

Touassilenoho, Michel. *L'oeil,* Paris, Sant-Germain-des-Près, 1980.

Tracy, H. "The problem of the future of Bantu music in the Congo," *Problemes d'Afrique Centrale,* no. 26, 1954, p. 272–277.

Van Loo, E. "Artistes africaines de Poto-Poto," *Géographie,* Feb. 1958, p. 30–35.

Whorf, B. L. *Masterpieces of the People's Republic of Congo,* New York, African American Institute, 1981.

Travel and Tourism

Baleine, Philippe de. *Voyage espiegle et romanesque sur le petit train du Congo,* Paris, Filipacchi, 1992.

Ballif, Noel. *Le Congo,* Paris, Harmattan, 1993.

Congo. Ministère du Tourisme et de l'Environnement. *Etude des besoins en formation dans le secteur hotelier en République Populaire du Congo.* Brazzaville, 1983.

Eyraud, Arlette. *Centrafrique, Congo, Gabon,* Paris, Hatier, 1979.

Franceschi, Patrice. *Au Congo jusq'au cou: chez les pygmées de la foret equatoriale,* Paris, F. Nathan, 1977.

Gosselin, M. *Brazzaville,* Paris, Hachette, 1958.

Gosselin, M. *Pointe-Noire,* Paris, Hachette, 1958.

Guide de Brazzaville, Brazzaville, Havas, 1953.

Guide pratique de Brazzaville, Brazzaville, Amicale Nationale, 1953.

Guide to the People's Republic of Congo, Heidelberg, Editions Bantoues, 1984.

Houlet, Gilbert. *Brazzaville, Léopoldville, Pointe-Noire,* Paris, Hachette, 1958.

Petit, M. *Dix années de chasse d'un jeune naturaliste au Congo,* Evreux, Imprimerie de l'Eure, 1926.

Sodergren, Sigfrid. *Sweet smell of mangoes: an artist looks at the French Congo,* London, Deutsch, 1968.

Tiano, J. "Brazzaville du jour et de la nuit," *Balafon* (Paris), no. 82, May–June 1987, p. 38–45.

Uhl, Wolfgang. *Expedition zu den Pygmaen am Kongo,* Stuttgart, Pietsch, 1988.

Reference and Bibliographies

Africa Research Bulletin (Exeter), monthly, 2 series.

Africa South of the Sahara (London) annual.

Africa South of the Sahara; index to periodical literature, Washington, Library of Congress, 1985.

Blake, David and Carole Travis. *Periodicals from Africa: a bibliography and Union list of periodical publishers in Africa,* Boston, G. K. Hall. 1984.

Breton, J. M. "Bibliographie indicatif sur la République Populaire du Congo," *Revue Juridique et Politique,* vol. 38 no. 3, 1983, p. 833–38.

Carozzi, Carlo and Maurizio Tiepolo. *Congo Brazzaville: Bibliographie Générale,* Turin, Edizioni Libreria Cortina, 1991.

Congo. *Journal Officiel de la République du Congo,* Brazzaville, 1958– irregular.

"Congo," In: Sean Moroney (ed.), *Africa,* New York, Facts on File, p. 121–132.

"Congo," In: *Sources d'information sur l'Afrique noire francophone et Madagascar,* Paris, La Documentation Française, 1988, p. 194–198.

Le Congo, un partenaire commercial: guide des produits congolais, Brazzaville, Centre congolais du commerce exterieur, 1979.

Congo. Secretariat general du gouvernement. *Liste des gouvernements de la République depuis la loi-cadre à nos jours,* Brazzaville, 1983.

Germany. Bundestelle fur Aussenhandelsinformation. *Volksrepublik Kongo,* Cologne, several series.

Gorman, G. E. and M. M. Mahoney. *Guide to current national bibliographies in the Third World,* London, Hans Zell, 1983.

Herterfelt, Marcel d', and Anne-Marie Bouttiaux-Ndiaye. *Bibliographie de l'Afrique sud-saharienne,* Tervuren, Musée Royal de l'Afrique, 1990.

Jahn, Janheinz et al. *Who's Who in African Literature,* Tubingen (Germany), Erdman, 1972.

Lauer, Joseph J. *American and Canadian doctoral dissertations and master's theses on Africa,* Atlanta, Crossroads Press, 1989.

Legum, Colin (ed.) *Africa Contemporary Record,* New York, Africana, annual.

Lipschutz, Mark R. and R. Kent Rasmussen. *Dictionary of African Historical Biography,* Berkeley, University of California Press, 1986.

Liste des entreprises (organismes d'état et d'économie mixte) dans la République Populaire du Congo, Brazzaville, Centre National de gestion, 1980.

McDonald, Gordon C. et al. *Area Handbook for the People's Republic of Congo,* Washington, Superintendent of Documents, 1971.

Mamonsono, L. P. and S. Bemba. *Biobibliographie des écrivains congolais,* Brazzaville, Editions congolaises, 1979.

Perrot, C., and H. Sauvalle. *République du Congo-Brazzaville, Repertoire Bibliographique,* Paris, B.D.P.A., 1965.

Personnalités Publiques de l'Afrique Centrale, Paris, Ediafric, 1972.

Répertoires bibliographiques, Brazzaville, Bibliotheque Nationale, 1977.

Répertoires bibliographiques: bibliotheque nationale, Brazzaville, Ministère de la culture, des arts et des sports, 1978.

Répertoire des Centres de documentation et Bibliotheques, Abidjan, Service de documentation du Conseil de l'Entente, 1980.

Répertoire des entreprises congolaises de commerce extérieur, Brazzaville, Centre Congolais du commerce extérieur, 1988.

Répertoire des ouvrages conservés à la bibliotheque du Centre d'énseignement supérièur de Brazzaville, Brazzaville, Centre d'énseignement supérièur de Brazzaville, 1970.

Répertoire des pouvoirs publics africains, Paris, Ediafric, 1975.

Scheven, Yvette. *Bibliographies for African Studies, 1970–1986,* London, Hans Zell, 1988.

Sociétés et fournisseurs d'Afrique Noire, Paris, Documentation Africaine, 1987.

Soret, Marcel. "Bibliographie des régions Nord du Moyen-Congo," Brazzaville, Institut d'Etudes Centrafricaines, 1959.

―――. "Bibliographie ethnique abrégée de la République du Congo," Brazzaville, Institut d'Etudes Centrafricaines, 1958.

―――. "Notes de bibliographie sur la République du Congo," Brazzaville, Institut d'Etudes Centrafricaines, 1959.

―――. Répertoire des articles parus dans le Bulletin de la Société des Recherches Congolaises, 1922 à 1941," Brazzaville, Institut d'Etudes Centrafricaines, 1954.

West Africa (London), weekly.

Yaranga, Zofia. *Bibliographie des travaux en langue française sur l'Afrique au sud du Sahara,* Paris, Centre d'études africaines, 1985.

About the Authors

Samuel Decalo (B.Sc., Ottawa University; M.A. and Ph.D. University of Pennsylvania) is an Israeli citizen, long resident in the United States. He has taught at various universities including the University of Rhode Island; The Graduate Faculty, New School for Social Research; and Emory University, as well as at several universities abroad including at the University of Botswana and the University of the West Indies. He is currently Professor of Political Science at the University of Natal, South Africa, and Visiting Professor at the University of Florida in Gainesville. He has conducted research in some twenty African states, including Congo, on numerous occasions, and is the author of thirteen books and some seventy articles on Africa and the Middle East.

Virginia Adloff, a graduate of Vassar College, received her doctorate at Columbia University in 1932. After World War II, she and her husband, Richard Adloff, traveled extensively throughout Southeast Asia and were joint authors of The Left Wing in Southeast Asia. Beginning in 1953, they traveled through French-speaking Africa, south of the Sahara. Their first book on that area, French West Africa, was followed by The Emerging States of French Equatorial Africa as well as other titles. Virginia Adloff was a member of the Académie des Sciences Outre-Mer in Paris and was decorated by the French government with the order of L'Etoile Noir de Bénin. Virginia Adloff died in January 1990.

967.24
Dec

Decalo, Samuel.

Historical dictionary
of Congo.

DATE			

REFERENCE